STRATEGIC MANAGEMENT

Concepts, Processes, Decisions

STRATEGIC MANAGEMENT

Concepts, Processes, Decisions

LESTER A. DIGMAN
University of Nebraska

1995

PUBLICATIONS, INC.
Houston, TX 77074

Artist: Anita Hester
Desktop Publishing: Joe Marquez, III
Jan Tiefel

ISBN 0-87393-314-1

Printed in the United States of America.

To Ellen, Stephanie, Sarah, and Mark

PREFACE

This text is written for strategic management and business policy students at high-quality business schools, whether at the undergraduate or master's level. The strategy and policy fields have undergone significant changes during the past four years; those changes—both in substance and process—are incorporated in this text. Therefore, this text reflects both the academic and practitioner state of the art in these fields.

The viewpoint taken in this text agrees with that of Paul Cook and Joseph Bower of Harvard, that the policy field includes "all the messy, unsolved, and perhaps undefined problems" characterizing the management of an organization. As soon as such problems are sufficiently well understood, they can be incorporated as part of the subject matter in one of the functional disciplines.

THE ALL-NEW TEXT

This new book replaces my previous second edition of *Strategic Management*. Thus, this third effort represents my current view of this dynamic field. This latest version of *Strategic Management* is a modular text and case book for the Strategic Management and Business Policy course. The package is targeted toward the MBA-level course as well as the undergraduate-level course at "better" institutions.

The package consists of two volumes: *Strategic Management: Concepts, Processes, Decisions* (text material—Part I of the package), and *Strategic Management: Cases* (cases and case-related material—Part II of the package). The reason for breaking the package into two parts is to provide maximum flexibility for the instructor and minimum cost for the student.

The case portion of the policy/strategy course clearly lends itself to a customized, modular approach. Instructor preference, plus the issues of case timeliness and the development of student "files" have resulted in many instructors using packets of individually-selected cases, individualized custom-case books, and the like. Thus, the life of the case portion of a text and case book is much shorter than the text portion, and there is much more divergence of preference concerning the "ideal" complement of cases.

Instructors also exhibit some divergence of opinion concerning the treatment of topics comprising the text portion of the learning materials. Instructors vary regarding the order in which they prefer to cover certain topics. Also, some prefer to intersperse topical material with cases, while some prefer that cases follow the "theory and concepts" portion of the course. Others vary regarding the depth of coverage, some preferring greater depth and few cases, others preferring more breadth and more cases. Some use no cases at all, perhaps relying upon a simulation to provide the application portion of the course.

For the above reasons, this edition employs a modular approach for both the text and case learning materials for the policy/strategy course.

The text portion (Part I) contains a complement of twenty-three chapter-modules, 10-20 pages in length, covering the important topical areas of strategy and policy. The reason that the number of modules is greater than the number of chapters in most books is that most books combine certain topic-modules to create somewhat consistently-sized chapters of related material. Each module in this text contains a single topical area. Some instructors do not elect to cover all topics, and module topics can be selected by the instructor as he/she sees fit. Therefore, the instructor can custom-select text modules and cases to fit his/her own course, arranged in whatever order they prefer.

Secondly, the modules contain the very latest material relevant to the strategic manager. Major new topics and coverage in this text include:

- Strategies for global and transnational business.
- Virtual organizations, including alliances and outsourcing, and "boundaryless" organizations.
- Core competencies.
- Characteristics of successful organizations.
- Process improvements, including TQM and reengineering.
- Time-based competition and strategies.
- Chaos theory, including how to plan in unpredictable environments.
- Expanded treatment of vision and strategic leadership.
- Performance measurement, including the Balanced Scorecard and Economic Value Added concepts.
- Strategies for professional organizations and family businesses.
- Expanded material on enterprise strategies and governance.
- All new cases, thoroughly reviewed and tested, none more than three years old.

Third, the text portion can be utilized as a stand-alone for instructors who do not use cases or prefer to use other cases. Likewise, the stand-alone case book (containing only those cases selected by the instructor) is an option. Either option will result in lower student cost.

Fourth, the modules address concepts, organizational processes, and decisions (that is, strategy and policy options and choices). Numerous examples, profiles, vignettes, and the like are interspersed throughout.

This textbook is in the mainstream of the field in that it fulfills the integrative, capstone needs of the policy course, cast in a strategic management framework. It is state of the art in that it presents the very latest strategic management material cast in a strategic decision framework. The body of knowledge is tied to the essential viewpoints, tasks, and analyses required to *perform* the strategic management function. Thus, the reader will be required (and shown how) to perform strategy formulation, implementation, and control, rather than simply being exposed to text material that talks *about* strategic management. Included are data, guides, and checklists on: (a) which types of strategies are appropriate, (b) what a given strategy requires and consists of, and (c) probable outcomes. In short, the text pulls the field together for the masters or undergraduate class and instructor, and moves in the direction toward which the field and the course are evolving. This text presents the field in a natural framework while adding emerging concepts.

THE CASES

A critical factor in the case portion of a text on strategic management and business policy is the balance or complement of the cases selected. The cases included in Part II were selected from a review of hundreds of cases, screened from a list of several thousand strategy- and policy-related cases. Careful consideration was given to the quality of the case, a balance of strategic issues and decisions, a wide representation of industries, varying company sizes, cases of varying length and complexity, geographical balance, how current the case is, and organizations in which students and faculty are likely to have an interest.

A complement of thirty-seven "core" cases is provided for the instructor, backed by consistent, in-depth teaching notes. High-quality new cases will be added as they become available (likely 10 or so per year). Additional cases from which the instructor can choose will be listed, but will rely upon the case developer's teaching note.

Case selection reflects the full complement of strategy and policy issues, balancing industries, sectors (NFP, service, etc.), size, geography, domestic/international/global, and stage of growth. Several industry-analysis cases are included.

In addition, the cases reflect most major types of organizations competing in a number of different industries. Several of the cases have "industry pairs" for comparison purposes. Further, the geographical balance of the cases closely approximates the population of the various regions of the United States in which they are headquartered, and most are national and international in scope and recognition. Canadian, British, French, Italian, Irish, German, Chinese, Japanese, and Indian companies are also represented.

Also included in Part II is student-oriented material on learning by the case method—what it is, how it works, and how to analyze a case.

INSTRUCTOR'S MANUAL

An essential aid to the faculty member is a high-quality instructor's manual, particularly for a case-oriented course. Unlike many, the instructor's manual for this text was prepared by the book's author, ensuring consistency and high quality. Extensive classroom testing and student research has gone into the teaching note for each case, in many instances including direct input by the case authors themselves.

An instructor's module is available for each text module and each core case. These will be consistently organized and updated yearly to reflect any important changes or developments. The purpose of the instructor's modules is to make the instructor the knowledgeable expert on the material and the case, including current happenings.

The complete manual includes the following:

- Thorough, logical, and consistent analysis of each case, including a detailed update.
- Detailed course outlines and schedules.
- Extensive test bank, including objective and essay questions and answers.
- Transparency masters.
- Suggestions and hints for covering the material in each part/module.
- Detachable pages, for ease of classroom use.

STRATEGY NEWSLETTER

It is important that the instructor keep abreast of significant developments in the field, both theory and practice. Sometimes this is a difficult task, given the preparation and grading demands of a case-oriented course. Likewise, it is important and always of interest to students to know the "latest scoop" concerning the cases they are analyzing. This is particularly true regarding dynamic organizations, industries, and individuals—the situation facing many of the cases in this book. For this reason, adopters will receive a periodic "Strategy Newsletter," providing synopses of important new developments in the field plus the latest happenings and results experienced by the case organizations. In this way, faculty members will be able to keep themselves and their students as current as is possible on the field and the cases.

SIMULATION

The final part of the package is a computerized, interactive simulation game, in which teams of students act as management of a simulated company. The teams will be able to make both corporate-level and business-level strategic decisions. At the corporate-level, they will choose which of up to six businesses in which to compete, including how to enter (start-up, purchase) and how many resources to allocate to each. At the business-level, they will choose how to compete (largely based upon generic strategies and distinctive competencies), plus the relative emphasis on functional areas. Instructors will be provided with game disks, and students will purchase game packets. The simulation will be available by Spring 1996.

NOTE FOR THE INSTRUCTOR

This textbook does *not* utilize a special computer package for case analysis—an approach currently popular with some authors and faculty members—even though such programs are useful in helping students analyze finances, ratios, and alternatives using spreadsheets. Why not? One of the current major trends in strategic management is toward creative, intuitive solutions to strategic problems, and away from step-by-step "mechanical analytical" approaches. Improper reliance on analytical aids can have several side effects:

1. By structuring the situation for the students, they are less likely to learn the most valuable aspects of strategic decision-making (creative problem solving).
2. They can leave students with the misconception that the primary aspect of strategic management and policy decisions is numerical analysis and manipulation.

While quantitative financial analysis *is* important to strategy and policy decisions, and is *necessary*, it is not *sufficient*. In strategy and policy courses, the goal is not to *teach* financial analysis, but to *use* it. To the extent that computer packages *reduce* the students' preoccupation with quantitative manipulations, allowing and assisting them to focus on key strategic issues, they are valuable. To the extent that they overstructure case situations and reduce creative, intuitive thinking, they do the student a disfavor. At present, the benefits of the former do not outweigh the risks of the latter, in my estimation.

In summary, it is my view that data should not be preorganized for students. They should be required to pull important financial and other data from the case (using *their* judgment); this data can be analyzed using independent spreadsheet computer packages on PCs at virtually all quality institutions of higher education.

ACKNOWLEDGMENTS

One can never adequately thank everyone who played a role in the completion of a textbook. With that in mind, let me single out the authors of the cases included in this book, both for their outstanding work and their permission to use the cases. Second, special mention is due for the authors of the many cases that were graciously sent to me for review, but which I was not able to include. I am especially indebted to adopters of the first and second editions—the people *really* responsible for the existence of this vastly improved new text. Their faith and confidence will not be forgotten. Special mention must also be made of the researchers and practicing managers who have advanced the state of the art of the field to its present level, and of those who will continue to do so in the future, leading the field into its second generation.

I will be forever grateful to my academic cohorts and professional society colleagues from various institutions who have helped and assisted my academic career progression. Special thanks are due to my friends and colleagues at the University of Nebraska: Fred Luthans, for encouraging my return to academics and for encouraging me to undertake this task; Sang Lee, for his continuing support and encouragement; and Gary Schwendiman and Jack Goebel for resources and a supportive environment.

My former and present doctoral students are due a debt of gratitude for the challenge and research assistance they provide, as well as for the feedback and impetus to keep current in one's field. Special mention should go to the following former doctoral students who contributed significantly in the form of examination questions, comments, and suggestions:

> *Mary E. Barton*—California State University/Northridge
> *Larry Cox*—Florida International University
> *Philip P. Crossland*—University of Missouri/Kansas City
> *Patricia M. Feltes*—Southwest Missouri State University
> *Todd Finkle*—University of North Carolina-Charlotte
> *Karen L. Fowler*—University of Wyoming, Colorado State University, San Diego State University, University of Northern Colorado
> *Neil Gilchrist*—Northeast Missouri State University
> *Phillip D. Hall*—University of Nebraska
> *Thomas G. Henricks*—Kansas State University
> *James J. Hoffman*—Florida State University
> *Paul M. Mallette*—Colorado State University
> *Rebecca J. Morris*—University of Nebraska at Omaha
> *Paul Poppler*—St. John's University
> *Robert G. Spagnola*—University of Denver, Colorado State University
> *Neil E. Swanson*—Arizona State University, Southwest Missouri State University
> *Jack Teh*—Utah State University, Nebraska Wesleyan University

Soen Eng Tjan—Creighton University, Indonesian Institute for Management Development
Brad Wagner—University of South Carolina at Beaufort
Yim Yu Wong—Indiana State University

Karen Fowler deserves special mention. She did an outstanding and thorough job of editing the final manuscript for this book. In addition, she prepared and contributed a major portion of the test bank questions found in the instructor's manual. I am sincerely proud of each of my doctoral students, both as individuals and as scholars, but Karen's teaching, research, and service contributions have been particularly noteworthy. Credit must also be given to Marina Onken, one of my current doctoral students, for her work in preparing the index and contributing answers to a number of the essay questions for the Instructor's Manual.

My present doctoral students at Nebraska include:

Jan Hansen	*Dale Henderson*
Sheng-Chyung Jou	*Joong Wha Kim*
Marina Onken	*Michael Ruback*
Mike Wakefield	

I am indebted to the many reviewers of the first and second editions for their insightful comments and suggestions. First edition reviewers include:

Richard Bettis Southern Methodist University	*R. Duane Ireland* Baylor University
H. Kurt Christensen Northwestern University	*Kenneth E. Marino* University of Kentucky
Joel Cook Texas A&M University	*Hugh M. O'Neill* University of Connecticut
Raymond L. Cook University of Texas	*Richard L. Pyle* University of Massachusetts at Boston
Arnold C. Cooper Purdue University	*William R. Soukup* University of San Diego
Tim Davis Cleveland State University	*John M. Stengrevics* Boston University
Roger Evered Naval Post Graduate School	*Gerardo Ungson* University of Oregon
Edward Freeman University of Minnesota	*D. Robley Wood, Jr.* Virginia Commonwealth University
Harvey Hegarty Indiana University	

Second edition reviewers include:

B.R. Baliga
Texas Tech University

Joseph Rosenstein
University of Texas at Arlington

Geoffrey R. Brooks
University of Oregon

E.K. Valentin
Weber State College

Phillip D. Jones
Xavier University

Jean M. Lundin
Northern Michigan University

Marshall Schminke
The University of Iowa,
Creighton University

J. Michael Geringer
University of Western Ontario

James B. Thurman
George Washington University

Ken Thompson
DePaul University

In addition, I gratefully acknowledge the case authors:

1. **United Colors of Benetton: Shock Ads, Social Responsibility and Specialty Retailing**
    James T. Strong, University of Akron

2. **Bridgestone-Firestone, Inc.**
    Stephen A. Allen, Babson College

3. **Industry Note: The Waste Industry**
    Joe G. Thomas and *Robert Mattix*, Middle Tennessee State University

4. **Browning-Ferris Industries**
    Ronald A. Coker, Dana M. Dieckman, Robert F. Mattix, and *John A Parnell*, Middle Tennessee State University and North Carolina Central University

5. **Carrier Corporation—Strategy Evolution for the Small Commercial Rooftop**
    Michael Zimmerman, Mark R. Eaker, Andrew C. Boynton, University of Virginia (Darden School)

6. **Clearly Canadian Beverage Corporation**
    Frank J. Fish III, Panasonic Division, Matshushita Corp.

7. **Club Med, Inc.**
    Robert P. Vichas, Texas A&M International University

8. **The Coca-Cola Company—The Carbonated Soft Drink Industry**
    Robert J. Mockler, St. John's University; *Dorothy Dologite*, Baruch College—CUNY; *Narasimhaswamy Banavara* and *Bridgett Brown*, St. John's University

9. **Cyrix Corporation**
   Beau Bruce, Marianne Burns, Li-Yen Chien, Kim Misemer, F. Gene Winfield, Sexton Adams, University of North Texas; and *Adelaide Griffin*, Texas Woman's University

10. **DB Software GMBH**
    James M. Gampper, Independent Consultant

11. **Managing Maturity at Deere & Company**
    Peter G. Goulet and *Lynda L. Goulet*, University of Northern Iowa

12. **A Prospective Acquisition at Figgie International**
    James J. Dowd, Jr., Michael D. Atchison, and *John H. Lindgren, Jr.*, University of Virginia (McIntire)

13. **Going Global: The Ford "Mondeo"**
    Barra O'Cinneide, University of Limerick

14. **Health Care in the Fox Valley: Competition or Cooperation?**
    Angeline W. McArthur, University of Wisconsin-Parkside; and *Alla Wilson*, University of Wisconsin-Whitewater

15. **Fresh Kills Landfill: New York City**
    James W. Clinton, University of Northern Colorado; *Steven H. Corey*, New York University

16. **Global Marine (B): A Company's Search for Profit in an Industry in Upheaval**
    James W. Clinton, University of Northern Colorado

17. **Goodyear: Beyond Goldsmith—An Update from 1988 to 1991**
    Bernard A. Deitzer, Alan G. Krigline, and *Thomas C. Peterson*, University of Akron

18. **Greyhound Lines, Inc.: The Intercity and Rural Bus Industry**
    Robert J. Mockler, Narasimhaswamy Banavara, Chanhorng Lin, and *Scott Alan Stepp*, St. John's University

19. **IBM Reborn: Restructuring a Sluggish Computer Industry Giant (1994)**
    William C. House, University of Arkansas, and *Walter E. Greene*, University of Texas—Pan American

20. **IKEA: An International Retailer Penetrates the U.S. Market**
    James T. Strong, University of Akron

21. **India Rubber Company, Limited**
    James W. Lawson, St. Peter's College

22. **John Labatt Limited and Birra Moretti**
    Arthur Sharplin, Institute for International Business Studies, Pordenone, Italy

23. **L.A. Gear, Inc.**
A.J. Almaney, DePaul University

24. **Bill Gates and the Management of Microsoft**
Philip M. Rosenzweig, Harvard University

25. **Mobil Chemical and the VPP**
Sue Greenfeld and *Harold Dyck*, California State University—San Bernardino

26. **Monsanto Enviro-Chem Systems, Inc. (A)**
Gerard F. Carvalho, Ohio University

27. **Occupational Safety and Health Administration**
Joe G. Thomas, Middle Tennessee State University

28. **Packman's Books: Profiting as an Independent Bookstore**
James T. Strong, University of Akron

29. **PepsiCo, Inc.: Marketing Soft Drinks in a Mature Economy**
William G. House, University of Arkansas and *Walther E. Greene*, University of Texas—Pan American

30. **PIP, Inc.**
Paula M. Sanders, Herbert E. Brown, Nabil Hassan, Wright State University

31. **Rubbermaid: Beyond Stanley Gault (1993)**
Bernard A. Dietzer, Susan Hanlon, Alan Krigline, and *Thomas Peterson*, University of Akron

32. **The U.S. Airline Industry**
Don M. Parks, Southwestern University and *Ivar H. Noer*, University of Wyoming

33. **Southwest Airlines: Expanding Beyond the Southwest**
Don M. Parks, Southwestern University and *Ivar H. Noer*, University of Wyoming

34. **Tandy Corporation**
Bill Brooks, Fei-Fen Cheng, Ed Dietz, Natalie Yue, and *Sexton Adams*, University of North Texas; *Adelaide Griffin*, Texas Woman's University

35. **Wall Lenk Corporation (A)**
Donald B. Boldt, East Carolina University

36. **Waterford Crystal, Ltd.**
Philip H. Anderson, University of St. Thomas

37. **Westlake Shopping Center: Economic Development vs. Quality of Life**
James W. Clinton, University of Northern Colorado

Mention must be made of the team at Dame Publications, Inc., a group which has been professional, cooperative, efficient, and friendly in creating a first-class product from my draft manuscript. Specifically, my most freqent inter-actions were with Cliff Francis, Jan Tiefel, and Joe Marquez.

Finally, I owe a debt to the office staff at the University of Nebraska, partic-ularly Linda Rohn, Cathy Watson, Debbie Burns, and Thyra Lowe (who are largely responsible for this new book). Again, my wife Ellen deserves special mention for her assistance and understanding, as do our children, Stephanie, Sarah, and Mark for putting up with—and often without—me while the book was being written and revised.

January 1995   *Lester A. Digman*

ABOUT THE AUTHOR

Lester A. Digman, Ph.D.

Les Digman is the Metropolitan Federal Bank professor of Management at the University of Nebraska, where he also serves as Director of Graduate Studies in Management and Director of the Center for Technology Management and Decision Sciences (now the Gallup Research Center). A graduate of the University of Iowa, Professor Digman specializes in strategic management, strategic decision-making, management of technology, and executive development.

He has written five books, made contributions to twelve others, published eighty-three journal articles and conference papers (including those in *Harvard Business Review, Organizational Dynamics, Operations Research*, and others), presented seventy-eight professional papers, and authored thirty-one reports and monographs. He has consulted with scores of private and governmental organizations in the United States, Russia, Sweden, Germany, Korea, Albania, Macedonia, China, Malaysia, and others.

Dr. Digman is a member of the Strategic Management Society, the Planning Forum, the Academy of Management, the Decision Sciences Institute, the Institute for Organizational Research and Management Science, the Pan Pacific Business Association, and others. He is a Fellow of the Decision Sciences Institute, served as national vice-president, and has served as program chair and president of the Midwest region, as well as coordinator of the Institute's Doctoral Student Consortium. He has also been singled-out as one of five top "developers and teachers" in the book, *Writers on Strategy and Strategic Management*, by J.I. Moore of England. In all, the book profiles the work of twenty-four top contributors to the strategy literature. He is listed in six editions of *Who's Who*.

TABLE OF CONTENTS

PART I
Strategic Management:
Concepts, Processes, Decisions

MODULES:

1   Strategic Management: An Overview **1-3**

Learning Objectives. Profile: The Institute of Electrical and Electronic Engineers (IEEE). Profile: Frances Hesselbein. Strategic Management Today. Types of Strategies. Enterprise Strategy. Interorganizational Strategy. Corporate Strategy. Business-Unit Strategy. Functional and Operations Strategies. *Organizational Planning Processes.* Strategic, Tactical, and Operational Planning. Statements of Strategy. *Strategic Versus Operating Management.* The Environmental Interface. *Value of Strategic Management.* Strategic Planning Pays. Strategic Planning Doesn't Always Pay. What Have We Learned?

2   Strategic Management: What it is and How it Developed **2-1**

Learning Objectives. What is Strategic Management? Versus Strategic Planning and Long-Range Planning. A Military Analogy. Characteristics of Strategic Decisions. *The Essence of Strategy.* "Schools" of Strategic Management. *History and Evolution of Strategic Management.* Need for Planning has Increased. More Areas Require Strategic Attention. Time Compression and Instability. Increased Rate of Change. Strategy as a Field. *Conclusions.*

3 Strategic Management: Processes and Practices **3-1**

Learning Objectives. Profile: ConAgra's Simplified Planning System. The Value of Strategy Processes. Planning Systems Stages. The Strategic Management Process. An Integrated Model. Overview of the Process. *Elements of the Strategic Process.* Vision. The Organization's Mission or Purpose. Goals and Objectives. Assessing the Strategic Situation. Strategy Formulation. Strategy Implementation and Planning. Strategic Control. *High-Performance Strategic Planning.* Make Planning Distinctive. Keep it Simple Flexible, and Workable. Take an Action Orientation. Make the Process Fit the Culture. Don't Hang Up on Order and Rationality. Top-Down or Bottom Up? Group Approaches. *Conclusions.*

4 Characteristics of Successful Organizations **4-1**

Learning Objectives. Profile: The GE Revolution. What Makes a Business Successful? Four Factors Essential to Success. Tom Peters: Search, Passion, Chaos, and Liberation. Enter Renewal. *Defining Critical Success Factors.* Critical Failure Factors. *PIMS Data.*

5 Planning for Uncertain Futures **5-1**

Learning Objectives. Profile: Swatch. The Future: Predictable or Chaotic? Coping with Chaos. *Planning Under Risk and Uncertainty.* Forecasting. Forecasting Techniques. Contingency Planning. Surprise and Crisis Management. *Organizational Learning: The **Real** Purpose of Planning.* Creating Order Out of Chaos. Scenario Planning. Issues Analysis.

6 The Key Players: Strategic Managers and Stakeholders **6-1**

Learning Objectives. Profile: NCR Manages for its Stakeholders. Who are the Strategic Managers? Managers and Strategic Decisions. The Team at the Top. Line and Staff Involvement. But Who is Responsible? *Skills and Approaches that Work.* Conceptual and Synthesis Skills. Technical and Analytical Skills. Combination of Skills. Organizational Effects. *Stakeholder Values and Expectations.* Who are the Stakeholders? Satisfying Stakeholder Wants.

7   Organizational Direction: Vision, Mission, Goals, Culture **7-1**

Learning Objectives. Profile: "Sharing the Vision" at US West. Creating the Vision. Effective Vision Statements. *Defining the Mission.* Defining and Redefining the Business. Multimission Organizations. Relationship to Goals, Objectives, Strategies, and Policies. Properties of Effective Mission Statements. Are Mission Statements of Value? *Determining Goals and Objectives.* Hierarchy of Objectives. Management's Goals and Objectives. *Organizational Culture.* Climate and Culture.

8   Strategic Advantage: Competencies, Resources, Timing, and Process Improvement **8-1**

Learning Objectives. Profile: Union Pacific Railroad. Achieving Competitive Advantage. Distinctive and Core Competencies. Resources. The Resource Audit. *Timing.* The Experience Curve. Experience Curve Pricing. Some Cautions. *Process Improvement.*

9   Real and Virtual Organizations: Structures, Alliances, and Outsourcing **9-1**

Learning Objectives. Profile: CUC International: A Virtual Retailer. Organizational Types and Stages. Types of Organizations. Patterns of Organizational Evolution. Newer Forms of Organization. *Virtual Organizations.* Outsourcing. Alliances.

10   The Relevant General Environment **10-1**

Learning Objectives. Profile: Kustom Electronics. Profile: Deere & Company. The Importance of Environmental Influences. The Need for Environmental Analysis. Which Factors are Important? *The Economy.* Microeconomic Factors. Macroeconomic Factors. International Factors. *Technology.* Management's Role. Service Technology. Process Technology and Productivity. Corporate-Level Responsibilities. *Social Factors.* Demographic Influences. Income, Employment, and Influence. Values, Attitudes, and Preferences. *Political/Legal Considerations. Conclusions.*

11   The Competitive Environment **11-1**

Learning Objectives. Profile: The Video Rental Industry. Determinants of Competition. Competitive Forces. Competitor Analysis. *The Effect of Market and Industry Structure.* Defining the Market. Defining the Industry. *The Product/Market Life Cycle.* Introductory and Growth Stages. Shakeout Stage. Maturity Stage. Decline Stage. Some Cautions.

12   Enterprise Stategies and Governance **12-1**

Learning Objectives. Profile: Managing by Values at Levi Srauss. Enterprise Strategies. Organizational Governance. The Role of the Board. Role of the CEO. Roles of the Consultant.

13   Business-Unit/Level Strategies **13-1**

Learning Objectives. Profile: Motorola, Inc. Profile: Berbiglia Liquors. Positioning the Business. Distinguishing the Business. Porter's Generic Strategies. Strategies of Differentiation. Strategies of Scope. *Increasing Scope: Strategies for Growth.* Penetration Strategies. Product Development Strategies. Market Development Strategies. Geographical Expansion Strategies. Combined Factors. *Strategies for Redefining and Reducing Scope.* Defense and Renewal Strategies Retrenchment and Turnaround Strategies. Strategies for Aging and Declining Markets. *Conclusions.*

14   Strategies for Global Competition **14-1**

Learning Objectives. Profile: USX Corp. Profile: Ford Motor Co. What is Global Competition? International Strategies. Strategy Types. Strategy Patterns. *Entering International Markets.* Stages of Internationalization. *Global Trends and Risks.* World Scenarios. *Conclusions.*

15   Functional, Value Chain, and Quality Strategies **15-1**

Learning Objectives. Profile: 3M Corporation. Functional Strategies. The Value Chain. Quality Strategies. *R&D/Technology Strategies.* Technology Strategies. *New Product Development Strategies. Flexibility.*

16   Corporate and Multibusiness Strategies **16-1**

Learning Objectives. Profile: ITT Corp. Managing the Multibusiness Organization. Strategic Business-Units. Core Competencies vs. SBUs. Corporate-Level Processes. *Corporate Portfolio Models.* The Growth/Share Matrix. GE's Business Screen. Business Profile Matrix. Portfolio Models: A Critique. *Entering New Businesses: Diversification Strategies.* Entry Strategies. Acquisition-Related Strategies. Internal Development and Venture Strategies. Diversification and Performance. *Corporate Concentration and Restructuring Strategies.* Divestiture Strategies. Corporate Restructuring. *Conclusions.*

17   Strategic Alternatives and Decisions **17-1**

Learning Objectives. Profile: Should GE Sell NBC? Strategic Decision-Making. High-Velocity Environments. Decision Speed and Quality. Analytical vs. Political Decisions. Decision "Blind Spots." *Evaluating the Strategic Situation. Developing Strategic Alternatives.* The Process. *Evaluating Alternatives and Selecting a Strategy.* Evaluation of Alternatives. Selecting a Strategy. *Conclusions.*

18   The Strategic Infrastructure:
      Information and Planning Systems **18-1**

Learning Objectives. Profile: The President's Information System. Strategic Decision Support Systems. Strategic Information Needs. Strategic Information Sources. Environmental Scanning and Monitoring. Intelligence Information. Strategic Information Systems. *Strategic Planning Systems.* A System of Plans. Characteristics of Successful Systems. *Conclusions.*

19   Implementation and Detailed Planning **19-1**

Learning Objectives. Profile: AM International, Inc. Profile: Monsanto. Implementing Strategic Planning Processes. Phases in System Implementation. Measures of System Effectiveness. Problems and Pitfalls. *Implementing Strategic Decisions.* Key Implementation Tasks. Reward Systems. The Manager as an Organization Builder. *Implementing Strategic Plans.* The Plan Itself. The Plan's Process and Content. *Strategy and Structure Relationships.*

20   Strategic Evaluation and Control **20-1**

Learning Objectives. Profile: Office Depot. Profile: Mike Walsh and Union Pacific. Strategic Control. Basic Control Elements. Levels of Control. A Contemporary View of Strategic Control. Strategic Control Processes. *Measuring and Analyzing Performance.* Activity-Based Management. Economic Value Added. The Balanced Scorecard. Benchmarking. Corrective Action: When to Pull the Plug. *Strategic Audits.* Measures of Organizational Health. Strategy Audits. *Conclusions.*

21   Entrepreneurial Start-Up and
Small Business Strategies **21-1**

Learning Objectives. Profile: Nebraska Furniture Mart. Profile: Gateway 2000. Smaller Organizations. Types of Smaller Firms. *Internal New Ventures. Start-Up Ventures.* New Venture Strategies. New-Venture Problems. *Small Businesses.* Characteristics of Small Business. Small Business Strategy Formulation. How Small Businesses Plan. Problems of Small Businesses. Family Business. *Conclusion.*

22   Service, Not-for-Profit, and
Professional Applications **22-1**

Learning Objectives. Profile: The HMO Industry. Service Organizations. Role in the Economy. Types and Characteristics of Service Organizations. Types of Service Organizations. *Not-for-Profit Organizations.* Types and Characteristics of Not-for-Profit. Differences between NFPs and for-Profits. Strategic Management in NFPs. Pubic-Sector Management. *Professional Services Organizations. Service Sector Lessons.*

23   Strategic Management Trends and Directions **23-1**

Learning Objectives. Current State of the Art. Creating a Vision. Fostering Organizational Learning. Interorganizational Strategies. Flexible Planning Processes. Restructuring and Internal Growth. Strategic and Operational Harmony. Improved Strategy Frameworks. Better Information and Tools. Focus on Core Competencies and Competitive Advantage. *Emerging Trends.* Rewarding Srategic Performance. Development of Strategic Managers. Contingent Strategy Processes. Managing Global Integration. Strategies for NFPs and Services. Improved Performance Measures. Activity-Based Management. *As the Field Matures.* . . Practical, Contingent Research Data. Contributions from DSS/AI/ES. Sustaining Networks and Cooperation. Virtual Organizations. Hypercompetitive Markets. *Conclusions.*

APPENDICES:

A   Financial Ratios **A-1**

B   Strategic Planning Worksheet **B-1**

C   How to Value a Business **C-1**

Index **I-1**

STRATEGIC MANAGEMENT

Concepts, Processes, Decisions

Module
1

Strategic Management:
An Overview

LEARNING OBJECTIVES

After reading Module 1, you should be able to:

1. Define the five levels or types of strategies.
2. Understand that strategic management is undergoing significant changes.
3. Realize that strategic thinking, not analytical strategic planning, is the important variable.
4. Appreciate the differences and relationships between strategic and operational management.

Why is it that some organizations perennially seem to be more successful than others, typically leaving the competition in the dust? It may be, as one expert observes, that there are three types of people in this world—those who *make* things happen, those who *watch* things happen, and those who *wonder* what happened. Which are you? Time management expert Alan Lakein and the well-known entrepreneur Ted Turner have similar analogies. Lakein says you can either decide, drift, or drown; Turner says, "Do something! Lead, follow, or get out of the way!" A common element among the leaders, doers, movers, and shakers is the ability to make effective strategy and policy decisions. These organizations are also able to turn those decisions into reality—to implement them—and to operate the organization efficiently, as well. How they do it is what this book—and this course—is all about.

PROFILE

The Institute of Electrical and Electronic Engineers (IEEE)

In recent years, the IEEE has experienced a massive growth in membership, expanded to true worldwide status, substantially broadened the technologies it encompasses, and significantly broadened and improved the quality of services it provides to its membership. At the same time, other professional societies seem to be struggling to maintain members and to remain financially solvent. What has IEEE done differently?

For one thing, IEEE has developed a coherent strategy. The society's plan consists of clear and appropriate statements of the following:

1. Our Mission.
2. Our Organization and its Members.
3. The Environment.
4. Our Vision.
5. Our Goals.
6. Reaching Our Goals.

The plan consists of the essentials of a good strategic plan, and is described in sufficient specifics to make the plan meaningful. It addresses the key challenges and issues of today and the future, and has been shared with all members of the society; in fact, the society's strategic planning committee specifically solicited input and feedback from all members.[1]

---

[1] "A Strategy for the Future: The IEEE in the 21st Century," *The Institute* (July/August 1993), 8-9.

PROFILE   **Frances Hesselbein**

Frances Hesselbein is past Chief Executive Officer (CEO) of the Girl Scouts of America, and is currently President and CEO of the Peter F. Drucker Foundation for Nonprofit Management. She is widely-respected as a nonprofit manager, and is a sought after speaker on management, leadership, and strategy topics. In fact, Peter Drucker himself has singled her out as one of the country's best executives. So, what does Frances Hesselbein have to say? She offers several steps to successful strategic leadership, including the following:

- *Understanding the Environment.* The first step is understanding the environment—global to local. This includes identifying major trends and their implications for the organization, as well as understanding the strategic context for planning decisions.
- *Have a Clear Mission.* A powerful and shared purpose is essential.
- *Answer Fundamental Questions.* Borrowed from Drucker, there are three fundamental questions that successful organizations ask themselves and have a clear understanding of. They are:

  —What is our business?
  —Who is our customer?
  —What does the customer consider value?

- *Communicate a Vision.* Effective leaders have agendas and are results-oriented. They adopt new visions of what is desirable and possible, communicate their visions, and persuade others to commit to the achievement of the vision. The more committed to the vision the people become, the more eager, motivated, and powerful they become as a force for change and progress.

Hesselbein espouses other suggestions, but these are key *and* directly related to effective strategic management. And, as her experience shows, they tend to work in all types of organizations—nonprofit as well as profit-making.[2]

---

[2] Francis Hesselbein, "Driving Strategic Leadership Through Mission, Values, and Goals," *The Planning Forum Network*, 7, No. 6 (Summer 1994), 4.

STRATEGIC MANAGEMENT TODAY

Writers introducing *Business Week's* new feature, "Corporate Strategies," in 1978 posed the question, "What is the business concept that has become the major thrust and emphasis in the management of U.S. corporations today?" Their answer was *strategic planning*, and their reason: "the discipline helps corporate officers anticipate and cope with a variety of forces beyond their operating control."[3]

While we saw tremendous growth in strategic planning in the 60s and 70s, the 80s have seen a reaction to this growth. A number of companies reduced their strategic planning staffs, creating the appearance of a decline in the field. It became "in" to say that strategic planning was "out"—"dead"—that this buzz-phrase had come and gone, and now was on the decline. Perhaps as a reaction to its earlier growth, pundits told the story of how strategic planning had even penetrated the Kremlin! In fact, at one May Day parade a few years ago, Mikhail Gorbachev and his staff were reviewing the latest Soviet weapons as they paraded by the reviewing stand. The weapons grew steadily more threatening; beginning with small arms, followed in order by jeeps, howitzers, combat vehicles, tanks, tactical missiles, intermediate-range missiles, ICBMs, and finally multiple-warhead ICBMs. Lastly, to everyone's confusion, came a cadre of fifty or so men in suits, carrying briefcases. Who were these people; the KGB? No, they were the new strategic planners; everyone *knows* how much damage *they* can do!

Skeptics of strategic planning would point out that the above story was very apropos—the Soviet Union fell apart a few years later. But is strategic planning the cause? Is strategic planning in decline? Nothing could be further from the truth; in fact, the old adage, "failing to plan is like planning to fail," still holds.[4] But it has changed, and changed significantly in recent years. We do have fewer strategic planners today in many organizations, just as we have fewer mainframe computer operators. But has computing declined? No, it has been decentralized. Strategic planning has also been decentralized and dispersed throughout the organization, with many of its functions being performed by the people who should have been doing them all along—line managers and their immediate staffs.

Managers today realize that every organization is in a constant process of change. The message is clear: "Be the best or go out of business. It is a cruel world with no medals for second place." So, how can organizations survive in today's turbulent environment? They must do more than "do things right." Vi-

---

[3] "Publishers Memo," *Business Week* (January 9, 1978), 5.

[4] Yut Keong Kan, "You and Your Business: Failing to Plan is Like Planning to Fail," *Sunday Times* (Singapore, May 29, 1994), 5.

tally important is "doing the right things," and only then concentrating on doing them well.[5]

Today, line managers, the people who run the companies, are themselves becoming more deeply involved in *strategic decisions*. As an example, strategic decision-making is the focus of a month-long executive development seminar AT&T conducts for all of its future top managers. Why? The program coordinator explains that strategic decision-making is "the most crucial aspect of managing, particularly in higher-level positions where the kinds of decisions a manager is called upon to make usually are complex and multifaceted."[6] The 1984 breakup of the Bell System—obviously a major strategic move—reinforces the need for such training.

Writers, such as Tom Peters, delight in making disparaging remarks about strategic planning, citing as an example Henry Mintzberg's new book, *The Rise and Fall of Strategic Planning*.[7] But despite the book's title, Mintzberg's message is *not* that planning has died, but that certain approaches to strategy formation are ineffective. Mintzberg points out that analytically-oriented strategic planning is ineffective, but *strategic thinking* is essential. Strategic thinking is about synthesis, not analysis, and involves intuition and creativity. Strategy formation does not result from analysis; it is in fact the synthesis of a vision. But the role of analysis is to provide input into strategy development and to assess the results. The role of analytic planning is largely to translate intended strategies into realized ones. In other words, strategic *planning follows* strategy formation, which demands synthesis, intuition, and creativity. Analysis can help us understand changes and the possible results of strategy alternatives. Thus, what has died is a strategic planning process devoid of synthesis and strategic thinking.[8]

These examples reflect the changing role of *strategic management* (of which strategic decision-making and planning are a part) and typify what is happening in business. Strategic management is in a refinement phase, similar to what happened with operations management a generation ago, management science in the 1950s and 60s, and human resource management in the 60s and 70s. According to Michael Kami (a pioneer and well-known consultant in strategic planning), as recently as 1952 only two companies did any type of formal strategic plan-

[5] R. Christopher Taylor, "Coping With a Changing Agenda," *Planning Review*, 20, No. 5 (September/October 1992), 5.

[6] "Where Will All the Leaders Come From?" *Bell Telephone Magazine*, 6 (1980), 2.

[7] Tom Peters, "On Excellence: Book Shows Strategic Planning Has Become Today's Dinosaur," *Lincoln Journal* (April 6, 1994), 4.

[8] Henry Mintzberg, *The Rise and Fall of Strategic Planning* (New York, NY: The Free Press, 1994).

ning: General Electric and IBM.[9] The technique began to grow rapidly during the late 1960s, and since then has been installed as a formal management process in most large companies and in many medium-sized and smaller companies.[10] Today, the *practice* of strategic management (its use in organizations) is in some ways ahead of the *teaching* of its concepts in most colleges and universities. Nonetheless, students of management wanting to adequately prepare for the future should learn all they can about the concepts and practice of strategic management.

TYPES OF STRATEGIES

Organizations, particularly multidivisional, multinational corporations, are complex entities. Management—strategic and operational—of these complex entities is a complicated and difficult task. As the saying goes, for every complex problem there is a simple solution, and it's almost always wrong. Strategic management is not a simple matter. Every organization must address several levels, types, or areas of strategic management. For example, each organization has to determine its place in society: what its contribution will be, which sector of the economy it will be part of, whether to be profit or not for profit, and so on. Decisions must be made regarding how the firm will compete in its market or markets. Also, the firm must decide how the functional areas of the business need to be managed to support its market strategy most effectively and efficiently. Along with this, strategic guidelines must be developed to ensure that the firm's line, or operating, management manufactures and delivers the products and services in a cost-effective manner. For firms competing in more than one business area or market, a strategy of integration and interrelationships between the various businesses must be developed. Finally, firms need a strategy for dealing with other firms on a competitive, cooperative, or collective basis. Various authors have described these areas, types, or levels of strategies differently, but the essential issues can be addressed using five categories: an enterprise strategy, an interorganizational strategy, a corporate-level strategy, a business-unit strategy, and functional/operational strategies, as described in Table 1.1.

---

[9] Michael Kami, *Strategic Planning for Changing Times* (Dayton, OH: Cassette Recording Co., 1984).

[10] William D. Guth, ed., *Handbook of Business Strategy* (Boston, MA: Warren, Gorham & Lamont, 1985), vii.

Table 1.1 Strategy Types

Strategy	*Applies to*	*Focus*
Enterprise	All organizations	Mission, purpose, role in society
Interorganizational	Relationships with outside organizations	Competitive, cooperative, and collective behavior
Corporate	Multibusiness organizations	Which businesses and their interrelationships
Business Unit	All organizations	How to compete most effectively
Functional/Operating	All organizations	Functional and operational business-unit support

Enterprise Strategy

Every organization, regardless of size or sector of the economy, has an institutional or societal-role strategy. This strategy may not be implicitly or formally stated, but it exists nevertheless. Called "enterprise" strategy by Ansoff,[11] this strategy concerns the organization's mission, purpose, and role in society. It addresses questions, such as: Why does this organization exist? What is it attempting to provide to society? What sector(s) of the economy is it part of? How does it function in society as a not-for-profit or profit-making firm, in a regulated or unregulated industry? What form of ownership exists? Who comprises the board of directors?

The firm's enterprise strategy also influences its relationships with its environment, particularly its relationships with those who have an interest in what the organization does and how it conducts its business. Sometimes called "stakeholders" (having a stake in the firm), these include investors, creditors, suppliers, customers, management, employees, and local governments and citizens, to name a few. One reason organizations are regulated to various degrees is that the government has accepted the role of representing the interests of the relatively powerless small stakeholders in the firm.

---

[11] H.I. Ansoff, "The Changing Shape of the Strategic Problem," paper presented at a special conference on Business Policy and Planning Research: The State of the Art (Pittsburgh, PA: May 1977).

An enterprise needs a clear, unambiguous concept of its mission and purpose—its role in society—to guide the formation of corporate policies and strategies in other areas. Thus, the enterprise strategy acts as a framework or envelope
within which other, more specific types of strategies will operate. For example,
the 1982 antitrust agreement between AT&T and the Justice Department significantly changed the societal role of that organization—from a regulated provider
of local and long-distance telephone service and equipment to an unregulated,
high-technology provider of long-distance voice and data communication services, equipment, and anything else it wishes to provide. AT&T's enterprise
strategy guided it in the decisions to accept a relatively unregulated growth opportunity while giving up the regulated, lower-profit, local phone businesses.

Interorganizational Strategy

Interorganizational strategy is concerned with the types of relationships that exist
between the organization in question and outside organizations, such as partners,
competitors, suppliers, customers, and associations. Most writers have not
singled-out interorganizational strategy as a separate area of focus, concentrating
instead on the types of substrategies making up the firm's interorganizational
strategy. For example, relationships with competitors can be treated as a business
unit strategy, or business unit relationships with outside firms could be considered as corporate strategies. But most interorganizational strategies—collective,
cooperative, joint ventures, networks, alliances, and the like—have typically been
considered as ad hoc strategies, not necessarily related to the firm's overall strategic framework.

Faced with intensifying competitive pressure, globalization, and other challenges, many firms are making changes in all strategy areas to improve their performance. For example, many are now pursuing *cooperative* actions with other
firms. By trying to affect the environment of the business through cooperative
advertising, lobbying, and the like, firms hope to create a more favorable external environment for themselves. For example, many industries have trade groups
which lobby for tax relief, legislation, trade restrictions, or loan guarantees.[12]

Another interorganizational strategy involves *collective* behavior with outside
businesses. For example, many firms are entering into joint ventures, alliances,
or networks to improve their performance, with competitors as well as noncompetitors. Businesses engaging in outsourcing actions as well as just-in-time
supplier relationships have highly-developed interorganizational strategies.

---

[12] Charles J. Fombrun, "Envisioning Strategic Change," in P. Shrivastava, A. Huff, and
J. Dutton, eds., *Advances in Strategic Management*, Vol. 9 (Greenwich, CT: JAI Press,
1993), 157.

Lastly, *competitive* behavior in the form of rivalry, whether it be "civil" or "cutthroat" is a manifestation of an interorganizational strategy. Most competitive relationships will be treated in specifics under business level strategies.

Corporate Strategy

Corporate strategy addresses the questions: What set of businesses should the firm compete in? and How should they be integrated? While this type of strategy is most applicable to organizations competing in more than one market—the multibusiness firm—in a sense it applies to all firms. That is, the single-business firm is pursuing a corporate-level strategy by choosing to compete in only one business, rather than several.

The primary concerns of corporate strategy are: What should the firm's "portfolio" of businesses be, now and in the future? How do the businesses complement or reinforce one another, and how are corporate-level resources to be allocated to the various business units? Corporate-level strategy deals with questions of diversification, acquisition/divestiture, and the starting of new ventures or divisions, for example. Its basic concern is with the current and future rationale for deciding which businesses comprise the total corporation. Techniques helpful in developing corporate-level strategies will be discussed in a later module.

Business-Unit Strategy

For single-business companies and for each business unit or market comprising the multibusiness corporate portfolio, a strategy must be developed focusing on how to compete in that product or market or industry segment. The focus of business-unit strategy is on what is appropriate for the product's stage in the life cycle, on the competitive environment, on the firm's distinctive competencies to develop or pursue, and on the niches it should seek, as well as on how to integrate the various functional areas of the business (notably, product design, manufacturing, and marketing) to produce a competitive advantage. The focus is also on the relative emphasis placed on each functional area and the level of resources each one is allocated. Numerous strategic factors important to business-unit success are presented in later modules.

Functional and Operations Strategies

The success of the individual business strategy depends not only on how well the firm positions itself and competes in the given market segment, but also on how well it coordinates the various functions and operations required to design, manufacture, market, deliver, and support the product or service. Functional strategy involves what should be done in each of the key functional areas, given the relative emphasis placed on them and the resources allocated to each. For example, if the firm's business-unit strategy is to broaden its offerings in a particular market, how should the products complement one another with regard to cost, quality, features, and other factors? If a strategy of expanding market share is to be followed, will the marketing strategy involve increased advertising? Will quantity discounts, expansion of outlets, or the use of manufacturers representatives be necessary? How will this strategy affect the manufacturing, distribution, and finance functions?

Operations strategies also are needed to manage operating units and line areas, such as manufacturing plants, sales offices, retail outlets, and parts and distribution warehouses, in a cost-effective manner. At both the functional and operating levels, the major emphasis is on maximizing resource productivity by capitalizing on any possible synergies and distinctive competencies that the firm may possess. The goal is to support the business-unit, corporate, and enterprise strategies. At the corporate level, management, and strategies, tend to be financially oriented; at the business-unit level, strategies are often marketing oriented. At the functional and operations levels, these strategies are implemented, and it is here that the people, for example, the R&D, sales, manufacturing, and plant managers, are found who many times make the difference in whether or not a higher-level strategy will be successful.

ORGANIZATIONAL PLANNING PROCESSES

A strategic planning system (SPS) is a structured way of formulating, implementing, and controlling the firm's strategies. Strategic planning systems are formalized approaches for doing the job of strategic planning. While some may be less structured and less formal than others, they still provide management with a *systematic approach* to planning.

One of the important decisions management must make is how formal this systematic approach should be. Research has shown that tailor-made planning systems tend to be the most effective. However, the design and operation of the planning system must be consistent with the organization's structure and processes in general. In addition, planning systems typically cannot be transplanted from one firm to another, but must be adapted to the needs of each firm.

Strategic, Tactical, and Operational Planning

The difference between strategic and operational planning, that of the future (strategic) versus the short-term (operational), is discussed in this module. In addition, planning is done at the tactical, scheduling, and dispatching levels. Table 1.2 illustrates the relationships between the four major levels of planning.

Table 1.2 Relationships between Planning Levels

Strategic planning

> Which business should the firm be in?
>
> How should they be financed?
>
> How should scarce resources be allocated across business sectors?

Tactical planning

> What are the optimal patterns of capital investment and divestment for implementing some longer-range plan?
>
> What decisions about facility location, expansion, or shutdown will maximize profitability?
>
> What products should be added to or deleted from the product line?
>
> What is the optimal product pricing pattern?

Operations planning

> What is the optimal operating plan (raw material acquisition, product sources, inventory levels, distribution system configuration, route and mode of distribution, and so on) to meet specified system objectives, consistent with some longer-term plan, with existing facilities in the next planning period (e.g., month, quarter, year)?
>
> What is the best operating plan on which to base plans for production and dispatch?

Scheduling and dispatching

> What specific operations or sequences of operations should be performed with which existing facilities, to meet specified output requirements in the next operational period (for example, hour, day, week)?

Source: Adapted from D.S. Hirshfield, "From the Shadows," *Interfaces*, 13, No. 2 (April 1983), 74. Copyright 1983 The Institute of Management Sciences.

Strategic planning typically involves issues significantly affected by elements in the organization's external environment. It also includes decisions that can greatly change the character or direction of the organization.[13] It deals with what the firm is to be in the future, reflecting the firm's role in the environment, and includes what businesses the firm should be in, how they should be financed, and how scarce resources should be allocated.

Tactical planning deals with the implementation and support of longer-range (strategic) plans. It includes capital budgeting, facility expansion or shut down, price setting, and product-line and market development decisions. Tactical plan-

---

[13] W.R. King and D.I. Cleland, *Strategic Planning and Policy* (New York, NY: Van Nostrand Reinhold, 1978), D9.

ning is often concerned primarily with future facilities or product planning, and its time horizon is related to the lead time for new, major facilities or products.

Operational planning allocates tasks to specific existing facilities to achieve particular objectives in each planning period.

The most specific form of planning, *scheduling and dispatching*, involves the assignment and sequencing of specific existing resources (people, machines, raw materials, and so forth) to manufacture or deliver given quantities of products, consistent with a longer-interval operating plan (such as a quarterly operations plan).

As can be seen in Table 1.2, strategic planning involves the greatest scope and the least specificity or detail, while the opposite is true for scheduling and dispatching.

People at all levels of the organization have strategic, tactical, and operational views of the environment within which they work. As shown in Figure 1.1, upper-level management's concerns are primarily long range and strategic, but management at this level must also think in terms of tactical and operational matters. Middle-level managers' concerns are primarily medium range and tactical, while at lower levels, the emphasis is primarily short range and operational. Therefore, each level of the organization has strategic, tactical, and operational concerns, but the relative proportion devoted to each and their time horizon varies by level.

Statements of Strategy

Differences of opinion exist on how explicitly an organization's strategies should be stated and how widely they should be disseminated. Researchers have found that firms may operate with several versions of a strategy, some widely publicized and some confidential. For example, a firm may employ the following:

1. *Corporate strategy for the annual report.* This is usually a "sterilized" and edited version, intended to convey to shareholders a sense of direction and an assurance that management knows where it wants to take the company.
2. *Corporate strategy for the board of directors, financial analysts, and middle managers.* More explicit than the previous version, this is still a relatively simple, camouflaged statement of strategy.
3. *Corporate strategy for top management.* Since the CEO needs top management's support, they are usually privy to and participate in a full discussion of potential strategic moves and countermoves by the firm.

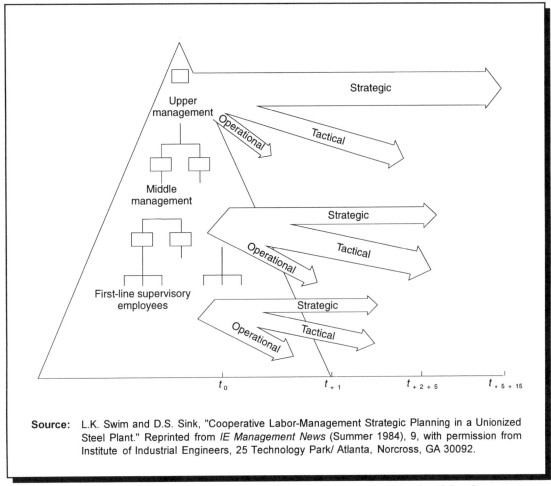

Source: L.K. Swim and D.S. Sink, "Cooperative Labor-Management Strategic Planning in a Unionized Steel Plant." Reprinted from *IE Management News* (Summer 1984), 9, with permission from Institute of Industrial Engineers, 25 Technology Park/ Atlanta, Norcross, GA 30092.

Figure 1.1   Strategic, Tactical, and Operational Views at Various Organizational Levels

4. *The CEO's private corporate strategy.* If the CEO is a strategic thinker, he or she may be mulling over a range of strategic moves that are, as yet, disclosed to almost no one.[14]

---

[14] Arnoldo Hax and N.S. Majluf, *The Strategy Concept and Process* (Englewood Cliffs, NJ: Prentice-Hall, 1991), 7-8.

From this breakout, one can see the CEO's strong influence in creating the vision and shaping the strategies of the company. The CEO also controls the flow of information and the degree of participation in the process.

STRATEGIC VERSUS OPERATING MANAGEMENT

Most of us are more aware of the operational than of the strategic aspects of a business. Operating management deals with the ongoing, day-to-day "operations" of the business. It involves producing, marketing, and selling the goods and services the organization provides. The organization chart, management information system, plant management, supervisory activities, sales meetings, and other functions are all focused on delivery of the firm's goods and services as efficiently as possible. Thus, when you "see" the organization, you see it *operating*, and you see the structure, systems, procedures, and facilities employed to permit it to operate as efficiently as possible.

On the other hand, the strategic function of the organization is more difficult to observe. The strategic function may be performed by some of the same people, but is separate and distinct from the operating function. Strategy is typically not reflected on the organization chart, nor can it be seen by studying operating systems and procedures, departments, plants, and facilities. However, it is linked to operations in that its main purpose is to ensure that the organization is capitalizing on its comparative advantages and distinctive competencies to take advantage of any opportunities the environment may provide, thus creating a competitive advantage. To accomplish this end, all of the operating elements of the organization must function *effectively*, the organization must "do the right things," as well as *efficiently*, "doing things right." Effectiveness means that the firm is producing the goods and services that the market wants; efficiency merely means that the firm is producing its goods and services at minimum cost. As an illustration of the relative importance of these two management responsibilities, ask yourself the following question: What good is it to be an efficient producer of Edsels? On the other hand, for seventeen years, Polaroid held an exclusive patent on the instant camera. How critical is efficiency when you have a monopoly on a product? In certain types of markets and stages of the product life cycle, efficiency may be *very* important and may, in fact, constitute a strategy—that of being the lowest-cost producer, as is discussed later.

As shown in Figure 1.2, the strategy is the primary determinant of success or failure in fulfilling the mission and achieving the organization's goals and objectives. The choice of strategy is based on comparative advantages and distinctive competencies of the firm (its strengths) and provides a framework or envelope for the effective and efficient tactics and operations necessary to carry out the strategy.

To summarize, remember that there are two essential areas of management responsibility: strategic management and operating management. Neither can be

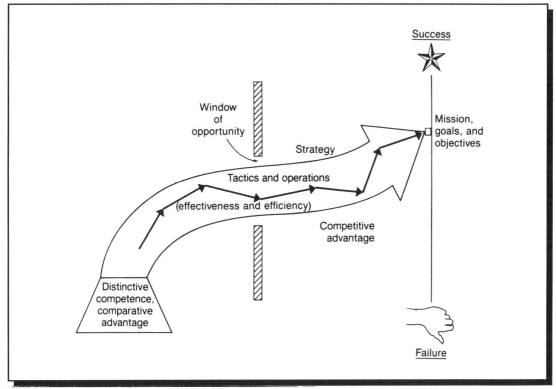

Figure 1.2 **Strategy is the Primary Determinant of Success or Failure**

neglected and they complement one another. However, our concern here is primarily with the strategic element.

The Environmental Interface

In the previous discussion, strategic management was defined as effectively matching or fitting the organization to its environment. Actually, the strategic process is an attempt to achieve a productive fit between the organization's *external* environment (economic, competitive, social, political/legal, technological) and its *internal* situation (structure, systems and procedures, climate, and physical, financial, technical, and human resources). This is shown schematically in Figure 1.3. In doing this, the organization must consider the threats and opportunities present in the external environment, and the strengths and weaknesses present internally.

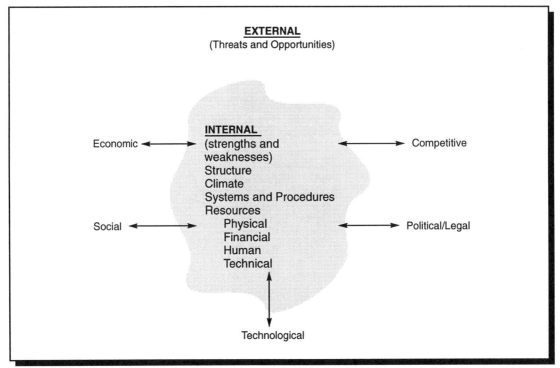

Figure 1.3 The Environmental Fit

The concept of environmental fit implies that there are certain things the organization may want to accomplish, but may not be able to or may choose not to, because of internal weaknesses or external risks. The strategic manager must carefully assess the marketplace, the competition, laws and regulations, taxes and interest rates, the business cycle, customer needs and desires, and any other pertinent factors in an attempt to locate opportunities for the organization. At the same time, it must be recognized that opportunities and threats often are opposite sides of the same coin; any change in the environment *at the same time* presents opportunities and threats. No opportunity is risk free; the strategic manager must weigh the risks against the rewards of any potential action. In addition, opportunities not recognized or seized by your firm may be taken by your competitors, turning them into very real threats. Thus, timing is important; opportunities must be recognized and taken advantage of when appropriate, and not too early or too late. Opportunities decay with time; on the other hand, an idea whose time has not yet come is not a viable opportunity.

Through planning, the firm ideally tries to *induce* change, or cause changes to occur that will put the organization in a relatively better position vis-à-vis the competition. Thus, the firm seizes or creates opportunity for itself and creates a threat for the competition, forcing the competition to react, much as Philip

Morris did by applying advanced marketing techniques to its Miller Beer subsidiary. The firm does not always have this luxury, however, but nonetheless should strive to *control* change, or through advance planning, have some influence over what happens, even though the firm may not have induced the change. As a minimum, the organization must be able to *react* effectively to changes over which it has no influence or control. This is a decidedly less desirable situation for the firm.

What the organization is able to do in the way of seizing opportunities or responding to threats depends on its internal strengths and weaknesses. It must *realistically* assess its management skills and depth, finances, production facilities, marketing abilities, technological base, structure and systems—in other words, perform a resource audit—to determine what it can or cannot do. Not all things are possible. For example, Braniff chose to expand rapidly after airlines were deregulated. However, the carrier's accompanying increases in fixed and operating costs greatly exceeded the added revenues and forced the company into bankruptcy. IBM, however, with its superior resources, was able to enter the microcomputer market and successfully move into a leadership position in a very short time.

In general, management should strive to build on, improve, and broaden its strengths and reduce its weaknesses. This usually is the result of effective strategic management and opens the door for a broader range of strategic alternatives in the future. In general, those who succeed seem to be those who select a niche in the market and build from there.

VALUE OF STRATEGIC MANAGEMENT

We have made a case, conceptually at least, that strategic management is important to the success of a company, and becomes more important as organizations and their environments become more complex. The bottom line, however, is whether or not the increased effort expended on strategic management can be shown to produce improved performance. Do firms that plan experience better levels of sales, growth, return on investment, or earnings?

This is a difficult question to answer. First of all, organizations may show mixed results depending on the criteria selected to measure performance: sales might be increasing while ROI decreases, growth rate might be diminishing while ROI and earnings improve, and so on. Also the company's performance is subject to a number of nonstrategic—or operating—factors, such as the effectiveness of its sales force, manufacturing efficiencies, accounting policies, and performance of its people. In addition, the economy, competitive actions, interest rates, tax rates, accidents (such as airplane crashes), acts of nature, product safety concerns (such as with nuclear reactors and Tylenol), and other environmental influences can significantly affect performance.

However, strategic management involves forecasting and developing an effective fit with the environment. Firms practicing strategic management should be in a better position to forecast and cope with (or at least react to) the types of environmental conditions just mentioned. So they should exhibit better performance, at least on the average and in the long run. What do the studies tell us?

Strategic Planning Pays

A number of early studies indicate that strategic planning pays. Using a number of commonly accepted criteria, most of these studies examined the performances of companies in various industries. Companies using formal planning systems or approaches were compared with companies that did not. A study by Thune and House, for example, matched eighteen medium-to-large companies on the basis of industry, size, and growth rate.[15] One member of each pair used formal planning systems and one did not. Over the seven years of the study, the formal planners significantly outperformed the informal planners in every area measured—sales growth, earnings per share, stock price, return on equity, and ROI. In addition, those adopting formal systems for the first time significantly bettered their previous performance in the areas observed—sales, earnings per share, and stock price. A study by Herold extended the drug and chemical portion of the Thune and House study for four more years and found similar results.[16] In fact, formal planners increased their lead over the others.

Studies by Ansoff et. al.,[17] Karger and Malik,[18] and Wood and LaForge[19] produced further indications that formal planners outperform the others in a variety of industries.

Some of the more recent studies began to investigate types and degrees of sophistication of planning systems, not just the oversimplified formal versus informal dichotomy. Several of these studies showed the degree of formality and comprehensiveness of the planning system to be related to improved performance measures.

---

[15] Stanley Thune and R. House, "Where Long-Range Planning Pays Off," *Business Horizons* (August 1970), 81-87.

[16] D.M. Herold, "Long-Range Planning and Organizational Performance: A Cross-Validation Study," *Academy of Management Journal* (March 1972), 91-102.

[17] H.I. Ansoff, J. Avner, R.G. Brandenburg, F.E. Portner, and R. Radosevich, *Acquisition Behavior of U.S. Manufacturing Firms, 1946-65* (Nashville, TN: Vanderbilt University Press, 1971).

[18] Delmar W. Karger and E.A. Malik, "Long-Range Planning and Organizational Performance," *Long-Range Planning* (December 1975), 63.

[19] D.R. Wood, Jr. and R.L. LaForge, "The Impact of Comprehensive Planning on Financial Performance," *Academy of Management Journal* (September 1979), 516-26.

A 1994 investigation by Hart and Banbury found that the *process* through which strategy is formed holds the potential for competitive advantage; that is, the strategy process can give the business a "leg-up" on competition. Specifically, the greater the skill the firm has in developing strategies in different modes (or conditions), the higher the firm's performance. Further, the benefits of this capability seem to make the most difference for larger firms operating in turbulent environments—where they're most beneficial. Smaller firms in more stable environments do not benefit as much from strategy-making process capability.[20]

Strategic Planning Doesn't Always Pay

On the other hand, a few of the early studies cast doubt on the value of formal planning. Rue and Fulmer found that planning paid off in certain industries but not in others, and paid off more for larger firms than for smaller ones.[21] In durable goods industries, manufacturers using formal planning outperformed the others in each case; however, the reverse was true in service industries. Whether the effect of planning varies from manufacturing to service industries, or whether the three-year study produced erroneous results is open to question. However, a Canadian study by Sheehan found that growth rate declined as the degree of planning increased from nonplanners to low, medium, then high.[22] It should be noted that Sheehan used growth rate alone as a performance measure; it may well be that firm size was an overriding factor, because, for example, small firms tend to have higher-percentage growth rates and employ less formal planning systems than do their larger counterparts. Thus, the results of the Sheehan study are somewhat open to question.

Several of the late studies showed no consistent relationship between planning measures and performance, and one study found a *negative* relationship between a plan's level of comprehensiveness and performance, as measured by a five- year return on assets and sales growth. This research by Fredrickson and Mitchell studied the comprehensiveness versus performance relationship under varying environments. Specifically, comprehensive approaches did not lead to improved performance under uncertain environmental conditions, but they did

[20] S. Hart and C. Banbury, "How Strategy-Making Processes Can Make a Difference," *Strategic Management Journal*, 15, No. 4, (May 1994), 251.

[21] L.W. Rue and R.M. Fulmer, "Is Long-Range Planning Profitable?" *Academy of Management Proceedings* (1973), 66-73.

[22] G.A. Sheehan, "Long-Range Planning and Its Relationship to Firm Size, Firm Growth, and Firm Growth Variability," Ph.D. dissertation (University of Western Ontario, 1975).

in relatively certain environments.[23] To add additional fuel to the controversy, however, several just-completed studies have found that high performers in fast-changing environments tend to use more thorough, structured approaches. These contemporary results will be discussed in more detail later.

What Have We Learned?

We have not proved conclusively that planning pays, but only that most well-conducted research studies suggest that planning pays. Even those studies did not *prove* that planning improved performance, but only that the two are correlated. It could be just as likely that high performers have the resources and time to engage in strategic planning, although the Thune and House, and Herold studies would suggest otherwise. If better-controlled studies can more closely identify the planning-performance link, a stronger case will emerge for the value of planning.

In addition, many studies largely dealt with formal versus informal planners, *not* planners versus nonplanners, as one might mistakenly conclude. "Every business enterprise from the smallest partnership to the largest corporation has a planning process. It may be informal and unstructured, but planning must be done if rational decisions are to be made. The mechanics reflect the nature of the industry, its management style, and systems peculiar to individual companies."[24] So the comparison is *how*, not *whether*, planning is done. Further, many formal planning systems serve as a means for *implementing* rather than *formulating* strategy; therefore, strategy formulation still may occur on an informal basis in firms utilizing a formal planning system. If this is the case, the studies of formal versus informal planning have merely shown that more systematized *implementation* of strategies tends to yield better performance—a conclusion worth noting on its own.

Other writers have reported a vague discontent with strategic planning among top managers. The managers question the value added by strategic planning processes that are increasingly more time-consuming and sophisticated. J. Quincy Hunsicker, of the management consulting firm McKinsey & Company, observes that top management is most frustrated by the "disproportion between the time and money expended on the strategic planning effort and the substantive

[23] J.W. Fredrickson and T.R. Mitchell, "Strategic Decision Processes: Comprehensiveness and Performance in an Industry with an Unstable Environment," *Academy of Management Journal*, 27 (1984), 399-432.

[24] D.R. Welsh and R.W. Lee, "Adapting Systems to Cope with Multiple Futures," *Management Focus*, 26, No. 1 (January/February 1979), 6.

value of the resulting strategies."[25] This should not be surprising since top management is more directly involved in strategy formulation than in strategy implementation, and formal planning aids implementation more than it assists in formulation.

Finally, most of the studies focused on "bottom-line" measures—profits, growth, and so on—measures which are subject to a variety of powerful influences in addition to planning systems and approaches. In addition, most firms today "plan;" any simple planner versus nonplanner dichotomy has long since vanished, forcing researchers to look for other factors. The evaluation measure should probably *not* be firm performance, but should be the following:

1. The *development* of high-quality *strategies*, regardless of the type of system employed.
2. The *appropriateness* of the planning *system*, given the firm's industry, size, diversification, and the like.

In sum, the deciding factor is the *quality* of the strategies implemented by the firm, not the degree of formalization of the planning process. It is reasonable to conclude that larger, more complex firms are likely to require a more formalized planning process, even if it is directed primarily toward the implementation of strategies. On the other hand, if increasing formalization of any step of the process, formulation or implementation, causes the firm to become less flexible and less responsive to a dynamic environment, the firm will be defeating the very purpose of strategic management; that is, achieving a beneficial fit with the environment. More *formalized* planning is not necessarily more *effective* planning, although formalization tends to ensure that the process will not be ignored.

Lastly, remember that the concept behind strategic management is quite simple. We are merely seeking the answers to four questions:

1. Where are we now?
2. Where would we like to be in the future?
3. What is the best way to get there?
4. How much can we afford to spend on the trip?

These questions and the strategy process will be addressed fully in subsequent modules.

---

[25] J. Quincy Hunsicker, "The Malaise of Strategic Planning," *Management Review* (March 1980).

Module
2

Strategic Management:
What it is and How it Developed

LEARNING OBJECTIVES

After reading Module 2, you should be able to:

1. Define and understand strategic management and its purpose.
2. Understand the elements, components, and analysis required for effective strategic management.
3. Describe the reasons for increasing strategic management and planning by organizations.

WHAT IS STRATEGIC MANAGEMENT?

Conceptually, strategic planning is very simple. Stripped of its complexities, a strategy consists of the *means* an organization chooses to move it from point A (where it is now) to point B (where it must be at some time in the future). As shown in Figure 2.1, the organization must first assess where it is at present. In reality, this step is not so simple; "where we are" includes defining the market; the industry; the competitors; our resources, strengths, and weaknesses; technology; economic factors; customer needs and preferences; demographics; international effects; regulatory influences; and a host of other factors. Determining "where we must be" and "when we must be there" is even more difficult, because it requires us to predict changes in all of the previously mentioned factors. Choosing the "best way to get from A to B" is obviously a judgmental matter, and is only as good as our ability to assess points A and B.

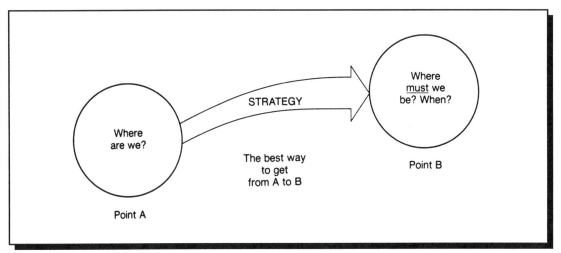

Figure 2.1 The Essence of Strategy

A continuing difficulty in teaching students about strategy is the proliferation of the term—almost everything today is "strategic." When a term achieves "buzz-word" status, it tends to lose precise meaning. With this problem in mind, Arnoldo C. Hax of MIT set out to go back to the fundamentals and to provide basic definitions of strategic management. He states that the concept of strategy embraces the overall purpose of the organization and has the ultimate objective of addressing stakeholder benefits—linking the firm to its stakeholders.[1] Hax states that six "critical dimensions" must be included in any definition of the concept of strategy. Strategy, then:

1. Is the coherent, unifying, and integrative pattern of decisions a firm makes.
2. Determines and reveals the organization's purpose in terms of its long-term objectives, action programs, and resource allocation priorities.
3. Selects the businesses the organization is in or is considering entering.
4. Is the attempt to achieve a long-term sustainable advantage in each of a firm's businesses by responding properly to both the environmental opportunities and threats and the strengths and weaknesses of the organization.
5. Engages all the hierarchical levels of the firm—corporate, business, and functional.
6. Defines the nature of the economic and non-economic contributions the firm intends to make to its stakeholders.[2]

From a practitioner's perspective, Alan Smith, Executive Vice President of General Motors, sees the focus of strategic management as a method to "help you prepare for unforeseen opportunities as well as adversity—rather than to give you a neat and clean blueprint based on past and current strengths and successes."[3]

Versus Strategic Planning and Long-Range Planning

In the previous discussion, the terms *strategic management* and *strategic planning* were used as if they were interchangeable. While they are related, in reality there are differences between them. Strategic planning describes the *periodic* activities undertaken by organizations to cope with changes in their *external* environments. Strategic management is a *continuous* process that involves attempts to match or fit the organization with its changing environment in the most advantageous way possible. It clearly includes adapting the organization itself (via internal changes) to fit the external environment.

In this light, strategic management is a broader, more encompassing concept than is strategic planning. Strategic management focuses on strategic decisions—whenever they are required—as well as on the strategic planning required to put

[1] Arnoldo Hax, "Redefining the Concept of Strategy and the Strategy Formulation Process," *Planning Review*, 18, No. 3 (May/June 1990), 34.

[2] Arnoldo Hax and N.S. Majluf, *The Strategy Concept and Process* (Englewood Cliffs, NJ: Prentice-Hall, 1991), 6.

[3] "Strategic Planning at General Motors," *The Planning Forum Network*, 1, No. 2 (March 1989), 1.

them into practice. Thus, strategic management represents the intersection, or marriage, of organization theory, microeconomics (the theory of the firm), and industrial organization. Organization theory joins the roles of individuals and the goals of the organization at the enterprise level. Theory of the firm, in turn, brings goal-oriented enterprises together at the market level. Strategic management deals with both the behavior of the organization within its external market *and* its internal roles, processes, structure, and decisions, to enable the organization to function as best it can within that external environment.[4]

Many people use the terms *strategic management*, *strategic planning*, and *long-range planning* interchangeably. This is unfortunate. Just as management consists of much more than planning, strategic management encompasses more than strategic planning.

Strategic planning involves formulating and evaluating alternative strategies, selecting a strategy, and developing detailed plans for putting the strategy into practice. In contrast, strategic management, as a minimum, includes strategic planning *and* strategic control, because plans at any level—operating management, or strategic—are not likely to be accomplished without effective controls. *Strategic control*, then, consists of ensuring that the chosen strategy is being implemented properly and that it is producing the desired results. Plans without effective controls are like a ship without a navigator; the captain may plan to sail from point A to point B, but the navigation process (controlling) is what actually gets him or her there. Controlling is the process of comparing actual conditions with planned conditions, analyzing the differences, and making necessary changes.

Long-range planning, planning for events beyond the current quarter or year, is not synonymous with strategic management (or strategic planning, for that matter). Certain strategic actions and reactions can be relatively short range and may include more than just planning aspects. Furthermore, not all long-range planning is strategic. It is perfectly reasonable to have long-range operating or technical plans that are not strategic. As an example of this distinction, several years ago, Bendix attempted to acquire Martin-Marietta. As a result, Martin-Marietta had to make a number of unplanned strategic decisions within a very short time frame in response to the takeover threat. While Bendix began acquiring Martin's shares, Martin decided to fight by trying to acquire Bendix— a move known as a "Pac-Man" strategy. In fact, both companies ended up holding controlling interest in the other, and deeply in debt. Bendix, however, made a tactical error in that it had to wait 30 days before assuming control of Martin, while Martin (incorporated in a different state) could assume control of Bendix in ten days. More short-term strategic decisions were required—this time

---

[4] J.C. Spender, "The Business Policy Problem and Industry Recipes," in *Advances in Strategic Management*, Vol. 2, ed. R. Lamb (Greenwich, CT: JAI Press, 1983), 215.

by Bendix—which sought out a "white knight" (a firm willing to take over Bendix on friendly terms) and which it found in Allied Corp. In this complicated situation, one can see a number of strategic decisions and actions being taken on an unplanned basis by all three of the firms involved. However, it should be noted that most strategic decisions—those that change the character or direction of the organization—have long-term ramifications, even if they were not planned in advance, although they usually are.

Ned Bowman, of The Wharton School, describes long-range planning as essentially a look *within* the firm, strategic planning as looking outside, and strategic management as treating all elements of the firm (people, skills, technology, information, finance) to see if they are consistent with strategy and if the firm can be made more competitive.[5]

Simply put, strategic decision-making involves determining how to get from point A (where we are now) to point B (where we need to be at some time in the future). Strategic planning involves determining the details of getting from A to B, and strategic management consists of controlling the entire process and its accomplishment.

The key concept in the definitions given above is *strategy*, the organization's preselected means or approach to achieving its goals and objectives while coping with current and future external conditions. A strategy is a pattern in the organization's important decisions and actions, and consists of a few key areas or things by which the firm seeks to distinguish itself.[6] *Tactics*, on the other hand, are specific actions the organization might undertake in carrying out its strategy. These terms will be explained more fully later in the text, but first some background information may be helpful.

A Military Analogy

The terms *strategy* and *tactics* have been borrowed directly from the military. In the military sense, strategy involves the overall approach or means used to combat the enemy, such as defending enclaves or large areas of the countryside, or using complementary deployments of air, sea, and land forces to attack the enemy.

Tactics, on the other hand, relate to specific means of carrying out a strategy: how to defend the enclaves or the countryside; how to carry out the land,

[5] Edward H. Bowman, "Strategy Changes: Possible Worlds and Actual Minds," in J.W. Frederickson, ed., *Perspectives on Strategic Management* (New York, NY: Harper Business, 1990), 9-39.

[6] Michael Kami, *Strategic Planning for Changing Times* (Dayton, OH: Cassette Recording Co., 1984).

sea, or air attack; how many planes, ships, or tanks to employ; the conduct of each skirmish or battle.

"Now, this one is a tactical rock, and that big one is a strategic rock."

Source: *Datamation*, 29, No. 11 (November 1983), 178.

Much can be learned from the military when applying strategy and tactics to the management of organizations, whether in the business sector, in government, health care, or in other areas. For example, World War II General George Patton reportedly said that it is virtually impossible to win a war using the wrong strategy, even though your tactics may be perfectly carried out. On the other hand, tactical errors may not cause you to lose the war if the correct overall strategy is being employed. In a business sense, attempting to market the wrong mix of products may not succeed, even though the marketing plan for each product is executed with precision. In turn, the organization with the correct product mix can be successful, even if errors are made in the individual marketing plans.

Characteristics of Strategic Decisions

A strategic decision can be defined as one that significantly affects what an organization does and how it does it. That is, a strategic decision would involve changes in one or more of the following: the organization's basic concept; its role in society; the mix of markets in which the organization competes; the choice of products and services within those markets; or how the firm competes within its markets. As the definition suggests, strategic decisions are complex and wide ranging.

In addition, there are several interrelated factors that contribute complexity and uncertainty to strategic decisions. As examples, firms typically pursue multiple objectives; strategic decisions have long time horizons; there are a number of interested (and often opposing) groups in each firm; strategic decisions by definition involve values, risks, and uncertainties, and involve many intangibles, assumptions, and judgments. In addition, strategic decisions tend to involve high stakes and are difficult to evaluate; and there also tends to be no individual or group possessing an overall expertise in a given decision area.[7] For these reasons, strategic decisions are seldom simple or clear-cut at the time they are made, and often not in retrospect, either.

As defined by Henry Mintzberg of McGill University in Montreal, Quebec, a strategy is a *pattern* in a stream of actions. This pattern is the result of strategic decisions made by the firm. The firm's strategy, however, is not always completely preplanned. As Figure 2.2 illustrates, the *intended* strategy may not be fully realized. For one reason or another, portions of the intended strategy may not materialize, while other patterns may emerge despite or in the absence of management's intentions.[8] Mintzberg's intent is not to suggest chaos, but "unintended order." It is frequently the means by which deliberate strategies change, and organizations adapt and learn.

As an example of this, as well as an illustration of how strategies must be flexible, consider the following case. Valcom, Inc.—now InaCom—began as a division of Valmont Corporation, the largest manufacturer of center pivot irrigation systems for agriculture. The Valcom strategy was to sell IBM® personal computers and software to farmers through Valmont's dealers. Within three months, sales had exploded, but not for the reasons anticipated. A sales analysis showed that less than 1 percent of sales were to farmers; the customers were bankers, small businesses, and so on, in small towns—areas without a PC outlet. So Valcom changed its strategy, selling computers to everyone in nonurban areas through company-owned and franchised stores. A subsequent sales analysis caused a further strategy refinement—a focus on businesses in smaller communities largely through franchised dealers.[9]

---

[7] Gus W. Grammas, "Quantitative Tools for Strategic Decision-Making," in *Handbook of Business Strategy*, ed. W. Guth (Boston, MA: Warren, Gorham & Lamont, 1985), 15-5.

[8] Henry Mintzberg, J.P. Brunet, and J.A. Waters, "Does Planning Impede Strategic Thinking?" in *Advances in Strategic Management*, Vol. 4, eds. Robert Lamb and Paul Shrivastava, (Greenwich, CT: JAI Press, 1986), 4; also see Mintzberg's article, "Crafting Strategy," *Harvard Business Review*, 65, No. 4 (July/August 1987), 66.

[9] William L. Fairfield, Keynote Address to the Third Nebraska Conference on Productivity and Entrepreneurship (Lincoln, NE, April 11, 1988).

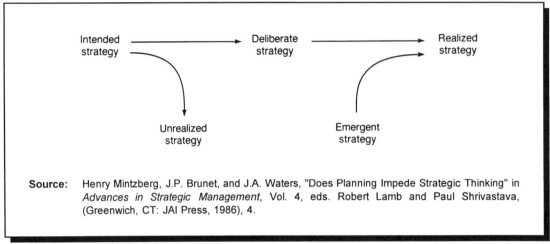

Source: Henry Mintzberg, J.P. Brunet, and J.A. Waters, "Does Planning Impede Strategic Thinking" in *Advances in Strategic Management*, Vol. 4, eds. Robert Lamb and Paul Shrivastava, (Greenwich, CT: JAI Press, 1986), 4.

Figure 2.2 **Intended versus Realized Strategy**

Strategy Making Requires Vision and Creativity. Unfortunately, some writers have tended to describe strategic management and strategic planning as a "rational," specific step-by-step process. While we do attempt to systematize elements of the process in large organizations, the most effective strategic decision-makers tend to be intuitive and creative, employing an adaptive, flexible process. In fact, the majority of strategic decisions are "event driven" rather than programmed in advance; therefore, they are "unplanned." Thus, strategy is often less an exercise in applied logic than it is "an exercise in preferences, choices, and matches."[10] The significance of this statement will become clearer as our discussion of strategy progresses.

An important key to effective strategic decision-making is the proper integration of analysis and intuition. Formal planning can help in developing strategy, particularly in complex organizations, but it's not the whole story. In fact, formal planning tends to drive out creative strategic thinking.[11] The reason we do formal planning is that we *have* to in order to manage the process in complex organizations, even though it is somewhat detrimental to the making of the most effective strategic decisions—it is a necessary evil. The goal is to make the correct strategic decisions, not the development of detailed plans.

---

[10] A Van Cauwenbergh and R. Martens, "Simplicity Behind Strategy: A Reflection on Strategic Management Theory versus Practice," in *Advances in Strategic Management*, eds. R. Lamb and P. Shrivastava (Greenwich, CT: JAI Press, 1983), 118.

[11] Henry Mintzberg, J.P. Brunet, and J.A. Waters, "Does Planning Impede Strategic Thinking? Tracking the Strategies of Air Canada from 1937 to 1976," in *Advances in Strategic Management*, Vol. 4, eds. Lamb and Shrivastava (Greenwich, CT: JAI Press, 1986), 3.

The best strategists tend to have a *vision* of their organization—a clear understanding of what the firm is about and where it is headed. This vision is the "glue" that holds things together through turbulent times and business fluctuations. It guides competitive strategy, and does not require exhaustive analysis.[12] In fact, some managers consider this vision to be at the very core of strategic planning—defining it as helping your organization "create," maintain, and implement a long-term or strategic vision.[13]

Control versus Breakthrough. It is also helpful to look at strategic decisions from the perspectives both of planning and of control. Most of what are considered problem-solving activities are related to the control function; that is, an attempt to bring the organization's performance back "under control." The other side of the control coin involves Juran's "breakthrough" concept.[14] Briefly, this concept holds that management's goal, once things are "under control," is to attempt to achieve a higher level of performance through conscious efforts. This means making certain changes that may reduce control in the short run, but are designed to improve performance (quality, output, effectiveness, efficiency, and cost) when things are brought under control at the new, but higher, level of performance. Again, this approach involves risk and short-term disruption, but it recognizes that "control" is not the manager's ultimate goal; performance improvement is. This type of planning decision requires that the manager be able to realistically assess and evaluate the risks of the attempted breakthrough strategy. Also, the managerial action required is more positive. The manager engages in "opportunity finding" activities, rather than in the more reactive "problem-solving" approach.

THE ESSENCE OF STRATEGY

Given the previous discussion, how can we determine whether or not an organization has a "strategy?" More pointedly, how can we describe or evaluate the viability of an organization's strategy. At its core, a strategy statement must answer four questions—questions one must seek answers to when attempting to describe or evaluate a strategy. Bill Rothschild, a former General Electric strate-

---

[12] Amar Bhide, "Hustle as Strategy," *Harvard Business Review*, 64, No. 5 (September/October 1986), 65.

[13] Major General Perry M. Smith (USAF), "Creating a Strategic Vision: The Value of Long-Range Planning," *Air University Review*, 37, No. 6 (September/October 1986), 16.

[14] J.M. Juran, *Managerial Breakthrough: A New Concept of the Manager's Job* (New York, NY: McGraw-Hill, 1964).

gist, consultant, and author, states that a company's strategy must answer four questions:

1. *What is our current business definition and what should it be in the future?* This includes the organization's *mission*—what the business does and who its customers are—and its *vision*—what it wants to be in the future. It also relates to *scope*—the domain of action within which the organization tries to achieve its objectives.
2. *Where shall we focus our energy, attention, and resources?* Here the organization is setting priorities and utilizing *distinctive competencies*—skills and resources that the organization will use to outperform its competitors and achieve its objectives.
3. *How can we create a sustainable competitive advantage?* Competitive advantages are advantages the firm expects to achieve over its competitors through its skills and resource deployments, including its distinctive competencies and comparative advantages.
4. *How will each of our functional units contribute to the implementation of the strategy?* The implementation strategy includes any synergies that will result from the way the organization deploys its skills and resources.[15]

In order to "win" in the competitive arena, a firm does not need to be superior to its rivals in every way. Actually, it does not *have* to be superior in *any* way. How can this be? In business, as in sports, a firm needs to create a mismatch, which can enable it to outperform its opponent. For example, assume that two basketball teams have fairly comparable players at each position. One team can gain an advantage by using plays pitting a quicker player against a slower player from the other team (recognizing that as a result of this tactic a potential mismatch also exists for the opposing team, but it may be meaningless *because the opposing team does not have the ball*). Another example, from tennis, involves a practice called "stacking." If two tennis teams have fairly equal players, the coach of one team may select a player most likely to lose; for example, no. 2 singles. By switching this player with another player also likely to lose—say, no. 6 singles, the coach may have picked up one more win for the team. That is, the former number two player will probably win playing at number six.

Therefore, a "cardinal feature of each strategy is the selection of a few relationships on which the company seeks to distinguish itself."[16]

---

[15] William E. Rothschild, *Risktaker, Caretaker, Surgeon, Undertaker: The Four Faces of Strategic Leadership* (New York, NY: John Wiley & Sons, Inc., 1993), 16-17.

[16] W.H. Newman, "Commentary," in *Strategic Management*, eds. D. Schendel and C.W. Hofer (Boston, MA: Little, Brown, 1979), 46.

At the business level, the company can choose to compete either selectively in one or more niches, or across the board. It can choose to compete in the same way that the rest of the industry competes, or it can try to change the rules. If the firm is a market leader, and if its competitive advantage is sustainable, playing the same game as the rest of the industry tends to be the best strategy. If it is not a market leader, the firm can explore ways to gain an advantage—either by focusing on a niche in which it has an advantage, or by exploring ways to change the game to its advantage.[17] For example, Miller Brewing marketed Lite, a low-calorie beer, as a new market segment and changed the way the industry competed.

"Schools" of Strategic Management

Just as Hax discovered six partially-correct definitions of strategy, Henry Mintzberg describes ten "schools of thought" describing strategic management. Each of the schools of thought appears to be correct and is, in fact, partially correct. While none is "incorrect," neither is any of the schools sufficiently, or completely, correct; except, perhaps, the Configurational School. Three of the schools are prescriptive in nature:

*   *Design School*—strategy formulation as a *conceptual* process.
*   *Planning School*—a *formal* process.
*   *Positioning School*—an *analytical* process.

Six are descriptive. Two of these relate to the individual strategist:

*   *Entrepreneurial School*—a *visionary* process.
*   *Cognitive School*—a *mental* process.

Three of the descriptive schools relate to the organization:

*   *Learning School*—an *emergent* process.
*   *Political School*—a *power* process.
*   *Cultural School*—an *ideological* process.

The sixth descriptive school is externally oriented:

*   *Environmental School*—a *passive* process.

---

[17] F.W. Gluck, "The Dilemmas of Resource Allocation," *Journal of Business Strategy*, 2, No. 2 (Fall 1981), 67.

Mintzberg's final school is integrative in nature, combining elements of the three prescriptive and six descriptive schools:

- *Configurational School*—where strategy formulation is an *episodic* process;[18] that is, the appropriate strategy and its resulting performance depend upon the interaction of a variety of variables.

For example, the interaction between various environmental (general and competitive) conditions, organizational variables (resources, competencies, characteristics), and strategies (types, levels) interact in multiple ways to affect and determine the organization's performance (quantitative and qualitative). In this light, strategic analysis—attempting to specify the "optimal" combinations of factors (environmental, organizational, and strategic) may appear mind-numbing because of the variety of possible permutations. It is no simple task.

HISTORY AND EVOLUTION OF STRATEGIC MANAGEMENT

Though much of the terminology and many of the concepts of strategic management are taken from military history, specific recognition of the strategy concept in management theory and practice is relatively new. As we will see later, the growth in size, complexity, and diversity of our economic and social organizations has created an increased need for formal strategic management. In the late 1800s, most businesses were relatively small, simple, and specialized. The rate of environmental change was also relatively slow, and major discontinuities in the environment were uncommon. For this type of organization and situation—a relatively simple organization in a relatively stable environment—the task of achieving a productive match or fit with that environment (the essence of strategic management) was relatively easy. Most firms followed an *implicit* type of strategy, since strategic decisions were relatively uncomplicated and were required relatively infrequently. Today, many small businesses still operate this way; however, the increased rate and abruptness of environmental change requires increased use of strategic management by small as well as large firms.

Need for Planning Has Increased

Figure 2.3 indicates that as organizations grow in terms of size, product line, diversity, geographical coverage, organizational complexity, and vertical integration (as well as operating in a less stable environment), their need for formal

---

[18] Henry Mintzberg, "Strategy Formation: Schools of Thought," in Fredrickson, *op. cit.*, 105-236.

strategic management increases—perhaps exponentially. If change is slow and predictable, it is easy to plan for the future, and the plan is likely to remain valid for extended periods of time. Planning can be a simple and infrequently needed function. On the other hand, in a rapidly changing and discontinuous environment, valid plans are difficult to develop and are likely to have short life spans. Unfortunately, some managers become frustrated by the likelihood that their plans will be outmoded, and in certain instances perhaps invalidated, soon after the plans are completed. The managers conclude that planning is an impossible task. But planning is much more important and critical in this situation, even though the process is more difficult and the resulting plans may be imprecise and short lived.

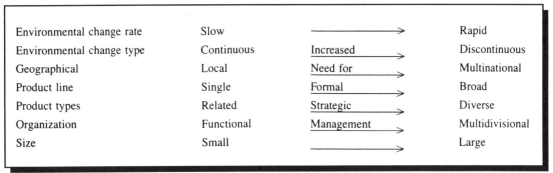

Figure 2.3 Conditions Requiring Formal Strategic Management

Through the first half of the 20th century, U.S. businesses and their environment grew steadily more complex, requiring progressively more attention to strategic management. But gradual change tends not to be noticed until it is perhaps too late (as in the case of the person who puts on two pounds a year and then discovers that an old army uniform no longer fits). We may have a gnawing feeling that things aren't working as well as they should (or once did), but may not be aware of the change or the need for a new approach because of the very gradual nature of the change.

Discontinuous changes, however, such as World War II, are readily apparent, even if the appropriate response to the change isn't. You know that things are different, and a new approach is required on your part. The years following World War II saw a dramatic increase in diversification and geographical (multinational) expansion by U.S. firms. There was an abrupt move toward the right side of the chart in most of the areas shown in Figure 2.3. In response to this shift, firms began to devote increasing effort to planning and strategy formulation to enable them to compete more effectively in their various markets. In the late 1960s, another rapid (if not discontinuous) change occurred in many of the organizations themselves. The trend toward multibusiness organizations (whether diversified firms or conglomerates) became evident, and in modified form continues today as cash-rich firms such as Philip Morris seek acquisition and buy-out candidates. As will be seen later, the multidivisional company needs to consider strategic alternatives not only at the individual business, product, or market level, but also at the corporate level. That is, in what businesses (products, markets) should the company compete, and how should these businesses be integrated to meet *corporate-level* goals and objectives?

More Areas Require Strategic Attention

Several researchers in the field of strategic management have developed models describing the evolution of the external environment and the strategic responses of organizations. Ansoff, as an example, analyzed the changing environmental challenges facing organizations during this century and the managerial responses, competitive strategies, and entrepreneurial strategies employed to cope with them.[19] Ansoff's major conclusions are summarized in Figure 2.4, which shows that markets, products, and technology progressively have become more diverse and complex. We have gone from trying to satisfy basic unfilled demands for goods and services (a production economy) to a situation where basic needs long since have been met, and "needs" must be created through product differentiation, planned obsolescence, and consumer manipulation (a marketing economy). More recently, increased environmental turbulence has necessitated resource conservation and contingency or surprise preparedness strategies. The firm now spreads its risks through diversification and a search for new areas for expansion, such as through products that conserve resources, ecology markets, and Third World markets. Strategies are needed to cope with a much larger number of environmental influences today than was true in the early 1900s, when a strategy of meeting existing unfulfilled demand was sufficient. Today, more strategies are required as progressively more areas become problems.

Additional environmental trends, threats, and opportunities are likely to appear in the future, and specific strategies will be required to cope with them. Real or artificial constraints on growth (rate and size) may require a limited-growth strategy. Challenges to the firm's right to compete in certain markets may require the firm to prove that it should be permitted to do so, necessitating a legitimacy strategy. The increasing rate of environmental change in general, when the rate exceeds the firm's ability to respond, may require an explicitly flexible response or surprise management strategy.

The point is: as more and more environmental constraints—and opportunities— emerge, more and more explicit areas of strategic attention are presented

[19] H. Igor Ansoff, "The Changing Shape of the Strategic Problem," in *Strategic Management: A New View of Business Policy and Planning*, eds. D. Schendel and C.W. Hofer (Boston, MA: Little, Brown, 1979), 30.

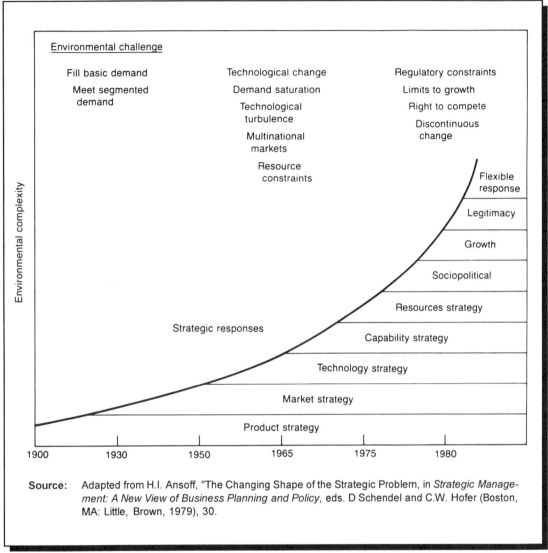

Figure 2.4 Increasing Challenges Require Additional Strategies

to the firm. This clearly increases the need for, the importance of, and the complexity of a firm's strategic management activities.

Time Compression and Instability

In the past, fluctuations in the variables affecting strategic decisions were relatively small and infrequent. As shown in Figure 2.5, the size of the fluctuations has increased, and they occur more frequently than in the past. This trend is likely to continue into the future, making the environment even more dynamic than it has been.

One obvious example of this phenomenon is interest rates. The prime rate during the 1950s and 60s was typically in the neighborhood of 5 percent, with a range from 4 to 6 percent. In the mid-1970s, the prime rate averaged over 10 percent, and typically ranged from 7 to 12 percent. In the 1980s, it was as high as 17 percent while averaging about 11 or 12 percent. So far in the 1990s, it has been as low as 6 percent. Another example is the price of gold, which has been as high as $800 per ounce and as low as $285 in the past few years. Similar instances have involved fluctuations in other interest rates, the value of the dollar, stock prices, the demand for and prices of many products such as gasoline, farm equipment, lumber, airline tickets, and others. Motor-home demand was once as high as 500,000 units per year. With the energy crisis, demand dropped to 40,000 units, later rose to 400,000, and more recently was in the neighborhood of 200,000 units.[20]

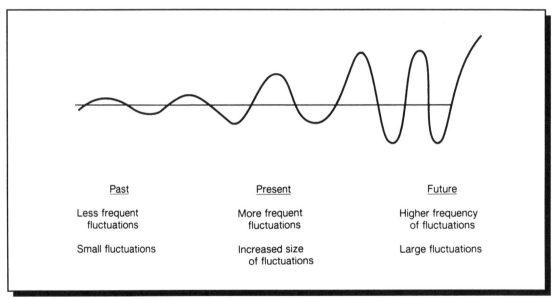

Past	Present	Future
Less frequent fluctuations	More frequent fluctuations	Higher frequency of fluctuations
Small fluctuations	Increased size of fluctuations	Large fluctuations

Figure 2.5 Increasing Frequency and Amplitude of Change

How does a company plan under such circumstances? First of all, as pointed out earlier, planning is at once more important and more difficult in such an environment, and requires a change in strategic response. With greater fluctuations

[20] Kami, *Strategic Planning for Changing Times*.

in sales, a firm must lower its break-even point to remain profitable, even if its average level of sales does not change. It will be operating at lower levels of output than before, which will result in lower profits or greater losses during those increasingly more frequent periods of low output. On the other hand, the higher peak demands necessitate more, not less, maximum capacity. These two phenomena may require more flexible, automated plants, outside sources of supply, producing to inventory, or other strategies. The point is that a greater number of strategic decisions must be made more frequently, and with less time for analysis than in the past. This trend is likely to continue or even accelerate in the future, making the organization's strategic management activities and decisions even more essential than they are today.

Increased Rate of Change

In describing "future shock" some years ago, Alvin Toffler pointed out that the last 50,000 years of human existence could be represented by some 800 sequential life spans of sixty-plus years each. Of those 800 life spans:

- The first 650 were spent in caves.
- Only the last seventy saw communication from one lifetime to another.
- Only the last six saw the widespread printed word.
- Only the last four saw time measured with precision.
- Only the last two saw the electric motor.
- Only the current lifetime has seen the overwhelming majority of material goods we take for granted today.[21]

This rate of change can be illustrated for a manufacturing firm as it adopts new technology, as shown in Figure 2.6. In the past, as a firm adopted a new technology or production method, it could expect to employ that method for an appreciable period of time before it fell behind the latest methods. At present, that period of time has shortened, and the amount of change required at each step has increased. In the future, it is likely that even more dramatic (and risky) changes will be required, with increasing frequency. Again, we can see that more significant strategic decisions must be made more frequently and with greater risk because of the rapidity and magnitude of change.

As General Motors' Michael Naylor points out, business is analogous to a race. But it is a race that never ends; winning today *only* earns you the right to compete again tomorrow!

---

[21] Alvin Toffler, *Future Shock* (New York, NY: Random House, 1970), 14.

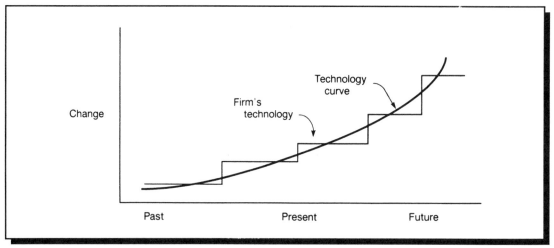

Figure 2.6 **Increasing Rate and Magnitude of Change**

Strategy as a Field

Strategic management is a coherent body of knowledge for practitioners and as a field of study for academics and researchers had its genesis in the concept of corporate strategy developed in the early 1960s. Researchers, such as Edmund P. Learned, C.R. Christensen, and Kenneth R. Andrews of the Harvard Business School[22] and H. Igor Ansoff of Carnegie Tech,[23] worked to understand why some companies with very different approaches could be equally successful. On the other hand, others following similar approaches showed very different results.[24] The answer can be found in the realm of strategic management; most notably, competitive advantage, distinctive competencies, and implementation.

CONCLUSION

Formal strategic planning has been with us since the early 1950s, even though organizations have always made strategic decisions. As organizations have grown larger and more complex, and as environments have become more

---

[22] E.P. Learned, C.R. Christensen, K.R. Andrews, and W.D. Guth, *Business Policy: Text and Cases*, 2 (Homewood, IL: Richard D. Irwin, Inc., 1965).

[23] Igor Ansoff, *Corporate Strategy* (New York, NY: McGraw-Hill, 1965).

[24] Richard G. Hamermesh, "Strategic Management," in H.E. Glass and M.A. Hovde, eds., *Handbook of Business Strategy: 1993/1994 Yearbook* (Boston, MA: Warren Gorham Lamont, 1993), 292.

dynamic and unstable, firms have tended to turn increasingly to formal strategic management activities. A strategy is defined as a means, approach, or pattern of actions designed to achieve goals and objectives, focusing on a few key or critical areas. A strategy attempts to achieve a productive fit between the organization and its environment, and exists at several different levels of organizational activity.

Strategic decisions are those that tend to change the character or direction of an organization or one of its units, and strategic management is the continuous process of formulating, analyzing, evaluating, selecting, implementing, and controlling strategies by the organization, whether by formal or informal means. The value of the process depends on the quality of the implemented strategies, rather than on the formality of the process.

Module
3

Strategic Management: Processes and Practices

LEARNING OBJECTIVES

After reading Module 3, you should be able to:

1. Realize that effective strategic management is a continuous, regular, planned process.
2. Understand the strategic management process, including its role and key components.
3. Understand the roles of strategic planning and control in strategic management.
4. Describe the specific steps in formulating and analyzing strategies.
5. Describe the relationship between strategies and policies.
6. Realize that effective strategic management is a flexible, adaptive, and creative process.

We have already explored the growing importance of strategic management by organizations competing in today's increasingly complex environments. Strategic management involves the match, or fit, the organization achieves with its environment, using its distinctive competencies to achieve competitive advantages and synergies. This module explores the process and key components of strategic management from an overall, or integrated, perspective. Specific steps in the process will be elaborated on in later modules.

PROFILE

ConAgra's Simplified Planning System

Many firms follow relatively simple and flexible planning approaches with excellent results. More detail and structure at the expense of flexibility and ease of use is not necessarily an improvement, and may even be a detriment. Flexibility, simplicity, and ease of use *are* important characteristics of planning systems. Planning systems should be no more formal, structured, or detailed than necessary.

One example of a company that stresses simple planning is ConAgra, a highly successful food processor located in Omaha, Nebraska. Mike Harper, former CEO and architect of the company's growth, states that "simplicity is the key to planning at ConAgra," and the goal is to become the best-earning food company in the United States, with a number 1 objective of "making shareholders rich." The company wants to earn an average return of over 20 percent after taxes. ConAgra has deliberately located its independent divisions away from Omaha to reinforce their independence. Some of ConAgra's credos include:

1. Outside directors should offer advice, but not be too involved in planning.
2. The basic test for acquisitions is whether they fit strategically. Much time and money is spent on research, using outside consultants, before making an acquisition decision.
3. A system of thirty-minute, Monday morning conference calls keeps the divisions in touch.
4. Executives are given adequate incentives to meet company goals.

An example of simple, clear thinking is illustrated by how the company decided to become a major force in raising chickens. Two pounds of feed are needed to produce one pound of meat on a chicken. Three pounds of feed are required for a hog, and seven to eight pounds for cattle. Thus, chickens are cheaper, more efficient sources of food. An important strategic factor in this emphasis on chickens was also government attempts to improve citizens' diets.[1]

The $25 billion giant's current CEO, Philip Fletcher, inherited ConAgra at the time the company's growth began to sag. He had to apply stricter top-down cost controls to ConAgra's sixty-plus operating units. The goal was to force the independent units to cooperate on purchasing, warehousing, and the like. But, Fletcher insists that each unit remain independent and nimble enough to respond to changes in consumer tastes and to moves by competitors.[2]

THE VALUE OF STRATEGY PROCESSES

Organizations rely on several key processes to determine and accomplish their goals. Strategy then, is the outcome of three processes which contribute to its formation and implementation. They are:

- Cognitive processes of individuals, where the understanding of the business, its external environment, and its internal competencies and resources reside.
- Social and organizational processes, which enable communication of information in formulating, selecting, and implementing strategies.
- Political processes, where power and influence affect decisions at all stages of strategic management.[3]

One of the tasks of the CEO, as we will explore in more detail later, is to draw from and harness these basic organizational processes in the development and implementation of strategies. The specific components and actions in formulating strategy are our focus in this module—the strategic management process.

This is an area of legitimate concern for organizations, because a recent study of *Fortune* 500 firms showed that only 35 percent of U.S. companies felt that their strategic planning process was effective. Thus, even though 93 percent utilize a formal process, only 25 percent stated that it was "effective," according to the Planning Forum/American Productivity & Quality Center joint study.[4]

---

[1] D.C. Beeder, "Fastest-Growing Food Company: Simplicity Helps ConAgra Grow," *Omaha World-Herald* (April 20, 1983), 18.

[2] Greg Burns, "How a New Boss Got ConAgra Cooking Again," *Business Week* (July 25, 1994), 72.

[3] Arnoldo Hax and N.S. Majluf, *The Strategy Concept and Process* (Englewood Cliffs, NJ: Prentice Hall, 1991), 7.

[4] "Survey Results Available on Strategic Management and Planning Practices," *The Planning Forum Network*, 7, No. 5 (May/June 1994), 11.

So, are planning systems worth the effort? Do they work? Thomas C. Powell of Bryant College argues that they have serious shortcomings. He argues that strategic planning does not provide a firm with a sustainable competitive advantage. The reason, Powell feels, is that a strategic planning process is easily imitated by competitors, even though it may produce economic value. Thus, if an organization successfully uses a strategic planning process, it will soon be adopted by competitors, affording no long-term advantage.[5] On the other hand, the University of Michigan's Stuart L. Hart has proposed an integrative framework of strategy-making processes that *does* show performance benefits. Hart's framework consists of five modes—command, symbolic, rational, transactive, and generative—that top managers and others play in the strategy-making process.[6] His subsequent research results show that capability counts: the greater the number of modes of strategy-making in which the firms had capabilities, the higher their performance.[7] Thus, strategy-making processes *do* appear to constitute a resource that offers the potential for competitive advantage.[8] Writing with Kate Banbury, Hart further found that this high capability is robust: that is, there appear to be few, if any, "costs" associated with accumulating/multiple strategy-making capabilities.

Specifically, Hart and Banbury write that high strategy-making capability makes the most difference for large firms in turbulent environments (small firms in stable environments do not seem to benefit). Looking even more closely, however, yielded some very interesting information: in *turbulent* environments, the best performers were those with high or low process capabilities; the worst performers were those with moderate capabilities. It may be that turbulent environments require a quick response above all else. The quickest responders are likely to be those with high process competence or those who "throw process to the wind" and focus on strategy content.

The findings have clear managerial implications: the *process* by which strategy is made can provide competitive advantage, and *requires purposeful design.*[9]

---

[5] Thomas C. Powell, "Strategic Management as Competitive Advantage," *Strategic Management Journal*, 13, No. 7 (October 1992), 551.

[6] Stuart L. Hart, "An Integrative Framework for Strategy-Making Processes," *Academy of Management Review*, 17, No. 2 (April 1992), 327.

[7] Stuart L. Hart and Catherine Banbury, "How Strategy-Making Processes Can Make a Difference," *Strategic Management Journal*, 15, No. 4 (May 1994), 265.

[8] Jay Barney, "Firm Resources and Sustained Competitive Advantage," *Journal of Management*, 17 (1991), 99-120.

[9] Hart and Banbury, *op. cit.*, 266.

PLANNING SYSTEMS STAGES

Glueck, Kaufman, and Walleck of McKinsey & Company found that planning systems employed by firms tend to go through an evolutionary process. The systems are likely to be found in one of four evolutionary stages, as shown in Figure 3.1.

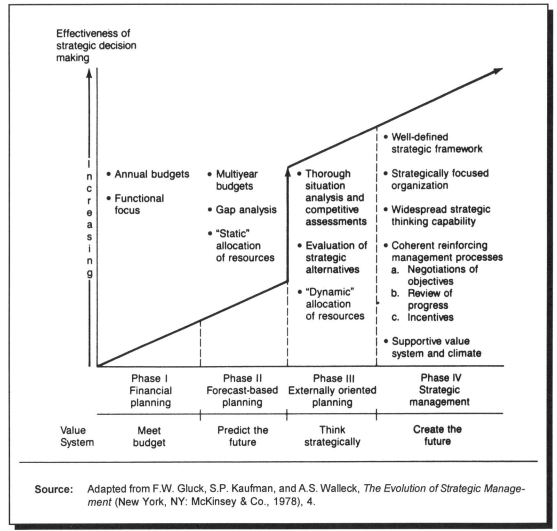

Source: Adapted from F.W. Gluck, S.P. Kaufman, and A.S. Walleck, *The Evolution of Strategic Management* (New York, NY: McKinsey & Co., 1978), 4.

Figure 3.1 **Phases in the Evolution of Strategic Planning**

Phase I-Basic Financial Planning. Most companies begin their formal planning with the annual budgeting process, where financial considerations dominate. The company's goal is to meet the budget, and a one-year time frame is usually used. Strategies are rarely formalized, but this does not mean that effective strategies are *not* employed.

Phase II-Forecast-Based Planning. Most of what we know as long-range or strategic planning is in reality forecast-based planning. At this stage, firms try to foresee or predict the future impact of environmental forces, since basic financial planning on a yearly basis has proved inadequate. While more effective resource allocation plus portfolio analysis may be included here, Phase II primarily attempts to extend Phase I into the future; the company is still essentially *reacting* to the environment, rather than changing the organization to fit the environment more productively.

Phase III-Externally Oriented Planning. This is the beginning of true *strategic* planning, where the firm focuses on changing its strategic thrusts to respond more effectively to markets and competition. In Phase I, the focus was operational control—attempting to control deviations from budgets. In Phase II, the emphasis was on more effective planning for growth by anticipating the environment. In this phase, strategic change, given *understanding* (rather than anticipation) of the causes of environmental changes, results in the firm looking for opportunities. Phase III employs the strategic business unit (SBU) concept, and represents a basic change in management style from those in Phases I and II. The planners are expected to offer strategic alternatives to management, including the risks and rewards associated with each.

Phase IV-Strategic Management. Phase IV attempts to merge the scenario-based approach of Phase III with the management system of the firm. Strategic planning and operational decision-making are linked for the first time. Not only does the firm think in terms of strategic alternatives and thrusts, but it also attempts to change its strategic *capabilities* by orchestrating its resources to *create* competitive advantages. In other words, the firm attempts to generate its own strategic alternatives. It does this through the use of: (1) a planning framework, which cuts across organizational units and levels, resulting in an integrated planning system; (2) a planning process that stimulates and rewards entrepreneurial thinking; and (3) a corporate value system that is geared to creating the firm's own future.[10]

---

[10] F.W. Gluck, S.P. Kaufman, and A.S. Walleck, "Strategic Management for Competitive Advantage," *Harvard Business Review*, 58, No. 4 (July/August 1980), 154.

Ansoff carries this progression to a "real-time" approach shown in Table 3.1. Ansoff feels that certain environmental changes occur too rapidly for management to either react to them or build them into the firm's plans. The firm may not have the luxury of waiting for the next annual planning cycle to respond, and it may not be possible to anticipate some of the changes, no matter how strategically oriented the firm's management may be. For these reasons, firms may need to think in terms of strategic issues (which may or may not arise) to prevent strategic surprises and to respond quickly to threats and opportunities. Even so, all issues or events are not forecastable. The firm will need a response mechanism *in place* to react to these unknown events as they occur (in real time) to minimize damage to the firm. Techniques for treating such uncertain and risky events are discussed later.

THE STRATEGIC MANAGEMENT PROCESS

In complex organizations, formal processes are necessary to ensure that strategic analyses and decisions are made and carried out in a coordinated, integrated manner. In addition, a certain degree of structure is required so that the firm maintains its sense of purpose, focus, and direction. Ideally, the organization's planning processes will allow the CEO's vision to flow from the top down, and strategic plans incorporating that vision to emanate from the operating divisions.[11] Doing so requires a balance between formal, or synoptic, planning processes and less-structured, or incremental, processes. Recent research has shown that more formal processes result in better strategic decisions when the organization faces a relatively turbulent environment, and incremental approaches work best in stable environments.[12] At this point, it is appropriate to investigate an overall model of the process, which can be implemented with the appropriate degree of formality or flexibility to fit the organization and its environment.

In studying the process of strategic management and its components, various authors have developed models representing their view of the process. For example, Kenneth Andrews[13] and his co-workers at Harvard, William F. Glueck,[14]

---

[11] Ray Stata, "The Role of the Chief Executive Officer in Articulating the Vision," *Interfaces*, 11, No. 3 (May/June 1988), 3.

[12] Rebecca J. Morris, "The Effect of Environmental Turbulence on the Design of Effective Strategic Information Systems," Ph.D. dissertation, University of Nebraska (1988).

[13] Kenneth Andrews, *The Concept of Corporate Strategy*, rev. ed. (Homewood, IL: Richard D. Irwin, Inc., 1980).

[14] W.F. Glueck, *Business Policy: Strategy Formation and Management Action*, 2nd ed. (New York, NY: McGraw-Hill, 1976); and W.F. Glueck, *Business Policy and Strategic Management*, 3rd ed. (New York, NY: McGraw-Hill, 1980).

Table 3.1 Ansoff's Modern Management Systems

	Management Orientation					
	Control	Long-Range Planning	Strategic Planning	Strategic Management	Strategic Issue Management	Surprise Management
Purpose	Control deviations and manage complexity	Anticipate growth and manage complexity	Change strategic thrusts	Change strategic thrusts and change strategic capability	Prevent strategic surprises and respond to threats/opportunities	Minimize surprise damage
Basic assumption	The past repeats	Past trends continue into future	New trends and discontinuities	Expect resistance New thrusts demand new capabilities	Discontinuities faster than response	Strategic surprises will occur
Limiting assumption	Change is slower than response	The future will be "like" the past	Past strengths apply to future thrusts Strategic change is welcome	Future is predictable	Future trends are OK	Future trends are OK

←————— Periodic —————→ ←————— Real time —————→

Source: H. Igor Ansoff, "Strategic Issue Management," *Strategic Management Journal*, 1 (1980), 132. Copyright ©1980. Reprinted by permission of John Wiley & Sons, Ltd.

George Steiner,[15] A.A. Thompson and A.J. Strickland,[16] and D.E. Schendel and C.W. Hofer[17] have all made major contributions in furthering the development of a comprehensive model of the strategic management process. The model described below integrates and incorporates the best features and major contributions of previous models.

An Integrated Model

As discussed earlier, strategic management includes both strategic planning and strategic control. Strategic planning, in turn, includes formulating and evaluating alternative strategies, choosing a strategy, and developing plans for putting it into practice. To formulate a strategy, the decision maker must take into account values and expectations of the stakeholders, the organization's mission and purpose, goals and objectives, the external environment and the internal capabilities of the firm, as well as major policies. Taken together with those of strategic control, these tasks comprise the strategic management process, and are described in the following paragraphs and illustrated in Figure 3.2. Its key elements are examined in depth in later modules.

Overview of the Process

Briefly, the process begins with top management's vision and a value analysis. The values and expectations of external stakeholders (e.g., stockholders, customers, suppliers, society, the community, and creditors) and the internal stakeholders (e.g., top management, other management, staff, and other employees) most importantly affect the organization's mission or purpose. They also affect the firm's policies, or the guidelines within which it operates, as well as the goals and objectives the firm sets for itself, and the strategies proposed and selected by the firm.

The firm's mission, goals and objectives, policies, and analyses of the external and internal environments provide the major bases for strategy formulation, including development, evaluation, and choice of strategic alternatives.

While certain authors define policies as dealing with implementation of strategies, it is more correct to consider them as constraints guiding strategy formulation and selection. For example, if a firm has a policy of not diversifying into

---

[15] G.A. Steiner, *Strategic Planning: What Every Manager Must Know* (New York, NY: Free Press, 1979), 17.

[16] A.A. Thompson, Jr., and A.J. Strickland II, *Strategy Formulation and Implementation* (Plano, TX: Business Publications, Inc., 1980).

[17] D.E. Schendel and C.W. Hofer, *Strategic Management: A New View of Business Policy and Planning* (Boston, MA: Little, Brown, 1979).

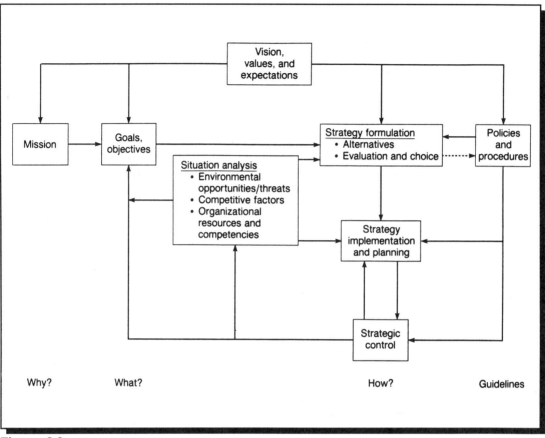

Figure 3.2 Integrated Model of Strategic Management

unrelated businesses, this policy would obviously affect the growth strategy alternatives open to the company; that is, it would cut down the number of strategies available if no such policy existed. On the other hand, strategies can, at times, result in policy changes. Using the same example, if a particularly desirable opportunity arose for the company to diversify into an unrelated business, it is entirely possible that the company would reevaluate the policy prohibiting it from taking this advantage. In general, however, the major direction of influence is from policies to strategies, rather than vice versa.

Just as tactics can be thought of as actions taken within a strategic framework, procedures can be considered to be specific expressions of policies. That is, procedures are guides to the day-to-day activities of the firm, designed to ensure that the firm operates within the broader guidelines of its policies. For example, if a firm has a policy of strongly protecting employee privacy, this will be reflected in procedures governing how the company's personnel records are prepared, disseminated, and stored. Obviously, a firm will have many levels of policies and many levels of procedures, but generally procedures can be thought of as supporting, implementing, or ensuring adherence to certain policies. Unfortunately, however, many employees are not aware of or do not see the connection between certain procedures that impinge on their work and the policies the procedures support. In addition, procedures have a tendency to remain in place long after their reason for being has expired, sometimes even after the policy they were designed to support has been changed. Both situations should be guarded against because, as indicated, policies guide strategy formulation, as well as strategy evaluation and choice. Likewise, procedures guide the strategy evaluation and choice process, and, perhaps to a greater degree, strategy implementation and planning.

Strategic control completes the process shown in Figure 3.2, answering the questions of: (1) whether the strategy implemented is the one that was chosen (or has it been changed in the implementation and detailed planning processes), and (2) whether the results are those that were expected. If the answer to either of these questions is negative, corrective action must be taken. The action can be directed to those areas where changes are required or appropriate, starting with modifications of detailed plans, and progressing through changing or modifying the strategy selected, selecting an entirely new strategy, or perhaps even modifying the goals and objectives of the firm (if it is judged that *no* strategy is likely to result in their accomplishment).

ELEMENTS OF THE STRATEGIC PROCESS

In general, following the framework of Figure 3.2, the organization's mission or purpose, a result of its enterprise strategy, defines why the organization exists and why it competes in certain sectors or industries. Within this mission or purpose, the firm addresses *what* it intends to accomplish, both in the long and short run. *Goals* are the broad directions or results the firm wants to accomplish, while *objectives* relate to more specific targets. Goals tend to involve longer-term or continuing results, and may not have a specific time frame for their accomplishment. Objectives, on the other hand, are more specific ends to be met within the framework of the broader goals, and usually relate to a given period. That time frame, however, can be long and/or short run. Thus, goals tend to be unrelated to time, but objectives include a time horizon. For example, a firm may have the goal of becoming a "leader in the industry." To support this, a long-term objective of having the largest share of the market by 2000 may be chosen, with shorter-range objectives of increasing market share by 2 percent in each of the next five years.

Defining why the organization exists and competes as it does and what it attempts to accomplish is not enough. The organization must decide *how* it plans to do this. The "how" question is the basis of the firm's strategy—its general approach and its specific plans. Just as there are many ways to skin a cat, there may be several strategies that could achieve the desired goals and objectives. Guidelines in the form of policies help to define which strategic alternatives mesh with the organization's value system and its general philosophies of doing business. Each of these areas will be addressed in greater detail in the following paragraphs.

But first, let's look at a real-world historical example of how some of the parts of the process fit together. Quaker Oats states that its mission is "to create shareholder value by consistently achieving our financial objectives of superior returns and growth."[18] In line with this mission, the company publicly stated its goals and objectives in 1981. The goals, strategies, actions, and results are as follows:

1. Goals and objectives:

   a. Maintain return on equity of 20 percent.
   b. Achieve real earnings growth averaging 5 percent.
   c. Increase dividends.
   d. Maintain strong bond and paper ratings.

2. Strategies:

   a. Remain a leading marketer of strong consumer brands.
   b. Achieve better than average real growth in grocery and Fisher-Price brands.
   c. Improve profitability of low-return businesses or divest.

3. Actions:

   a. Divestitures: 1982—restaurant division; 1983—chemicals division; 1987—specialty retailing.
   b. Acquisitions: 1982—Ardmore Farms (food service); 1983—European Pet Foods; 1984—Stokely-Van Camp; 1987—Golden Grain, Gaines.
   c. New product introductions: 1982—chewy granola bars; 1983—Fisher Price toys for older kids; 1984-87—various food products.

4. Results:

   a. By 1985: 8.5 percent compound growth; growth categories represent 52 percent of grocery sales.
   b. By 1986: ROE exceeds 20 percent; 63 percent of grocery sales from market-leading brands.
   c. By 1987: returns reach all-time high in grocery products.[19]

[18] *Annual Report 1987*, Quaker Oats Co., Chicago, inside cover.
[19] *Ibid.*

An important part of Quaker's success was and is effective strategic management. Again, the following paragraphs and chapters provide the fundamentals necessary to achieve successful results.

Vision

A vision of the future is vital to an organization. The vision describes what the organization aspires to be and do in the future. For example, the Gallup Organization aspires to be "the world's preeminent collector and disseminator of quality information." The vision is intertwined with the firm's *mission* (*why* it is doing what it is doing), its *goals and objectives* (what it hopes to accomplish), and its *culture* (its organizational values, attitudes, and beliefs). The organization's vision, which is most often the product of the CEO and top management, is its driving force; it instills meaning and excitement into the organization. The vision is the "dream" that people in the organization can relate to and commit their time and efforts to achieve.

The Organization's Mission or Purpose

The starting point in formulating an organization's strategy is its mission or purpose; that is, the definition of the organization's role in society and the economy. The firm's mission defines why it exists and why it competes in certain selected sectors or industries and not in others. The mission flows from the values of stakeholders, the people and groups with an interest in the organization, including the public and their representatives (the government). For any but a newly formed organization, the past plays a major role in the current mission or purpose of the firm; the basic mission reflects previous competitive practices and performance.

A firm's mission is a broad statement, providing a general direction for business activities and a basis for the coherent selection of desired ends (goals and objectives) and means to achieve them (strategies). Institutions in our society may have missions that relate to charitable, religious, social, or economic realms. Within these realms, an organization may have a more specifically focused mission, such as providing transportation products, communication services and equipment, and financial services. For example, Control Data Corp.'s mission statement reads as follows:

"Control Data is in the business of applying micro-electronics and computer technology in two general areas: computer-related hardware; and computing-enhancing services, which include computation, information, education and finance."[20]

---

[20] John A. Pearce, II and Fred David, "Corporate Mission Statements: The Bottom Line," *The Academy of Management Executive*, I, No. 2 (May 1987), 111.

Firms without specified mission statements can run into difficulties similar to those experienced by the conglomerates of the late 1960s. Many of these firms began wild and unrelated diversification moves into businesses and industries with profit and growth being the only reasons. If they had a mission, it seemed to be solely "to make money" or "to grow." While profits are essential to business and growth may be a desirable goal, they do not define purpose. History has shown that many firms without statements of mission encountered serious difficulties in later years, because they had no clear concept of what their business was.

In this context, all U.S. federal government agencies must develop a mission statement that guides and limits their activities and defines their role. Unfortunately, many firms in the private sector have not given sufficient attention to this critical area. The mission or purpose of most small firms and new ventures may be readily apparent (even though not formally stated). But when these firms are able to grow and diversify, a mission statement becomes important to guide and focus the direction of that growth and diversification. We will discuss development of the mission statement, as well as goals and objectives, in more depth in Module 7.

Goals and Objectives

Once a firm has defined its purpose, the next step is to define what it attempts to accomplish. Goals are broad directions the firm wishes to pursue or results it wishes to accomplish within its mission. Statements of goals might include the following:

1. Becoming a leading producer in the construction equipment industry.
2. Realizing a continuing high level of profits and return on investment.
3. Steady, stable growth in sales, profits, and dividends.
4. Maintenance of a stable, productive work force through all phases of the business cycle.

Many other goals could be cited. The point is that they are broad and general, and can be pursued on a continuing basis—they may never be satisfied completely. Goals provide direction for the firm and its employees.

However, goals are not sufficient. Statements of intentions and directions that are never really (or specifically) achieved make it difficult to assess and evaluate corporate and individual performance. Thus, objectives provide more specific ends to be met within the framework of the broader goals, and they involve specific time frames for accomplishment. An organization's objectives should cover varying time frames, ranging from general, long-range objectives to quite specific short-term objectives. The number of objectives (or targets) is likely to increase as the time frame becomes shorter and shorter.

It is important that goals and objectives be consistent and support one another. Goals must be developed within a defined mission, and objectives must be developed to support specific goals.

Goals and objectives provide the targets for which strategies are developed, and, particularly in the case of objectives, become important in the implementation of those strategies. Goals and objectives exist at the enterprise, corporate, business-unit, and functional and operational levels of a firm; in other words, all areas in which the firm is involved.

Assessing the Strategic Situation

To create a productive match between an organization and its external environment, the firm must understand both the general external environment and its competitive environment, in addition to organizational factors (and by implication, its values and the resulting mission, goals and objectives, and policies). These areas are outlined briefly here and treated in more depth in later modules.

The General Environment: Opportunities and Threats. The external environment consists of factors over which the organization has little direct control. For most firms, this would include a number of economic factors, social factors, political-legal factors, and technological factors. A firm may have *some* influence in one or more of these areas; for example, an invention by one firm may help it change its technological environment. Some firms also may exert greater control than others over certain environmental factors. However, environmental factors are typically beyond direct control of most firms.

Environmental analysis is important because the environment is constantly changing, and the organization may need to change, as well, to maintain its productive fit. To keep up with the external environment, management must watch for changes and trends of strategic significance. The changes and trends are brought into and disseminated within the organization by means of a strategic information system, which probably functions separately from the firm's operating or management information system. Since responding to change requires a certain amount of lead time, forecasting those changes is an important organizational activity. Numerous quantitative as well as qualitative approaches to environmental forecasting have been developed and are discussed later.

The more rapid and discontinuous the change, the greater the need for environmental analysis and forecasting so that the firm can anticipate and react. In a stable, unchanging environment, there is less need for analysis and forecasting; these tasks are relatively simple and can be performed with great precision and little risk of error. A turbulent environment, however, puts a premium on analysis and forecasting, but makes the tasks very difficult, imprecise, and risky.

Any change creates, simultaneously, both threats and opportunities. But whether a given change is a threat or an opportunity depends on how accurately the firm diagnoses and understands the change and its significance, as well as what the firm decides (and is able) to do about it. Thus, management must be aware of changes, interpret their impacts (the most difficult task), and take appropriate action. Obviously, a firm with limited resources that prevent it from capitalizing on new situations will find changes creating more threats than opportunities.

The major environmental forces affecting most firms include:

1. The economy, including tax rates, interest rates, price controls, business cycles, inflation, and general overall condition. Some sectors and products (such as housing, autos, and resorts) are more susceptible to economic factors than are others (such as food, medical care, and other necessities).
2. Technology, including product design, production processes, related cost factors, product quality, the general rate of technological change and innovation, and raw materials.
3. Social factors, including consumer preferences, values, demands for product safety, demographics, lifestyle changes, roles of women and minorities, career expectations, and others.
4. Political/legal considerations, including government regulations, restrictions, the political climate (in Washington, the statehouse, and overseas), antitrust legislation, import/export restrictions, environmental and consumer protection laws, product liability, and OSHA regulations.

Changes in any one of these areas can have significant impacts on the firm, its products, its markets, its ability to compete, and its methods of doing business. Analyzing the environment is not an easy task. It is often easier to forecast the changes themselves than to accurately determine their effects, or the timing of those impacts. American Motors foresaw the change to smaller cars as early as the 1950s and produced compact cars well in advance of the competition. The public, however, was not yet ready to buy them in sufficient quantities to support the company.

The Industry Environment: Competitive Factors. In addition to its general economic environment, competitive factors within the organization's industry or sector of the economy provide a number of more specific opportunities and threats. For example, direct and indirect competition from other firms, the market structure, market size, costs of entry and exit, market changes and niches, and distribution channels all are important determinants of the strategic situation facing the firm.

Industry structure—whether the market is local, regional, national, or global—as well as the number and composition of *strategic groups* (firms following similar strategies) within the industry are important considerations. Also important are factors relating to the product life cycle, such as whether the market is in a rapid growth, shakeout, or maturity stage. Last, factors relating to capital intensity as well as experience curve effects must be considered.

The Organization: Resources and Competencies.
The internal situation must be analyzed, as well. Three dimensions affect the capabilities of an organization and influence its strengths and weaknesses: (1) the values and expectations of stakeholders, (2) the goals and objectives of management, and (3) the organization's resources and competencies. Influencing these factors are the size, type, and stage of development of the organization (e.g., whether it is large or small, concentrated or diversified, young or mature, and the like).

Many stakeholders may actually be external to the firm (such as society, the community, suppliers, creditors, customers, and the government). Others clearly are internal (top and other levels of management, staff, and other employees), while a third external group can be considered quasi insiders (investors). Whether the stakeholders are internal, external, or on the boundary, their collective impact determines the set of values and expectations directing and guiding the firm, which is an element of the internal situation. As was shown in Figure 3.2, the resulting values and expectations ultimately define the mission, goals and objectives, and policies of the firm.

In the short run, the stakeholders having the most immediate impact on the firm's strategies are management, particularly top management. Strategies are formulated by people (primarily top management) within the existing environment, and management's individual and collective goals and objectives are a potent and direct influence on strategic decisions.

Strategy Formulation

Strategy formulation, described more fully in Modules 12 through 17, is a decision-making process that builds on the analysis of the strategic situation, as determined by the general, industry, and internal factors. It involves a determination of strategic alternatives, or the means by which the organization is able to meet its goals and objectives, given its available resources and competencies. Strategy formulation essentially is problem solving in unstructured situations, and most important, involves selecting the right problems to solve.

The key to effective strategy formulation lies in finding the major variables the firm can manipulate to improve its match with the environment. This requires an understanding of which strategic directions and alternatives are appropriate for the current and future situation facing the firm. At the business level, for example, this would include strategies for positioning and distinguishing the business, plus strategies for increasing, refining, or reducing its scope. At the corporate level, strategies of business integration, diversification, concentration, and restructuring are included. It includes analyzing factors for each level of strategy—enterprise, interorganizational, corporate, business, and functional—and is both a social/political and analytical/conceptual process. That is, strategy formulation may employ analytical tools such as financial analysis and management science techniques, but is still the result of the values, goals, and judgments of the group of individuals comprising the firm.

Two categories of strategies may be required, depending on the environment. Our concern so far has been with *initiating actions* (sometimes called action strategies) that define means of dealing with expected environmental circumstances. On the other hand, if the environment is too complex or changes too rapidly to develop meaningful action strategies to cope with it, *response actions* (sometimes called preparedness strategies) may be necessary. These are predetermined contingency plans that can be implemented in the event a certain set of circumstances occurs in the environment. The result is a strategy for coping with unforeseen events, or a preparedness strategy, which consists of contingency plans that can be implemented when and if needed.

In general, strategy evaluation consists of first making sure that no obvious strategic alternative has been overlooked, then systematically narrowing down the list to the "best" alternatives based on factors critical to the firm's success. Procedures for doing this are discussed in Module 17.

It is not unusual for seemingly obvious alternatives to be overlooked during strategy formulation. One such alternative, always present, is to *not* change strategy at all. If certain proposed strategies are no more likely than the current strategy to accomplish the firm's goals and objectives, they should be rejected.

Evaluating strategic alternatives requires criteria for acceptance or rejection. These may be "go/no go," absolute criteria for acceptance or rejection; for example, that all alternatives must result in a certain level of return on investment and not require that the firm borrow more than a given amount of money. Any alternative not meeting these criteria will be rejected and dropped from further evaluation. Other criteria may not be so clear-cut. In these instances, a "scorecard" for each alternative may be developed and used as a basis for selecting the strategy with the best overall score. In evaluating alternatives, as in quality control testing, candidates should be subjected to the most demanding criteria first, with as many alternatives as possible rejected as early as possible. Examples of how to perform these tasks are given in Module 17.

Strategy Implementation and Planning

After a strategy has been evaluated and selected, the critical implementation phase begins. Implementation is vitally important because a brilliant strategy poorly put into action may be no more effective than a well-implemented but otherwise less desirable strategy. In short, a strategy is only as good as its implementation.

While strategy formulation and evaluation are sometimes performed apart from the organization's operating structure, processes, and systems, implementation is largely an administrative task that occurs within these functions. Consequently, individuals who are not involved in formulation and evaluation (operating managers and staff at various levels), and who use existing organizational procedures are largely responsible for implementation. This transfer of responsibility is critical to the success of a strategy.

In the implementation phase, a master plan is required to turn strategy into reality. Module 18 shows how a master plan is developed and outlines the major actions and schedules required to implement the strategy. A master plan becomes the basis for more detailed and shorter-term planning and scheduling at progressively lower operating levels of the firm. It also includes any structural, system, process, or personnel changes required for implementation, as well as resource requirements and budgets. Resource allocation decisions are made at this time, and are reflected in the budgets and schedules of the implementing units of the firm.

Most of what we have come to know as strategic planning, including the use of formal planning systems and techniques, occurs in this implementation phase. It is here, also, that alternative, or contingency, plans are developed, in case actual events do not correspond to the assumptions of the master strategic plan.

Strategic Control

Strategic control involves evaluation of whether or not a strategy is being implemented as intended, and whether or not the desired results are being achieved. If not, corrective action may be required to modify the implementation activities or even the strategy itself. In addition, the internal situation and external environment of the firm likely will change with time, and their impacts must also be periodically reevaluated as part of the strategic control process.

A critical element in strategic control, as well as in strategy formulation, is the strategic information system, which is described in Module 18. A strategic information system is vital to determining strategic results (some of which may be determined by the organization's management information system), as well as to be aware of important environmental changes, trends, and "surprises."

HIGH-PERFORMANCE STRATEGIC PLANNING

We have already learned that not all strategic planning improves profitability or creates a sustainable competitive advantage. But certain types of strategic planning in certain types of situations *do* show results. Also, it should be obvious by now that any organization needs strategies. The question then, is how can this process be made more effective? How can we engage in "high performance strategic planning?"

Make Planning Distinctive

We have already heard that strategic planning will not provide a firm with a sustainable competitive advantage if the process is easily imitated. Performance advantages can accrue if the process is valuable, scarce, and not easily copied. How can a firm make it so? One way is to focus on producing information with "firm-specific value." For example, information resulting from personal relationships and face-to-face interactions is likely to be more firm-specific, and therefore more valuable, than general information from published sources.[21]

Keep it Simple, Flexible, and Workable

The cost of a planning system is multiplied by its complexity and its reliance on detail and "completeness." Often, however, its value is unrelated, perhaps even inversely related, to its complexity and completeness; simplicity and timeliness are more critical. The important strategic questions are simple: Who are our customers? What do they value? How well are we serving them?

Unfortunately, many companies fall into the trap of allowing their strategic plans to become massive documents. Phillip Caldwell, former Ford CEO, cautions that "planning is basically a thought process. It is not a paper mill." Ford's final corporate plan may run only thirty to thirty-five pages, with key issues covered on a single page.[22] Michael Kami agrees, stating that the plan should be short and cover only a few really key areas, perhaps in six pages or so for a typical business unit. The emphasis should be on the thought process, not methodology. In fact, Kami feels that elaborate methodology plus "paralysis-by- analysis" kills effective planning.[23]

Another example of a less formal, flexible approach to planning was that used by Honda in entering the U.S. motorcycle market in 1959. Honda began by importing primarily heavyweight bikes to compete with the then-dominant Harley-Davidson. However, they had severe problems with clutches and oil leaks, and withdrew. They were forced to replace the big bikes with their light-

---

[21] Thomas C. Powell, "High-Performance Strategic Planning for Competitive Advantage," in H.E. Glass and B.E. Cavan, eds., *Handbook of Business Strategy* (New York, NY: Faulkner and Gray, 1994), 392.

[22] "Some Better Ideas from Ford Motor's CEO," *Planning Review*, 12, No. 5 (September 1984), 9.

[23] Michael Kami, *Strategic Planning for Changing Times* (Dayton, OH: Cassette Recording Co., 1984).

weight 50cc Supercub, which they initially felt wouldn't do well here because of Americans' preference for "macho" cycles. To Honda's surprise, the smaller bikes became an immediate hit. The point is that a business should remain flexible and not overplan.[24]

Michael Kami suggests a simple, action-oriented approach to developing strategic plans:

1. Assemble a team of six or so people knowledgeable about the industry and the business, and put them in a conference room for two or three days.
2. Have them brainstorm 100 factors that will affect the organization in the next three years.
3. Categorize the factors by their level of importance (such as critical, very important, not so important, and so on).
4. Arrive at a consensus about the ten most important factors, and assign priorities to them.
5. Brainstorm 50 to 100 alternative actions for dealing with each important factor.
6. Pare this list down to five to ten clever, innovative actions.
7. Reconcile the actions and take steps to begin implementation right away.[25]

IBM uses a similar approach, called process quality management (PQM) for certain of its strategic planning activities, relying heavily on the critical success factor concept in determining what the company must accomplish to achieve its mission and what must be done to meet the critical success factors. PQM—like Kami's approach—demands an intensive one- or two-day session attended by *all* key managers and employing a brainstorming and consensus-building approach.[26]

Another suggestion for simplification by Gary Hamel of the London Business School involves the following approach:

1. Of the top 100 people in your company, pick 25 or so and ask them the following question: "How will our industry be different in the future?" Give them a week or a month, but insist on a one-page response.
2. Analyze the responses:

   a. Do they have a sufficiently long-term view (10 years or so)?
   b. Is their industry view broad enough to see shifting boundaries?

---

[24] Milton Moskowitz, "Honda's Market Conquest Not Entirely Planned," *The Media General Financial Weekly* (June 25, 1984), 6.

[25] Kami, *Strategic Planning for Changing Times.*

[26] M. Hardaker and B.K. Ward, "How to Make a Team Work," *Harvard Business Review*, 65, No. 6 (November/December 1987), 112-20.

c. Is there consensus on the most important changes?

d. Would their answer surprise competitors? Are they competitively unique; do they have their own viewpoint?

e. Can you distill an action plan from there answers? Is there a path linking the short-term to the long-term?[27]

Take an Action Orientation

Executives should determine the firm's sources of competitive advantage and define its mission and vision in those terms. The vision should drive the strategy and its implementation. The goal is to produce actions that serve customers and improve performance, not to produce plans.

Make the Process Fit the Culture

Formalized planning processes may be incompatible with a culture of rapid innovation and informality. The planning system must fit the organization's culture, or the system will be ignored, bypassed, or tolerated at best.

Don't Hang Up on Order and Rationality

It is important to generate creative, innovative strategies; the kind associated with *strategic thinking*. To the extent that planning processes drive out strategic thinking because of an overemphasis on order and logic, they are doing the organization a disservice. Effective leaders ensure that long-range planning and prediction do not sabotage intuition, experimentation, and learning (see Figure 3.3).[28]

Strategic planning does not have to be a complex, voluminous, methodologically threatening, time-consuming process. The emphasis should be on clear thinking, not on format and sophisticated analysis.

Top-Down or Bottom Up?

Strategic planning in U.S. corporations is primarily a bottom-up process for implementing the CEO's vision of the future. In this way, division managers responsible for an individual business-unit develop the strategies and plans for that unit. This approach has some well-known advantages. However, recent research

---

[27] Bernard C. Reimann, "Gary Hamel: How to Compete for the Future," *Planning Review*, 22, No. 5 (September/October 1994), 43.

[28] Powell, "High Performance Strategic Planning for Competitive Advantage," 393-97.

Traditional Strategic Planning	Strategic Management
• Generic	• Firm-specific
• Formal	• Relationship-based
• Complex	• Simple, focused on competitive advantage
• Expensive	• Inexpensive
• Periodic	• Manager's ongoing work
• Systematic data collection	• Constant, unsystematic data collection
• Analysis-oriented	• Action-oriented
• Plan-oriented	• Performance-oriented
• Planner-driven	• Executive-driven
• External changes a threat	• External changes an opportunity
• Mechanistic	• Flexible
• Diffuses commitment and enthusiasm	• Generates commitment and enthusiasm
• Assumes orderly environment	• Assumes chaotic environment
• Assumes predictable environment	• Assumes unpredictable environment

Source: Adapted from Thomas C. Powell, "High Performance Strategic Planning for Competitive Advantage," in H.E. Glass and B.E. Cavan, eds, *Handbook of Business Strategy* (New York, NY: Faulkner and Gray, 1994), 398.

Figure 3.3 High Performance Strategic Planning

shows that this approach is not *always* the best, nor should it be used under all conditions. For diversified corporations, interrelationships between businesses become an important factor, requiring more top-down strategy making. Michael Porter's research indicates that "multipoint competition," in which firms are challenged on many industrial fronts, requires top-down strategy and a lot of initiative from the top levels of the firm. Stellar performances from individual business-unit managers are no longer enough to assure the success of this type of firm, and senior executives must take a proactive role in strategy development and implementation.[29]

This view is corroborated and expanded by a recent study of ten leading British companies, which found that there are conditions under which either method—top-down or bottom-up—may be preferable. For example, if corporate development and coordination of individual businesses is the key objective of the firm, headquarters should make the strategy and accept the fact that the motivation of managers and performance of their units may suffer. If unit financial performance matters most, headquarters should let unit managers determine strategy,

---

[29] Donald F. Heany, "Porter's Competitive Advantage Revisited," *Planning Review*, 14, No. 1 (January 1986), 27.

and accept less coordination between the businesses. Also, if a balance of the two is sought, be prepared to accept increased ambiguity.[30]

Group Approaches

An interesting set of alternative ways of making group strategic decisions involves the dialectic inquiry, devil's advocate, and group consensus approaches. The dialectic inquiry approach involves debates between managers backing diametrically opposed sets of recommendations. Devil's advocacy relies on critiques of single sets of recommendations and assumptions (where an individual or group plays the "devil's advocate" role). Consensus approaches involve an interactive sharing of information and evaluation of assumptions, alternatives, and recommendations, with challenge likely to occur only when there is lack of agreement. Recent research results show that both the dialectic inquiry and devil's advocacy methods led to higher-quality recommendations and assumptions than did consensus. Dialectic inquiry was more effective than devil's advocacy in surfacing assumptions. However, consensus groups expressed more satisfaction and harmony within the group, as well as greater acceptance of the group's decisions.[31] Again, a trade-off seems to exist, depending upon which factor or set of factors is more important to the firm.

CONCLUSIONS

Understanding and following a logical and complete process of strategic management helps to ensure that no important factors will be overlooked in formulating and implementing strategies. This increases the likelihood that the organization will employ the best strategies that it possibly can—those that result in the best possible fit between the firm's external environment, its distinctive competencies and resources, and the values and expectations of its stakeholders. Following a regular schedule for the process further ensures that the firm's strategic management activities will yield maximum benefits. Remember, *too much* planning may lead to chaos, but so would too little, and more likely so.

---

[30] Michael Goold and Andrew Campbell, "Many Best Ways to Make Strategy," *Harvard Business Review*, 65, No. 6 (November/December 1987), 70-76.

[31] D.M. Schweiger, W.R. Sandberg, and J.W. Ragan, "Group Approaches for Improving Strategic Decision-Making," *Academy of Management Journal*, 29, No. 1 (March 1986), 51-70.

Module
4

Characteristics of
Successful Organizations

LEARNING OBJECTIVES

After reading Module 4, you should be able to:

1. Describe the main factors essential to business success.
2. Understand the concept and importance of critical success factors to an organization's strategic decisions.
3. Appreciate the various methods of determining critical success factors.
4. Describe the PIMS project and understand its major findings.

The search for organizational "success" is a virtually universal goal. There are numerous anecdotes which proponents claim will improve organizational performance and ensure success. Unfortunately, until recently we had very little generalizable hard data to confirm what it is that *really* determines the performance of an organization. The critical success factor (CSF) concept and the Profit Impact of Market Strategies (PIMS) data base have gone a long way toward answering this question.

In addition, many prescriptions for organizational success have tended to be overly general or too limited in their focus. That is, some are so general that they are almost "truisms;" they are not incorrect but they are so general that they offer little value to managers. Secondly, there are the current fads or "buzz word" management approaches which proponents claim will answer all management problems. The past generation has seen a number of these approaches come and go, such as total MIS, PERT, PPBS, Management Grid, zero-based budgeting, T-groups, JIT, TQM, and the like (some *do* have value, but not as much as is claimed by their advocates).

PROFILE

The GE Revolution

General Electric, founded by Thomas Alva Edison in 1889, commercialized widely-used products such as the light bulb, electric fan, phonograph, TV, refrigerator/freezer, and much more. With record financial performance in 1981, many GE employees thought the rock-solid company would be their meal ticket throughout their lives.

Little did they know, however, that their new CEO, Jack Welch—dubbed "Neutron Jack" by *Newsweek*—deliberately planned to destroy the old GE and create a new, more prosperous company. Welch saw that many of GE's businesses had become commodities and many were in decline.

Welch quickly set out to "fix, sell, or close" every GE business that was not No. 1 or 2 in its market globally. Welch divested $11 billion worth of businesses (including 130,000 employees), laid off 170,000 more, and added 150,000 employees via $21 billion in acquisitions. Welch pushed a common vision and evolving values, reflected in his "six rules: (1) control your own destiny; (2) face reality; (3) be candid; (4) don't manage, lead; (5) change before you have to; and (6) if you don't have a competitive advantage, don't compete."

Since 1988, Welch has been promoting GE as a "boundaryless" company. His view is that walls separating internal units should be knocked down, as should those between GE and its key outside constituencies. There should be no distinction between "domestic" and "foreign," and, in the new GE culture, labels like "management, salaried, and hourly" should not exist.[1]

WHAT MAKES A BUSINESS SUCCESSFUL?

Recent studies have shown that companies succeed when "management balances long-term risk taking with near-term commitment to make small improvements in what works, and ignores tempting opportunities that are peripheral to its core technology." One of the researchers, Joseph G. Morone of Cal-Berkeley, goes on to say that "general business and management strategy is the most significant, but least examined, factor in determining a company's ability to compete effectively. . ."[2]

Four Factors Essential to Success

What can management do to increase the likelihood that their business will be successful? While it is difficult to *guarantee* success, it is unlikely that any business will be very successful for very long without observing the following four factors:

1. *Choose the Correct Business.* The single most important decision one can make is to choose the right business to be in: that is, one with growth, profit, and diversification potential. Many firms do not define their business correctly; for example, "transportation" is not a business, it is a sector of the economy that contains more than 100 businesses. Growth potential is the most important factor in business success, closely followed by profit potential. Without growth and profit potential, the business is essentially trying to "swim upstream." Later on, when the business matures, diversification potential comes to the fore. Where will the new growth come from, and how will the transition occur?

2. *Create the Correct Strategy.* The correct strategy takes maximum advantage of the business' potential. To do so, management needs to understand the concept of strategy and its process. This includes analyzing the industry, developing strategy alternatives, and evaluating and selecting the appropriate

---

[1] "Neutron Jack and the GE Revolution," *The Real World Strategist*, 1, No. 5 (July/August 1994), 8.

[2] Chris Raymond, "What Makes a Business Successful? A Willingness to Take Risks While Focusing on What Works, Say Two Management Scholars," *The Chronicle of Higher Education* (November 14, 1990), A11-A12.

strategy. Again, the mission and vision are important both in strategy formation and implementation.

3. *Design and Develop the Correct Infrastructure.* The firm's infrastructure (systems and structure) is sometimes overlooked. Systems are important because they represent routine ways of handling information, decisions, incentives, and the like. As such, they *must* focus on the desired outcomes. Structure can affect systems and strategies, so having a supportive structure is important. The ideal structure should be linked directly to the firm's strategy and systems, and must support and facilitate them, rather than vice versa.

4. *Acquire the Correct Resources.* While there are a variety of resources an organization needs and uses (human, physical, financial, information, time, and technology), in the long run people seem to make the most difference. That is, they can determine the other resource types and how well these resources are used. Having the right people can make the difference between success and failure. In addition, success breeds success; firms that are strong in the first three factors (business, strategy, and infrastructure) tend to be better able to attract the best people.[3]

Tom Peters: Search, Passion, Chaos, and Liberation

Thomas Peters, formerly of McKinsey & Company and Stanford University, conducted a study of well-managed companies to determine the common factors that contribute to their successes. Peters' study (conducted in conjunction with Robert H. Waterman, Jr.) initially looked in-depth at ten companies that had been successful over long periods of time and continued to lead their industries: IBM, Texas Instruments, Hewlett-Packard, 3M, Digital Equipment, Procter & Gamble, Johnson & Johnson, McDonald's, Dana, and Emerson Electric. While the companies differ in many ways, Peters found eight common attributes that they adhere to and work hard to maintain:

1. *Bias toward action.* The companies are action oriented; their approach is "do it, fix it, try it." They don't analyze a problem to death before acting (paralysis by analysis), and make progress in small steps rather than through sweeping, grand plans. In this way, if the action turns out to be a mistake, they reverse the action quickly and do something else. They are flexible, incremental, and responsive. They focus quickly on problems, typically appointing a "czar" or a task force (of *line* managers) to solve them.

2. *Simple form and lean staff.* The structure or form of an organization is not an end in itself; it is a *means* to an end. The best organization structure is the simplest structure that works, regardless of how it looks on paper. Many

---

[3] Dan Thomas, *Business Sense* (New York, NY: The Free Press, 1993), v-viii.

of these companies are divided into small, entrepreneurial units that manage to get things done. Staffs are kept as small as possible to avoid bureaucracies. (Staffs have a way of growing and generating their own workload—for example, reports and analyses—that sap line managers' energies if not kept in check.)

3. *Closeness to the customer.* Successful companies tend to view the customer as an integral part of their businesses, rather than as an outsider. The companies are "customer driven." Their goods and services are designed, above all, to satisfy the customer's needs. Contrast this with the technology-, product-, or strategy-driven companies that produce products because they can be built, then try to convince customers to buy them. A classic example of a product/technology-driven company is Polaroid. Its "instant movie camera" could be built, but customers decided they did not need it. In fact, IBM does not allow managers to hold staff jobs for more than three years, because they tend to lose touch with customers.

4. *Productivity improvement through people.* The companies surveyed believe that productivity can be improved by motivating and stimulating employees, largely through giving them autonomy, feedback, and recognition programs. In fact, much of the feedback and recognition programs—for example, progress charts in the plant, badges, pins, medals, and slogans—may sound simplistic, but they work.

5. *Operational autonomy.* Well-managed companies authorize their managers to act like entrepreneurs, giving them the authority to make a wide range of decisions on their own. These companies do not unduly constrain their managers by making it impossible for them to fail—or succeed. The managers know they are in charge, and the companies rarely force them to go against their best judgment.

6. *Stress on a key business value.* The companies studied by Peters focus on a corporate value that is important to their success, yet simple enough to be clearly understood—and internalized—even by the lowest-level employees. The value may involve customer service or productivity improvement. At Iowa Beef Processors, the focus is on being the lowest-cost producer, a value that gives the company a definite strategic advantage over the competition and "drives" other decisions.

7. *Doing what they know best.* All of the companies surveyed have been able to define their strengths and build on them. They resist the temptation to move into attractive businesses that require skills the company does not have. One executive states, "Never acquire any business you don't know how to run." A cigarette company diversifying into high-technology or land development or motion pictures may be asking for trouble; on the other hand, marketing beer may be a natural extension of the company's consumer-product strengths.

8. *Simultaneous loose/tight controls.* At first glance this may appear inconsistent; how can controls be both loose *and* tight? Successful companies control

a few variables tightly, but allow flexibility and leeway in others. They do not control everything tightly, nor do they give their managers free rein on everything. There are several measures—such as return on sales or output per employee—that top management uses for control and that subordinate managers *must* meet. The subordinate has the flexibility, autonomy, and leeway he or she needs by *not* being closely measured on other variables.[4]

Reevaluating "Excellence:" Peters and Waterman expanded their research and published it in book form in 1982.[5] The book was wildly successful—hitting a management nerve—and sold over five million copies. The book was largely an attack on managers who rely too heavily on financial analysis and controls. As time went on, however, the book's message began to lose some of its luster. By 1984, several of the "excellent" companies were experiencing serious financial difficulties. Peters' response was to write a sequel, *A Passion for Excellence*, with Nancy Austin.[6] The new book attempted to identify the sources of longer-term excellence, rather than the broadbrush approach of the first book.

Critics pointed out that the entire thrust of the book is on doing things right, without examining whether the companies were doing the right things.[7] Further questions were raised by academic studies which showed that "nonexcellent" companies outperform the "excellent" ones—at least in terms of shareholder returns.[8] In reality, all this may illustrate is that the "excellent" companies had this fact reflected in their stock prices at the beginning of the study, making them vulnerable to any bad news. In any event, Peters became increasingly pessimistic about the ability of American corporations to compete in foreign markets, reflected in his book, *Thriving on Chaos*,[9] but offers potential solutions in *Liberation Management*.[10]

---

[4] Thomas J. Peters, "Putting Excellence into Management," *Business Week* (July 21, 1980), 196.

[5] Thomas J. Peters and Robert H. Waterman, Jr., *In Search of Excellence* (New York, NY: Harper & Row, 1982).

[6] T.J. Peters and Nancy Austin, *A Passion for Excellence* (New York, NY: Random House, 1985).

[7] Milton Leontiades, "Editorial: A Memo to the CEO," *Planning Review*, 14, No. 2 (March 1986), 4.

[8] W.G. Simpson and Timothy Ireland, "Managerial Excellence and Shareholder Returns," *The Journal of the American Association of Individual Investors* (August 1987).

[9] T.J. Peters, *Thriving on Chaos* (New York, NY: Alfred A. Knopf, 1987).

[10] Tom Peters, *Liberation Management* (New York, NY: A.A. Knopf, 1992).

Enter Renewal

If Peters thinks that American industry cannot compete globally, his original cohort, Robert Waterman, does not share his view. Waterman says that *In Search of Excellence* merely *described* the excellent company, and his book—*The Renewal Factor*—tells managers what is needed to become excellent and to stay there. Renewal involves retaining the best of the past, but changing with the times. It involves moving from strength to strength, effectively managing change, adapting company cultures, strategies, systems, products, and structures to survive and prosper—even through severe crises. Eight themes underlie effective renewal:

1. *Informed Opportunism.* Information is their main strategic advantage, and flexibility is their main strategic weapon. Renewing companies assume opportunity will keep knocking, but it will knock softly and in unpredictable ways.
2. *Direction and Empowerment.* Managers at renewing companies define the boundaries, and their subordinates figure out the best way to do the job within them. Managers give up some control to regain results.
3. *Friendly Facts, Congenial Control.* Renewing companies love information that provides context and removes decision making from the realm of mere opinions. Their people regard financial controls as the benign checks and balances that allow them to be creative and free.
4. *A Different Mirror.* Leaders are open and inquisitive. They get ideas from almost anyone in and out of the hierarchy, such as customers, competitors, and even next-door neighbors.
5. *Teamwork, Trust, Politics, and Power.* Renewers stress the value of teamwork and trust their employees to do the job. While relentless at fighting office politics, they acknowledge politics are inevitable in the workplace.
6. *Stability in Motion.* Renewing companies undergo constant change against a base of underlying stability. They understand the need for consistency and norms. But they also realize that the only way to respond to change is to deliberately break the rules.
7. *Attitudes and Attention.* Visible management attention, rather than exhortation, gets things done. Action may start with the words, but it has to be backed by symbolic behavior that makes those words come alive.
8. *Causes and Commitment.* Commitment results from management's ability to turn grand causes into small actions so that everyone can contribute to the central purpose.[11]

---

[11] R.H. Waterman, *The Renewal Factor: How the Best Get and Keep the Competitive Edge* (New York, NY: Bantam Books, 1987).

DEFINING CRITICAL SUCCESS FACTORS

An important step in the strategic process is to identify the critical external factors, largely uncontrollable by the firm, that have an impact on effectiveness. Similarly, *critical success factors* (CSFs), typically pertaining to the industry and the firm, must be identified. Once these external and internal factors are identified, their impact can be assessed. Critical success factors for any business are the limited number of areas in which satisfactory results ensure successful competitive performance. Studies have shown that three to six factors are usually critical to success in most industries; these are the areas where things must go right if the firm is to flourish. If they do not, the firm's performance is likely to be disappointing, regardless of its performance on other factors.[12] Thus, these factors are of paramount importance in formulating and evaluating strategies.

CSFs apply more broadly than just to business success; they apply to almost any human endeavor—family life, school work, marriage, sports, and so on. A recent survey asked moviegoers which factors were most critical in their choice of a particular movie. One-third cited favorable reviews, 20 percent responded to TV ads, and 20 percent based their decision on a friend's suggestion. On the other hand, show time convenience influenced only 1 percent, and newspaper ads only 10 percent.[13]

Critical success factors can be examined at several levels; those relating to the firm, to the industry, and to the general environment. Obviously, all three levels are important.

More specifically, CSFs can be influenced by the *sector* of the economy of which the business is a part. For example, for-profit businesses would typically have different CSFs than not-for-profit businesses and public-sector organizations. Other factors could be influenced by the *industry*; for example, industry structure and type of market (whether perfectly competitive, or monopolistic, for example). Also, the *strategic group* would exert an influence, depending on the types of strategies and focus pursued by the group. Internally, the firm's distinctive competencies and competitive advantages would impact the relative importance of CSFs. As a final point, critical success factors are also likely to change with the stage of the product/market life cycle, as well as with changes in strategic group membership, competition, and focus.

Table 4.1 lists CSFs for several industries, while Table 4.2 takes a closer look at CSFs for four firms in the semiconductor industry. The point is that the industry factors would apply to all firms in the industry, but individual firms

---

[12] J.E. Rockart, "Chief Executives Define Their Own Data Needs," *Harvard Business Review* (March/April 1979), 81.

[13] "A Thumbs Up' Pulls in the Audience," *The Wall Street Journal* (March 23, 1994), C1.

Table 4.1 Critical Success Factors for Selected Industries

Automotive	Semiconductor	Food Processing	Life Insurance
Styling	Manufacturing process, cost efficient, innovative, cumulative experience	New-product development	Development of agency personnel
Perceived quality			
Strong dealer network		Good distribution	Effective control of clerical personnel
Manufacturing cost control	Technological competence, adequate technical product development	Effective advertising	Innovation in policy development
Ability to meet EPA standards	Capital availability		Innovative advertising
			Marketing strategy

Source: Adapted from *Long-Range Planning*, 17 (February 1984), J.K. Leidecker and A.V. Bruno, "Identifying and Using Critical Success Factors," 24. Copyright 1984, Pergamon Press, Ltd. Reprinted with permission.

may have unique CSFs because of their relative positions and thrusts within the industry.

Looking at CSFs another way, as Table 4.3 shows, the degree of criticalness of certain factors varies by industry. And, as shown in Table 4.4, they also vary for firms within the same industry.

In general, at least five criteria tend to determine which factors are critical to the business and their relative importance:

1. Impact on performance measures, such as market share, profits, cash flow, etc.
2. Relationship to strategic thrusts, such as differentiation, costs, segmentation, preemptive, turnaround, renewal, and the like.

Table 4.2 Critical Success Factors for Selected Firms in the Semiconductor Industry

National Semiconductor	Intel	Advanced Micro Devices	Avantek
Broad product line	Innovator and leader in technology	Proprietary innovative products	Strong transistor line
Large efficient production capacity	Strong product development and customer service capability	Does not compete in price-sensitive markets	Solid customer range High-yield manufacturing
Vertically integrated		Effective location of fabrication and assembly	
Innovative packaging and assembly operations	High-margin proprietary devices	Operations; strong technical marketing capabilities	

Source: Reprinted with permission from *Long-Range Planning*, 17 (February 1984), J.K. Leidecker and A.V. Bruno, "Identifying and Using Critical Success Factors," 24. Copyright 1984, Pergamon Press. Ltd.

3. Relationship to life-cycle stage; that is, introduction, growth, maturity, and aging and decline.
4. Relates to a major activity of the business, such as marketing at IBM.
5. Involves large amounts of money relative to other activities of the firm.

There are several techniques for identifying CSFs for a business, its industry, and its general environment. They include environmental scanning, industry structure analysis, opinions of experts in the industry, analysis of competitors, analysis of the industry's dominant firm, a specific assessment of the company, intuitive judgment or "feel" of insiders, and profit impact of market strategy

Table 4.3 Importance of Selected CSFs for Four Industries

	Industry			
Factor	Soft-drink Bottlers	Semiconductor Manufacturers	Ferrous Metals Distribution	Tax Preparation
Basic R&D	Slight	Major	Unimportant	Unimportant
New-product development	Secondary	Major	Slight	Unimportant
Manufacturing	Major	Major	Secondary	Unimportant
Distribution	Major	Secondary	Major	Slight
Customer service	Major	Secondary	Major	Major
Advertising	Secondary	Unimportant	Unimportant	Secondary
Post-sales service	Secondary	Slight	Slight	Major

*Classifications are for purposes of discussion.

Source: Reprinted with permission from *Long-Range Planning*, 17 (February 1984), J.K. Leidecker and A.V. Bruno, "Identifying and Using Critical Success Factors," 31. Copyright 1984, Pergamon Press. Ltd.

(PIMS) data.[14] The focus, sources, advantages, and disadvantages of each of these techniques are listed in Table 4.5. Remember that these techniques are to be used in conjunction with one another, not in place of one another.

Finally, keep in mind that the way the dominant firm in an industry conducts business can provide insights into an industry's CSFs. Figure 4.1 is an illustration of this approach based upon the leading firm in the electronic components distribution industry. This figure also illustrates how the CSF concept fits in with the firm's goal structure. Expert input is required to judge those elements in the hierarchy that are critical, as well as unique relationships that may exist. Keep in mind, however, that blindly copying the leading firm in an industry may be counterproductive and a recipe for disaster; less-dominant firms may need to carve out their own niche, which, along with different competitive advantages, may produce a very different set of CSFs.

---

[14] J.K. Leidecker and A.V. Bruno, "Identifying and Using Critical Success Factors," *Long-Range Planning*, 17 (February 1984), 26-31.

Table 4.4 Importance of Selected CSFs for Four Semiconductor Manufacturers

	Firm			
Factor	National Semiconductor	Intel	Signetics	Texas Instruments
Basic R&D	Slight	Major	Slight	Secondary
New-product development	Secondary	Major	Secondary	Major
Manufacturing	Major	Major	Major	Major
Distribution	Major	Secondary	Secondary	Major
Customer service	Major	Secondary	Secondary	Major
Advertising	Slight	Slight	Slight	Secondary
Post-sales service	Unimportant	Unimportant	Unimportant	Secondary

*Classifications are for purposes of discussion.

Source: Reprinted with permission from *Long-Range Planning*, 17 (February 1984), J.K. Leidecker and A.V Bruno, "Identifying and Using Critical Success Factors," 31. Copyright 1984, Pergamon Press, Ltd.

Critical Failure Factors

As important as critical success factor analysis may be, it is also helpful to examine those factors critical to *failure*—those which must be avoided. Contrasting the two lists—CSFs vs. CFFs—can be interesting and even more informative. Many of us are familiar with recent product failures, but we may be unaware of the reasons for their failure.

- BIC Perfume: Customers did not respond to perfume resembling a cigarette lighter.
- NEXT Computer: Job's black box used an optical drive customers didn't want.
- Cadillac Allante: GM rushed the introduction, leaving "bugs" aplenty.
- Dry Beer: Consumers were never quite sure what it was.
- Pepsi A.M.: Consumers preferred the traditional Pepsi taste.

Table 4.5 Techniques for Identifying Critical Success Factors

Technique	Focus	Sources	Advantages	Disadvantages
Environmental analysis	Macro	Environmental scanning (corporate staff) Econometric models Sociopolitical consulting services	Future orientation Macro orientation: analysis goes beyond industry/firm focus Can be linked to threats/opportunity evaluation	More difficult to operationalize into specific industry or firm CSFs Results may not lend themselves to incorporate usage in current time frame (today's CSFs)
Analysis of industry structure	Industry Macro	A variety of industry structure frameworks	Specific focus is on industry Frameworks allow user to understand interrelationships between industry structural components Can force more macro level focus (beyond industry boundaries)	While excellent source for industry wide CSFs, not as useful in determining firm specific CSFs
Industry/business experts	Industry Micro	Industry association executives Financial analysts specializing in industry Outsider familiar with firms in industry Knowledgeable insiders who work in industry	Means of soliciting conventional wisdom about industry and firms Subjective information very often not discovered with more objective, formal, and analytical approaches	Lack of objectivity often leads to questions of verifiability/justification
Analysis of competition (focus is limited to the competitive environment, how firms compete)	Industry Micro	Staff specialists Line managers Internal consultants External consultants	Narrowness of focus, offers advantage of detailed, specific data Depth of analysis leads to better means of justification	Narrowness of focus, CSF development limited to competitive arena (as opposed to industry structure approach)

Table 4.5 (Concluded)

Technique	Focus	Sources	Advantages	Disadvantages
Analysis of the dominant firm in the industry	Industry Micro	Staff specialists Line managers Internal consultants External consultants	Dominant competitor may in fact set industry CSFs Understanding of number 1 may assist in corroborating firm specific CSFs	Narrow focus may preclude seeking alternative explanations of success May limit individual firm's strategic response and focus
Company assessment (comprehensive, firm specific)	Micro	Internal staff line organizations (detailed analyses by organization function—checklist approach)	A thorough functional area screening reveals internal/strengths and weaknesses that may assist CSF development	Narrow focus of analysis precludes inputs of more macro approaches Checklist approach can be very time-consuming and become data bound
Intuitive judgment (firm specific)	Micro	Internal staff Brainstorming CEO/General management observation	More subjective and not limited to functional analysis approach Leads to identification of important short-run CSFs that may go unnoticed in more formal reviews	Difficulty in justifying as CSF if of short-term duration Important factors may be overstated, if, in fact, a short-run phenomenon
PIMS data	Industry Micro	Articles of PIMS project results	Empirically based Excellent starting point	General nature Applicability to your specific firm or industry Determination of relative importance

Source: Reprinted with permission from *Long-Range Planning*, 17 (February 1984), J.K. Leidecker and A.V. Bruno, "Identifying and Using Critical Success Factors," 26. Copyright 1984, The Pergamon Press, Ltd.

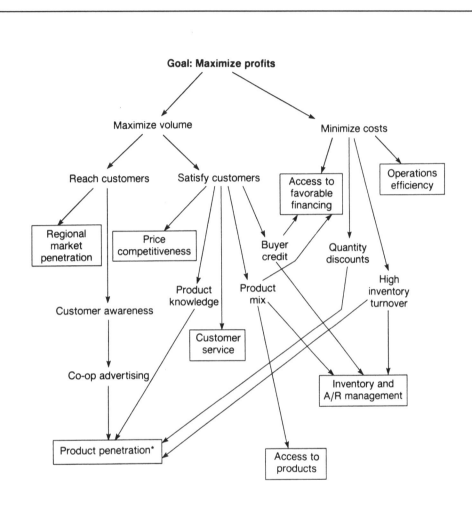

Goal: Maximize profits

*Production penetration = all the sales and/or marketing activities that make the distributor the preferred supplier for the customer by creating awareness of the firm's product mix, depth, and potential to benefit the customer through dissemination of product knowledge, value-added, and purchase discounts.

Source: J.K. Leidecker and A.V. Bruno, "Critical Success Factor Analysis and the Strategy Development Process," in *Strategic Planning and Management Handbook*, eds. W.R. King and D.I. Cleland (New York, NY: Van Nostrand Reinhold, 1987), 343.

Figure 4.1 **Electronic Component Distribution Industry CSFs**

Numerous other flops abound, from the Edsel to New Coke to Corfam to Polavision.[15] One of the few research efforts to isolate CFFs focused on failure factors for TQM implementation. The results are shown in Table 4.6.

Table 4.6 Failure Factors for TQM Implementation

Rank	Problem	Frequency	(%)
1	Lack of upper management involvement	59	30.1
2	Resistance to change	43	21.9
3	Poor middle-management attitudes	41	20.9
4	Lack of team concepts	40	20.4

Source: Adapted from Kwansik Cho, *Impact of Total Quality Management on Organizational Performance in the US: An Empirical Investigation of Critical Success Factors*, unpublished doctoral dissertation, University of Nebraska (April 1994), 150.

PIMS DATA

The profit impact of market strategy (PIMS) program began in 1960 as an internal project at GE in an attempt to discover the consequences of strategic business decisions. The goal was to discover the "laws of nature" that operate in the marketplace—the relationship between business-level decisions and their consequences. Using regression models, GE attempted to explain how return on investment (ROI) varied for its businesses in diverse markets and industries; in other words, which variables affect ROI, and what is their relative contribution?

The PIMS program was transferred to the Harvard Business School in 1972 and enlarged to include other companies, as well. In 1975, the member companies formed a nonprofit corporation, the Strategic Planning Institute (SPI), to manage the PIMS project. Currently, the PIMS data base includes information on over 3,000 "businesses" (SBUs) from over 450 medium to large organizations in the United States and Europe. In return for submitting about 100 proprietary data items to SPI, the member firms receive feedback indicating how their strategic decisions and results compare with those of the other companies, and what strategic changes hold promise for improving their future performance.

---

[15] Christopher Power, "Flops," *Business Week* (August 16, 1993), 31-37.

Despite some criticism, the PIMS project has been a valuable source of concrete data on the results of strategic decisions, and has benefited the member companies. The fundamental PIMS concept is that there are certain strategic characteristics that companies and their markets have in common and that tend to determine profitability and cash flow. SPI has identified 37 key variables that together explain about 80 percent of the variance in ROI, for example. The following key findings summarize the PIMS results to date:

1. Business situations are generally regular and predictable. The performance of a business can be predicted with reasonable accuracy by the factors PIMS has identified.
2. Business situations obey common laws of the marketplace. This makes strategic management more of an applied science, and enables trained strategists to recommend strategies to the business.
3. Laws of the marketplace explain about 80 percent of the variance in business performance, as described above.
4. There are a number of important linkages between strategy and performance. For example:

   a. In the long run, the most important single factor affecting a business unit's performance is the *quality* of its products and services relative to those of its competitors. Higher quality boosts performance in two ways:

      (1) In the short run, superior quality yields increased profits via premium prices (on average, businesses with superior quality products have costs about equal to competitors').
      (2) In the long run, superior and/or improving quality is the most effective way for a business to grow, leading to market expansion and increasing market share.

   b. *Market share* and profitability are strongly related, since large-share businesses tend to have lower unit costs.[16]

   c. *Investment intensity* (investment as a percent of sales) is inversely related to profitability and cash flow. Investment is working capital plus fixed capital at book value.

   d. *Vertical integration* (making rather than buying components, for example) favorably affects performance only in mature, stable markets; in growing, declining, or unstable markets, the opposite is true.

   e. *Productivity* is directly related to profitability and cash flow.

---

[16] R.D. Buzzell and B.T. Gale, *The PIMS Principles: Linking Strategy to Performance* (New York, NY: The Free Press, 1987), 1-15.

    f.   *Growth of served market* is positively related to profitability in terms of dollars, indifferent to percent of profitability, and negatively related to cash flow.

    g.   *Innovation and/or differentiation* activities produce positive effects on performance if the firm already has a strong market position; otherwise, they usually do not.

    h.   *Cost-push factors*, such as wages, salaries, material costs, and the presence of unions depend on how the company is positioned; that is, whether or not it can pass along the costs.

    i.   *Current strategic efforts* may have effects opposite to those just described; for example, a high market share increases cash flow, but attempts to increase share drain cash.

5. Interaction of the factors is complex. Sometimes they offset, sometimes they reinforce one another, and sometimes they produce temporarily opposite effects.

6. Product characteristics do not matter; *business* characteristics, such as the nine described above, do matter.

7. The characteristics make their effects felt over time.

8. Business strategies tend to be successful if their fundamentals (the laws of the marketplace) are sound; unsuccessful if their fundamentals are not.

9. Most clear strategy signals are robust; that is, the above-mentioned effects usually override small-to medium-sized errors (such as in measuring one of the variables) and are therefore not sensitive to relatively minor errors or misinterpretation.

The major PIMS findings are summarized in Tables 4.7 and 4.8. Keep in mind that the findings represent average or typical relationships; there are exceptions. For example, while market share correlates highly with return on investment (ROI) and return on sales (ROS), there are some very successful low-share businesses. While some confusion can creep in depending on how the market, and, therefore, its shares are defined, businesses that are not typical tend to have their own critical success factors that may differ from the average.

Despite criticism, recent studies have tended to uphold the basic PIMS relationships. For example, Mark Chussil systematically tackled each of the arguments against the role of market share in determining organizational performance, and concluded that "the statistical evidence in favor of a positive relationship between market share and ROI is too compelling to dismiss. . . but, the data don't show an indisputable causal relationship. . ."[17]

---

[17] Mark J. Chussil, "Does Market Share Really Matter?" *Planning Review*, 19, No. 5 (September/October 1991), 31-37.

Table 4.7 PIMS Findings Regarding Competitive Position, Strategy, and Profitability

| | Impact on | |
| | ROI | ROS |
Competitive Position/Strategy Factors	+ = Positive	− = Negative
Share of served market	+	+
Relative product/service quality	+	+
New products, percent of sales	−	−
R&D expense, percent of sales	−	−
Marketing expense, percent of sales	−	−
Value added, percent of sales*	+	+
Fixed assets, percent of sales (at capacity)	−	−
Newness of plant and equipment	+	+
Labor productivity	+	+
Inventories, percent of sales	−	−
Capacity utilization rate	+	+
FIFO inventory valuation	+	+

*Value added is adjusted to remove above-average or compensate for below-average net profits.

Source: Adapted from R.D. Buzzell and B.T. Gale, *The PIMS Principles: Linking Strategy to Performance* (New York, NY: The Free Press, 1987), 46. Used with permission.

Joachim Schwalbach in Germany sheds some additional light on the market share-profitability relationship. His PIMS study found that small share businesses were not less profitable, per se. In services and raw or semi-finished materials, they were at least as profitable as large-share businesses. In some markets— services, retail, wholesale—the most profitable were either large or small, not mid-range. Lastly, very-large-share businesses (over 65-70 percent) were often less profitable.[18]

One problem with the market share data is the imprecision in defining market share. For example, market share is not merely percent of industry sales; most industries contain multiple markets. Mercedes has a small share of the automobile industry, but a strong share of the luxury car market.[19]

---

[18] Joachim Schwalbach, "Profitability and Market Share: A Reflection on the Functional Relationship," *Strategic Management Journal*, 12, No. 4 (May 1991), 299-306.

[19] Chussil, *op. cit.*, 34.

Table 4.8 PIMS Findings Regarding Market/Industry Influences on Profitability

	Impact on	
	ROI	ROS
Market/Industry Profit Influences	+ = Positive	− = Negative
Real market growth rate (annual %)	+	+
Stage of market evolution		
Growth stage	+	+
Decline stage	−	−
Rate of inflation in selling prices	+	+
Concentration of purchases with few suppliers	+	(+)*
Typical customer purchase amount		
Small	+	+
Large	−	−
Importance of product purchase to customer		
Low	+	+
High	−	−
Percent of employees unionized	−	−
Industry exports	+	+
Industry imports	−	−
Standardized products (versus custom produced)	+	+

*Relationship not statistically significant.

Source: Adapted from R.D. Buzzell and B.T. Gale, *The PIMS Principles: Linking Strategy to Performance* (New York, NY: The Free Press, 1987), 47. Used with permission.

Module
5

Planning for
Uncertain Futures

LEARNING OBJECTIVES

After completing Module 5, you should be able to:

1. Realize that the future is in many ways unpredictable.
2. Relate ways to cope with and plan in chaotic environments.
3. Describe the primary forecasting techniques and their features and applicability.
4. Understand the role of risk analysis in making strategic decisions.
5. Realize the importance and roles of contingency and scenario-based planning, as well as issue and surprise management.

To reiterate a point made earlier, effective planning and strategic management are flexible, adaptive processes. Successful organizations adapt themselves to the business environment; they are successful because they have managers who learn quickly and cause their organizations to respond effectively. However, most organizations "learn" more slowly than individuals do. Therefore, an important aspect of the corporate planning function is to cause the company to speed up its learning processes; that is, recognizing environmental change, digesting the new information, confirming it, and acting on it. Some companies—Shell Oil, for example—consider the prime value of the planning function to be speeding up the organizational learning process, not just "making plans." Shell does this through changing the way executives see and think about their markets, competitors, and businesses, using what-if scenarios, computer models, and other techniques to be discussed in later modules. Many times, the ability to learn faster than competitors is the only real sustainable advantage a company has.[1] On the other hand, frequent strategy shifts may cause an organization to lose its focus or direction.[2] Balancing the need to respond quickly while maintaining a sense of direction is no easy task.

PROFILE

Swatch

The Swiss have traditionally set the standard for the world's watchmakers. With names like Rolex and Patek Phillipe, the Swiss dominated the industry with 43 percent of the world's market in 1970. Over the years, they had successfully blunted competition from low end products such as Timex and other competitors. But one of their own inventions—which they pooh-poohed as not being a "real watch"—was nearly their undoing. Their invention, the quartz watch, was picked up by Japanese competitors like Casio, Citizen, and Seiko, and caused sales of traditional Swiss watches to plummet. These new quartz watches could keep better time than the very best mechanical watches, and at a fraction of the price. As a result, Swiss exports fell by more than half and their market share dropped to as low as 15 percent.

This unforeseen event sent the Swiss scrambling. Some recommended withdrawing from all but the luxury end of the market, as numerous companies were going bankrupt or merging. But Nicolas Hayek saw another possibility. Using a strategy of product originality, quality, and carefully targeted marketing, his company—Societe Suisse Microelectronique et d'Horlogerie (SMH)—created the

---

[1] Arie P. DeGeus, "Planning as Learning," *Harvard Business Review*, 66, No. 2 (March/April 1988), 70.

[2] Robert Lamb and Paul Shrivastava, eds., *Advances in Strategic Management*, Vol. 5 (Greenwich, CT: JAI Press, 1988), xi.

Swatch line in 1982. The initial Swatches were highly accurate, waterproof, shock resistant, and low cost (because they are made with synthetic materials). Swatch created a new market—the inexpensive, "fun" watch. As a result, Switzerland once again accounts for the majority of the watches sold in the world.[3] Who said an industry like watchmaking was predictable and unexciting?

THE FUTURE: PREDICTABLE OR CHAOTIC?

Traditional "strategic planners" put a heavy premium on forecasting the future in order to formulate their detailed plans. Often, they made assumptions concerning the future that ended up being far off the mark, rendering their plans useless. In response, critics have said that the future is unpredictable, so it is useless to try to predict it; and it is useless to try to plan for it. In reality, the future is not likely to fall at either extreme; it is not going to be perfectly predictable, nor is it likely to be totally chaotic. There will be varying degrees of risk and uncertainty in all future happenings. How to cope with unpredictability is an essential skill for the strategic manager.

Coping With Chaos

Chaos theory holds that many complex phenomena are inherently unpredictable. Even nature, once viewed as inherently orderly, is coming to be viewed by many scientists as inherently disorderly. Chaos theory holds that the long-term behavior of a system (the weather, the universe, etc.) cannot be predicted with certainty unless the initial conditions of that system are known with certainty—which is impossible.[4]

Scientists have recently discovered that systems in nature are capable of endless variety because their dynamics are *chaotic*—unpredictable new patterns emerge through a process of spontaneous self-organization. Human organizations are also dynamic feedback systems. Therefore, these new discoveries—chaos and self-organization—apply to *organizations* and provide managers with totally new ways of understanding their change and development.[5] Table 5.1 compares the traditional and chaos theory frames of reference—paradigms—for strategic man-

---

[3] Andrew Rosenbaum, "Switzerland's Watch Industry: Changing with the Times, *Hemispheres* (June 1994), 39.

[4] Dennis Farney, "Chaos Theory Seeps into Ecology Debate, Stirring Up a Tempest," *The Wall Street Journal* (July 11, 1994), A1.

[5] Ralph Stacey, "Strategy as Order Emerging From Chaos," *Long-Range Planning*, 26, No. 1, (1993), 10-17.

Table 5.1 Changing the Frame of Reference for Strategic Management

Traditional	Chaos Theory
Long-term future is predictable.	Long-term future is unknowable.
Visions and plans are central to strategic management.	Dynamic agendas of strategic issues are central to effective strategic management.
Vision: single shared organization-wide intention. A picture of a future state.	Challenge: multiple aspirations, stretching and ambiguous. Arising out of current ill-structured and conflicting issues with long-term consequences.
Strongly shared cultures.	Contradictory counter-cultures.
Cohesive teams of managers operating in state of consensus.	Learning groups of managers, surfacing conflict, engaging in dialogue, publicly testing assertions.
Decision-making as purely logical, analytical process.	Decision-making as exploratory, experimental process based on intuition and reasoning by analogy.
Long-term control and development as the monitoring of progress against plan milestones. Constraints provided by rules, systems and rational argument.	Control and development in open-ended situations as a political process. Constraints provided by need to build and sustain support. Control as self-policing learning.
Strategy as the realization of prior intent.	Strategy as spontaneously emerging from the chaos of challenge and contradiction, through a process of real time learning and politics.
Top management drives and controls strategic direction.	Top management creates favorable conditions for complex learning and politics.
General mental models and prescriptions for many specific situations.	New mental models required for each new strategic situation.
Adaptive equilibrium with the environment.	Non-equilibrium, creative interaction with the environment.

Source: Adapted from Ralph Stacey, "Strategy as Order Emerging from Chaos," *Long-Range Planning*, 26, No. 1 (1993), 13.

agement. Remember, these frames of reference represent end points on a continuum, so most situations contain varying elements of each.

Concerning business organizations, the biggest causes of financial problems are severe, random changes in the environment, plus the firm's inability to respond adequately. Top performers, in contrast, tend to be those who can "reinvent" themselves in response to these unpredictable changes. While chaos theory acknowledges apparent randomness in many phenomena, it also recognizes "inherent unpredictability that can't be removed by a simple process of collecting and analyzing data." However, this randomness occurs within limits; within constraints, patterns, or boundaries. Therefore, things may be chaotic or unpredictable at the *local* level, but can still be part of a stable pattern at the global level; there is *disorder within order*.[6] For example, any single roll of the dice may be unpredictable, but after a large number of rolls, a predictable pattern will emerge.

A few properties of chaotic systems would include the following:

- Non-linearity. In chaotic non-linear systems, a seemingly small force may have an astounding effect, such as the "straw that breaks the camel's back."
- Sensitivity to initial conditions. Future events can be "infinitely" sensitive to the past; two seemingly identical systems (e.g., organizations) will eventually be very different because of small initial differences. These differences don't cancel each other, but can multiply, like microphone feedback. An example is the relatively insignificant lawsuit against AT&T by MCI that had worldwide ramifications.
- Bifurcations, or unexpected catastrophic changes. Chaos often hides under apparently smooth-running systems, appearing suddenly, like an earthquake. Examples are the fall of the Berlin wall, the Soviet Union, and erupting problems with products like Halcion or Dow Corning's silicone breast implants.[7]

What Does it All Mean? One lesson is that randomness is rampant. Everything (at the micro level) has a stochastic element; unexpected, "irrational" events *will* occur. Secondly, more information does not ensure better predictions. In a random series, previous numbers give no clue as to the next number in the series. Thirdly, successful organizations operate with "positive feedback loops," which recognize unexpected happenings as *opportunities* for growth and transformation.

---

[6] Richard Daft and Robert H. Lengel, "The Challenge of Chaos," *The Owen Manager*, (Spring 1993), 1.

[7] *Ibid.*

In short, chaos "adds up to a new way of managing." The new way is "decentralized, encourages trial and error," rewards positive feedback loops, and "lets the organization get lucky." In this new world, managers don't need more and more data, can't control random events, but should rely on their vision of the overall pattern at the global level.[8] In fact, the key to competitive advantage may lie in being the one producing the chaos through innovation, thus forcing competitors to react.

PLANNING UNDER RISK AND UNCERTAINTY

Ansoff has repeatedly pointed out that predicting the future is becoming progressively more difficult for firms, since the future is becoming less and less predictable. As shown in Figure 5.1, events are becoming more discontinuous and novel, change is occurring faster than the firm's ability to respond, and the future contains more surprises. Prior to the mid-1970s, there was little need to anticipate crises such as inflation, materials shortages, and similar dilemmas. The current era, however, seems to be characterized by a nervous uncertainty. How to deal with this uncertainty causes uneasiness among strategic planners, and has led to a search for new methods to cope with unexpected events. Risk and uncertainty may be anticipated and responded to, and surprises avoided by increasing awareness of the environment and by preparing reactions to possible circumstances *in advance*. Multiple scenarios (which assume alternative sets of future conditions) and contingency planning are employed in some firms to mitigate the effect of future surprises.

In the past, managers were able to rely on judgment and intuition if analytical techniques were unavailable or in dealing with areas that the techniques were not able to treat. Problems, situations, and decisions are becoming progressively more complex and interrelated, however, and a manager needs progressively more help in dealing with those problems, situations, and decisions. It is not that judgment and intuition are no longer necessary; they are no longer *sufficient*.

Risk Analysis. The essence of managerial action today involves dealing with risks. Risk is inherent in any activity, because we live in a probabilistic world— one where nothing is absolutely certain. The successful decision maker is one who understands the existence of risk, is able to ascertain the degree of risk that exists, evaluates the potential desirable and undesirable outcomes and their ratio, limits assumed risks to tolerable levels (given the situation and resources), and is able to make decisions in this context. Much of the above is included in what

---

[8] *Ibid.*

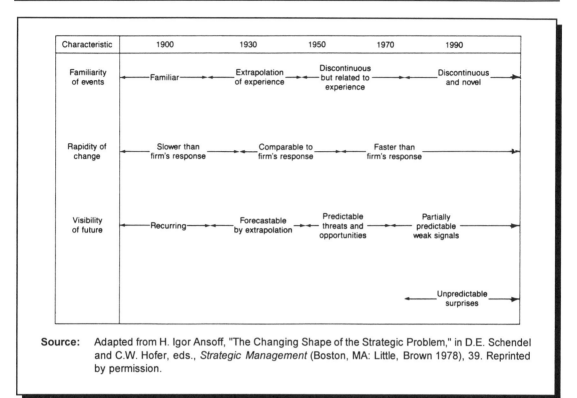

Characteristic	1900	1930	1950	1970	1990
Familiarity of events	←——Familiar——→	←— Extrapolation of experience —→	←— Discontinuous but related to experience —→	←—	Discontinuous and novel —→
Rapidity of change	←— Slower than firm's response —→	←— Comparable to firm's response —→	←— Faster than firm's response ———————→		
Visibility of future	←——Recurring——→	←— Forecastable by extrapolation —→	←— Predictable threats and opportunities —→	←— Partially predictable weak signals ——→	
				←— Unpredictable surprises ——→	

Source: Adapted from H. Igor Ansoff, "The Changing Shape of the Strategic Problem," in D.E. Schendel and C.W. Hofer, eds., *Strategic Management* (Boston, MA: Little, Brown 1978), 39. Reprinted by permission.

Figure 5.1 Decreasing Predictability of the Future

we typically call *judgment*, knowing when and when not to pursue certain courses of action.

Simply stated, risk analysis involves determining the unfavorable outcomes possible as the result of a decision or action, and evaluating how likely it is that one or more of these undesirable events will occur. The likelihood that a venture will fail, and to what degree, is information every manager and planner needs to make decisions. If the needed information does not exist, it must be judged, guessed at, appraised by experts, or estimated by other means—but it cannot be ignored.

The prudent manager will weigh the risk-to-reward ratio, ensuring that the favorable outcomes and their likelihood (return) clearly exceed the unfavorable outcomes and their likelihood (risk), as Figure 5.2 illustrates. Before proceeding, this manager will make sure that the organization can afford the worst possible case since the most unfavorable set of outcomes *does* sometimes occur.

One of the major risks and uncertainties facing multinational firms today, for example, is that of political changes in the host country. Surveys of corporate executives, dating back to the 1960s, have found that managers rank political in-

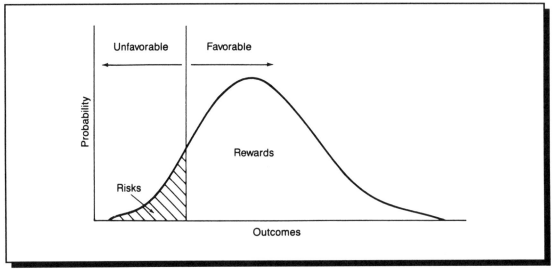

Figure 5.2 Risk Analysis

stability as one of their major considerations when making foreign investment decisions.

Regardless of whether the risk is foreign or domestic, predictable or unpredictable, however, logical processes can be followed to identify these risks and incorporate them into the strategic decision process.

Certain risks arise from the occurrence of surprise events, some of which may be anticipatable (such as strikes, wars, technological breakthroughs, and the like), while others may be unanticipatable (such as acts of God, fires, earthquakes, timing of stock market crashes, and plane crashes). By studying emerging issues and employing possible future scenarios, anticipatable surprises can be spotted and perhaps prevented or minimized by early action. On the other hand, the best we can do for unanticipatable surprises is to study them on a "what if" basis using future scenarios, and develop contingency plans to enable us to react as effectively as possible in the event the surprise scenario does occur. Figure 5.3 illustrates these relationships.

Forecasting

Strategic management deals with the future. In attempting to decide what a firm can and should do to fit into its environment, three things are necessary: (1) strategic decision-makers must be able to *forecast* what that environment will be like in the future (which is when strategic decisions made today will be implemented); (2) managers must be able to assess the firm's ability to implement strategic decisions in the future; and (3) the firm must be able to react and adapt

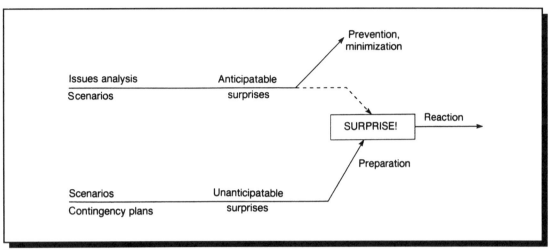

Figure 5.3 **Anticipatable and Unanticipatable Surprises**

to unforeseen or unpredictable environmental conditions which it is unable to predict. While all three are essential, the focus here is on predicting the future environment and being able to satisfactorily respond to the unpredictable. Forecasting techniques for the most predictable events, as well as techniques and approaches for dealing with the risks and uncertainties presented by less predictable happenings, will be examined. Techniques for contingency planning, possible future scenarios, and downright surprises are discussed in a later section of this module. Surprises, or sudden environmental changes, pose perhaps the greatest threats, but also offer the best opportunities for firms to change their relative positions in the market.

Strategic forecasting primarily involves *predictions*—assumptions about the future—not projections. Projections are extensions of the past into the future, and may be appropriate for forecasting (or predicting) changes if the future does not radically or drastically depart from the present or the past. If changes occur suddenly, or if there are drastic breaks with the present and the past, change is discontinuous. With discontinuous change, projections do not make very good predictions, and most common forecasting techniques prove inadequate. Figure 5.4 shows that projection-based forecasting techniques fall short in predicting surprise events, and should be supplemented with approaches designed to predict discontinuities.

A forecasting technique that projects very precisely but misses surprise events is definitely of less value to a strategic decision maker than is a less precise approach that signals the likelihood of events that may result in discontinuities. It is better to be "roughly right" than "precisely wrong." Furthermore, it is more important for the strategist to correctly predict and assess the impact of

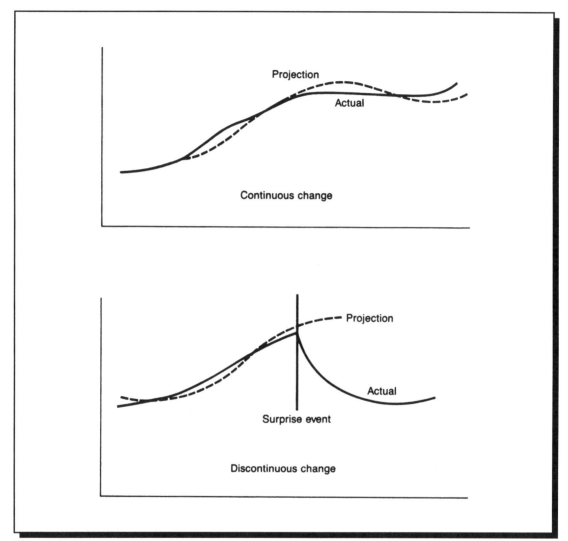

Figure 5.4 Projection Techniques with Continuous and Discontinuous Change

major or broad changes than it is to predict specific changes that may be over-ridden by the broader trends. Predicting such trends, unfortunately, may be the easy part. The difficult task is predicting their effects and timing. For example, it may well be that the United States is in the process of restructuring itself from an industrial society to one based on information and knowledge, but what does this mean in terms of specifics? What effect will that phenomenon have on particular industries? And over what time frame and at what rate will changes take place?

Forecasting Techniques

Almost every strategic decision involves some sort of forecast. Therefore, the more the executive knows about forecasting techniques—including their strengths, weaknesses, and general applicability to specific types of forecasting situations—the better and more reliable his or her decisions will be. Selection of appropriate forecasting methods depends on a number of factors, including: the type of decision to be made, the availability of pertinent data, the required degree of accuracy, the length of the forecast period, the amount of time available for analysis, the importance of the forecast to the firm, and the stage of the product's life cycle. In general, four questions need to be answered *prior* to selecting a forecasting technique:

1. How is the forecast to be used? The purpose of the forecast determines its required accuracy and precision. A basic trade-off exists between the cost of producing the forecast and its accuracy. More accurate forecasting methods typically consume more resources, and less accurate methods cost less. Most strategic decisions do not require absolute accuracy. However, as accuracy declines, the cost of inaccuracy (the cost of making forecasting errors) increases, making a midrange level of accuracy the least-cost choice for many decisions.
2. What are the relationships between the variables to be forecast and the variables dependent on them? Specifically, what are the causal and interaction effects of the environmental variables to be forecast and company performance?
3. Can the past and present be reliably used to predict the future? To what degree?[9]
4. What decisions are the forecasts intended to support, and how do they relate to the product life cycle? Certain types of decisions tend to be made at various stages of the product life cycle (and before introduction, during the product development phase). Certain types of techniques support decision needs in each life-cycle stage. Further, it must be realized that no technique can accurately predict specific surprises, but it may predict average or aggregate events with precision.

---

[9] J.G. Chambers, S.K. Mullick, and D.D. Smith, "How to Choose the Right Forecasting Technique," *Harvard Business Review*, 49, No. 4 (July/August 1971), 45.

Qualitative Techniques. Qualitative techniques are likely to be used when data are scarce, such as prior to or during product introduction. These forecasts are based on opinion, judgment, and "feel" or personal experience, and generally represent the opinion or advice of some person or group knowledgeable in the area. Such forecasts are difficult to prove or disprove, and faith in them is largely a function of the reputation and track record of the forecaster. Sometimes, visionary forecasts, historical analogies, and panel consensus methods are classified as qualitative techniques. Many times, qualitative approaches are used in conjunction with more objective or quantitative approaches, with expert judgment (qualitative) used to interpret the results of the more formal methods.

Opinion Quantification Techniques. These techniques attempt to quantify the qualitative forecasts of experts. Examples of such approaches are the Delphi method, the Nominal Group technique, and market research. In general, these techniques use rating schemes to turn qualitative information into quantitative estimates.

Extrapolation of Trends. Most "traditional" forecasting methods attempt to project the past and present into the future in one way or another. Statistical techniques such as time-series analysis and projection are included here. Some specific approaches include moving averages, exponential smoothing, seasonal adjustments, trend projections, and Box-Jenkins techniques.

Simulation and Cause and Effect Techniques. Simulation models attempt to relate environmental variables and constraints to end-result variables that affect the firm. Econometric models are examples; by "plugging" certain values for independent (environmental) variables into the models, a prediction of the effects on the firm is obtained. Related to simulation techniques are certain causal methods that can be used when historical data are available and enough analysis has been performed to specify the relationships between the dependent variable (the factor to be forecast) and the predictive factors. A causal model usually is the basis of a simulation model, although not all causal models are simulations.

Contingency Planning

Contingency plans are alternative plans that can be put into place if events are not as expected. The more turbulent, discontinuous, and unpredictable the environment, the more likely this is to happen. Strategic plans are based on "most likely" events, those that have the highest probability of occurring. But because those events are most likely does not mean they are "certain." Other, less favorable, events *could* occur, creating serious problems for the firm. Interest rates could be higher than forecast, key executives could die or leave the firm, inflation could accelerate, prices could be frozen, imports of raw materials could be curtailed, a strike could occur, and a host of other events *could* materialize. Contingency plans are preparations to take certain actions when and if an event or situation that was not included in the strategic plan occurs.

There are four reasons for, or advantages of, contingency planning: (1) it helps the firm get into a better position to cope with unexpected developments; (2) indecision, uncertainty, and delays are reduced when something unusual happens; (3) the firm's responses are likely to be better thought out and more rational; and (4) managers are forced to think in terms of *possible* outcomes, rather than just the most likely outcome.

In general, the purpose of contingency planning is to prescribe *in advance* the actions a firm should take *if* some of the key assumptions or forecasts are not accurate. It provides alternatives, changing objectives, options, and strategy revisions to be implemented if the key assumptions and/or forecasts fail to hold. For example, *if* a firm's divestiture strategy is not successful, *then* the firm may opt (contingent on this unfavorable outcome) to: sell segments of the business; phase out unsold segments; close down certain segments; or withdraw from the business.[10] Thus, contingency plans can be a series of actions to be implemented in the event certain situations materialize.

The key elements in contingency planning include:

1. Identify contingent events. What less-than-likely events would cause serious damage to the firm? What is the "worst case" for interest rates, competitor actions, and the like? What events could render your plans ineffective? As an example, sales may be higher than planned, nullifying existing manufacturing schedules. While events can be negative *or* positive, in general, firms focus on the likelihood of unfavorable events. A company probably should focus on no more than five to ten critical events, to keep the contingency planning process manageable.

2. What if? What if the critical event occurs? What strategies or actions can be put into place to deal with, offset, capitalize on, or neutralize the critical event? These actions should be specifically stated. The response is planned *in advance* should one or more critical events occur.

3. Trigger points. Specific "trigger points" should be specified in advance. These indicate *when* the contingency actions should be implemented. The question here is, what will trigger implementation of the plan? For example, a company may specify that a contingency plan is to be put into practice if sales are 10 percent below forecast for two consecutive months. The plan may include a production slowdown, increased advertising, reduction of in-

---

[10] King and Cleland, *Strategic Planning and Policy*, 55.

ventories, a cutback in raw material purchases, and other steps in response to the unexpected low sales.

Contingency plans, then, are reactions planned in advance if things do not go according to forecast. Most companies prepare such plans for a few critical events after the basic strategic plan has been completed.[11] During 1982, for example, many companies had prepared contingency plans in the event that the Reagan administration's "riverboat gamble," Reaganomics, failed. In fact, automakers, among others, were forced to trigger their contingency plans, including postponing new models and new plants, and slashing the number of salaried employees.[12] More recently, many firms developed contingency plans to cope with possible changes in health care programs.

In fact, months before Iraqi tanks rumbled into Kuwait in 1990, General Colin Powell had the Pentagon develop contingency plans for a crisis in the Mideast. The old plan of halting a Soviet drive through Iran to the Gulf was replaced by one to defend Saudi Arabia's oil fields against threats from neighboring countries. In July of 1990, General H. Norman Schwarzkopf used the contingency plan to run elaborate, computerized war games matching 100,000 U.S. troops against Iraqi armored divisions. In August, Kuwait fell to the Iraqis, and the pre-tested contingency plan was implemented with little change and amazing results.[13]

Surprise and Crisis Management

Contingency planning is designed to reduce the number of potential "surprises" facing a company. However, not all surprises can be forecast. Therefore, the firm must be able to react effectively to, as well as anticipate, such events. In addition, there are surprises that are not really issues, such as natural disasters, accidents, and wildcat strikes. Such events, including totally unpredictable chance events, are impossible to deal with effectively in the firm's planning cycles.[14] An example would be Union Carbide's December 1984 tragedy in Bhopal, India, where a leakage killed thousands of residents. Other examples would include the Exxon Valdez oil spill and the unrest in the former Soviet Union.

---

[11] G.A. Steiner, *Strategic Planning: What Every Manager Must Know* (New York, NY: The Free Press, 1979), 235.

[12] R.E. Winter, "Supply-Side Sighs: Business Leaders Begin to Express Skepticism about Reaganomics," *The Wall Street Journal* (January 29, 1982), 1.

[13] Andy Pasztor and Gerald P. Seib, "Force in Gulf Reflects Colin Powell's Vision; It's Big and It's Mobile," *The Wall Street Journal* (October 15, 1990), A1.

[14] Ansoff, "Strategic Issue Management," 131.

> Unanticipated events may occur because management either did not make the necessary efforts to anticipate them, or because the events could not be forecast effectively on the basis of existing knowledge, intuition, and wisdom. Such surprises often lead to crisis situations, where the organization's objectives, plans, intentions, and assumptions are profoundly modified. . . . They also usually produce increased uncertainty, greater disorder, and higher costs. Over the last few years, there have been many such surprises in Western societies, including the rapid deterioration of the international monetary system, the inflationary wave, the oil crisis, and the explosion of political violence.[15]

The reason for such surprises is that most human situations involve both forces of change and forces of continuity.

> Surprises tend to occur when the forces of change move much faster and become stronger than the forces of continuity (which are themselves never completely stable). For instance, a currency might enjoy a solid position for a while because of adequate reserves and a favorable balance of payments. However, a sudden flow of capital in or out can completely alter the situation and create both surprise and crisis.
>
> Such surprises and crises can originate either within the organization (e.g., the sudden death of a general manager) or outside of it (e.g., a takeover bid). Because such crises are costly in all respects (money, morale, etc.), some effort should be made to locate the areas where surprises may occur. (Note: While it may be possible to identify the general areas in which a surprise may occur, it is seldom possible to identify the surprise itself, which by its nature can hardly be forecast, otherwise it would not be a surprise.) One way to identify such areas is by analyzing in as much detail as possible the circumstances in which surprises would seem most likely to take place. In this regard, it has become an important aspect of management, both in business and in the military, to build so-called surprise matrixes. In such matrixes, potentially destructive events are identified . . . according to the areas from which they originate and the strategy elements and/or functional activities of the firm that they may affect.[16]

Such a matrix could resemble the one shown in Table 5.2. Of course, different forms may be appropriate depending on the environment, the industry, and the firm involved.

[15] C.W. Hofer, *Instructor's Manual to Accompany Strategic Management* (St. Paul, MN: West Publishing, 1981), 191.

[16] *Ibid.*, 191-93

Table 5.2 Surprise Matrix

Sources of Surprise Events / Functional Areas of the Organization Affected by the Surprise	Outside the Organization					Within the Organization		
	Customers	Suppliers	Political Environments	Economic Environments	Technological Environments	Physical Events	Psychological Events	Social Events
Marketing	Boycotting of a customer	Become competitors	A revolution	Price controls	Product obsolescence through competitor's innovation	Fire in warehouse	Corruption in sales personnel	Strike of salespeople
Finance	Bankruptcy of a product	Take-over bid	Increased taxes	Rapid increase in interest rates	—	Errors in computer system	Stealing of cash	Organized falsification of data
Personnel	Corruption by customers	Stealing of trade secrets	Terrorist action for political reasons	General strike	Technological unemployment	Epidemics	Sabotage	Factory occupation
Production								
R&D								
etc.								
etc.								

Source: Reprinted by permission of C.W. Hofer, *Instructor's Manual to Accompany Strategic Management*, 192. Copyright © by West Publishing Company. All rights reserved.

> The exact construction will also depend on the perception and realism of the builder. Nevertheless, every firm should try to build such a surprise matrix, even if only in the most simplified way.
>
> Once a surprise matrix has been constructed, the next step in the surprise management process is to plan countermeasures (contingency plans) for the most probable [and most important surprises]. In some cases (e.g., fires or strikes), detailed plans can be set up. [For less precise events,] only relatively broad responses may be possible. However, in every area some individual should be assigned responsibility for dealing with such surprises should they occur.[17]

An example of effective scenario analysis and contingency planning relates to the October 19, 1987 stock market crash. Weeks before the crash, Federal Reserve Board Chairman Alan Greenspan asked his key aides to pinpoint weak spots in the U.S. economy and financial system, and to preplan responses, should the weaknesses develop into crises. They identified three areas: how to deal with major bank failures; how to respond to a free-fall of the dollar; and, most important, as it turned out, how to handle a stock market collapse. The team considered all of the "flash points" that could cause a breakdown, including scenarios of how each could occur. When the stock market actually did crash, Greenspan and his aides followed the contingency plan prepared weeks earlier which outlined the emergency actions to take.[18]

ORGANIZATIONAL LEARNING: THE *REAL* PURPOSE OF PLANNING

It has been stated that the only real sustainable competitive advantage a firm has is its ability to respond faster and stay ahead of the competition. In relatively chaotic, unpredictable environments, this means being able to diagnose and respond to what is really happening—in other words, to *learn*. Also, *organizational* learning is not the same as individual learning; getting a group to change its viewpoint and paradigm is much more difficult, as is changing the course of an entire organization. Two approaches toward this end are steps that help the organization create order out of chaos and the use of decision scenarios. The key is for the organization to become a "learning planner:" to identify the crucial uncertainties of the future and to learn to formulate robust goals and strategies.

---

[17] *Ibid.*, 193.

[18] Alan Murray, "Fed's New Chairman Wins a Lot of Praise on Handling the Crash," *The Wall Street Journal* (November 25, 1987), 1.

Creating Order Out of Chaos

On the one hand, chaos is good; it permits spontaneous self organization, making it possible for innovation and new strategic direction to occur. This, of course, assumes that the organization can learn to operate in less-predictable environments. Ralph Stacey, of Great Britain's Hertfordshire University Business School, suggests eight steps for managers:

1. *Develop New Perspectives on Control.* Group learning prospers under the self-organizing, self-policing control, characteristic of political systems. We can apply this notion to organizations, resulting in controlled behavior, even though no one is "in control."
2. *Design the Use of Power.* Group dynamics conducive to complex learning occur when win/lose conditions are removed and open questioning and public testing of assertions is encouraged.
3. *Encourage Self-Organizing Groups.* To do so, a group must discover its own challenges, goals, and objectives; the role of top management is to create the atmosphere by which this can happen.
4. *Provoke Multiple Cultures.* Create cultural diversity by rotating people between functions and business units.
5. *Present Ambiguous Challenges.* Self-organizing groups respond best to ambiguous challenges rather than clear long-term objectives.
6. *Expose Them to Challenges.* Managers who avoid taking chances face stagnation and a high probability of collapse in the long term.
7. *Improve Group Learning Skills.* Managers must spend time explicitly exploring how they interact and learn together.
8. *Create Resource Slack.* The organization which is 100 percent efficient (using all of its resources) will not be effective because it cannot respond to new challenges. Learning and political interaction are hard work, requiring time and effort.[19]

Scenario Planning

Scenario planning encourages decision makers to imagine working in various possible futures, and to develop strategies that would be successful even in the event of a radical change in the industry. It requires managers to think about alternative futures, showing them that situations other than the conventional wisdom *can* occur. The process also alerts managers to the events which must happen in order for the alternative futures to occur, enabling them to spot these

---

[19] Stacey, *op cit.*, 15-17.

trends or changes earlier than they would have otherwise (and earlier than competitors).

Peter Schwartz states that scenarios are about "making sense out of chaos." They are devices for ordering one's perceptions about alternative environments within which one's decisions might be played out. They get at the heart of good planning, which is creating "maneuvering room" for management.[20]

Briefly, a scenario is a possible future situation. Obviously, one scenario is the future that would occur if current events and trends continue—usually, the "most likely" scenario. But, the most likely scenario often does not occur; at least not in its entirety. So, how can management prepare itself, and the organization, for what else might happen? Creating one or more alternative scenarios is often the best answer.

Basically, creating a scenario requires the writer to envision him/herself in an alternative future situation, and to describe in detail what that future entails, much as if we were able to "Quantum Leap" into a new time period. Once the alternative scenario is described in detail, key events and drivers leading up to it can be identified and watched for in real life. Usually, it is best to plan in detail for the most likely future, or scenario, and to also prepare for a distinct alternative to this. This second scenario is also a possibility, but not as likely as the number one scenario and its minor variants. Scenarios are, very simply, exploratory learning tools; hypotheses—or stories—about the future. They are a way of learning about the future.

A Generic Example. Scenarios are "attempts to describe in detail a sequence of events which could plausibly lead to a prescribed end state, or alternately, to consider the possible outcomes of present choices."[21] Scenarios enable the firm to plan for specific situations, or scenarios, and attempt to answer two kinds of questions: (1) How might the situation (favorable or unfavorable) come about? (2) What alternatives exist for preventing, facilitating, or altering the process leading to the situation? Scenarios may be low-probability events with high impact, such as a plane crash, nuclear power station melt down, corporate takeover attempt, or new technological breakthrough.

Michael Naylor of General Motors has described seven steps firms should follow in a scenario analysis.

---

[20] Peter Schwartz, "The Art of the Long View: Using Scenarios to Plan for an Uncertain Future," *The Planning Forum Network*, 4, No. 12 (December 1991), 1-4.

[21] J.H. Grant and W.R. King, "Strategy Formulation: Analytical and Normative Models," in *Strategic Management*, eds. D. Schendel and C.W. Hofer (Boston, MA: Little, Brown, 1979), 11.

- **Step 1:** Develop a pair of scenarios—most likely and alternate. This forces consideration of more than one outcome. What are the key determinants and principal impact factors of each?
- **Step 2:** Write down the basic strategy options that can be pursued. Many times, strategy options fall into four categories: business as usual (no changes in present programs, organization, or personnel); reorganize the present business (regroup, transfer people, relocate plants, etc.); adjust the level of integration (more, or less, vertical or horizontal integration); or diversify into new businesses.
- **Step 3:** Evaluate the outcomes of the various strategies, assuming the most likely scenario. Each strategy should be evaluated and ranked relative to the other strategies. This ranking and evaluation should be in terms of how favorable the outcome will be to the firm.
- **Step 4:** Follow the same procedure for the alternative scenario.
- **Step 5:** Combine the two strategy evaluations into a scenario-strategy matrix such as the one shown in Table 5.3. The key here is to examine the spread in desirability for each strategy between the optimistic and pessimistic scenarios. For example, the business-as-usual strategy has the highest spread (+ + to − −) and thus the highest uncertainty. It also has the highest risk, since it has the most negative outcome if the alternate scenario occurs . Furthermore, the strategy of more integration dominates the business-as-usual strategy (it has the same most-likely results but a better alternate outcome), and reorganize dominates the less-integration strategy. If the firm is not willing to tolerate the moderately negative risk of the more-integration strategy, only reorganize or diversify remain. These are "robust" strategies, since the outcome is favorable under either scenario. However, the diversify strategy appears to dominate the reorganize approach, and appears to be the best option for the firm.

Table 5.3 Scenario-Strategy Matrix

Most likely scenario	+ +	+	+ +	−	+
Alternate scenario	− −	+	−	+	+ +
Strategy	Business as usual	Reorganize	More integration	Less integration	Diversify

Source: Adapted from M.E. Naylor, "Planning for Uncertainty—The Scenario-Strategy Matrix," in K.J. Albert, ed., *The Strategic Management Handbook* (New York, NY: McGraw Hill, Inc., 1983), 22-9.

- **Step 6:** Evaluate the strategies against pairs of scenarios for other factors. The example in steps 1 to 5 represented one set of critical factors for the firm. The same approach should be used for several other critical factors or areas.
- **Step 7:** Compare results for each of the critical factors analyzed. Using decision rules (perhaps similar to those in step 5), strategies are progressively eliminated, and the remaining strategies are examined in closer detail. In summary, the scenario-strategy matrix approach is useful in strategic planning because it depends less on the accuracy of specific forecasts than do traditional methods. In addition, it forces people to think in terms of a range of outcomes and emphasizes flexibility.[22]

A scenario can be described as "a slice of future history." It is also a model used to examine relationships between the environment and an organization. The scenario is a hypothetical sequence of events designed to draw attention to causal processes and decision points.[23] Scenarios will probably be more widely applied in an increasingly more turbulent environment.

For example, the October 19, 1987 stock market crash caused some analysts to consider possible future scenarios. In reality, the Wall Street plunge should not have been totally unexpected, given the debtor status of the United States, the huge budget deficits brought on by tax cuts and military spending, high interest rates and strong dollar, and chronic trade deficit. Thinking in terms of three scenarios—the worst case, or "hard landing;" a less drastic outcome; and the most desirable, or "soft landing"—the market drop may have signaled that the United States was initially on the path toward the "hard landing" scenario.

The three plausible scenarios were as follows:

1. *The worst case.* A wave of selling of dollars occurs within a few weeks, dropping the value to about the 130 yen range. Interest rates skyrocket and inflation fears lead Japanese institutional investors to pull away from their U.S. investments. That sends the dollar lower and freezes consumer spending. The U.S. Congress enacts a protectionist trade package.
2. *Less drastic.* In this case, the market, disappointed with inability of the United States to cut its deficit, puts more pressure on the dollar. Selling depresses the dollar even lower than 130 yen by mid-1988. Anxiety over creeping inflation and rising interest rates causes a worldwide recession in 1988.

---

[22] M.E. Naylor, "Planning for Uncertainty—The Scenario-Strategy Matrix," in K.J. Albert, ed., *The Strategic Management Handbook* (New York, NY: McGraw-Hill, 1983), 22-9.

[23] A.W. Smith, *Management Systems: Analyses and Applications* (Hinsdale, IL: Dryden Press, 1982), 193.

3. *The most desirable, but the most complex.* Stock prices edge lower, but a tight money supply stabilizes the dollar, limiting the trade deficit. Reagan and Congress cooperate on an aggressive combination of budget-tightening cuts and higher taxes. The combination convinces central banks in Japan and West Germany that they should ease their own monetary policies. The effectiveness of such measures would depend upon the changes during the first six months, when the growth rate would be expected to be nearly zero.[24]

Thus, government policymakers need to determine in which direction the economy is headed, and try to steer it toward favorable outcomes and minimize the negative effects of worst case outcomes, if they materialize.

Another current example of scenario analysis is the approach used by research institutes and business firms to plan for possible impacts of the "greenhouse effect." Battelle Pacific Northwest Labs is developing a computer model to predict possible impacts on various regions of the United States, because the firm expects a demand for such information for business planning in the 1990s. In fact, companies such as Archer Daniels Midland (barge lines), Weyerhaeuser (lumber), and Travelers Corp. (insurance) are already developing "what-if" plans based upon the greenhouse scenario.[25]

Issues Analysis

A more recent approach, called *issues analysis*, is related to contingency planning and scenario analysis. The purpose of issues analysis is to alert management to emerging political, social, and economic trends and controversies and to mobilize the company's resources to deal with them. An issue "is a condition or pressure, either internal or external to an organization, that, if it continues, will have a significant effect on the functioning of the organization or its future interests."[26]

Issues analysis supplements other forecasting approaches. Atlantic Richfield (ARCO), for example, felt that its planning was too numbers oriented, and created a team of issues managers. Their task is to spot trends, a job previously done somewhat haphazardly by top executives, government relations people, planners, and public relations staffs. Recently, ARCO was tracking 140 issues,

---

[24] Yoichi Funabashi, "Stock Plunge Hint of Hard Landing," *Sunday Journal-Star* (November 1, 1987), 1.

[25] "When the Rivers Go Dry and the Ice Caps Melt," *Business Week* (February 13, 1989), 95.

[26] J.K. Brown, *This Business of Issues: Coping with the Company's Environments* (New York, NY: Conference Board, 1979), 1.

including such government matters as state tax rates, the Clean Air Act review, natural gas decontrol, and state legislation on hazardous wastes.

Other companies with issues managers include S.C. Johnson & Company, Sears, and the Bank of America. Johnson removed fluorocarbons from its aerosol sprays three years before federal action forced others in the industry to do so. Sears became aware of the flammable nightwear controversy and placed non-flammable goods on its shelves before it was required to do so. Sears also realized that a cancer issue was building over Tris (a flame retardant used in clothing) and removed affected garments from its shelves early. Issues managers alerted Bank of America about a likely controversy over redlining of loans (avoiding certain neighborhoods). Bank of America changed its lending policies two years before Congress required banks to do so.[27]

Today, over seventy companies have issues staffs and use varying techniques to rank issues. One way is to assign an "impact index" to each issue, reflecting its potential effect on the firm. Multiplying this index by its probability of occurrence gives an estimate of the expected effect, which can be used to rank the issue's importance.[28] An example of this procedure is shown in Table 5.4.

Table 5.4 Procedure for Ranking Issues

Issue	Impact*	Probability of Occurrence†	Expected Effect‡	Ranking of Issue
A	8.8	0.3	2.64	4
B	6.7	0.7	4.69	1
C	4.4	0.9	3.96	2
D	3.8	0.8	3.04	3
E	2.1	0.5	1.05	5

*Rated on a scale of 1 to 10, from least to greatest.
†From 0, improbable, to 1, certain.
‡Impact multiplied by probability.

[27] E.C. Gottschalk, Jr., "Firms Hiring New Type of Manager to Study Issues, Emerging Troubles," *The Wall Street Journal* (June 10, 1982), 21.

[28] Brown, *This Business of Issues*, 32.

Module
6

The Key Players:
Strategic Managers
and Stakeholders

LEARNING OBJECTIVES

After completing Module 6, you should be able to:

1. Understand the roles and responsibilities of various management levels in the strategic process.
2. Define the term *general manager*, and appreciate the general manager's perspective.
3. Understand the roles of line and staff managers, including those in corporate planning, in the strategic process.
4. Realize that an organization is made up of and influenced by a number of stakeholder groups with varying values and expectations.

Organizations are run by people; strategies and policies are formulated by people; strategic and operational decisions are made by people; and the decisions are implemented and planned by people. Those primarily responsible for strategic decisions are the managers overseeing the organization and its major divisions—the general managers. This module examines the essence of managerial roles and responsibilities, with particular emphasis on strategy and policy-related aspects.

Finally, the groups having an interest in the organization—the stakeholders—are studied in terms of the values they bring and the expectations they have of the business.

PROFILE NCR Manages for its Stakeholders

Some experts claim that companies not managed to maximize returns to shareholders are vulnerable to attack. NCR Corp., however, attempted to manage with all of its *stakeholders* in mind—employees, customers, suppliers, and communities where NCR has plants—not just shareholders. NCR's CEO, Charles E. Exley Jr., felt that it was his responsibility to balance the shareholders' interest in the long-term prosperity of the company against their understandable interest in yearly dividend increases and steady quarterly earnings increases. He believed that considering the interests of all stakeholders was the best way to do this, which in turn maximizes value over the long run, even for shareholders.[1] His approach seemed to work. NCR had one of the higher returns on equity in the EDP industry, had relatively low debt, and saw its stock and earnings rise significantly during the past several years. In 1992, acting in what some would say was the best interests of all stakeholders, NCR agreed to be acquired by AT&T.

WHO ARE THE STRATEGIC MANAGERS?

To understand strategic management, we must know where strategic decisions are made in organizations, what levels of management are involved, the roles of line and staff, and the skills required.

Managers and Strategic Decisions

In large organizations, several levels of management may be involved in strategic decision-making at any given time. The majority of strategic decisions, how-

---

[1] George Melloan, "NCR's Exley Manages for His 'Stakeholders'," *The Wall Street Journal* (June 16, 1987), 27.

ever, will emanate from both the corporate level and the division or business-unit level. Does this mean that others have little or no role in such decisions?

To answer this question, one must understand how decisions are made in organizations. In reality, very few decisions are made *totally* by one person. A "decision" is the result of a stream or sequence of inputs and actions by a number of people. For example, a salesperson may inform the sales manager that a competitor is working on a "new and improved" line of products (according to information gleaned informally from a customer or other source). The sales manager may recommend to the division managers that a similar product should be developed, and research and engineering will likely be asked for feasibility and schedule estimates. Assuming that the effort is a major one, with effects on the product lines of other divisions (and needing funding from the corporate level), corporate staff input and analysis will be required. Finally, a recommendation will be made to the corporate president, who decides either to go ahead or drop the new line. The president *made* the decision—or did she? This decision was shaped by everyone involved in the process, from the salesperson who gathered the intelligence information, to the functional and staff people at division and corporate levels who performed the analyses, to those at various levels who made the recommendations, and finally to the president, who made the "choice." Thus, many people and levels can be involved in a significant strategic decision made by top management.

Henry Singleton, the well-respected former chief executive officer of the Teledyne Corporation, believes that a CEO's most important function is to foresee trends and act on them to help his company. When facing strategic decisions, Singleton demands maximum flexibility and the right to change his positions when the external environment warrants it. For his efforts and successes, *Forbes* has concluded that "when the history of this era is written, Dr. Henry E. Singleton will probably be one of its towering figures."[2] The point is that top managers are less responsible for *making* strategic and other decisions than they are for *managing* the decision process—making sure that the right decisions are made.

The Team at the Top

The people *responsible* for major strategic decisions, of course, are the board of directors, the chief executive officer (CEO), the chief staff officer (CSO), the chief operating officer (COO), and the division managers—the team at the top (see Figure 6.1). The board's role is rather limited in most strategic decisions. Truly major decisions, however—such as those involving mergers, acquisitions, or divestitures—typically may require board input and approval. Most lesser stra-

---

[2] Robert J. Flaherty, "The Singular Henry Singleton," *Forbes* (July 9, 1979), 45.

tegies, particularly at the business unit or division level, do not. The CEO's prime strategic function, perhaps even more than *making* such decisions, is to provide strategic leadership to other executives and managers—shaping the premises offered by other executives, calling for changes, and focusing the attention of the organization on what he or she feels is important.[3]

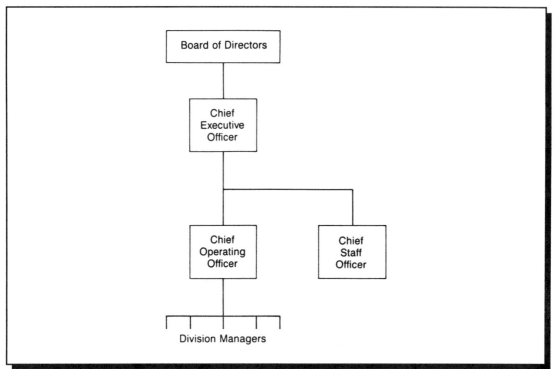

Figure 6.1 **The Team at the Top**

A good leader pulls together the right people and sets the agenda; then lets people make their own decisions.[4] Even so, the role of the CEO has changed in the past five years. A recent study of 897 chief executives indicated that more than one fifth say they plan to become more involved in strategic planning in the

[3] L. Bower and Yves Doz, "Strategy Formulation: A Social and Political Process," in *Strategic Management: A New View of Business Policy and Planning*, eds. D.E. Schendel and C.W. Hofer (Boston, MA: Little, Brown, 1979).

[4] Alan M. Webber, "Gerald R. Ford: The Statesman as CEO," *Harvard Business Review*, 65, No. 5 (September/October 1987), 76.

next five years. As Harvard's Andrall Pearson states, "If top managers don't get involved in the details of the markets they compete in, they're going to get killed by people who do."[5]

John Kotter of Harvard points out that leadership and management are two distinctive, complementary—and necessary—systems in organizations. He states that leadership is about coping with change, while management is about coping with complexity. Strategic leadership, then, would appear to be closely aligned with vision—deciding how to cope with change, and which changes to initiate.[6]

The essence of strategy is the purposeful management of change, so that the firm can achieve competitive advantages in each of the businesses in which it competes.[7] In this regard, the job of top management is becoming more one of *changing things* (strategic) than *running things* (operational).[8]

The corporate planning staff under the CSO coordinates the analytical functions of the organization and manages the planning process. Included in this function are the analysis of environmental information, assessments of the firm's capabilities, the generation of strategic alternatives, and the review of implementation plans for completeness. The responsibility for strategic *decisions* lies with *line* managers, such as the CEO, COO, and division or business unit managers. Table 6.1 highlights the relative roles and responsibilities of the key decision levels for various organizational strategies.

Line and Staff Involvement

Planning staffs in U.S. and United Kingdom corporations typically *do not* decide on strategies, at least not at the corporate level. In fact, in their study of corporate planning, Taylor and Irving found that *planning is a line job*. "The role of the planner, therefore, is not to *do* the planning, but to design, sell, and direct the planning effort" or process.[9] However, at the divisional or functional levels,

---

[5] "A CEO's Life: Money, Security, and Meetings," *The Wall Street Journal* (July 7, 1987), 27.

[6] John Kotter, "What Leaders Really Do," *Harvard Business Review*, 68, No. 3 (May/June 1990), 94-111.

[7] Arnoldo C. Hax and N.S. Majluf, "The Concept of Strategy and the Strategy Formation Process," *Interfaces*, 18, No. 3 (May/June 1988), 102.

[8] Derek F. Abell, "Keynote Address," 20th Annual Conference, Decision Sciences Institute (November 1988).

[9] Bernard Taylor and P. Irving, "Organized Planning in Major U.S. Companies," *Long-Range Planning* (June 1971).

Table 6.1 Strategic Decision-Making Roles and Responsibilities

	Decision Level			
Hierarchy of Strategy	Board of Directors	CEO	Corporate Management	Division Management
Enterprise strategy				
Formulation	Primary			
Assessment		Primary		
Implementation		Primary	Contributory	
Monitoring	Primary			
Corporate strategy				
Formulation	Contributory	Primary		
Assessment	Primary			
Implementation			Primary	
Monitoring	Contributory	Primary		
Business strategy				
Formulation			Contributory	Primary
Assessment		Contributory	Primary	
Implementation				Primary
Monitoring			Primary	

Source: R.H. Rock and Marv Eisthen, "Implementing Strategic Change," in *The Strategic Management Handbook*, ed. K.J. Albert (New York, NY: McGraw-Hill, 1983), 16-7. Reproduced with permission.

the planner's role may be somewhat different. He or she may be more of a "doer" than a manager of the process.

McGill University's Henry Mintzberg suggests that planners' most important role has nothing to do with planning, per se; their most important role is *finding* emerging strategies (which often originate with line managers). This requires snooping, sorting, investigating, generalizing, interpreting, and recognizing patterns. Planners are catalysts, encouraging strategic thinking and the creation of strategies by others. The planners do not generate strategies, but they must be active and involved, to make sure the line managers develop the best strategies.[10]

The emphasis on the line aspects of planning is indicated by recent cutbacks. An article in *Business Week* pointed out that the trend recently has been to cut

---

[10] Henry Mintzberg, *The Rise and Fall of Strategic Planning* (New York, NY: The Free Press, 1994).

back sharply on the number of staff jobs in organizations—a trend that is likely to be permanent. In fact, in 1982, GE cut its corporate-level strategic planning department from sixty to twenty-five people.[11] A study by Arthur D. Little of twelve major corporations also showed a general cutback in corporate staff, including corporate strategic planning staffs. Some of the planners have been transferred to division levels, with other positions eliminated completely.[12]

Such cutbacks often are meant to emphasize that strategic planning must be performed *by* line managers, not *for* them. In fact, large centralized planning groups may have interfered at times with planning by line managers. Michael Kami, for example, feels that one to two planners per business unit is sufficient.[13] The view now is that if implementation is to become part of the plan, the planners must be the same people who will be responsible for carrying out the plan.[14] Given this line emphasis, the role of corporate planning, then, includes the following:

1. Developing a framework for strategic planning and providing the data base.
2. Identifying and evaluating new product and market opportunities.
3. Monitoring, reviewing, and revising the strategic plan.
4. Forecasting economic conditions and trends.
5. Developing contingency plans and alternate scenarios.
6. Predicting the uncertain future.[15]

But Who is Responsible?

The General Manager. Earlier, the statement was made that general managers are the people primarily responsible for strategic decisions. Who are these people and how do their jobs differ from those of other types of managers?

A general manager is someone responsible for the totality of an organization, a division of the organization, or a significant operating element (such as a subsidiary). A functional manager, by contrast, is responsible only for certain activities of that organizational element, such as marketing, manufacturing, finance, or engineering. The general manager, in turn, is responsible for *all* activities of

---

[11] "A New Era for Management," *Business Week* (April 25, 1983), 50.

[12] R.M. Tomasko, "Subbing Division, Line Work for Corporate Staff," *The Wall Street Journal* (March 28, 1983), 14.

[13] Michael Kami, *Strategic Planning for Changing Times* (Dayton, FL: Cassette Recording Co., 1984).

[14] S.G. Brandt, *Strategic Planning in Emerging Companies* (Reading, MA: Addison-Wesley Publishing, 1982), 54.

[15] "Corporate Planning: Piercing Future Fog in the Executive Suite," *Business Week* (April 28, 1975), 46.

his or her (usually multifunctional) organizational unit. Business policy and strategic management, of necessity, take the view of the general manager because they are concerned with the total organization (or a complete division or subsidiary).

Their Unique Responsibilities. General managers, particularly those at the corporate level of an organization, tend to have responsibilities that differ from those of other managers. They are primarily responsible for managing other managers. No longer can this person function as a "playing coach" or expert practitioner. Many people get by in middle-level management jobs by working harder and longer. At the corporate executive level, however, this approach will not succeed for long (if at all) because the job is just too big. The time demands are very much greater than they are at lower levels, and a different approach is required. The need to delegate is critical—not just assigning work to people, but defining responsibilities and delegating responsibility (not tasks). Inherent in this is recognizing which issues are important, which and how much risk to take, and how much challenge a subordinate is capable of accepting and carrying out. There are qualitative, rather than quantitative, differences between executive and middle-level jobs; it is not a case of more of the same and broader responsibilities.

Key corporate-level general management functions include:

1. *Managing the strategic process.* This level of management is responsible for creating the appropriate structure and systems so that the organization's objectives are met effectively and efficiently, and so that resources are allocated properly. At lower levels, these things are largely "givens"; at upper levels, very little is given, especially in the long run. The main focus is what should the objectives be, rather than how they should be met. It is by creating the appropriate structure and systems that corporate management influences strategic and operational decisions, not by making or controlling those decisions directly.

2. *Managing relationships.* While division-level managers must successfully manage a number of relationships, the thrust of this task changes at the corporate level. Here the relationships between and among the corporate level and the division level units is a key concern. The issue again becomes more of what the roles and relationships should be, rather than how to live with them. In addition, the corporate level must develop a productive relationship with the board of directors. Further, the executive's use of corporate staff must be specified, as must the important relationship between corporate staff and division management.

3. *Managing executive development.* In the final analysis, the quality of the organization's managers—corporate and divisional—determines the success of the firm. What kinds of executives are needed? How should and can they be developed or acquired? What is the executive succession plan? How are can-

didates identified and their performance evaluated? Corporate-level management is responsible for these vital decisions.[16]

Some experts liken the job of the general manager to that of the wagon master, the leaders of the westward movement. Like wagon masters, effective general managers realize that their own success is inseparable from that of their fellow travelers. In this light, the leaders must realize that they have two important jobs—to reach the goal and to maintain morale along the way.[17]

SKILLS AND APPROACHES THAT WORK

The skills required for effective strategic management can be looked at in two ways. One is to focus on the general skills required to analyze, formulate, and implement strategies, and these are addressed here. The second is to focus on the skills required to function effectively with certain strategies. This second element, along with a more detailed treatment of specific strategy-related skills, is addressed in a later module.

Conceptual and Synthesis Skills

Upper levels of management must be adept at conceptualizing. They must possess *vision*; they must be able to see the enterprise as a whole and how the organization fits (and *can* fit) into its overall environment. This skill is critical for strategic managers. Strategic decision makers must visualize things that do not yet exist. They must have a vision of what their organization or division can become and can do. Required is an ability to see the situations in their entirety—a synthesis skill. This includes being able to understand the role of the organization in its environment and how environmental changes can and will affect the company. Synthesis skill is required to assess what the various functions and divisions of the company must do to successfully implement a strategy, and what the effects will be on each division and function. Conceptual and synthesis skills are difficult to teach, unlike specific technical and analytical skills, such as accounting, engineering, and effective writing and speech making.

---

[16] H.E.R. Uyterhoeven, R.W. Ackerman, and J.W. Rosenblum, *Strategy and Organization*, rev. ed. (Homewood, IL: Richard D. Irwin, Inc., 1977).

[17] Jack S. Ninomiya, "Wagon Masters and Lesser Managers," *Harvard Business Review*, 66, No. 2 (March/April 1988), 84.

Technical and Analytical Skills

Nonetheless, strategic decision making requires more than conceptual/synthesis skills. Technical and analysis skills are required, as well, and may be important elements in synthesizing and conceptualizing. Just as an artist must be able to work with paints, brushes, and the like to put what he or she conceptualizes on canvas, the strategic manager must be able to analyze trends, prepare plans and budgets, make presentations, sell his or her ideas, and implement them. In either case, having the vision or the concept is necessary, but not totally sufficient.

In addition, the skills needed vary by level in the corporate hierarchy. At lower levels of administrative responsibility, the major need is for technical skills and for human skills in working with, for, and leading others. At higher levels, managerial effectiveness depends largely on human and conceptual skills. At the top, conceptual skill becomes the most important of all for successful performance.[18] This identification of the skills most needed at various levels of responsibility is important in the selection, training, and promotion of managers. Technical skills may enable a person to be promoted to first-line management; for example, supervisor. Technical *plus* human skills can get you to middle-level management, but conceptual skills are required for effective performance in general management and executive-level positions. The primary responsibility at the executive level in an organization is that of policy formulation. In other words, the direction in which the organization is going to proceed and how it will conduct its activities are the prime executive-level concerns. Middle management, in turn, is primarily responsible for interpreting and implementing these goals and policies, while the supervisory level is responsible for accomplishment, producing the goods or delivering the services.

Combination of Skills

Strategic decision makers also must be able to function in the political environment of organizations, which requires well-developed human skills. They must have a willingness and desire to make decisions by integrating and balancing elements, assessing risks, communicating and enlisting support, and employing a sense of timing. Also required is a combination of analysis and synthesis skills— a diagnostic ability—since strategic and organizational situations do not present themselves as concretely and neatly as do technical or financial facts. Making strategic decisions in complex organizations is a delicate art, requiring a balance of vision, entrepreneurship, and politics. The strategic decision maker must be able to sense needs, build awareness, broaden support, create pockets of commit-

---

[18] Robert L. Katz, "Skills of an Effective Administrator," *Harvard Business Review* (July/August 1975), 49.

ment, crystallize a developing focus, obtain increased commitment, and keep the process moving forward.[19]

Organizational Effects

As shown in Table 6.2, organizations can employ several approaches to strategy making. In the various strategy-making modes, the relative roles of top management and organizational members vary. That is, the role of top management is much greater than others in the organization in the Command mode, while the reverse is true in the Generative mode. While many might think that the organic style Generative mode might be ideal, this is not the case. As Table 6.3 suggests, the highest performance is likely to occur in the mid-range modes. The reason for this is the role imbalance likely to exist at the extreme positions on the process style continuum.

A current organizational topic is diversity; how does diversity affect strategy making? Susan Jackson of New York University posits that the most effective top management teams are those: (a) that are diverse with regard to both personal attributes and abilities, and (b) which assign subgroups to tasks in accordance with the task requirements. Specifically, (b) requires that creative and judgmental tasks be carried out by groups that are heterogeneous—diverse—with regard to personal attributes and technical skills. It also requires that implementation activities be carried out by subgroups that are homogenous with respect to personal attributes and *heterogeneous* with regard to technical skills.[20]

In summary, strategic management requires the perspective of the general manager. General managers must act both as strategists and as organization builders, and many times must sail through uncharted waters, managing when no precedent exists. Strategic decisions are evaluated by the board of directors, but are the responsibility of *line* general managers, supported by corporate planning staffs that perform analyses and manage the planning processes. Successful, respected companies tend to keep their processes flexible and simple; they do not use long-term plans as straitjackets, but as guides.

---

[19] J.B. Quinn, "Strategic Goals: Process and Politics," *Sloan Management Review*, 19, No. 1 (Fall 1977), 21.

[20] Susan E. Jackson, "Consequences of Group Composition for the Interpersonal Dynamics of Strategic Issue Processing," in *Advances in Strategic Management*, Vol. 8., eds. P. Shrivastava, A. Huff, and J. Dutton (Greenwich, CT: JAI Press, 1992), 368.

Table 6.2 Framework of Strategy-Making Modes

Descriptors	Command	Symbolic	Rational	Transactive	Generative
Style	*Imperial* strategy driven by leader or small top team	*Cultural* strategy driven by mission and a vision of the future	*Analytical* strategy driven by formal structure and planning systems	*Procedural* strategy driven by internal process and mutual adjustment	*Organic* strategy driven by organizational actors' initiative
Role of top management	*Commander* provide direction	*Coach* motivate and inspire	*Boss* evaluate and control	*Facilitator* empower and enable	*Sponsor* endorse and sponsor
Role of organizational members	*Soldier* obey orders	*Player* respond to challenge	*Subordinate* follow the system	*Participant* learn and improve	*Entrepreneur* experiment and take risks

Source: Adapted from Stuart L. Hart and Catherine Banbury, "How Strategy-Making Processes Can Make a Difference," *Strategic Management Journal*, 15, No. 4 (May 1994), 254.

STAKEHOLDER VALUES AND EXPECTATIONS

Two important parts of creating a firm's enterprise strategy include analyses of the firm's stakeholders and their values and expectations. As defined earlier, stakeholders are individuals and groups with a positive "stake" in how well the organization performs, including investors, directors, managers, employees, unions, customers, suppliers, creditors, the community, the state and region, society in general, and perhaps others, all of whom provide resources to the organization. Many of these people and interest groups have differing expectations of the firm; top management's responsibility is to deal with, and satisfy, as many of them as possible. Obviously, management will not be able to fully meet or even reconcile all expectations. At best, an uneasy equilibrium may exist that temporarily accommodates conflicting demands. Nonetheless, management should remember that the price of resource inputs from stakeholders is a certain degree of satisfaction of their needs, conflicting as they might be. William Dill of New York University observed that environmental turbulence is less of a threat for companies that spent time listening to and assessing what stakeholders

Table 6.3 Strategy Making Mode and Firm Performance

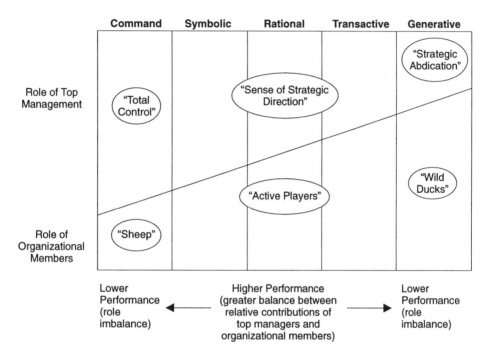

Source: Adapted from Stuart L. Hart, "An Integrative Framework for Strategy-Making Processes," *Academy of Management Review*, 17, No. 2 (April 1992), 340.

say about the powers they are and are not willing to delegate to corporations and corporate management.[21]

Who are the Stakeholders?

Again, stakeholders are those individuals or groups who have a stake, or claim, against the firm. As shown in Table 6.4, this group is extensive, although many of the stakes are dissimilar and even conflicting. Satisfying their expectations

---

[21] W.R. Dill, "Commentary," in *Strategic Management: A New View of Business Policy and Planning* (Boston, MA: Little, Brown, 1979), 49.

and incorporating their values is an important management task, part of the firm's social and economic responsibilities. From one perspective, management *must* satisfy stakeholder wants, because—collectively, if not individually—stakeholder groups have a great impact on a firm's performance. Although various stakeholder groups can exert their influence in different ways, an obvious example involves stockholder power. In fact, choosing the firm's CEO may be the ultimate decision the stockholders (through the board of directors) can make, because the CEOs' values and beliefs shape the way their companies operate, and the CEO's aspirations mold the corporate environment.[22]

Satisfying Stakeholder Wants

Again, some writers have said that the overriding purpose of management is to maximize stockholder wealth. While this is a major management concern, the needs of other stakeholders must be met, as well, and balanced against the interests of stockholders. However, public corporations clearly have obligations to present and potential shareholders, including disclosure of information about their firms, such as the nature and activities of the business, financial and policy matters, tender offers, special problems, and opportunities facing the firm. Disclosure should be frequent and the information should be pertinent to the shareholders' investment decisions.

But stockholders are only one group of stakeholders. Organizations have been described as collections of internal and external stakeholders. Given this view, the task of management—including strategic management—becomes one of satisfying stakeholders' wants and needs and of managing the relationships between, and often conflicting demands of, various stakeholders. In fact, some authors feel that the ultimate objective of strategy should be to address stakeholders' benefits.[23] How can this be done? Two writers in the field, Richard Mason and Ian Mitroff, have proposed a strategic assumption surfacing and testing technique (SAST) to assist management in this task.[24] The first step in their approach is to identify the full range of relevant stakeholders. This is necessary because whether or not an organization achieves its goals depends inevitably on the assumption it makes about its stakeholders and their behavior.

[22] Alan M. Webber, "The CEO Is the Company," *Harvard Business Review*, 65, No. 1 (January/February 1987), 114.

[23] Arnoldo C. Hax and N.S. Majluf, "The Concept of Strategy and the Strategy Formation Process," *Interfaces*, 18, No. 3 (May/June 1988), 102.

[24] R.O. Mason and Ian Mitroff, "A Telelogical Power-Oriented Theory of Strategy," in *Advances in Strategic Management*, Vol. 2, ed. R. Lamb (Greenwich, CT: JAI Press, 1983), 31.

Table 6.4 A Claimant View of Company Responsibility

Claimant	Nature of the Claim
Stockholders	Participation in distribution of profits, additional stock offerings, assets on liquidation; vote of stock, inspection of company books, transfer of stock, election of board of directors, and such additional rights as established in the contract with the corporation.
Creditors	Legal proportion of interest payments due and return of principal from the investment. Security of pledged assets; relative priority in event of liquidation. Participate in some management and owner prerogatives if certain conditions exist within the company (such as default of interest payments).
Employees	Economic, social, and psychological satisfaction in the place of employment. Freedom from arbitrary and capricious behavior on the part of company officials. Share in fringe benefits, freedom to join union and participate in collective bargaining, individual freedom in offering up their services through an employment contract. Adequate working conditions.
Customers	Service provided with the product: technical data to use the product; suitable warranties; spare parts to support the product during customer use; R&D leading to product improvements; facilitation of consumer credit.
Suppliers	Continuing source of business: timely consummation of trade credit obligations; professional relationship in contracting for, purchasing, and receiving goods and services.
Governments	Taxes (income, property, and so on), fair competition, and adherence to the letter and intent of public policy dealing with the requirements of fair and free competition. Legal obligation of businesses; adherence to antitrust laws.
Unions	Recognition as the negotiating agent for employees. Opportunity to perpetuate the union as a participant in the business organization.
Competitors	Norms established by society and the industry for competitive conduct. Business statesmanship on the part of peers.
Local communities	Place of productive and healthful employment in the community. Participation of company officials in community affairs, regular employment, fair play, purchase of reasonable portion of product of the local community, interest in and support of local government; support of cultural and charity projects.
The general public	Participation in and contribution to society as a whole; creative communications between governmental and business units designed for reciprocal understanding; bear fair proportion of the burden of government and society. Fair price for products and advancement of state of the art technology which the product line involves.

Source: From W.R. King and D.I. Cleland, *Strategic Planning and Policy* (New York, NY: Van Nostrand Reinhold, 1978), 153. © by Litton Educational Publishing, Inc. Reprinted by permission of Van Nostrand Reinhold Company.

success of a strategy than are those of others, the various stakeholders should be rated on a scale of importance. Next, each strategic assumption should be rated on a scale of certainty; that is, how certain are you of the validity of each assumption? The result of these two ratings—importance and certainty—reveals the likely impact of each assumption on the organization and its strategy. Finally, implementation becomes a matter of developing an action plan for each important stakeholder.

A simpler and perhaps more practical approach to assessing stakeholder positions on issues is the Strategic Assumptions Analysis technique, developed at the Wharton School. This approach simply requires management to judge each major stakeholder group's position on the issue, consider the strength and importance of their position, and arrive at an overall assessment and decision, as Table 6.5 illustrates.[25] Whether this approach or the more involved SAST approach is used, each is a systematic means of specifically incorporating stakeholder wants, needs, and desires into the strategic planning process. In fact, consideration of the claims of inside and outside stakeholders is an important input to determination of the company's mission, as shown in Figure 6.2.

Table 6.5 **Strategic Assumptions Analysis**

Issue: Joint Venture in Manufacturing

Stakeholder	Position
Senior management	Yes
Direct customers	Strong yes
End-product customers	Yes
Plant management	Weak yes
R&D management	No
Investment bankers	Strong yes
Overall assessment	Yes

Source: Adapted from James R. Emshoff and Arthur Finnel, "Defining Corporate Strategy," *Sloan Management Review* (Spring 1979), 41-52.

---

[25] James R. Emshoff and Arthur Finnel, "Defining Corporate Strategy," *Sloan Management Review* (Spring 1979), 41.

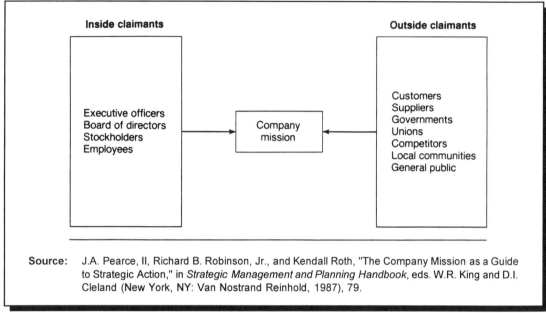

Source: J.A. Pearce, II, Richard B. Robinson, Jr., and Kendall Roth, "The Company Mission as a Guide to Strategic Action," in *Strategic Management and Planning Handbook*, eds. W.R. King and D.I. Cleland (New York, NY: Van Nostrand Reinhold, 1987), 79.

Figure 6.2 Inputs to the Company Mission

Module
7

Organizational Direction: Vision, Mission, Goals, Culture

LEARNING OBJECTIVES

After completing Module 7, you should be able to:

1. Understand the key role of vision in setting the direction and acting as a unifying force.
2. Describe the important features and characteristics of effective mission statements.
3. Relate the importance of goals and objectives to achieving the vision and setting the stage for developing strategies.
4. Understand how organizational culture, climate, and related social factors impact strategic management.

Referring back to the strategic management process, we learned that top management's vision and the values and expectations of stakeholders set the stage for most other elements in the process. They affected and interacted with the organization's mission, or purpose, and its goals—what it hopes to achieve. Also important as an influence guiding all organizational activities is the organization's culture: the values, attitudes, and beliefs held in common by its members.

PROFILE

"Sharing the Vision" at US West

One of the "baby Bells," US West, has found itself in a changing and unsettled environment. Realizing that competing and prospering in the new information industries requires being in the right businesses and working together as one team to achieve important goals, US West embarked upon two key programs in 1993. The first, "Sharing The Vision," and its follow-up, "Connecting People," provide in-depth information company wide on specific strategies and focus on how the company's guiding principles and total quality system will help achieve its vision. Dick McCormick, US West Chairman and CEO, says: "Worldclass companies achieve alignment in every department and at every level around customer and employee needs. That consistency is driven by a connected vision, mission, strategy, values, and guiding principles."

US West's program appears to be a textbook, state-of-the-art strategic management approach. The US West model begins with an analysis of its environment, which shapes the direction in which the company is headed. Vision, mission, and strategies describe what the company attempts to do, and is explicitly guided by the US West culture. These elements are defined as follows:

Vision: By the year 2000, US West will be the finest company in the world connecting people with their world.

Mission: US West will be a leading provider of integrated communications, entertainment and information services over wired broadband and wireless networks in selected local markets world-wide.

Strategies: US West has three strategy areas:

1. Revitalize the core business, via:
   a. Increase customer satisfaction/loyalty.
   b. Develop and deploy broadband network.
   c. Package and deliver information, communication, and entertainment services.
   d. Reduce costs to achieve competitiveness.

2. Expand into new regions:

   a. Establish domestic and international wired broadband network positions.
   b. Build strong wireless positions.
   c. Package and deliver information, communication and entertainment services.

3. Utilize "enablers:"

   a. Deploy Total Quality System.
   b. Achieve capital structure appropriate to new needs.
   c. Shape public policy to support strategies.
   d. Implement people strategies, provide skills needed and drive transformations.
   e. Form strategic alliances to secure skills and market positions.
   f. Identify & deploy technology to achieve strategic objectives.

The US West culture focuses on four areas:

- Total Quality System, incorporating company values of: delight our customers, succeed through people, deliver outstanding shareowner value, support our communities, and continually improve our performance.
- Guiding Principles: Customer focus, quality driven system, people partnership, and leadership commitment and alignment.
- Total Quality Operating System, made up of: policy management, process management, and team work.
- Transformation Levers: education, rewards and recognition, involvement, and communications.[1]

CREATING THE VISION

Simply put, *vision* is what the business wants to become in the future; it is what the firm aspires to be and to accomplish. The vision serves to "build a dream" for people in the organization, and can serve to focus and inspire them. To do so, a vision must include a sense of the future; that is, a recognition that the future entails change and opportunity, and the company has set its sights on improving its lot and achieving significant progress.

---

[1] "Connecting People: An Experience That Ties it all Together," *US West Today*, 6, No. 15 (September 13, 1993), 1-3.

The terms "aspire" and "inspire" suggest that the organization should reach a bit in developing its vision of the future. Business as usual—described by terms such as "continue to"—do not suggest growth or improvement, nor do they tend to inspire or excite people. Therefore, a vision should not be a "sure thing;" it should entail some risk of failure because we are setting our sights high in terms of new markets, challenging goals, transforming business, and the like. On the other hand, the vision should not be a "pie-in-the-sky" dream or hallucination; it is something definitely worth working toward that has a reasonable chance of success.

For example, when President John F. Kennedy in 1960 committed the US to put a person on the moon and return by the end of the decade, he had created a challenging vision for the country. In 1960, many people may have doubted the likelihood of his goal being achieved, but it served to unite, uplift, and inspire the country to greatness. A good vision can do the same thing for a company.

A vision depends upon and incorporates three important components. It builds upon the mission or purpose (why the organization does what it does), includes goals and objectives (what we aspire to), and incorporates culture (the firm's core values and beliefs). It becomes the basis for developing strategies and plans for how to achieve the vision, as shown in Figure 7.1.

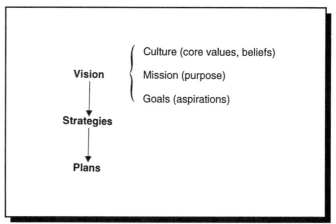

Figure 7.1 The Role of Vision

A good vision statement acts as a clear and powerful overall aim. This aim acts as a beacon, or "guiding star," on which people in the organization can sight. It can provide meaning for people; their efforts are actually contributing to something important and significant. Whether this goal is to go to the moon, build a national championship team, build a new personal computer, elevate your company to industry leadership, or whatever, it adds this element of meaning and excitement to people's work. This quest for meaningful work is unsatisfied for many people, and is a powerful driving force. Work with meaning and purpose is a powerful motivator, and a strong vision may solve many organizational direction, effort, and motivation problems.[2]

Effective Vision Statements

Vision is not necessarily a grand, sweeping plan on how to respond to major changes in the world. Mostly, effective vision is conceptual in nature; it is the intuitive ability to see the potential in opportunities right in front of you. Typically these are opportunities that others don't see or don't understand their significance and potential. Vision, then, isn't about forecasting the future, it is about creating a positive future for your firm by taking action in the present.[3]

The vision of the Gallup Organization is to "position itself to be the world's preeminent collector and disseminator of quality information."[4] It is this vision that has led Gallup beyond polling to providing customer feedback information for management decision purposes. In general, it has been shown that effective vision statements are leader-initiated, shared, positive and inspiring, and detailed. Some have said that "building a dream" for people is the essence of good leadership; it is also the essence of a good vision statement. Also critical is the ability of the leader to "sell" the vision—to get others to "buy-into" the vision. This will not occur without the vision being shared so that others can take their part of the vision and be responsible for it. Lastly, visions must be detailed enough to lend specifics and realism to their plans for accomplishment. As Fred Glueck, President of McKinsey & Co. management consultants has said, vision is a specific concept of what a company is trying to become. It should be based "not only on a clear notion of the markets in which they would compete, but also on specific concepts of how they would establish an economically attractive and sustainable role or position in that market. . . not mere wishful thinking as is the case with so many incomplete visions.[5]

[2] James C. Collins and Jerry I. Porras, "Making Impossible Dreams Come True," *Stanford Business School Magazine* (July 1989), 12-19.

[3] *Ibid.*

[4] "UNL Business Dean Brings International Perspective to Gallup, Inc., Board," press release dated September 10, 1993, The Gallup Organization, Inc.

[5] Richard G. Hamermesh, "Strategic Management," in H.E. Glass and M.A. Hovde, eds., *Handbook of Business Strategy: 1993/1994 Yearbook* (Boston, MA: Warren Gorham Lamont, 1993), 292.

DEFINING THE MISSION

The organization's mission defines *why* the organization exists and guides *what* it should be doing. It specifies what the organization's business is now or will be in the future. It also states the kind of organization the firm is or wants to be.

It includes the firm's "driving force," or reason it is in business. For example, Madonna Rehabilitation Hospital in Lincoln, Nebraska is in business "to serve the needs of people with physical disabilities." This is Madonna's driving force, or core reason for being. Its full mission statement elaborates on this core purpose. It is also part of the Madonna vision: "to become the regional system for children and adults with chronic or potentially chronic physical disabilities who require medical rehabilitation and medical care."[6]

Without a mission, there is no clear statement of why the company exists. More and more companies are developing formal mission statements, because such statements can provide management and personnel with a shared sense of opportunity, direction, significance, and achievement. Unfortunately, it is not easy to develop an effective mission statement. Some organizations work a year or two before they come up with an adequate one. But in the process of developing a mission statement, a company will learn more about itself and its latent opportunities.[7]

More than 50 percent of large companies have mission statements now, twice as many as five years ago. Cities, schools, and not-for-profits are taking stock of what they do, and creating mission statements. In fact, every Marriott hotel has its *own* mission statement, developed by each hotel's top managers and refined by the staff. Marriott feels that the involvement of virtually every employee in the process was "incredibly powerful."[8]

Some organizations endeavor to conceal their true purpose beneath obscure and all-inclusive terminology. An umbrella statement such as "our purpose is to serve the food needs of the nation" can refer to anything from farming in Nebraska, to delivering bread, to running a Boston Chicken franchise. It is simply too broad to guide management action. Since mission statements are not carved in stone, there is no real danger of the organization locking itself in by being too specific. A statement is properly dynamic and may, from time to time, be fine tuned. This is particularly true of mission statements for diversified organizations expanding into many businesses. Even without diversification, however,

[6] *Strategic Vision: 1993 Through 2000*, Madonna Rehabilitation Hospital (October 21, 1993), 4.

[7] A.A. Thompson and A.J. Strickland III, *Strategy and Policy: Concepts and Cases*, rev. ed. (Plano, TX: Business Publications, 1982), 7.

[8] Gilbert Fuchsberg, "Visioning' Missions Becomes Its Own Mission," *The Wall Street Journal* (January 7, 1994), B1.

a well-conceived mission statement seldom will stay current for more than a decade or two.

Defining and Redefining the Business

However, unless a firm has a clear definition of purpose, it is impossible to design a mission statement with sharply focused objectives, strategies, and policies. Managerial effectiveness begins with clarity of purpose—with a clear concept of the business.

Purpose defines for whose benefit the organization exists. A central issue of purpose is to define why the organization is in business: to make money for its shareholders, to create lasting products for its customers, or to provide interesting and fulfilling work for its employees, or whatever. Matsushita of Japan, for example, states that "profit comes in compensation for contribution to society."[9] Profit, then, is Matsushita's reward for achieving its corporate purpose—contributing certain products and services to society.

At least three questions must be answered when defining or redefining a business:

1. Which groups of customers or clients does the firm wish to attract?
2. Which functions does the business wish to perform?
3. What technology will the firm use? (In other words, how will the needs of the customers and clients be satisfied?)[10]

The answers to these questions determine how broadly or narrowly focused the firm's mission should be, as well as the degree of differentiation of its products and markets. AT&T, for example, was forced to redefine its business after it agreed to divest its operating telephone companies. According to its new mission statement, "AT&T's business is the electronic movement and management of information—in the United States and around the world."[11] This revised mission statement puts AT&T clearly in the information industry via electronic media. The stated mission would seem to preclude it from handling written information (a basic mission of the postal service), but would not prevent AT&T from entering computer information systems markets. Actually, AT&T's mission is somewhat more limited than its stated mission would seem to imply; it can provide long-distance service but not local phone service.

---

[9] Andrew Campbell, "The Power of Mission: Aligning Strategy and Culture," *Planning Review*, 20, No. 5 (September/October 1992), 10.

[10] Derek F. Abell, *Defining the Business: The Starting Point of Strategic Planning* (Englewood Cliffs, NJ: Prentice-Hall, 1980).

[11] *AT&T 1984 Annual Report*, 5.

The mission of the U.S. Postal Service (USPS), in turn, is stated as follows:

> The function of the United States Postal Service, an independent establishment of the Federal Government, is to provide prompt, reliable and economical services to customers in all urban, suburban, and rural areas through the collection, transmission and delivery of personal, educational, literary and business communications and parcels.[12]

This statement identifies the USPS as part of the public sector, describes the breadth of its customer base, limits the types of items it will handle, and indicates a desired quality of service.

Multimission Organizations

It is sometimes important to distinguish between the mission of a *business* and the mission of a *firm*. This distinction becomes important when an organization is engaged in more than one business, sometimes known as a "multibusiness" or "multimission" organization. Usually an organization grows by expanding or diversifying into additional businesses at some point. Obviously, the mission which described why the company was engaged in its original business will no longer be adequate for the entire firm as it expands into additional businesses. But, if the mission statement is broadened to include the new businesses, will it have much real value for any of the individual businesses?

For this reason, multibusiness organizations often have two types of mission statements: one for each business, and one for the firm as a whole. As we defined earlier, the mission for an individual *business* provides an overall sense of direction and purpose for that business. The mission of the *firm*, on the other hand, is more a statement of which businesses the firm competes in and how it does so. It includes the present and future scope of businesses, including products, markets, geographical areas and technologies, as well as distinctive competencies the firm is applying across business units to achieve long term sustainable advantage. The firm's mission statement provides guides to corporate strategy decisions—which business should we be in and how are they related? As such, determining the mission and vision of the *firm* usually precedes planning activities at the business unit level.

---

[12] Stan Payne, Letter to Omaha Division Employees, USPS Field Division (Omaha, NE: November 17, 1988).

Relationship to Goals, Objectives, Strategies, and Policies

The mission should be a company's driving force, a sort of "invisible hand" that guides it. The mission combines with objectives and goals to define exactly what an organization seeks to achieve through its activities. Strategy is the master plan for achieving the desired results, while policy sets up the framework for implementing the strategy. Over time, circumstances inevitably change and complications arise. These prompt the organization to modify its purpose, as well as its objectives, strategies, and policies. Developing a consistent, compatible relationship among these four items is a continuous task.

Amid changes and complications, purposes, desired results, and the means of achieving them take on different meanings for various levels of an organization. The CEO tries to provide benefits for stakeholders by fulfilling the firm's mission, while his or her management team also tries to fulfill that mission by meeting goals and objectives.

Properties of Effective Mission Statements

To be effective, a mission statement must be: (1) market oriented, (2) feasible, (3) motivating, and (4) specific.

Market Oriented. A clear mission statement defines the business domain in terms of the market to be served. Business domain here refers to product class, technology, customer group, market need, or any combination of these. A well-defined, market-oriented mission statement would state that the business is formed to serve a particular customer group, meet a particular type of need, or both.

Feasible. The mission statement must not define a market too narrowly or too broadly. For example, a product-oriented statement such as "we manufacture slide rules" is too narrow. It leaves no room for expansion when such items as the electronic calculator are developed. On the other hand, a mission statement such as "we manufacture communication equipment" is too broad for a company that makes pencils. The mission statement has to determine the middle path for operations, to allow for growth while not getting the company into unrealistic business ventures beyond its capabilities. For example, a prune company can be described as a dried fruit company, as a fruit company, or ultimately as a food company. (It may be a bit farfetched, however, to label it a laxative company or a pharmaceutical company).[13]

Motivating. A successful mission statement motivates. It inspires employees to work by making them feel that their efforts are significant and a contribution to the betterment of society. If possible, the mission should be stated as an accomplishment external to the firm. In this way, the employees can feel that they are producing a product or service for the benefit of the target consumer group. Workers are inclined to be more productive if they feel they are helping the consumer rather than just making a larger profit for the company.

Specific. The mission statement must be specific enough to include major policies, and it must give specific guidelines enabling management to choose from among alternative courses of action. The policies in the mission statement should express the value system of the company and the tone of its dealings with customers, suppliers, distributors, competition, and other market participants. On the other hand, a mission statement should not be overly specific. An effective mission statement should serve the company for many years. It should not have to be updated every few years just because the environment has changed or because a new, unrelated opportunity has come up. However, a company should revise its mission statement if the statement is no longer appropriate or does not define an optimal course for the company.[14]

Are Mission Statements of Value?

In reality, many corporate mission statements are of little value, consisting of pious platitudes and necessities. Of what value is stating "We hope to provide products of the highest quality?" A mission should not describe what a firm *must* do to *survive*; it should describe what the firm *chooses* to do in order to *thrive*.

Mission statements by themselves are of very little value. The mission *statement* is not the critical issue—creating a management team with a *sense of mission* is critical.[15] If a mission statement helps to create a sense of mission, it is valuable.

To be of value, a mission statement should include statements such that progress or performance in achieving the mission can be measured. Second, a mission statement should differentiate the company from other companies, and

---

[13] Philip Kotler, *Principles of Marketing*, (Englewood Cliffs, NJ: Prentice-Hall, 1980), 74-76.

[14] *Ibid.*

[15] Andrew Campbell, *op. cit.*

should define the business the company *wants* to be in—not merely the business it is in. In addition, a mission statement should be relevant to a wide range of stakeholders and, most importantly, it should be inspiring and motivating.[16]

A recent study of *Fortune* 500 firms attempted to determine if the mission statements of the high performers differed from those of the low performers. The study found a significant difference; the higher performers prepared publicly available *written* mission statements that included the organization's:

• Company philosophy—including the firm's basic beliefs, values, and broad aspirations.
• Self-concept—the company's view of itself, including its competitive strengths.
• Desired public image.

In other words, significantly more of the high-performing organizations had mission statements that addressed the above three areas. The conclusion is that the high performers have more comprehensive mission statements, and the three areas (corporate philosophy, self-concept, and desired image) are especially important components to include in an organization's mission statement.[17] The implication is that the successful firms are clear on these three issues, which somehow translate into improved performance. Every person in the organization should have a full understanding of the firm's mission.

DETERMINING GOALS AND OBJECTIVES

Another important aspect of strategic management involves goals and objectives which define *what* it is the organization hopes to accomplish, both over the long and short term. They are expected results, or targets, that support the organization's purpose. Goals and objectives are typically applied in certain specific areas, including:

1. Growth—including corporate growth rate, eventual size and growth, as well as relative size of business units.
2. Financial—including profits, cash flow, return on investment, dividends, and ratios.

---

[16] Russell L. Ackoff, "Mission Statements," *Planning Review*, 15, No. 4 (July/August 1987), 30.

[17] John A. Pearce II and Fred David, "Corporate Mission Statements: The Bottom Line," *The Academy of Management Executive*, 1, No. 2 (May 1987), 112.

3. Product/service—including development of new products/services, innovation, and quality.
4. Marketing—including customer base, advertising, sales, market penetration, market expansion, and customer service.
5. Operating—including inventory, cost control, production processes, and plant operations.
6. Personnel—including human-resource planning, management development, turnover, and labor relations.
7. Social responsibility—including regulations, pollution control, and community involvement.

A look at the goals and objectives of the postal service shows the inclusion of a number of the seven areas, even though the postal service is a public sector organization. Specifically, the overall goals of the USPS are:

1. Respond to the needs of postal customers by providing a full range of services that are prompt, reliable, and economical.
2. Maintain the integrity of the postal service on the basis of sound fiscal and operational policies.
3. Provide postal employees with career opportunities, working conditions, and compensation comparable to generally accepted practices in the private sector.[18]

In support of these overall goals, the postmaster general has developed a set of general objectives to be achieved by the year 2000:

1. To manage our resources in such a way to obviate the need for future rate increases.
2. To restore public and customer confidence and satisfaction in the postal service and return service levels (as defined by the overnight, second-, and third-day service, Express Mail, and so on) to at least those levels experienced in 1986-87.
3. To provide a workplace climate which recognizes the value of the individual and stimulates participation and individual initiative.[19]

While these goals and objectives are largely in the product/service, operating, and personnel areas, they are appropriate to the postal service's situation and support its mission.

---

[18] Payne, Letter.
[19] *Ibid.*

Hierarchy of Objectives

An important responsibility of management at each level of the organization is ensuring that lower-level goals reinforce one another. That is, the goals and objectives of division A must complement those of division B so that the organization is working toward the same ends and not at crosspurposes.

The important point is that all goals and objectives must support the organization's mission and must complement those of other departments of the firm—they must be consistent. Also, goals and objectives of lower-level departments must support those at higher levels of the organization. For this reason, it is helpful to think in terms of a hierarchy of objectives: primary, secondary, and subobjectives.

Primary objectives for the firm are typically finance and profit related, and may include: (a) return on capital employed; (b) return on shareholders' capital; and (c) levels of sales, profits, and rate of growth. These are typically broken down into specific targets for each division and profit center.

Secondary objectives are additional targets the firm and its divisions wish to attain, but are considered to be less important than the primary objectives. Examples would be customer satisfaction goals, equal opportunity targets, product quality levels, and the like.

Subobjectives support the achievement of the firm's primary and secondary goals. For example, one objective of a firm may be to achieve a 15 percent ROI after taxes. Subobjectives that support this goal may include increasing manufacturing efficiency to a certain level, reducing sales and distribution costs, and bringing higher-margin products on-line by a certain date.

In short, goals and objectives are required at every level of the organization and for each level of strategy: enterprise, corporate, business unit, and functional.

Further, goals and objectives must be achievable. They should *not* be so high that achievement is unlikely. Success breeds success: therefore, achievable goals tend to result in more divisions (and people) feeling that they are winners rather than losers—an important climate for the successful firm.

Also, while short-term accomplishments are important, long-term goals and objectives are even more important. Recent popular opinion holds that American managers pay undue attention to short-term financial results (and that business school graduates are trained this way, as well). However, a recent study of top executives at leading U.S. industrial firms indicates that this is not true—the overriding objective is long-term self-sustaining growth. Managers are most concerned with the long-term survival of their companies, and with minimizing their dependence on external sources of funds and on narrow product lines.[20] This is as it should be.

Management's Goals and Objectives

Managers are human, and, like most human beings, tend to put self-interest before anything else. This includes preserving their jobs. Instead of trying to maximize corporate earnings, managers *satisfice*, that is, attempt to meet a satisfactory performance level for themselves and for the corporation, while doing whatever it takes to ensure their job tenure and promotion chances. Much of their behavior, then, is directed toward maximizing not stockholder returns or wealth, but returns to themselves in the form of money, promotions, satisfaction, and security. In this context, you should *not* assume that outside directors truly represent stockholder interests and can effectively "control" management. Even outside directors owe their board seats to inside directors (management), and many will act to preserve their tenure on the board.[21]

In general, managers attempt to meet certain thresholds in areas such as profitability, to ensure survival of the firm and permit the pursuit of other goals, as a means of furthering their careers. Thus, long-term profit satisfaction, rather than maximization, and the satisfaction of other corporate needs, best describe the goals and objectives of both management and the organization.

ORGANIZATIONAL CULTURE

The organization is a minisociety (or not so "mini" in the case of the old AT&T, which employed 1 percent of the total U.S. work force). An organization has assorted internal constituencies (departments, divisions) attempting to influence the direction of the organization and to achieve a favorable share of its resources. External stakeholders attempt to influence the organization, as well. It is not surprising, then, that power and influence play major roles in organizational decisions—strategic perhaps even more than operational. Nothing is inherently wrong or "bad" about this situation; politics are a fact of organizational life. As a result, managers of today's large organizations may be less economic decision-makers than they are "governors of a social and political strategic management process."

The management of power is an explicit CEO function; in large, complex organizations we cannot talk about the process of strategy formulation *except* in

---

[20] Gordon Donaldson and Jay W. Lorsch, *Decision-Making at the Top: The Shaping of Strategic Direction* (New York, NY: Basic Books, 1983), 7-10.

[21] Paul Solman and Thomas Friedman, *Life and Death on the Corporate Battlefield* (New York, NY: Simon and Shuster, 1983).

social and political terms."[22] The task of the CEO in strategy formulation is twofold: he or she must develop a broad vision of what the firm's future position in its environment should be; the CEO must also manage a network of organizational forces to refine and implement the attainment of that vision. Strategy can be viewed as the outcome of cognitive, social and organizational, and political processes, and it is the CEO's task to *administer* these processes.

One of the CEO's key responsibilities is to forge a degree of agreement on the organization's goals (ends) and strategies (means), within the broad vision of the future of the organization. This is no easy task; in fact, it is sometimes easier to get parties in the organization to agree on means rather than ends. This is particularly true in the case of large organizations with multiple goals because not everyone will agree on all of them. The important thing is to find something to agree upon, such as means, that results in action toward the multiple goals. In fact, studies have shown that agreement on means is actually more important than agreement on goals. While agreement on both was associated positively with economic performance, agreement on means is significantly more important. In fact, agreement on goals without agreement on means was found to correlate with *poor* performance. Therefore, strategy makers should concentrate more strongly on reaching consensus concerning means than concerning ends. Agreement on means enables people to commit themselves to those strategies, while lack of such agreement (regardless of the end being pursued) reduces their commitment to action.[23]

Climate and Culture

All organizations must make changes continuously to resolve three basic dilemmas in dealing with their mission, objectives, policies and strategies. These dilemmas involve: (1) The technical design problem—in the face of environmental threats and opportunities, social, financial, and technical resources must be arranged to produce a desired output. (2) The political allocation problem— organizations must allocate power and resources. The uses to which the organization will be put, as well as the people who will reap the benefits, must be determined. (3) The cultural problem—organizations are in part held together by the

[22] J.L. Bower and Yves Doz, "Strategy Formulation: A Social and Political Process," in *Strategic Management: A New View of Business Policy and Planning*, ed. D. Schendel and C.W. Hofer (Boston, MA: Little, Brown, 1979), 165.

[23] L.J. Bourgeois III, "Performance and Consensus," *Strategic Management Journal* (1980), 227.

normative glue that is called *culture*. Culture consists of the values, attitudes, beliefs, principles, and objectives shared by organization members.[24]

These three dilemmas form three strands of a "strategic rope" in the sense that the strands must be interwoven and mutually supportive for an organization to be effective. And strategic management requires attention to all three strands. This is carried out by adjusting the organization's (1) mission and strategy, (2) structure, and (3) human resources to balance technical, political, and cultural concerns.[25]

There is not as yet a firm agreement on exactly what is meant by the culture of a business firm. Ansoff and Baker, however, offer a particularly attractive definition consisting of two aspects:

1. A shared *commitment* to norms and values. This common commitment to a set of behavior norms, for example, is an important contributor to the consistency of the firm's behavior. It also contributes to the energy and enthusiasm level of the individuals, plus the performance discipline within the firm. But culture can be more than values, beliefs, and norms; it also includes.
2. A shared *understanding* of what needs to be done to assure the firm's success. Participants must also know the success model and critical success factors for the firm, its niche, its industry, and its environment.[26]

What a business is able to accomplish may be determined as much, if not more, by its culture than its strategic plan. But a match or agreement between strategy and culture is important. In Korea, a study analyzed how organizations with fitted strategy and culture types perform differently from those with unfitted ones. An important picture emerged from this analysis: organizational performance in organizations with fitted strategy and culture types tend to far exceed those with unfitted strategy and structure.[27] Strategies are only as good as the culture that exists to encourage and support them. This culture is, in large measure, the product of the CEO's behavior over time. And, if there is no way of translating strategy moves into culture change, little change in subordinate behavior is likely, regardless of the strategy. Sophisticated planning and strategy

[24] R. Henry Migliore and Rinne T. Martin, "Use of a Corporate Culture Index for Strategic Planning," *Journal of Strategic Change*, 3 (April 1994), 95-105.

[25] Noel M. Tichy, "The Technical, Political, and Cultural Keys to Managing Change," *Organizational Dynamics* (Fall 1982).

[26] H.I. Ansoff and T.E. Baker, "Is Corporate Culture the Ultimate Answer," in *Advances in Strategic Management*, eds. Robert Lamb and Paul Shrivastava (Greenwich, CT: JAI Press, 1986), 83.

[27] Man Kee Choe, "An Empirical Study of Strategy Types, Culture Types, and Behavioral Performance in Korean Organizations," *Proceedings of Pan Pacific Conference XI* (1994), 29.

changes don't, by themselves, produce performance changes. *Implementation* is what counts, and is profoundly influenced by the corporate culture.[28] In fact, a firm's culture can be a source of sustainable competitive advantage, if that culture has economic value, is rare, and is not easy to imitate. To the extent that a firm's culture is hard to describe (as is usually the case) and is valuable, it is difficult to describe what it is about some firms that makes them more successful than others.[29]

In a multifaceted business world, it becomes vital to match the internally held (cultural) model of success with the realities of the external environment and the organization's resources, strengths, and weaknesses. On the one hand, therefore, culture can be a powerful motivator and contributor to success—when the cultural model of success *matches* the realities of the marketplace. But a strongly entrenched culture can be a major deterrent to success if the external requirements for success change.[30]

For example, IBM has been known for years for its strong culture. After experiencing problems in the early '90s, IBM hired a new CEO from the outside to turn the company around. The new CEO shelved the three "basic beliefs" that had guided the company for decades: pursuit of excellence; provide outstanding customer service; and respect for individual employees. These were replaced by eight goals that had worked for the new CEO, Louis V. Gerstner, Jr., in previous jobs at RJR Nabisco and American Express. Needless to say, longtime IBM employees, and the company itself, were shocked by this attempt to change its deeply ingrained culture.[31] It may be much easier and quicker to change the company's strategy than to change its culture.

[28] Leonard R. Sayles and R.V.L. Wright, "The Use of Culture in Strategic Management," *Issues and Observations*, 5, No. 4 (November 1985), 1-9.

[29] Jay B. Barney, "Organizational Culture: Can it Be a Source of Sustained Competitive Advantage?" *Academy of Management Review*, 11, No. 3 (July 1986), 656-65.

[30] Ansoff and Baker, "Is Corporate Culture the Ultimate Answer," 84.

[31] Laurie Hays, "Blue Period: Gerstner is Struggling as He Tries to Change Ingrained IBM Culture," *The Wall Street Journal* (May 13, 1994), A1.

Module 8

Strategic Advantage: Competencies, Resources, Timing, and Process Improvement

LEARNING OBJECTIVES

After completing Module 8, you should be able to:

1. Relate the critical importance of competitive advantage to strategic success.
2. Describe the sources of comparative and competitive advantage.
3. Realize the importance of distinctive and core competencies.
4. Appreciate the major resources on which an organization relies and how they relate to organizational strengths and weaknesses.
5. Discuss the role of time as a resource and source of competitive advantage.
6. Appreciate the growing role of process improvements in organizational performance.

From earlier discussions, we learned that firms desire to create competitive advantages. We said that a competitive advantage is critically important to any strategy; in fact, firms should probably *not* compete in markets in which they do not have a competitive advantage. Competitive advantage relates to how well a business is able to conduct the activities along its value-added chain, and includes any number of factors, such as technological advantages, marketing superiority, productive efficiencies, brand images, customer loyalty, superior service, and the like.

Competitive advantage results from the strategies of the business, any comparative advantages the business may possess, distinctive competencies, excellence in areas critical to success, and any productive synergies between businesses. Contributing to competitive advantage through the above-mentioned factors are resource deployments, time response, and improvements in organizational processes.

This latter area, dubbed "business process reengineering," is looked to by many as their potential source of competitive advantage. Writers such as Gary Hamel note that many organizations experiencing a crisis first try restructuring as a solution. If restructuring doesn't suffice, they turn to reengineering. If that doesn't solve the crisis, they look to a strategy change. As Hamel points out, this approach is backwards; the firm should *start* by examining its strategy to see if that is the cause of the crisis. Restructuring and/or reengineering will not solve an organization's problems *unless* its strategy is correct in the first place.[1]

So Peter Drucker states, most businesses face crises not because things are being done poorly. Therefore, "how to do it" tools—such as downsizing, TQM, reengineering, and the like—will not turn things around *if* the firm's "theory of the business" is wrong. That is, if the assumptions about markets, customers and competitors, their values and behavior, technology, the company's strengths and weaknesses, and the like no longer fit reality, problems will result. The problem is not that things are being done poorly; the wrong things are being done.[2]

PROFILE

Union Pacific Railroad

During the 1980s, the U.S. rail industry's freight revenues were flat, but intercity trucking revenues grew by 76 percent. This, plus the fact that the railroads had to cut prices to maintain their market share, has caused the railroad industry to

---

[1] Bernard Reimann, "Gary Hamel: How to Compete for the Future," *Planning Review*, 22, No. 5 (September/October 1994), 41.

[2] Peter F. Drucker, "The Theory of the Business," *Harvard Business Review*, 72, No. 5 (September/October 1994), 95.

reengineer itself around improved information systems. The new goal is to improve customer service radically.

The railroads are broadening their outlook from that of "managing trains" to managing their customers' shipments; eventually, "they'll be managing customers' inventories." Managers at companies such as Union Pacific have recognized that their fragmented information networks are a competitive disadvantage; there hasn't been a way to tell a customer where a rail car is as it passes from one carrier to another. The rail companies are involved in an effort to create "seamless service" for the customer; an interline system where the railroads share data on shipments. Therefore, the customer will have to deal with only one carrier.

The rails are going so far as to coordinate with trucking companies, which are beginning to shy away from long-haul shipments because of driver problems and shortages. With computer links between companies, customers will be able to order and even determine the location of shipments—including intermodal—with a single call.[3]

ACHIEVING COMPETITIVE ADVANTAGE

Competitive advantage is enjoyed by those companies which are appealing to the largest number of customers in a target market. In order to be sustainable, the product/service and related aspects need to be the result of some type of capability difference, vis-a-vis competitors, which will endure.[4]

It is important that businesses possess *sustainable* competitive advantages; a temporary competitive advantage is of little value. For example, competitors secure detailed information on 70 percent of all new products within a year of their development, and can soon offer competing products. New production processes are even harder to protect than are new products. Competitors often can quickly respond to marketing strategies, such as prices and advertising. What steps can be taken to ensure that a competitive advantage can be sustained? The difference between advantages that will endure and those that won't is often a matter of degree, partly dependent upon the industry, the competitors, and the relative strength of the advantages. Harvard's Pankaj Ghemawat holds that sustainable competitive advantage results from certain "commitments" (the tendency for strategies to persist) which should be the main focus of strategy choice. He feels that there are four possible sources of competitive advantages. The first is

[3] John Verity, "They've Been Working on the Railroad," *Business Week* (August 29, 1994), 73.

[4] Richard Hall, "A Framework Linking Intangible Resources and Capabilities to Sustainable Competitive Advantage," *Strategic Management Journal*, 14, No. 8 (November 1993), 610.

"lock-in," which occurs when firms commit to durable, specialized, non-tradeable assets, which he calls "sticky factors." The second—"lock-out"—is the opposite; since sticky factors are not easy to acquire. Therefore, firms may be locked-out of certain options by virtue of earlier commitments. The third and fourth factors are lags in adjusting asset stocks (changing commitments) and organizational inertia.[5]

In earlier writings, Ghemawat suggested four factors which enable a firm to sustain a competitive advantage through commitments. These factors include:

1. *Large-Scale commitments.* Investing in larger scale and more diverse operations can preempt competitors and result in great power in a given market.
2. *Experience.* Use of superior knowledge and reputation to improve quality, reliability, superior service, and marketability can be difficult for competitors to overcome (analogous to distinctive competencies).
3. *Comparative advantages.* Access to resources, information, or markets on favorable terms—protected by contracts or other mechanisms—can provide a long-term advantage.
4. *Competitor restraints.* Anything which limits competitors' options and prevents or slows their response (such as government regulations, resource limitations, previous commitments, and other weaknesses) can provide your business with a head start which may be sustainable.[6]

Others have suggested some similar and some additional factors contributing to sustainable advantages. Margaret Peteraf of Northwestern concludes that superior resources, limits to competition *after* a firm gains an advantage, imperfect resource mobility, and limited competition *before* gaining the advantage, all contribute.[7]

It seems that firms will enjoy a competitive advantage only if their resources and capabilities are unique in some way. Factors which increase the difficulty of imitation (and the potential for sustained competitive advantage) are:

1. *Time.* Continuous investments over many years are difficult to replicate.
2. *Asset mass efficiencies.* Possessing a relatively high level of an asset makes subsequent additions to that asset easier (e.g., Notre Dame has an advantage over many other universities in recruiting football players).

---

[5] Pankaj Ghemawat, *Commitment: The Dynamic of Strategy* (New York, NY: The Free Press, 1991).

[6] Pankaj Ghemawat, "Sustainable Advantage," *Harvard Business Review*, 64, No. 5 (September/October 1986), 53-59.

[7] Margaret Peteraf, "The Cornerstones of Competitive Advantage: A Resource-Based View," *Strategic Management Journal*, 14, No. 3 (March 1993), 179.

3. *Asset stock interconnectedness.* If adding to one asset depends upon having another asset (e.g., technological capability depends upon investment in R&D facilities), this asset is hard to replicate.

4. *Asset erosion.* Resources and capabilities decay with time and must be replenished.

5. *Causal ambiguity.* If it is difficult to determine the cause of a firm's advantage, it will be difficult to copy.[8]

Finally, Harvard's Rosabeth Moss Kanter concludes that success comes from the capacity to respond and act, not from product or market characteristics. As such, she lists four bases for sustainable competitive advantage that should guide the actions of a company. First, the *core competence* of the firm must be considered. Companies compete based on what they do best—Goodyear's ability to build tires, Honda's knowledge of engines, or 3M's competence in adhesives. Successful companies remain focused on their core strengths and de-emphasize activities that do not add value.

Next, *time compression* becomes much more important in today's society. The ability to be first to market, reduce production times, and respond rapidly to changes in market needs are important factors to competitive advantage.

Third, *focus on continuous improvement.* Today "quality" means much more than zero defects. The total quality movement must include a program of continual improvement of the firm's product. The firm must base these improvements on measures, feedback, and learning.

Lastly, *relationships* provide a source of competitive advantage. Collaboration across company boundaries allows a company to stretch its own capacity through adding a partner's competencies to theirs. These collaborations also can lead to new synergies from ventures with other firms, whether in adding distribution channels, supply channels, or new product innovation.[9]

In general, one can take a resource-based view to determine the degree and sustainability of a firm's competitive advantage. As shown in Table 8.1, a resource must be valuable, rare, difficult to imitate, and without substitutes to result in a sustained advantage. As the figure shows, the resource's value is most important, followed by rarity, inimitability, and substitutability.

Many of the analyses of factors determining competitive advantage have centered around distinctive competencies and resources. Another contributor can be the existence of a comparative advantage vis-a-vis competitors.

---

[8] J.L. Stumpert, "Competitive Advantage Research: A New Perspective," *Decision Line* (July 1994), 6-7.

[9] Rosabeth Moss Kanter, "How to Compete," *Harvard Business Review*, 68, No. 4 (July/August 1990), 7-8.

Table 8.1   Resource Properties and Advantage

Valuable?	Rare?	Difficult to Imitate?	Without Substitutes?	Competitive Implications?
No	—		—	Competitive Disadvantage
Yes	No	—	—	Competitive Parity
Yes	Yes	No	—	Temporary Competitive Advantage
Yes	Yes	Yes	No	Competitive Parity
Yes	Yes	Yes	Yes	Sustained Competitive Advantage

Source: Adapted from Jay Barney "Integrating Organizational Behavior and Strategy Formulation Research," in *Advances in Strategic Management*, Vol. 8, eds. Paul Shrivastava, Anne Huff, Jane Dutton (Greenwich, CT: JAI Press, 1992), 43.

Comparative advantage depends upon the costs of inputs to the business. A firm with access to superior or lower cost inputs necessary to produce its goods or services is said to have a comparative advantage. These inputs can include labor, equipment, raw materials, management and other personnel, financing, and the like, and can depend upon and vary from region to region (e.g., between cities, areas, countries, and so on). Comparative advantages can be significant factors in determining the competitive advantages of a business along with the firm's distinctive competencies and its resources. In short, as shown in Figure 8.1, a number of factors interact to determine the level of competitive advantage a business possesses—an important determinant of which business strategies it should pursue. For example, market/industry factors and environmental influences contribute to comparative advantages and factors critical for success in a particular market. Combined with an accurate and thorough analysis of competitive advantages, these factors are important determinants of competitive advantages. Multibusiness firms have additional influences. For example, the corporate portfolio of businesses and corporate resources can add to comparative advantages, plus create the possibility of synergies with other businesses in the portfolio—another possible source of competitive advantage. Depending on the positions of competitive advantage that exist (or lack thereof) the firm may attempt to resegment the market or industry, or may take action to restructure its corporate portfolio to improve advantages and synergies.

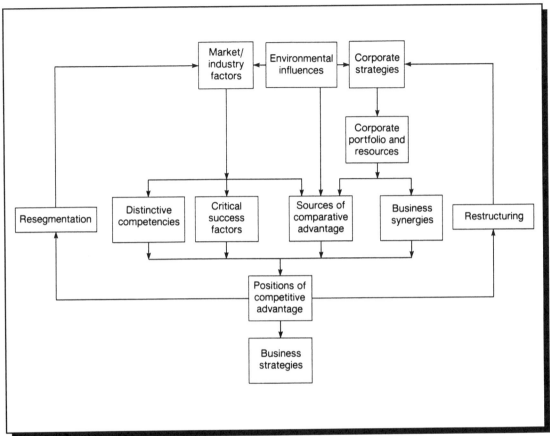

Figure 8.1 Competitive Advantage and Strategies

DISTINCTIVE AND CORE COMPETENCIES

Regardless of the type, developmental stage, and size of the organization, a firm is able to do only what it has the knowledge, skill, ability, and resources to accomplish. In other words, its capabilities are determined by its competencies and its resources. An organization's *distinctive competencies* are those relatively few things that the organization does particularly well, and if properly focused, can enable it to achieve competitive advantages and successfully achieve its goals and objectives.[10] Typical sources of distinctive competence include financial, managerial, functional, and organizational capabilities, as well as the company's reputation and history.[11] In short, if a company has superior abilities in producing or marketing a product or service, or has superior skills or resources in other competitively important areas, it may have a source of competitive advantage which can be an important part of its strategies.

These capabilities—the skillful performance of organizational processes—provide the basis for the firm's distinctive competencies. One cannot discuss capabilities without discussing core competencies; capabilities are the mechanisms by which core competencies are made real. As consultant George Stalk observes, however, "most customers don't see core competencies; instead, they see the capabilities that deliver them. They see Acuras on the market five or six years earlier than Saturns, although both companies were formed within a year of each other."[12]

Core competencies are those capabilities central to the business and its strategy. Michigan's C.K. Prahalad, along with Gary Hamel, holds that core competencies must meet three requirements: they provide potential access to a wide variety of markets; they contribute directly to the value the customer receives from the product or service; and they are difficult to imitate.[13] Core competencies—the set of competencies that create a firm's competitive advantage—define the firm's "core business."[14] This is the business that is central to the firm, which cannot be outsourced or divested. Core business skills (core competencies) need to be constantly exercised to maintain corporate fitness (competitive advantage).[15] As we will discuss later, a company trying to be a "world class" competitor must have exceptional competence in all areas; however, it is not possible to be world class in all functions and processes. Therefore, such companies are often urged to focus on what they do best—their core businesses and core competencies—and outsource the rest to high quality providers of those non-core activities.

---

[10] Mark R. Hurwich and Richard A. Furniss, Jr., "Measuring and Rewarding Strategic Performance" in *Handbook of Business Strategy*, ed. W.D. Guth (Boston, MA: Warren, Gorham & Lamont, 1985), 24:22.

[11] Kenneth R. Andrews, *The Concept of Corporate Strategy*, rev. ed. (Homewood, IL: R.D. Irwin, Inc., 1980), 69.

[12] George Stalk, Jr., "True-Based Competition and Beyond: Competing on Capabilities," *Planning Review*, 20, No. 5 (September/October 1992), 27.

[13] C.K. Prahalad and Gary Hamel, "The Core Competence of the Corporation," *Harvard Business Review*, 68, No. 3 (May/June 1990), 79.

[14] David J. Teece, "Contributions and Impediments of Economic Analysis to the Study of Strategic Management," in *Perspectives in Strategic Management*, ed. J.W. Fredrickson (New York, NY: Harper Business, 1990), 67.

[15] *Ibid.*

RESOURCES

A final consideration in any assessment of a firm's strengths and weaknesses is *resources*. In general, organizations possess six types of resources that they can employ toward the achievement of objectives:

1. *Financial resources*, such as cash flow, debt capacity, the availability of new equity, and cash and other liquid resources on hand.
2. *Physical resources*, such as plants and equipment, buildings, land, inventories, vehicles, and other facilities.
3. *Human resources*, such as management, supervisors, production employees, staff specialists, salespeople, and engineers.
4. *Technology*, such as patents, licenses, designs, production methods, proprietary information, and technological skills.
5. *Organizational resources*, such as systems, procedures, management techniques, decision-making models, company reputation, and goodwill.[16]
6. *Information*, such as knowledge of markets, the competition, the economy and other environmental influences, customer and supplier data and plans, technological advances, internal operating data, and the like.

One reason many small businesses fail and strategies in larger firms do not succeed is that management has attempted to do more than the firm's resources will permit or support. The business that tries to grab a large market share when it does not have sufficient capital, people, or experience is likely to fail. For this reason, strategies must be evaluated in terms of their resource requirements and the ability of the organization to support those requirements—spreading a firm too thin is a recipe for failure. In addition, resources are relative. American Motors had more financial assets than General Mills and Armstrong Cork, and outsold National Cash Register and Campbell Soup, but it did not compete in those industries; it competed in the automotive industry. Chrysler had ten times the assets of AMC, Ford twenty times, and GM forty times. In the auto industry, AMC's otherwise substantial assets were marginal, at best. A company's strengths and weaknesses must be evaluated not in absolute terms but in relation to its competitive environment, including other companies pursuing similar strategies.

One must also keep in mind that it is how productively the resources are used, not just the amount of resources, that is most important. An organization can waste resources as well as leverage resources to multiply their value. Obviously, management should try to leverage, or "stretch," its resources. Toyota,

---

[16] Charles W. Hofer and Dan Schendel, *Strategy Formulation: Analytical Concepts* (St. Paul: MN: West Publishing, 1978), 145.

CNN, British Airways, and Sony, for example, bypassed competitors with deeper pockets. How? Through greater ambition and better use of resources.[17]

The Resource Audit

In terms of internal strengths and weaknesses, the resource audit provides the best assessment. A resource audit can determine which external opportunities can be exploited. According to Harvard's Hugo Uyterhoeven, the resource audit encompasses three main dimensions:

1. *Operational*, focusing on what it takes to succeed in a particular market, industry, or field of endeavor. What are the key requirements for success?
2. *Financial*, focusing on assets, earnings, cash, and sources and uses of funds. What are the current financial resources of the firm and what can the firm afford to commit to a given strategy from internal as well as external (debt and equity) sources?
3. *Management*, focusing on human resources, particularly the ability to plan and implement strategies. Does the firm have enough of the necessary skills and abilities, given the requirements of the external environment and the strategy?[18]

The operational dimension consists of what it takes to succeed in a particular business or market. Does the company possess the technological capability to compete? Can it produce and distribute the product in sufficient volume at an acceptable level of quality? Are its costs competitive? Are the products aimed at the proper segments, and does the company possess distinctive competencies in important areas? In other words, will the company be able to effectively compete in this market? Out of this analysis will come an assessment of what the company *can* and *cannot* do.

The financial dimension focuses on money, such as cash flow and debt capacity. Ratio analysis, funds flow analysis, computer-based financial models, and other similar measurements are helpful in determining a business's intermediate- and long-term financial resources and requirements. The strategist is primarily interested in the following financial elements:

---

[17] Gary Hamel and C.K. Prahalad, "Strategy as Stretch and Leverage," *Harvard Business Review*, 71, No. 2 (March/April 1993), 75.

[18] H. Uyterhoeven, R.W. Ackerman, and J.R. Rosenblum, *Strategy and Organization: Text and Cases in General Management*, rev. ed. (Homewood, IL: Richard D. Irwin, Inc., 1977).

1. What are the asset requirements per dollar of sales? If the company's strategy calls for an increase in sales, how much will have to be invested in operating assets to support those sales?
2. What does the company earn? What will be its return on sales and on the assets required to support those sales?
3. How much cash is generated? Cash flow in broad terms is defined as cash receipts minus cash disbursements—it equals profits plus depreciation minus dividends. This figure determines how much *internally* generated cash will be available to support future investments.
4. How has the company committed its resources? How much of the internally generated cash is already committed? The *remainder* is the amount available for reinvestment. This figure should be compared to the reinvestment required to support the strategy. If sufficient funds are not available internally, how much can be gotten externally, from loans or additional equity? The company's debt capacity must be analyzed if external funding will be required.

The management dimension centers on the company's human resources. In many ways, a company's management is its most critical resource and perhaps the most constraining. Certainly, management is the most difficult resource to assess. However, the company's management capabilities must be equal to environmental requirements and to the demands of strategies chosen, and management must be able to use the firm's operational and financial resources effectively. As Bob Daugherty, chairman of Valmont Industries (supplier of agricultural products and services, and largest producer of center-pivot irrigation systems) states: "We want to have a management team capable of running a company ten times as large as we are now."[19] The strategy, in Daugherty's view, ensures that management is not his company's constraining resource. If it is, what good is having all the other resources to permit growth?

TIMING

The issue of time as a source of competitive advantage has been appearing ever more frequently. In fact, the theme of the November/December 1990 issue of the *Planning Review* was "Time: The New Strategic Frontier," claiming that time-based management can enable a firm to "achieve an enormous competitive advantage." The reason is that once a firm has established a time gap by being first and winning brand loyalty, market share, and cost advantages, the competition will find it difficult to catch up.

---

[19] R. Daugherty, visiting executive speech, (University of Nebraska, April 1983).

Joe Vesey, of Unisys concurs, stating that for manufacturing firms, time-to-market may be the "single most critical factor for success."[20] George Stalk, of the Boston Consultant Group (BCG), cites The Limited as being a master of time-based competition with an apparel acquisition system substantially faster than its competitors.[21] The Limited's system gives the company a competitive advantage in several ways. The Limited owns an apparel supplier with world-wide manufacturing connections as well as its own transportation network. The Limited can totally bypass importers, wholesalers, independent buying offices, and shippers (The Limited owns its own planes to rush finished goods to the U.S.). As a result, The Limited can respond much more quickly to buying trends of customers. This enables the company to buy in smaller quantities (reducing the risk of buying too much of the wrong merchandise) and enables the company to replenish its shelves and racks more quickly with hot-selling merchandise. Compared to competitors, The Limited is less likely to have to discount over-bought slow-selling merchandise and less likely to be short of popular items. Thus, quick time response gives The Limited a competitive advantage which flows directly to the bottom line. Other companies with time-based strategies are Federal Express, Toyota, Toys "R" Us, and Sun Microsystems. The specifics of time-based strategies are discussed in the module dealing with business-unit strategies.

The Experience Curve

Pricing strategies offer another source of competitive advantage. One possible source of cost advantage to a business results from experience effects, enabling the firm to price its product more attractively than competitors. For example, the price of a four-function, hand-held calculator produced by Texas Instruments was about $150 in 1971. Five years later, an equivalent model was priced in the $15 range, and by 1990 cost less than $5. In inflation-adjusted terms, the price of calculators dropped 99 percent in nineteen years. Why? One of the main reasons is the learning or "experience" curve, as its use in strategic analysis is called.

The learning-curve concept was first observed in 1925 when the commander of Wright-Patterson Air Corps Base noticed that the number of direct labor-hours required to assemble each plane decreased as more and more aircraft were assembled. With further study, it was found that as production doubled, labor-hours tended to decrease by a relatively stable amount. If the decrease was, for

[20] Joseph T. Vesey, "The New Competitors: They Think in Terms of 'Speed to Market,'" *Academy of Management Executive* (May 1991), 23.
[21] George Stalk, Jr., "Time Replaces Cost-Cutting as Strategic Weapon," *The Planning Forum Network* (November 1990), 2.

example, 15 percent, the result would be an 85 percent learning curve. This means that the time required to assemble the 20th plane is 85 percent of the time required to assemble the 10th plane, the 40th requires 85 percent of the time for the 20th, and so on. Table 8.2 lists times for various units, assuming a value of 100 for the 10th unit.

Figure 8.2 shows the learning curve graphically, and Figure 8.3, shows the same data plotted on double log paper (logarithmic scale for each axis), in which case the relationship becomes a straight line.

The learning curve, with labor costs falling with cumulative volume, has important implications for competitive strategy. Firms with marketing and pricing strategies geared to accumulating experience much faster than do their competitors may be able to achieve significant cost advantages over their competitors. For example, if one firm has produced a total of 320 units, its cost per unit will be at a labor index of 44, which is 15 percent less than the cost for a competitor

Table 8.2 Percent Curve Values

Unit	Labor Index
10	100
20	85
40	72
80	61
160	52
320	44
640	38

that has produced only 160 units. The first producer can make more profit than the second (assuming that they charge the same price), or can price product lower, pick up additional sales, and lower labor costs even more.

According to the Boston Consulting Group, the learning-curve concept applies not only to direct labor but to all costs, such as production, marketing, and economies of scale. BCG studies indicate that most cost elements, including nonlabor items, decline in such a way that total cost follows a composite "experience curve." Of course, all costs must be expressed in real terms (constant dollars) to observe the effect. Inflationary effects can be added to determine actual cost. BCG has found that the costs of most value-added items decline in the 20 to 30 percent range each time cumulative experience doubles. Factors contributing to this effect include:

1. Labor efficiency (indirect as well as direct labor).
2. Improved processes and methods, such as innovations and process improvements.
3. Product redesigns that result in faster production, less consumption of material, and lower costs.
4. Product standardization, such as the use of components common to other products.

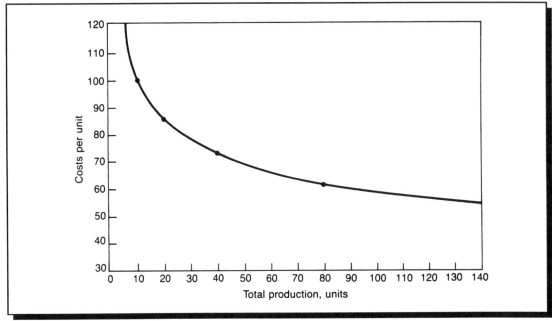

Figure 8.2 The Learning Curve

5. Economies of scale; the cost per unit of capacity increases less rapidly than does the level of capacity.
6. Substitution, including less expensive processes and cheaper materials.

Experience Curve Pricing

If a firm prices its product at a fixed percentage over costs, prices should decline at the same rate as the experience curve. However, the producer with the highest cumulative production will be rewarded with the lowest costs, encouraging some producers to price initial items below cost. In this way, the lower price will encourage more customers to purchase the product, resulting in a faster growth in sales, which puts the producer farther out on the experience curve than its competitors. This "dominant producer" greatly influences average costs for the industry. If the dominant producer's costs are declining, for example, at an 80 percent rate, so must the costs of other producers, if they are to survive. The other producers must be able to match the experience effects. Furthermore, the dominant producer will be able to set prices lower than those of others because of the position on the curve, making production less profitable (or even unprofitable) for competitors. This is shown in Figure 8.4. Competitor A, having greater cumulative production and lower costs, has a higher profit margin. In fact, C is break-

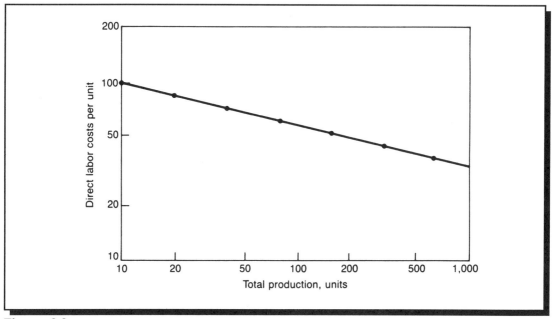

Figure 8.3 The Learning Curve on Log-Log Scales

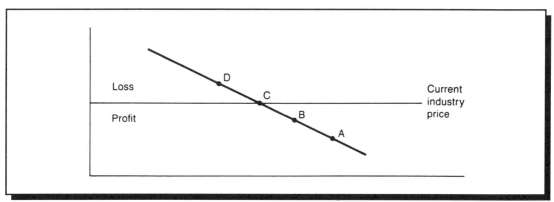

Figure 8.4 Profit Effects of Experience Curve

ing even and D is losing money. Only by catching up in cumulative production can C and D compete, unless they are able to place themselves on a separate experience curve with a greater slope than those of the competitors (which may be possible).

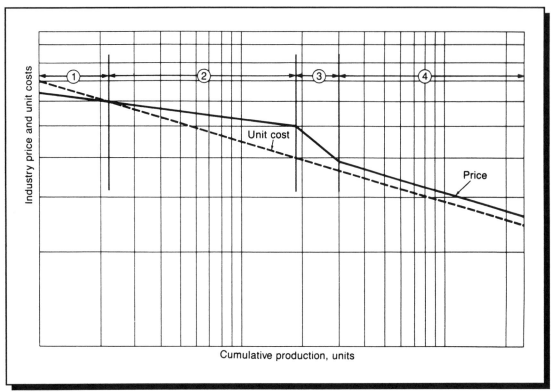

Figure 8.5 Common Price versus Cost Relationships

As Harvard's G. B. Allan observed, prices and costs often exhibit relationships similar to those shown in Figure 8.5. In Phase 1, prices may be less than average costs if firms base their prices on anticipated costs to gain an early volume and experience lead.

These prices often remain stable for a period of time (Phase 2) if production is less than demand. As supplies increase, however, this temporary situation is likely to change. One or more producers will try to increase their revenues by lowering prices and increasing their sales volume. Or others will be attracted by the high profit margins, producing a degree of overcapacity, usually resulting in price reductions. The typical result is Phase 3, where prices decline faster than costs, causing marginal producers to be shaken out of the market. When profit margins return to "normal" levels, the shakeout ends, and prices follow costs down the experience curve (Phase 4). Such shakeouts occurred in chemicals in the late 1950s and in semiconductors in the early 60s.[22]

The experience curve concept can be employed to determine strategies appropriate to the life-cycle stage and competitive position. In the growth stage (15 percent or greater growth per year, where experience doubles in five years or less), gaining and holding a dominant market position is the most desirable strategy. A firm may accomplish this position through price reductions, improved service, quality or support, or by concentrating on a market segment or niche in which dominance can be obtained.[23] Table 8.3 provides guidelines for experience-based strategies for several combinations of competitive position and growth rate (indicated by life-cycle stage).

Table 8.3 Experience Position and Stage Strategies

Experience Curve Position	Life-Cycle Stage		
	Growth	Maturity	Decline
Cumulative output exceeds competitors'.	Reduce prices to discourage new entrants and maintain capacity utilization.	Innovate, improve quality, and increase sales efforts to hold share.	Cut expenses by attempting to improve efficiency.
Cumulative output trails competitors'.	Attempt to increase share or seek a niche that can be dominated.	Innovate to create a new experience curve, or maintain share through low costs and prices. If not able, withdraw.	Withdraw.

[22] G.B. Allan, *Note on the Use of Experience Curves in Competitive Decision-Making*, Case No. 9-175-174 (Boston, MA: Harvard Business School, 1976), 9-10.
[23] *Ibid.*

Some Cautions

If experience curve effects hold, eventual market dominance should be determined early in the product life cycle, since trailing firms will find it difficult to overtake the market leader. How, then, was IBM able to enter the personal computer market late and rapidly catch Apple and Radio Shack? Because IBM was able to transfer its substantial experience in larger computers to the microcomputer market. In addition, product or process innovations can both change the shape of the curve and make it obsolete. For example, a significant product innovation by a previous follower can force an entire industry "back to zero,'' putting the innovator in the lead with the new product. And not all firms follow the same experience curve. A firm with a more steeply sloping curve (such as an 80 percent versus the 85 percent experience factor we are using) can reach a lower cost position with less total production than can a firm with a flatter experience curve. Finally, Hax and Majluf of MIT, report that experience effects vary with different activities in the firm, and the total effect depends on the *relative* influence of these activities. For example, their experience suggests the following typical learning effects:[24]

Activity	Experience Factor (percent)
R&D	95%
Manufacture of parts and components	75
Subassembly	70
Marketing	90
Distribution	85
Retailing	95

Thus, in our microcomputer example, IBM was able to transfer its considerable experience in R&D, manufacturing, assembly, and marketing. It was at a disadvantage in distribution and retailing of small computers. But this was outweighed by IBM's previous experience in the other areas.

Finally, the use of experience curve strategies depends upon how easy it is for firms to protect (or acquire) experience from competitors. When a firm is able to protect its proprietary experience, entry barriers for others are high. As diffusion of learning increases, entry barriers erode rapidly, however, making

[24] Arnoldo C. Hax and N.S. Majluf, "Competitive Cost Dynamics: The Experience Curve," *Interfaces*, 12, No. 5 (October 1982), 58.

late entry feasible for competitors. In addition, experience curve pricing is a viable strategy only when there is little or no diffusion of experience. Also, the Strategic Planning Institute has found that changes in product quality have a far more potent—and lasting—effect on market share than do changes in price. Therefore, it may be time to swing the pendulum away from the experience curve drive for market share and toward effective quality control and customer perceived quality improvements.[25] These findings underscore the danger of simple strategy prescriptions based on the experience curve. Only rarely is it in a firm's best interests to attempt experience curve pricing.[26]

PROCESS IMPROVEMENT

When the quality revolution caught on in the late 1980s, one of its key tenets was continuous improvement. The implication for most people was that continuous improvement meant incremental improvement. While continuous incremental improvement is a noteworthy goal, critics soon pointed out that it did not go far enough. Business process reengineering, which became popular in the early '90s, focused on radical redesign of business processes to achieve breakthrough results. Actually, TQM and reengineering are not at odds; they are complementary. They both seek a continuous search for improvement; one major, one incremental.

The concept behind business process reengineering (BPR) is that one should first seek out opportunities for major improvements through radical redesign of key business processes. Where that is not possible, one should continue to strive for incremental progress.

The key question behind reengineering is: "If we could start from scratch, how would we do this process?" Many processes have evolved over time, first being automated, then computerized. Certain processes were converted from manual processing to machine-aided to computerized. Even though they are much faster now, they still herald back to a manual process; in essence, we have "paved the cowpaths" into four-lane highways. If, however, we were to start from scratch, given today's computer technology, would the reinvented process be the same as the previously manual, but currently computerized, process? If not, it is a candidate for reengineering.

An additional rub is that many current business processes lose efficiency because they cross several functional departments of an organization. Therefore, no one individual bears complete responsibility for a single process. Some orga-

---

[25] Gale and Klavans, *Formulating a Quality Improvement Strategy*, 9.

[26] M.B. Lieberman, "The Learning Curve, Diffusion, and Competitive Strategy," *Strategic Management Journal*, 8, No. 5 (September/October 1987), 451.

nizations are seeking to overcome this situation by reorganizing along process lines. These new organizational forms reflect key processes. Some processes touch the external customer, like billing, order fulfillment, complaint handling, and the like. Others are solely internal, like hiring, purchasing, budgeting, and so on. One large store fixture manufacturer has decided to reorganize around four core business processes: strategy development, product and process design, customer relations, and order fulfillment. It has additional managers for the processes supporting the core processes, such as human resources, public relations, facilities, legal, and the like. The key is to focus on those processes and tasks *adding value for the customer*, and seriously questioning the rest.

Numerous dramatic examples of improved results exist. A pharmaceutical manufacturer cut its time to develop and test a new drug from eight to four years. A telephone company was able to offer same-day phone installation, down from thirty days previously. An insurance company found that an application for a policy took twenty-four days to process through underwriting, billing, etc., but was being actively worked on for only a fraction of that time. Now, a single caseworker handles the entire process and is able to deliver a policy in one week.

While such results are legend, one caution exists, however. One should focus on core business processes for reengineering, and only after making sure the business is pursuing the correct strategy. Only in this way will optimal results accrue from improvement activities, whether radical, as with BPR, or incremental, as with TQM.

Module
9

Real and Virtual Organizations: Structures, Alliances, and Outsourcing

LEARNING OBJECTIVES

After completing Module 9, you should be able to:

1. Describe the major types of business organizations and how they differ.
2. Understand typical growth and evolutionary patterns of organizations.
3. Realize that organizations have differing needs and opportunities at different stages in their development.
4. Define unitary, multidivisional, and professional forms of organization.
5. Describe the reasons for and characteristics of virtual organizations.
6. Realize the tie-in between core competencies and outsourcing of organizational functions.
7. Understand the important means of outsourcing, such as strategic alliances and networks, including collaborative and cooperative strategies.

This module looks first at traditional organizations, especially the growth and development patterns through which organizations typically progress, because organizations face different strategic concerns at different stages in their life cycle. In addition, the size and diversity of an organization are important determinants of which strategies the firm can and should pursue. Modern trends in organizational structure, such as multidivisional forms and professional partnerships, are important forms of organization in our society today.

Many business school graduates find themselves working for and with professional-based organizations, such as accounting firms, law firms, consulting firms, and advisory services, in the growing knowledge and services-based sector of our economy. The future portends rapid growth in even less-traditional forms of organization; the "virtual organization." While numerous examples of virtual organizations already exist in varying degrees, the growing use of outsourcing and strategic alliances as interorganizational collaborative strategies will make this type of organization much more common in the future. That is, many organizations are already engaging in some number of virtual activities and the percentage of their activities managed in this way is likely to be much larger in the future.

PROFILE

CUC International: A Virtual Retailer

CUC International has no inventory, no stores, and no warehouses. But in 1993 its revenues were $879 million. How? By brokering sales of consumer products and sales. CUC sells memberships that allow its thirty million members to shop for discounted products and services by telephone. CUC was founded on the vision of interactive home shopping via home computers, not the passive cable TV approach of Home Shopping Network and QVC.

CUC is the only large player that can deliver interactive home shopping services today. Until interactive cable is widely available, CUC practices its virtual retailing in a more traditional way; members order merchandise by phone from one of 5,000 sales agents. If the item isn't in a CUC on-line catalogue, the agent taps the company's extensive database. Once the customer makes a purchase, the company selects the fastest and cheapest vendor to deliver the item to the customer. As more and more communities acquire interactive TV, the customers themselves will be able to scan the product catalogues and databases at will and place their own orders.

Eventually, retailers like Macy's and others will enter interactive home shopping as well. But CUC should have a competitive advantage, since they have no investment in inventory, overhead, or risk of cannibalizing in-store sales. CUC is in the lead on "the cusp of a retail revolution," one which will likely reward virtual retailers like CUC.[1]

ORGANIZATIONAL TYPES AND STAGES

Defining the business—including development of goals and objectives, as well as assessing the organization's resources and competencies—is affected by the organization's current characteristics. That is, organizations face different strategic and policy concerns at different stages in their life cycles; start-ups, high-growth firms, mature businesses, and shrinking organizations face very different strategic situations. Also, the size and diversity of a firm are important determinants of which strategies the firm can and should pursue from this point on. Therefore, it is important to understand basic organizational growth and development patterns as they impact the strategic situation.

The process and content of strategic planning are affected by the size, maturity, and diversification of an organization. Such things as how to grow, how rapidly to grow, how much and what type of diversification, internal versus acquisition growth and diversification, horizontal or vertical integration, forward versus backward integration, domestic versus international growth, the type of departmentation, all are, in fact, strategic decisions.

These factors apply to all types of organizations, from traditional medium-to-large business firms to public-sector organizations, other not-for-profit organizations, new ventures, small businesses, international businesses, and even to professional and service organizations such as CPA firms. The focus in this section is on strategy processes and content as applied to organizations in general, concentrating on those aspects applicable to traditional medium-to-large business firms. For certain other kinds of organizations, unique characteristics, features, and needs that may affect strategic decisions and processes are treated in detail in a later module.

Types of Organizations

There are many types and sizes of organizations. Appropriate strategies for organizations not only vary with their relative size (large businesses and agencies *are* different from small businesses and agencies), but also with the *type* of organization. One major strategic decision involves the type of business an organization wishes to become (or is at present). Here, strategic issues facing four generic types of business (the single-product business, the dominant-product business, the diversified company, and the multi-industry company), shown in Figure

---

[1] Stephen Barr, "The Future of Retailing," *CFO Magazine* (June 1994), 49-54.

Figure 9.1, will be examined.[2] (The term *business* is used broadly and is not limited to private-sector organizations.)

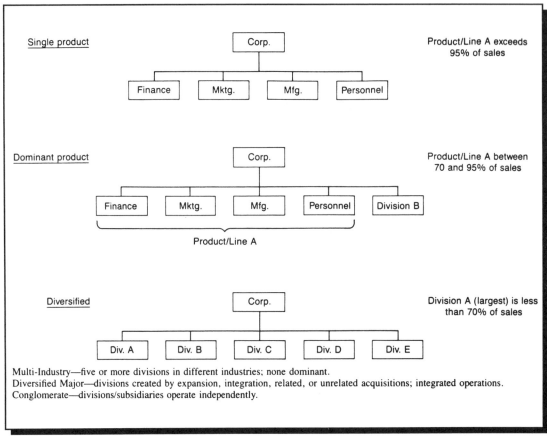

Figure 9.1 Types of Businesses

Single-Product Businesses. The single-product business receives over 95 percent of its revenues from a single line of goods or services. This type of business is almost always departmentalized along functional lines, regardless of its size. Many small businesses are of this type, although some single-product firms, such as Caterpillar, as well as banks and insurance companies, are relatively large. The major corporate-level strategic decision in this type of company deals with

---

[2] Leonard Wrigley, "Divisional Autonomy and Diversification," Ph.D. dissertation, Harvard Business School (Cambridge, MA, 1970).

how to grow—within the single product line (for example geographically), or by broadening the line and ceasing to be a single-product firm.

Dominant-Product Businesses. This type of business is somewhat diversified, but a single line of goods or services still accounts for 70 to 95 percent of revenues. The dominant-product business is usually managed along functional lines. A separate subsidiary division, or divisions, is often created for the remaining product or services lines—a partial move to a multidivisional structure. Again, financial institutions typify larger dominant-product businesses, but another example is Deere & Company, where farm equipment dominates, yet industrial equipment, lawn equipment, and recreational products also are manufactured.

Dominant-product businesses may be vertically integrated, diversified into products linked in some way to the dominant product, diversified to exploit a particular advantage they possess, or diversified on an unrelated basis. The corporate strategic questions here are how much to diversify, into which areas, and the relationship (if any) to the dominant product.

Diversified Businesses. Diversified organizations typically receive over 30 percent of their revenues from products outside their main business. This type of business is typically large and organized along divisional lines, sometimes called M-form (for multidivision form) structure. The product lines relate to one another in many ways that are the same as in the dominant-business firm. Yet no one business dominates to the degree that it does in the dominant-business firm. Corporate-level strategy relates largely to the "portfolio" of businesses comprising the firm, and to their relationships. For example, diversification moves can lead the firm into businesses that are *related* in some way, or *unrelated*, or some combination.

Multi-Industry Firms. This type of business is a subtype of the diversified firm. The multi-industry, or multimission, organization is characterized by a relatively large number of businesses, none of which is significantly bigger than the others. While the diversified company might have three divisions accounting for, say, 50, 30, and 20 percent of sales, the true multi-industry firm might have five or more divisions in a number of *different* industries.

Multi-industry firms, then, have diversified into a number of *related or unrelated* industries, and no one product line comes close to dominating the others. Multi-industry corporate strategies typically deal with managing the portfolio of businesses, as well as the type of diversification methods to be followed. Some multidivision firms, called *diversified majors*, manage their divisions on a closely related basis—sharing technology, for example, and transferring employees between divisions. Others manage the divisions separately, acting as a holding company for the divisions, which operate quite independently. A *conglomerate* tends to treat its subsidiaries not so much as divisions but as independent companies owned by the parent corporation; in fact, each subsidiary typically has its own president and CEO. While this arrangement appears similar to the holding company, conglomerates typically treat their subsidiaries as investments that can be bought or sold and are acquired through aggressive financial transactions.

The diversified company (including the multi-industry company) is the most important form of industrial organization in the United States in terms of sales and assets. This type of company comprises about 80 to 85 percent of the *Fortune* 500 industrials, which account for two thirds of the output, investment, and employment, and three fourths of the profits of U.S. industry.[3]

Patterns of Organizational Evolution

As organizations increase in size, they often change from a single-product firm to a dominant business, a diversified major, or a multi-industry firm. In addition, at any stage in this progression, the firm can expand geographically into foreign markets, becoming progressively more global or multinational. There are, however, typical patterns, or stages of development, that organizations pass through as they grow, develop, and mature.

It is important to understand these stages, because strategies and modes of operation appropriate for one stage may be inappropriate for another. Goals, objectives, strategies, organization structure, and management styles tend to differ from stage to stage.

A number of researchers have proposed models depicting these growth patterns. For example, Downs[4] studied the life cycle of government bureaus. Lippitt and Schmidt[5] proposed a three-stage model of development for companies, as did Scott.[6] While each of these models approaches organizational growth and development somewhat differently, there is a degree of commonality. The models usually progress from the start-up stage through various intermediate stages to that of a large mature organization, often a multidivisional (perhaps multinational) corporation. Two models that are particularly helpful in understanding an organization's growth patterns are Greiner's evolution and revolution model and Galbraith and Nathanson's model.

---

[3] Norman Berg and R.A. Pitts, "Strategic Management: The Multi-Business Corporation," in *Strategic Management*, eds. D. Schendel and C.W. Hofer (Boston, MA: Little, Brown, 1979), 339.

[4] A. Downs, "The Life Cycle of Bureaus," in *Inside Bureaucracy*, ed. A. Downs (San Francisco, CA: Little, Brown, and Rand Corp., 1967), 296.

[5] G.L. Lippitt and W.H. Schmidt, "Crises in a Development Organization," *Harvard Business Review*, 45, No. 6 (November/December 1967), 102.

[6] W.R. Scott, *Stages of Corporate Development—Part 1*, Case No. 9-371-294 (Boston, MA: Intercollegiate Case Clearing House, 1971).

Greiner's Evolution and Revolution Model. Greiner suggests that organizations progress through five sequential stages as they grow and mature.[7] There is a distinct strategy, structure, and management style appropriate for each phase, but inappropriate for other phases. Further, the approach appropriate for each phase has certain limitations that prevent the organization from growing beyond a certain size. When this limit is reached, the organization must change in certain ways to progress to the next phase. That is, it must make certain "revolutionary" or dramatic changes, or its growth will be effectively halted.

Greiner's model begins with a small, informal organization growing because of the creative ideas of its founders (Phase I). If the firm grows and prospers, this informal, entrepreneurial approach may begin to cause problems. A need arises for a strong, professional manager to take charge and lead the firm toward unified objectives. If this happens, the firm can grow through Phase II under strong, centralized leadership.

However, this approach also has its limits. As the firm grows and expands, centralized decision-making becomes a bottleneck and subordinate managers begin to demand more autonomy. The firm becomes too large and diverse for a few top managers to make all the important decisions. Only by increased delegation of authority and responsibility can the burden on top management be eased, and the firm can grow through the third phase. Again, this approach eventually reaches its limit as diverse, autonomous divisions begin to drift apart. In fact, the divisions may begin to function almost as separate companies, with differing financial, personnel, and operating policies as well as differing strategies. There is a need to regain control over these diverse subunits, which is usually met by creating corporate staff groups to coordinate and control planning, decision-making, and operations of the units.

However, a large organization with too much coordination and control can become bureaucratic, and faces a "red-tape" crisis. Greiner suggests that this can be overcome by collaborative approaches, such as matrix management, team building and group rewards, project teams, and the like, to create increased motivation, purpose, and excitement. The next crisis may be one of information overload and psychological saturation ("burnout"). In short, firms face very different problems and need different solutions as they grow and mature through the five phases. Again, structure, strategies, and management approaches must be appropriate to the firm's current phase.

The Galbraith and Nathanson Model. Galbraith and Nathanson also studied organizational growth patterns in some depth, and offer models that shed addi-

---

[7] Larry Greiner, "Evolution and Revolution as Organizations Grow," *Harvard Business Review*, 50, No. 4 (July/August 1972), 37.

tional light on the growth process and the strategies it requires.[8] Their model focuses more on organizational types and characteristics at various stages of development. Figure 9.2 shows likely growth patterns based upon the Galbraith and Nathanson model.

In their model, as the simple (analogous to the single-product) firm grows (in sales volume, assets, and employees), it almost always adopts a simple functional structure. At this point, however, the type of growth strategy it pursues dictates the type of structure the firm will adopt in the next stage of its evolution. The firm can grow in two ways—internally, or by acquisitions. If growth is internal, related diversification is usually the pattern, and the firm becomes multidivisional. This is also the case if related lines are acquired. If unrelated acquisitions are made, the firm becomes a holding company. The predominant path, however, is to pursue a strategy of vertical integration, which calls for a centralized functional form of organization. After reaching this stage, the typical firm begins related diversification strategies (either through internal growth or by acquisition), taking the company to the point where a multidivisional (M-form) structure is called for. As one might suspect, companies can move between organization types at this point, depending on their strategies and actions.

The next major strategy is almost always international expansion, which results in the firm requiring a global structure (functional, holding company, or, typically, multinational). Figure 9.2 describes a number of characteristics (including corporate-level strategies) that typify the major organizational types in this framework. This figure can be used in two ways; to identify the characteristics appropriate for a particular type of organization, or to identify the type of organization by studying its characteristics.

Further Observations. You should bear in mind that growth models such as the above describe paths that organizations typically follow and stages they typically go through *if they progress to the final stage.* Not all (or even most) organizations progress to the final stages; some stop at various stages or types of structure along the way. Some even regress to previous stages or types. Some fail and cease to exist at some point. Some are acquired and exist as divisions of other companies, and some lose their identity entirely after an acquisition or merger.

A model developed by Miller and Friesen at Canada's McGill University takes these factors into account. Their model incorporates a birth phase (in which a new firm is attempting to become a viable entity), a growth phase (after the

---

[8] Jay R. Galbraith and D.A. Nathanson, *Strategy Implementation: The Role of Structure and Process* (St. Paul. MN: West Publishing, 1978), 118.

Type Characteristic	(S) Single	(F) Functional	(H) Holding	(M) Multidivisional	(MN) Multinational	(G) Global
Strategy	Single product	Single product and vertical integration.	Growth by acquisition, unrelated diversity	Related diversity of product lines—internal growth, some acquisition.	Multiple products in multiple countries.	Standard products worldwide
Organization Structure	Single functional	Central functional.	Decentralized profit centers around product divisions Small headquarters	Decentralized product or area division profit centers.	Decentralized profit centers around worldwide product or area divisions.	Same
Performance Measurement	By personal contact Subjective	Increasingly impersonal based on cost, productivity, but still subjective.	Impersonal based on return on investment and profitability	Impersonal based on return on investment profitability with some subjective contribution to whole.	Impersonal with multiple goals like ROI, profit tailored to product and country.	MN centralized by product
Strategic Choices	Need of owner versus needs of firm	Degree of integration. Market share. Breadth of product line.	Degree of diversity. Types of business. Acquisition targets. Entry and exit from businesses.	Allocation of resources by business. Entry and exit from businesses. Rate of growth.	Allocation of resources across businesses and countries. Exit and entry into businesses and countries. Degree of ownership and type of country involvement.	Which products, regions, location

Source: Adapted from *Strategy Implementation: The Role of Structure* by Jay R. Galbraith and D.A. Nathanson; copyright © 1978 by West Publishing Company, 118. All rights reserved.

Figure 9.2 Characteristics of Organizational Types

firm has established its distinctive competencies and enjoys some initial product-market successes), and a maturity phase (which follows growth as sales levels stabilize, the level of innovation falls, and a more bureaucratic structure is established). In addition, they include a decline phase (which results from stagnation as markets dry up and the firm declines with them. Profitability drops because of external factors and a lack of innovation.) Further, they include a revival phase, which is typically a phase of diversification and expansion of product and market scope. In this phase, firms typically adopt divisionalized structures to cope with more complex and heterogeneous markets and emphasize more sophisticated planning and control systems.[9] While elements of decline and revival are inherent in some of the earlier models (such as Greiner's crises and revolutionary changes), treating them explicitly, as Miller and Friesen have done, adds to understanding of the processes.

Miller and Friesen's revival phase is analogous to corporate *renewal*, which is characteristic of many firms from time to time. In fact, most established (and many young) firms go through significant periods of decline and renewal, some externally caused and some internal. Figure 9.3 illustrates this process.

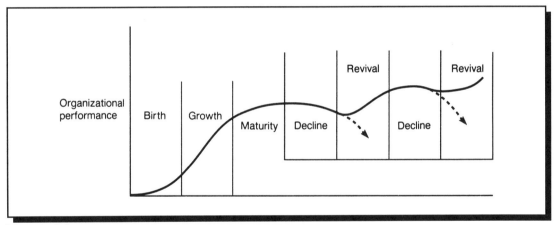

Figure 9.3 Organizational Growth and Renewal

Also, nothing was said about the *rate* of progression from stage to stage; some firms progress rapidly, some slowly, some in spurts, and so forth. What is important to realize, however, is that patterns of development seem to be somewhat consistent, and that structures, strategies, and other characteristics at one stage or type are not the same as the characteristics at other stages. It is also

[9] Danny Miller and Peter H. Friesen, "A Longitudinal Study of the Corporate Life Cycle," *Management Science*, 30, No. 10 (October 1984), 1161.

worth noting that our understanding of *how* organizations of varying types and sizes function is incomplete. Some observers have suggested studying small businesses, implying that there is more knowledge of larger businesses. This may be true if "big business" is defined as anything larger than a "small business." However, most organization studies tend to focus on medium-sized organizations or a department or division of a large organization. In reality, relatively little is known about the way the *very large* businesses function.[10] The point is that there are qualitative as well as quantitative differences among organizations of different sizes and types.

Newer Forms of Organization

M, H, and P^2-forms. The traditional functional form of organization is sometime referred to as the U-form (for Unitary). Organizations which have diversified and decentralized their operations to separate divisions are sometimes called M-form (for Multidivisional) organizations. Organizations patterned after holding companies can be referred to as H-form organizations. Recently, researchers have begun to study the characteristics of professional partnerships, or P^2-form organizations. Professional partnerships would typify accounting, legal, some medical services, consulting firms, and the like.

Table 9.1 compares key strategic characteristics of the M, H, and P^2-forms of organization. Briefly, M-form organizations clearly separate strategic and operating responsibilities, with corporate strategy and financial controls centralized. Division strategy and operations are decentralized to the divisional level. The H-form tends to treat its divisions as separate entities, much like a conglomerate, and views them as investments. Therefore, corporate strategy integration is weak, with business level strategy and operations decentralized to the divisional level.

The P^2-form resembles the M-form in some ways, but differs in others. It differs largely in the area of strategic direction (weak), and its strategic process is one of negotiation, consensus building, and negotiation. Successful implementation depends upon acceptance and professional agreement, not authority and the typical corporate manipulation of resources, rewards, and controls.[11] The professional relationship between colleagues is an important characteristic of the P^2-form of organization.

---

[10] David S. Brown, *Managing the Large Organization*, (Mt. Airy, MD: Lomond Publications, 1982), jacket.

[11] R. Greenwood, C.R. Hinings, and J. Brown, "P2-form Strategic Management: Corporate Practices in Professional Partnerships," *Academy of Management Journal*, 33, No. 4 (December 1990), 725-55.

Table 9.1 Strategic Comparisons of Organizational Forms

Form	Control Dimensions		
	Strategic	Market-Financial	Operating
1. Multidivisional: M-Form	Corporate centralized, Business decentralized	Financial and nonfinancial targets, Precise targets, Tight accountability, Multiyear orientation	Decentralized
2. Holding Company: H-Form	Weak Corporate, Business decentralized	Financial targets, Tight accountability, Precise targets, Short-term orientation	Decentralized
3. Professional partnership: P²-form	Weak to modest, Consensus orientation	Financial targets, Precise targets, Tolerant accountability, Explicit short-term and implicit long-term orientation	Decentralized, Centralized control of standards and quality.

Source: Adapted from R. Greenwood, C.R. Hinings, and J. Brown, "P²-form Strategic Management: Corporate Practices in Professional Partnerships," *Academy of Management Journal*, 33, No. 4 (December 1990), 749.

Horizontal Corporations. The traditional hierarchical, or vertical, organization has not been performing up to par in today's faster-paced environment. A traditional organization spends a major amount of energy internally—managing relations between departments and pushing information up and down the hierarchy. Some, such as AT&T, DuPont, GE, and Motorola, began to change the way they work, adopting what is called the "horizontal corporation."

The horizontal corporation organizes the company based upon its key processes and creates teams from different departments to run them. The multidisciplinary teams, overseen by a top management team, perform core processes, such as product development or sales generation, reducing the hierarchy to three or four layers of management. The results have been promising. Chrysler used a process approach to turn out its Neon in 1994, quicker and at a fraction of the typical development cost. General Electric, calling itself a "boundaryless company," has reduced costs, shortened cycle times, and increased responsiveness to customers. To create greater allegiance to a process (vs. to a single boss), the company utilizes "360-degree appraisals," in which an employee's performance is appraised from all sides—peers, above, below, etc.

The key steps in creating and operating a "horizontal corporation" include the following:

1. **Identify** strategic objectives.
2. **Analyze** key competitive advantages to fulfill objectives.
3. **Define** core processes, focusing on what's essential to accomplish your goals.
4. **Organize** around processes, not functions. Each process should link related tasks to yield a product or service to a customer.
5. **Eliminate** all activities that fail to add value or contribute to the key objectives.
6. **Cut** function and staff departments to a minimum, preserving key expertise.
7. **Appoint** a manager or team as the "owner" of each core process.
8. **Create** multidisciplinary teams to run each process.
9. **Set** specific performance objectives for each process.
10. **Empower** employees with authority and information to achieve goals.
11. **Revamp** training, appraisal, pay, and budgetary systems to support the new structure and link it to customer satisfaction.[12]

As can be seen from the steps, the horizontal corporation embodies the concepts of competitive advantage, core processes, reengineering, empowerment, customer satisfaction, and others.

The Integrated Organization. Advances in information technology (IT) enable enterprises to have a *high performance team* structure, to function as *integrated businesses*, and to become *extended enterprises* by developing new relationships with external organizations. As shown in Figure 9.4, certain "enabling technologies" permit certain changes which, in turn, yield the promise of organizational advancements. Information technology, in the form of workgroup computing, facilitates business process redesign (reengineering), promising high-performance teams. Integrated systems permit an organizational transformation, resulting in an integrated organization. Interenterprise computing is one of the technologies making it possible to recast external relationships, permitting extended enterprises—virtual organizations—to operate.

Federal Express is an example of an integrated organization. Federal Express strives to maintain positive control of each package through "real-time electronic tracking and tracing systems" by using integrated computing architecture. Fed Ex has solved the problem facing most organizations; they are not integrated—in part, because their computer systems are not integrated. They have highly frag-

---

[12] John A. Byrne, "The Horizontal Corporation," *Business Week* (December 20, 1993), 76-81.

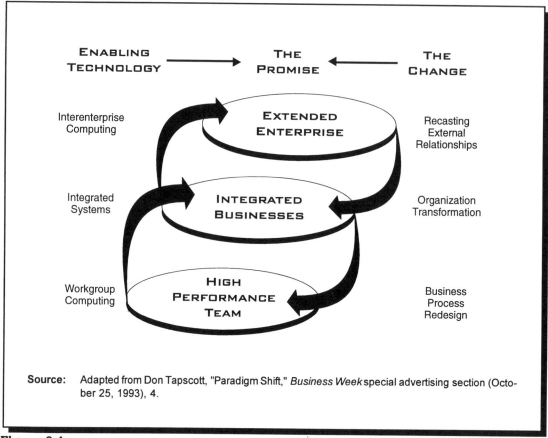

Figure 9.4 Technology, Change, and Organizational Progress

mented, isolated systems that overlap but do not function in an integrated manner. Integrated systems provide the backbone for the new, open, networked enterprise. Such systems permit the enterprise to function as a "cohesive organization, providing corporate-wide information for decision-making and competitive enterprise applications that transcend autonomous business units."[13]

---

[13] Don Tapscott, "Paradigm Shift," *Business Week* special advertising section (October 25, 1993), 3-4.

VIRTUAL ORGANIZATIONS

The next step in organizational evolution permits the extended enterprise, or *virtual organization*, to exist. What is a virtual corporation? Popularized by William Davidow and Michael Malone in their book of the same name,[14] a virtual corporation is a temporary network of independent companies—suppliers, customers, even competitors—linked by information technology to share skills, access to markets, and costs. Typically, collaborators will unite to exploit a specific opportunity; once realized, the venture will likely disband. Each company contributes only its core competencies. As shown in Figure 9.5, a manufacturer will contribute its manufacturing capability, while relying on design houses to design the product, other manufacturers to produce components and assemblies, distributors, and marketing companies to sell the product. Some virtual companies can endure indefinitely, depending upon the life of the product line or service, becoming extended enterprises through systems such as American Airlines SABRE reservation system or American Hospital Supply's customer order system.

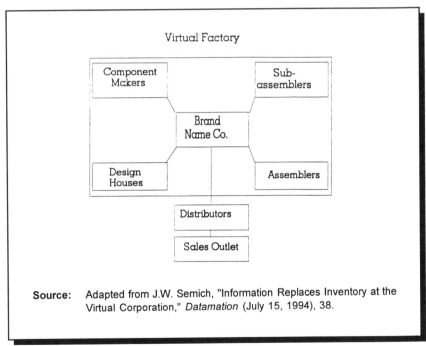

Source: Adapted from J.W. Semich, "Information Replaces Inventory at the Virtual Corporation," *Datamation* (July 15, 1994), 38.

Figure 9.5 A Virtual Corporation

---

[14] Wm. H. Davidow and Michael S. Malone, *The Virtual Corporation* (New York, NY: Harper Business, 1992).

The number of virtual corporations operating through strategic alliances between partners is growing rapidly. For example, AT&T used Marubeni Trading Co. and Matsushita Electric Industrial to produce its Safari notebook computer, designed by Henry Dreyfuss Associates. IBM, Apple, and Motorola are allied to develop an operating system and microprocessor for a new generation of computers. Ambra Computer, solely owned by IBM, contracts out all phases of design, production, distribution, and sales. Apple's partnering is one reason that its revenues per employee are nearly four times those of DEC and twice those of IBM. For example, Sony manufactures the least-expensive version of Apple's Power-Book computers. Corning Inc. has nineteen partnerships, accounting for 13 percent of earnings, "providing size and power without the bulk."[15]

Virtual corporations bringing world-class skills together in every key area clearly have the opportunity to hold the competitive advantage. But virtual enterprises have risks as well. A company joining a network loses control of the functions its partners perform. Proprietary information and technology may dissipate, and management skills are different. Virtual managers will have to build relationships, negotiate "win-win" deals, find partners with the right skills and compatible goals and values, and provide the right balance of control and freedom. It is likely that a company's desirability as a partner "will be a strategic requirement to remaining competitive."[16] Therefore, whether a firm wins or loses *and* how it plays the game will both be important. Finally, infrastructure changes are needed. Most virtual corporation partners are turning to Supply Chain Management (SCM) systems to help run the show. SCM systems are an integrated class of distributed business software; a large distributed client server application. In a completely virtual corporation, the information systems function, through the SCM system, would be the only production part of the factory still up and running.

Outsourcing

Outsourcing and alliances make the virtual corporation work. Both are key elements of virtual organizations, but have important roles for more traditional firms as well. The practice of outsourcing has flourished in certain industries, such as apparel, electronics, construction, movie-making, and others. Again, organizations cannot perform "everything in their value chain at a best-in-world level. Companies that perform an activity internally at less than best-in-world levels give up a competitive edge. If they do not outsource to best-in-world ser-

---

[15] John A. Byrne, "The Virtual Corporation," *Business Week* (February 8, 1993), 98-103.

[16] *Ibid.*

vice providers, they are actually upping their cost and decreasing their value-added."[17] Each value chain element must be analyzed as a service. Companies should not spend time and resources trying to be world-class at something customers don't care about. Any element that does add customer value that can't be performed internally at or close to best-in-world levels is a candidate for outsourcing.

By concentrating on their strengths—designing and marketing high-tech, fashionable sport footwear—Nike and Reebok each earned a return on assets of over 16 percent in 1992. The two outsource virtually all production to suppliers in Asia, primarily Taiwan and South Korea. Dell Computer prospers by concentrating on marketing and service; areas where its vertically integrated competitors are vulnerable. Dell owns no plants, having only $55 million invested in fixed assets, and returns 35 percent on shareholders' equity. Chrysler buys 70 percent of its parts from outside, similar to Toyota. Chrysler's new LH cars are designed in modules; the interior consists of four easy-to-install units that arrive ready-built from different suppliers.[18] Boeing outsources most of its functions, but not avionics and control systems—the "core intellect" of the aircraft.[19]

Alliances

Strategic alliances make it possible for two companies to "reach out together for a mutual objective and create more value together than is ever possible in an over-the-fence, commercial transaction."[20] In most industries, the strongest firms are leaders in the use of alliances. Examples are Merck and Glaxo in pharmaceuticals, Motorola and Northern Telecom in telecommunications, and American and United in airlines. Glaxo Holdings is one of the world's largest pharmaceutical companies. However, it knew that its marketing capability was no match for that of SmithKline Beecham, producer of Tagamet, the drug that dominated the stomach ulcer market. Glaxo had just developed Zantac, an ulcer medication with enormous potential. To overcome its marketing disadvantage, Glaxo formed an alliance with competitor Hoffman LaRoche to market Zantac.[21]

---

[17] James Brian Quinn, "Managing the Intelligent Enterprise: Knowledge and Service-Based Strategies," *Planning Review* (September/October 1993), 14.

[18] Shawn Tully, "The Modular Corporation," *Fortune* (February 8, 1993), 106-114.

[19] Quinn, *op. cit.*, 15.

[20] Jordan D. Lewis, "The New Power of Strategic Alliances," *Planning Review*, 20, No. 5 (September/October 1992), 45.

[21] Christopher Elias, "Glaxo is Swallowing Market for Prescription Drugs in U.S.," *Insight* (November 12, 1990), 36.

KLM Royal Dutch Airlines recently bought a 57 percent stake in Northwest Airlines, giving both greater access to international markets as well as codesharing—linking the two carriers' flights in computer reservations systems and coordinating flight schedules. American recently bought 25 percent of cash-strapped Canadian Airlines International, and United entered into a marketing alliance with Air Canada, also struggling. Delta, SwissAir and Singapore formed a "world partnership" that includes some codesharing and frequent flyer transferability.[22]

Realistically, however, many alliances do not work. For an alliance to work, three conditions for success must be present: mutual objectives, complementary needs, and shared risks. *Trust* must also exist. Trust depends upon responsibility, equality, and reliability. In order to make alliances work, partners must focus on choosing a partner and sharing a strategic objective.

Choosing a partner should focus on three criteria: combined strength through complementary abilities, similar levels of commitment, and compatibility. Motorola, for example, no longer picks its suppliers on the basis of price, product design, or company attributes. It picks them on the basis of their corporate values; are they driven to constantly lower price and improve quality? McDonald's looks for "alliance partners" (franchisees) whose personal values stress customer service, not food business experience.

Sharing a strategic objective requires that the only things that go into the alliance are those things that are best for the alliance; no politics or power issues. The allocation of control in a strategic alliance should depend upon which partner is best qualified to make a given decision, not which is bigger or more powerful.

---

[22] Lisa Sanders, "Let's Make a Deal," in H.E. Glass and B.E. Cavan, eds., *Handbook of Business Strategy* (New York, NY: Faulkner and Gray, 1994), 13-15.

Module 10

The Relevant General Environment

LEARNING OBJECTIVES

After completing Module 10, you should be able to:

1. Appreciate the importance of the impact of the general environment.
2. Delineate the major environmental influences affecting the firm.
3. Realize that general environmental conditions may have a significant bearing on the choice of strategic alternatives.
4. Understand the major macro- and microeconomic influences on the firm.
5. Describe basic technology and productivity-related influences.
6. Describe social, political, legal, and regulatory influences and processes.

PROFILE   Kustom Electronics

Kustom Electronics of Kansas City is the nation's leading producer of police radar systems. Until the mid-1970s, Kustom's markets were mature and experiencing little growth, and the company was flirting with losses. However, the OPEC oil embargo changed all that. How? To save oil, Congress mandated a nationwide 55 MPH speed limit in 1974, which gave birth to a new industry—the radar detector—and also gave new life to the CB-radio industry. To combat the "fuzzbusters," "super snoopers," and other radar detectors motorists were using, the police were interested in purchasing new, more advanced radar equipment that the motorists' fuzzbusters could not detect. The police also were interested in longer-range, more powerful equipment to thwart the CB warning network the drivers had developed. Kustom, therefore, began producing and selling radar equipment that operated on a higher frequency band than the motorists' detectors were able to intercept.

Electrolert (which manufactured fuzzbusters) and other manufacturers of detectors then added multiband capability to their equipment, generating more sales for themselves in the process. Radar manufacturers, in turn, again modified their products to counter the more sophisticated detectors. In fact, the situation became a continual game of countermeasures.

Thus, a new U.S. industry was created, and new life was given to a stable, mature company—by a seemingly unrelated political event in the Middle East. Each competitive response, in turn, gave a shot in the arm to the opposition by creating the demand for new products.

Subsequent changes in the international political and economic environments—such as competition between OPEC countries, plus creation of an energy conservation ethic—have increased oil production and reduced relative demand. This has led to increased supplies of oil, lower prices, and the raising of interstate highway speed limits to 65 MPH—an event in the legal environment which *reduced* the demand for radar detectors, and in turn, police radar units.

PROFILE   Deere & Company

During the 1970s, the revenues of Deere & Company grew faster than those of Xerox and nearly twice as fast as those of IBM and Texas Instruments. Earnings kept pace, increasing almost sixfold during the same period. This record of performance, particularly for a large corporation, would satisfy all but the most ardent growth enthusiasts. But Deere is a farm and construction equipment company, not an electronics, semiconductor, or other high-tech business. What caused this outstanding record?

According to industry observers, Deere is the industry's most efficient producer, has the strongest dealer network, the newest factories, and boasts the lowest inventory-to-sales ratio in the industry. This enviable position was achieved largely as a result of perceptive strategic decisions made since the mid-1950s, when Deere was operating in the shadow of the industry leader, International Harvester.

Deere had conducted extensive research into the future of farming. Management concluded that long-run trends would result in a reduction in the number of and an increase in the size of farms, requiring larger equipment and fewer—but larger—dealers. Deere capitalized on this trend away from labor toward heavy machinery by spending twice as much on R&D as its competitors (4 cents of every sales dollar) to design larger tractors and equipment. At the same time, Deere began to focus on the 20 percent of farmers who earn most of the cash income. These strategies paid off, with Deere passing IH in the mid-1960s.

Thus, innovation, service, and efficiency have been the strategies that contributed to Deere's success. In fact, more than half of its manufacturing facilities are less than ten years old. Deere's new tractor plant in Waterloo, Iowa, for example, is one of the most modern in the world, with the latest in manufacturing technology and computer control. Deere is the industry's lowest-cost producer, and can break even operating at 45 percent of capacity at the Waterloo plant.

However, the strong dollar of the mid-80s and agricultural self-sufficiency in more and more foreign markets dramatically reduced U.S. farm exports, causing a crisis in the U.S. farm economy. Even though Deere is the dominant U.S. producer and has been increasing its market share, the demand for farm equipment dropped, causing Deere's sales and profits to fall as well. Thus, the company took advantage of environmental changes and appropriate strategies to achieve its dominant position, but recently has fallen victim to a lengthy decline by its industry, caused by other environmental influences.

Bioengineered seeds, no-till farming (brought on by the 1985 and 1990 farm bills requiring farmers to protect against soil erosion), and other changes mean less tractor use and less-frequent replacements. The result is a threat to the traditional business of farm equipment companies like Deere.

THE IMPORTANCE OF ENVIRONMENTAL INFLUENCES

A number of factors have major bearing on the *content* of the strategies of an organization. These factors dictate the types of strategies the firm should pursue. This module examines the role of general factors external to the firm (the economy, technology, social factors, and political/legal considerations).

Key to this process is the ability to identify early those social, technological, political, economic, competitive, legal, and other issues that may significantly affect the operation and strategic success of the firm. (An *issue* is a "condition or pressure, either internal or external to an organization, that, if it continues, will have a significant effect on the functioning of the organization or its future interests.")[1]

Strategic issues are those major trends, developments, and progressions of events that materially affect the strategy and operations of the organization. Strategic issues tend to be broad, multifaceted, and closely interrelated; examples include the women's movement and civil rights. Normally, such issues affect both the external environment in which the organization must operate and the internal activities of the organization.[2] Such issues must be considered in the strategic planning process, in the operational execution of those plans, and whenever the strategy is confronted by an external trend or event. They can emerge at virtually any time and with little prior notice. Customarily, strategic issues pose basic questions in four general areas:

1. *The external environment:* How to gain better understanding of the sociopolitical, technological, and economic changes affecting the organization's strategic and operating environment.
2. *Resource capabilities:* How to determine the organization's human resource needs and responsibilities while following the present strategy or change in strategy.
3. *The alignment of business units:* How to organize and position the product and market groups to best support the strategy.
4. *Communication:* How to get the strategy and/or issues fully communicated, understood, and applied throughout the organization.

Strategic issues can include such concerns as energy shortages and embargoes, pollution control, industry deregulation, consumerism, equal rights, employee safety and privacy, unstable foreign economies and governments, and changing consumer tastes, to name just a few.[3]

The Need for Environmental Analysis

Environmental analysis has become a key task in strategic planning in the last two decades. The match, or fit, between the internal strengths and resources of the firm and the opportunities in its environment is the crux of strategic management. Knowledge of the environment becomes critical as the firm seeks these

---

[1] James K. Brown, *This Business of Issues: Coping with the Company's Environments* (New York, NY: The Conference Board, 1979), 1.

[2] J.E. Dutton and Edward Ottensmeyer, "Strategic Issue Management Systems: Forms, Functions, and Contexts," *Academy of Management Review*, 12, No. 2 (April 1987), 355.

[3] James B. Farley, "Winners and Losers in the Eighties," *World Business Weekly* (April 28, 1980), 5.

propitious matches with the opportunities in its environment. The firm must also analyze its environment to avoid, to the extent possible, any problems or threats that might arise. Michael Kami, former head of planning for IBM and head of his own firm, Corporate Planning, Inc., has stated that successful organizations plan from the outside in—not from the inside out—because the environment shapes the future of the organization. Furthermore, Kami contends a company can influence changes in internal issues or trends, and can, in effect, manage them.[4] External issues and trends, however, remain far less amenable to management control. In fact, the firm's environment can be looked on as the product of the strategic decisions of others: government, competitors, customers, society, and a host of other outside influences. Events external to the firm have important effects on future results.

During the 70s and 80s, there has been a growing recognition of the need to understand environmental influences and changes in order to devise successful strategies for the firm. Several indications of this recognition include:

- An increased realization that organizations are *open*—not closed—systems. Systems theory tells us that an open system is *dependent* upon input from its environment for survival and growth. Therefore, an organization is dependent upon its environment, and should look upon this interaction as a necessity and an opportunity, not merely as a threat.
- An increased awareness of environmental change and turbulence and their impact upon a firm, the industry, and society in general. Coupled with this realization is the notion that management needs to study and *understand* the environment in order to think strategically.
- Along with the previous points, increased efforts to include environmental analysis in the organization's strategy formulation processes, in order to ensure that important external changes and information are included in the firm's strategic decisions.[5]

Environmental analysis, then, is the process of seeking information about relationships and events *outside* the company that will help management chart the company's future actions. Environmental analysis helps identify those parts of the environment the firm can concentrate on and attack competitively—the orga-

---

[4] Michael J. Kami, *Kami Strategic Assumptions: Fall '82 Update* (Lighthouse Pt., FL: Corporate Planning, 1982).

[5] Liam Fahey and V.K. Narayanan, *Macroenvironmental Analysis for Strategic Management* (St. Paul, MN: West Publishing, 1986), 1.

nization's *domain.*[6] One problem in such analysis is that environmental influences often are complex and sometimes unpredictable. However, the mere fact that the environment is changing does not mean that it is unpredictable. For example, demographic changes due to the baby boom and their effects on retirement plans, population aging, and the like are predictable. On the other hand, environmental changes that don't follow known patterns, such as oil embargoes, natural disasters, and political changes are more difficult to anticipate, and are less predictable.

In addition, a quickening *pace* of change requires a firm to focus more directly on the environment, since the firm will experience more changes (even if they are predictable) in a given period of time. As a result, the firm will find itself making more strategic decisions in a given time frame. The more dynamic the environment, the greater the impact on the firm's strategies.

Igor Ansoff, sometimes called "the father of corporate planning," has conducted research confirming that an organization's performance is optimized when its strategy and management capabilities fit the environment. Specifically, as Figure 10.1 shows, both the strategic aggressiveness of a firm's behavior and the responsiveness of its general management capabilities should match the turbulence of its environment in order to achieve top performance. Lack of a match between the three factors yields less-than-optimal performance.

Which Factors are Important?

Which environmental factors are most important for a firm to analyze? Figure 10.2 shows a model for environmental analysis which suggests that the firm, the XYZ Company, should direct its environmental analysis toward five major directions: economic, technological, competitive, social, and political/legal forecasting.[7] Michael Kami, on the other hand, gears his environmental analysis toward five major areas as well, but with a somewhat different focus on economic, government, business, social, and international environments.

Other authors distinguish between the *general* environment (economic, technological, social, political, regulatory, and others) and the *industry* or operating environment (the market, industry structure, and suppliers, customers, and others with whom the firm deals directly).

---

[6] Sol Levine and P.E. White, "Exchange as a Conceptual Framework for the Study of Interorganizational Relationships," *Administrative Science Quarterly*, 5 (1961), 583-601.

[7] Ian H. Wilson, "Socio-Political Forecasting: A New Dimension to Strategic Planning," *Michigan Business Review* (July 1974), 19-20.

Environmental Turbulence Level				
	1 (LOW)	*2*	*3*	*4*	*5 (HIGH)*
CHARACTER OF TURBULENCE	REPETITIVE No Change	EXPANDING Slow Incremental Change	CHANGING Fast Incremental Change	DISCONTINUOUS Discontinuous Predictable Change	SURPRISEFUL Discontinuous Unpredictable Change
STRATEGIC AGGRESSIVENESS	STABLE Stable Based on Precedents	REACTIVE Incremental Change Based on Experience	ANTICIPATORY Incremental Change Based on Extrapolation	ENTREPRENEURIAL Discontinuous New Strategies Based on Observable Opportunities	CREATIVE Discontinuous Novel Strategies Based on Creativity
RESPONSIVENESS OF GENERAL MANAGEMENT CAPABILITY	STABILITY SEEKING Rejects Change	EFFICIENCY DRIVEN Adapts to Change	MARKET DRIVEN Seeks Familiar Change	ENVIRONMENT DRIVEN Seeks Related Change	ENVIRONMENT CREATING Seeks Novel Change

Source: Adapted from H. Igor Ansoff and Patrick A. Sullivan, *Empirical Support for a Paradigmic Theory of Strategic Success Behaviors of Environment Serving Organizations* (San Diego, CA: United States International University, 1993), 7.

Figure 10.1 **Matching Turbulence/Aggressiveness/Responsiveness**

Fahey and Narayanan[8] offer a clear and cogent framework of the relevant environments surrounding an organization: the general environment, the competitive or industry environment, and the task environment. At the broadest level lies the general environment, or macroenvironment, which influences all industries functioning within it. Again, the macroenvironment includes the economic, technological, social, and political/legal segments. However, not all aspects of the general environment may be relevant to the firm; analyzing *all* aspects of the macroenvironment would be impossible and unnecessary. The firm should focus on those aspects of the general environment judged *relevant* to the firm's strategic situation, as shown in Figure 10.3.

Within the general environment lies the competitive or industry environment, which includes those businesses of a firm competing in a particular industry. The

---

[8] Fahey and Narayanan, Macroenvironmental Analysis, 25.

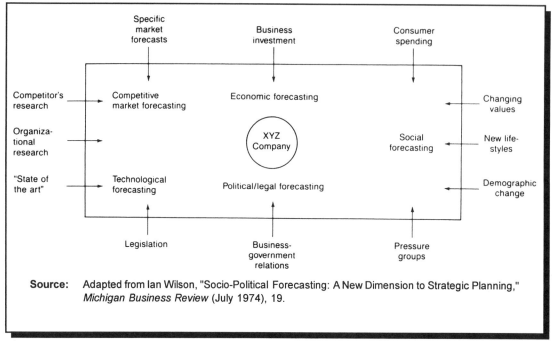

Source: Adapted from Ian Wilson, "Socio-Political Forecasting: A New Dimension to Strategic Planning," *Michigan Business Review* (July 1974), 19.

Figure 10.2 **A Model for Environmental Analysis**

firm's most specific environment is the task environment, which refers to the customers, suppliers, competitors, agencies, and so on, directly related to the firm. The task environment is specific to the firm and is not necessarily shared by all competitors within an industry. This chapter examines factors comprising the general environment, while the industry environment is treated in another module.

Recent studies have shown an important link between environmental analysis and *critical success factor (CSF)* analysis. These success factors are key areas in which the business must be satisfactory to survive and in which it must excel to competitively flourish; they might include low costs, high quality, innovation, diversification, and flexibility. Identifying critical success factors for a business is a key basis for structuring environmental analysis. The environment is scanned for opportunities or threats in terms of CSFs, and competitors are analyzed with regard to these factors.[9]

---

[9] J.R. Leidecker and A.V. Bruno. "Identifying and Using Critical Success Factors," *Long-Range Planning*, 17, No. 1 (1984), 23-32.

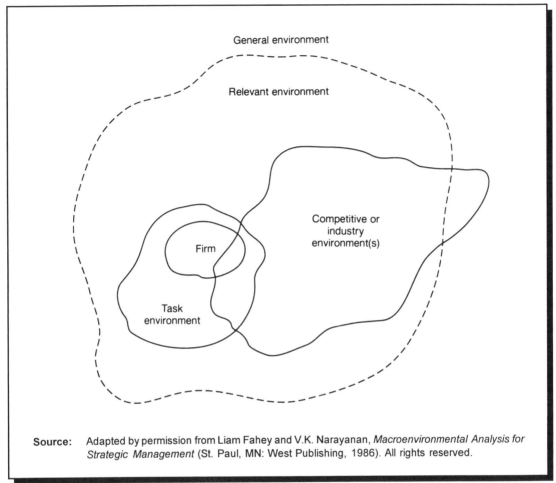

Figure 10.3 Levels of Environment

potential *changes* occurring in the environment. It provides important *intelligence* for strategic decision makers, and therefore should precede attempts at strategy formulation and implementation. Last, the analysis has implications for both the content and the process of strategic management. Concerning content, it should foster *strategic thinking* by managers, increasing their understanding of the context within which the firm operates and sparking ideas for strategic actions. In the process area, the analysis and strategic actions can affect the organization's structure and ways of doing business.

THE ECONOMY

The economy is very important to the success of a firm or an industry. Assume, for example, that an objective of management is to maximize the wealth of its stockholders. Research by Martin Zweig, a well-known stock market analyst, has shown that roughly two thirds of the movement in a stock's price is explained by the movement of the stock market in general, and another fourth is explained by the action of the firm's industry. Therefore, the bulk of management's objective is affected by factors external to the firm and beyond its control. Further, the market is significantly influenced by economic variables, such as interest rates, corporate profits, and gross domestic product (GDP).

But how does the economy affect the firm's sales and profits? The level of the economy directly influences these factors in several important ways. The stage of the economic cycle has a direct bearing on GDP, disposable income, the level of investment, and sales. It is easier to increase sales in an economic upturn than during a recession. Therefore, strategies that may be successful in prosperous times may well fail in a recession. On the other hand, it takes time to implement a strategy. Waiting until an economic expansion is under way to build a new plant may mean that the firm will have added capacity late in the expansion, perhaps just in time for the next downturn.

In addition, inflation, interest rates, and currency valuations have much to do not only with the total economy and customer behavior, but also with the decisions a firm makes. A strategy promising a rate of return of 15 percent may be very attractive with inflation at 3 percent and interest rates at 7 percent, but totally unacceptable with inflation at 12 percent and interest rates at 16 percent. Inflation forces strategists to adopt a shorter-term perspective, focusing on asset growth rather than on inflation-dominated profits. As an example, many firms had difficulty adapting to the inflationary period of the 1970s, with high interest rates, little real investment, and inflation-eroded profits. The resulting low equity prices forced firms to forgo the stock and bond markets as sources of capital, or accept them as very expensive sources. The alternative, short-term borrowing, was even more expensive. In the early 1980s, inflation decelerated abruptly, again catching many firms unprepared for a "disinflationary" economy. Firms could no longer repay debts with money that would be cheaper in the future, so many began to focus on sharply reducing expenses and the ratio of debt to capital. In periods of disinflation, when the value of assets is declining, companies with real assets, such as natural resources, fare less well than those with consumer products and other items with high "value added." The opposite was true during the inflationary 1970s.

Such factors not only affect the performance of a given business unit, but also directly influence corporate-level strategies, such as in which industries to compete. In a stagnant economy, companies compete more fiercely to maintain sales, inevitably putting pressure on profits. Fiscal policies, such as tax rates and depreciation allowances, also exert significant pressures on profits and dividends.

Economists refer to factors relating to the general state of an economy as *macroeconomic* factors. Such influences on a business would include inflation, fiscal and monetary policies (including taxes, government spending, and interest rates), unemployment, consumption, investment, tariffs, and the like. *Microeconomic* factors, on the other hand, typically deal with firm behavior in various types of markets, including production, pricing, and distribution decisions. *Industrial organization* economists, however, typically concern themselves with industry structure, competition, and competitive behavior of firms.

Becoming increasingly important—critically so since the mid-80s—are international economic influences. Included here are factors such as the relative productivity of the economies of our trading partners and competitors, the effects of currency exchange rates on imports and exports, and trade and tariff policies of the countries. Microeconomic, macroeconomic, and international economic factors are part of the general environment and are discussed in the following paragraphs. Competitive factors are part of the industry environment and are discussed in another module.

Microeconomic Factors

At the microeconomic or firm level, the economic models available to guide decision-makers in most industries are insufficient. While relatively well-developed models exist to guide firms in perfectly competitive and monopolistic markets, models of monopolistically competitive and oligopolistic markets are less well defined. As Table 10.1 shows, perfectly competitive markets account for only 4 percent of total U.S. GNP and 6 percent of private-sector GNP. (Perfectly competitive markets are those in which no single supplier is able to exert any effect on prices or quantities, and products are perfect substitutes for one another. Agricultural products are an example.)

Monopolistic markets—where there is only one supplier (even though substitutes may exist, such as gas for electricity)—also account for a small percentage of output.

Monopolistic competition exists in markets where there are a number of producers, but the products are differentiated in some way and are close substitutes for one another. Many consumer products have these characteristics, including soaps, cigarettes, beer, and soft drinks. Such products account for 28 percent of total GNP and 44 percent of private-sector output.

Oligopolies are characterized by few suppliers, with possibly one dominating the market. Examples would be autos, computers, and perhaps oil companies. Such markets total 24 percent of total GNP and 38 percent of the private sector. Although monopolistic competitions and oligopolies represent 52 percent of total GNP and 82 percent of private-sector production, models of their behavior are

Table 10.1 Market GNP Contribution

Market Type	Example	Percent of GNP	Percent Private-sector GNP
Perfect competition	Agricultural products	4%	6%
Monopolistic competition	Soap, beer, cigarettes	28	44
Oligopoly	Autos, computers	24	38
Monopoly	Utilities	7	11
Other	Government, education	37	—

Source: Adapted from "Domestic Business Report," *Commerce America*, 1, No. 10 (May 10, 1976), 12.

inferior to models of perfectly competitive and monopolistic markets, and offer little to corporate decision-makers.

As an added point, at first glance it might appear that microeconomic factors would apply only to traditional, private-sector, for-profit firms. On closer analysis, however, it becomes evident that most organizations in our economy and society are subject to similar influences. For example, many government programs, such as medicare, social security, and postal services, have close substitutes or even competitors in other sectors of the economy. The postal service competes with Federal Express, United Parcel Service, Western Union, and even fax machines and the telephone companies. To a degree, even the military departments (army, navy, air force, and marines) compete with one another. Thus, many government and other services are not truly monopolies, but find themselves in oligopolistic or even monopolistically competitive markets—a realization that may have important strategic implications in offering, targeting, and pricing their services.

Macroeconomic Factors

The type of economy in which a firm competes—laissez-faire, managed capitalistic, or socialistic—has a great influence on strategic decisions. The first decision in this context is whether or not to compete in certain countries or industries. Within the U.S. economy, for example, various degrees of regulation exist. Transportation, utilities, drugs, hospitals, and other industries have been highly regulated, while other industries have not. Deregulation of the airline, financial services, trucking, and natural gas industries has dramatically changed the environment for many companies, creating a new set of opportunities and threats in their industries.

In other capitalistic economies, the environment may be very different from that in the United States. In the 1980s, Sweden, for example, taxed the typical blue-collar worker at a marginal rate of 55 percent and an executive at 85 percent. In fact, the rate could go as high as 99 percent. Individuals actually could *lose* money as a result of a salary increase, because of the loss of government allowances for such things as housing, coupled with the high tax rates. One Swedish company calculated that it would cost the company the equivalent of $255,000 to provide each of its top five executives with a $1,000 after-tax raise.[10]

Sweden's expensive "cradle-to-grave" welfare system became more than the country could afford, plunging the economy into a deep recession in the early 1990s. As a result, Sweden introduced new market incentives and trimmed unemployment benefits, sick leave, and health care, along with lowering taxes. But Sweden's overall tax burden remains the highest in Europe.[11]

Japan also has a managed capitalistic economy, but one that is distinctly different from Sweden's. After World War II, Japan adopted economic policies that fostered economic growth. These involved a mix of macro-level monetary and fiscal policies coupled with micro-level industrial policies. Macroeconomic planning includes projecting economic growth and setting goals for the economy. These plans are an important means of achieving national consensus on long-range economic goals and the direction of the economy. Following World War II, the Economic Planning Agency was created to prepare national economic plans that were approved by the Japanese legislature. These plans initially focused on economic recovery.

Japan's economic development since the occupation can be categorized into four stages. The first stage, 1951 to 1954, centered on reconstruction and rebuilding basic industries. In stage two, 1955 to 1964, the focus was on catching up with other industrialized countries through development of heavy and chemical industries, creation of an "open economy," improving the balance of payments, and closing gaps in the development of areas within the country. In stage three, 1965 to 1974, the emphasis was on social development and welfare, including urban development, housing, pollution control, computer technology, and power generation. The current fourth stage continues stage three's targets, with a focus on adjusting to stable growth, conserving resources, improving the qual-

---

[10] L.A. Digman, Personal Interview with Leif Philippson, MoDo KP AB Personnel Director (March 3, 1981).

[11] Steve Coll, "Sweden's Once-Proud Welfare State Retreats as Economy Unravels," *International Herald Tribune* (May 4, 1994), 1.

ity of life, and further developing technology.[12] Thus, the Japanese seem to have had a logical set of economic goals in place, which guided their economic policies and became the basis for the development of more detailed strategies and plans.

An additional example of macroeconomic influence involves the complicated domestic effects of fiscal and monetary policies on selected industries, such as agricultural production and equipment. Because of the large federal deficits in the early to mid-1980s, the Federal Reserve Board held interest rates relatively high to reduce inflationary pressures. According to some, this attracted foreign investment, which greatly strengthened the dollar, making exports expensive and imports cheap. This encouraged imports and discouraged exports, such as farm products. In turn, farm prices, receipts, and land values declined, causing farm bankruptcies, low sales of farm equipment, and bank failures due to nonperforming loans. Others have held, however, that these events resulted more from increased farm production in South America, China, India, and the Soviet Union, greatly reducing demand for U.S. farm products. Whatever the cause, during the latter 80s and early 90s, interest rates declined and the value of the dollar dropped significantly, encouraging exports.

Finally, economic cycles are important to a firm's strategies. The timing of plant expansions, new product introductions, and financial investments should consider whether the economy is in the early or late stages of an economic expansion, as well as the likely occurrence and severity of the next recession. Again, government fiscal and monetary policies, as well as the ability of the federal government to take corrective action in the event of a downturn, can be important considerations.

International Factors

It is apparent that international factors are closely woven into the fabric of the economic environment, and are becoming even more so. In recent years, much of our national debt has been financed by foreign investors, as have our stock market operations. Low wage rates and increasing foreign productivity made it desirable for manufacturing facilities to be located in foreign countries, accelerating our trend to a service economy. In addition, such factors increase the trade deficit, as more and more such products are imported into the United States. To attract these funds back into the United States in the form of investments, interest rates must be kept relatively high, further discouraging domestic investment.

A declining dollar, however, tends to offset wage rate differentials, as does increasing reliance on high technology and automated manufacturing. In fact, in

---

[12] U.S. General Accounting Office, *Industrial Policy: Japan's Flexible Approach*, GAO/ID-82-32 (June 23, 1982).

1986, the United States was the only major nation to cut its labor costs, resulting from increases in manufacturing productivity and a decline in the value of the dollar. Since October 1987, factory workers in West Germany, Norway, and Switzerland received *higher* average hourly pay than in the United States, with Sweden and the Netherlands close behind. Japan's $11.20 was 85 percent of U.S. wages, with Brazil, Mexico, Hong Kong, South Korea, Singapore, Taiwan, and Portugal all less than 20 percent of the U.S. figure.[13] When compared with economic output, the U.S. position appears favorable. Workers in the United States produced an average of $38,900 of output in 1987, 23 percent more than the higher-paid German workers, and 41 percent more than Japanese workers.[14]

In fact, the early 90s saw a "wave" of announcements by foreign corporations to build or expand plants in the U.S. The reason is a dramatic rise in U.S. competitiveness. Because of the dollar's drop since 1985, and because of wage restraint and faster productivity growth, U.S. labor costs have declined sharply in comparison to those of the twelve major industrial nations. Specifically, U.S. labor costs rose from an index of 100 in 1979 to 140 in 1985 before dropping to 80 in 1992 (therefore, trade-weighted U.S. labor costs are 80 percent of those in the twelve other industrialized countries).[15]

But, hourly labor costs may not tell the total picture. In Mexico, the minimum wage is about 65 cents per hour, vs. $4.25 in the U.S. in 1994. The average pay of factory workers is $1.50 to $3 per hour in Mexico vs. about $10 in the U.S. But, the Mexican government has mandated an extensive list of employee benefits that rachet up labor costs by 60 to 80 percent in Mexico vs. about 37 percent in the U.S., narrowing the gap somewhat. In fact, consultants say that pay for technical and administrative staffs in Mexico sometimes exceeds that in the States.[16]

In addition, the changing costs of manufacturing in the United States versus foreign countries have reversed much of what we have only recently learned. In the early 80s, Japanese auto manufacturers, for example, were able to build a car in Japan for $2,400 less than U.S. companies could build one here. By 1987, however, as the dollar depreciated from 240 to 140 yen per dollar, and to 100 yen per dollar by 1994, this cost relationship was reversed; that is, it became cheaper to build cars in the United States. For this reason, Japanese manufacturers began importing U.S. components and parts. Japanese car models in the mid-90s average over $2000 more than comparable American cars, even though the Japanese are trying to temper price increases by cutting costs and moving

---

[13] Gene Koretz, "Economic Trends," *Business Week* (November 23, 1987), 26.

[14] "Losing the Lead," *The Wall Street Journal* (October 24, 1988), A1.

[15] Gene Koretz, "Economic Trends: U.S. Factories Should Be Humming Next Year...," *Business Week* (November, 22, 1993), 28.

[16] Stephen Barr, "Is Mexican Labor Really Cheaper?" *CFO* (March 1994), 63.

some manufacturing operations to the U.S.[17] Japanese trade publications cited numerous cases of this, including companies such as Yamaha, Mitsubishi Electric, NEC, Honda, Toyota, Mitsubishi Motors, and Hitachi Construction Machinery Co.[18] The point is that changing currency values can dramatically change the relative costs of manufacturing in one country versus another, complicating international marketing and production decisions.

Another international economic influence has to do with demand for capital. In the 1990s—for the first time—virtually all of the world's economies are market-oriented. The increased demand for capital to fund growth throughout the world, including ventures in China, Russia, and others, has contributed to rising global interest rates. This phenomenon is exacerbated by Japan's increasing reluctance to supply capital, because of their recession. Thus, some expect interest rates to remain high for some time.

Also, countries new to the market system have experienced drastically different results. Russia, for example, has experienced high inflation, unemployment, and a plummeting ruble. A survey by the *Economist* shows that 82 percent of respondents in the Commonwealth of Independent States countries were dissatisfied with free markets. On the other hand, 71 percent *support* market reforms in Albania, the country with the "purest" form of communism headed by a Stalinist-type dictator from World War II to 1990. In fact, of all the transforming countries of Eastern Europe, Albania is recognized by most as being the most successful. In two years since becoming a democratic market-oriented economy, inflation has dropped to 30 percent, unemployment has declined from 50 to 25 percent, and output is growing at over 10 percent per year. All agriculture and housing has been privatized, as have many small-scale enterprises.[19]

In conclusion, like international factors, the macroeconomy and related policies have much to do with how a firm can and should compete. They influence both the freedom to pursue certain strategies and the effect of government monetary and fiscal policies on the firm and its customers. As we discussed earlier, microeconomic factors, such as the economic structure of the market, also play an important role in strategic management.

---

[17] Valerie Reitman, "Global Money Trends Rattle Shop Windows in Heartland America," *The Wall Street Journal* (November 26, 1993), A1.

[18] "Japan's Manufactured Imports Rise Sharply in First Half of 87," *JETRO Monitor* (October 1, 1987), 4.

[19] "Business Eastern Europe," *Crossborder Monitor* (March 23, 1994), 4.

TECHNOLOGY

The role of technology in corporate and business-unit strategy is extremely important, yet is poorly understood by many writers on strategic management. "High technology" has become a buzz phrase in our society, and is looked on by many to solve a country's growth, development, productivity, and balance-of-payments problems. Yet technology receives short shrift in many discussions of strategic management. Nonetheless, it is the high-tech companies, such as Texas Instruments, IBM, Hewlett-Packard, Genentech, Merck, Teledyne, Apple Computer, and many others—that have become the focus of attention by strategic analysts, even though the role of technology is underdeveloped and ignored relative to other important strategic areas such as marketing and finance.[20] Technology *creates* many of the products and advances that must be strategically financed and marketed. It helps a firm produce its products more efficiently than does its competition. Technology creates not only new products, but also entire industries. For these reasons, strategic planning is of little value if technology isn't taken into account.

However, many misconceptions abound concerning technology. For example, most people would probably consider computers to be a high-technology industry and automobile manufacturing to be a lower-technology, "smokestack" industry. Lester Thurow of MIT, however, observes that while computers may be high-technology *products*, their *manufacture* is not; it requires lower-level skills and is more labor intensive than many people realize. Autos, on the other hand, now employ sophisticated processes and robotics in their manufacture, and the industry has many high-technology characteristics. In addition, autos themselves have become much more technologically complex in recent years with the addition of sophisticated electronic engine controls and sensors, nonskid braking systems, and electronic instruments and displays.

Management's Role

The strategic implications of technology are not limited to high-tech industries, however. New methods have greatly reduced the size required for steel mills to produce efficiently, automated teller machines and electronic funds transfer are transforming much of banking, radial treads have revolutionized the tire industry, and so on. Management must therefore be able to *understand* the technology of the products and processes it manages. Otherwise, it cannot make strategic and operational decisions about those products and processes. The critical decisions are: (1) which technology to pursue and when to pursue it, (2) how to manage

---

[20] H. Dudley Dewhirst, "Strategic Management of Research and Development," presented at national meeting of American Institute for Decision Sciences (1982).

the transition from one technology to another, and (3) how to prepare the corporation for technological change. Managers must be able to assess the limits of their firm's technologies, as well as those of alternative approaches, before they can answer questions about which areas to pursue. In this light, technology is too important to be left only to engineers. Development of technologies and innovations is the responsibility of scientists and engineers, just as fighting a war is the responsibility of the generals. But generals should not decide whether or not we will fight, just as engineers should not decide which technologies should be incorporated into products or processes; these are strategic decisions that management must understand and make.

Managers must understand that technological breakthroughs result in more rapid obsolescence of existing products, which can be either an opportunity or a threat. It may be wise for a firm to postpone introducing an innovation because of its effect on existing products. Also, all innovations—technological or other-wise—should be put into their proper perspective; they create a degree of uniqueness. How and when this uniqueness, or distinction, is exploited is the basis for a strategic decision.

The selection of technology is a major element in business strategy. While it is not as strategically important for some firms as for others, for many firms, it is *the* central element of strategy.[21] In a study of rapidly growing firms, *INC.* magazine found that an increase in R&D spending of 1.5 percent (measured in percent of sales) translated into a 10 percent sales gain eighteen months later.[22] In a study of the larger firms in the pharmaceutical and chemical industries, Bruce Old found that R&D expenditures over Years 1-10, plus capital expenditures in Years 5-15, correlated 0.85 with increases in profits in Years 1-20.[23] Thus, R&D pays off for large companies as well as for smaller firms.

Managers of firms may choose to achieve growth through technology in one of three ways:

1. Internally, by a strategically managed R&D program.
2. By a mix of internal and external means. Internally, by scanning the technological environment plus establishing a limited R&D program; externally, by providing venture capital for new technology, or licensing or acquiring firms with promising technology.

---

[21] R.A. Burgelman and M.A. Maidique, *Strategic Management of Technology and Innovation* (Homewood, IL: Richard D. Irwin, Inc., 1988), 12.

[22] "The More They Spend on R&D, the Faster They Grow," *INC.* (August 1981), 44.

[23] Bruce S. Old, "From the Boardroom: Corporate Directors Should Rethink Technology," *Harvard Business Review* (January/February 1982), 6.

3. By acquiring or licensing technology only after its acceptance and feasibility have been demonstrated.[24]

Again, the choice is often broader in scope than it might initially appear; the ramifications extend beyond the R&D functional-level strategy.

Service Technology

In addition to products, technology affects the delivery of services as well. In fact, technologies have restructured the service industries extensively in recent years. For example, new technologies have created economies of scale in services by making larger organizations possible and efficient, as in rental cars, brokerage clearinghouses, and medical care. Second, technology permits increased economies of scope, or the offering of new or additional services to customers with little added cost. Examples include Federal Express's Zap Mail, resulting from its advanced electronic communications network (even though the venture was not competitive with proliferating facsimile machines), and the insurance companies' new products, also arising from their electronic networks.

In addition, technology in services permits new levels of complexity to be managed (as in computerized legal research), the breaking down of traditional boundaries between industries (such as banks, insurance companies, and brokerage houses), and an increase in international competitiveness. Services are a critical factor in manufacturing competitiveness, including items such as transportation, communication, financing, insurance, health care, and other costs. Overall, Japanese productivity has consistently lagged behind the United States because of our more productive service sector, even though they excel in certain mass-manufacturing fields.[25]

Process Technology and Productivity

Products and services are directly affected by technology, as are manufacturing and service processes and their relative productivity. Productivity is defined as output (products produced or services delivered) per unit of resource input (labor and capital). Much has been written about the productivity growth in countries such as Japan versus the United States. In reality, the value of output per labor hour in the United States as a percentage of Japan in 1980 was as follows:[26]

---

[24] Dewhirst, "Strategic Management."

[25] J.B. Quinn and C.E Gagnon, "Will Services Follow Manufacturing into Decline?" *Harvard Business Review*, 64, No. 6 (November/December 1986), 95-103.

[26] *Ibid.*

Sector	Percent
Private domestic business	167%
Agriculture	771%
Electricity, gas, water	129%
Transportation and communication	232%
Trade	175%
Finance and insurance	68%
Business services	211%
Manufacturing	127%

In 1994, productivity data (GDP per employed person based on purchasing-power parities) showed the U.S. as the world's productivity leader with France trailing at about 90 percent of the U.S. Britain was third and rising, at about 72 percent, with Japan fourth and flat at 70 percent. In fact, U.S. automakers have caught up to their Japanese rivals (from 14 percent behind in 1990), and lead by 17 percent in nine key industries.[27]

Thus, while Japanese productivity had been increasing more rapidly than the United States in recent years, that is no longer the case, and the absolute level of U.S. productivity is above that of Japan, even in manufacturing. Granted, manufacturing employment in the United States has declined slightly in recent years; however, the share of manufacturing output has not changed. This increased productivity has caused the manufacturing sector to *appear* to decline, because its share of employment and total spending have declined; but its output has not declined.[28]

On the other hand, there are those who say that the U.S. advantage in productivity may erode, partly because of social factors. For example, we have a large number of young people entering the legal and finance fields (versus science, engineering, and manufacturing) as compared to other countries. As some have observed, this results in a society adept at *administering* wealth, rather than *creating* it.[29] Other social factors, such as demographic changes, may have impacted productivity, as well. The U.S. economy has had a tremendous increase in labor supply during the 70s and 80s, due to the baby boom and the increasing numbers of women entering the work force. As Figure 10.4 shows, an increase in labor supply lowers its cost relative to capital, resulting in

---

[27] Christopher Farrell, "Is the Japanese Dynamo Losing Juice?" *Business Week* (June 27, 1994), 44.

[28] J.A. Tatom, "Why Has Manufacturing Employment Declined?" *The Review*, Federal Reserve Bank of St. Louis (December 1986), 15-23.

[29] Allan Murray, "The Outlook: The U.S. Economic Role May Face Long Decline," *The Wall Street Journal* (August 17, 1987), 1.

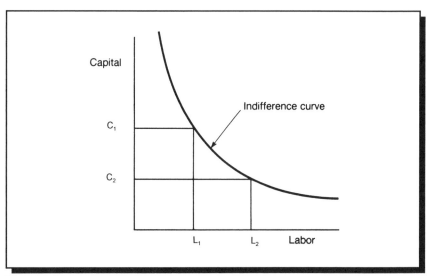

Figure 10.4 Labor, Capital, and Productivity

lower capital expenditures. Productivity, which is often defined as output per labor-hour, appears not to grow as a result.

But the possibility of massive increases in productivity is on the horizon. Carver Mead, a professor of computer science at Cal Tech and a long-time expert in the field, points out that the entire Industrial Revolution enhanced productivity 100-fold. The microelectronic revolution has already enhanced productivity in information-based technology by a factor of more than a million, with the promise of yet another 10,000-fold increase in the cost-effectiveness of technology in the next decade. The important point, however, is not the increasing productivity of computing; it is that these advances are spilling over into other industries, increasing their productivity as well. For example, people in other industries—computers, telephones, office equipment, autos, toys, transportation, and many more—will be able to *design* their own custom chips, which will be *manufactured* by the semiconductor industry. Major productivity enhancements will come about because of this custom-designed chip software, the greatest source of its added value.[30]

Based upon the writings of Joseph Schumpeter, there is growing realization that three things really propel growth: technology, innovation, and knowledge. As the Industrial Era gives way to the Information Age, we see a "gathering web of technological and commercial innovations revolutionizing the economy, much

---

[30] George Gilder, "You Ain't Seen Nothing Yet," *Forbes* (April 4, 1988), 89.

as steam power did in the late 1700s and electricity did in the late 1800s.[31] Such revolutions can totally change normal patterns of economic development and corporate growth. Why, for example, do the new market economies of Eastern Europe have to develop an industrial infrastructure before progressing to a knowledge economy. With their already well-educated workforce, they can write software for Microsoft, communicating electronically. A company like Microsoft can utilize this relatively low-cost resource benefitting both itself and the Eastern European economy in the process.[32]

Corporate-Level Responsibilities

To this point, we have been discussing technology strategies independent of the levels of strategic decisions faced by the organization. Technology represents one of several functional-level strategies for the organization. At the business level, the various functional strategies must be integrated and coordinated; that is, the technology, marketing, financial, and other strategies must relate and reinforce one another. So, most of what we have been discussing would apply to the technology of a given business unit or product line—in short, business-unit technical planning.

However, corporate-level strategies must integrate business-unit strategies; corporate-level technical planning is more than the sum of the technical plans of the business units. Technical planning at the corporate level must realize and strive for synergies from related technologies across business units; a corporate technology portfolio should exist and must involve planning. Key technologies that must be supported and pushed forward by the corporate level rather than by business units must be identified at the corporate level. In addition, technological considerations may require that the firm evaluate its business units, possibly adding or divesting certain units. For example, NBI of Boulder, Colorado, was a strong competitor in the word processing industry. Industry experts, however, felt that companies not competing in integrated office systems (including word processing, computers, message systems, and the like) would be at a definite disadvantage in this industry. Since NBI lacked the technology to compete across the board in office automation (versus dedicated word processing), they attempted to acquire a company with the required technology.[33]

---

[31] Christopher Farrell, "Why Are We So Afraid of Growth?" *Business Week* (May 16, 1994), 62-72.

[32] Esther Dyson, "Micro Capitalism: Eastern Europe's Computer Future," *Harvard Business Review* (January/February 1991), 26-38.

[33] William Celis, III and Hank Gilman, "NBI Sets Offer for Computer Consoles, Inc.," *The Wall Street Journal* (January 14, 1985), 5.

Technology is important because it is an organizational resource as well as an environmental influence. Technology takes on varying degrees of centrality in the strategies of different companies, as well as within companies. And it can be a key corporate strategic weapon that drives the other strategic actions of the firm.

SOCIAL FACTORS

Social factors in the environment involve issues and information that are essentially people oriented. They are the broadest and least specific factors the firm must consider. Social factors, while including social issues affecting the firm, are not synonymous with social responsibility. Social responsibility has been described as the "obligation of businessmen to pursue those policies, to make those decisions, or to follow those lines of action which are desirable in terms of the objectives and values of society."[34] While social factors and issues arise from the environment and may affect a firm's social responsibility, the resulting social responsibility actions more properly become part of the firm's societal role, or enterprise, strategy. As part of our discussion of social factors, we will examine demographic factors; income, employment, and influence factors; and values, attitudes, and preferences.

Demographic Influences

Demographic factors can have significant impacts including, for example, the baby boom of the late 1940s and 1950s and the subsequent decline in birthrates which have resulted in a progressively aging work force. As the population bulge moves through the years—like a pig through a python—there are many effects. People fortunate enough to be born during low-birthrate years go to uncrowded schools and colleges, and experience high demand for their services in terms of job opportunities and relatively rapid promotions. For the baby-boom generation, the opposite is true.

Other demographic factors have important impacts as well. When the baby-boom generation entered the work force in the 1970s, many more women also chose to work and pursue new career opportunities. These two factors, as discussed earlier, have caused the work force to grow more rapidly than normal, resulting in relatively high unemployment and cheaper labor. When labor is cheap relative to capital equipment costs, productivity tends to grow less rapidly,

---

[34] Howard R. Bowen, *Social Responsibilities of the Businessman* (New York, NY: Harper & Row, 1953), 6.

with attendant side effects. Also, increased mobility of the work force tends to accentuate growth in certain geographical areas and declines in others.

In addition, because of healthier lifestyles, improved health care, and a declining birthrate, our society's average age is steadily increasing. In fact, by the year 2000, it is anticipated that there will be 100,000 Americans aged 100 years or older. Many will be in good health and able to work well past traditional retirement ages. This phenomenon is occurring worldwide, and has a number of important implications for retirement plans and health-care services.

Two opposing trends are also occurring. The baby-boomers are having babies of their own, creating an "echo" of the original baby boom. This boomlet will have a considerable effect on youth-related products and services. On the other hand, our society is seeing more and more singles; therefore, fewer children will result, and more money will likely be spent on adult luxuries, amusements, and conveniences.

Income, Employment, and Influence

Some experts have concluded that standards of living have been dropping for up to twenty years, requiring either two wage earners per household, or a reduced living standard. Further, Americans traditionally have expected to move up the social and economic ladder with each generation. Not only is that no longer the case, but the middle class is being squeezed. Between 1973 and 1985, there was a 9 percent drop in households with incomes between $20,000 and $50,000, with gains at the high and low ends. One reason is a cut in the middle-management ranks of many companies, making it increasingly difficult for lower- and middle-level employees.[35]

An often overlooked social factor is that countries with less population growth than others can expect to have declining global influence. It is difficult to compete militarily (in terms of troops and defense expenditures), as well as economically for small countries or those with below-average population growth.[36]

Values, Attitudes, and Preferences

Another important social factor is people's attitudes, both as employees and as consumers. What people want, demand, and are able to get from their jobs depends on a host of factors, including supply of and demand for their skill. Few

---

[35] Jonathan Peterson, "Much-Heralded Service Economy Has Arrived," *Lincoln Journal* (September 24, 1987), 28.

[36] Alan L. Otten, "Some Thinkers Expect Population to Drop and Trouble to Result," *The Wall Street Journal* (June 18, 1987), 1.

would have thought a few years ago that unions would agree to wage reductions in the recessionary early 1980s.

Sometimes, people's values and attitudes change faster than companies can change products and services to accommodate them. For example, during most of the 1970s, people were chastising U.S. auto manufacturers for not producing enough smaller cars. But customers continued to purchase large cars over compacts. And Japanese automakers moved into the market for small, inexpensive automobiles. As Kotler and Fahey point out, sales of "Japanese cars were going nowhere in the United States until the price of oil shot up. Had fuel costs not escalated, most Americans would still be preferring and driving large cars."[37] This is borne out by Charles Hofer's observation that in 1978 Chrysler could not produce a sufficient number of full-sized cars to satisfy the demand. Scarcely a year later, that same public was "calling for Chrysler's head" and criticizing the company's management for "not building the small cars the public wanted."[38] Ford had a similar experience. To meet the corporate average fuel economy (CAFE) levels mandated by the federal government, the company had to artificially discourage buyers of their large-engined cars by adding a surcharge.[39]

After the second (Iranian) oil embargo in 1980, a great number of Americans shifted to the type of car the Japanese had been producing for years (in fact, the *only* size car they had been producing for export—the subcompact). Since Detroit had not been producing such cars for as long a time as the Japanese, or in the same quantities, the Japanese were much farther ahead on the experience curve, giving them a cost and quality advantage. Kotler and Fahey also observed that the "Japanese companies were doubly lucky that U.S. auto manufacturers responded slowly rather than swiftly to the increased demand for small cars—and triply lucky that Detroit's first small cars were poorly designed."[40]

The United States traditionally has been called the "melting pot," because of its diverse immigrant heritage. During periods of high immigration and for perhaps several generations thereafter, people seem to have a desire to join, to be accepted, and to be like everyone else. This behavior creates mass markets. Increasingly, however, U.S. citizens seem to have been searching for their heritage, their identity, and uniqueness. The resulting mass of subcultures, or diversity, is the opposite of a melting pot, and breaks the mass market down into

---

[37] Philip Kotler and Liam Fahey, "The World's Champion Marketers: The Japanese," *The Journal of Business Strategy*, 3, No. 1 (Summer 1982), 3-13.

[38] C.W. Hofer, "New Frontiers in Strategic Management," visiting scholar speech, University of Nebraska (November 12, 1980).

[39] Fred Secrest, "The Automobile Industry," visiting executive speech, University of Nebraska (February 1981).

[40] Kotler and Fahey, "The World's Champion Marketers," 4.

smaller segments, with important implications for producers of goods and services.[41]

Another change sweeping the United States involves neotemperance: it is becoming "in" *not* to drink, or to drink very sparingly. Based on the perceptions that drunk driving had increased and that drinking-related auto deaths were increasing, people began demanding tougher laws. Coupled with the physical fitness craze and attempts to stamp out teenage drug abuse, people began to look more closely at their own drinking habits, resulting in a reduction of the use of alcohol. While drinking is much lower than it has been throughout most of U.S. history, the *perception* that it is higher and affecting people's safety and well-being parallels a more basic change in society; Americans "have overcome their post-Prohibition distaste for meddling with other people's personal behavior." In fact, "the evidence is overwhelming that Americans are finding it increasingly acceptable—and sometimes desirable—to try to alter other people's behavior." It seems that concern with community rights outweighs the ideal of absolute personal liberty.[42]

Another major social behavior change, with ramifications for industries as well as workplace policies, concerns smoking. In 1995, the adult smoking rate dipped below 25 percent, and to many Americans, the habit is not only unhealthy but unfashionable (perhaps the stronger influence of the two). In an attempt to arrest the rate of decline in this industry, R.J. Reynolds announced plans to introduce Premier, a cigarette with "little smoke, no ash, no odor, and no tar."[43] The product may make smoking safer, but not more fashionable. In fact, the cigarette was pulled off the shelves after only five months of test marketing, making it one of the most expensive new product flops in decades.[44]

Lastly, the world seems to be trending toward a more homogeneous society, as communication and travel become more widespread. One analyst observed that there is less difference between teenagers in New York, Tokyo, and Geneva than there is between the teenagers and their parents.

In conclusion, between 1965 and today, corporations were hit with a succession of social changes (minority rights, consumerism, environmentalism, women's rights); by the politics of oil, Vietnam, Watergate, and sentiment against institutions and multinational corporations; by changes in consumer tastes and be-

---

[41] Michael Kami, *Strategic Planning for Changing Times* (Dayton, OH: Cassette Recording Co., 1984).

[42] "The Sobering of America: A Push to Put Drinking in Its Place," *Business Week* (February 25, 1985), 112.

[43] John Helyar, "RJR Unveils Cigarette that Produces Little Smoke; Marketing May Be Tricky," *The Wall Street Journal* (September 15, 1987), 2.

[44] Peter Waldman, "RJR Nabisco Abandons 'Smokeless' Cigarette," *The Wall Street Journal* (March 1, 1989), B1.

havior ("natural" foods, health consciousness, conservation, emphasis on value); and by new work-life values (individual rights, assertiveness, participation, and diversity). But coping with social change is not simply corporate social responsibility; it is related to work force productivity and availability, as well as to costs and profitability. It is also related to corporate credibility, acceptance, and support, resulting in a firm's freedom to act and implement its strategies. It is better to adopt a proactive stance concerning social change than to adopt a reactive one. As social issues intensify, corporate options decrease. Furthermore, social issues can quickly become political and even legal issues,[45] as will be discussed in the following section.

POLITICAL/LEGAL CONSIDERATIONS

Government is often the major factor in the political and legal environment of a firm or industry. Laws and regulations are usually formulated by government bodies and can have dramatic effects on a company's strategic alternatives, as our previous discussions of deregulation pointed out. Further, firms must comply with antitrust laws, pollution laws, safety regulations, EEO programs, and a host of other constraints. However, other regulations and guidelines also constrain firms; industries and professions sometimes enforce standards of conduct and practice over and above those imposed by any government body. For this reason, and because regulations and constraints are the *result* of a political/legal process, the strategist needs a framework for analyzing political activity that may have an effect on the company.

Figure 10.5 describes a model of the political processes affecting company strategy. Obviously, political factors influence government and other regulatory policies, which can affect the company's distinctive competence, competitive positions, and even its values. A company can use several options to forge a corporate political strategy. The purpose of the strategy is influencing the political factors and, in turn, the regulatory policies that affect the company. Instead of thinking only of competitors, managers should view their company as one of a number of *players* in a political arena, and should assess the agendas of all the other players. These may include—in addition to competitors—unions, legislative bodies, government agencies and officials, trade and industry groups, consumer groups, other interest groups, and the media. All of the players, while pursuing their own agendas, create issues that may affect the company. These issues are not raised and dealt with in the marketplace, but in *forums*, such as the legislature, the media, or others. Managers must be aware that in such environments,

---

[45] Ian Wilson, "Evaluating the Environment: Social and Political Factors," in *Handbook of Business Strategy*, ed. W.G. Guth (Boston, MA: Warren, Gorham & Lamont, 1985), 3-3.

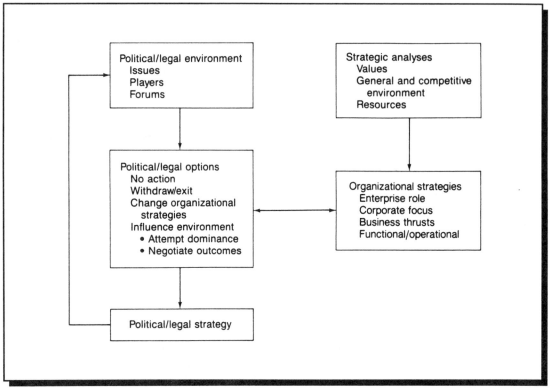

Figure 10.5 Political/Legal Strategy Process

strategy is not simply formulated but is in large measure *negotiated* with the other players.

In dealing with or confronting issues, two things must be addressed: (1) the issue's potential for political dramatization by one or more of the players; and (2) the pattern of cooperation and conflict that the issue encourages—in other words, who is likely to line up on which side of the issue. This requires assessment of who the players are with regard to the issue, as well as what motivates them. Who the players are, what their agendas are, what alliances and adversaries are likely to emerge, and how powerful they are must be considered. The manager must know the setting and rules of the forum in which the players will deal with the issue. "Facts" may count less than how well a player is able to utilize a particular forum.

How can managers respond to or influence political activity? Four basic options exist: do nothing and suffer the consequences; exit the business or market; modify the firm's strategy to offset or capitalize on the issue; or seek greater influence over the political environment. The latter can be done by attempting to dominate the other players (a high-risk approach) or by attempting to negotiate a relatively desirable outcome with them.

The result of this process is the firm's political strategy, which attempts to achieve a balance or fit between the company and its political environment. Some specific goals for this strategy should include:

1. Attempting to frame an issue in a favorable way.
2. Assembling a coalition of players with similar to overlapping agendas.
3. Seeking to choose the most favorable forum for the company and the coalition.[46]

Political strategy is not usually thought of when discussing the topic of competitive advantage. However, Japan has aggressively pursued a strategy of political superiority and has developed a distinct competitive advantage in this area. By spending on political influence, Japanese companies have influenced U.S. decision-making processes in their favor. For example, in the 1980s, the Japanese auto industry successfully won a political battle by convincing the Treasury department to override a U.S. Customs Service decision concerning light trucks from Japan. The Japanese consequently were able to import their light trucks as passenger cars, thus paying low tariffs, and then reclassifying them once in the U.S. to sell as light trucks. The second reclassification allows them to have the best of both worlds; low import tariffs and lower pollution standards for trucks— a win-win situation for the Japanese.

Japan's government and leading companies together spend $400 million annually running an ongoing political campaign in the United States. Japan spends more on its lobbying than the five most influential American business organizations combined. Also, Japan spends more on lobbying in America than the twelve nations of the European Community combined.[47]

CONCLUSIONS

In conclusion, the general environment can have a significant impact on an industry, a firm, and its task environment. As an example, the financial services industry has experienced revolutionary changes since the 60s. Several interacting forces, such as economic, international, regulatory, and technological, have drastically changed the type and degree of competition within the industry (as

---

[46] J.L. Badaracco, Jr., *Note on Corporate Strategy and Politics*, Case No. 9-382-151 (Boston, MA: Harvard Business School, 1982).

[47] Pat Choate, "Political Advantage: Japan's Campaign for America," *Harvard Business Review* (September/October 1990), 87.

well as the definition of the industry itself). As a result, the industry no longer faces the "3-6-3 environment" (pay depositors 3 percent interest, lend money at 6 percent, and tee off at 3 p.m).

What caused the change? In the macroeconomic arena, declining industry growth, double-digit inflation, and volatile interest rates have all introduced major instabilities in the industry, tending to shift the focus of financial investments from long term to short term. In the regulatory area, increased deregulation has caused the lines separating the various segments of the financial services industry (between banks, S&Ls, credit unions, securities firms, and the like) to be increasingly blurred. Technologically, computerized telecommunications and electronic technology have increased the scope, scale, and volume of transactions. In the process, it has integrated geographical markets, reduced labor intensiveness, and facilitated networking, such as fund transfer and automated teller machines (ATMs). Lastly, internationalization has been a factor as well. Increased competition from foreign lenders, the growth of multinational firms and international financial markets, electronic technology, and related factors have contributed to this trend. The end result of these environmental changes has been to make the financial services industry more competitive than ever before.[48]

Assessing the strategic situation is the first phase in determining the content of the proper strategies for a firm. This assessment often begins with an analysis of the general environment of the firm, in terms of economic, technological, social, and political/legal influences. They are important collectively as well as individually, and often override industry or organizational variables and strategies.

---

[48] David Rogers, "Environmental Change in the Financial Services Industry," in *Advances in Strategic Management*, eds. Robert Lamb and Paul Shrivastava, Vol. 5 (Greenwich, CT: JAI Press Inc., 1988), 90-94.

Module
11

The Competitive
Environment

LEARNING OBJECTIVES

After completing Module 11, you should be able to:

1. Describe the primary determinants of the intensity of competition facing a business unit.
2. Appreciate the differences between businesses, markets, and industries.
3. Understand the role of strategic groups and market structure.
4. Realize the importance of stage of the product/market life cycle in strategy formulation.

The third major aspect in assessing the organization's strategic situation involves analyzing the industry, or competitive, environment. The effects of competition and market structure, including industry and strategic-group memberships, are part of this environment. As was mentioned earlier, the competitive or industry environment affects those businesses of a company which compete within a particular industry. Therefore, the individual businesses comprising a corporation may face very different competitive environments, depending on the characteristics of the industries in which they compete. In this light, *businesses*—not companies or firms—face competitive environments. A diversified company may face a number of competitive environments, ranging perhaps from relaxed to hyper-competitive in nature.

In addition, firms and businesses face task environments, directly related to the firm or business and not necessarily to the industry as a whole. Our focus in this chapter is to address those aspects of the industry and task environments *relevant* to the competitive situation facing the business. As such, we may touch upon elements of a business's task and industry environments in analyzing the impact of the industry, markets, and competitors upon the focal business. Industries and markets can range from local to global, and can progress through definite life-cycle stages, as can products.

PROFILE

The Video Rental Industry

Revenues of the videocassette rental industry skyrocketed to $5.6 billion in 1986 from $76 million in 1981, and reached $10 billion in the early 90s—obviously a high-growth industry. Yet, with video rental outlets cropping up in convenience stores, record shops, electronic outlets, book stores, supermarkets, and discount stores to compete with the neighborhood video specialty shops, the video rental industry became overcrowded. In fact, rental rates in many areas are off sharply and profits are slim to nonexistent for many outlets—a case of "profitless prosperity."

Why was this the case in an obvious high-growth industry? It is an industry with very low and inexpensive barriers to entry; thus, competitors expanded faster than the market. The industry is undergoing a "shakeout," whereby marginal outlets will be forced to close. In addition, the industry is further threatened by "rack jobbers"—firms which set up and service displays of 200 or so cassettes in convenience stores and other high-traffic locations and then share the revenue. On the other end, video "superstores" are emerging, with 7,500 or so tapes, serviced by central distribution centers. In the process, the medium-sized outlet, unable to match neither the selection and prices of the superstores nor the convenience and prices of the rack jobbers, will continue to be forced out.[1]

DETERMINANTS OF COMPETITION

Competition can be defined as vying for customers or resources. Often, however, people concentrate on firms competing for buyers or customers when describing the competitive environment, ignoring the equally important competition for resources that may occur. As Figure 11.1 shows, however, competition can (and does) arise from either source. In Case 1, two businesses compete intensely for customers, but do not compete for resources. In Case 2, however, two businesses do not compete for customers (as in the case of a monopoly), but compete intensely for resources. Which case contains the greater degree of competition? We cannot answer this question, but we should realize that both can describe relatively competitive environments. As Figure 11.2 illustrates, the two cases just discussed would likely represent situations of moderate total competitive pressure on the business. In Case 1 (competing for customers), significant marketing-oriented competition is apt to exist, but little purchasing-oriented competition. In Case 2 (competing for resources), the reverse is true. The most intensely competitive situation would exist where a business competes for *both* customers and resources, and the least competitive would be where minimal competition exists for customers and resources.

Competitive Forces

The terms *competition* and *rivalry* are often considered to be synonymous. Harvard's Michael Porter points out, however, that rivalry is but one of a number of factors, or forces, determining the degree of competition within an industry. Porter's studies of structural factors and strategic groups within industries concluded that the state of competition in an industry depends on the five basic competitive forces shown in Figure 11.3. The combined strength of these forces determines the profit potential in the industry, in terms of return on invested capital.

Threat of New Entrants. New entrants bring increased competition to an industry. Entry depends on the barriers existing—economies of scale, product differentiations, capital requirements, access to distribution channels, cost advan-

---

[1] W.M. Alpert, "What's Wrong with This Picture?" *Barrons* (September 21, 1987), 8.

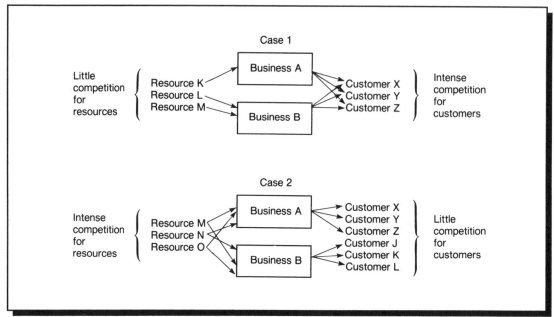

Figure 11.1 Firms Compete for Customers and Resources; Two Cases

Competition for Resources		Competition for Customers	
		Intense	Minimal
	Intense	Intense competitive pressure	Moderate pressure (purchasing) —Case 2
	Minimal	Moderate pressure (marketing) —Case 1	Little competitive pressure

Figure 11.2 Intensity of Competition

tages for established competitors, and certain government and legal constraints—as well as on the possible reactions of existing competitors.

Rivalry among Existing Firms. Rivalry, or attempts to improve the firm's position within the industry, can have noticeable effects on the firm's competi-

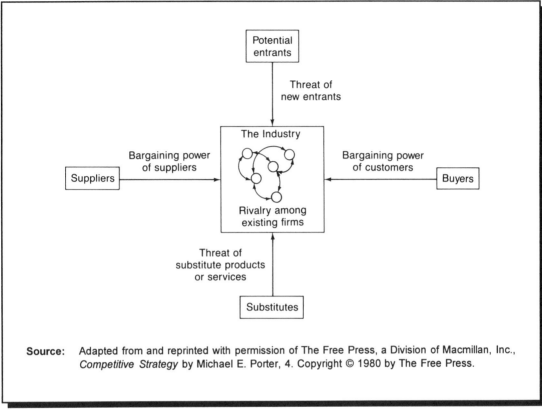

Source: Adapted from and reprinted with permission of The Free Press, a Division of Macmillan, Inc., *Competitive Strategy* by Michael E. Porter, 4. Copyright © 1980 by The Free Press.

Figure 11.3 Forces Driving Industry Competition

tors, because firms in an industry are mutually dependent. The intensity of the rivalry is greatest when the following factors are present:

1. Competitors are numerous and roughly equal in size and power.
2. Industry growth is slow.
3. Fixed or storage costs are high.
4. The product or service is not differentiated from those of competitors.
5. Capacity normally is added in large increments.
6. Competitors have diverse goals, objectives, strategies, origins, and "personalities."
7. Companies rate the need to succeed in the industry as high.
8. High exit barriers exist, based on costs, interrelationships with other divisions, company commitment, or legal restrictions. Obviously, the worst case exists in an industry with high exit but low entry barriers, while the reverse would be the ideal.

More intensive rivalry may exist between some competitors in an industry than between others. We are well aware of the rivalries that exist between certain sports teams—such as between Texas vs. Oklahoma, Army vs. Navy, and Notre Dame vs. Michigan in college football. Recent intense rivalry has erupted between Ford and Chrysler in automobiles. As the Japanese threat has receded and GM's previously dominant position has eroded, Ford and Chrysler more and more have come to regard themselves as chief rivals.[2]

Threat of Substitution. All firms in an industry, even monopolies, compete with industries and companies producing substitute products. Saccharin, fructose, aspartame, and sugar are examples of substitute products, as are heat pumps, furnaces, and air conditioners.

Bargaining Power of Customers. Buyers attempt to force down prices as well as to demand higher quality, better services, and other concessions. The need to make such concessions to buyers with bargaining power increases rivalry and reduces profits.

Bargaining Power of Suppliers. Suppliers can increase rivalry and reduce profits by their ability to raise prices, reduce services, and allocate purchases.[3]

The five forces determine the attractiveness of an industry, because their collective strength determines industry profitability. They determine profitability because they influence the elements of return on investment—prices, costs, and required levels of investment. The main point is that each of the forces is a function of industry *structure*, which is relatively stable. However, businesses—through their strategies—can influence the five forces, and industry structure can change over time. In short, industry profitability is a function of industry structure—the five forces—not product, process, or technological characteristics, per se. For example the forces are favorable in pharmaceuticals and soft drinks, and industry participants can earn high returns. Returns are inherently low in industries where one or more of the forces is unfavorable, such as steel, rubber, and video games. Thus, when the forces are favorable, returns are likely to be attractive; when they are unfavorable, returns are likely to be disappointing, *despite management's efforts.*[4]

---

[2] Douglas Lavin and Jacqueline Michell, "Ford and Chrysler Bicker Like Siblings Over Which is Better," *The Wall Street Journal* (March 1, 1994), A1.

[3] Michael Porter, *Competitive Strategy* (New York, NY: The Free Press, 1980), Chapters 1 and 7.

[4] Michael Porter, *Competitive Advantage* (New York, NY: The Free Press, 1985), 4-7.

Competitor Analysis

It is important to evaluate competitive advantages of the firm, but it is equally important to evaluate the capabilities of competitors. In large measure, a competitor analysis closely resembles the analysis of a firm's strengths and weaknesses. Figure 11.4 illustrates the major components of a competitor analysis. This information, presented in a form such as that shown in Table 11.1 permits a comparative evaluation of competitors based on key factors and criteria. This form can be used to evaluate relative strength, as well as to compare the strengths and weaknesses of competitors with those of your firm.

Table 11.1 Competitor Evaluation Form

Item	Competitors			
	A	B	C	D
Name				
Estimated sales ($000)				
Estimated share of market				
Price advantage*				
Quality advantage*				
Technology base*				
Sales force base*				
Distribution advantage*				
Cost advantage*				
Overall				
Standing in industry (today)*				
Standing in industry (next year)*				
Seriousness of competition (today)*				
Seriousness of competition (next year)*				
Seriousness of competition (two years ahead)*				
Anything special to which we must react?				
Soon				
Next year				
Longer range threat				

*Evaluate on the following scale: 1 = great, highest, best; 2 = above average; 3 = average; 4 = below average; 5 = worst, no threat, very poor.

Source: Reprinted with permission of The Free Press, a Division of Macmillan, Inc., from *Strategic Planning: What Every Manager Must Know* by G.A. Steiner, 139. Copyright © 1979.

Source: Reprinted with permission of The Free Press, a Division of Macmillan, Inc., from *Competitive Strategy* by M.E Porter, 49. Copyright ©1980.

Figure 11.4 The Components of a Competitor Analysis

Another method of analysis is to compare the position of the business with that of its competitors with regard to relative quality and price—in other words, relative value. As Figure 11.5 shows, the interaction of customers and suppliers in the marketplace tends to align products along a "price-performance curve," so that strong competing products offer roughly the same perceived value. For example, economy products offer both low price and low quality, and better products command higher prices. Products offering less value than those on the curve are likely to lose out, while those offering greater value are likely to win. Research has shown that products (and businesses) offering greater value have a far better chance of gaining market share and growing than do the rest. Further, changes in relative quality have a more potent effect on market share than price changes do, and quality improvements are harder for competitors to follow than are price changes.[5] In summary, it is important to compare and analyze the position of your business relative to competitors in the industry to determine relative positions with respect to the industry's price-performance curve.

THE EFFECT OF MARKET AND INDUSTRY STRUCTURE

Another factor in the firm's competitive environment involves the type of market and industry structure it faces. For example, the scope of the market and industry within which the firm competes are very important considerations. Is the firm competing in a broad market, such as General Motors in automobiles, or does it compete in certain segments of that market, as Mercedes Benz does and Checker did? Is the industry or service area local, regional, national, international, or even global? What is the intensity of the rivalry between the competitors? What strategic groups (firms following similar strategies) exist?

These factors, discussed in this section, are related to industrial organization and microeconomics. However, they are sufficiently different from the general economic environment and related closely enough to the firm to warrant a separate and more detailed look. Also, these factors are not fixed—they can change. Remember our previous discussion of banking. For years, banking was a relatively stable, protected industry. Bank charters were difficult to acquire, and change in the industry was slow. The advent of savings and loans provided some competition for deposits, but each financial institution had its own market niche. Then came high interest rates and money market accounts. Financial institutions such as Dreyfus and Fidelity permitted customers to write checks on their accounts, and started to compete with banks. Deregulation blurred the distinction between savings and loans and banks, and both found themselves in a more competitive environment. Many banks were ill prepared for life without the shelter of regulation.

Not only did deregulation permit price competition for deposits, but it also increased the range of services that nonbank institutions could offer. For the first time in banking history, institutions other than banks were able to offer checking deposits and have broader lending powers. And the Depository Institutions Act of 1982 changed the regulations governing deposits, allowing savings and loans

---

[5] Bradley T. Gale and Richard Klavans, *Formulating a Quality Improvement Strategy*, PIMS Letter No. 31 (Cambridge, MA: The Strategic Planning Institute, 1984), 3-6.

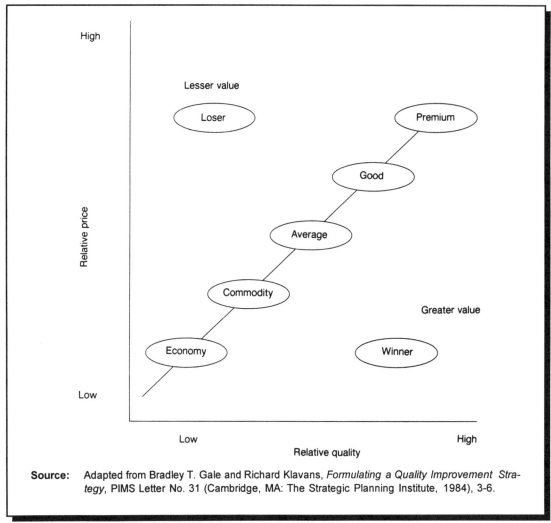

Source: Adapted from Bradley T. Gale and Richard Klavans, *Formulating a Quality Improvement Strategy*, PIMS Letter No. 31 (Cambridge, MA: The Strategic Planning Institute, 1984), 3-6.

Figure 11.5 Value and the Price-Performance Curve

to act more like banks, thus creating another competitive force. The financial effect on the industry has been an increase in the cost of funds due to more permissive interest rate ceilings plus increased competition from financial service institutions other than banks. The net effect of this is a squeezing of profits from both ends for banks.

This trend can already be observed. Intensified competition (including that from other types of financial institutions, insurance companies, brokerage-based firms, and giant retailers) will increase the number of bank consolidations and buyouts. Many banks have found themselves unprepared and financially crippled by the competitive environment and have had to sell out. Larger banks (realizing the loss in market share and/or profitability) and nonbank financial institutions are seeking acquisitions to add to their portfolio to increase market share.

Furthermore, the size of most banks' markets is changing. It used to be that a bank in Sioux Falls, South Dakota, for example, competed only with other banks in the same city. Then came savings and loans. Then competition with national organizations such as General Motors Acceptance Corp. (GMAC) for auto loans. Then money market funds and total investment packages such as those offered by Sears (through Allstate and Dean Witter) and Merrill Lynch (through its cash management account). Finally, de facto interstate banking has been offered by Citibank and First Interstate, and is likely to intensify greatly when and if banking laws are further relaxed.

Defining the Market

Market characteristics can change, markets themselves can change, and measures such as "market share" and "market growth" can depend on how one defines the market. Thus, there is no one way to define a market. But markets tend to be described, if not defined, in terms of several dimensions.

1. *Products.* Products or services comprising a market can be defined narrowly (the market for microwave ovens) or broadly (the market for all ovens, or even all appliances). In general, useful ways of categorizing products in terms of their markets would include groupings relating to similar functions and/or similar technology.
2. *Customers.* Are the products sold to similar or different types of customers?
3. *Geography.* Markets often are defined in terms of geographical regions.
4. *Components versus goods.* Is the product a raw material, component, or sub-assembly sold to other producers, or is it sold to end users?
5. *Multidimensional factors.* While a market may be defined in terms of each of the four factors above, it may also be defined in terms of combinations of factors.

In general, as Harvard's Robert Buzzell states:

Market definition is an important and difficult step in the process of strategy formulation. For the management of a business unit (BU), determining the scope of the *served* market is a basic strategic decision. In most cases, there are choices to be made about what kinds of customers to serve, what types of products to offer, the geographic scope of the BU's market, and the level(s) of production/distribution on which to operate. The strategy employed by a BU is largely determined by the definition of its served market. To complicate matters, an appropriate served market definition at one point in time may not be appropriate later on, because of changes in customer needs, technology, or competitors' activities. . . . managers may need to use several different definitions of "the market" to satisfy different purposes. To summarize this point, . . . Assume that the BU sells . . . [150 units] to only two customer or product segments, with market shares of 50 percent in Segment A and 67 percent in Segment B—or 60 percent for the two segments combined. Beyond these two served segments, there is an "immediately adjacent" market in which the BU makes no sales—but into which it could expand by directing marketing efforts to new types of customers, broadening its product offering, etc. If the size of this unserved portion of the market is 500 units, then the BU's share of its "total market" is (150/750) or 20 percent.

For purposes of evaluating the BU's competitive effectiveness, it seems reasonable to say that *all* of the "market shares" just cited—share in each served segment, combined share in both segments, and share of total market including unserved segments—are relevant measures.

Finally, for purposes of evaluating possible future growth opportunities and potential competitive threats, a still broader view of "the market" will be necessary. Potential competitors may include firms selling in the "immediately adjacent" market; firms operating in related cost sectors; those in other geographic regions, including overseas markets; and producers of functionally related products whose offerings might be modified so as to compete directly with those of the business unit. All of these possibilities are, furthermore, two-way streets—and each represents a potential direction for the BU's future growth as well as a possible source of new competition.[6]

Thus, while General Motors may appear secure in the fact that it controls over 30 percent of the U.S. auto market, it competes against not only Ford and Chrysler, but against a number of Japanese and European automakers. Since GM is a full-line producer, and foreign companies compete in the United States, perhaps it should consider its share of the *world* market. On this score it would not fare so well (even in comparison to Ford, which is a major producer in Europe). In fact, the Big 3 U.S. producers control only one-third of the world's

---

[6] From Robert D. Buzzell, *Note on Market Definition and Segmentation*, 9-579-083, 27 (Boston, MA: Harvard Business School, 1978). Reprinted by permission.

market. In contrast, Mercedes Benz has a very small share of the total market, but it does not compete across the board. If one defines its market as luxury sedans and coupes, its share of this *served* market is much greater.

On the other hand, some markets, such as those for laundries and bakeries, are inherently local. Some are regional, such as cement production (limited by transportation costs). And some are national, international, and even global.

Furthermore, markets are not fixed; they can be expanded. Herb Kelleher, CEO of Southwest Airlines, does not see other airlines as his principal competition. He says Southwest competes against other forms of travel, such as autos, on many of its routes, particularly the shorter ones. With its low fares, Southwest has often doubled or tripled air traffic on certain routes, as travelers are lured out of their cars and into the air.[7]

Defining the Industry

Equally important and related to the definition of the market is the definition of the industry. An *industry* is a group of firms offering products or services that are close substitutes for each other.[8] An industry is also a group of producers and sellers of close substitute outputs who supply a common group of buyers. An industry, then, is defined in terms of both product or service and of customers.

In analyzing industry structure, economists often consider the basic determinants of supply and demand because an "industry" tends to involve common factors that affect both. Supply-related factors include: (1) raw materials, (2) technologies, and (3) the type of work force. Demand-related factors are: (1) price elasticities of products and services, (2) rates of growth, (3) cyclical characteristics of demand, and (4) the method of purchase. These supply and demand factors interacting over time produce an industry structure with several key strategic aspects:

1. The number and size of buyers and sellers.
2. The degree of product differentiation.
3. Requirements and conditions for entry into the industry, for exit from the industry, and for positioning within the industry.

---

[7] S.N. Chakravarty, "Hit'em Hardest with the Mostest," *Forbes* (May 9, 1994), 107-112.

[8] Arnoldo C. Hax and N.S. Majluf, *Strategic Management* (Englewood Cliffs, NJ: Prentice-Hall, 1984), 261.

4. Cost structure, particularly the relationship between fixed and variable costs.
5. The degree of vertical integration, both backward and forward.[9]

While industry structure may change over the product life cycle, structural factors are important in determining the appropriate corporate, business, and functional strategies; the purpose of these strategies is to provide a strong position for the firm relative to its competition and market environment.

For example, the airline industry is going through much the same trauma that older industries, such as steel, autos, and others, have earlier. That is, fundamental changes, requiring new ways of doing things and new ways of organizing. The airlines, however, have yet to face up to their restructuring. The airline industry is becoming more commodity-like and price sensitive, particularly on shorter flights. Before the end of the century, American, United, Delta, Northwest, and US Air will likely change radically in the way they operate. The restructured airlines will define their function and markets more narrowly, tailoring their costs to that narrower function. Those insisting on full service will find their fares rising sharply.[10]

Strategic Groups. While it is important to define the market and the industry, a more useful concept than total industry definition is often the identification of "strategic groups" within industries. The most relevant unit of industry analysis may be the strategic group to which the business belongs.

As an example, Figure 11.6 shows the variation in the relationship between return on equity (ROE) and market share for three industries. Only brewing seems to adhere to the across-industry trend of ROE rising with increased market shares. However, a different picture emerges from a closer look at the brewing industry if it is divided into three strategic groups—local, regional, and national firms. As Figure 11.7 shows, ROE declines with increasing share *within* each of the groups, but increases *between* groups. A regional brewer, for example, attempting to pick up market share may find a lower ROE *until* the firm goes national.

As this example illustrates, looking only at the industry can be misleading; you need to look further. Michael Porter points out that "the first step in structural analysis within industries is to characterize the strategies of all significant competitors along these dimensions. This activity then allows for the mapping of the industry into strategic groups. A strategic group is the group of firms in

---

[9] Abraham Katz, "Evaluating the Environment: Economic and Technological Factors," in *Handbook of Business Strategy*, ed. W.D. Guth (Boston, MA: Warren, Gorham & Lamont, 1985), 2-6.

[10] Howard Banks, "A Sixties Industry in a Nineties Economy," *Forbes* (May 9, 1994), 107-112.

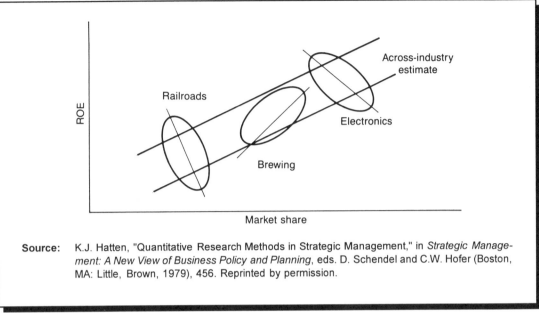

Source: K.J. Hatten, "Quantitative Research Methods in Strategic Management," in *Strategic Manage-ment: A New View of Business Policy and Planning*, eds. D. Schendel and C.W. Hofer (Boston, MA: Little, Brown, 1979), 456. Reprinted by permission.

Figure 11.6 **Relationship between Market Share and ROE**

an industry following the same or a similar strategy" and having similar strategic characteristics. "An industry could have only one strategic group if all the firms followed essentially the same strategy. At the other extreme, each firm could be a different strategic group. Usually, however, there are a small number of strategic groups which account for the essential strategic differences among firms in the industry."[11]

Strategic groups, then, can be defined as the set of firms competing within an industry which pursue similar strategies and employ similar combinations of scope and resource commitments.[12] They are essentially inhabitants of similar niches in the marketplace. The reason that the strategic group concept is impor-tant is that the major issue in industry analysis involves which strategies will best suit organizations with particular resource capabilities—a good strategy for

---

[11] Porter, *Competitive Strategy*, 129.

[12] K.O. Cool and Dan Schendel, "Strategic Group Formation and Performance: The Case of the U.S. Pharmaceutical Industry, 1963-1982," *Management Science*, 33, No. 9 (September 1987), 1106.

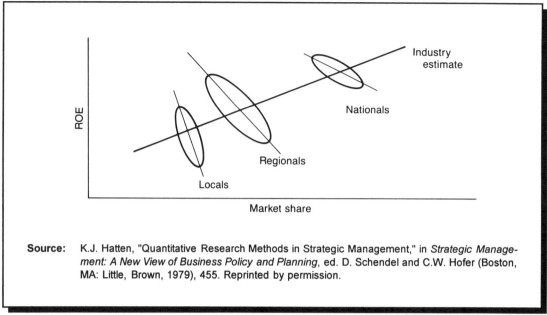

Source: K.J. Hatten, "Quantitative Research Methods in Strategic Management," in *Strategic Management: A New View of Business Policy and Planning*, ed. D. Schendel and C.W. Hofer (Boston, MA: Little, Brown, 1979), 455. Reprinted by permission.

Figure 11.7 ROE and Market Share for Brewing Industry

one firm may not suit another.[13] Strategic groups identify firms which have chosen to utilize similar resource capabilities in similar ways. Table 11.2 defines six strategic groups within the U.S. pharmaceutical industry as an example, based upon scope and resource commitments.

Based upon inventive activity, however, a somewhat different set of strategic groups emerges for the pharmaceutical industry. As shown in Table 11.3, the industry can be grouped into "core firms" (firms "typical" of the industry in terms of inventive activity); "related firms" (those significantly different from but still related to the technical core, either positively or negatively); and "unrelated firms" (those which vary markedly from the core firms, either positively or negatively). Thus, strategic group membership can be defined in a variety of ways.[14]

In Porter's view, both the industry and strategic group membership determine a firm's profitability; these underlying factors include:

---

[13] K.J. Hatten and M.L. Hatten, "Strategic Groups, Asymmetrical Mobility Barriers and Contestability," *Strategic Management Journal*, 8, No. 4 (July/August 1987), 341.

[14] Philip D. Crossland and L.A. Digman, "Using Time-Series Analysis to Identify an Industry's 'Inventive Strategic Groups'," *Proceedings of the 20th Annual Conference*, Decision Sciences Institute (November 1988).

Table 11.2 Strategic Groups in the U.S. Pharmaceutical Industry

Group Description	Firms
1. Large, R&D-intensive, prescription products, broad range of products, competing in many segments.	Abbott American Home Bristol-Myers Pfizer SmithKline Warner-Lambert
2. Large, advertising intensive, prescription and nonprescription products, fewer prescription segments, and narrower product range than (1).	Lilly Merck Upjohn
3. Medium-sized, ''me-too'' product strategy, heavy promotion.	Johnson & Johnson Schering-Plough Squibb Sterling Drug
4. Medium-sized, lacking R&D competence, otherwise like (3).	Searle Syntex
5. Small, prescription products, narrow product range, selective market participation, me-too development, heavy professional promotion.	Carter-Wallace Marion Morton-Norwich Richardson-Vicks Robins Rorer
6. Small, very focused product line, narrow scope, negligible R&D.	Lederle

Source: Adapted from K.O. Cool and Dan Schendel, "Strategic Group Formation and Performance: The Case of the U.S. Pharmaceutical Industry, 1963-1982," *Management Science*, 33, No. 9 (September 1987), 1115.

1. Common industry characteristics.

   a. Industry-wide structure elements that determine the strength of competitive forces and that apply equally to all firms. These traits include rate of growth of industry demand, overall potential for product differentiation, structure of supplier industries, and aspects of technology, which provide the overall context of competition for firms in the industry.

2. Characteristics of strategic group.

   a. The height of *mobility barriers* protecting the firm's strategic group.

   b. The *bargaining power* of the firm's strategic group with customers and suppliers.

Table 11.3 Inventive Strategic Groups in the Pharmaceutical Industry

Core Firms	Related Firms	Unrelated Firms
Abbott Labs	Johnson & Johnson	American Home
Becton-Dickinson	SmithKline	C. R. Bard
Lilly	Sterling Drug	Baxter-Travenol
Pfizer	Warner-Lambert	Bristol-Myers
Schering-Plough		Marion Labs
Squibb		Merck
Upjohn		Robins
		Syntex

    c. The vulnerability of the firm's strategic group to *substitute products*.

    d. The exposure of the firm's strategic group to *rivalry from other groups*.

3. The firm's position within its strategic group.

    a. The degree of competition *within* the strategic group.

    b. The *scale* of the firm relative to others in its group.

    c. *Costs of entry* into the group.

    d. The ability of the firm to execute or *implement* its chosen strategy.[15]

Upon observation, it is apparent that many of the factors listed above are related to Porter's five-forces model of industry competition. Therefore, the factors which determine competition apply to strategic groups within industries as well as to industries as a whole. For example, entry barriers depend on the particular strategic group the firm wishes to join, and can vary from group to group within an industry. In addition, there may be barriers to shifting from one strategic group to another. Therefore, an important element of formulating competitive strategy within an industry is choosing the strategic group or niche in which to compete.[16]

Financial Services: A Changing Industry. At the beginning of this section, we discussed the changing financial services industry in terms of the effects of those changes on banks. Earlier, we pointed out that a number of environmental forces have been at work since the 60s to cause revolutionary changes for the

---

[15] Porter, *Competitive Strategy*, 42.

[16] Sharon M. Oster, *Modern Competitive Analysis* (New York, NY: Oxford University Press, 2nd ed., (1994), 80-97.

entire industry, not just for banks. As we mentioned, these converging forces were macroeconomic, regulatory, international, and technological in nature. It appears that the forces of change are still at work, as one of the "rescue plans" proposed for the savings and loan industry would abolish many of the remaining distinctions between commercial banks and thrift institutions.[17]

Whatever the outcome of the latest crisis, the forces for change are forcing major changes in the industry, resulting in a new market structure and an industry much more competitive than ever before. As a living example of industry change, let us take a glance at the dynamics of industry change that commercial banks and S&Ls are facing as they attempt to reposition themselves, both to survive and to enhance their performance.

The regional banks, for example, are being challenged by newly merged, larger regional banks, sometimes called *superregionals*. One consequence of these mergers may be a change in the balance of power in commercial banking, because the superregionals possess advantages over both the regionals and the national money center banks. For example, they can still claim their regional identification, autonomy, and attraction by customers, which the nationals do not have. In addition, they have fewer bad loans, more access to mid-size corporations, and operate in more protected markets than the nationals. Vis-a-vis the regionals, the superregionals possess new economies of scale and scope, and are no longer easy takeover targets.

Foreign banks are another vigorous new competitor. Not subject to U.S. regulations and anxious to penetrate American markets, foreign banks operate with a big advantage. The Japanese, for example, are radically altering the industry by following the approaches that made them strong competitors in automobiles and electronics.

Last, the "nonbank banks" are becoming big players in consumer lending; in fact, only two of the largest five consumer lenders are banks. The largest is the General Motors Acceptance Corporation (GMAC), with Sears fourth and Ford Motor Credit fifth. Other big players include General Electric, American Express, Merrill Lynch, JC Penney, and Prudential Bache. Some of the factors enabling the nonbanks to approach dominance of the consumer lending market include their merchandising skills, their ability to segment markets and package services, and their effectiveness at lobbying in Washington.

In summary, commercial banks are finding themselves competing in a drastically changed market. As Citibank's former CEO Walter Wriston observed, "We had a monopoly and it was lovely; now there's a market and we're losing mar-

---

[17] Alan Murray and Paulette Thomas, "The Bush Bailout Plan for Savings and Loans Could Spell Extinction," *The Wall Street Journal* (February 7, 1989), A1.

ket share."[18] We will return to the financial services industry in a later module, as we examine some of the strategic options appropriate to its new competitive environment.

THE PRODUCT/MARKET LIFE CYCLE

As students of marketing are aware, products, markets, and entire industries go through definite life cycles of the type shown in Figure 11.8 from the introductory, embryonic, or development stage to a more rapid growth stage—including a resulting shakeout—to a low-growth maturity stage, and finally to an aging or actual decline stage. Another important factor in achieving competitive advantage involves developing strategies appropriate to the life-cycle stage of the product/ market/industry, since appropriate strategies vary from stage to stage. Important stages and their recommended strategies are discussed in the following paragraphs.

Introductory and Growth Stages

In the introductory stage, sales growth tends to be slow due to buyer unfamiliarity and inertia. This stage requires heavy start-up investments in research, manufacturing, and marketing. It tends to be unprofitable and involves a negative cash flow and high risks. At this stage, there tend to be few competitors. The strategic objectives should be to achieve a commanding competitive position, if possible, including elimination of design, product, and marketing defects, development of awareness of the product and its benefits, and sales to early adopters.

In the growth stage, the product begins to "take off" in sales. This attracts other producers. As sales of products such as cellular phones begin to grow more rapidly, the product starts to become profitable. Strategic objectives should be to establish a strong brand identity and develop a distribution system capable of meeting the rapidly growing demand. The goal of both objectives is to capture and maintain a large share of this demand, so that money invested during the introductory phase will begin (and continue) to pay off. The ideal situation is to have the customer identify the firm's product with the market, as was the case with Xerox copies and Nintendo video games. Cash flow remains negative during most of this phase, however, as investments are made in such areas as additional plant capacity.

---

[18] David Rogers, "Environmental Change in the Financial Services Industry," in *Advances in Strategic Management*, eds. Robert Lamb and Paul Shrivastava, Vol. 5 (Greenwich, CT: JAI Press, 1988), 94-98.

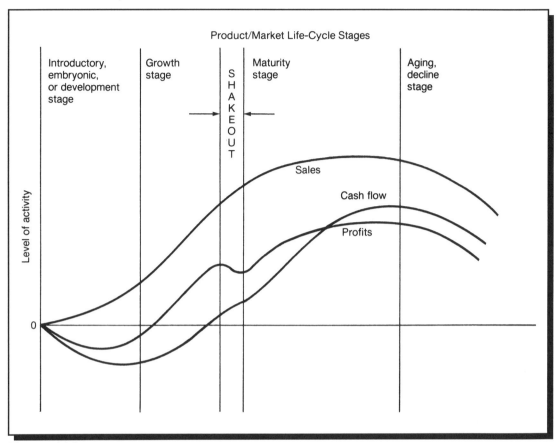

Figure 11.8 **Product/Market Life-Cycle Stages**

Shakeout Stage

As shown in Figures 11.8 and 11.9, a shakeout phase typically occurs toward the latter part of the growth stage. In the early growth stage, margins are such that relatively inefficient producers may survive and even prosper. Rivalry focuses on product performance, access to distribution channels, identifying market segments, and highlighting special product features to enable sales to grow with the rapidly expanding market. In the shakeout phase, however, the *rate* of growth begins to decline, although growth is still occurring. Margins begin to fall, and firms with inferior products, poor distribution, high costs, or inappropriate segmentation come under pressure. Weaker competitors begin to be cleared from the market; those with efficient production, selling, and distribution are likely to survive and prosper because of reduced competition caused by the shakeout. The strategic objective during shakeout is to maintain and strengthen market

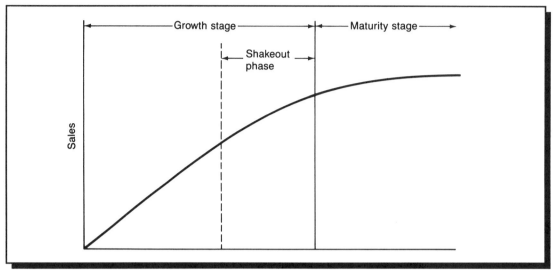

Figure 11.9 Growth/Maturity Transition

niches or segments through dealer and customer loyalty. In this stage, cash flow tends to turn positive for successful competitors. Keep in mind, however, that shakeouts can and do occur at *any* stage in the life cycle.

Maturity Stage

In the maturity stage, sales may continue to grow. But this growth is due mainly to replacement purchases of the product, new purchases owing to population growth or other stable factors, and inflation. In the maturity stage, relative stability reigns. Marginal producers have been cleared from the industry, and few (if any) new entrants are attracted because of the reduced growth rate. Profits peak in this phase, as do cash flows. Strategy shifts to a more defensive posture, as the firm attempts to protect itself from competitor erosion of market share and profits. This is done by paying constant attention to product improvement and refinement, as well as to trying new or refined promotional and distribution efforts.

In a mature market, without innovation or distinct changes in the environment, the primary way a firm can pick up major improvements in market share is through the mistakes of its competitors. Attention should be focused on efficiency—becoming the low-cost producer—through operations management approaches such as productivity improvement, cost control, and backward integration. The firm's product differentiation and pricing strategies are designed to *preserve* the firm's competitive position and to put pressure on competitors. This will enable the firm to take advantage of any strategic mistakes competitors make. As the maturity stage progresses, growth in sales to new customers may fall below the growth rate of the new-customer population, leaving largely replacement sales. Eventually, even replacement sales may begin to decline, resulting in an actual decline in total sales. However, profits and cash flow still may be strong, because expenditures and capital investments are minimal.

Decline Stage

Finally, it becomes clear that the product's future is limited. Buyers are shifting to newer products, and definite signs of old age and decline are evident for the industry—thus, the decline stage. Beset by declining sales and excess capacity, producers begin to drop out of the industry; the business can, however, extend its life span through product refinements and pricing strategies. The basic strategy now should be to milk the business of all possible profits and cash flow, using this money for investment in other products in earlier stages of the life cycle. But staying with products in the decline phase can have some advantages. If the firm is well established in the market and is a low-cost producer, it is likely that some competitors can be enticed to leave the market, leaving voids the remaining producers can capture. Philip Morris, for example, continues to increase its cigarette sales by picking up sales from others who have departed.

Tables 11.4 and 11.5, adapted from Wasson[19] and Fox,[20] outline a number of descriptors and appropriate business strategies for the various stages in the product life cycle. These tables provide guidelines for business and functional-level actions and strategies for each stage, although exceptions can and do occur.

Some Cautions

While the preceding section and tables present the typical life cycle, certain caveats must be kept in mind. One is that the duration of the stages varies widely from industry to industry, as can the rate and height of the growth curves.

Consider, for example, "fad" products such as hula-hoops or pet rocks, in which the whole cycle can be completed in one year or less. ATARI® video games seemed to have a two-year growth and maturity stage but Nintendo's success seems longer lasting. Also, an industry does not always go through each of the stages. Or it may spend very little time in any given stage. CB radios, for example, went through a very long introduction stage, a growth stage of one or two years, little (if any) maturity stage, then into decline. Industry growth sometimes revitalizes, or renews, after a period of decline (this was true in the motor-

---

[19] Chester R. Wasson, *Dynamic Competitive Strategy and Product Life Cycles* (St. Charles, IL: Challenge Books, 1974), 247-48.

[20] Harold W. Fox, "A Framework for Functional Coordination," *Atlantic Economic Review*, 23, No. 6, (1973), 10-11.

Table 11.4 Wasson's Hypotheses about Appropriate Strategies over the Product Life Cycle

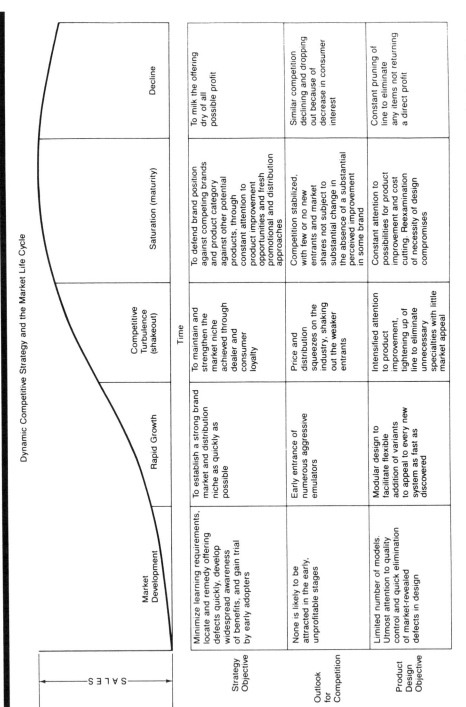

Dynamic Competitive Strategy and the Market Life Cycle

	Market Development	Rapid Growth	Competitive Turbulence (shakeout)	Saturation (maturity)	Decline
Strategy Objective	Minimize learning requirements, locate and remedy offering defects quickly, develop widespread awareness of benefits, and gain trial by early adopters	To establish a strong brand market and distribution niche as quickly as possible	To maintain and strengthen the market niche achieved through dealer and consumer loyalty	To defend brand position against competing brands and product category against other potential products, through constant attention to product improvement opportunities and fresh promotional and distribution approaches	To milk the offering dry of all possible profit
Outlook for Competition	None is likely to be attracted in the early, unprofitable stages	Early entrance of numerous aggressive emulators	Price and distribution squeezes on the industry, shaking out the weaker entrants	Competition stabilized, with few or no new entrants and market shares not subject to substantial change in the absence of a substantial perceived improvement in some brand	Similar competition declining and dropping out because of decrease in consumer interest
Product Design Objective	Limited number of models. Utmost attention to quality control and quick elimination of market-revealed defects in design	Modular design to facilitate flexible addition of variants to appeal to every new system as fast as discovered	Intensified attention to product improvement, tightening up of line to eliminate unnecessary specialties with little market appeal	Constant attention to possibilities for product improvement and cost cutting. Reexamination of necessity of design compromises	Constant pruning of line to eliminate any items not returning a direct profit

Source: Adapted from Chester R. Wasson, *Dynamic Competitive Strategy and Product Life Cycles* (St. Charles, IL: Challenge Books, 1974), 247–48.

cycle, bicycle, and radio broadcasting industries), as if an entirely new life cycle began at some point. Others appear to skip the introductory phase altogether.[21] Still others either abort during the introductory phase and never make it any further, or go directly into decline.

In general, many businesses expect in the neighborhood of seven years of losses plus an even longer period of negative cash flow in the growth stage for products now in the early embryonic stage. After that, profitable maturity can go on for a long time. The life-cycle theory suggests that, over time, every business drifts to the right—toward decline—and that its financial performance changes. A corporate strategy that expects large and rising profits from an embryonic or aging business is not realistic. Expecting high profits in the growth and maturity stages, however, is reasonable.

---

[21] Porter, *Competitive Strategy*, 158.

Table 11.5 Fox's Hypotheses about Appropriate Business Strategies over the Product Life Cycle

Stage	Functional Focus	Department		
		R&D	Production	Marketing
Precom-mercialization	Coordination of R&D and other functions	Reliability tests	Production design Process planning Purchasing department lines up vendors and subcontractors	Test marketing Detailed marketing plan
Introduction	Engineering: debugging in R&D production, and field	Technical corrections (engineering changes)	Subcontracting Centralize pilot plants; test various processes; develop standards	Induce trial: fill pipelines; publicity
Growth	Production	Start successor product	Centralize production Phase out subcontractors Expedite vendors output; long runs	Channel commitment Brand emphasis Reduce price if necessary
Maturity	Marketing and logistics	Develop minor variants Reduce costs through value analysis Originate major adaptations to start new cycle	Many short runs Decentralize Import parts, low-priced models Routinization Cost reduction	Short-term promotions Cooperative advertising Forward integration Routine marketing research; panels, audits
Decline	Finance	Withdraw all R&D from initial version	Revert to subcontracting; simplify production line Careful inventory control: stock spare parts	Withdraw most promotional support Selective distribution Careful phaseout, considering entire channel

Source: Reprinted by permission from *Atlanta Economic Review* (now *BUSINESS* Magazine), "A Framework for Functional Coordination," by Harold W. Fox (November/December 1973), 10-11.

| | Department | | | |
Physical Distribution	Finance	Other	Customers	Competition
Plan shipping schedules, mixed carloads Rent warehouse space, trucks	LC plan for cash flows, profits, investments, subsidiaries	Final legal clearances (regulatory hurdles, patents)	Panels and other test respondents	Neglects opportunity or is working on similar idea
Plan a logisitics system	Accounting deficit; high net cash outflow Authorize large production facilities	Help develop production and distribution standards	Innovators and some early adopters	(Monopoly) Disparagement of innovation Legal and extra-legal interference
Expedite deliveries Shift in owned facilities	Very high profits, net cash outflow still rising Sell equities	Short-term analyses based on return per scarce resource	Early adopters and early majority	(Oligopoly) A few imitate, improve, or cut prices
Reduce costs and raise customer service level Control finished goods inventory	Declining profit rate but increasing net cash inflow	Spearhead cost reduction, value analysis, and efficiency drives Price cuts bring price wars; possible price collusion	Early adopters, early and late majority, some laggards; first discontinued by late majority	(Monopoly competition) First shakeout; yet many rivals
Reduce inventory and services	Retrenchment Sell unneeded equipment Export the machinery	Accurate sales forecast very important	Mainly laggards	(Oligopoly) After second shakeout, only a few rivals

Module
12

Enterprise Strategies
and Governance

LEARNING OBJECTIVES

After completing Module 12, you should be able to:

1. Define enterprise strategies and describe their importance to the organization.
2. Discuss the role of the board of directors in strategic management.
3. Describe the role of top management in governance of the organization.
4. Understand the role of outside consultants.

This module elaborates on the firm's enterprise strategy, introduced briefly in an earlier module. Other modules deal with business unit strategies, corporate, functional, global, and interorganizational strategies. Thus, this and related modules deal with strategy *content* for the various types, or levels, of strategies. In addition, the topic of governance of the organization is discussed, focusing on the roles of the board of directors, top management, and external consultants in managing the strategic aspects of the firm.

PROFILE

Managing by Values at Levi Strauss

Levi Strauss has embarked on a grand social experiment; a "singular lofty vision of how to run a modern corporation. . ." This experiment is the vision of Chairman and CEO Robert D. Haas, the great-great-grandnephew of founder Levi Strauss. Haas calls Levi's approach "responsible commercial success;" no other company has pursued a values-based enterprise strategy to the extent Levi's has.

Specifically, Levi Strauss aspires to six enterprise goals:

1. *New Behavior.* Management must exemplify "directness, openness to influence, commitment to the success of others, and willingness to acknowledge our own contributions to problems."
2. *Diversity.* Levi's "values a diverse workforce (age, sex, ethnic group, etc.) at all levels of the organization. . . Differing points of view will be sought; diversity will be valued and honestly rewarded, not suppressed."
3. *Recognition.* Levi's will "provide greater recognition—both financial and psychic—for individuals and teams that contribute to our success. . . those who create and innovate and those who continually support day-to-day business requirements."
4. *Ethical Management Practices.* Management should epitomize "the stated standards of ethical behavior. We must provide clarity about our expectations and must enforce these standards throughout the corporation."
5. *Communications.* Management must be "clear about company, unit, and individual goals and performance. People must know what is expected of them and receive timely, honest feedback. . ."
6. *Empowerment.* Management must "increase the authority and responsibility of those closest to our products and customers. By actively pushing the responsibility, trust, and recognition into the organization, we can harness and release the capabilities of all our people."

Haas states that Levi's is not pursuing these goals because it makes them feel good, nor because it is politically correct. They are doing it because "we believe in the interconnection between liberating the talents of our people and business success."[1]

ENTERPRISE STRATEGIES

As defined in Module 1, enterprise strategies relate to the organization's role in society, including its mission and purpose. Sometimes called "institutional strategy," the enterprise strategy is concerned with "fitting the firm comfortably into the legal, political, and social environments in which it operates."[2]

An important question relating to the basic enterprise strategy is "How do we fit in?" to our general environment and society. Obviously, how we "fit in" would include all aspects of the environment—economic, social, political/legal, and technological. The main focus here is on organizational character—such as for-profit vs. NFP, corporation vs. partnership and the like—and institutional strategy, which would include the organization's culture. Implicit in enterprise strategy is an identification of which stakeholders the organization will try to serve and how it will try to serve them. In this light, the enterprise strategy pertains to society, stakeholders such as employees and customers, markets focused on, and guides to competing, as shown in Table 12.1.

Table 12.1 Enterprise Strategy Components

Focus	Descriptor
Society	Organizational form, concept, ownership
Customers	Key value offered to customer
Employees	Important aspects of work climate
Markets	Products, services provided to customers
Competitive Mode	Source of competitive advantage

---

[1] Russell Mitchell, "Managing by Values," *Business Week* (August 1, 1994), 46-52.

[2] Edward H. Bowman, "Strategy Changes, Possible Worlds and Actual Minds," in James W. Fredrickson, ed., *Perspectives on Strategic Management* (New York, NY: Harper Business, 1990), 18.

Ed Freeman and Dan Gilbert offer seven different conceptions, or alternatives, of enterprise strategy. That is, each of the seven strategies assumes different moral views and obligations, including whose interests the enterprise should serve and to whom the organization owes a moral obligation. The seven strategies are:

1. *Stockholder Strategy:* The corporation should maximize the interests of stockholders.
2. *Managerial Prerogative Strategy:* The corporation should maximize the interests of management.
3. *Restricted Stakeholder Strategy:* The corporation should maximize the interests of a narrow set of stakeholders, such as customers, employees, and stockholders.
4. *Unrestricted Stakeholder Strategy:* The corporation should maximize the interests of all stakeholders.
5. *Social Harmony Strategy:* The corporation should maximize social harmony.
6. *Justice Strategy:* The corporation should promote inequality among stakeholders only if inequality results in raising the level of the worst-off stakeholder.
7. *Personal Projects Strategy:* The corporation should maximize its ability to enable corporate members to carry out their personal projects.[3]

Remember, enterprise strategy is at once the organization's most basic and its most general strategy. Some organizations and many people within organizations may not have a clear idea of what their firm's enterprise strategy consists of. An organization needs a clear concept of the two questions, "How do we fit in?" and, What do we stand for?" Since the answers to these questions provide the guidelines for the firm's business, corporate, functional, and interorganizational strategies, it is easy to see why a firm with an unclear enterprise strategy could drift off course. Organizations need a clear idea of how they hope to serve society and their customers, how they will treat their employees, what their main markets are, and the source of their competitive advantage.

ORGANIZATIONAL GOVERNANCE

In an earlier module, we discussed the role of the "key players" in the strategic management process; largely the roles of line and staff top managers in formulating and implementing strategies. Here we take a closer look from the perspec-

---

[3] R. Edward Freeman and Daniel R. Gilbert, Jr., *Corporate Strategy and the Search for Ethics* (Englewood Cliffs, NJ: Prentice-Hall, 1988), Chapter 4.

tive of organizational governance—who is in charge of the organization? What roles do the board of directors, the CEO, and external consultants play in determining organizational direction?

But what is corporate governance all about? Professor John Pound of Harvard's Kennedy School of Government feels that corporate governance is actually pretty simple. It revolves around "two or three big decisions a year made at the very, very top levels" of the corporation. It sounds complex, but there really aren't all that many decisions that get made at the very top levels; it's not all that complicated. It is important, therefore, not to get involved in too many decisions—to be able to focus on and devote sufficient attention to the critical few.

In this light, effective corporate governance is essentially strategic, behavioral, political, and ethical in its focus. It is about the need to foster good decisions among the ten to twenty people at the top of the organization responsible for making those decisions; the decisions that affect the very character of the organization. It means assuring that the right decisions are made, and that if a poor decision is made it will be challenged and reversed quickly.[4]

The board of directors plays an important role in the long-term strategic, operational, and policy-related activities of any organization. The board does not act as management, although certain inside officers may be members. However, for larger organizations in particular, the bulk of board members are outsiders, thus the term *quasi insiders* is used when referring to them. Consultants—outsiders who may play an important advisory role in strategic management processes and content—are another group of important quasi insiders.

The Role of the Board

What is the role of the board of directors of an organization? More specifically, what is the board's role in strategic management? The first role of any board is legal. Under corporate laws, the board represents the owners' (i.e., shareholders) interest in a firm, by choosing a chief executive officer, evaluating and rewarding the CEO, and replacing the CEO if necessary. The board's loyalty must be to the stockholders rather than to management. There is a problem inherent in performing this function: the CEO also often chairs the board of directors. This makes ambiguous the role of the board and especially the role of the chair—when the board chair speaks, is he or she representing management or the board (thus indirectly the stockholders)? How can the board objectively evaluate the CEO's performance if he or she, in fact, chairs the board?

---

[4] John Pound, "Corporate Governance and Market Forces," in *Corporate Governance: The Need for a Long-Term Perspective* (St. Louis, MO: Emerson Center for Business Ethics, April 23, 1993), 49-56.

Make-up of the Board. A number of studies have been conducted concerning board make-up. A number have concluded that "too many" insiders on the board is not desirable, but "some" inside representation is good. Open to question, however, are the meanings of the terms "too many" and "some." Most experts would like to see a majority of independent outside directors on the board of a major corporation. Many feel that boards must take into consideration interests of a broader range of stakeholders—more than just shareholders. This means more academicians, politicians, and culturally-diverse group representatives, such as women and minorities. It also means more representatives from foreign countries as international and global competitiveness increases.[5]

Responsibilities of the Board. William Boulton of the University of Georgia sees the board as progressing through a series of transitions from legitimizing to auditing to directing. Using a survey of forty-five chief executives and directors, as well as in-depth investigations of boards in seven firms, Boulton attempted to trace the processes that boards had gone through in evolving to their current format. The first transition, from legitimizing to auditing, comes about partly due to increased legal pressures on directors, making them more insistent on being informed. As the board becomes more involved in decisions, it may then adopt a directing role in questioning the firm's long-term direction. At this point, the board develops a formalized statement of its role and function. Boulton considers providing continuity to be one of the most important functions of the board. Chief executive officers come and go, but the organization lives on: it is the role of the board to maintain a continuing philosophy of the firm. The board must ensure that management is carrying out the functions necessary for long-term viability.[6]

Involvement in Strategic Planning. Courtney Brown of the Conference Board has discussed the various responsibilities of the board and identified four areas in which the board should be involved: policy, personnel, procedures, and performance. Brown has contended that the only area being adequately dealt with is performance. He has stated, "the board of directors is the proper body for the establishment of broad policies and procedures . . . management personnel are selected by the chief executive officer in collaboration with the board and delegated to carry out these policies and procedures." The paradox seems to be that although boards are legally accountable for corporate affairs, they do not often

---

[5] John M. Nash, "Restructuring Corporate Leadership," in *Corporate Governance: The Need for a Long Term-Perspective* (St. Louis, MO: Emerson Center for Business Ethics, April 23, 1993), 21-28.

[6] W.R. Boulton, "The Evolving Board: A Look at the Board's Changing Roles and Information Needs," *Academy of Management Review*, 3. No. 4 (October 1978), 827-36.

involve themselves in the *planning* of such affairs. The two reasons most often cited for this noninvolvement are the directors' lack of time and of necessary expertise.[7]

Reasons for Involvement. Kenneth Andrews believes there are several reasons for the board of directors to become involved with corporate strategy. First, the involvement provides evidence that management has some process for evaluating alternatives. It also provides an understanding of the company's business and a means of evaluating management. Another, and perhaps the most important, reason for board involvement is that an understanding of corporate strategy provides a reference point for evaluating other decisions and their impact.[8] An effective board should require that management formulate a unique corporate strategy, should review it periodically, and should use it as the reference point for all other board decisions.

Another writer, Robert Mueller, has identified three areas in which he feels that the skills and objectivity of the board of directors would prove useful:

1. Determining new directions of growth.
2. Deciding when to make profound changes in the strategic approach to corporate objectives.
3. Choosing a philosophy and the timing for investments.[9]

If it is assumed that boards should be involved in strategic management in some way, the next question becomes: How involved? Should boards actually determine strategy or merely evaluate the strategy determined by management? Should the board examine the process by which the strategy has been formulated? Samuel Felton has identified three possible levels of board involvement.

1. Approve strategic recommendations, monitor the agreement between plans and performance.
2. Take part in the determination of objectives.

---

[7] Courtney Brown, *Putting the Corporate Board to Work* (New York, NY: Macmillan, 1976), 30.

[8] Kenneth J. Andrews, "From the Boardroom: Replaying the Board's Role in Formulating Strategy," *Harvard Business Review*, 59, No. 3 (May/June 1981), 18.

[9] Robert Mueller, "Criteria for the Appraisal of Directors," *Harvard Business Review*, 57, No. 3 (May/June 1979), 48.

3. Become completely familiar with the plans of management. By doing this, the board will be able to discriminate between external and internal causes of performance and results.[10]

Felton has defined the role of the board to include: deciding what business the firm is in (enterprise and corporate-level strategies), defining the principal quantitative and qualitative objectives of the firm, and reviewing the strategies the organization is going to employ.

Obviously, there are differences of opinion concerning board involvement. Some feel that if the board actually gets involved in planning, it would be a duplication of effort, since management would also be doing planning. This view holds that even if all the board did was approve plans, they would need to be experts to pass judgment. Thus, corporate boards should *not* be involved in the development and approval of business-level plans, but should rely on management. According to this view, the role of the director is to ensure that the premises for planning correspond to the board's shared views of the business. These premises should be audited when there are large discrepancies between planned outcomes and actual results, leading to conflicting assumptions about the causes. The board's role in this process is to synthesize the competing assumptions as well as to discuss diverging viewpoints. The board manages the discussion, commits the firm to a new direction, and ensures that those parties advocating defeated alternatives are not punished. It should be pointed out that this view does not explain how directors will gain the expertise for this task, but not the expertise to evaluate strategy.

It seems, then, that the board's responsibility is to evaluate strategy but not to formulate it. However, the level of strategy in question needs to be considered. For example, the board should be intimately involved in the formulation of and changes in enterprise strategy, as in the case of AT&T. In addition, it should probably be involved in any *major* changes in corporate-level strategy, such as the decisions to restructure ITT and Coca-Cola; at least in evaluating and approving the concept in advance. But business-level strategy is another matter, especially in multibusiness firms. When the board starts developing business-level strategy, it is usurping management's responsibility, which can lead to a disastrous relationship between management and the board.

Given that most board members have a great deal of business knowledge that can best be utilized by allowing them to analyze management problems and decisions, how does the board go about evaluating strategic alternatives? It must be remembered that board members are usually employed in high-level positions in other firms and cannot devote more than a small part of their time to board

---

[10] S.M. Felton, Jr., "Case of the Board and the Strategic Process," *Harvard Business Review*, 57, No. 4 (July/August 1979), 20.

activities. In addition, they cannot wait to evaluate a strategy based on the results obtained. Strategic management involves crucial, long-term decisions; if mistakes are made, the firm's existence may be put in jeopardy.

Felton has advocated evaluating strategy based on five criteria:

1. Does it exploit opportunity fully in terms of market share?
2. Is it internally consistent?
3. Is it feasible in terms of competence and resources?
4. Does it have the support of those who must carry it out?
5. Is it a clear stimulus to achievement?[11]

Committees of the Board. How a board performs its functions is partially a result of its structure. While this structure is affected by the laws of the state in which the firm is incorporated, most firms tend to show some similarities in the committees that comprise the board. Table 12.2 lists the committees used by 16 typical major corporations.

All of the firms included had an audit committee that serves as an intracompany watchdog to ensure that the affairs of the company are being handled competently and ethically. (Any company listed on the New York Stock Exchange *must* have an audit committee.) Another fairly universal committee is the executive committee. This is usually the most powerful, and typically is empowered to act for the total board between meetings. The compensation committee recommends compensation for senior management, while the nominating committee selects or evaluates candidates for the total board, for membership on board committees, for top corporate officers, and the like.[12]

Strategy Committees. Because of the importance of strategy and policy, some firms have created board committees to deal with these areas. Kenneth Andrews, for example, recommends formulation of a strategy committee that would be similar to an audit committee. The objective of the strategy committee is to encourage and strengthen the strategic planning process within the company. This committee first would become familiar with current strategy, then assess the current strategy's strengths and weaknesses and consider what measures would improve strategy. Another recommendation is the implementation of full-scale strategy reviews, which, at a minimum, should compare last year's results against planned performance. These reviews should also evaluate and mod-

---

[11] *Ibid.*

[12] Stanley C. Vance, *Corporate Leadership: Boards, Directors, and Strategy* (New York, NY: McGraw-Hill, 1983), 62.

Table 12.2 Committees of the Board in a Sample of Sixteen Companies

Company	Audit	Compensation	Executive	Finance	Nominating	Public Policy	Other
Allied Chemical	X	X	X		X	X	XX
American Airlines	X	X	X	X	X		XX
AT&T	X	X	X	X	X	X	XX
Armstrong World	X	X					X
Bethlehem Steel	X	X	X				
Boeing	X	X		X	X		
Champion International	X	X					XXX
Dow Jones	X	X	X				
Du Pont	X	X	X	X			
Exxon	X	X	X		X		X
Mobil	X	X	X		X	X	X
Textron	X		X		X		X
UAL	X	X	X				
Union Carbide	X	X	X	X	X	X	

Source: Adapted from Stanley C. Vance, *Corporate Leadership: Boards, Directors, and Strategy* (New York, NY: McGraw-Hill, 1983), 62.

ify long-range plans. The special skills and talents of directors can be fully utilized only by involving them in these critical issues.[13]

William Wommack also has suggested forming a corporate strategy committee composed of outside, independent directors. This would involve the board in the strategy of the company, something not done by many companies. If such a committee is formed, the chief executive officer should develop a set of objectives. Wommack suggested identifying someone in the organization as the chief strategic officer (CSO)—not to be confused with the chief staff officer—who would develop a strategic philosophy. The CSO should be at an organizational level at least equal to that of the chief operating officer (COO) and must

---

[13] Andrews, "From the Boardroom."

have control over resources necessary for change (e.g., capital funds). In this approach, the board reviews and approves corporate-level objectives (as determined by the chief executive officer) and broad strategic directions (as determined by the chief strategic officer). The chief strategic officer then provides the board objectives committee with strategic guidelines for each strategic business unit. With this information, board members can evaluate the soundness of decisions, such as capital allocations, by relating them to the strategic guidelines.

Wommack has provided some additional information on the job characteristics of the chief strategic officer. First, the job cannot be done by a group; if strategic change must occur, group consensus usually will not bring it about. In addition, success in effecting strategic changes is in inverse proportion to the number of duties the chief strategic officer has. The chief strategic officer also must make direct contact with every level at which strategic choices are considered rather than waiting for these ideas to filter up.[14] In practice, however, the CSO role has not materialized in many companies. Working counter to Wommack's concept is the growing realization that the CEO and CSO are in reality one and the same. Thus, a separate CSO may not appear to exist on paper, but one *does* exist in the form of the CEO.

Additional Board Approaches. Another suggestion in terms of board involvement in strategic management is having outside directors conduct a performance audit. This would involve appraising the results of management performance so that the board can evaluate the success of strategy and objectives. The problem with this technique is that the results of strategic decisions may not be known for many years, and it is foolish to wait that long before evaluating strategy. This would, however, begin to involve the board in the consideration and evaluation of strategic alternatives. An alternative would be for the board to set standards of performance for management and then evaluate management based on achievement of these standards. This suggests placing some levels of strategic planning in the hands of the board and leaving only the decisions as to what means will be used to accomplish these plans in the hands of management. The prevailing opinion, however, is that business-level strategy formulation is properly the management's domain.

In Summary. During the 1980s, there was strong interest in the United States in increasing the role of the board in strategy-related activities, for some of the reasons mentioned in the preceding paragraphs. In actuality, however, these ex-

---

[14] W.W. Wommack, "The Board's Most Important Function," *Harvard Business Review*, 57, No. 5 (September/October 1979), 58.

pectations have not been realized.[15] What we have seen, however, is increased "hands-on" involvement in select areas of responsibility, such as corporate control. That is, the board must be intimately involved in actions affecting corporate ownership (mergers, takeovers, LBOs, and the like), and in decisions likely to have a major impact on corporate control. Examples would be enterprise and corporate-level actions involving the corporate purpose, the corporate portfolio of businesses, and restructuring actions. This is because the board is responsible to the stockholders and has an obligation to maximize their welfare. In recent years, we have seen boards take their powers—and responsibilities— much more seriously in these areas.[16]

There are no concrete answers as to how deeply the board of directors should be involved in strategic management. However, board members have no choice but to get involved in some way in strategic management. They can no longer afford to act as a rubber stamp for managerial decisions when they should be protecting the interests of the owners. A challenge for the future may be to develop a means of involving directors in strategic management in such a way that the amount of time they devote to board matters is not increased.

Role of the CEO

We have already observed that the CEO's primary role in formulating strategy is at the corporate-level. We saw that business-unit strategies are formulated by division general managers, unless the company in question is a single-business firm; then, the CEO is responsible. The CEO is also the primary author of the corporate vision, and is responsible for garnering support for that vision by others.

Bill Rothschild suggests that the role of the CEO changes with the needs of the organization; there is no one leader for all seasons, situations, and times. He suggests that there are four types of strategic leaders:

1. *Risktakers:* Revolutionaries who can develop and lead new businesses or institutions during their birth, infancy, and early youth. They have the "passion and genius to make dreams happen."
2. *Caretakers:* The systematic, evolutionary "growers" who can move the organization from its youth to adulthood.
3. *Surgeons:* The "restructurers" who can clinically focus on the organization's critical and vital products, services, processes, etc., and discard those that

---

[15] Joseph Rosenstein, "Why Don't U.S. Boards Get More Involved in Strategy?" *Long-Range Planning*, 20, No. 3 (March 1987), 30-34.

[16] Arthur Fleischer, Jr., G.C. Hazard, Jr., and M.Z. Klipper, *Board Games: The Changing Shape of Corporate Power* (New York, NY: Little, Brown, 1988).

don't make the grade. Usually, surgeons are needed when the firm has begun to peak, in its mature stage.

4. *Undertakers:* Those who harvest, close down, or merge the enterprise with another, when a surgeon's approach is not sufficient to save the firm. While this group is usually not thought of as leaders, they show concern for those affected by the demise of the enterprises.[17]

Along the lines of the stages of organizational life, Don Hambrick has suggested that CEOs themselves go through certain stages or "seasons." Hambrick further postulates that these stages give rise to distinct patterns of executive behavior and, ultimately, organizational performance (see Table 12.3). Hambrick suggests that CEO performance will peak at sometime other than the very early or very late stages of their term.

Role of the Consultant

Outside consultants can be important in strategic management as they perform their customary roles of defining, analyzing, and solving problems for their clients. Despite the old adage that "a consultant is someone who borrows your watch to tell you what time it is, and then keeps the watch as payment," consultants *can* make a contribution in four areas of strategic management: corporate strategy formulation; business-unit strategy formulation; strategic planning system design; and general education and transfer of experience.[18]

Corporate Strategy Formulation. Corporate strategy issues essentially involve resource allocation, such as allocation of cash among existing business units and the proportion of assets invested in the various businesses. The pattern of resource allocation can be examined and evaluated by consultants. Sometimes outsiders can see situations and simple theories more clearly and objectively than can insiders. Consultants can often perform objective analyses for the company and advise it regarding practices and experiences of other companies.

Business-Unit Strategy Formulation. The predominant use of strategy consultants is in the area of analyzing and recommending strategies for individual business units.

---

[17] William E. Rothschild, *Risktaker, Caretaker, Surgeon, Undertaker: The Four Faces of Strategic Leadership* (New York, NY: John Wiley and Sons, Inc., 1993), 17-18.

[18] Peter Carroll, "The Role of the Consultant," in *Handbook of Business Strategy*, ed. W.D. Guth (Boston, MA: Warren, Gorham & Lamont, 1985), 28-11.

Table 12.3 Stages of a CEO's Tenure

Descriptive CEO Characteristics	1 Response to Mandate	2 Experimentation	3 Selection of an Enduring Theme	4 Covergence	5 Dysfunction
Commitment to a Paradigm	Moderately Strong	Could be strong or weak	Moderately strong	Strong; increasing	Very strong
Task Knowledge	Low but rapidly increasing	Moderate; somewhat increasing	High; slightly increasing	High slightly increasing	High; slightly increasing
Information Diversity	Many sources; unfiltered	Many sources but increasingly filtered	Fewer sources; highly filtered	Few sources; highly filtered	Very few sources; highly filtered
Task Interest	High	High	Moderately high	Moderately high but diminishing	Moderately low and diminishing
Power	Low; increasing	Moderate; increasing	Moderate; increasing	Strong; increasing	Very Strong; increasing

Source: Adapted from Donald G. Hambrick and Gregory D.S. Fukotomi, "The Seasons of a CEO's Tenure," *Academy of Management Review*, 16, No. 4 (1991), 729.

Strategic Planning System Design. Another area in which consultants can be helpful is in the process area, recommending, establishing, or modifying the strategic planning systems and techniques used by the organization.

General Education and Transfer of Experience. The body of strategic management is growing so rapidly that it is difficult for practitioners to keep up with it. Consultants—experts and specialists in the field—can brief and train practicing managers on the latest process and content knowledge in the field. Consultants are in a position to keep up with developing techniques, philosophies, and attitudes. It is especially important for top management to be aware of the latest philosophies and attitudes. Also, consultants can often act as facilitators, creating the consensus necessary for the formulation and implementation of strategic decisions.

In the final analysis, consultants, no matter how knowledgeable, cannot (and should not) *make* strategic decisions for management. Management must make its own decisions, using the consultants only for advice, training, analysis, and temporary assistance.

Module 13

Business-Unit/Level Strategies

LEARNING OBJECTIVES

After completing Module 13, you should be able to:

1. Describe the general strategic options available to business units.
2. Understand the importance of positioning the business.
3. Discuss key strategies for distinguishing the business, including differentiation and scope.
4. Describe strategies for increasing the scope of the business—growth— including penetration, market development, product development, and geographical expansion.
5. Relate strategies appropriate for redefining and reducing the scope of the business; that is, defense and renewal, retrenchment and turnaround, and endgame strategies.

Business-level strategies deal with how a given business unit of the organization should compete, as well as how the various functional strategies supporting the business—marketing, financial, production, research and development, and the like—should be integrated to support the business-level strategy. Concern in this module is with the basic business-level options; functional strategies other than innovation are not treated in depth here, since they are adequately covered in other courses in the business school curriculum and in another module. While there are numerous individual strategic options a business can pursue, the approach in this module is to group them into related or similar types or categories. Basic strategic thrusts for businesses are discussed, including the following:

1. Strategies for positioning the business at the proper point in the stream of product/service development activities.
2. Distinguishing the business; defining distinguishing characteristics in terms of differentiation, scope, and functions that enable the business to achieve competitive advantage.
3. Increasing the scope of the business; strategies for developing and growing the business through increased penetration, market development, product development, and geographical expansion.
4. Redefining and reducing the scope of the business; strategies for contraction, retrenchment, turnaround, and renewal, as well as retreat and product termination.

Strategies for extending the firm into other businesses are treated separately as multibusiness strategies in another module.

The approach in this module is not to present any single author's conceptualization of basic business strategies, even though a number of credible frameworks exist. Beginning with Miles and Snow's types of organizational adaptation (Defenders, Prospectors, Analyzers, Reactors)[1] at least five schemes deserve mention here. Notable contributions toward development of a conceptual framework of "generic" business strategies have been made in recent years by Derek Abell[2] and Michael Porter.[3] Most recently, however, authors have been judging the widely espoused framework of Michael Porter (cost leadership, differentiation, and focus strategies) to be deficient in important areas, and have proposed

---

[1] R.E. Miles and C.C. Snow, *Organizational Strategy, Structure, and Process* (New York, NY: McGraw-Hill, 1978), 29.

[2] Derek F. Abell, *Defining the Business: The Starting Point of Strategic Planning* (Englewood Cliffs, NJ: Prentice-Hall, 1980).

[3] Michael E. Porter, *Competitive Advantage: Creating and Sustaining Superior Performance* (New York, NY: Free Press, 1985).

improvements. Improved frameworks have been proposed by Chrisman, Hofer, and Boulton,[4] Hofer[5] again, and Henry Mintzberg.[6] The approach in this module is to consider the arguments behind each of the frameworks and to rationalize and incorporate the strongest points of each.

PROFILE

Motorola, Inc.

Motorola is a U.S. electronics and semiconductor company involved in a competitive struggle with the Japanese. The company has recently made several acquisitions and management changes designed to give it a strategically interrelated, yet reasonably diversified, corporate portfolio. Until the mid-1970s, the company was "simply reacting to the ideas that the operating guys had. Now we're strategizing. We're thinking about where we want the company to go," says Keith Bane, vice president and director of corporate strategy.

Motorola has developed a "library" of formal strategies, one for each of its more than forty businesses. The firm uses five-year and one-year plans, with monthly operating reports to let headquarters know whether a division is straying from its plan. Each business also develops a "technology road map" to forecast technologies that will be needed for the next two generations of products.

In 1982, Motorola was the top U.S. producer of the 64K RAM computer memory chip, and today is one of the leaders in the latest technology, the 64-bit 80 mhz RISC Power PC chip. The company has succeeded in the information-processing business, capitalizing on its unique combination of communications, data processing, software, and silicon foundry. Motorola's strategy was to manage that uniqueness into a leadership position.[7]

Motorola's fundamental stated objective is "total customer satisfaction." The company has several key initiatives to support this: producing products and services to a six-sigma standard (99.9997 percent defect free); reducing total cycle time in all activities; leading in the areas of product, manufacturing, and the environment; and providing a creative, cooperative workplace, with empowerment for everyone.[8] It appears as if the strategy is working.

---

[4] J.J. Chrisman, Charles W. Hofer, and W.R. Boulton, "Toward a System for Classifying Business Strategies," *The Academy of Management Review*, 13, No. 3 (July 1988), 413.

[5] Charles W. Hofer, *Generic Business Strategies: Some Topological Considerations*, paper presented at Midwest Decision Sciences Institute Meeting (April 1988).

[6] Henry Mintzberg, "Generic Strategies: Toward a Comprehensive Framework," in *Advances in Strategic Management*, eds. Robert Lamb and Paul Shrivastava, Vol. 5 (Greenwich, CT: JAI Press, 1988), 1-68.

[7] "Motorola's New Strategy," *Business Week* (March 29, 1982), 128.

[8] *Motorola Facts 94* (Schaumburg, IL: Motorola Corporate Communications, 1994).

PROFILE   **Berbiglia Liquors**

Michael Berbiglia started selling liquor in one of his two grocery stores immediately after the repeal of prohibition in 1933. Today, the fifteen-store Berbiglia chain in Kansas City does $20 million in sales annually, and is run by Mike's stepsons, Jack and Ralph Bondon. As Jack says, "In Missouri, anyone can sell spirits, wine and beer—any gas station, grocery store, or drugstore. It's a totally wide open market. We needed to establish our own niche—something we do better than anyone else—and that niche is one stop shopping for parties."

The key to Berbiglia's strategy, then, is to focus on its niche: parties. They sell the standard liquor and beers, and have an extensive wine selection. They have a deli that prepares meat and cheese trays and delivers them to the other stores. Corporations, especially, like to buy both wine and cheese for their office parties at one place.

Important to Berbiglia's market niche is their extensive inventory of over 2,000 different wines. To encourage people to try different varieties, Jack and Ralph hold a monthly gourmet wine dinner at the Italian Gardens Restaurant, another family business. The dinners cost $25, are open to the public, consist of eight courses and six or seven wines, and accommodate up to 140 people.

The Bondons' game plan is not to open more liquor stores but, in fact, to close some. They plan to increase the size of their stores by opening one new store for every two they close. Of course, the location of the new, larger stores is of critical importance. Thus, the Bondons' strategy is to continue to hone the chain's focus, build its selection, and strengthen its reputation for selection and services.[9]

POSITIONING THE BUSINESS

The initial business-level strategic question involves *position*; where should the business be positioned in the industry chain or stream. That is, where should its "center of gravity" be located in the industry chain from raw materials to primary manufacturer to fabricator to assembler to wholesaler/distributor to retailer? Should its primary focus be "upstream," "midstream," or "downstream" in the chain? Upstream (or primary) industries tend to be capital intensive, process oriented, standardization focused, and efficiency oriented. Further downstream, businesses tend to be more people intensive, concerned with product innovation, interested in segmentation, customization, and differentiation, and in search of

---

[9] Cheryl Ursin, "Berbiglia: Kansas City, MO," *Beverage Dynamics* (January/February 1992), 32-33.

marketing pull. Therefore, the decision as to where to position the business can strongly influence—even dictate—the strategies to be employed in distinguishing the business.[10]

DISTINGUISHING THE BUSINESS

Porter's Generic Strategies

Porter defines three business-level generic strategies: cost leadership, differentiation, and focus (or scope).[11] In Porter's framework, *cost leadership* strategies are where the business attempts to achieve and maintain a competitive advantage through lower unit costs of production and distribution. This advantage enables the business to either sell at a lower cost or make a greater profit than the competition. This is the type of strategy that Henry Ford employed to gain dominance in the automobile market during the 20s.

Competitors in commodity businesses (where the products or services are essentially the same and differentiation is on the basis of price) *must* strive to be low-cost producers. An example is Iowa Beef Processors, whose key corporate value—appropriately—is to be *the* lowest-cost producer. In addition, the business must be a low-cost producer in the total relevant market, which may be global. This may mean closing high-cost plants and opening others that are lower cost owing to either automation or location in areas where labor and distribution costs are low (e.g., in the South or in foreign countries).

Product or service differentiation strategies attempt to achieve competitive advantage by providing features that set your product or service apart from the competition. If a low-cost position is not possible, uniqueness—perceived or real value that causes customers to pay more—is essential. General Motors, under the leadership of Alfred P. Sloan, used differentiation strategies to build its market position during the 30s. Differentiation can be based on the product, service, quality, cost control, financing, or whatever. Examples of differentiated products are designer jeans, Izod sportswear, Corona beer, and Cabbage Patch dolls. Braniff tried to differentiate itself by painting its planes bright colors; unfortunately for them, this uniqueness was not enough to overcome an overly ambitious expansion program which forced the company into Chapter 11 bankruptcy.[12]

---

[10] Mintzberg, "Generic Strategies," 6-12.

[11] Michael E. Porter, *Competitive Strategy* (New York, NY: The Free Press, 1980), 35.

[12] Michael Kami, *Strategic Planning for Changing Times* (Dayton, OH: Cassette Recording Co., 1984).

Today, many successful businesses differentiate themselves from the pack by offering premium quality and superior service. One such business—Sewell Village Cadillac in Dallas—realizes that the service department is critically important in keeping customers satisfied, as well as in repeat business. In fact, they give customers biographical sketches of their mechanics (who averaged $80,000 a year in 1986) as well as their *home* phone numbers.[13]

Porter also discusses *focus* strategies, which attempt to gain competitive advantage by narrowing the competitive scope of the business to specific segments. In line with his cost leadership and differentiation strategies, the business would either attempt to employ a cost focus or differentiation focus within the targeted segment of the market.

Porter holds that a business should strive for either a strong cost-leadership position or a strong differentiation position. He contends that a strong position in either is necessary to create a competitive advantage, and is superior to a moderate position in each (being "stuck in the middle"), because doing so offers no clear competitive advantage. Recent studies have evaluated the effectiveness of cost leadership and differentiation strategies, alone and in combination. As Figure 13.1 shows, four possible types of competitive advantage are possible, given high and low levels of cost and differentiation. As the figure also shows, a favorable position in both cost and differentiation tends to yield the highest return on investment, with the pure individual strategies yielding somewhat less favorable results. As might be expected, businesses with neither fared much less well.[14]

More recent studies have lent credence to the possibility that a business *can* successfully pursue both cost leadership and differentiation strategies.[15] That is, the vigorous pursuit of any one generic strategy does not seem to preclude the pursuit of another; there seems to be no penalty associated with being "stuck in the middle."[16] The key seems to be that pursuing two generic strategies *by itself* does not cause one to be stuck in the middle: pursuing one or both of the two strategies *ineffectively* or *insufficiently* (halfway) may cause poor performance.

[13] Steve Jordon, "Author: Endless Service is the Means to Success," *Omaha World-Herald* (November 18, 1987), 58.

[14] R.E. White, "Generic Business Strategies, Organizational Context and Performance: An Empirical Investigation," *Strategic Management Journal*, 7, No. 3 (May/June 1986), 217-31.

[15] Ronald F. Green, James P. Jolly, and Alok Srivastava, "Differentiation and Cost Leadership Strategies: A Strategic Continuum of Alternatives," *Journal of Business Strategies*, 7, No. 1 (Spring 1990), 15.

[16] Danny Miller, "Generic Strategies: Classification, Combination, and Context," in P. Shrivastava, A. Huff, and J. Dutton, eds., *Advances in Strategic Management*, Vol. 8 (Greenwich, CT: JAI Press, Inc., 1992), 391-408.

		Differentiation Position	
		Low	*High*
Cost Position	*Low*	Pure cost strategy (ROI = 28.6%)	Cost and differentiation strategies (ROI = 30.2%)
	High	No competitive advantage (ROI = 4.9%)	Pure differentiation strategy (ROI = 22.1%)

Figure 13.1 Generic Business Strategies and ROI

Lastly, the generic low cost and differentiation business-unit strategies are actually the result of functional substrategies, or components, as Figure 13.2 shows. In recent years there has been a growing recognition that time (response time, speed, cycle time, etc.) has emerged as an important source of competitive advantage and, therefore, an important strategy component. Timing can clearly be a source of differentiation, and can affect costs through learning effects and labor costs.

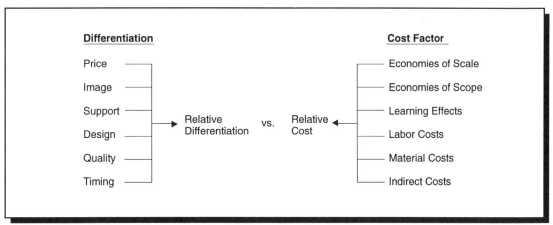

Figure 13.2 Generic Strategy Components

Strategies of Differentiation

Mintzberg, in evaluating Porter's framework, suggests that cost leadership is not really a competitive strategy, but is more a comparative advantage that makes a different strategy—*price differentiation*—possible. What attracts customers is the price, not the producer's cost position. Following this line of reasoning, Porter's cost leadership and differentiation strategies become one strategy—differentiation.[17]

Numerous examples of organizations attempting to distinguish themselves in the competitive marketplace exist. Maytag's investment in quality, resulting in products that last longer and need less service (thus, the lonely Maytag repairman) comes to mind. Upon closer examination, seven strategies of differentiation exist.

Price Differentiation. The most basic way to differentiate a product or service is to charge less for it than competitors do. This is often the major source of differentiation in commodity markets, where products are not differentiated in any other way.

Image Differentiation. Sometimes, differentiation can be created in the mind of the customer, even if no real basis for differentiation exists. Marketing and advertising attempt to create images of products to cause customers to want to buy those products. A few years ago, Smirnoff vodka raised its prices, enhancing its image as a premium product. The mystique behind Coors beer, Corona beer, and Chivas Regal scotch involves image differentiation, as does the branding of oranges as Sunkist and bananas as Chiquita. Cosmetic features and packaging, as well as many other real and perceived differences, can contribute to a product's image—both negatively and positively.

Support Differentiation. This type of differentiation attempts to set the product or service apart by offering something in addition to the basic purchase. That may be selling-related (credit, delivery, free assembly), service-related (free return policy, extended warranties, free repair), or inclusion of a complementary product or service (free lessons, a users' association, and the like).

Design Differentiation. Here we refer to "true" differentiation—the product or service is different from competitors by design. The differences can be minor or cosmetic (as designer jeans) or major (e.g., instant cameras).

---

[17] Mintzberg, "Generic Strategies," 14.

Quality Differentiation. Quality variations have to do with features of the product that make it "better"; no different by design, but better. Thus, the product can be essentially the same as competing products, but may possess greater reliability, durability, and/or superior performance.

Timing Differentiation. Being a market pioneer, an early entrant, or first-to-market with a product or service is an obvious source of differentiation.

Undifferentiated Products. The lack of differentiation is also a strategy, whether by choice or circumstance. Commodity products are by definition undifferentiated, as are "generic" products, medicines, and the like. The "copycat" strategy falls into this category, even though many businesses try to differentiate themselves in other ways even in commodity markets.

For example, observers have said that many products have become more commodity-like as the customer-perceived differentiation between different brands has declined. Brands of appliances, TVs, and other products seem to mean less to people than they once did. Some have suggested that personal computers have become more commodity-like, as well. However, results of a McKinsey & Co. study shows that brand name is still important to PC buyers, ranking second only to performance in importance (price ranks fifth). The brand image study shows the amount of premium buyers say they will pay or discount they would need to buy a certain brand:[18]

Brand	Premium	Brand	Discount
IBM	$295	Zeos	$15
Compaq	232	NEC	44
Apple	195	Everex	47
Digital	129	Packard Bell	69
AST	107		
Dell	92		
Hewlett-Packard	76		

Lastly, it is worth mentioning that differentiation strategies are often related to functional-level strategies. For example, price, image, support, design, and quality differentiation strategies are all rooted in some functional area. The source of these differences usually emanates from strategies in design, proc-

---

[18] Kyle Pope, "Computers: They're No Commodity," *The Wall Street Journal* (October 15, 1993), B1.

essing, sourcing, delivery, or support areas of the business. Supporting functional strategies are discussed further in another module.[19]

Looking more closely at timing as a strategy, recent studies have shown that first-mover or pioneer status may or may not result in sustainable advantages because of a combination of forces, as depicted in Figure 13.3. Each of the factors must be assessed to determine the overall desirability (if any) of being the pioneer, or first-mover. Other studies have yielded interesting results; for example, for industrial products, success is higher when a new product is launched during the introduction or growth stage of the product life cycle, and lower when launched during the maturity stage. Also, success tends to be lower for first and second entrants, higher for third and fourth, and lower for fifth and later entrants. What do these results suggest? First, entering *relatively* early is good (introductory or growth stage). Second, however, rushing a product to market too early (first or second entrants) or waiting too long will lower payback.[20] But in general, businesses that enter markets early tend to outperform later entrants.[21] First-mover advantages tend to arise from three primary sources:

1. *Technological leadership.* If a firm is able to build a favorable position on the experience curve and/or through patent or R&D success, it may be able to gain advantage through sustainable leadership in technology.
2. *Preemption of assets.* If the first-mover firm can preempt rivals in the acquisition of scarce assets (e.g., purchasing input factors at temporarily low prices, acquisition of desirable geographical and market segment locations, and preemptive investment in plant and equipment), it may gain advantage.
3. *Buyer switching costs.* Later entrants must invest extra resources to attract customers from the first-mover firm, and buyers often tend to stick with the first supplier that meets their needs satisfactorily.[22]

Other studies also confirm the above findings, that pioneers tend to have substantially larger market shares, even after a market has matured. Therefore, late entrants should recognize that the odds are against their receiving a large market share, and a niche strategy should be given serious consideration. Pio-

---

[19] Mintzberg, "Generic Strategies," 17-21.

[20] Gary L. Lilien and Eunsang Yoon, "The Timing of Competitive Market Entry," *Management Science*, 36, No. 5 (May 1990), 574.

[21] Mary Lambkin, "Order of Entry and Performance in New Markets," *Strategic Management Journal*, 9, special issue (Summer 1988), 127.

[22] M.B. Lieberman and D.B. Montgomery, "First Mover Advantages," *Strategic Management Journal*, 9, special issue (Summer 1988), 41.

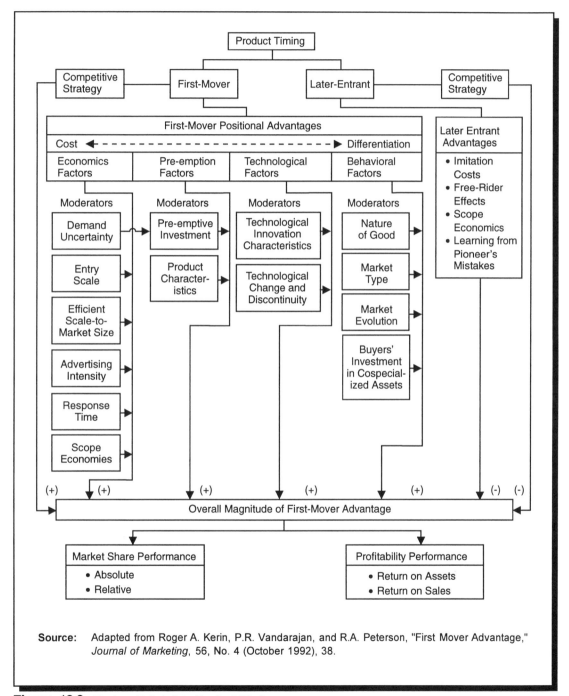

Figure 13.3 **Factors Related to Product Timing**

neers should continue to defend their position against late entrants through product-line extensions.[23]

Strategies of Scope

Strategies of differentiation identify what is distinct about a business's products and services in the marketplace. The orientation is toward the product and adopts the perspective of the customer, since differentiation has to be perceived by the customer to have any effect. Another set of strategies adopts the perspective of the producer, focusing on the served market. These latter strategies—strategies of scope—identify the markets the business is pursuing, as perceived by management. Scope (or focus, in Porter's terminology) pertains to market definition; how the business perceives its markets. Scope is related to market segmentation (in reality, segmentation is one aspect of the scope strategy of a business). As part of scope, segmentation refers to the business's approach to its markets; how it targets its various *types* of products to its markets. Differentiation, on the other hand, refers to distinctive product *characteristics*.[24]

Unsegmented Strategy. In the unsegmented approach, the business views the market as one large segment; a mass market of basically homogeneous buyers buying the same product. Typical of this approach would be general products, promoted by general advertising, and sold through mass merchandisers. An example is the brewing industry, particularly before the changes introduced by Philip Morris via its Miller division. The trend today is clearly away from unsegmented market strategies.

In recent years, U.S. markets have been undergoing a trend to extremes, or polarization. We see full service versus no service, top-of-the-line versus discount products, global versus local markets, and the like. Targeting one's products at the middle or average may miss both extremes, as Sears found out several years ago. The retailer was squeezed from above and below, with little distinctive competence or clear image.

Segmentation Strategy. In reality, segmentation is a continuous variable ranging—on the one hand—from very little segmentation (essentially unsegmented markets) to almost complete segmentation (customized products). Whatever the degree of segmentation, a business can choose to be *comprehensive*, attempting to serve all segments, or *selective*, carefully targeting only certain segments. De-

---

[23] W.T. Robinson and Claes Fornell, *"Market Pioneering and Sustainable Market Share Advantages,"* PIMS Letter No. 39 (Cambridge, MA: Strategic Planning Institute, 1986), 3-6.

[24] Mintzberg, "Generic Strategies," 25.

partment stores are an example of the comprehensive approach, offering a complete line of products, grouped by department. Another example is General Motors in automobiles, offering a product in every price range, size, and category. Companies pursuing selective segmentation would include Deere & Co. in tractors, targeting the large equipment market. Mercedes-Benz and BMW would be other examples, concentrating only on certain segments of the market.

Niche Strategies. Businesses that focus only on a single segment of the market are pursuing specialization or *niche* strategies. Porter's focus strategy is in one sense a niche strategy. An organization can specialize in a variety of ways—by product type, by type of customer or channel, by geographical area, or by function (such as oil exploration).[25] In general, then, a niche is a relatively small segment of a market, such as luxury automobiles, sports cars, specialty beers, generic products, no-frills airlines, limited geographical areas, and the like. Wal-Mart discount stores and InaCom computer stores both got their start pursuing market niches; they both focused on relatively small communities. George Mason University concentrates on two academic niches—conservative economics and information technology, and one athletic niche—basketball.[26]

A business should try either to be big, or focus on niches in the market. If the latter, the firm should always try to dominate the niche, whatever it is. However, a niche doesn't last forever; if the niche is growing, it will attract big competitors with superior resources, as Apple learned when IBM entered the PC market. It may be advisable for a firm to sell out if its niche or niches are growing too large.[27]

Guerrilla Warfare Strategies. In one light, niche strategies (pursuing a segment of the market small enough to defend) are the business equivalent of guerrilla warfare. Guerrilla warfare is often the only effective strategy for small, counterinsurgency movements. This approach is also appropriate for small, aggressive businesses that do not have the resources to slug it out head-to-head with the large competitors. The guerrilla's defensible niche could be geographic, or exceptional service, or some other aspect that a larger company may find difficult—or uneconomical—to attack. According to Columbia's Kathryn Harrigan, Rolls-Royce pursues a guerrilla/niche strategy in dominating the ultraluxury segment of the auto market.

---

[25] Mintzberg, "Generic Strategies," 29.

[26] Kae H. Chung, *Management: Critical Success Factors* (Boston, MA: Allyn and Bacon, 1987), 202.

[27] Kami, *Strategic Planning*.

For guerrilla strategies to be successful, several precepts are important:

1. *Choose a defensible guerrilla base.* Choose specialized marketplaces, ignored customers, offer customized, differentiated products, excellent service, and the like—all in areas that larger competitors are not likely to offer.
2. *Keep the base secure.* Focus on a limited span of activities geared to your base.
3. *Divert the enemy from your base.* Distract competitors with diversionary tactics, secondary product lines, and the like.
4. *Surprise the enemy.* Fall back, retreat, then turn and fight when competitors least expect it.
5. *Outwit the enemy.* Analyze market changes and move to capture new segments or niches before competitors realize that changes are taking place.
6. *Control information.* Again, use smokescreens, rumors, and disinformation to distract and confuse competitors.
7. *Build and sustain a strong corporate culture.* Take pains to maintain and reinforce your corporate values, which are different from those of your large competitors.[28]

Customizing Strategies. Finally, a business can pursue the ultimate in segmentation; products or services oriented to a single customer. In effect, each customer represents a unique market segment. Again, degrees of customization exist in actuality, ranging from pure customization through tailored customization to standardized customization. Examples of pure customization would be the architecturally designed house and any special project.

In tailored customization (sometimes called "mass customization"), a basic design is adapted to meet a customer's needs or specifications, such as a tailored suit or the typical custom-built house. In standardized customization, individualized end products are assembled from standard components. Thus, the product is customized, but from a limited set of choices or options.[29] Examples would include ordering a hamburger at Wendy's to selecting carpeting, fixtures, and wall covering for the typical tract house.

INCREASING SCOPE: STRATEGIES FOR GROWTH

The third business-level strategy area deals with strategies for increasing the scope of the business; ways to develop and extend the core mission of the busi-

---

[28] Kathryn R. Harrigan, "Guerrilla Strategies for Underdog Competitors," *Planning Review*, 14, No. 6 (November/December 1986), 4-12.

[29] Mintzberg, "Generic Strategies," 30-31.

ness. A core business can be elaborated in a number of ways, as shown in Figure 13.4. The organization can choose to expand with existing products in existing markets through *penetration* strategies, or in new markets via *market development* strategies. It can also choose to introduce new products in existing markets via *product development* strategies, or in new markets through *business development*.

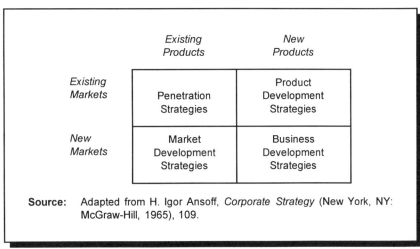

Source: Adapted from H. Igor Ansoff, *Corporate Strategy* (New York, NY: McGraw-Hill, 1965), 109.

Figure 13.4   Strategies for Increasing Scope

Actually, increasing the scope of a business is one path to growth for a firm. As Figure 13.5 shows, there are two major growth paths; expansion into existing businesses and diversification into new businesses. Expansion of existing businesses can take the form of vertical integration (expanding the value chain or positioning of the core business) and increasing the scope of the business. As was shown in Figure 13.4, changes in scope can occur through penetration, product development, and market development strategies (business development, along with vertical integration and diversification go beyond increasing the scope of—or growing—the core business, and are discussed in another module).

Penetration Strategies

Penetration strategies involve attempts to achieve a greater share of existing product sales in existing markets. This can be done by expansion, in essence taking share from existing competitors, or by taking over or acquiring all or part of a competing business. A firm must be careful not to merely attempt to "buy market share," because the real source of *profitable* growth in market share is sustainable competitive advantage—not just expansion.

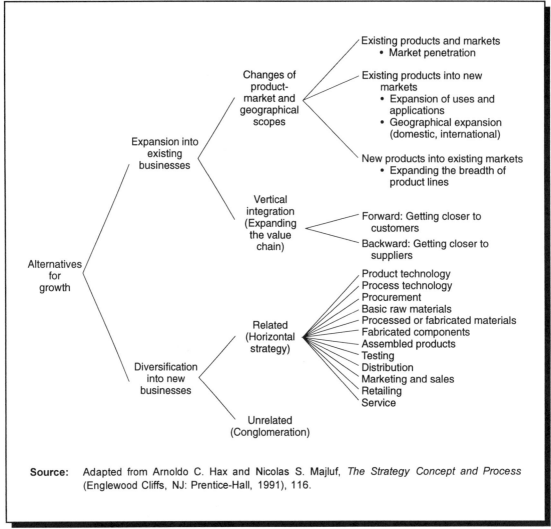

Figure 13.5 has the following structure:

Alternatives for growth

- **Expansion into existing businesses**
  - **Changes of product-market and geographical scopes**
    - Existing products and markets
      - Market penetration
    - Existing products into new markets
      - Expansion of uses and applications
      - Geographical expansion (domestic, international)
    - New products into existing markets
      - Expanding the breadth of product lines
  - **Vertical integration (Expanding the value chain)**
    - Forward: Getting closer to customers
    - Backward: Getting closer to suppliers
- **Diversification into new businesses**
  - **Related (Horizontal strategy)**
    - Product technology
    - Process technology
    - Procurement
    - Basic raw materials
    - Processed or fabricated materials
    - Fabricated components
    - Assembled products
    - Testing
    - Distribution
    - Marketing and sales
    - Retailing
    - Service
  - **Unrelated (Conglomeration)**

Source: Adapted from Arnoldo C. Hax and Nicolas S. Majluf, *The Strategy Concept and Process* (Englewood Cliffs, NJ: Prentice-Hall, 1991), 116.

Figure 13.5 Alternatives for Growth; Expansion and Diversification

Growth is a prime goal for most firms and businesses. Many compensation plans reward managers not only for profits but also for growth and increases in market share. But the product life-cycle curve shows that it is relatively easy to grow during the "growth" stage (although increasing market share may not be as easy), and that growth *and* share increases are much more difficult to achieve in the maturity and decline stages. However, growth can be *managed* by portfolio decisions at the corporate level: start up or acquire growth businesses and divest declining businesses. At the business-unit level, that luxury does not exist. Growth and share building must occur *within* a given business and industry.

What opportunities for growth and share building exist in the various life-cycle stages?

Share-building strategies are intended to strengthen the competitive position of the business. But such changes require heavy investment—investments far above those made by the typical firm in the industry. Therefore, access to capital (internally or from outside) is typically required. In addition, certain life-cycle stages are more likely to result in significant changes in share than are others. For example, the shakeout stage typically reduces the number of competitors, as does the decline stage, allowing others to pick up share. Also, different factors are more important in determining competitive strength in different stages. Early stages reward product design, quality, positioning, and availability; shakeout and later stages reward segmentation, service, pricing, and distribution. Thus, in the absence of merger-induced growth in share, the firm needs major advantages over competition to increase share, unless a competitor makes a strategic error.

Growth strategies, in turn, do not necessarily attempt significant gains in share, but try to enable the business to grow at least as fast as the market is growing—especially in the market's growth stage. Such strategies also require adequate resources to match market growth (and provide a defense against potential shakeout), as well as other weapons to continue growth in the latter stages of the market life cycle.

Managed Growth. Growth must be managed—a firm must have a strategy specifying *how rapidly* it plans to grow. Unmanaged growth can destroy a firm just as wildly growing cancer cells can destroy the body. A company must consolidate its gains to support future growth, just as the stock market needs to "back and fill" from time to time, even in a bull market. The question of how fast a business or company should grow depends on whether future profitability (such as return on equity—ROE) is greater or less than the cost of capital required to support the growth. If ROE can be expected to exceed the cost of capital, the more growth the business can achieve, the better. If, on the other hand, ROE is likely to be less than the cost of capital, financing additional growth does not make sense; it costs more than it returns. If a business in this position cannot sufficiently improve its profitability, it should reduce its size (perhaps by divesting low-profit businesses).[30]

Assuming that the business recognizes its long-term versus short-term growth potential, what are some specific approaches that can contribute to growth and share building in its markets? Research by Buzzell and Wiersema has shown that gains in market share are associated with improvements in product quality, new-product introductions, and marketing budget increases, but price reductions

[30] W.E. Fruhan, Jr., "How Fast Should Your Company Grow?" *Harvard Business Review*, 62, No. 1 (January/February 1984), 84.

seldom are used as a means for building share. Further, businesses with "high" market shares tend to lose share over time, while those with "low" share tend to gain.[31]

Growth through Franchising. Innovative companies, as they review their competitive position, may find themselves the worried owners of businesses with low market share. As they consider the strategies suggested to improve the situation, they are faced with the knowledge that to make a substantial change in their position as a follower in a high-growth industry, they must consider the dilemma of increasing market share while satisfying resource constraints. For firms requiring widespread outlets and convenient availability of service and production, one viable option is to create a franchise system. Franchising offers a company access to capital investment at little risk, as well as offering cost sharing, economies of scale due to increased size, motivated management, and widespread brand identification. The successful franchisor can then remain strictly in franchising, buy up the franchises as they become available to develop a wholly owned chain of company stores, or practice a combination strategy.[32]

Product Development Strategies

Unlike penetration strategies, product development strategies attempt to increase the scope of the business by bringing out new products within existing markets. One way of doing this is through a *product extension* strategy, which consists of offering new or modified products in the same basic business. Another approach is to engage in *product line proliferation*—virtually complete coverage of a given line of products. Again, this approach is related to market segmentation, intending to end up with comprehensive product segmentation (as with General Motors in automobiles). A variation of this strategy involves product line fortification, or attempts to fill voids in existing product lines, in effect preempting competitors' moves to do so.[33]

Preemptive Strategies. A preemptive strategy is one that attempts to disrupt the "normal" course of industry events and in the process change the rules—to create new industry conditions to the disadvantage of the competition. It is defined as "a major move by a focal business, ahead of moves by its adversaries, that allows it to secure an advantageous position from which it will be difficult

---

[31] R.D. Buzzell and R.D. Wiersema, "Successful Share-Building Strategies," *Harvard Business Review*, 59, No. 1 (January/February 1981), 135.

[32] Pat Feltes and L.A. Digman, "Franchising as a Share Building Strategy," *Proceedings of Midwest American Institute for Decision Sciences Meeting* (April 1986).

[33] Mintzberg, "Generic Strategies," 37-38.

to dislodge because of the advantages it has captured by being the first mover."[34]

An example of a preemptive move was Goodyear's decision to expand its capacity ahead of industry demand, hoping to gain market share by discouraging competitors from expanding. Another example of a preemptive move was Philip Morris' decision to segment the beer market and apply its advanced marketing skills to this formerly tradition-bound industry with its Miller brand. In the process, it changed the industry, forcing the industry to play by a new set of rules. With airline deregulation, the opportunity existed for new competitors to enter with new ways of operating. Early entrants, such as Southwest and expansion by others, preempted such moves by existing or potential competitors. Other examples involve introducing products before the competition, gaining early acceptance by customers, and perhaps even temporary monopolies. Polaroid, Frigidaire, Xerox, Hoover, and Kleenex were so successful at this that their brand names became synonymous with the product.

Preemptive Opportunities and Characteristics. There are several characteristics of preemptive strategies to keep in mind. First, they entail a degree of risk, as in game theory, since the strategist is making assumptions, which may not be correct, about the resulting behavior of competitors. Second, preemptive moves need not affect *all* competitors or their actions, only the major ones—enough to make a significant difference. Third, the results of preemptive moves are not permanent, and competitors will eventually respond. A good example of this is the brewing industry, where Anheuser-Busch changed its tactics in response to Miller's marketing strategies, and came back a much stronger competitor.[35]

Actually, preemptive strategies are not confined to direct moves against the competition. Opportunities exist along the entire product chain from raw material supply sources to distribution and service after the sale, as shown in Table 13.1. In addition, opportunities for preemption occur at all stages of the life cycle, from preintroduction to decline.[36]

Contrarian Preemptive Strategies. The best time to expand may be when the market is temporarily in decline, as long as the competition is cutting back. For example, recession may be the best time for businesses to pick up market share. During recessions, firms, particularly weaker competitors, often cut back. A recent study showed that the average surviving industrial business picks up 0.63 percent of share in recessions, and loses 0.10 percent during expansionary times (when new competitors arrive and competition expands, as well). Signifi-

---

[34] Ian C. MacMillan, "Preemptive Strategies," in *Handbook of Business Strategy*, ed. W.D. Guth (Boston, MA: Warren, Gorham & Lamont, 1985), 9-2.

[35] *Ibid.*

[36] *Ibid.*, 9-18.

Table 13.1 Sources of Preemptive Opportunities

Supply Systems

1. Secure access to raw materials or components.
2. Preempting production equipment.
3. Dominating supply logistics.

Product

1. Introducing new product lines.
2. Developing dominant design.
3. Positioning.
4. Securing accelerated approval from agencies.
5. Securing product development and delivery skills.
6. Expanding scope of the product.

Production Systems

1. Proprietary processes.
2. Aggressive capacity expansion.
3. Vertical integration with key suppliers.
4. Securing scarce and critical production skills.

Customers

1. Segmentation.
2. Building early brand awareness.
3. Training customers in usage skills.
4. Capturing key accounts.

Distribution and Service Systems

1. Occupation of prime locations.
2. Preferential access to key distributors.
3. Dominance of distribution logistics.
4. Access to superior service capabilities.
5. Development of distributor skills.

Source: Ian C. MacMillan, "Preemptive Strategies," in *Handbook of Business Strategy*, ed. W.D. Guth (Boston, MA: Warren, Gorham & Lamont, 1985), 9-9. Reprinted with permission. All rights reserved.

cant share gainers during recessions were those firms that increased their advertising by 28 percent or more, which resulted in a 1.5 percent increase in share. Big increases in advertising in normal or fast-growth periods, however, yielded only a 0.2 percent increase in share.[37]

Market Development Strategies

Market development strategies are attempts to promote existing products in new markets, in effect broadening the scope of the business by finding new market segments or new channels.[38] An example might be a manufacturer of brand name products agreeing to produce store-brand products. One particularly successful market development strategy is to enter "emerging" markets or industries.

Emerging industries are either newly formed or are industries reformed, as a result of technological change, changes in consumer needs, changes in cost structures, or similar factors. As Intel's Robert Noyce stated, get into unpopulated or underpopulated industries and markets if you want to grow.[39] One way (perhaps the most obvious way) to do this is to enter the market earlier than do competing firms, ideally in the embryonic or early growth stage.

Another way is through segmentation or reformulation. Most of the businesses achieving major gains in market share do so by focusing their efforts on selected segments—often segments that were relatively small at first. Philip Morris offers two examples: Merit cigarettes and Lite beer. Merit concentrated on a high-growth segment of a declining industry, and brought with it high growth. Lite beer did the same. In fact, one might conclude that such segments actually are new subindustries with their own life cycles. Creating or discovering such a segment enables the business to avoid often self-defeating attempts to gain share and growth in the perhaps mature or declining broader market. Other examples include Honda motorcycles, compact cars, fast-food restaurants, and other niches or segments that follow the characteristics of emerging markets and may be early in their life cycles.

Geographical Expansion Strategies

Geographical expansion is actually a form of market development which takes an existing product line to new geographical areas. Growth can come through geographic expansion—international or domestic. Philip Morris, Coca-Cola, and

---

[37] "Marketing . . . When to Gain Market Share," *The Wall Street Journal* (July 8, 1982), 17.

[38] Mintzberg, "Generic Strategies," 35.

[39] "Intel: The Microprocessor Champ Gambles on Another Leap Forward," *Business Week* (April 18, 1980), 92.

Pepsi achieved significant growth by expanding into countries where demand for their products was not as saturated as it was in the domestic market. Overseas, these firms were early in the market life cycle. The geographical growth strategies employed domestically by the makers of J&B and Cutty Sark scotches provide an interesting contrast. Cutty Sark went nationwide early and became the top-selling brand. J&B's parent, Paddington Corp., having fewer resources, meanwhile followed a different method—an "enclave" approach. Just as an army establishes a beachhead and branches out from there, J&B first concentrated on the New York market. In a short time, J&B—through intensive marketing— became the number 1 seller in New York with 40 percent of the market. Next, it concentrated on Chicago, then on the West Coast. In time, J&B, with its intensive, concentrated approach, overtook Cutty Sark, market area by market area. A similar approach was employed successfully by Vlasic Pickles. For firms not hampered by limited capacity or resources, the reverse approach may be best, as the Japanese have shown by entering domestic and foreign markets simultaneously.

Combined Factors

Successful share-building strategies often involve a combination of several competitive factors. Typically, better results are achieved by using a balanced, consistent marketing program or a mix of strategic factors. Buzzell and Wiersema have cited L'eggs pantyhose as an example. Hanes used a combined approach when it introduced L'eggs in 1971. Heavy advertising and promotion speeded up customer trial of the product. This facilitated acceptance by retailers. And direct distribution ensured that L'eggs seldom would be out of stock, allowing customers to develop repeat buying routines.[40]

STRATEGIES FOR REDEFINING AND REDUCING SCOPE

A quick glance at the product life-cycle curve yields an obvious conclusion: not all firms and businesses can be in growth markets. Additionally, the maturity and decline stages are often much longer than the growth phase. Therefore, a firm must face the possibility that many of its business units are likely to be in limited growth or even decline at any given time. How should firms handle this situation? What should their strategies be? While "growth" sounds more exciting than maturity, don't forget that profits and cash flow are greater during the maturity phase than in any other stage; even in the aging and decline phase profits and cash flows often equal or exceed those of the growth stage. In fact, recent

---

[40] Buzzell and Wiersema, "Successful Share-Building Strategies," 143.

research has shown that mature businesses that actively invested in highly differentiated positions, low-cost operations, or defensible niches performed significantly better than did those attempting to milk such businesses for diversification funds. In fact, the industry leaders produced *better* results than did the leaders in rapidly growing high-technology fields.[41]

The thirty years following World War II are often referred to as the golden years of economic growth. Not since the Industrial Revolution of the late 1800s had the United States seen such growth in the number and scope of businesses. With the booming economy of the 1950s and 1960s came an emphasis on growth and expansion. The main concerns of businesses were capital investments, expanding market share, and increasing sales. A company whose annual report did not show significant growth from year to year was viewed as stagnant and a poor investment. The prosperity of the time lulled people into a belief that the good times would last forever, and there would never be any need to worry about a business decline.

The rapidly changing, hostile environment of the 1970s burst the public's idealistic bubble, and suddenly survival, not growth, was the key word to industry. The attitude that a business which could not survive was simply poorly managed disappeared quickly. Suddenly, business was faced with high interest rates, increasing raw-material costs, and skyrocketing energy costs. After nearly 30 years of prosperity, many managers were in a situation where they did not know what to do. Little research had been done on the retrenchment and turnaround strategies needed by many businesses in the slower growth environment. In addition, many found themselves with excess capacity, having built for growth that failed to materialize.

Thus, businesses need to be redefined and possibly reduced in scope under certain conditions, usually due to changes in the competitive or general environments. Redefining, or reconceiving, the business may also be required because some firms lose sight of their essence—their vision, their distinctive competencies and competitive advantages. The question then becomes one of how to recapture, rediscover, or recreate this essence. Mintzberg suggests that three approaches are possible:[42]

1. *Redefining the business.* This approach requires the firm to reconceive the business, to use innovative means to redefine markets, functions, or products—the very concept of the business—to gain a new competitive advantage. Redefinition strategies are essentially creative, designed to change the rules,

---

[41] W.K. Hall, "Survival Strategies in a Hostile Environment," *Harvard Business Review*, 58, No. 5 (September/October 1980), 75.

[42] Mintzberg, "Generic Strategies," 54-61.

as Timex did with watches, Miller for beer, and cable for television programming.

2. *Recombining businesses.* In certain instances, it may be advantageous to combine various activities, either within or between existing businesses, in order to create a new concept of market scope, or segmentation. 3M was early to define the "coating and bonding" business, and Procter & Gamble the "personal care" industry. The recombination must exist in more than name only; critics question whether there ever was a " transportation" business.

3. *Relocating the core.* As changes in the industry, the business, and its strategic position take place, the firm may need to change the "center of gravity," or position in the stream, of the business. The business can be shifted further upstream or downstream, can change the relative emphasis of functions, or make relocation changes in conjunction with moves to redefine and recombine the business as described above.

In examining situations warranting scope redefinition and reduction actions, it is helpful to think in terms of defense and renewal strategies, retrenchment and turnaround strategies, and "endgame" strategies. These concepts are discussed in the remaining sections of this module.

Defense and Renewal Strategies

The further a firm progresses in the product/market life cycle, the more important defensive strategies become. There is less margin for error, and improvements in performance are likely to be incremental, rather than dramatic, as they were in the earlier stages. Put another way, businesses in mature markets may find the risk/reward ratio from a bold action less favorable than it was in earlier stages. Market-share improvements tend to be won in the trenches, by hard work and attention to detail day after day and year after year.

A serious strategic or even tactical error can cause hard-earned ground to be quickly lost, and it may take years to recover. For example, Schlitz switched to lower-cost ingredients for its beer in the 1970s, causing a rapid loss of market share. The company quickly corrected its mistake, but was never able to regain its sales even though some industry experts felt that their subsequent product was superior to the competition. In this context, the easiest and cheapest way to increase market share is through the mistakes of competitors. Thus, the patient firm that does not become overanxious and overambitious will likely be the long-term beneficiary, particularly in mature markets.

The maturity phase is also an opportune time for actions that may renew or revive the products and services of the business. Such actions can include product innovations, new technologies, service and distribution innovations, process innovations, management improvements, and the like, and may even serve to put the industry or a segment on a new growth curve. An obvious example of this was the creation of the fast-food segment of the already mature restaurant industry.

Segmentation Tactics. Numerous experts prescribe differentiation strategies for businesses in mature industries. One way to achieve differentiation is by segmenting the market in some productive way, such as by appealing to singles, Generation X, or the elderly, for example. Often products or services can be repositioned to appeal to such defined segments. Another approach is using multiple branding to promote similar products to different customers, as the cigarette industry has done. In general, segmentation tends to create identifiable market niches, one or more of which may be pursued by the business.[43]

Quality Improvements. Another major competitive strategy for mature industries centers on quality. Improving the quality of the product or service can result in improved sales and market share. This can be done by product improvements or by building in additional features or services (such as delivery, on-time service, quick repair, extended warranties, and the like). Actions taken to enhance the product's image and reliability—such as Ford's "Quality is Job 1" campaign—are obvious examples.

Efficiency Improvements. Low-cost strategies are important in mature markets, especially if a business does not have a dominant position or a defensible niche. Economies of scale, purchasing, common interchangeable parts, selective consolidations of facilities, automation, and the like can contribute to efficiency and lower costs.[44]

Defensive Responses. Suppose, however, that a new competitor is contemplating entering "your" market, such as McDonald's pizza entry. If you are Pizza Hut, for example, what should your response be? Table 13.2 lists guides to response actions, depending upon your level of competitive advantage and the new entrant's scale economies plus its access to resources. The aggressiveness of the retaliation depends upon the relative strength of the pioneer and the new entrant in both the product/market domain where entry is anticipated and in other product/market domains. The pioneer should respond in those product/market domains where it is strongest relative to the newcomer, which may not be in the newly-entered markets.

[43] R.G. Wilson, "Competitive Business Strategies," in *Handbook of Business Strategy*, ed. W.D. Guth (Boston, MA: Warren, Gorham & Lamont, 1985), 8-4.

[44] *Ibid.*, 8-7.

Table 13.2 Responses to New Entrants

	Your Response Action		
	Retaliate	*Accommo-date Entrant*	*Abandon Market*
Your Competitive Advantage	Clear Advantage	Equal	Inferior
Entrant's Scale Economies	Lower	Equal	Greater
Entrant's Resources	Inferior	Equal	Superior

Source: Adapted from Thomas S. Robertson and Hubert Gatignon, "How Innovators Thwart New Entrants Into Their Market," *Planning Review*, 19, No. 5. (September/October 1991), 7.

Retrenchment and Turnaround Strategies

Chrysler's recent turnaround is familiar to all and has made a folk hero of its architect, former CEO Lee Iacocca. Other more recent but less spectacular turnarounds were staged by Ford and Peugeot in automobiles, and Control Data in computers. Turnaround strategies are attempts to arrest and reverse the decline of a business. As in the case of Chrysler, reasons for the decline can be external (recessions, declining demand, competitive pressures, and the like), internal (largely mismanagement and poor planning), or both. Successful turnaround strategies typically have short- and long-term aspects, but the short term is clearly the most important in survival situations such as Chrysler's. Why? Because if the short-term actions fail, *there will be no long-term*—the survival of the business is at stake. Without this clear realization, turnaround strategies are not likely to succeed. In fact, actions may be required that are clearly detrimental in the long run. Without them, however, the firm may not exist to reap any long-term benefits.

Retrenchment Actions. The best turnaround is the one that does not have to happen; prevention is a lot better than the cure. On a personal basis, it is obviously better for an individual to exercise and follow a proper diet than to have coronary bypass surgery. The business that watches its general and competitive environments, thinks strategically, and regularly examines and redirects its use of resources is not likely to find itself needing a turnaround. The business has made a regular practice of controlling its resources and retrenching regularly.

Retrenchment involves defensive actions taken when the market is saturated or in actual decline, when the company is in financial or other trouble, or during recessions. During the 1980-83 recession, for example, Chrysler shrank (retrenched) in size to the extent that its break-even point was half of what it was before survival actions were taken, and also sold its profitable tank business. Chrysler used a retrenchment strategy and selective shrinking as part of its survival and turnaround actions. Braniff, on the other hand, was not so adept at retrenchment actions, and was forced to cease operations in 1982.

Retrenchment actions in some ways are the reverse of strategies for increasing scope. A negative penetration strategy, for example, would amount to *contraction*—cutting back on investment or service to reduce its commitment to a certain market and/or product. The opposite of a product development strategy is *product line rationalization*—actions taken to simplify or even eliminate a particular product line to get rid of unprofitable excesses or overlaps. The inverse of a market development strategy obviously involves *market contraction*, or reducing the number of segments. Again, the goal here is to periodically purge the excesses gained from proliferating market segments.[45] In reality, many organizations analyze and take actions to redefine and reduce business scope at the same time they are increasing scope in other areas.

Warning Signals. What are some of the danger signals that indicate impending trouble? John Harris of Booz Allen & Hamilton offers 12 danger signals that are remarkably similar for both industries and companies. Companies that are in turnaround situations typically exhibit one or more of the following characteristics.

1. *Decreasing market share.* This is perhaps the most telling signal of a major problem. It may be masked temporarily by sales increases due to market growth or inflation. However, the company's competitive position is eroding, portending future trouble.
2. *Declining constant dollar sales.* Inflation-adjusted declines in sales in comparison to industry criteria (such as sales per square foot of retail space) indicate trouble.
3. *Decreasing profitability.* This can show up as lower dollar profits, lower return on sales or investment, or similar measures.
4. *Increasing reliance on debt.* A substantial rise in debt or the debt-to-equity ratio, or a lowered credit rating can cause significant problems.
5. *Restricted dividend policies*, such as lowered or eliminated dividends. Do not confuse this with actions taken to effect a turnaround, however, once the need is recognized.

---

[45] Mintzberg, "Generic Strategies," 34-38.

6. *Inadequate reinvestment in the business.* Adequate reinvestment in plant, equipment, and maintenance is required for a business to remain competitive. Deferral indicates that the company is mortgaging its future for the short-term.

7. *Proliferation of new ventures.* Such actions, if done while ignoring the basic business, may be attempts to cover up problems and a search for a bailout. Diversification should supplement, not replace, the basic business of the firm.

8. *Lack of planning.* Unplanned growth or inattention to environmental changes and strategy is sure to create problems.

9. *CEO resistant to the ideas of others.*

10. *Management succession problems.*

11. *An overly passive board.*

12. *Inbred management.* Management that feels nothing can be learned from outsiders, professional conferences, competitors, and the like is headed for trouble.[46]

Action is Needed. While such danger signals may be present, they are valuable only if recognized and acted on. Many firms ignore such signals until it may be too late. Or management prevents action from being taken. At some point, however, the firm must face the music, and *someone* has to intervene and take charge. Once consensus has been achieved that trouble exists, the turnaround can begin. Figure 13.6 portrays actions typically required as part of a turnaround effort.

Extraordinary powers must be granted to those responsible for the turnaround. The "turnaround team" needs to select and focus on *one or two* activities offering the greatest opportunity to affect company performance. Singleness of purpose is crucial—the company cannot tolerate business as usual. The cause of the decline must be isolated, and corrective actions taken. In turnaround situations, achieving a positive cash flow, not profits, becomes all important. Profit-making, but cash-absorbing, assets may have to be sold to generate cash. In any event, cash outflows must be stopped in the short run, with a goal of restoring profitability as the next step. Curtailing investments and dividend payments are obvious ways to conserve cash. Others are price increases and cost and asset reduction programs.

Turnaround Options. Four major turnaround options exist. Depending on the firm's position in relation to its break-even point, the following actions may be taken:

---

[46] J.M. Harris, "Corporate Turnaround Strategy," in *The Strategic Management Handbook*, ed. K.J. Albert (New York, NY: McGraw-Hill, 1983), Chapter 20.

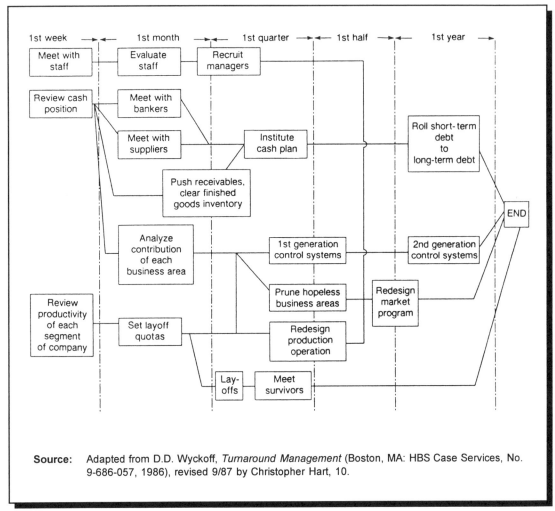

Figure 13.6 Schematic Diagram of a Turnaround Strategy

1. *Cost-cutting strategies.* If the firm has high direct labor costs, high fixed expenses, or is close to the break-even point, cost-cutting may be most appropriate. Such actions usually take effect relatively quickly.

2. *Asset-reduction strategies* may be needed if the firm is far from its break-even point, since there is no way to cut costs sufficiently. Assets or capacity unneeded in the next two years or so should be the first to go.

3. *Revenue-increasing strategies.* If the firm is close to covering its fixed costs and has low variable costs (such as direct labor costs), revenue increasing approaches such as price increases may be most beneficial. This option is an alternative to asset reduction strategies if the assets are likely to be

needed within the next year or two. Keep in mind that revenue-increasing strategies may not pay off as quickly as cost-cutting or asset-reduction approaches.

4. *Combination strategies.* If the firm is covering fixed costs but significantly below its break-even point, a combination of the previous three approaches may be most fruitful.[47]

Whatever action is pursued, the focus must be on short-term cash flow, while minimizing long-term damage. Whether or not a turnaround strategy is required, keeping a low break-even point should be considered essential for any business; therefore, periodic retrenchment may be warranted. Financial leverage can be increased by automation, such as the use of robotics or, in banking, automatic teller machines. Automation provides depreciation, which labor does not. From a human standpoint, it is better to have a thriving business with 30 percent fewer people, than a business with 100 percent fewer people because of bankruptcy.

However, one must keep a core of key, motivated, and talented people. Outsourcing all nonessential activities (such as janitorial, grounds keeping, maintenance, and the like) is one way to keep the organization lean. In addition, modern technology—such as shared data bases—can sometimes eliminate a whole layer of management. Honda Motors has only five levels of management, and the Roman Catholic Church with 1 billion members has only three; most large corporations have many more.[48]

In summary, firms would prefer never to have to use turnaround strategies. However, because of the dynamic nature of the environment in which firms must compete and mistakes on their part, they are sometimes forced to do so. The major factor causing a firm to use such strategies is declining demand. However, success is possible even in hostile environments, particularly if the firm can achieve the lowest delivered cost position and the highest product, service, and quality position in the industry. If possible, the firm should attempt to gain or defend a leadership position in the industry.

Strategies for Aging and Declining Markets

Aging and declining markets experience permanent (rather than temporary) declines in demand, for various reasons. An obvious current example is the cigarette industry (due to changing consumer habits), as is the Japanese aluminum

---

[47] C.W. Hofer and Dan Schendel, *Strategy Formulation: Analytical Concepts* (St. Paul, MN: West Publishing Company, 1978), 173.

[48] Kami, *Strategic Planning.*

industry (due to the high cost of producing electricity, critical to aluminum production).

One of the leading authors in strategies for declining businesses is Kathryn Rudie Harrigan of Columbia University. She uses the term *endgame* to describe the strategies businesses use in coping with declining demand. It is helpful to think of endgame as having rules, situations, strategies, and consequences.[49] Of course, in the real world, endgame—a condition of declining demand—is no mere "*game*" to the participants.

Characteristics of Declining Demand.

Before declining demand can be studied, it must first be defined and differentiated from temporarily sagging demand. It is a market condition in which demand will drop to and remain at a reduced level, or drop even lower. Sagging demand is a temporary dip in demand that will return to previous levels as soon as the condition causing the dip is gone. Declining demand necessitates retrenchment strategies.

Possibly the most important and most misunderstood aspect of endgame is: when does it start? History is littered with the stories of firms that folded or nearly folded because they failed to realize soon enough that they were playing in endgame. It is much easier for a company to take corrective measures early and avoid or minimize the effects of declining demand than it is to pick up the pieces after things are falling apart. One reason big firms realize too late that they are in endgame is that they can survive a long time before they feel its effects. Also, whether it is out of stubbornness or wishful thinking, many firms simply do not want to recognize that they are in a declining industry. But once a business has identified itself as being in endgame, it must decide whether or not it wants to "play." If the environment appears hostile, the company may decide to exit as quickly as possible and minimize its potential losses. Most businesses do not simply "jump ship" when things get rough. They stay in the fight and do everything possible to survive. It is the decision to stay in business and recover profits that creates the need for endgame strategies. But, again, recognizing whether declines in demand are permanent or temporary is fraught with the risk of error. For example, are farm products, agricultural equipment, beer, and liquor in a state of temporary or permanent decline? Such questions are of vital importance to dominant businesses in those industries, such as Deere & Company and Anheuser-Busch.

Endgame Strategies.

As in other areas of business strategy, there is no one absolute rule to follow in endgame. Industries are not homogeneous, and it would be impossible to come up with a contingency theory to handle every possible sit-

---

[49] K.R. Harrigan, "Strategic Planning for Endgame," *Long-Range Planning* (December 1982), 17-20.

uation. To further complicate matters, there may be several business strategies appropriate for a single firm experiencing declining demand. And what works for one firm may spell doom for another. In an attempt to conceptualize the strategies that firms seemed to follow in endgame, Harrigan has outlined five strategies.

1. Increase the investment (seek dominance).
2. Hold investment level.
3. Shrink selectively.
4. Milk the investment.
5. Divest now.[50]

Increase the Investment. The underlying theme behind this strategy is the firm's belief that enduring pockets of demand will remain, so the firm must reposition itself to serve these pockets. By reinvesting, the company is hoping to gain market dominance, becoming the market leader when demand stabilizes. Because of the additional investment involved, this is one of the riskier strategies in endgame, but it also offers the biggest rewards if it pays off.

Hold Investment Level. The hold-investment-level strategy means that a company is taking a defensive reinvestment position. It is interested in reinvesting only enough to maintain the level and tactics it has been following in the past. This strategy of matching competitors' price changes and marketing expenditures is a wait-and-see attitude designed to delay long enough to see whether the uncertainties of demand are resolved.[51]

A hold-investment-level strategy indicates that the firm is interested in remaining in the business, or that it is waiting for its exit barriers to lower so it can leave the industry in as orderly a manner as possible. The single-business firm is much more likely to use this strategy than is a multibusiness firm, since the alternative for the single-business firm is completely closing its doors, instead of shutting down one or more unprofitable divisions.

Shrink Selectively. A shrink selectively strategy is an attempt to reposition the firm within the industry. The objective is to identify the profitable market segments and then position the company and product to best serve this market niche. The firm is hoping to build a loyal customer relationship through some distinctive competence, either internal or external. Once a firm is serving this niche, it should try and raise barriers to entry, because, as the number of profitable niches decreases, there will be increased competition to serve the few profitable segments that remain.

[50] K.R. Harrigan, "Strategies for Declining Businesses" (Lexington, MA: D.C. Heath, 1980), 20-34.
[51] *Ibid.*

The three strategies mentioned so far—increase the investment, hold the investment level, and shrink selectively—all assume that there are still acceptable returns to be earned in endgame. Firms in endgame can be assumed to pursue aggressive strategies, since their additional investments will motivate them to protect their commitment to continued performance. It is only when acceptable returns on assets cannot be earned by remaining invested in the endgame that a company may wish to exit.

Milk the Investment. The idea behind a milk-the-investment strategy is to retrieve the value of earlier investments. This was commonly called a *harvest* strategy in the past.[52] Although participation in the industry still yields attractive cash flows, the firm has made a commitment to get out of the business as soon as: (1) the salvage value of its assets equals the expected value of cash flows generated, or (2) some other corporate criterion has been fulfilled.[53] Timing becomes critical with this strategy; the company drains its resources without regard for long-run positioning.

The objective of milking the investment is to either: (1) increase return on investment by surrendering market share; or (2) funnel as much cash as possible into other projects as quickly as possible.[54] The danger with this strategy comes from external or unforeseen forces inhibiting the planned actions of the company. An example of external factors would be customers or the government exerting pressure to keep the firm invested, even though the business is unprofitable.

Divest Now. Divest now is simply a get out strategy. The idea behind this strategy is, as the earning power of the endgame business shrinks, to sell off assets as quickly as possible before their value shrinks too much. Divesting can either be through the sale or simply the abandonment of assets; the decision often comes down to the depreciated worth of the assets.[55] In any event, the crucial element in divesting is timing. The longer a firm waits to divest, the greater the likely loss on assets. The ability to get rid of assets quickly supports the practice of keeping a flexible position and having a realistic assessment of the assets' salvage value.

Should a firm exit early? The advantage to early exit is that the firm will recover a substantial proportion of its cash, equivalent to the expected cash flows that would be realized from continued operation. An early exit often is motivated by fear and the belief that other strategies will not yield acceptable results. The disadvantage to early exit is that if the firm guessed wrong, it will have closed its doors to an industry that could yield very attractive profits in the future.

---

[52] *Ibid.*

[53] Harrigan, "Strategic Planning," 17-20.

[54] *Ibid.*

[55] Harrigan, *Strategies for Declining Businesses*, 20-34.

CONCLUSIONS

We have examined a number of business-level strategies, applicable primarily to single-business organizations or to an individual unit of a multibusiness or multimission organization. We grouped the strategic options into a framework consisting of several categories: strategies for positioning the business; distinguishing the business; increasing scope; redefining and reducing scope; and extending the core business (this latter category is discussed in another module as part of multibusiness strategies). Having delineated all these strategies, the question becomes when and under what conditions to use each? Research in this area is sketchy and uneven, but the body of strategic knowledge is steadily developing.

A note of caution is due, however, with regard to generic strategies. While a framework may help a firm see options more clearly, blind usage may put the business at a disadvantage vis-à-vis more creative competitors. If the use of generic approaches makes a firm's actions *predictable*, the strategy can be self-defeating. That is, predictable actions are easy to anticipate and relatively easy to defend against. For example, if a football team *always* runs the ball on "running downs"—such as 3rd and 2 yards to go—and *always* passes on "passing downs"—such as 3rd and 8 yards to go—the defending team has an easier task. Firms must have an element of unpredictability to their strategies, to keep the competition guessing and off guard. On the other hand, they need consistency to keep their strategic direction and focus.

Module
14

Strategies for
Global Competition

LEARNING OBJECTIVES

After completing Module 14, you should be able to:

1. Describe the differences between local, national, international, regional, multinational, global, and transnational business.
2. Discuss the primary means of entering international markets.
3. Define important global strategies.
4. Describe the major risks facing international business.

A few years ago, Coca-Cola found that it couldn't use the Chinese characters sounding like the product name because it would have translated into "bite the wax tadpole." In Taiwan, "Come Alive with the Pepsi Generation" translated into "Pepsi will bring your ancestors back from the dead." Coors tried to translate its slogan "Turn It Loose" into Spanish, only to find out that it came out as "Drink Coors and Get Diarrhea."[1] Needless to say, doing business in other cultures and languages creates unique problems.

In the U.S., many people subscribe to the "Buy American" philosophy. But, which product is "American?" Is it the Panasonic manufactured by U.S. workers in California; or the Zenith with parts from the Far East assembled in Mexico; or the RCA built with U.S. parts in a plant in Bloomington, Indiana owned by France's Thomson Consumer Electronics? Or, how about the town in New York that wanted to buy a Komatsu earth mover, but decided to buy a John Deere costing $15,000 more—only to learn that the Komatsu was built near Chicago by the Komatsu-Dresser joint venture, but the Deere was built by Hitachi in Japan?[2] There are a lot more examples; evidently, things have become more complex in today's "global" business environment.

PROFILE

USX Corp.

For years, U.S. Steel (now USX Corp.) dominated an oligopolistic industry with little foreign competition. In fact, the company continued to operate as if this were still the case long after it had become just another competitor in a rapidly changing international market.

J.P. Morgan put the company together in the early 1900s by merging ten companies to prevent Andrew Carnegie from expanding his steel empire. Put together for defensive purposes, the company maintained a centralized, autocratic climate for most of its history with a short-term focus. In recent years, however, problems have begun to surface. U.S. Steel's domestic market share dropped to less than 16 percent in 1982, down from over 50 percent earlier. Some of this was as a result of foreign competition; the firm was in a global market, and domestic market share became a meaningless statistic. Management reacted to changes and foreign competition defensively, pleading for government protection against imports. The company even mounted an advertising campaign against the Environmental Protection Agency.

---

[1] "In Chinese, Coca-Cola Means 'Bite the Wax Tadpole,'" *Omaha World-Herald* (July 11, 1994), 14.

[2] M. Carl Johnson, Jr. and Craig R. Johnson, "Ten Myths Used to Blame Japan for American Problems," *JETRO Monitor*, 7, No. 7 (October 1992), 3.

Here was a mature company in a mature industry undergoing major restructuring to adjust to a more competitive, global industry. Suddenly the firm was threatened by innovative foreign upstarts with no respect for its leadership position. Actually, while U.S. Steel may have been the leader of an oligopolistic *domestic* industry, it was merely another competitor producing a commodity product in a monopolistically competitive *global* industry.[3]

PROFILE   Ford Motor Co.

Until 1994, Ford operated largely separate vehicle engineering organizations in North America and Europe (in fact, Ford has two product-engineering centers in Europe). While the company's assembly plants are almost as efficient as the best Japanese factories, its high product-development spending in recent years has lowered financial results. Ford's pre-1994 structure saw Ford North America, Ford of Europe, and Ford Asia/Pacific operate as quasi-independent car companies, with largely different vehicles, engines, and components sold in each market.

Ford's new CEO, Alex Trotman, set out to change that in 1994, combining its North American and European auto operations into a single group, and launching a campaign to cut purchasing and product-development costs. Trotman wants Ford to be a "global company in primarily product development, manufacturing, and purchasing to optimize the strength Ford has in various parts of the world." In essence, Ford is betting its future on the proposition that it must "go global" and sell essentially the same vehicles around the world.

The reorganization, designed to let Ford avoid costly duplication of efforts in different parts of the world, will merge the two European engineering centers into a single "program center" devoted to designing small, front-wheel-drive cars. Midsize and larger cars, plus vans and trucks, will be developed by four new "program centers" in Dearborn, Michigan. The goal is to develop vehicles which, with minor modifications, can sell in different parts of the world. Ford has already developed and introduced such a car in Europe in early 1994 called the Mondeo (introduced later in the U.S. as the Ford Contour and Mercury Mystique).

While the Mondeo is the "world car" type that Ford aspires to, it cost $6 billion (4 times the cost of the Plymouth/Dodge Neon), because of expensive and time-consuming coordination between engineers in Dearborn and Germany. The

---

[3] "The Toughest Job in Business," *Business Week* (February 25, 1985), 50.

new structure hopes to make that process more efficient, saving time and money.[4]

WHAT IS GLOBAL COMPETITION?

To many, the terms "international," "multinational," and "global" mean essentially the same thing (with the possible exception that some people consider the term "global" to be merely the latest buzz-word for a company engaged in international activities). However, there are differences. Chris Bartlett and Sumantra Ghoshal have studied multinationals and have identified four forms of organizations used in managing international corporations: international, multinational, global, and transnational. However, since "multinational" is in reality a variation of international (selling or operating in a number of countries vs. a few), the term multinational is less descriptive than "multidomestic" or "multilocal," terms with a distinctly different meaning. That is, while there are multinational firms, the markets in which they compete and the strategies which they employ are not well described by the term.

An *international* competitor is typically one which is primarily a domestic company with foreign appendages. That is, the firm has expanded out of its domestic market to sell and/or manufacture its products in one or more foreign markets (the multinational, then, is an international competitor which competes in a number of foreign markets). The international firm's primary focus is toward the domestic market, and that is where its headquarters and most operations are centered. Technology and knowledge flow largely one way; from the parent organization to foreign operations.

A *multidomestic* competitor (sometimes called *multilocal*) is one which has geared its products, services, and operations to meet the unique needs of various markets around the world. The overall strategy is one of being responsive to unique national needs, with decentralized units operating in various parts of the world. Thus a multidomestic might be offering different products in the German market than in the U.S. or in Japan, for example. The various units are decentralized and self-sufficient, with their own resources. The overall strategy is one of exploiting opportunities, and knowledge is largely developed and retained at the subsidiary level. Distinctive competencies are usually manifested in "downstream" activities, such as marketing, service, distribution, and the like.

There is, however, one problem with the term "multidomestic." Domestic typically refers to a country—a political jurisdiction—and not a market. A market can be larger or smaller than a country. Thus, markets can be thought of as rang-

---

[4] Paul Ingrassia and Jacqueline Mitchell, "Ford to Realign with a System of Global Chiefs," *The Wall Street Journal* (March 31, 1994), A3.

ing from local to global in scope, with certain intermediate sizes between these two extremes. A market that is "regional" can be thought of as one that is larger than local but not a single global market. Therefore, regional could suggest a part of the U.S., for example, or North America, or Europe—it is a relative term. The point is, however, that its focus is on market-defining characteristics, not national boundaries. As Peter Drucker states, economies are national, markets are local, regional, or global.[5] Figure 14.1 suggests the relationships between the various international markets and appropriate strategies (which are discussed later).

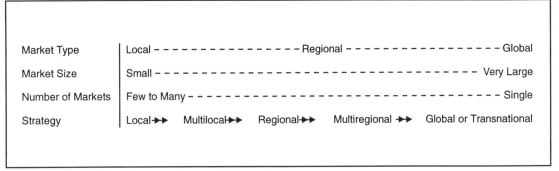

Figure 14.1 **International Markets and Strategies**

A *global* competitor is one which treats the world as a single market. A global market is one in which a standard product can be sold world-wide at a largely standardized price. Often, the economics of operating in certain parts of a global market depend not only on what a firm is doing in that part, but on its world-wide activities. The strategy here is to perform certain common activities— largely upstream, such as R&D, product design, proprietary manufacturing, and the like—and spread their cost over a large number of units sold world-wide. As such, the global competition is typically centralized and globally scaled, with knowledge developed and retained by the parent. Subsidiaries in various parts of the world usually are focused on implementing strategies and carrying out operations and logistics.[6]

---

[5] Peter F. Drucker, "The New World According to Drucker," *Business Month* (May 1989), 48-59.

[6] C. Bartlett and S. Ghoshal, *Transnational Management: Text, Cases, and Readings in Cross-Border Management* (Homewood, IL: Richard D. Irwin, Inc., 1992), 11-12.

INTERNATIONAL STRATEGIES

As we have already seen, "global" competition is one type of international business, and a "global" competitor is one type of "multinational" corporation, which is, in turn, a type of international business. Therefore, we are discussing various strategies for businesses competing internationally.

There are two basic reasons for companies to expand beyond local markets: comparative advantage and economies of scale. To the extent that these characteristics are favorable, larger operations will possess a competitive advantage and be rewarded. Some industries will function most effectively at the local level (such as dry cleaners, auto repair, and a host of inherently "local" industries), some at the regional level, and some at the global level of scope.

Some industries can be expanded in scope by the actions of competitors. Some previously local industries can be transformed into regionals and some regionals into global industries. For example, Philip Morris transformed the cigarette industry into a global entity through the marketing approach of its Marlboro brand. A senior-executive at Philip Morris has commented that too much national research would have prevented the cowboy campaign from being adopted globally. National market research would probably have identified a boxer as the best symbol in Britain, a bullfighter in Spain, a cyclist in France, and a sumo wrestler in Japan. The power of the common global identity would then have never been achieved.[7]

But Japanese firms have tended to take the lead as global competitors. The Japanese have tended to export one standardized world product to all markets; firms in the United States have tended to follow a product life-cycle strategy by first producing for the U.S. market and then exporting as demand by other countries for the product grew; and firms in Europe tended to focus on local market conditions and to view each market as a separate entity.[8] In fact, European- and American-based companies tended to have well-established networks of fairly independent and self-sufficient national subsidiaries, or "decentralized federations." Those with such organizations had little difficulty in responding to the increased demands from their host governments or adapting to shifts in consumer preferences world-wide, and their strategic posture was often literally "multinational"—multiple national positions, each highly sensitive to its local market. The problem with this strategy was that it was difficult to coordinate and control these world-wide operations in order to respond to the global forces.

---

[7] George S. Yip, "Implementing Total Global Strategy for World-wide Competitive Advantage," *The Planning Forum Network*, 6, No. 7 (September 1993), 11.

[8] P.W. Beamish, J.P. Killing, D.J. LeCraw, and H. Cookrell, *International Management: Text and Cases* (Homewood, IL: Richard D. Irwin, Inc., 1991), 39.

Most of the Japanese companies had the opposite problem. Their operations tended to be concentrated in the home country, and this gave them the ability to capture the opportunities presented by the global forces. The strategic posture of these companies was literally global—integrated whole. But, this approach made them less successful in building world-wide operating units sensitive and responsive to unique local or regional demands.[9]

Therefore, the Europeans pioneered the idea of far-flung autonomous foreign subsidiaries. The American multinational corporations (MNCs) gave foreign subsidiaries autonomy in handling local markets, but centralized technological and marketing expertise. Thus, the European and American MNCs have tended to pursue multilocal or multiregional strategies, while the Japanese MNCs have tended to pursue global strategies.

Strategy Types

As Figure 14.2 shows, the choice of international strategy varies with the number of markets entered and the degree of product integration and standardization from market-to-market. If the firm pursues a *local* strategy, it is in one or a few—likely domestic—markets, offering products and services largely unique to those markets. Even at this level, however, let us not forget that the business must have a sound core strategy. This core strategy is the basis for sustainable advantage, and a prerequisite for success at *any* level; it is an absolute necessity for internationalizing the business.

The basic reason for having an international strategy is that most product and factor markets extend beyond the boundaries of a single country. Thus, the competition that ultimately determines a firm's performance is not constrained to individual country markets. To be competitive, the strategic analysis for most firms must encompass threats and opportunities of both domestic and foreign origin.[10]

With this realization, the firm seeks to internationalize its core strategy through expansion of its activities to other markets and by adapting the core strategy, if necessary. Different ways of doing this constitute the different strategies of internationalization.

The conventional wisdom in international business is that companies should adapt their strategies when entering foreign markets, and should tailor their ways of doing business to local customs, needs, and preferences. But this local adaptation has hidden dangers and disadvantages. Total localization can result in a

---

[9] C.A. Bartlett and Sumantra Ghoshal, "Organizing for World-wide Effectiveness: The Transnational Solution," *California Management Review* (Fall 1988), 55.

[10] S.H. Robock and Kenneth Simmonds, *International Business and Multinational Enterprises*, 4th ed. (Homewood, IL: Richard D. Irwin, Inc., 1989), 196.

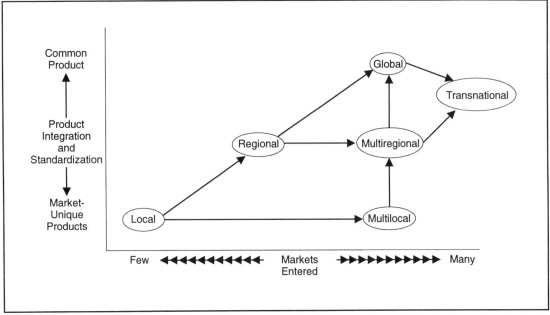

Figure 14.2 Types of International Strategy

fragmented business system that dissipates synergy between markets and economies of scale, and fails to exploit the advantages of a successful core strategy.[11]

In a regional strategy, product and service standardization has occurred across a region. Otherwise, it shares many of the same characteristics as the local strategy, except for a broader scope.

Determining which approach to choose, from local to multilocal, regional to multiregional, or global requires analysis along five dimensions. They are:

1. *Market participation:* the choice of markets in which to conduct business, and the level of activity, particularly in terms of market share.
2. *Products/services:* the extent to which an international business offers the same or different products in different markets.
3. *Location of value-adding activities:* where to locate each of the activities that comprise the entire value-added chain—from research to production to after-sales service.
4. *Marketing:* the extent to which a world-wide business uses the same brand names, advertising and other marketing elements in different markets.

---

[11] Yip, *op. cit.*, 1.

5. *Competitive moves:* the extent to which a world-wide business makes competitive moves in individual countries as part of a global competitive strategy.[12]

As we have seen, a multilocal strategy seeks to maximize world-wide performance by maximizing local competitive advantage, revenues, and profits. The products and services offered in each market are tailored to local needs. In the multiregional strategy, products and services are tailored to the needs of each region, and the goal is to achieve maximum world-wide performance by maximizing regional advantage and performance. In multilocal or multiregional strategies, markets are selected on the basis of their stand-alone potential in terms of revenues and profits. The next step in the progression is to globalize the strategy by integrating it across regions. In a global strategy, the ideal is a standardized core product that requires a minimum of local or regional adaptation. It seeks to maximize world-wide performance through sharing and integration. A business that has a fully globalized strategy would have fully global market participation, global products and services, global location of activities, global marketing, and global competitive moves.[13]

Current trends make it more likely that in many industries a global strategy will be more successful than a multilocal or multiregional one. An organization of highly autonomous local or regional business units, in which the managers from different countries seldom meet, is scarcely likely to be able to formulate a global strategy in the first place, let alone implement it.[14]

As the CEO of Whirlpool Corp., David Whitwam, states "Being an international company—selling global, having global brands or operations in different countries—isn't enough. In fact, most international manufacturers aren't truly global. They are what I call flag planters. They may have acquired or established businesses all over the world, but their regional or national divisions still operate as autonomous entities. In this day and age, you can't run a business that way . . . Our vision at Whirlpool is to integrate our geographical businesses wherever possible, so that our most advanced expertise in any given area—whether it's refrigeration technology, financial reporting systems, or distribution strategy—isn't confined to one location or division. We want to be able to take the best capabilities we have and leverage them in all our operations world-wide."[15]

Booz-Allen management consultants offers advice from CEOs who have gone through the globalization process:

---

[12] *Ibid.*

[13] *Ibid.*

[14] Yip, *op. cit.*, 11.

[15] David Whitwam, "The Right Way to Go Global," *Harvard Business Review*, 72, No. 2 (March/April 1994), 136.

- Know the fundamentals that really drive your business. If you do, you'll know when it's time to go global.
- Forget about in what country "headquarters" is located.
- Bring foreign nationals onto the board of directors.
- Use the same language (probably English) for all top-level communication.
- Foreign posting should be required for advancement.
- Much of the value-added lies in tightly coordinating company operations.

The final international strategy type is the *transnational* approach, which hopes to combine the best of all worlds. It attempts to combine the economies of scale of the global behemoth with the market responsiveness of the local or regional company; in essence, taking the best of the Japanese, European, and American approaches. It is an often-complex mixture of local and global power centers, centralizing (globalizing) those functions and processes that are common across markets, and decentralizing those that add net value by being unique to local and regional markets.[16] Transnational organizations, then, become more responsive to individual market needs while retaining global efficiency. An example might be the Ford Mondeo, which is essentially the same vehicle worldwide; however, it incorporates certain design variations and marketing approaches which appeal to consumers in the major regional markets of the world. The fundamental planning challenge for an MNC, then, is one of balancing the economic imperative of global integration with the market imperative of customer wants and the political imperative of stakeholder satisfaction.

Strategy Patterns

Research at the Universities of Western Ontario and South Carolina has revealed four dominant patterns or combinations of strategies for international businesses. As Figure 14.3 shows, two main strategy dimensions were examined: degree of internationalization and competitive positioning. The four most common strategy types within each dimension were surfaced, which yield four top combinations, or clusters. The results, shown in Table 14.1, seem to suggest that certain strategy combinations yield higher performance and, in general, the international/ innovation and the quasiglobal/manufacturing and marketing leadership clusters outperform the domestic/ niche and the exporting/quality strategies.[17]

---

[16] R.L. Hudson and J.S. Lublin, "Power at Multinationals Shifts to Home Office," *The Wall Street Journal* (September 9, 1994), B1.

[17] A.J. Morrison and K. Roth, "A Taxonomy of Business-Level Strategies in Global Industries," *Strategic Management Journal*, 13, No. 6 (September 1992), 399-418.

Strategy Dimensions	Internationalization		Competitive Positioning
Strategy Clusters	1. Domestic 2. Exporting 3. International 4. Quasi-global	+ + + +	Product Niche High Quality Product Innovation Combined Manufacturing and Marketing Leadership

Figure 14.3 Common International Strategies

Table 14.1 Performance Ranking of Clusters

	Performance Measure		
	ROA	ROI	Sales Growth
Cluster Ranking	4	3	3
	3	4	4
	2	2	1
	1	1	2

ENTERING INTERNATIONAL MARKETS

Companies typically internationalize in stages. Companies usually begin by concentrating on local, domestic markets. If successful, they subsequently reach limits to growth in their home markets. To grow further, they have to expand. At this point they commonly go into *export mode*, operating from a central office in the home market.

If successful at exporting, many companies next seek to achieve greater proximity to markets abroad. At this point, they replicate their approach by the creation of autonomous regional operations. Manufacturing, marketing, and sales are decentralized, but key decisions are still made at the head office in the home region. These are clearly *international companies*, typically multilocal.

Today, many successful companies are finding that being an international company by this definition is not a long-term formula for profitable growth. International companies face the need to optimize their businesses by adopting the global model of operation. In a *global company*, no one geographic area is assumed to be the primary base for any function. R&D, sourcing, and manufacturing are situated in the most suitable locations, anywhere in the world. They take on regional, multiregional, perhaps global, and in a few cases, transnational strategies.

Stages of Internationalization

From an organizational perspective, there are a number of ways of conducting international business. As shown in Figure 14.4, the degree of parent company control increases as a firm goes from licensing agreements to branch operations to joint ventures to subsidiary operations. In addition to increasing control, the amount of required capital, risk, and profit potential also increases.

Licensing grants a foreign firm the right to handle specified products in the country. Most companies begin foreign sales, however, by establishing a branch office in the foreign market. With this approach, sales offices and warehouses must be established, but manufacturing is performed elsewhere. Sometimes, a joint venture with a foreign firm (or a consortium with several firms) is used, enabling the companies to share investment, skills, and profits. The advantage of this method is that the distribution and marketing skills of the firm can be helpful in a foreign country, and these skills increase the likelihood of successful operations. Laws in some countries (such as Mexico) effectively *require* joint ventures. The most predominant method, however, is to form a wholly-owned subsidiary incorporated under the laws of the host country. For example, Seagram Co. Ltd. of Canada operates a wholly-owned subsidiary in the United States—Joseph E. Seagram & Sons. Sandoz, the large Swiss multinational pharmaceutical company, has subsidiaries in a number of countries, including Sandoz, Inc. (prescription drugs) and Dorsey Labs (over-the-counter drugs) in the United States.

Most businesses that operate in foreign countries evolve into international, multinational, or global operations over time. They tend to begin with low stakes in foreign operations, then develop a growing corporate dependence on foreign operations, and finally evolve into global corporate structure (as opposed to domestic plus international divisions). The three typical phases, including typical corporate viewpoints, organizational arrangements, and managerial emphasis for each, are shown in Figure 14.5.

GLOBAL TRENDS AND RISKS

Inherent in the previous discussion was the suggestion that doing business in foreign countries is a different ball game. It involves more than just deciding to pursue an international or multinational strategy, or recognizing that an industry requires global strategies. It involves more than selecting the specific type of

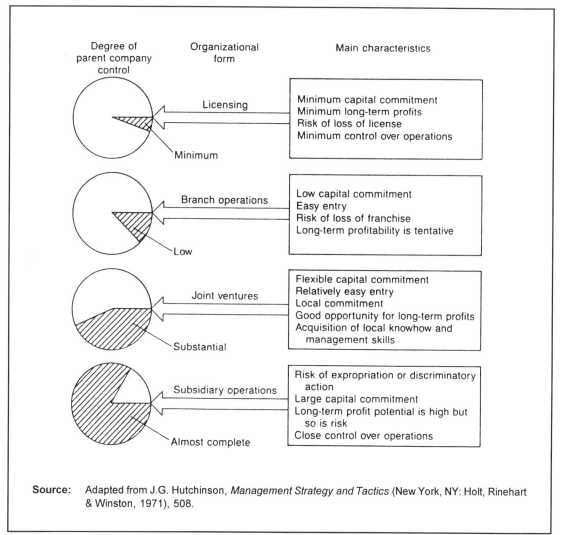

Source: Adapted from J.G. Hutchinson, *Management Strategy and Tactics* (New York, NY: Holt, Rinehart & Winston, 1971), 508.

Figure 14.4 Basic Organizational Forms for Multinational Operations

strategy by which the firm will compete internationally. Attention must be given to the risks unique to international business—risks over and above those that must be analyzed in evaluating domestic strategies. Three such risks relate to areas critical to the success of international operations: currency fluctuations and foreign risks (political turmoil, financial instability, expropriation or confiscation of assets, or increasing tariffs).

1. *Currency Fluctuations.* A strong dollar sounds attractive. However, this usually means that other currencies are weaker in relative terms. And, an in-

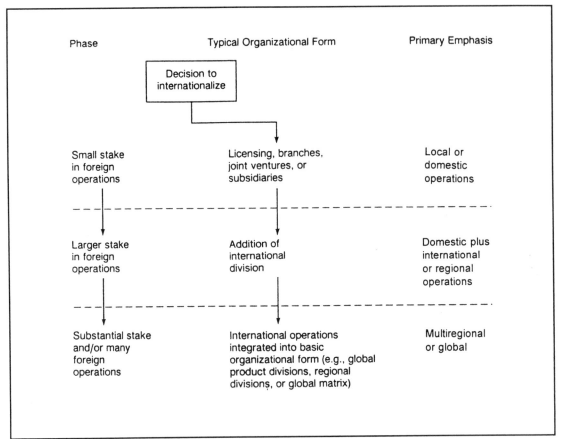

Figure 14.5 Typical Phases in the Internationalization of Organizations

crease in the value of the dollar relative to foreign currencies adversely affects a firm's earnings in two ways. First, foreign assets on the firm's balance sheet are worth fewer dollars; this is a one-time charge against earnings and lowers profits. Second, there is an ongoing profit and loss effect as sales and profits generated abroad continue to represent fewer dollars. Furthermore, a stronger dollar makes U.S. exports relatively more expensive to foreigners, and imports to the United States cheaper. Of course, the reverse is true when the dollar weakens. The implications of such changes can be enormous. In 1981, the net effect of currency translations on IBM's balance sheet and income statement was a charge against earnings of nearly 35 cents a share for the first nine months; this works out to about $200 million.[18] Anyone with a calculator can figure out what happened to companies with assets in Mexico, where the value of the peso dropped from 22 per dollar to 4,000 per dollar since 1976. For a multinational company, even the amount of cash and inventories located in various countries can have a substantial effect on assets and profits. Thus, currency fluctuations can greatly affect the success or failure of an international strategy.

2. *Political Risks.* In 1960, Texaco lost a $60 million refinery (costing the equivalent of $340 million in 1995 prices) when the Castro government seized all foreign assets in Cuba. For firms with assets in foreign countries, the risk of government instability, political turmoil, and other risks are *major* considerations, and can wipe out years of work and investment almost overnight. For this reason, it is of critical importance to consider such risks when engaging in international strategies. But how does one evaluate or quantify such possibilities? The prudent firm would be wise to employ a surprise matrix and contingency planning approach to cover such events, as described in another module. In addition, business information firms such as Frost and Sullivan, Business International, and others attempt to assess such risks. As an example of such an analysis, Table 14.2 provides eighteen-month and five-year forecasts for a number of countries. When a firm is involved in international operations, its profits must reflect these added risks. In addition, international expansion is not always (or even usually) more profitable. A recent research study found that high-technology firms employing domestic, export, or direct foreign investment strategies showed no significant difference in financial performance. Thus, international strategies did not improve their performance, nor did these strategies hurt the firms' performance.[19]

3. *Trade Risk.* As we have seen, quite elaborate analyses accompany the evaluation of political risk. The case can be made, however, that expropriation— while dramatic—presents a much smaller financial risk over time than does the cost of protectionism. Lost and reduced sales and profits due to import quotas, tariffs, and the like affect not only producers but consumers as well.[20]

---

[18] J.A. White, "IBM Earnings Dropped 22 Percent in Third Period," *The Wall Street Journal* (October 14, 1981), 4.

[19] P.M. Feltes and L.A. Digman, "The Effect of International Trading Strategy on Financial Performance," *Proceedings of Pan Pacific Conference*, VI (May 1989).

[20] Larry W. Cox and L.A. Digman, "The New Face of Political Risk Assessment," *Proceedings of the Second Decision Sciences Institute International Meeting* (June 1993).

Table 14.2 Political Risk and Economic Forecast Chart

NOTE: Next to each country name is the date of Political Risk Services last update or report, followed by the eighteen-month (2nd line) and five-year (3rd line) political forecasts, the REGIMES most likely to hold power and their PROBABILITIES, risk rating for TURMOIL (low to very high), and risk ratings (A+ the least, to D-the most) for financial TRANSFER direct INVESTMENT, and EXPORT to the country. Parentheses indicate a recently changed forecast. An asterisk means a non-incumbent regime. The list of ECONOMIC INDICATORS contains the most recently issued economic data and forecasts, including a previous five-year average, a one-year forecast or estimate, and five-year forecast or estimate, and five-year forecast average. REAL GROWTH of GDP and INFLATION are expressed as percentages, and CURRENT ACCOUNT figures are in billions of U.S. dollars.

Country Regimes & Probabilities	Turmoil	Transfer	Investment	Export	Date	Real GDP Growth	Inflation	Current Account
Argentina 12/93					1989-1993	3.1	1119.2	-3.71
Menem 70%	Moderate B-	B	B-		1994	6.5	5.0	-6.50
*Menemist 60%	Moderate B-	A-	B		1995-1999	5.5	4.0	-5.00
Australia 11/93					1989-1993	2.0	4.0	-17.56
Keating 75%	Low	A	A+	A+	1994	3.2	3.5	-12.00
Keating 55%	Low	A	A+	A+	1995-1999	3.5	4.0	-9.00
Austria 6/93					1989-1993	2.6	3.3	+0.09
Grand Coalition 75%	Low	A+	A+	A+	1994	1.5	2.7	-0.50
Grand Coalition 70%	Low	A+	A+	A+	1995-1999	2.5	3.0	-0.20
Brazil 12/93					1989-1993	0.3	1533.0	+1.02
Centrist 40%	Moderate	D+	B-	C+	1994	3.5	1200.0	+1.00
*Center-Right 45%	Moderate	C	C+	C	1995-1999	3.0	100.0	+2.50
Canada 12/93					1989-1993	0.8	3.9	-22.97
*Liberals 85%	Low	A-	A	A	1994	3.2	2.8	-22.00
*Liberals 50%	Low	A	A+	A+	1995-1999	3.5	3.5	-20.00
China 1/94					1989-1993	8.2	8.8	+3.97
Pragmatists 75%	Low	A-	B+	A--	1994	9.0	12.0	-1.60
Pragmatists 65%	Low	A-	B	B	1995-1999	9.0	11.0	+0.30
Cuba 1/94					1989-1993	-12.0	5.2	-0.41
Castro 60%	Low	B	A-	B	1994	-5.0	12.0	+1.00
Castro 60%	Low	A-	A-	B+	1995-1999	2.0	15.0	+1.00
Czech Republic 12/93					1989-1993	-1.5	19.4	+0.29
Center-Right 65%	Low	A-	A	A	1994	2.8	12.0	+0.50
Center-Right 60%	Low	A	A	A+	1995-1999	3.5	6.0	+0.60
Egypt 12/93					1989-1993	3.4	16.1	+1.12
Mubarak 65%	Moderate	C+	B+	C+	1994	2.5	8.5	+1.50
Mubarak 45%	Moderate	B-	C-	C-	1995-1999	3.2	7.0	+1.20
France 6/93					1989-1993	1.6	2.9	-4.68
Center-Right 60%	Low	A+	A+	A+	1994	1.5	2.0	+1.00
Center-Right 60%	Low	A+	A+	A+	1995-1999	2.5	3.0	+1.20
Germany 10/93					1989-1993	2.3	3.5	+6.04
CDU/CSU-FDP 45%	Moderate	B+	A	A	1994	1.0	4.0	-30.00
CDU/CSU-FDP 45%	Low	A	A	A	1995-1999	2.5	3.5	+5.00
Greece 11/93					1989-1993	1.5	16.2	-2.16
Pasok 40%	High	B-	B	B	1994	1.5	14.0	-1.50
Leftist Coalition 40%	High	C+	B	C+	1995-1999	2.0	12.0	-1.80
Haiti 10/93					1989-1993	-1.4	16.4	-0.06
*Compromise Coalition 40%	High	C	B	C-	1994	-4.0	18.0	-0.10
*Authoritarian 40%	Low	B+	B-	C+	1995-1999	1.0	20.0	-0.12

Table 14.2 Political Risk and Economic Forecast Chart Continued:

Country Regimes & Probabilities	Turmoil	Transfer	Investment	Export	Date	Real GDP Growth	Inflation	Current Account
Hong Kong 11/93 Routine Transition 85% *Accelerated Democracy 50%	Low Moderate	A A-	A A-	A+ A-	1989-1993 1994 1995-1999	3.9 4.5 5.0	10.1 8.5 10.0	+2.99 +1.50 +2.00
Hungary 1/94 Center Coalition 65% Center Coalition 55%	Moderate Low	C+ B-	A A-	B B	1989-1993 1994 1995-1999	-3.5 1.0 2.2	25.0 20.0 15.0	-0.39 -1.50 -0.50
India 12/93 Congress (I) Party 55% Congress (I) Party 55%	Moderate Moderate	B- C+	B C	C+ C-	1989-1993 1994 1995-1999	4.2 4.5 5.0	9.9 6.0 8.0	-5.56 -4.20 -3.00
Indonesia 12/93 Suharto 75% Suharto 45%	Low Moderate	B B-	A- B-	B C+	1989-1993 1994 1995-1999	7.9 6.2 6.5	7.6 8.0 9.5	-3.01 -3.50 -3.80
Iran 9/93 Rafsanjani-Khamenei 60% Rafsanjani-Khamenei 45%	Moderate Low	C B	B- B+	B- B	1989-1993 1994 1995-1999	8.1 7.0 5.0	26.0 50.0 25.0	-2.51 -2.50 -1.50
Iraq 8/93 Saddam 65% *Military 50%	High Moderate	D C+	C C+	C C+	1989-1993 1994 1995-1999	-2.9 0.0 2.0	61.0 100.0 60.0	-2.65 -2.00 -1.00
Ireland 11/93 Fianna Fail-Led 45% Fianna Fail-Led 55%	Low Low	A- A+	A+ A+	A+ A+	1989-1993 1994 1995-1999	4.6 3.5 3.8	3.4 3.0 2.8	+1.25 +2.50 +2.00
Israel 10/93 Labor Coalition 65% Labor Coalition 50%	Moderate High	C+ C	A- B+	B- B-	1989-1993 1994 1995-1999	4.8 4.5 5.0	15.7 10.0 9.0	+0.21 -0.50 -0.80
Italy 12/93 Center Left 40% Center Left 40%	Moderate Moderate	A- B+	A A-	B+ B	1989-1993 1994 1995-1999	1.5 1.2 2.0	6.0 4.5 4.0	-18.63 -19.00 -15.00
Japan 11/93 Reformist Coalition 45% *Reformist Coalition 45%	Low Low	A+ A+	A+ A+	A+ A+	1989-1993 1994 1995-1999	3.4 2.2 3.5	2.4 1.8 2.2	+82.67 +110.00 +65.00
Kuwait 7/93 Al-Sabah Family 65% Al-Sabah Family 55%	Low Low	B B	B+ B-	A- C+	1989-1993 1994 1995-1999	-3.1 10.0 7.5	13.3 5.0 5.0	-1.41 +6.00 +6.50
Libya 12/93 Qaddafi 70% Qaddafi 50%	Low Moderate	B- B+	C+ B-	C+ B-	1989-1993 1994 1995-1999	1.8 0.5 2.5	8.0 7.0 10.0	-0.35 -1.50 -0.80

Table 14.2 Political Risk and Economic Forecast Chart Continued:

Country Regimes & Probabilities	Turmoil	Transfer	Investment	Export	Date	Real GDP Growth	Inflation	Current Account
Malaysia 11/93 Mahathir 65% Mahathir 45%	Low Low	A- A-	A- A+	A- A	1989-1993 1994 1995-1999	8.9 8.2 7.0	3.8 4.3 5.8	-1.50 +0.50 +0.40
Mexico 1/94 PRI/Technocrat 55% PRI/Technocrat 55%	Low Low	B- C+	B+ A	B+ B-	1989-1993 1994 1995-1999	3.1 2.5 3.8	19.0 6.0 5.0	-14.00 -25.00 -20.00
Netherlands 7/93 CDA-Labor 50% *CDA-Labor-D'66 50%	Low Low	A+ A-	A A	A+ A-	1989-1993 1994 1995-1999	2.7 2.4 2.8	2.7 3.1 3.0	+7.93 +6.30 +6.00
Nicaragua 9/93 Chamorro 60% *Center-Left Coalition 55%	High Moderate	B- B-	B+ B	C+ B-	1989-1993 1994 1995-1999	-0.6 1.0 2.5	2459.3 20.0 25.0	-0.36 -0.40 -0.50
Panama 2/93 Endara 60% *Populist 45%	High Low	A A-	A- B+	B+ A-	1989-1993 1994 1995-1999	5.7 5.5 5.0	1.4 3.0 5.0	+0.01 -0.05 +0.10
Philippines 12/93 Ramos 75% Ramos 60%	High Very High	B C-	A- C-	B- D+	1989-1993 1994 1995-1999	1.9 2.0 2.8	12.4 7.0 8.0	-1.62 -1.00 -0.50
Poland 11/93 Center-Left 55% *Shifting Coalitions 45%	Moderate Moderate	B B-	A B+	B- B-	1989-1993 1994 1995-1999	-3.7 2.0 2.2	196.0 30.0 20.0	-1.21 -1.00 -0.75
Puerto Rico 9/93 Rossello 85% Rossello 50%	Low Low	A+ A	A+ A+	A+ A	1989-1993 1994 1995-1999	2.2 2.9 3.0	3.7 3.5 4.5	+0.06 +0.06 +0..05
Russia 1/94 Yeltsin 45% (55%) Yeltsin 40% (45%)	Moderate Moderate	C+ C+	C(C+) C	C+ C-(C)	1989-1993 1994 1995-1999	-7.2 0.5 1.5	779.2 800.0 100.0	-5.24 -6.00 -3.00
Saudi Arabia 12/93 Fahd 80% Fahd 55%	Low Low	A- B-	B a	A+ B-	1989-1993 1994 1995-1999	5.1 5.0 5.7	2.0 2.5 3.0	-10.64 -5.00 -4.50
Singapore 1/94 Goh Chok Tong 75% (65%) Goh Chok Tong 55% (45%)	Low Low	A+ A+	A+ A+	A+ A+	1989-1993 1994 1995-1999	7.7 8.0 6.5	2.8 2.4 2.8	+2.53 +2.20 +2.00
South Africa 12/93 *Unstable Transition 45% *Pragmatic ANC 45%	High High	B+ B-	B- B-	C+ B-	1989-1993 1994 1995-1999	0.0 2.5 4.0	13.6 12.0 9.0	+1.68 +1.00 -1.00

Table 14.2 Political Risk and Economic Forecast Chart Continued:

Country Regimes & Probabilities	Turmoil	Transfer	Investment	Export	Date	Real GDP Growth	Inflation	Current Account
South Korea 1/94 DLP 65% DLP Base 45%	Low Low	B+ A+	A- A-	A- A	1989-1993 1994 1995-1999	6.7 4.5 5.2	7.3 5.0 7.0	-2.71 -3.00 -2.50
Spain 1/94 Centrist PSOE 55% Centrist PSOE 55%	Low(Moderate) Low	A(A-) A	A A+(A)	A+(A-) A+(A)	1989-1993 1994 1995-1999	2.2 1.0 3.2	6.0 4.5 3.8	-15.83 -18.00 -15.00
Sweden 4/93 Nonsocialists 45% Nonsocialists 45%	Low Low	 A+	A+ A+	A+ A	1989-1993 1994 1995-1999	-0.5 1.5 2.0	6.8 3.6 4.0	-3.91 +1.00 +2.00
Switzerland 3/93 Centrist Coalition 85% Centrist Coalition 75%T	Low Low	A+ A	A A+	A+ A+	1989-1993 1994 1995-1999	0.9 1.5 2.0	4.3 2.0 3.0	+11.08 +15.25 +10.00
Taiwan 12/93 Collective KMT 60% Collective KMT 50%	Low Moderate	A A-	A- A	A+ A+	1989-1993 1994 1995-1999	6.4 5.2 6.0	4.1 3.8 5.0	+9.02 +5.00 +7.00
Thailand 12/93 Chuan 45% *Civilian-Military 70%	Low Low	A- A-	A+ A+	A A	1989-1993 1994 1995-1999	9.0 8.0 7.2	50 4.0 4.4	-6.21 -7.20 -6.00
Turkey 1/94 DYP-SHP 60% *Center Right 50%	Moderate Low	C B-	B+ B+(B-)	B B-(C+)	1989-1993 1994 1995-1999	4.4 6.0 5.5	66.5 70.0 50.0	-1.51 -3.00 -2.00
Ukraine 1/94 Kravchuk-Kuchma 55% *Democratic 45%	Moderate High	C B-	B B+	C B	1989-1993 1994 1995-1999	-7.6 -5.0 1.0	558.1 400.0 200.0	-1.92 -3.00 -2.00
United Kingdom 7/93 Conservatives 75% Conservatives 55%	Low Low	A+ A	A A+	A+ A	1989-1993 1994 1995-1999	0.3 2.9 3.0	6.0 3.5 4.0	-25.00 -30.00 -16.00
United States 3/93 Democratic Majority 60% Democratic Majority 60%	Low Low	A A	A+ A	A+ A	1989-1993 1994 1995-1999	1.3 3.1 3.0	4.1 2.8 3.5	-69.49 -93.00 -75.00
Vietnam 11/93 CPV Mainstream 75% CPV Mainstream 65%	Low Low	C+ B-	B+ A	B- B+	1989-1993 1994 1995-1999	5.3 7.5 7.0	40.3 18.0 25.0	-0.34 +0.20 +0.10
Zaire 12/93 *Unstable Democratic 45% *Limited Democracy 40%	Very High Very High	D D-	B- D+	D+ D	1989-1993 1994 1995-1999	-5.8 -8.0 2.0	1893.7 1000.0 100.0	-0.80 -1.00 -0.20

Source: Adapted from W.D. Coplin and M.K. O'Leary, "Annual Five-Year Political Risk Forecast," *Planning Review*, 22, No. 2 (March/April 1994), 50-56.

World Scenarios

What kind of future do experts see for the world over the foreseeable future? Peter Schwartz, internationally renowned futurist and president of Global Business Network, sees four main scenarios. They are:

1. *New Empires Protectionist Scenario.* In this scenario, free trade begins to decline in an increasingly protectionist world. Politicians such as Pat Buchanan, Jerry Brown, and H. Ross Perot express a "strong, protectionist, isolationist sentiment that resonates in the heart of America."
2. *New Empires Open Trade Scenario.* This scenario, like the first, sees an increasingly regionalized world. In this one, however, regionalization, such as the EEC, is simply a form of organization preceding globalization.
3. *Market World Scenario.* Here, regionalization is trivial, short-lived, and not particularly significant in the long-term. Instead, the significant development is likely to be the evolution of MNCs on a global scale and/or the evolution of global institutions, like new trading or telecommunications systems.
4. *Global Incoherence Scenario.* This is the dark scenario. There are enormous quantities of weapons in the world, with the breakup of the Soviet Union. Anyone can buy a T-72 tank for $50,000 or a MIG-29 for $1.5 million. We might see a decade of international conflict, partly because the source of stability and control of the past—the Cold War—has ended.[21]

For the future, where does the world turn for leadership? The U.S.? Big-time borrowers are not particularly good leaders. Europe? Europe is headed in several different directions at the same time; integration a'la EEC and disintegration a'la Yugoslavia and Czechoslovakia. Asia? Southeast Asia is beginning to organize itself separately from North America and Europe. Therefore, we may see three great trading blocks: North America, Europe, and Asia. A world broken into regional trading blocks—which will become political blocks—would be primed for conflict over the long run. Therefore, the new world order of the next century may be one we do not like very much.[22]

[21] Peter Schwartz, "Re-Perceiving the Future Through The Lens of the Past," *Planning Review*, 20, No. 5 (September/October 1992), 36-38.

[22] *Ibid.*

CONCLUSIONS

In summary, a strategy of international expansion holds an inherent attractiveness and mark of success for many firms. For many whose domestic markets are saturated, it may be a requirement for future growth, and certain industries effectively demand global strategies. But international expansion is not without a number of problems and significant risks. A firm should look hard when deciding whether or not to pursue an international strategy to determine if the benefits truly outweigh the costs.

Module
15

Functional, Value Chain, and Quality Strategies

LEARNING OBJECTIVES

After completing Module 15, you should be able to:

1. Understand the primary functional strategy areas and how they support business-unit strategies.
2. Describe the role of the value chain in supporting business-unit strategies.
3. Relate the importance of quality-based strategies to functional and business strategies.
4. Discuss research and development and technology-based strategies.
5. Relate new product development and innovation strategies to strategies of the business unit.

As we discussed earlier, functional strategies are vitally important to the business unit, because, through competencies emanating from the firm's internal processes, they are a major determinant of the competitive advantage of the business. So these internal processes which add value—the *value chain* of the business—provide the firm with the ability to carry out certain business-unit strategies. The value chain and functional strategies are supported by techniques such as total quality management, reengineering, and time-based competition. These tools, however, are not strategy tools in themselves, because they only support—not determine—what the firm's unique and sustainable competitive advantage will be.

Our intent here is not to discuss all functional strategies, since many of these strategies are addressed in other courses in the typical business curriculum. Those that are not, however—notably research and development (R&D)/ technology strategies as well as new product development/innovation strategies—are discussed in this module.

PROFILE   3M Corporation

Minnesota Mining & Manufacturing Co. (3M) is celebrated year after year as one of the country's most respected companies. Business schools commonly make 3M a case study in new-product development and good management; 3M stands apart as a smooth-running innovation machine.

New-product development and innovation are key elements of 3M's business strategy. Illustrating the importance of new-product development to 3M's business strategy is the corporate guideline requiring that 25 percent of a division's sales must come from products introduced within the past five years. To meet this goal, 3M spends a lot on R&D (over 6% of sales) and works to reward innovative behavior. For example, a 3M employee who develops a new product gets the chance to manage it as if it were his or her own business. The person with an idea for a new product forms an action team by recruiting people from R&D, manufacturing, marketing, sales, and possibly finance. The team designs the product and a plan for producing and marketing it. If successful, team members are given raises and promoted. When sales hit $5 million, the originator becomes a project manager; at $20-30 million, a department manager; at $75 million or so, a division manager.

As a result, 3M turns out new products faster and better than almost any other company. It boasts over 60,000 products, with nearly one-third introduced during the past five years. The company has created a culture which rewards success but considers it OK to fail—a culture that has given 3M a sustainable competitive advantage.[1]

---

[1] Russell Mitchell, "Masters of Innovation," *Business Week* (April 10, 1989), 58-63.

FUNCTIONAL STRATEGIES

As was stated earlier, the bulk of the sources for product or service differentiation are functional in nature. That is, differentiation by price, image, support, design, timing, and quality are each based on one of the functional strategy areas, as shown in Figure 15.1.

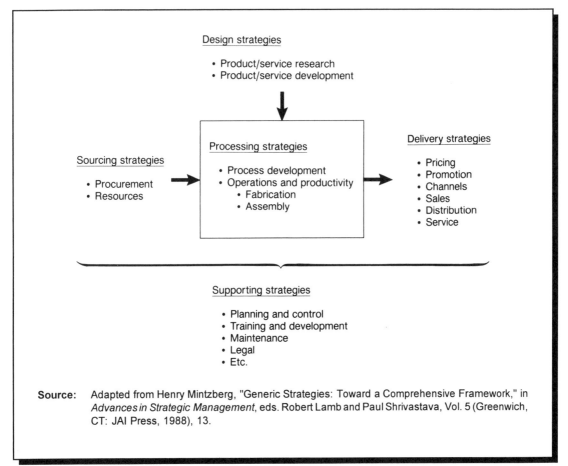

Source: Adapted from Henry Mintzberg, "Generic Strategies: Toward a Comprehensive Framework," in *Advances in Strategic Management*, eds. Robert Lamb and Paul Shrivastava, Vol. 5 (Greenwich, CT: JAI Press, 1988), 13.

Figure 15.1 Functional Strategy Areas

One of the important aspects of business-level strategy involves determining the proper integration of functional-level strategies (product design, manufacturing, marketing, and finance, in particular) for the business. With the exception of product design and development—or innovation—functional strategies are treated in other courses in the business school curriculum. As Richard Cyert, president of Carnegie-Mellon University has observed, business schools do not do an adequate job of educating MBAs about new technology and its management. They are led to think that "the key to management is finance and marketing, when in fact it is new technology. Managers don't have the background to make decisions" in this vital area.[2] The management of technology involves planning and strategies concerning entrepreneurship, research, technology development, invention, and innovation.

Even in international competition, companies gain competitive advantage by innovating. Michael Porter conducted a four-year, ten-nation study of the factors which contribute to "world-class" status for certain industries. Porter found that world-class industries are built by innovative acts of companies comprising those industries. To the extent that those innovative acts make several or more competitors in a given country world-class, the result becomes a world-class industry centered in that country. What causes this to happen, this grouping of world-class competitors in a given country? The answer lies in four interrelated attributes of the nations which define the firms' environment. They are:

1. *Factor Conditions.* These are factors of production, such as a skilled labor pool, resources, etc. A nation must not rely only on its existing resources but must actively create and nourish applicable factors of production to be successful. Disadvantages in Factor Conditions may force a company to innovate to compensate for the disadvantages.
2. *Demand Conditions in the Home Market.* A company is more competitive if the home market is especially demanding or competitive. Environmental circumstances in the home market may force innovation. Also, home market trends or concerns may indicate trends that will emerge in foreign markets.
3. *Related and Supporting Industries.* An organization is more competitive if there are strong suppliers and related industries that create an infrastructure. Information and technical support speed up innovation. The suppliers should be global competitors themselves.
4. *Firm Strategy, Structure, and Rivalry.* A firm will be erroneously preoccupied with short-term profits if capital moves too frequently in the home market. Firm organizational structures should match the products manufactured. Strong rivalry in home markets can even stimulate competitive advantage.[3]

---

[2] "U.S. Business Schools Criticized for Failing to Educate MBAs about New Technology," *The Chronicle of Higher Education* (June 24, 1987), 16.

[3] Michael Porter, *The Competitive Advantage of Nations* (New York, NY: The Free Press, 1990).

THE VALUE CHAIN

Competitive advantage is the advantage a firm gains over its competitors because it is better able to transform resources, or inputs (labor, capital, raw materials, purchases) into goods and services at maximum profit. To do so, a company must either be able to transform these inputs into goods and services at a lower cost, or perform them in a way that leads to differentiation (greater value) and a premium price.[4] Competitive advantage, however, should not be confused with comparative advantage, which is derived from the relative costs of the inputs between countries, regions, states, cities, and other location factors. Obviously, comparative advantage is a contributing factor to a firm's competitive advantage,[5] as are its distinctive competencies.

Competitive advantage influences the decision in which of the activities and technologies along the *value-added chain*—the chain of activities a firm performs in creating the value that causes customers to buy the product or service—that the firm should concentrate its investment and managerial resources. The value chain is the process by which technology is combined with material and labor inputs, and then the resulting product or service is assembled, marketed, and distributed.[6] Ideally, maximum value, in the eyes of the consumer, is added by this process at low cost, resulting in the firm's competitive advantage.

The value chain is the basic tool for systematically examining the activities a business performs and how they interact, and is necessary in order to determine its sources of competitive advantage. That is, one cannot understand competitive advantage by studying a business as a whole; it must be dissected into its "strategically relevant activities" to understand the *sources* of competitive advantage (cost leadership or differentiation, according to Porter).[7]

As Figure 15.2 shows, value-producing activities fall into nine categories: five primary activities and four support activities. Primary activities are those involved in producing the product or service, its marketing and delivery, and its post-sale service and support. Support activities provide the resource inputs and company infrastructure so that the primary activities can occur. Also, the way the activities are linked together often affects the cost or effectiveness; a sort of interaction effect.[8]

[4] M.E. Porter and V.E. Millar, "How Information Gives You Competitive Advantage," *Harvard Business Review*, 63, No. 4 (July/August 1985), 150.

[5] Bruce Kogut, "Designing Global Strategies: Comparative and Competitive Value-Added Chains," *Sloan Management Review* (Summer 1985), 15.

[6] *Ibid.*

[7] Porter, *Competitive Advantage*, 33.

[8] Porter and Miller, "How Information Gives You Competitive Advantage," 150.

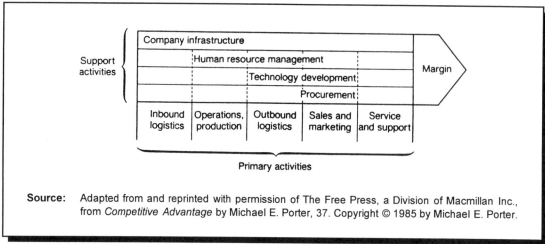

Source: Adapted from and reprinted with permission of The Free Press, a Division of Macmillan Inc., from *Competitive Advantage* by Michael E. Porter, 37. Copyright © 1985 by Michael E. Porter.

Figure 15.2 **The Generic Value Chain**

Competitive advantage can be created in the value-added chain by actions which lower costs, enhance differentiation of the product or service, and optimize the firm's competitive scope—the breadth of activities performed. In some instances, broadening the competitive scope (broadening product lines, more vertical integration selling in more markets, and the like) may increase value added (and profits). In other instances, narrowing the competitive scope (targeting and focusing on particular market segments, customers, or regions) may add more value and provide a competitive advantage.[9]

While it is important that companies add value for customers via core competencies along the chain, leading companies today are doing more—they are inventing and redefining value. That is, instead of just *adding* value, they are *creating* value in ways that previously did not exist or of which customers were not aware. For example, companies such as IKEA are combining products and services into activity-based "offerings" from which customers can create value for themselves. IKEA customers take on tasks traditionally performed by manufacturers and retailers, such as transporting the furniture to their home and assembling it themselves—for a reduction in price. Therefore, IKEA has reconfigured the value chain to permit *customers* to create their *own* value from the company's product offerings—at a savings in cost.[10]

[9] Porter and Millar, "How Information Gives You Competitive Advantage," 151.

[10] Richard Normann and Rafael Ramirez, "From Value Chain to Value Constellation: Designing Interactive Strategy," *Harvard Business Review*, 71, No. 4 (July/August 1993), 65-77.

QUALITY STRATEGIES

Total Quality Management (TQM) or some variation was the dominant "buzz-word" for managers in the early 90s. Virtually every organization professed to focus on providing "quality" products and services to its customers. But terms like quality control, quality assurance, reliability, statistical quality control, zero defects and the like have been around during the period of the 40s through the 80s. No one seemed too interested in them until the Japanese began using quality as a differentiation strategy during the 1980s. Prior to that, marketing, finance, and human resource management were all the rage.

Even though many companies have been emphasizing quality in recent years, some are still uncertain as to how quality fits into their business strategy. This confusion is due partly to the many definitions of the term "quality." Four primary definitions of quality include the following:

1. *Quality is "Excellence."* Quality is defined as meeting uncompromising standards and high achievement. However, "excellence" is difficult to measure and may change dramatically and rapidly.
2. *Quality is "Value."* This definition incorporates multiple attributes, but is still subjective, difficult to measure, and implies that cost affects quality.
3. *Quality is "Conformance to Specifications."* While easy to measure, this definition focuses on predictability and consistency, not "excellence." Thus, Gallo wine and McDonald's could be considered of the highest quality, because they exhibit the least variation from a standard.
4. *Quality is "Meeting and/or Exceeding Expectations."* This definition recognizes that "beauty is in the eye of the beholder (or customer)," and provides an all-encompassing definition. But it is difficult to define, measure, depends on image, is relative, and a variety of other complicating factors.[11]

Given the varied meanings of quality, it is reasonable to ask, how does quality fit into the long-run success of the organization? What role does it play in business strategy? The answer is that the level of quality directly influences competitive position, which in turn determines the range of business strategies available to the organization and the firm's long-run competitive performance.[12]

[11] Carol A. Reeves and David A. Bednar, "Defining Quality: Alternatives and Implications," *Academy of Management Review*, 19, No. 3 (July 1994), 419-445.

[12] James A. Belohlav, "Developing the Quality Organization," *Quality Progress* (October 1993), 119-122.

R&D/TECHNOLOGY STRATEGIES

Some writers suggest that the three main causes of change are "technology, technology, and technology."[13] Others would add that technology strategy must be a key facet of the overall strategy for the business. That is, the management of a firm's technology must be integrated with the management of its other functions as part of an overall business strategy.[14]

But what is "technology" and how can it be integrated into business strategy and managed effectively? One broad definition is that it is all of the products, processes, tools, methods, and systems employed in the creation of goods or in the provision of services. In fact, a key to America's success in services lies in using technologies to increase the value-added by other functions and processes.

But in many organizations, technology is not well-managed. A recent study suggests that only 20 percent of companies enjoy a positive payback on R&D expenditures.[15] Why is that? Perhaps part of the reason lies in the fact that many managers do not possess the academic or experiential know-how necessary to understand the technology they are managing. Firms need the ability to maintain internally developed technology over time to foster corporate vitality. This "transformative capacity" depends on the ability to accomplish three tasks: to choose the correct technology; to maintain these technologies over time; and to reactivate and synthesize technologies when required. All of these tasks require judgment, understanding, and timing, since not all technologies developed by firms can or should be utilized immediately. These judgments must be made by managers and strategists, not technical people. As one of the directors in Japan's Ministry of International and Industry (MITI) stated, if U.S. firms started making better use of their vast storehouse of technology "we would not be able to compete with them."[16]

Technology Strategies

A firm can employ four broad strategies with regard to technology, according to Maidique and Patch:[17]

---

[13] Catherine Swift, "On Becoming a Change Junkie," *The Planning Forum Network* (March 1994), 4.

[14] Chris Raymond, "What Makes a Business Successful?" *The Chronicle of Higher Education* (November 14, 1990), A6.

[15] Otis Port, "Developments to Watch: Rating R&D," *Business Week* (July 5, 1993), 98.

[16] Raghu Garud and P.R. Nayyar, "Transformative Capacity: Structuring by Intertemporal Technology Transfer," *Strategic Management Journal*, 15, No. 5 (June 1994), 365.

[17] M.A. Maidique and Peter Patch, *Corporate Strategy and Technological Policy*, Case No. 9-679-033 (Boston, MA: Harvard Business School, 1978), rev. 1980.

1. *First to market.* This offensive strategy attempts to get the product to market before the competition does, creating a temporary monopoly. A strong commitment to applied research and development is required. Users of this strategy were Cray Research (in large computers) and Apple (in microcomputers). A major risk with this strategy is that there may not be a market for the product, as was the case with Polaroid's instant movie camera.

2. *Second to market.* The "fast-follower" strategy involves entry in the early growth stage of the life cycle and quick imitations of innovations developed by a competitor. This strategy may involve lower R&D expenditures, but requires flexibility and responsiveness. Zenith (versus RCA) and Japan (versus the United States) have used this strategy, as has IBM in both mainframes and microcomputers. This somewhat more defensive strategy lets the first-to-market pioneers test the market and perhaps develop it to the point warranting entry on a larger scale.

3. *Cost minimization.* This late-to-market approach involves market entry in the later growth stages and attempts to avoid development costs and to exploit cost advantages through economies of scale, joint product lines, and process efficiencies. U.S. manufacturers of small cars have taken this approach, as did Wendy's in fast-food restaurants (versus McDonald's and Burger King).

4. *Market segmentation.* This specialized strategy attempts to serve niches or pockets of demand through special applications of the basic technology. Entry can occur in almost any stage of the life cycle, and is often practiced by smaller, lower-volume producers.

These technology strategies and their primary functional requirements are shown in Table 15.1.

NEW PRODUCT DEVELOPMENT/INNOVATION STRATEGIES

The goal of technology is either product, service, or process improvement. Despite innovations in office work like typewriters and word processors, neither produced any measurable increase in productivity among white-collar workers. But technological innovations cause dramatic shifts within the industries producing the products. As technology changes, so do the industry leaders, because each innovation represents a different approach and requires a different set of skills from producing firms (for example, office machines leadership evolved from Remington to Underwood to IBM to Microsoft and Intel). It is rare to find an industry-changing innovation coming from the current leaders in an industry (remember how the quartz watch affected the Swiss watch industry). Most major

Table 15.1 Technology Strategy and Functional Policy

Technology Strategy	Policy Requirements					
	R&D	Manufacturing	Marketing	Finance	Organization	Timing
First to market	Requires state of the art R&D	Emphasis on pilot and medium-scale manufacturing	Emphasis on stimulating primary demand	Requires access to risk capital	Emphasis on flexibility over efficiency; encourage risk taking	Early—entry inaugurates the product life cycle
Second to market	Requires flexible, responsive and advanced R&D capability	Requires agility in setting up manufacturing, medium scale	Must differentiate the product; stimulate secondary demand	Requires rapid commitment of medium to large quantities of capital	Combine elements of flexibility and efficiency	Entry early in growth stage
Cost minimization late to market	Requires skill in process development and cost-effective product	Requires efficiency and automation for large-scale production	Must minimize selling and distribution costs	Requires access to capital in large amounts	Emphasis on efficiency and hierarchical control; procedures rigidly enforced	Entry during late growth or early maturity
Market segmentation	Requires ability in applications, custom engineering, and advanced product design	Requires flexibility on short to medium runs	Must identify and reach favorable segments	Requires access to capital in medium or large amounts	Flexibility and control required in serving different customers' requirements	Entry during growth stage or later

Source: Adapted from Modesto Maidique and Peter Patch, *Corporate Strategy and Technological Policy*, Case No. 9-679-033 (Boston, MA: Harvard Business School, 1978), 24. Reprinted by permission.

innovations occur in unexpected ways, causing current leaders to lose their dominance.[18]

We do know, however, that successful corporate innovators—such as 3M, Rubbermaid, Hewlett-Packard, Dow Corning, Merck, G.E., and the like—follow a few simple rules. 3M, for example, does the following:

1. *Keep divisions small.* When a division exceeds $250-300 million in sales, it is split up.
2. *Tolerate failure.* By encouraging experimentation and risk-taking, chances for successful new products are increased.
3. *Reward the champions.* Successful innovators share in the product's success.
4. *Stay close to customers.* Researchers, marketers, and managers routinely visit with customers and brainstorm product ideas.
5. *Share the wealth.* Wider use of new technology and innovations by other divisions for spin-off products is encouraged.
6. *Encourage persistence.* Employees can spend 15 percent of their time on pet projects, for which they can apply for corporate grants.[19]

FLEXIBILITY

In the turbulent 90s, a company should try to develop multiple capabilities. The company will likely have to be able to switch gears—for example, from rapid product development to low-cost to product differentiation—fairly quickly and with limited resources. Therefore, the goal of competitive strategy is not merely choosing the correct strategy, but possessing the strategic flexibility to switch to another strategy as conditions change.[20]

---

[18] James M. Utterback, *Mastering the Dynamics of Innovation* (Cambridge, MA: Harvard Business School Press, 1994).

[19] Mitchell, *op. cit.*, 62.

[20] Robert H. Hayes and Gary P. Pisano, "Beyond World Class: The New Manufacturing Strategy," *Harvard Business Review*, 72, No. 1 (January/February 1994), 161.

Module
16

Corporate and Multibusiness Strategies

LEARNING OBJECTIVES

After completing Module 16, you should be able to:

1. Understand that organizations may be structured differently for strategic versus operational purposes.
2. Define strategic business units.
3. Understand the major strategic alternatives available for corporate-level decisions.
4. Understand the role of portfolio models in corporate-level strategy, as well as the strategies appropriate for each segment of the models.
5. Appreciate the role of mergers, acquisitions, and new ventures in diversifying and entering new businesses.
6. Understand how companies restructure their portfolios and exit from businesses, including divestitures.
7. Appreciate conditions under which the various strategic alternatives are appropriate.

In previous modules, we investigated strategies for individual businesses. Many organizations compete in essentially a single market, industry, or business. Others, however, have diversified or expanded into more than one business and are, therefore, "multibusiness" companies. Sometimes called *multimission* organizations, these firms are faced with corporate-level strategic decisions; that is, which businesses should the organization compete in, and what should be the relationship between the businesses?

In short, the major focus is on what to do *with* the business units, whereas what to do *within* the business unit—how to compete—is the focus of business-level strategies. Corporate-level performance is influenced by at least four general factors:

1. *Performance of existing business units.* A firm will grow if its business units grow (as a result of business-level strategies).
2. *The number of business units.* Corporate-level growth can occur by employing corporate resources to increase the number of business units. This can be done by acquiring existing businesses or by creating new ventures internally. The reverse is also true; corporate size can be reduced by divesting or liquidating business units.
3. *The mix of business units.* Corporate performance can be improved by divesting, retrenching, or liquidating poorly performing businesses, and by acquiring or starting better performers with the additional resources provided.
4. *A combination of actions.* The three actions listed above are not mutually exclusive. Firms can and often do use them in conjunction as part of their corporate-level strategies.

The focus in this chapter is on how multibusiness organizations organize and align their individual businesses, including how they decide to enter new businesses and retreat from existing businesses. Keep in mind, however, that diversified *companies* don't compete in individual markets; only their *businesses* do. Therefore, competition occurs at the business-unit level; unless a corporate-level strategy focuses on the success of each unit, the strategy will fail, no matter how clever or elegant.[1]

PROFILE   ITT Corp.

During the 60s and 70s, the legendary Harold S. Geneen turned the ailing International Telephone and Telegraph Co.—whose business was mainly overseas—

---

[1] Zane N. Markowitz, "Hidden Sector Competitor Analysis," *Planning Review*, 15, No. 5 (September/October 1987), 20.

into the world's foremost conglomerate, with some 2,000 units. In the late 70s, Geneen's star dimmed with revelations of bribery in Chile and Italy, "accounting gimmickry," declining profits, high debt, declining stock price, and low morale. Geneen retired in 1979, and was replaced by the current CEO, Rand V. Araskog.

Since 79, Araskog has sold off 240 companies in an attempt to focus and restructure the company, changing its sights from size and growth to earnings and return on equity. The sell-offs have changed ITT dramatically. With only a few businesses left, ITT bounced back from a loss in 1992 and earned close to $1 billion in 93. Its stock is up 140 percent from its 1990 low.

In the early 80s, raiders were circling as the company's stock price fell below $22 per share, with some estimates of a breakup value of close to $100 per share. So, Araskog began selling off parts of the company, keeping the more promising, efficient businesses with synergy and which fit his new corporate focus.[2] As a result, ITT focused on four lines of business: manufactured products, insurance and financial, Rayonier forest products, and Sheraton hotels. Rayonier, having no synergy with the rest of ITT, was spun-off to shareholders in March of 1994.

Today's conglomerates, it seems, are focusing on a relatively few businesses, rather than many. They are working harder at improving business-unit performance and on synergies between businesses.[3]

MANAGING THE MULTIBUSINESS ORGANIZATION

Running a diversified company is different than managing an individual business company; the main difference arises from the need to manage diversity. As SCM Corporation's George Hall observes, three points need to be kept in mind:

1. In the diversified company, each separate unit has to carry its own weight, as if it were an independent business. To a large extent, such units should do their own planning (business-unit planning) and run themselves.
2. Some operational and staff functions, such as personnel matters, coordination of information networks, and external relations, are best left to the parent.

---

[2] Leslie Eaton, "Getting the Message: Investors Start to Appreciate a New ITT," *Barron's* (August 31, 1987), 13.

[3] William M. Bulkeley, "Conglomerates Make a Surprising Comeback—With a 90s Twist," *The Wall Street Journal* (March 1, 1994), A1.

3. The parent must forge a sense of group identity in the units, judging their performance through review and budget processes and rewarding business-unit managers for good performance.[4]

But why diversify? The fundamental question is whether "rents" (excess profits) can be generated by combining businesses, vertically integrating, or using forms such as joint ventures. The strategic question is not just *whether* a firm should diversify, but *how*.

As Figure 16.1 shows, the reasons for diversification have changed over the years. From the general management skills of the 60s, to the portfolio planning of the 70s, the restructuring of the 80s, to the core competencies and virtual organizations of the 90s, there has been an evolution in the reasons for creating multibusiness organizations.

But what kind of structure works best for diversified firms? Recent research has shown that the M-form structure (multidivisional) increases the rate of return for unrelated diversifiers—companies diversified into unrelated businesses. However, this structure decreases the rate of return for vertically integrated firms, and results in no significant change for related diversifiers (companies diversified into related businesses).

As shown in Table 16.1, unrelated diversifiers improve their performance by being able to take advantage of resource allocation efficiencies in the M-form structure. For vertically integrated firms, however, performance declines, possibly because interdependence between businesses now in separate divisions compromises the vertically integrated firm's ability to allocate resources. Although related diversified firm's performance also declined (again, possibly because of divisional interdependence), the drop was not statistically significant. Keep in mind that the related diversified firms outperformed the other two, regardless of the type of structure. The results indicate that unrelated diversifiers *should* adopt the M-form structure, bringing their performance closer to the others, while vertically integrated firms should not. Regardless of the corporate structure, however, related diversified firms are the top performers.[5]

Strategic Business Units

In order to focus their planning efforts, companies have created the strategic business unit (SBU) to describe the businesses or markets in which they compete

---

[4] George E. Hall, "Reflections on Running a Diversified Company," *Harvard Business Review*, 65, No. 1 (January/February 1987), 84.

[5] R.E. Hoskisson, "Multidivision Structure and Performance: The Contingency of Diversification Strategy," *Academy of Management Journal*, 30, No. 4 (December 1987), 625-44.

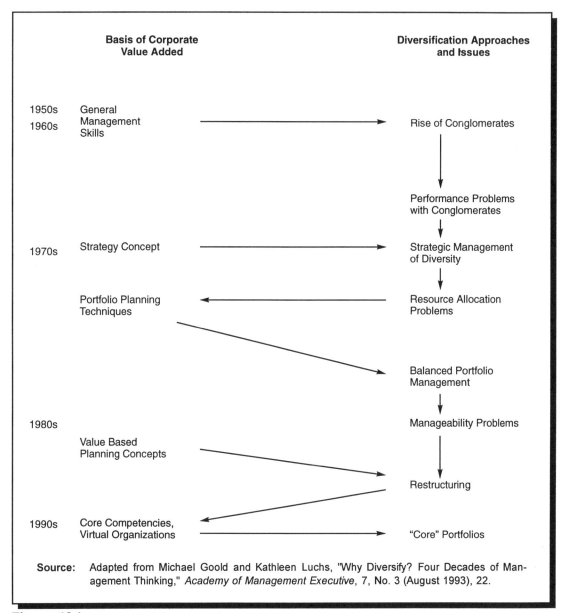

Figure 16.1 Evolution of Corporate Strategy

and to provide the structure for their strategic decisions. Thus, while a single plant may at the same time be *operationally* producing products for different business units, one of the business units—say, building products—may be supplied by more than one plant (such as those manufacturing wood and aluminum prod-

Table 16.1 ROA before and after M-form Structure

Firm Type	Before M-form	After M-form
Unrelated diversified	4.11%	5.16%
Vertically integrated	6.85	5.86
Related diversified	7.60	7.11

ucts). One organization structure may exist for strategic *purposes* and another for *operational* purposes. Still, the organization structure should represent the simplest, easiest, and most effective means of accomplishing the operational and strategic tasks.

The ideal organizational arrangement obviously would be to have the strategic structure and the operational structure coincide with one another—but this is not always possible, as our example has shown. The key building block in organizing the firm's strategic planning activities is the *strategic business unit*. A strategic business unit can be defined as an operating unit or a focal point for planning that provides a distinct set of products or services to a distinct group of customers and competes within an identifiable group. It is the point at which business-level strategy is focused and developed.[6]

The strategic business unit concept was developed by General Electric in the 1970s as a solution to its previous "profitless growth" and other problems it was experiencing with its planning processes. GE is perhaps the most widely diversified nonconglomerate company in the world. (In the late 1970s, it consisted of 170 separate departments grouped into forty-nine divisions. The divisions, in turn, reported to ten group executives, who reported to the CEO.) The basic unit of organization in GE was the department—the profit center within which goods and services are manufactured and distributed. The reason for the division and group levels in GE's hierarchy was to make the organization manageable; a span of control of 170 departments reporting to a single CEO obviously would be unworkable. To reduce the span of control, related departments were grouped into the forty-nine divisions, and related divisions were gathered into the ten groups.

GE's diversification put it into product lines ranging from toaster ovens to nuclear reactors, and from jet engines to construction equipment, chemicals, light bulbs, electric motors, transformers, turbines, space products, and more. While GE's organization in the early 1970s worked well in managing the diversified

---

[6] A.C. Hax and N.S. Majluf, *Strategic Management* (Englewood Cliffs, NJ: Prentice-Hall, 1984), 294.

operations, it did little to facilitate effective planning. This was because, as you know, a strategic plan requires an analysis of the environment—competitive, technological, and so on—but widely divergent products are beset by very different environmental influences. There is no *common* conclusion that can be drawn concerning the technological environment and competitive environment for refrigerators and jet engines, for example. Therefore, a single strategic plan for GE would be useless and 170 strategic plans would be unwieldy. Developing strategic plans for the ten groups or forty-nine divisions would make more sense. But the departments comprising them were joined for operational effectiveness and efficiency, and typically included product lines in differing markets. For example, the consumer-products group encompassed home entertainment products as well as light bulbs. Obviously, such products are different in terms of many competitive, technological, and purchase-decision aspects.

So how does one plan in such a setting? If one plan is meaningless, 170 plans are unwieldy, and many of the ten groups and forty-nine divisions did not share the homogeneous environments required to develop meaningful plans. GE's solution was to reorganize for planning purposes only, around the markets it serves rather than around production or other functions. In the process, GE created forty-three strategic business units, one for each of the "businesses" it competed in, and for which a meaningful and separate strategic plan could be developed. Many of the SBUs cross traditional group, division, and departmental profit-center lines. For example, food preparation appliances had been located in three separate divisions for operational efficiency. For strategic-planning purposes, these appliances were merged into a single SBU serving the housewares market.[7]

GE Update. A company that is just starting a formal strategic planning process may find the identification of SBUs very taxing. Normally, a temporary definition of SBUs is suggested at an early stage; as the planning system evolves, major redefinitions may be required.[8] For example, in 1977, GE reorganized its SBUs into six sectors of the economy (consumer products and services, industrial products and components, technical systems and materials, international power systems, and the since-sold Utah International Inc.). The sectors consisted of related groups and divisions. GE felt that one level of business-unit planning was not enough. In the early 80s, GE used forty-nine SBUs with a plan developed for each. The strategies of each of its six to ten businesses (SBUs) were reviewed and resources allocated to them at the sector (industry) level. This was then reviewed at the corporate level, where allocations were also approved. So,

---

[7] W.K. Hall, "SBUs: Hot, New Topic in the Management of Diversification," *Business Horizons* (February 1978), 17.

[8] *A System for Managing Diversity* (Cambridge, MA: Arthur D. Little, 1974), 10.

GE essentially created a two-level business-unit planning structure by grouping similar SBUs into sectors.[9]

In the late 80s, GE significantly restructured its portfolio, selling off several of its businesses (including consumer electronics) and sectors and adding several new businesses, notably RCA and its subsidiary, NBC. GE replaced its sector-form of organization, dropping a layer of top management and effectively merging its strategic and operational organizations.

Currently, GE is organized around thirteen "core businesses" which are led by Chief Operating Officers. The COOs of the thirteen core businesses report to the following top executives:

Chair, John Welch:	NBC, Medical Systems, Major Appliances.
Vice Chair:	Aircraft Engines, Aerospace, Locomotives.
Vice Chair:	Plastics, Power Systems, Lighting, Motors, Electrical Distribution, Communications, Financial Services.[10]

Therefore, GE now plans and operates on the basis of key "businesses." It has gone to the ideal of having the planning structure the same as its operating structure, minimizing the differences between its planning and operating units to the point that the company plans by businesses, not separate SBUs. This decision on GE's part involves a trade-off; its ideal planning units do not *exactly* coincide with its ideal operating units, but merging the two creates fewer problems than having two structures. This is not the case for all organizations or situations.

Process-wise, GE top managers keep in touch with one another through a series of top management meetings, designed to foster cross-fertilization. For example:

January:	GE's 500 top managers meet for two and one-half days in Boca Raton, Florida for the purpose of facilitating informal and formal "cross-pollination" between divisions and functions.
October:	The top 100 managers meet in Phoenix for two and one-half days, engaging in "strategic and generic discussions."
Quarterly:	The Corporate Executive Council (30-40 senior GE executives) meet for a corporate update, review, and discussion.[11]

---

[9] R.F. Vancil, *Implementing Strategy: The Role of Top Management* (Boston, MA: Harvard Business School, 1982), 83.

[10] S.W. Quickel, "Welch on Welch," *Financial World* (April 3, 1990), 62-70.

[11] *Ibid.*

Core Competencies vs. SBUs

C.K. Pralahad and Gary Hamel suggest that companies should organize around core competencies rather than around strategic business units. They agree that diversified companies must have a portfolio of businesses and products, but feel that corporate structure for such companies must also focus on core competencies. The five or six fundamental competencies in which the firm should attempt to build world-class abilities underlie core products, business units, and end products, and determine how successful the business units and their products will be. Pralahad and Hamel's message is to ensure that the company's structure recognizes and guides the causal factor for business success—core competencies.[12]

Corporate-Level Processes

Again, the main goal of corporate-level strategies is to find and manage the right combination of businesses, so that the corporation can achieve its goals and objectives. In the past, growth has been a dominant corporate objective; more recently, the balance has swung toward return on investment. Equally important to having business units in which the company has a competitive advantage is the coordination of those businesses. For example, a number of functional strategies and actions may benefit the company, but are beyond the scope of and may not be presently feasible for any one business. Technology development and innovative activity is one such case, where the corporate level can coordinate business-level technology strategies and actions for the benefit of other businesses of the company. The corporate level can fund, for example, the development of an advanced technology by one business unit (or in a corporate laboratory) that may have application across several businesses, and would be too costly or risky for any one business to undertake on its own. Thus, coordination and funding of functional activities (technology, marketing, and the like) between businesses are responsibilities of corporate management in multibusiness firms.

CORPORATE PORTFOLIO MODELS

One tool many corporations use to aid in corporate-level strategic decision making is corporate portfolio models. These models illustrate the relationship between business units and aid corporate resource allocation decisions, and even suggest strategies for the business units. They also highlight which businesses

---

[12] C.K. Prahalad and Gary Hamel, "The Core Competence of the Corporation," *Harvard Business Review* (May/June 1990), 79-91.

should be retained or divested, and which types of businesses should be acquired or started. Three commonly used and related portfolio models will be examined: the growth/share matrix, the GE business screen, and the business profile matrix.

These models were developed in the late 1960s because, understandably, corporate management usually didn't know as much as the division general managers did about the firm's operating divisions. Portfolio models provided corporate management with a mechanism for comparing the relative strength and attractiveness of each SBU without being familiar with each in detail. The purpose of portfolio analysis, then, is to encourage a more rational allocation of corporate resources to SBUs based on their attractiveness and strengths.[13]

The Growth/Share Matrix

The Boston Consulting Group (BCG) proposed a new way to visualize the role played by each SBU in a diversified organization, as well as the relationships of SBUs. The BCG matrix plots market growth rate on the vertical axis and the business's relative market share on the horizontal axis, as shown in Figure 16.2. Actually, market growth rate is used as a proxy to indicate the attractiveness of the industry in which the SBU competes, and the market share in relation to the leading competitor is used to indicate the competitive strength of the business. This matrix is divided into four cells, with some figure (an arbitrary 10 percent market growth, the firm's target growth rate, the inflation rate, or whatever is meaningful) used to distinguish between high and low industry attractiveness. High competitive strength, in turn, is typically indicated by a relative market share over 1.0, with low strength below that level. (Relative market share is the SBU's sales divided by those of the largest competitor in the market.) The growth/share matrix visually portrays a company's SBUs in relationship to one another on these two axes.

Cell Categories. Business units positioned in the upper-left cell of the grid are *stars*, and are strong competitors (they have the largest market share) in high-growth markets. Stars usually require large amounts of cash to sustain their growth, but their strong position in the market makes them highly profitable. Thus, their cash flow is typically close to being in balance and is usually positive.

Cash cows are SBUs in the lower-left cell, and usually are large net providers of cash for the firm. Their leading market position usually makes them highly profitable, and because their needs for cash are less than those of stars, the net result is a healthy positive cash flow.

---

[13] R.F. Vancil, *Implementing Strategy: The Role of Top Management, Teacher's Manual* (Boston, MA: Harvard Business School, 1982), 6.

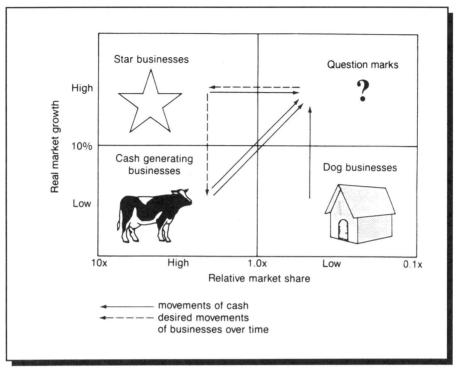

Figure 16.2 BCG Growth/Share Matrix

Question marks—sometimes called wildcats, sweepstakes, or problem children—are those in the upper-right cell. They are in high-growth industries and therefore require large amounts of cash. However, because of their relatively weak position competitively, they tend not to be very profitable, meaning that they require cash from outside (borrowing from the corporation "bank" or from other SBUs).

Dogs are businesses in the lower right—those in low-growth industries and in a weak competitive position. They usually are not very profitable (if at all), but do not require a lot of cash because of the low growth of their industry. In fact, they are typically providers of small amounts of cash.

Matrix Observations. Several points concerning the matrix should be kept in mind. One is that the product life cycle indicates that growth declines with maturity. Thus, over time, stars can be expected to become cash cows (which is *not* undesirable) and question marks may turn into dogs (which *is* undesirable). The company should be continually striving to move its SBUs farther to the left, in effect turning question marks into stars and possibly dogs into cash cows. Remember from the discussion of the life cycle in an earlier module, however, that it is difficult to gain market share in the maturity and decline stages. The best action may be to "spruce up" the dogs for the purpose of divesting them. (Keep in mind that a dog to one company may be a cash cow to a stronger competitor, and thus, an attractive purchase.) Ideally, question marks are in the preshakeout stage of the life cycle and market share possibly can be gained, so they may become stars. However, the risks may be high (hence, the term *wildcat*).

The largest amount of cash flow is from cash cows to question marks, so the company needs a balance of these types of SBUs. While a preponderance of stars may appear ideal, they typically do not produce enough cash to fund many future growth products, such as new stars. Thus, a few cash cows may be necessary to create new stars. Likewise, a predominance of cash cows may generate high profits and cash now, but what about the future as these businesses go into the decline stage? Too many question marks mean too much risk and the need for too much cash, and too many dogs may signify a company approaching serious trouble.

GE's Business Screen

In the early 1970s, GE and McKinsey & Company, consultants, developed a nine-cell "business screen" that is more complex than the simple growth-share matrix. While the screen is conceptually similar to the matrix, it defines industry attractiveness and business strength in terms of composite measures, determined and weighted by the company. As Figure 16.3 suggests, a number of factors besides market growth may determine attractiveness. These factors can be weighted according to their relative importance to the company, assigned a relative value, and combined into an overall index of industry attractiveness.

The same approach can be used for business strength, which obviously depends on more than just relative market share, especially when the future is considered. Other factors beyond those in Figure 16.3 might include breadth of product line, patents and other proprietary factors, newness and efficiency of plants, level of capacity, and experience-curve effects.

Like the growth-share matrix, the business screen is a portrayal of a company's SBUs, providing a visual display of its portfolio. GE divides its screen into nine cells, which becomes the basis for its "stoplight strategy." What this means is that the three cells in the upper left get the "green light" and are considered to be "invest-grow" businesses. The three in the lower right get a "red light," and are slated for "harvest-divest" action. The middle three on the diagonal from upper right to lower left get a "yellow light," or caution, and are held for a closer, more selective look. SBUs are typically portrayed on the screen as circles, with the size of the circle representing the SBU's size, and the shaded area representing its market share.

GE's current goal is to compete only in those businesses where it can be either the number one or two competitor; in other words, only in those businesses where it has a clear competitive advantage. This would result in GE having businesses only in the left third of the matrix, on anything but a short-term basis.

While the GE screen offers some refinements over the BCG matrix, it also has some shortcomings. Its refinements come at a cost of increased complexity. The individual firm must decide whether using the screen is worth the additional effort. Second, as with the BCG matrix, the business screen does not adequately depict new-growth industries and businesses. For these reasons, many companies couple either the BCG or GE matrix with a business profile matrix.

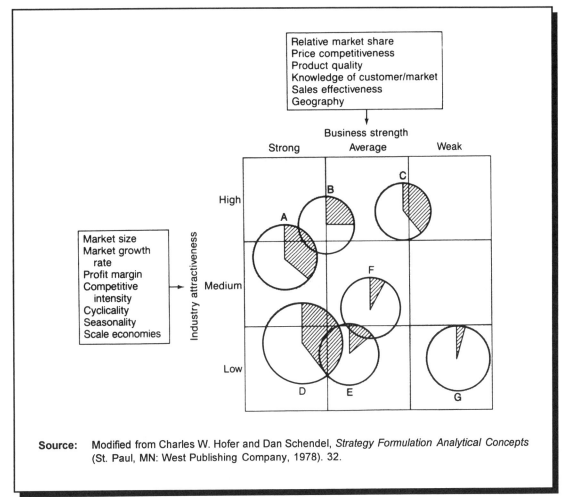

Source: Modified from Charles W. Hofer and Dan Schendel, *Strategy Formulation Analytical Concepts* (St. Paul, MN: West Publishing Company, 1978). 32.

Figure 16.3 General Electric's Nine-Cell Business Screen

Business Profile Matrix

The business profile matrix plots the SBU's competitive position against its life-cycle stage. The purpose is to portray the relative strength of SBUs in the embryonic and growth stages. Plotting the SBUs on the matrix, using circles as in the business screen, provides several types of information:

1. The relative strength of the company's business portfolio.
2. The likely future prospects for the company, as indicated by where the SBUs fall on the life-cycle axis.
3. Which relatively weak SBUs are targets for actions to improve the company's position (since the embryonic, shakeout, and decline or aging stages are those in which major changes in competitive position can occur most easily).
4. What type of generic strategy is most appropriate for the businesses falling in each of the twenty cells of the matrix.

Suggested strategic guidelines for each of the cells are shown in Figure 16.4 (Some companies portray the turbulent shakeout stage separately, giving the matrix 25 cells.)[14]

Portfolio Models: A Critique

Business portfolio models can be helpful in arraying the corporation's business units, and in showing the relative balance between them, or lack thereof. Using such tools helps the company decide on future corporate actions: which businesses should grow, which should be divested, where voids and overrepresentations exist, and the like. They also highlight the rationale for transactions between business-units, such as cash throw-off and absorption.

Such models do have weaknesses, however. They are static and don't represent trends; they depict, at best, the present performance of business units. But strategic decisions relate to the future, so care must be taken to realistically estimate where SBUs are likely to be in the future. As an example, investment in a high-potential question mark should be continued, while one with low star potential should be dropped. Keep in mind, however, that such assessments (particularly the latter case) can become self-fulfilling prophecies as a result of the firm's subsequent actions.

---

[14] Peter Patel and Michael Younger, "A Frame of Reference," 6-10.

Strength of Competitive Position	Life-Cycle Stage			
	Embryonic	Growth	Maturity	Aging
Dominant	Hold position All-out push for share	Hold position Hold share	Hold position Grow with industry	Hold position
Strong	Attempt to improve position All-out push for share	Attempt to improve position Push for share	Hold position Grow with industry	Hold position or Harvest
Favorable	Selectively attempt to improve position Selective or all-out push for share	Attempt to improve position Selective push for share	Custodial or Maintenance Find niche and attempt to protect it	Harvest Phased withdrawal
Tentative	Selectively push for position	Find niche and protect it	Find niche and hang on Phased withdrawal	Phased withdrawal or Abandon
Weak	Up or out	Turnaround or Abandon	Turnaround or Phased withdrawal	Abandon

Source: Adapted from Peter Patel and Michael Younger, "A Frame of Reference for Strategy Development," *Long-Range Planning*, 11 (April 1978), 8.

Figure 16.4 Business Profile Matrix

In addition, the portfolio models say nothing about another important variable—the relationship between headquarters and the business unit. In reality, it takes more than portfolio-dictated actions to succeed; one of the corporation's key roles is establishing the proper intracompany environment for each of its SBUs. Factors such as the degree of autonomy of an SBU, including its responsibility for its own functional decisions, as well as how much of division management's compensation is based on the unit's performance, all weigh heavily on its success.[15]

There are mechanical problems with some of the models, particularly the growth/share matrix. First, any SBU with less than 1.0 relative market share is a dog or wildcat. In any given market, only *one* business can have a relative share of greater than 1.0—all the others are dogs or wildcats! Second, most SBUs are likely to fall closer to the middle of the matrix than to the ends; there is likely to be relatively little difference between SBUs falling close to the dividing lines, but on opposite sides. Blind use of the matrix prescriptions, however, would suggest very different treatment of these businesses. Finally, comparing *extreme* stars, cash cows, wildcats, and dogs (corner cells of the nine-cell matrix) indicates that *all* tend to have positive ROI, as shown in Table 16.2. However, wildcats have the least favorable cash flow, with even extreme dogs close to self-sufficiency.[16] Remember, portfolio planning can improve corporate strategy, but only when used with other techniques for analyzing industries, competitors, and core competencies.

Table 16.2 Performance of Corner Cell Businesses in a Nine-Cell Matrix

Measure	Wildcats	Stars	Cash Cows	Dogs
Return on investment	14.90	32.94	27.40	14.66
Cash flow on investment	−4.20	5.14	8.03	-0.69

[15] R.G. Hammermesh and R.E. White, "Manage beyond Portfolio Analysis," *Harvard Business Review*, 62, No.1, (January/February, 1984), 103.

[16] N.E. Swanson and L.A. Digman, "Organizational Performance Measures for Strategic Decisions: A PIMS-Based Investigation," in *Handbook of Business Strategy: 1986/1987 Yearbook*, ed. W.D. Guth (Boston, MA: Warren, Gorham & Lamont, 1986), 17-19.

ENTERING NEW BUSINESSES: DIVERSIFICATION STRATEGIES

Growth and profitability are goals of most, although not all, organizations, at least those in the private sector. While satisfying a need or performing a level of service may be the primary mission and even the number-one goal for most organizations, even those in the public and not-for-profit sectors most often want to grow—to offer more and better service, for example. However, in the private sector, some for-profit organizations make a conscious decision as to size and do not attempt growth beyond that. Typical examples are smaller firms, family-run businesses, and service firms (such as hospitals, schools, law firms, clinics, and the like).

Given that *whether* to grow is a basic decision, the majority of organizations doggedly pursue growth—in sales, market share, geographical area, and more. There are three generic strategies usually employed in the pursuit of growth, in this order:

1. *Horizontal growth of existing businesses*, including more volume, greater market share, geographical (even international) expansion, a broader product line, and the like.
2. *Vertical integration*, both forward and backward. This strategy is typically followed as additional horizontal growth becomes more difficult.
3. *Diversification.* After approaching the limit of vertical integration opportunities, firms typically seek out new business opportunities via diversification. Diversification can be into related products, markets, industries, or technologies, or into unrelated areas.

Diversification, the opposite of concentration, usually results from several pressures. One is that the business cannot grow beyond its present size, because either the market is not large enough, or gaining additional shares of the market is not feasible. Another is the emergence of new markets that the firm sees as attractive. New technologies or new applications of existing technologies may also lure the firm into new markets. Finally, firms may diversify for legal reasons, such as tax laws that reward the firm for reinvesting profits as opposed to distributing them to shareholders. But, whatever the reason for diversification, the firm must define the role of each business within the enterprise— successful diversification is not mere aggregation (which may come as a surprise to certain conglomerates).[17]

Firms successfully grow into related markets if they can duplicate existing skills (core competencies) in the new business. It is also necessary for them to

---

[17] Peter F. Drucker, *Management: Tasks, Responsibilities, Practices* (New York, NY: Harper & Row, 1974), 683-97.

adopt the M-form structure to efficiently manage subsidiaries. Companies that grow into unrelated businesses typically do so because they lack suitable related diversification opportunities and because a slack capital market permits them to do so.[18]

Some diversification moves result in real synergies. For example, Metropolitan Financial Corporation of Minneapolis has three major subsidiaries; Metropolitan Federal Bank (facilities in nine states), Edina Realty (49 offices and 2,000 sales associates) and Equity Title Services (eight offices). Edina Realty creates significant fee income through realty commissions and services, and provides Metropolitan Federal access to an important source of assets through mortgage loan referrals. In 1993, Edina Realty completed 26,000 closings with Equity Title.[19]

As Peter Drucker states, "attempts to diversify without either a foundation in common markets or in common technology are doomed to frustration." He further concludes that diversification to make a business "countercyclical"— balancing the cycles of one industry with those of another—rarely works, nor do attempts to marry businesses with high demands for capital with those having a high cash throw off; the balance tends to change with time, invalidating the reason for the diversification. There is one absolute requirement for successful diversification: unity of values. The business unit's climate and values must be compatible and there must be "respect" for the businesses.[20]

Entry Strategies

There are a variety of mechanisms for entering new businesses. Each is described briefly below, and the advantages and disadvantages of each are summarized in Table 16.3.

1. *Acquisitions.* Purchase of an existing business.
2. *Internal development.* Establishing a business new to the company, using internal resources, operating as an internal part of the company.
3. *Licensing.* Acquiring products or technology through licensing is an alternative to purchasing an entire company, and avoids the risks of product development.
4. *Internal ventures.* Entering markets different from the existing base businesses by setting up a separate entity within the existing corporate structure.

---

[18] Michael Ollinger, "The Limits of Growth of the Multidivisional Firm: A Case Study of the U.S. Oil Industry From 1930-90," *Strategic Management Journal*, 14, No. 7 (September 1994), 503-20.

[19] *1993 Annual Report* Metropolitan Financial Corp., 8.

[20] *Ibid.*, 706-10.

Table 16.3 Entry Mechanisms: Advantages and Disadvantages

New Business Development Mechanisms	Major Advantages	Major Disadvantages
Acquisitions	Rapid market entry.	New business area may be unfamiliar to parent.
Internal developments	Use existing resources.	Time lag to break even tends to be long (on average eight years). Unfamiliarity with new markets may lead to errors.
Licensing	Rapid access to proven technology. Reduced financial exposure.	Not a substitute for internal technical competence. Not proprietary technology. Dependent upon licensor.
Internal ventures	Use existing resources. May enable a company to hold a talented entrepreneur.	Mixed record of success. Corporation's internal climate often unsuitable.
Joint ventures or alliances	Technological/marketing unions can exploit small/large company synergies. Distribute risk.	Potential for conflict between partners.
Venture capital and nurturing	Can provide window on new technology or market.	Unlikely alone to be a major stimulus of corporate growth.
Educational acquisitions	Provide window and initial staff.	Higher initial financial commitment than venture capital. Risk of departure of entrepreneurs.

Source: Adapted from E.B. Roberts and C.A. Berry, "Entering New Businesses: Selecting Strategies for Success," *Sloan Management Review* (Spring 1985), 8. Used with permission. All rights reserved.

5. *Joint ventures or alliances.* Either formation of third corporations involving several or more companies, or "mutual pursuit" alliances between two companies (often a small company with new technology and a larger company with marketing capability).

6. *Venture capital and nurturing.* Securing closeness to (and possible later entry into) new technologies by making minority investments in young and growing enterprises.

7. *Educational acquisitions.* Acquisitions for the purpose of obtaining people familiar with a new business area, which can complement one of the other methods.[21]

The entry alternatives fall into two main types—acquisitions and internal developments and ventures—which are discussed in the following sections.

Acquisition-Related Strategies

Acquisitions are one way a firm may attempt to grow in size and sales, to increase its economies of scale, or to spread its risks. Divestitures, in turn, are attempts by a firm to eliminate "dogs" or other businesses that do not fit the firm's portfolio for one reason or another. Here, the types of acquisitions and reasons for acquiring businesses are examined.

There are five basic reasons for acquiring businesses:

1. To strengthen or protect the core business. An acquisition may provide key personnel, assets, and purchasing power that aid an existing business. An acquisition may provide economies of scale or entry to additional markets (such as G. Heileman's acquisitions of various regional and local brewers), making the firm a stronger and more viable competitor.

2. To diversify, for the reasons discussed previously.

3. To avoid a takeover by acquiring a competitor of a company desiring to take over your business. For example, Ryder Systems (truck rental) intended to take over Frank B. Hall Company (insurance brokerage), which acquired Ryder's competitor Jartran as a defensive move. Thus, antitrust laws prevented Ryder from acquiring Frank B. Hall.

4. To improve financial returns by, for example, improving return on excess capital or purchasing tax credits owned by the acquired firm.[22]

---

[21] E.B. Roberts and C.A. Berry, "Entering New Businesses: Selecting Strategies for Growth," *Sloan Management Review* (Spring 1985), 3-17.

[22] L.L. Fray, J.W. Down, and D. Gaylin, "Acquisitions and Divestitures," in *Handbook of Business Strategy*, ed. W.D. Guth (Boston, MA: Warren, Gorham & Lamont, 1985), 12-4.

5. To alter the company's business mix (perhaps coupled with divestitures). For example, Gould changed from an electrical equipment to an electronics company through acquisitions.

Types of Acquisitions. There are four types of acquisitions: (1) vertical, (2) horizontal, (3) concentric diversification, and (4) unrelated diversification, as shown in Figure 16.5.

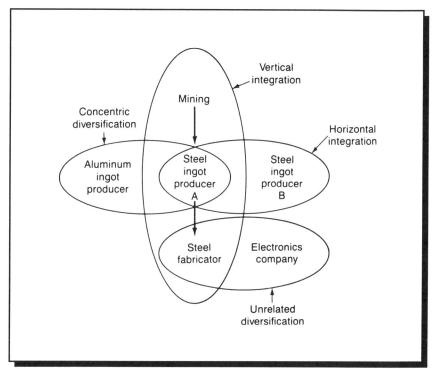

Figure 16.5 Types of Acquisitions

According to George Steiner, "vertical acquisitions are those in the same product-line (or line of business) and involve integration from basic raw materials to the ultimate sale to consumers."[23] For example, a producer of steel ingots may acquire an iron mine or a steel fabricating company. The company can proceed "upstream" toward the source of supply by acquiring supplies of raw materials, or components, or subcontractors, or "downstream" through the chan-

---

[23] George Steiner, *Top Management Planning* (New York, NY: Macmillan, 1969), 641.

nels of distribution toward the final customer.[24] Vertical acquisitions can reduce costs and increase a firm's competitive market position.

Although vertical acquisitions can improve a firm's market position, they have two major drawbacks. The first is that the firm is still dependent on its particular market and on the business fluctuations of its industry. The second is the possibility of social repercussions, primarily government intervention on antitrust grounds. A major example of government intervention in vertical-control firms was the antitrust decision that led to the breakup of AT&T.

In a horizontal acquisition, a competitor or a business in the same field of endeavor is purchased. Functional skills and resources are expanded and market share is increased. One example is the acquisition of Metropolitan Federal Bank by First Bank of Minneapolis. The same two drawbacks of vertical acquisitions—the firm is still confined to the same industry and the possibility of government antitrust intervention—also affect horizontal acquisitions.

A concentric acquisition occurs when two businesses in different industries have a common thread of interest. An example would be the acquisition of a cake mix producer by a shortening manufacturer. Another form is the acquisition of a business in a separate industry that uses the same marketing channels.

Another type of acquisition involves diversification into unrelated industries. The firm expands not into similar fields but into totally unrelated markets. This decreases the firm's dependence on a particular product or market.

These multi-industry firms are typically either diversified majors or conglomerates. The two styles of firms have dissimilar functions and strategies at the corporate level.[25] The diversified major attempts to bring a synergistic approach to the business units. A conglomerate treats each unit as a complete and independent, or even as a separate, company. In a diversified major, the corporate level is involved in R&D, marketing, manufacturing, and purchasing. A conglomerate, however, is rarely involved in these functional areas. Some examples of diversified majors are GE, Du Pont, and Union Carbide—firms that expanded internally and through acquisition of technologically and market-related businesses. Two examples of conglomerate firms are Textron and Teledyne. Textron expanded from the wool market into a wide range of consumer and industrial goods.

---

[24] N.A. Stacey, *Mergers in Modern Business* (London, England: Hutchinson, 1970), 33.

[25] Norman Berg and R.A. Pitts, "Strategic Management: The Multi-Business Corporation," in *Strategic Management*, eds. D.Schendel and C.W. Hofer (Boston, MA: Little, Brown, 1979), 339.

Internal Development and Venture Strategies

In addition to acquisition strategies, internal actions are also a means of diversification. Business-unit strategies appropriate for the growth, maturity, and decline stages, as well as the judicious use of strategies pertaining to positioning, distinguishing, and determining the desired scope of the businesses can be employed to achieve corporate-level objectives. A corporate-level strategy, the creation of new business units either internally or by joint ventures, is discussed in the following paragraphs.

Internal/Joint-Venture Strategies. There are two main types of new ventures: those intended to function as a separate company and those created *within* a larger company. The latter are often called *intracorporate ventures*, or *internal new ventures*, and function within a distinctly different environment than does the totally separate venture.

The internal venture is many times a "question mark" or "wildcat" in the corporate portfolio, and has the financial backing of the corporation. The price it pays for this backing, however, is often a lack of independence and an element of corporate "meddling" and control over its activities. Often, the internal new venture is unduly constrained by the parent, because corporate management may not fully appreciate the unique needs of the venture: for entrepreneurial people, flexibility, avoidance of conformity, and risk-taking behavior. Separate ventures do not have these potentially inhibiting constraints, but often possess inadequate financial backing, which inhibits their growth.

As Peter Drucker has said, "it is widely believed that large companies cannot innovate. That is simply not true: Merck, Citibank, and 3M are but three examples of highly innovative corporate giants. But it is true that to innovate successfully, a company has to be run differently from the typical "well managed" business, whether large or small."[26] Innovative companies have a separate "innovation budget" to support potential new ventures; they do not expect returns in the short run; they closely control new ventures; and they do not hesitate to abandon obsolete products.

Venture Characteristics. Inadequate capital remains an important source of failure for new ventures. Ralph Biggadike found this to be a problem even for internal ventures.[27] In his study, he found, for example, that the median ROI was minus 40 percent for the first two years of operation, and minus 14 percent

---

[26] Peter F. Drucker, "The Innovative Company," *The Wall Street Journal* (February 26, 1982), 22.

[27] Ralph Biggadike, "The Risky Business of Diversification," *Harvard Business Review* (May/June 1979), 103.

for the next two years. According to Biggadike, it takes *eight years* on the average for new ventures to reach profitability, and *ten to twelve years* before their ROI equals that of mature businesses. Furthermore, the highest ROI tends to go to businesses with high market shares. So the strategic objective for the early years should be to build share, regardless of short-term profitability. In fact, the biggest risk is entering *too small*. Entering on a large scale leads to better financial results earlier than does entering on a small scale. From this it can be seen that the venture with a high chance of succeeding requires a large amount of capital—enough to enter on a large scale and enough to stand negative profits and cash flow for eight years or so. It is better not to enter at all than to enter without adequate backing and fail before the corner is turned. For larger firms, then, it is better to adequately finance fewer ventures than to "test the water" (and likely fail) with a larger number of ventures. Big losses are rare events; small losses are numerous and more likely. As a result, for a start-up, it is not uncommon for a provider of venture capital to give *more* money to the entrepreneur than was requested, to improve the likelihood of survival.

Venture Strategies. Figure 16.6 displays the range of alternative strategies for launching new ventures, ranging from low to high corporate involvement. At the left, *venture capital* involves the investment of money in the stock of one company by another. The capital source may be an existing industrial firm, or a firm specializing in venture capital, which underwrites a stock issue.

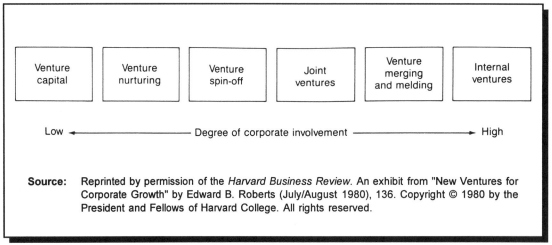

| Venture capital | Venture nurturing | Venture spin-off | Joint ventures | Venture merging and melding | Internal ventures |

Low ◀——————— Degree of corporate involvement ———————▶ High

Figure 16.6 Spectrum of Venture Strategies

In *venture nurturing*, the investing company contributes more than just capital, usually, managerial assistance in such areas as research, manufacturing, and marketing.

A *venture spin-off* is a new company created by a larger firm to capitalize on its R&D efforts. The new company can pursue an idea or technology that does not fit the developing firm's interests or risks or may be better developed in an outside "entrepreneurial" company. Exxon pursued this approach with its Solar Power Corp.

In a *joint venture*, two companies—typically, one large and one small—enter jointly into a new project or venture. The smaller company provides enthusiasm, vigor, flexibility, and technology, and the larger one provides capital and channels of distribution, marketing, and service. In this way, the benefits of both the large and small firm can be realized by the joint venture. IBM employed this approach in conjunction with Rolm and Intel in recent years. A current example of two large companies pursuing joint ventures is the New United Motors Manufacturing, Inc. (NUMMI), undertaken by General Motors/Toyota. Also, in 1988, Motorola and Toshiba entered into a 50-50 joint venture. Called Tohoku Semiconductor Corp., the venture was created to combine Motorola's advanced microprocessor designs with Toshiba's manufacturing knowhow.[28]

Venture merging and melding attempts to piece together similar ventures (e.g., having similar technologies) into a "critical mass" to increase their marketing and technological strengths. This improves the success rate of otherwise small ventures. The semiconductor industry's joint research consortiums, Sematech and Microelectronics and Computer Technology Corp. (located in Austin, Texas), are prime examples. Another, less successful, example was Exxon Enterprises.

Internal ventures, as discussed previously, are situations in which a firm sets up a separate internal group to develop a new product line or to enter a new market; 3M has been consistently successful using this approach. Additional examples include IBM's personal computer division and General Motors' Saturn Corp.[29]

Successful Internal Ventures. A number of companies have begun to stress "intrapreneurship"—encouraging entrepreneurial behavior within the corporate structure—with varying degrees of success. IBM, for example, recognized the personal computer market as a separate business, and set up independent engineering, marketing, and distribution for the product. Companies without such an approach typically try to "find a home" for new products and technologies in existing business units. Most often, the new product represents a small market, and suffers accordingly in comparison to "bread and butter" products, or is

---

[28] Larry Armstrong, "A Chipmaking Venture the Gods Smiled Upon," *Business Week* (July 4, 1988), 109.

[29] E.E. Roberts, "New Ventures for Corporate Growth," *Harvard Business Review* (July/August 1980), 130.

poorly understood, or does poorly because it doesn't fit the existing structure and strategies.

Recent studies have shed some light on how internal entrepreneurial activities can succeed. Successes mainly occur in firms that are able to delicately balance the need for diversity and order; the diversity results from operational-level innovation and strategic initiatives, while order flows from imposing a strategy concept on the organization. Top management's critical task is to balance these conflicting demands for diversity and order, controlling the level and rate of change, rather than the specific content of entrepreneurial activity.[30] Typically, a few key people in an organization are the indispensable entrepreneurs and innovators. Management should know clearly who they are, and go to great pains to keep them by overriding seniority systems, and by providing big rewards, freedom, and responsibility.[31]

Diversification and Performance

Under what conditions should a company employ the various methods of diversification to assure maximum success? In general, new business development should be constrained within areas related to a company's base (present) businesses in order to ensure highest performance and likelihood of success. Given this criterion, either internal developments *or* acquisitions may be successful diversification methods. But, there are degrees of familiarity a firm may have with both the market and the technology represented by the products and services of the new business. If the market or technologies (or both) are not part of the firm's present businesses, different entry strategies may be called for to maximize entry success, depending on the degree of familiarity. Figure 16.7 highlights strategies appropriate for various situations.

Diversification Results. In a well-publicized study (1987), Michael Porter found that more than half of the diversification efforts by large companies since 1950 have ended in failure. Diversification—whether through acquisition, joint venture, or start-up—has not generally brought the competitive advantages or profitability sought by management. Why? Companies undertaking diversification typically fail one of three key tests: they overspend for the new business; they rationalize rather than analyze the attractiveness of the new industry; or they don't demonstrate how the new business will fit with the company's strategy and existing businesses. In contrast, successful companies transfer skills and

---

[30] R.A. Burgelman, "Corporate Entrepreneurship and Strategic Management: Insights from a Process Study," *Management Science*, 29, No. 12 (December 1983), 1349.

[31] Michael Kami, *Strategic Planning for Changing Times* (Dayton, OH: Cassette Recording Co., 1984).

share activities between businesses; this is the practical essence of effective corporate-level strategy.[32]

One company—Nordson Corporation—calls its successful related-diversification approach the "lily pad" strategy. As a frog jumps to the nearest lily pad (which it can see, and from which it can hop back to safety if necessary), Nordson has focused on internal growth into businesses that are very close to, or make good use of, its core capabilities. Nordson does this by introducing new technologies in its existing markets, or existing technologies in new markets.

		Joint Ventures	Venture capital or venture nurturing or educational acquisitions	Venture capital or venture nuturing or educational acquisitions
	New Unfamiliar			
Market Factors	New Familiar	Internal market developments or acquisitions (or joint ventures)	Internal ventures or acquisitions or licensing	Venture capital or venture nurturing or educational acquisitions
	Base	Internal base developments (or acquisitions)	Internal product developments or acquisitions or licensing	Strategic alliances
		Core	New Familiar	New Unfamiliar

Technologies or Services Embodied in the Product

Source: Adapted from E.B. Roberts and C.A. Berry, "Entering New Businesses: Selecting Strategies for Success;" *Sloan Management Review* (Spring 1985), 13. Used with permission. All rights reserved.

Figure 16.7 **Optimum Entry Strategies**

Other recent studies show somewhat inconsistent and even conflicting results. There seems to be some indication, however, that related diversifiers (e.g., horizontal and concentric expansions) earn higher returns than unrelated diversi-

---
[32] M.E. Porter, "From Competitive Advantage to Corporate Strategy," *Harvard Business Review*, 65, No. 3 (May/June 1987), 43-60.

fiers.[33] Another study suggests that firms attempt related diversification in order to exploit operating synergies, and attempt unrelated diversification to increase leverage due to greater stability of cash flows. The study found that related diversification tends to yield higher profitability than does unrelated, but pure financial diversification (unrelated) results in more stable cash flows, higher leverage, and lower profitability.[34]

On the other hand, some kinds of relatedness may prove detrimental. Researchers at Clemson University found, predictably, that firms diversifying into products using similar marketing channels had higher profitability without incurring higher risk. Conversely, however, diversification into products sharing mostly the same technologies yielded lower profitability and higher risk. These results suggest that expanding beyond a narrow range of technologies can spread the risk and increase financial returns.[35]

So, what can we conclude at this point? England's Andrew Campbell suggests that diversification is not wrong; over-diversification is the danger. Problems arise from getting into businesses managers do not fully understand. Managers wrongly believe that diversification reduces risks. Unfortunately, diversification to achieve balance often increases risk to the company because it can introduce inefficiencies and opportunities for mismanagement. Corporate performance and survival is improved by increases in competitive advantage, which can be dissipated by a loss of focus on core businesses. Also, many managers believe that their role is to grow the company, and see growth through diversification. But, growth for growth's sake "is dumb."[36]

Acquisition Results. In a late study of 64 Fortune 1,000 firms, it was found that conglomerate, technology-related, and marketing-related acquisition strategies *all* were associated with a decline in market position; however, the marketing-related strategy was superior to the other two. Therefore, managers may want to consider internal growth as an alternative to acquisitions.[37] On the other hand, some acquisitions create value—some more than others. A recent

---

[33] R.M. Grant, A.P. Jammine, and H. Thomas, "Diversity, Diversification, and Profitability among British Manufacturing Companies, 1972-84," *Academy of Management Journal*, 31, No. 4 (December 1988), 774.

[34] R. Amit and J. Livnat, "Diversification Strategies, Business Cycles, and Economic Performance," *Strategic Management Journal*, 9, No. 2 (March/April 1988), 99.

[35] J.S. Harrison, E.H. Hall, Jr., and L.G. Caldwell, "Assessing Strategy Relatedness in Highly-Diversified Firms," *Journal of Business Strategies*, 7, No. 1 (Spring 1990), 34-46.

[36] Andrew Campbell, "Why Do Companies Over-Diversify?" *The Planning Forum Network* (September 1992), 3.

[37] H.D. Hopkins, "Acquisition Strategy and the Market Position of Acquiring Firms," *Strategic Management Journal*, 8, No. 6 (November/December 1987), 535-47.

Harvard/Booz, Allen & Hamilton-sponsored study found that value is created by acquisitions in which the assets of either the target or the bidder are used more intensively (e.g., identical, vertical, or concentric). But those that permit acquisition into new markets (concentric) or within the same business (identical), create the *most* value.[38] Therefore, horizontal and concentric acquisitions are preferred over vertical moves, and unrelated acquisitions appear least desirable. Another study found that acquiring firms tend to outperform nonacquirers in the years *prior* to the acquisition, but underperform the others *after* the event. In addition, this study raised the point that firms may acquire others because of their prior superior performance, as an investment. Interestingly, the remuneration of the acquiring firms' managers significantly outpaced the others, indicating that firm performance may not be the only factor motivating acquisition behavior.[39]

Finally, in a study of 297 large mergers, it was found that *all* types of mergers—single business, vertical, related, and unrelated—were associated with *increases* in the risk (variance) resulting from the firm's individual businesses. Further, only related mergers significantly reduced the sensitivity (risk) of returns to variations in the aggregate returns of the marketplace.[40]

Supporting this finding, Alok Chakrabarti of Georgia State found that corporate prior understanding of the acquired business was significantly related to all six of his measures of firm performance. Those who look upon acquisitions as a quick way to improve financial performance are not likely to spend the time and money to familiarize themselves prior to the acquisition, with less than satisfactory results.[41]

All in all, these studies seriously question the desirability of unrelated diversification strategies via acquisitions. Perhaps corporate managers should concentrate on building competitive advantage in each business rather than pursuing new markets to spread their risk. If diversification is desired, internally developed related businesses seem to be the superior choice.

[38] L.M. Shelton, "Strategic Business Fits and Corporate Acquisition: Empirical Evidence," *Strategic Management Journal*, 9, No. 3 (May/June 1988), 284.

[39] K.L. Fowler, D.E. Schmidt, and L.A. Digman, "The Effect of Tender Offer Acquisitions on the Bidding Firm: Overall Performance, Managerial Gain, and Gains to Shareholders," *Proceedings of the 18th Annual Conference, Decision Sciences Institute* (November 1986).

[40] Michael Lubatkin and H.M. O'Neill, "Merger Strategies and Capital Market Risk," *Academy of Management Journal*, 30, No. 4 (December 1987), 665-84.

[41] Alok Chakrabarti, "Acquisition Performance," *IEEE Transactions on Engineering Management* (November 1990), 259-68.

CORPORATE CONCENTRATION AND RESTRUCTURING STRATEGIES

Given the pessimistic results concerning diversification strategies, it is understandable that many firms have undertaken restructuring actions, designed to *reduce* their diversification and focus their companies on a few key-related businesses. Sometimes companies are forced by the threat of takeover to divest and restructure, and some have done so at a loss. The French oil service company Schlumberger acquired Fairchild Semiconductor Corp. in 1979 for $425 million. In 1985, Fairchild had a $627 million loss, and Schlumberger sold Fairchild to National Semiconductor in 1987 for $122 million in stock and warrants.[42]

Recent studies support the trend toward more concentrated, restructured firms. Because different markets require different skills for success, firms which concentrate in one market area (e.g., consumer or industrial), at a given level of diversification, achieve superior performance.[43]

Divestiture Strategies

Divestiture involves selling a business unit, subsidiary, division, or product line as a going business. In contrast to the situation in the 1960s when acquisitions and takeovers were the rage, in recent years there has been a growing desire on the part of many companies to go the other way; to divest themselves of unrelated, unprofitable, or unmanageable operations.[44] In fact, sometimes the two strategies are coupled; one company acquires or takes over another, and then divests the unwanted businesses, perhaps retaining the business units or assets it wanted at little cost.

Portfolio models can give an indication of business units that are potential candidates for divestment. In most cases, however, it is not clear that a unit should be divested immediately. Management usually must decide whether or not a business unit should be retained and possibly reduced in size or turned around, or whether it should be divested. In addition, even if the decision is to divest, timing the divestment is a major concern. An important aspect of the decision to divest is the amount and timing of the cash recovery from the divestiture. In addition, the decision to divest may entail appreciable costs.

[42] R.B. Schmitt, "Schlumberger Reaches Accord to Sell Fairchild," *The Wall Street Journal* (September 1, 1987), 2.

[43] N. Capon, J.M. Hulbert, J.U. Farley, and L.E. Martin, "Corporate Diversity and Economic Performance: The Impact of Market Specialization," *Strategic Management Journal*, 9, No. 1 (January-February 1988), 61.

[44] Laurie Meisler, "Mergers and Divestitures: A Forbes Special Supplement," *Forbes* (November 5, 1984), 4.

In general, however, studies have shown that divestitures linked to corporate or business-level strategies tend to be valued positively by the market; those perceived as the sale of unwanted units in the absence of defined strategic goals tend to be valued negatively.[45] A company can have several reasons for divesting itself of a division: unsatisfactory earnings performance, expansion needs that the parent company cannot afford, a need to diversify that the segment does not meet, receipt of an attractive offer, lack of synergy with the company's other businesses, government antitrust action, and debt reduction.

Exit Barriers. Kathy Harrigan has described problems associated with divesting an SBU. Once the decision is made, a company may find divestment is not easy, especially in the case of a failing business. Even trying to sell the assets, let alone the entire unit, may be impossible if there is no market. Paradoxically, entry barriers that the divesting company helped put in place to protect its own market niche from competition may now become barriers to exit. Exit barriers include:

1. *Economic.* These factors could induce the firm to continue operating a subsidiary even while earning a below-normal return from it. Exiting a business may be blocked by the high cost of dismantling assets, such as plants, or the lack of an adequate resale market. For relatively new businesses, it may be better to recapture the value of the assets through depreciation over several years than to sell them at a loss immediately. A simple formula can aid in making this decision: the discounted expected value of future operations is divided by the expected salvage value. A ratio greater than one would indicate that it is better to continue operations.
2. *Strategic.* If a synergy exists between the unattractive business and the company's other units, the firm may be reluctant to divest itself of the "lemon." These exit barriers include: customer service obligations; the possibility of hurting the quality image of the firm and its other products; physical facilities shared by businesses the corporation wants to keep; and the loss of strong customer industries that have relied on the products that will be discontinued. This last factor could damage the firm's competitive posture in other markets.
3. *Expectations.* If a company expects demand to pick up, it may decide to weather the storm instead of giving up on a failing business. Also, if one

---

[45] Cynthia Montgomery, A.R. Thomas, and R. Kamath, "Divestitures, Market Value, and Strategy," *Academy of Management Journal*, 27, No. 4 (December 1984), 830.

niche of the product market is still attractive, the firm may not want to lose the assets that serve that niche.[46]

It is suggested that companies plan their exit from a business at the time of entry. If a company keeps these exit barriers in mind, and realizes that any business's attractiveness can decline as fast as its profits, the company can be more prepared to hurdle these barriers.

Thus, divestitures are not always clear-cut or simple procedures. Barriers to exit and tax considerations easily can override decisions that appear straightforward up to that point. Some alternatives to divestiture or liquidation, including defense, renewal, retrenchment, or turnaround, were discussed earlier as business-unit strategies.

Corporate Restructuring

Many companies—such as ITT, Allied-Signal, and others—have recently undertaken restructuring actions, at least partly to increase shareholder value. In fact, some experts see restructuring as "the biggest issue in corporate America today," downsizing and simplifying corporations to focus their businesses more clearly.[47] Many corporate restructurings have been undertaken because of the threat of a corporate takeover; the firm is valued by the stock market at less than its book value and its breakup value (the *parts* are worth more than the whole—a *negative* synergy exists). Raiders tend not to be interested in companies whose stock prices reflect their true value; therefore, a real takeover defense "requires developing the perspective of a corporate raider and learning to act like a turnaround artist."[48]

A 1988 study of top executives and financial professionals revealed that 97 percent saw restructuring as an *ongoing* process, rather than as a single event, and felt that either they or their clients were likely to execute major restructuring moves in the near future. Also of interest are the major reasons for restructuring, which the respondents ranked as follows:[49]

---

[46] K.R. Harrigan, "Deterrents to Divestiture," *Academy of Management Journal* (June 1981), 306.

[47] W.B. Shaffir, "Focus and Simplicity: Today's Strategic Priorities," *Planning Review*, 15, No. 3 (May/June 1987), 44.

[48] B.C. Reimann, "Realizing Shareholder Value," *Planning Review*, 15, No. 4 (July/August 1987), 42.

[49] Martin Sikora, "Corporate Restructuring," undated promotional material for *Corporate Restructuring* newsletter (Spring 1988).

To increase shareholder value 83%
Change in corporate strategy 66
To meet increasing competition 33
Defense against hostile takeover threat 30
To redeploy funds more productively 30
Decline of important markets 26
Diversification 20
Loss of synergies 14

Studies bear out the trend toward restructuring. Even going back to the 1975-84 time period, managers of multibusiness firms were reducing the complexity of their enterprises by decreasing the number of businesses managed as well as by increasing the relatedness of their portfolio of businesses.[50]

How to Avoid Being Acquired. While mergers, acquisitions, and takeovers may be good or bad for the stockholders of the acquired company, they frequently are detrimental to the acquired's management. To reduce the likelihood of a takeover, management should reduce as many as possible of the factors favoring the action. Management has little control over the firm's desirability as a target for horizontal or vertical integration or diversification. But it can reduce the firm's vulnerability through the following actions:

1. Remain as efficient and profitable as possible, contenting stockholders and reducing attractiveness to a firm looking to purchase turnaround situations.
2. Acquire a competitor of the acquirer.
3. Keep liquidity to low but safe levels to discourage cash-hungry firms.
4. Follow innovative, aggressive strategies and policies that, coupled with good earnings and growth, result in a high stock price/earnings ratio.
5. Broaden and splinter outside ownership of stock through timely splits.
6. Adopt antitakeover amendments.

Since all of these moves are not possible at all times, management should monitor stock ownership by pension and investment funds and potential arbitrageurs (third-party speculators hoping to profit from a takeover attempt), as well as by potential acquirers. In the event that a takeover attempt does occur, the company can denounce the offer and urge stockholders not to accept it, seek to block it through legal action or government intervention, or even acquire another firm in the interim. If all else fails, management can look for a "white knight," or favorable acquiring company. A recent study of antitakeover amendments showed that they had no significant strategic, managerial, or organizational ef-

---

[50] J.R. Williams, B.L. Paez, and L. Sanders, "Conglomerates Revisited," *Strategic Management Journal*, 9, No. 5 (September/October 1988), 403.

fects on firms adopting them. While the relationships may be complex, there is no evidence that the amendments affect a firm positively or negatively.[51]

Leveraged Buyouts. A practice which recently attracted a lot of attention and some controversy is the leveraged buyout. In general, a leveraged buyout (LBO) is a financial transaction in which the buyer (either an individual or a group, management or outsiders) takes over the company by using its assets as collateral. In a typical LBO, management borrows against the firm's assets or issues junk bonds to buy all of its outstanding stock. Once the LBO has occurred, the new owners usually take bold actions to pare the resulting debt down to a more manageable, less-risky size.[52] One of the key questions concerning LBOs is why managers who can't maximize shareholder value while the company is publicly traded seem to be able to do so as soon as it goes private. Perhaps the main forces at work are those of corporate control and personal gain.[53]

CONCLUSIONS

Multibusiness organizations often find the need to depart from their operational structures to accomplish their strategic planning tasks. Focusing on markets and strategic business units rather than on operational divisions or departments has facilitated this task in a number of companies. However, SBUs and operating units should be aligned as closely as possible.

Various portfolio models, if properly used, can aid in formulating corporate level strategies, highlighting the portfolio of businesses and their interrelationships. Corporate-level growth strategies most often involve growth and diversification decisions, particularly after horizontal and vertical expansion options have been exhausted. At this stage, adjusting the mix of business units through acquisitions, divestitures, internal and joint ventures, and combination strategies takes center stage. Recently, studies and practice have found diversification results to be disappointing, forcing many companies to sharpen their focus by restructuring and divestitures. For some, these actions have been taken in self defense to avoid being taken over.

---

[51] Paul Mallette, *An Empirical Examination of the Strategic, Managerial, and Organizational Consequences of Antitakeover Amendments*, Ph.D. dissertation, (University of Nebraska, 1988).

[52] Joe Queenan, "The ABCs of LBOs," *Barron's* (September 5, 1988), 58.

[53] Phillip D. Hall, *An Investigation of the Strategic Use of Leveraged Management Buyouts*, Ph.D. dissertation (University of Nebraska, 1988).

Module 17

Strategic Alternatives and Decisions

LEARNING OBJECTIVES

After completing Module 17, you should be able to:

1. Describe the characteristics of strategic decision situations, including high-velocity environments.
2. Discuss the major corporate- and business-level strategies and options available to management.
3. Describe the major steps involved in evaluating alternatives and selecting a strategy.
4. Identify the major criteria strategic alternatives must meet.

To this point, the strategic situation has been assessed in terms of the general and competitive environments, the firm's resources, distinctive competencies, and vision, and the values and expectations of the stakeholders. Corporate-level and business-level strategic options have also been explored. At this point, we are ready to begin the process of selecting a strategy. As part of the process of making this strategic decision, the situation assessment based on critical success factors for the organization, development of final strategic alternatives, evaluation of those alternatives, and selection of a strategy will be discussed.

The first section of this module will examine the strategic decision process, particularly in organizations facing rapidly changing environments, followed by ways to ensure that the proper strategic decision is made.

PROFILE

Should GE Sell NBC?

In 1994, General Electric was toying with the idea of selling its subsidiary, the National Broadcasting Company (NBC). And, if GE should decide to sell NBC, should they sell all or part of it, and to whom?

NBC has been in third place among the major networks. The major networks, once viewed as dinosaurs compared to "narrowcasting" competitors like Turner Broadcasting System and cable programmers, seem to be enjoying a resurgence, with a recent upturn in ad rates. So, should GE hold on for the future, or sell now that the value of networks has improved? Also, how does NBC fit the GE business portfolio?

Several companies have expressed interest in NBC. One, Time Warner Inc., has been talking with GE about purchasing part of NBC for about $2.5 billion. Time Warner would buy 49 percent of NBC's programming operations, leaving GE with 51 percent and its seven TV stations. One problem facing the Time Warner alternative is its cable system ownership, which would create regulatory hurdles if it attempted to buy the TV stations. Another potential purchaser is Walt Disney Co., which may pay as much as $5 billion for all of NBC. Disney owns no cable systems, so the sale would not face major regulatory hurdles. Disney has a strong balance sheet, and has talked in the past with NBC about a joint programming venture. Also, studios are increasingly viewing the acquisition of a network as a way to ensure future distribution of their programming.

NBC is likely to be in demand, because its third-place status is sure to make it the cheapest network to acquire. In addition, as a unit of GE, no stockholder approval or protracted bidding war are likely. So, should GE sell NBC and, if so, to whom?[1]

STRATEGIC DECISION-MAKING

The process of strategic decision-making was discussed and described in detail and modeled in earlier modules. To recap this model, the process begins with the vision of top management and the values and expectations of important stakeholders. These factors affect the firm's mission, goals and objectives, policies and procedures, and—relevant to this module—strategy formulation. Remember, strategy formulation consists of developing strategy alternatives, evaluating those alternatives, and selecting a strategy for implementation and detailed planning. On the surface, the decision-making portion of the process (formulating, evaluating, and choosing from alternatives) appears similar to the making of other decisions. In actuality, however, it is more complex because the situations are often ill-structured, the decisions are often complex and momentous, and it occurs in an atmosphere of organizational politics.

High-Velocity Environments

It may be helpful to examine the process in one of its most demanding circumstances—that of a high-velocity environment. Such environments—where the rate of technological and competitive change is so extreme that market information is often unavailable or obsolete, where strategic windows (opportunities) are opening and shutting quickly, and where the cost of error may be involuntary exit from the industry—may describe the limiting case of strategic decision-making; other situations may seem relatively simple by comparison. High-velocity environments are characterized by rapid, frequent, and discontinuous change, and may characterize today's microcomputer, airline, and banking industries. A recent study of microcomputer firms found that high performers make major decisions carefully, but decide quickly; they have both a powerful, decisive CEO *and* a powerful top-management team; and they seek bold, innovative strategies but follow safe, incremental implementation. These complex relationships are shown in Figure 17.1.

Several of the points may need further explanation. First, high performers deal with their extremely uncertain world by structuring it, using a thorough, analytic process similar to a "classic textbook strategic planning effort." Second, while the analytic approach provides order to their fast-moving world, they prevent premature commitments to irreversible actions by using "threshold-triggered

---

[1] Elizabeth Jensen and Richard Turner, "Disney Weights $5 Billion Offer for GE's NBC," *The Wall Street Journal* (September 14, 1994), A3.

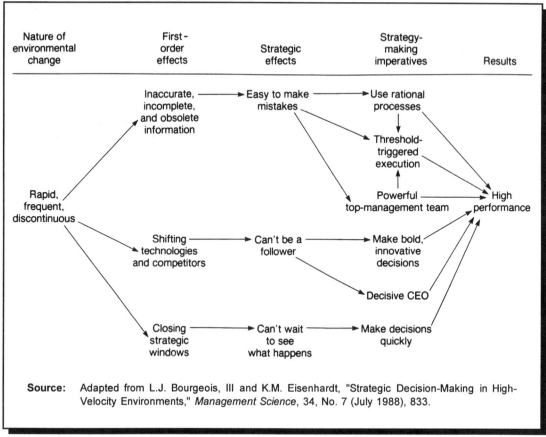

Figure 17.1 **Strategic Decision-Making in High-Velocity Environments**

execution decisions." Thus, they keep their implementation options open as long as possible. As more industries face high-velocity environments in the future, this model of decision-making may take on increasing importance.[2]

Decision Speed and Quality

As the high-velocity discussion indicated, many strategic decisions must be made more rapidly than before. Therefore, decision-makers don't have the luxury of time, and some would expect that the quality of strategic decisions would decline as a result. Wrong! Practitioners and researchers alike have discovered that speed

[2] L.J. Bourgeois, III and K.M. Eisenhardt, "Strategic Decision-Making in High-Velocity Environments," *Management Science*, 34, No. 7 (July 1988), 817-35.

enhances decision quality; "good management is distinguished from mediocre management by the speed with which it does the obvious. *Great* management is distinguished by the speed with which it acts based on creative thinking."[3]

Stanford's Kathleen Eisenhardt has found that the companies making fast decisions were the most profitable. The question is, how can quality decisions be made rapidly? Eisenhardt's studies show that the fast decision-makers review as much and sometimes *more* information than their slow counterparts; the difference lies in the *type* of information. Slow decision-makers rely on general trend and futuristic information, while fast decision-makers look at real-time information, focusing on the present instead of the past or future. That is, the focus is on what is happening, versus what happened in the past (accounting information) or what is likely to happen (long-term forecasts). Real-time information allows organizations to spot real problems and opportunities faster, which enables managers to better develop their intuition and pattern recognition skills.

Secondly, fast decision-makers evaluate *more* alternatives than their slower counterparts, and they evaluate these alternatives *simultaneously*, not sequentially. Thirdly, fast decision-makers seek expert counsel from anyone whose opinion is relevant and from experienced business counselors (efficient information sources).

Fourth, fast decision-makers are adept at resolving conflict; they don't wait for consensus, but refer non-consensus decisions to the relevant top executive to make the choice. Finally, fast decision-makers do not treat each decision as a "big, isolated, scary" event; they tend to make frequent, quick, integrated decisions. They tend to see individual decisions as part of a larger framework than as discrete issues. The fast decision-makers attribute their success to their speed, feeling that "the worst decision is no decision."[4]

Analytical vs. Political Decisions

Political behavior suggests the use of power and influence in making decisions. Often, people contrast "political" behavior from "rational" behavior, implying that the two are opposite in some way. Rational, however, merely means behavior that is sensible or logical in pursuing one's goals—which may mean that "it can be rational to be political and politic to be rational." By rational, however, most people mean "analytical," implying objectivity, use of appropriate information, seeking the "best" alternative, etc. Political, in turn, would suggest the use of power, negotiation, individual preferences and goals, and the like. Given this

---

[3] Peter A. Michael, "Making Smarter Decisions Faster," *The Planning Forum Network*, 7, No. 6 (Summer 1994), 6.

[4] Kathleen M. Eisenhardt, "Speed and Strategic Choice: Accelerating Decision-Making," *Planning Review*, 20, No. 5 (September/October 1992), 30-38.

terminology—political vs. analytical approaches—recent strategic decision research has shown that high analytical/low political decisions resulted in the most successful outcomes. Low analytical/high political approaches yielded the most failures, and either low/low or high/high combinations of analytical procedures and politics resulted in modestly successful outcomes. Therefore, it appears that an analytical, objective approach is critical to strategic decisions, and the political approach tends to compromise decision quality.[5]

Decision "Blind Spots"

Ed Zajac and Max Bazerman at Northwestern suggest that decision-makers often have specific "blind spots" when they make decisions in the competitive arena. In fact, these blind spots may explain persistent and common conditions such as industry overcapacity, new business failures, and overpaying for acquisitions. As Figure 17.2 shows, the strategic decisions of capacity expansion and entering new businesses can be adversely affected by certain "competitive blind spots," which yield poor decision outcomes. These blind spots are: overconfidence in judgment (overly-optimistic expectations); "winners curse" (tendency to overbid for acquisitions); limited frame (seeing the situation from too narrow a perspective); and escalation of commitment[6] (taking small disputes to a higher level, or raising the stakes). The result is often industry overcapacity, new business failures, and acquisition premiums.[7] Each of these outcomes is detrimental to the firm and lowers its profitability, and—most importantly—is caused by a weakness in the strategic decision-making process.

EVALUATING THE STRATEGIC SITUATION

The first step in evaluating and choosing a strategy is to review the results of the strategic situation assessment (consisting of an analysis of the general and competitive environments, and the firm's distinctive competencies and resources in terms of factors critical to the success of the business which create competi-

---

[5] James W. Dean, Jr. and Mark P. Sharfman, "The Relationship Between Procedural Rationality and Political Behavior in Strategic Decision-Making," *Decision Sciences*, 24, No. 6 (November/December 1993), 1069-1083.

[6] Paul Poppler, *An Empirical Investigation of Escalatory Strategic Decision-Making: A Prospect Theory Interpretation*, unpublished doctoral dissertation (University of Nebraska, 1992.)

[7] Edward J. Zajac and Max H. Bazerman, "Blind Spots in Industry and Competitor Analysis: Implications of Interfirm (Mis) perceptions for Strategic Decisions," *Academy of Management Review*, 16, No. 1 (January 1991), 50.

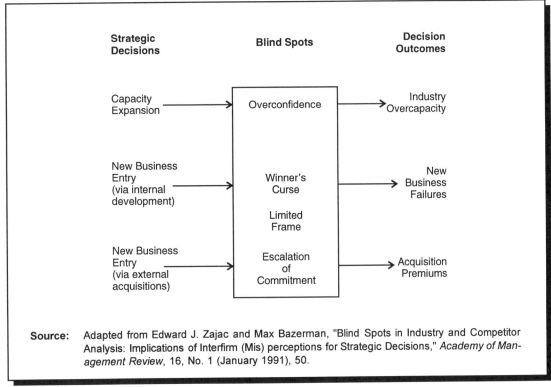

| Strategic Decisions | Blind Spots | Decision Outcomes |

Capacity Expansion → Overconfidence → Industry Overcapacity

New Business Entry (via internal development) → Winner's Curse → New Business Failures

Limited Frame

New Business Entry (via external acquisitions) → Escalation of Commitment → Acquisition Premiums

Source: Adapted from Edward J. Zajac and Max Bazerman, "Blind Spots in Industry and Competitor Analysis: Implications of Interfirm (Mis) perceptions for Strategic Decisions," *Academy of Management Review*, 16, No. 1 (January 1991), 50.

Figure 17.2 Strategic Decision Blind Spots

tive advantages). Sometimes called the *strategic position* or *strategic profile*, the strategic situation involves an analysis of the firm's external opportunities and threats and its strengths and weaknesses.

George Steiner stated that three types of data are required to perform a *situation audit* identifying opportunities, threats, strengths, and weaknesses:

1. Past performance of the firm.
2. Data about the current situation, including:

   a. Analysis of customers and markets.
   b. Resources of the company.
   c. Competition.

    d. Environmental setting.

    e. Other performance measures or areas of interest.

3. Forecasts of the future.[8]

Concerning analysis of the competition, Dartmouth's Richard D'Aveni suggests that we are entering a new age of "hypercompetition." He says that competitive moves, responses, and countermoves escalate so rapidly that traditional sources of competitive advantage are no longer sufficient. In hypercompetitive industries, such as computers, software, autos, soft drinks, toys, and the like, companies succeeded by disrupting the status quo and creating a continuous series of temporary competitive advantages. Therefore, there may be no lasting or sustainable competitive advantage, other than the ability to create temporary advantages.[9]

DEVELOPING STRATEGIC ALTERNATIVES

Strategy formulation is a complex task. It begins with the development of major strategic directions, sometimes called generic strategies. Within a given generic thrust, however, several options or alternative approaches may be possible. For example, a company may embark on a high-profit strategy, only to find that this generic strategy can be pursued via three alternatives—focusing on high volume, high asset utilization, or aggressive financing. Thus, strategic alternatives exist not only at the broad generic level, but within major strategic directions as well.

Strategy formulation is basically problem solving of a highly unstructured nature. The basis of any such problem-solving activity is to first recognize a changing situation. Whether the situation presents a threat or opportunity is the key question. Next, the situation must be clarified. How can it be classified, structured, or redefined in terms of more familiar subproblems?

The primary function of developing a strategic thrust is not to "solve" the situation in its entirety, but to structure the situation so that subproblems (or strategies) are solvable and manageable.[10] Solving the *right* problem is the most important task.

It is commonly felt that one set of generic strategies is not appropriate for all stages of the product/market life cycle. That is, different strategies may be called for as the market moves from the embryonic or introduction stage through

[8] G.A. Steiner, *Strategic Planning* (New York: Macmillan, 1979), 129.

[9] Richard A. D'Aveni, *Hypercompetition: Managing the Dynamics of Strategic Maneuvering* (New York, NY: The Free Press, 1994).

[10] R.P. Rumelt, "Evaluation of Strategy: Theories and Models," in *Strategic Management*, eds. D. Schendel and C.W. Hofer (Boston, MA: Little, Brown, 1979), 196.

the growth, maturity, and finally the aging or decline stage. Various authors have given a myriad of names to these prescribed strategic options. However, recent studies have shown that the options may not be appropriate for all types of businesses and industries, for all types of markets and competitive situations, and for all business objectives. What this means is that appropriate strategies are *contingent* on certain conditions, shown in Figure 17.3, and fall within the *range* of available strategic options.

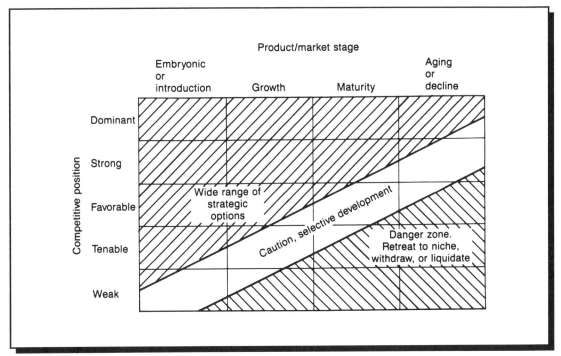

Figure 17.3 Strategic Options and the Life Cycle

Going beyond the general to the specific, certain studies have shown that appropriate strategies not only depend on the life-cycle stage, but are also influenced by the business's goals—whether long term (such as to increase market share) or short term (such as increasing cash flow)—and depend on the type of business and industry/market conditions. In fact, there tends to be conflict between long- and short-term goals, suggesting a trade-off. As an example, market share tends to increase with increases in investment and assets. However, cash flow improves as investment and assets are cut. Thietart and Vivas found this to be true regardless of the life-cycle stage or type of business.[11] Their study looked at 1,100 industrial goods versus consumer-products businesses in the growth, maturity, and decline stages of the market. In general, their findings are as follows:

1. A trade-off *does exist* between long-term measures of performance (e.g., change in market share) and short-term measures (e.g., cash flow).
2. There is a set of strategic actions for each of these two performance measures that *does not* depend on the life-cycle stage, type of business, or market structure. These actions are:

    a. To increase market share, one should increase investment (but at a decreasing rate), increase capacity utilization, and increase assets.
    b. To improve cash flow, one should decrease investment and decrease assets.

3. There are strategic actions that depend on life-cycle stage (growth, maturity, or decline).
4. There are strategic actions that depend on the type of business (generally, industrial versus consumer products).
5. The relative impact of strategic actions changes with life-cycle stage.[12]

Thus, although life-cycle stage is not the only determinant of business-level strategy, it is an important factor.

In earlier modules, we observed that the financial services industry has been experiencing a high-velocity environment due to macroeconomic and technological changes, plus deregulation and globalization. We also concluded that these environmental changes were affecting the industry's market structure, favoring superregional and foreign banks, plus nonbank competitors. But what should the strategies of commercial banks be, given these changes? What should they do to reposition themselves to survive and prosper? The banks need to make many changes, but perhaps two are primary: to lobby for relief from regulatory constraints which put them at a competitive disadvantage, and to seek expanded power in new fields (e.g., securities).[13] Thus, political/legal strategies may be their most promising avenue.

---

[11] R.A. Thietart and R. Vivas, "An Empirical Investigation of Success Strategies for Businesses along the Product Life Cycle," *Management Science*, 30, No. 12 (December 1984), 1405.

[12] *Ibid.*, 1421.

[13] David Rogers, "Environmental Change in the Financial Services Industry," in *Advances in Strategic Management*, eds. Robert Lamb and Paul Shrivastava 5 (Greenwich, CT: JAI Press), 98-102.

The Process

James Quinn has pointed out that strategy is usually developed incrementally. That is, strategies are changed in small steps by modifying previous strategies.[14] Thus, the starting point in developing strategic alternatives is always the past and current strategies of the firm. Any modifications are reviewed as time goes on to see what new changes may be required or desirable. The process is one of continuous refinement and adjustment, with an occasional major change. In general, this process seeks answers to the questions listed in Table 17.1. What are we doing, what is happening externally, and what should we be doing?

Another step must be taken in the formation of strategy. It involves identification of major strategies, followed by an identification and later evaluation of substrategies. (All strategies must be broken down into substrategies for successful implementation.)

As Table 17.2 illustrates for eight common (or generic) strategic alternatives, adoption of a given strategy alternative requires certain actions for its success. In addition, there is typically a desired outcome for each strategy alternative, but there is also a *required* outcome—an absolute accomplishment which must be achieved for the strategy to succeed.

Generic strategies often will be suggested by a business unit's position on the industry attractiveness/competitive position matrix shown in Figure 17.4. However, this is only the first phase of strategy formulation. The next stage is developing more specific competitive position objectives and investment strategies, as shown in Table 17.3. The generic strategies permit the development of broad internal and external action programs (substrategies) of the type shown in Table 17.4. At this stage, the broad action programs must be turned into very specific tactical plans, including detailed financial analyses. Here, specific quantitative projections of elements such as sales, prices, market share, costs, interest rates, and taxes are required to determine how attractive the proposed strategy might be.

In summary, remember that strategic options—whether corporate or business level—flow from the enterprise strategy (including the mission and societal-role) of the firm. The strategies are means to achieve the firm's goals and objectives, within its chosen mission. At the corporate level, the primary strategic decision is whether to diversify or concentrate the firm, and to what degree. Diversification leads to acquisition, internal development, and venture-related decisions, while concentration points to divestiture and restructuring decisions.

---

[14] J.B. Quinn, *Strategies for Change* (Homewood, IL: Richard D. Irwin, Inc., 1980).

Table 17.1 Process for Formulating a Competitive Strategy

What is the business doing now?
  Identification
    What is the implicit or explicit current strategy?
  Implied assumptions
    What assumptions about the company's relative position, strengths and
      weaknesses, competitors, and industry trends must be made for the current
      strategy to make sense?
What is happening in the environment?
  Industry analysis
    What are the key factors for competitive success and the important industry
      opportunities and threats?
  Competitor analysis
    What are the capabilities and limitations and probable future moves of existing
      and potential competitors?
  Societal analysis
    What important government, social, and political factors will present
      opportunities or threats?
  Strengths and weaknesses
    Given an analysis of industry and competitors, what are the company's strengths
      and weaknesses *relative to present and future competitors*?
What should the business be doing?
  Tests of assumptions and strategy
    How do the assumptions embodied in the current strategy compare with the
      analysis above?
  Strategic alternatives
    What are the feasible strategic alternatives given the analysis above? (Is the
      current strategy one of these?)
  Strategic choice
    Which alternative best relates the company's situation to external opportunities
      and threats?

Source: Reprinted with permission of The Free Press, a Division of Macmillan, Inc., from *Competitive Strategy* by M.E. Porter, 19-20. Copyright © 1980.

At the business level, the basic strategies are related to positioning and distinguishing the business (including differentiation and scope). Other appropriate
moves include increasing scope (penetration, product development, market development, and geographical expansion), or redefining and reducing scope (defense
and renewal, retrenchment and turnaround, and endgame strategies).

Table 17.2 Strategic Alternatives, Actions, and Outcomes

Strategic Alternative	Action Required	Desired Outcomes	Required Outcomes
Build aggressively	Build share on all fronts as rapidly as possible.	Rapid growth in share—all markets. Leadership in technology, service.	Limits on losses and negative cash flow.
Build gradually	Steady sustained increase in share of entire market.	Sustained growth in share—all markets. Leadership in quality, service.	Limited losses. Sustained cost reductions.
Build selectively	Increased share in carefully selected markets.	Share growth in selected markets. Leadership in customer satisfaction. Superiority in market research.	Growth in profits and profitability. Growth in cash flow.
Maintain aggressively	Hold position in all markets and generate profits.	Hold market share in all markets. Relative cost leadership—fixed and variable. Technology leadership—in product and process.	Improve asset utilization. Growth in profitability and cash flow. Improve expense-to-revenue ratio. Reduce force levels.
Maintain selectively	Select high-profit markets and secure position.	Overall share reduction. Hold market share in selected markets. Improve relative profitability. Distribution, service leadership.	Minimum investment. Improve asset utilization and cash flow. Reduce fixed cost/sales.
Prove viability	If there are any viable segments, maintain selectively, divest rest.	In this exhibit, see the sections to the left called "Maintain Selectively" and "Divest or Liquidate."	Minimize drag/risk to organization. Growth in profits and cash flow.
Divest or liquidate	Seek exit and sell off at best price.	Reduce share except for highly selective segments. Enhance value added via technical leadership.	Minimize investment. Reduce fixed costs. Improve profitability. Maximize selling price. Reduce work force levels.
Competitively harass	Use as vehicle to deny revenues to competitors.	Attack competitor's high-share business but do not gain share. Relative price never above that of target competitors.	Minimize fixed costs. Sustained reduction of variable costs. Limits on losses and negative cash flows.

Source: Adapted from I.C. MacMillan and P.E. Jones, "Designing Organizations to Compete," *Journal of Business Strategy*, 4 (1984), 13. Reprinted with permission.

		Competitive Position		
		Strong	*Average*	*Weak*
Industry Attractiveness	*High*	Grow Seek dominance Maximize investment	Evaluate potential for leadership via Segmentation Identify weaknesses Build strengths	Specialize Seek niches Consider acquisitions
	Medium	Identify growth segments Invest strongly Maintain position elsewhere	Identify growth segments Specialize Invest selectively	Specialize Seek niches Consider exit
	Low	Maintain overall position Seek cash flow Invest at maintenance levels	Prune lines Minimize investment Position to divest	Trust leader's statesmanship Sic on competitor's cash generators Time exit and divest

Source: C.W. Hofer and M.J. Davoust, *Successful Strategic Management* (Chicago, IL: A.T. Kearney, 1977), 52. Reproduced by permission.

Figure 17.4 **Attractiveness/Competitive Position Strategies**

EVALUATING ALTERNATIVES AND SELECTING A STRATEGY

The development and evaluation of alternatives should be two separate and distinct steps. Separating the two seems to produce a broader range of alternatives. As our experience with the brainstorming technique suggests, evaluation during the generation stage appears to limit the development of alternatives.

Evaluation of Alternatives

Suppose that one objective of an organization's grand strategy is to achieve a 15 percent sustainable growth rate. This objective can be reached in three very different ways, as Table 17.5 illustrates. Each alternative is workable, but requires a very different way of operating the company. Which, if any, should the firm adopt? The answer can depend on a host of factors and criteria.

Table 17.3 Competitive Position Objectives and Investment Strategies

Generic Strategy	Competitive Position Objective	Investment Strategy
Share increasing		
Development stage	Increase position	Moderate investment
Shakeout stage	Increase position	High investment
Other stages	Increase position	Very high investment
Growth	Maintain position	High investment
Profit	Maintain position	Moderate investment
Market concentration and asset reduction	Reduce (shift) position to smaller defensible level (niche)	Moderate to negative investment*
Liquidation or divestiture	Decrease position to zero	Negative investment
Turnaround	Improve positions	Little to moderate investment*

*Usually, some new assets are required while others are sold off. The net level of investment depends on the relative proportion of these two activities in each specific case.

As the above suggests, in a large firm, evaluating and selecting a strategy usually involves a sequence of analyses and decisions, rather than a single decision. The requirements for an effective strategy will probably undergo frequent modification because change is continuous, both outside and inside the firm.

The evaluation should take place at the corporate, divisional, and business-unit levels, with close scrutiny of the policies and plans at each of these levels. Two basic questions must be asked during strategy evaluation: (1) Has the existing strategy been satisfactory? (2) Will the existing or proposed strategies be satisfactory in the future?

Evaluation of an existing strategy requires the following steps:

1. An identification of the existing strategy in terms of its components, including its underlying goal structure and environmental assumptions.
2. A comparison of the results achieved against goals that have been established.

Table 17.4 Example of Broad Action Programs

Broad action programs based on controllable internal factors

Maintain R&D and technical standing above leading competitor level.

Implement an automation program leading toward significant increases in labor productivity.

Improve the distribution network worldwide, developing a sense of priorities according to the attractiveness of each individual market.

Reduce manufacturing costs through proper rationalization in every stage of the production process.

Increase number of qualified managers via proper hiring, developing, and promotional procedures.

Maintain market positioning by the allocation of financial and human resources compatible with competitive challenges.

Broad action programs to deal with external environmental forces

Profit from a possibly temporarily favorable currency situation by taking advantage of a strong purchasing power in terms of:

Switching from national to foreign suppliers.

Engaging in an active acquisition of manufacturing facilities abroad.

Set up a task force to study the legal, financial, and sales implications of currency transfer.

Use local manufacturing, distribution, and marketing facilities whenever possible, seeking partnerships to neutralize trends toward nationalization.

Stockpile raw materials on critical items, and firm up long-term contracts for the procurement of those raw materials, taking advantage of the temporary strong currency situation.

Address the issue of labor shortage by:

Internal development of qualified labor at all levels.

Seeking increased government support.

Establish the base for a systematic information gathering conducive to a better understanding of competitors and market opportunities.

Source: A.C. Hax and N.S. Majluf, "The Use of the Industry Attractiveness-Business Strength Matrix in Strategic Planning," *Interfaces*, 13, No. 2 (April 1983), 67. Copyright © 1983. The Institute of Management Sciences.

3. A comparison of environmental assumptions included in the strategy with the changes currently expected, based on an analysis and forecast of the future environment.

Table 17.5 Three Alternatives Yielding 15 Percent Sustainable Growth

	Strategy Alternatives		
Growth Factor	Efficiency	Balanced	Aggressive Financing
After-tax return on assets (ROA)	18.7%	17.3%	12.0%
Debt/equity ratio (D/E)	0.5	0.4	1.5
After-tax interest on debt (i)	6.0%	7.0%	10.0%
Percentage of earnings retained (p)	60.0%	70.0%	100.0%
Sustainable growth*	15.0%	15.0%	15.0%

*Where sustainable growth $= p \left[\text{ROA} + \frac{D}{E} (\text{ROA} - i) \right]$.

4. A determination of whether the strategy appears capable of meeting its goals in light of the existing and expected environment.[15]

The firm's planning department, CEO, and other staff and division executives play important roles during evaluation. The planners review and critique strategy alternatives, while others involved typically are required to submit a one-page critique of the alternatives to the CEO, spelling out several strategic issues thought to be critical to the division's business. The CEO then must prepare a list of strategic issues for discussion, as well as chair the strategy review session.[16] While strategy evaluation, like strategy formulation, is still very much an art, there are certain objective evaluation criteria or factors, including:

1. *Goal consistency.* Is the strategy an attempt to achieve goals or objectives that conflict with other goals, objectives, values, or even the mission of the

---

[15] Dan Schendel and C.W. Hofer, eds. *Strategic Management* (Boston, MA: Little, Brown, 1979), 16.

[16] Ram Charan, "How to Strengthen Your Strategy Review Process," *Journal of Business Strategy*, 2, No. 3 (Winter 1982), 55.

firm? If so, the process should go no further until this inconsistency is re-solved.

2. *Strategy content.* Does the strategy satisfy important criteria such as:

    a. Is it acceptable to the stakeholders of the firm in terms of their values, expectations, and goals?

    b. Does it support the organization's mission and comply with its policies?

    c. Will it achieve the goals and objectives of the firm, and to what degree?

    d. Is it consistent with the environmental assumptions within which the firm must operate?

    e. Does the firm have the necessary resources and competence to carry out the strategy?

    f. Is the strategy likely to be successful? That is, does it create or exploit an advantage for the firm?

3. *Implementation.* Can the strategy be implemented successfully by the firm? The considerations here include resource requirements and availability; the organization's systems, structure, and processes; and the skills, abilities, mo-tivation, and dedication of the firm's people.

Some additional questions that might be asked include: Does the strategy rely on areas in which the firm is weak or do anything to reduce weaknesses? Does it exploit major opportunities? Does it avoid, reduce, or mitigate major threats? If it does not, are there adequate contingency plans? Does it meet criti-cal success factors for the industry and the business?

In addition to the above general criteria, more quantitative criteria and ques-tions relating to the firm should be considered. Alfred Rappaport has suggested that the ultimate test of a strategy is whether or not it creates value for share-holders. Therefore, the following questions must be answered: (1) Will the cor-porate plan create value for shareholders? If so, how much? (2) Which business units are creating value and which are not? (3) How would alternative strategies affect shareholder value?[17]

Quantitative factors are important in evaluating strategies. They provide a solid basis for decision-making. In analyzing quantitative data, the firm's results must be compared with those of its competitors or its own history. Often, profit is the starting point for many decisions in the strategic plan, but should not be the only criteria used in evaluation of strategic alternatives; degree of risk is also a critical factor. Nonetheless, the strategy chosen must be capable of meeting profit targets within a reasonable degree of likelihood.

---

[17] Alfred Rappaport, "Selecting Strategies that Create Shareholder Value," *Harvard Business Review*, 59, No. 3 (May/June 1981), 139.

Evaluation Techniques. Several quantitative techniques have been proposed to aid in strategy evaluation. One, STRATPORT, developed by Jean-Claude Larreche of INSEAD in France and V. Srinivasan of Stanford, uses a decision support system to evaluate and formulate business portfolio strategies. Strategies are expressed in terms of market share objectives to be achieved in each of the business units in the corporate portfolio. STRATPORT evaluates a strategy in terms of the net present value of after-tax cash flows in the long as well as the short run.[18] Another, previously mentioned, technique is Rappaport's approach to calculating the shareholder value contributed by a strategy.[19] While such techniques may assist in evaluating alternative strategies, it should be obvious that while, at best, they can provide additional information to the strategic decision-makers, such techniques will not *make* the decision.

Selecting a Strategy

In the final analysis, formulating, evaluating, and selecting strategies remains more an art than a science, and may continue to be so for the foreseeable future. Even after thorough evaluation of strategic alternatives, the "best" one still may not be clear. The process will rule out alternatives that do not satisfy important criteria, but several alternatives may remain which are essentially equal. One may be favorable according to certain criteria, another may be favorable on other criteria, and so on. But, regardless, a decision must be made.

In deciding between the remaining alternatives, the decision-maker should reexamine all major assumptions on which they are based. Care should be taken to ensure that participants in the formulation and evaluation process have been dealing with similar assumptions and speaking a common language. Then, in the final analysis, the decision may come down to the risks inherent in the alternatives as opposed to their potential return. Risks can be categorized as those you can expect to happen, those that you are willing to accept, those that you are *not* willing to accept, and those that you *must* accept.

For each major risk, the following questions should be answered:

1. What are the consequences?
2. Will the "worst case" scenario seriously hurt the company, the division, or finances?
3. What level of risk am I willing to accept?

---

[18] J.C. Larreche and V. Srinivasan, "STRATPORT: A Model for the Evaluation for Formulation of Business Portfolio Strategies," *Management Science*, 28, No. 9 (September 1982), 979.

[19] Rappaport, "Selecting Strategies," 149.

4. What if I do not accept the risk? Will the competition accept it?
5. How can the risks be reduced?

In general, the firm must examine its attitude toward risk—is it a "risk avoider" or is it willing to gamble? The amount of risk versus the potential rewards must also be compared for each alternative. In no case should an alternative be selected that involves undue risk, regardless of the reward. The decision-maker must determine how much of the company or division he or she is willing to bet on the outcome of the strategic decision.

CONCLUSIONS

Numerous factors affect both corporate- and business-level strategies. Consideration must be given to the external environment—the economy, the competition, the market, technology, social factors, and political/legal considerations—as well as to internal influences, including stakeholder values and expectations, management's vision, goals and objectives, and the firm's level and types of resources. Critical success factors *must* be included in the strategy, as well as whether or not the strategy is likely to create a sustainable competitive advantage. Strategy formulation, evaluation, and choice is no simple or easy task.

Module 18

The Strategic Infrastructure: Information and Planning Systems

LEARNING OBJECTIVES

After completing Module 18, you should be able to:

1. Understand the roles of scanning and monitoring the environment in strategic decision-making.
2. Appreciate the types and sources of information required for strategic decision-making.
3. Relate the important characteristics of a strategic information system, especially in contrast to the MIS.
4. Understand strategic planning systems and the interrelationship between various types of plans.

In earlier modules, decision-making, including formulating, evaluating, and selecting strategies, was discussed. Various corporate and business-level options and alternatives were also dealt with as were factors critical to their evaluation and selection. In this module, the focus changes. Here, the systems and techniques for providing the information supporting those decisions, and then systems and techniques helpful in planning activities are studied. This module also describes the systems managers need to help them make strategic decisions. It addresses how information and systems aid in strategy formulation and planning, and examines levels of planning, and how "formalized" planning systems and approaches tend to be in practice.

These planning and decision support systems constitute what might be called the "strategic infrastructure" of the firm. These are the processes, systems, and techniques that enable the firm to manage strategically, just as highways, bridges, airports, communication systems, and the like enable our economy to function. This strategic infrastructure works with what some have called the "strategic architecture" of the firm to enable it to successfully form and implement winning strategies. Strategic architecture includes mechanisms for organizational learning, innovation and experimentation, empowerment, corporate sustainability, and strategic change, for example.[1]

As was pointed out earlier, some organizations use formal systems that require strategies to be explicitly stated, while others follow less formal approaches, with more implicit strategies. Smaller organizations tend to use the latter. In contrast, leading large firms tend to use more extensive, formal systems. In addition, the larger firms tend to use more formalized systems and procedures for both strategy formulation and selection, as well as for strategy implementation planning.

Whether simple or complex, formal or informal, the process by which an organization develops its strategies is its *strategy formulation system*. Regardless of the degree of formality or complexity of the process, the strategy formulation system's purposes are the same: to help structure the unstructured problems the organization faces, and to assist in choosing the best strategies for the firm.

PROFILE

The President's Information System

Even when important information exists and is known by the organization, it may be misinterpreted or mishandled. Newspaper columnist Jack Anderson observed that the president of the United States has professionals who produce "stunningly accurate assessments" of world events of momentous importance,

---

[1] Matthew J. Kiernan, "The New Strategic Architecture: Learning to Compete in the 21st Century," *The Executive* (February 1993), 7-21.

which seem to be routinely ignored because of system breakdowns. He cites the following examples:

- President Nixon could have prevented the 40-fold jump in oil prices.
- President Carter could have prevented the takeover of the U.S. embassy in Iran, the Soviet invasion of Afghanistan, and the deportation of Cuban criminals and undesirables to Florida.
- President Reagan might have averted the Falkland Island seizure, and could have dealt more effectively with the Lebanon crisis.[2]
- Perhaps the Gulf War could have been averted, had the U.S. State Department not sent Saddam Hussein mixed signals, resulting in Iraq's invading Kuwait.

According to Anderson, in each of these cases, the presidents had access to information *in advance* that would have enabled them to take preventive actions. Why didn't they? Because the information was misinterpreted and misrepresented at several steps along the way; in other words, the president's strategic information system malfunctioned due to human error. So, even a sophisticated, highly developed intelligence system does not guarantee success.

STRATEGIC DECISION SUPPORT SYSTEMS

Effective strategic decision making and planning require having access to vital information. This information includes: technological, social, economic, political, legal, and environmental facts; information on the market and competition; information on the firm's strengths and weaknesses; information on past performance; information on current opportunities, problems, and contingencies; and information on the risks and uncertainties of current and proposed strategies. *Strategic information*, then, is the information necessary to make strategic decisions at either the corporate or business level of the organization. This information can be an important resource to the company if it is used to achieve a strategic competitive advantage.[3] To do this requires analysis of critical information needs and acquisition, as well as proper storage and dissemination, of that information.

But how does the firm acquire and handle such diverse information? Some of it may be available within the organization, but a good share of it is not. Furthermore, much of it may be subjective, impressionistic, and possibly unreliable.

---

[2] Jack Anderson, "Why Presidents Stumble," *Parade* (March 13, 1983), 4.

[3] Charles Wiseman, *Strategic Information Systems* (Homewood, IL: Richard D. Irwin, Inc., 1988).

Much information exists in unrelated, unevaluated "bits and pieces" that are difficult for the decision maker to use. As a result, much information goes unused.

It may be beneficial to define and relate some of the relevant information-related terms commonly used in organizational and decision contexts. As Figure 18.1 shows, *data* is a quantification or description reflecting reality. This data is classified and analyzed, providing *information* needed for insight. This insight becomes the basis for *intelligence*—relevant and insightful information of interest to potential users. The users are typically interested in creating and using *knowledge* to help make *policy*, or wise decisions for the organization.[4]

Most companies have less sophisticated systems for handling strategic information. In fact, many try to rely on their management information systems (MIS). However, as information expert Stafford Beer has noted, the information top management really needs must be separately collected and processed and must follow separate pathways from information required for operations. In addition, top management cannot rely on lower levels of management to pick out and provide the information needed for strategic purposes.[5] King and Cleland point out that the MIS is almost exclusively concerned with the past, with the *control* function applied to the operational activities of the firm; few focus on the *planning* function or strategic decisions critical to the company's future.[6]

What is required is a separate strategic information system (SIS) designed to support the company's competitive strategies. Such systems are increasingly required for success and survival in the dynamic and turbulent environment of the 1990s.[7] The SIS should provide for "scanning" the business environment to pick up new signals, and "monitoring" to track previously identified trends singled out as important to the firm. An important part of an SIS is establishing responsibility for acquiring and handling such information within the firm, following systematic procedures. In doing so, it is necessary to specify the firm's information needs, the sources, and the systems necessary to handle the data and information.

It must be noted that the term "strategic information system" does not mean the same thing to strategists and information systems people. To strategists, as we have seen, an SIS is a system which provides relevant information to a manager to help make a strategic decision. To information systems people, however,

---

[4] Vincent P. Barabba and Gerald Zaltman, "The Inquiry Center," *Planning Review*, 19, No. 2 (March/April 1991), 4-9.

[5] "The Shorter Catechism of Stafford Beer," *Datamation* (February 1982), 146.

[6] W.R. King and D.I. Cleland, *Strategic Planning and Policy* (New York, NY: Van Nostrand Reinhold, 1978), 221.

[7] N.E. Swanson and L.A. Digman, "Conceptual Framework for a Modular Data-Based Strategic Information System," paper presented at 14th Annual Conference, American Institute for Decision (November 1982).

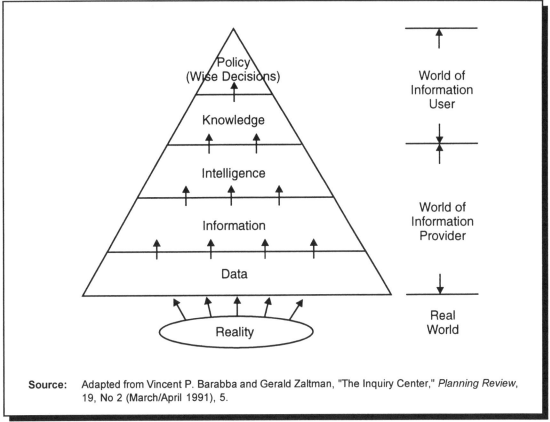

Source: Adapted from Vincent P. Barabba and Gerald Zaltman, "The Inquiry Center," *Planning Review*, 19, No 2 (March/April 1991), 5.

Figure 18-1 Information Pyramid

strategic information systems are those information-related systems which give the organization a strategic, or competitive advantage.[8]

Strategic Information Needs

What kinds of information do strategic decision-makers need? Studies have shown that a number of environmental and organizational variables are of major importance in determining the content of specific business strategies, as listed in Table 18.1. Actually, there probably are additional important variables, such

---

[8] Joong Wha Kim and L.A. Digman, "Information Technology vs. Strategic Management Perspectives," *Proceedings of 23rd Annual Meeting of Midwest Decision Sciences Institute* (Atlanta, GA: Decision Sciences Institute, May 1992).

as stakeholder values and social responsibility of the firm, which have not been studied adequately by researchers. While the fifty-four variables in the table can be grouped logically, as shown, the fact remains that monitoring each of them constitutes a major task.

John Rockart of MIT proposed a way of making masses of information more manageable. He suggests that firms use critical success factors (CSFs) to define the *significant* information needs of the organization.[9] As we saw in an earlier module, studies have shown that three to six factors usually are critical to success in most industries, and these key factors must be met exceedingly well if the firm is to be very successful. By starting with the CSFs and using them to determine our primary information needs, we will be specifying the *critical data set* needed to run the business.

Grayson Manufacturing Company, a British and U.S. textile firm with sales of about $500 million, uses the CSF method to determine the information it needs and who should receive it. As shown in Table 18.2, Grayson starts with its mission, then develops supporting goals, objectives, and strategies. Next, the strategic success factors are developed. As Table 18.3 illustrates for one of the strategic success factors, key performance indicators for each factor are developed, and the individuals critical to successful performance in terms of that factor are specified. The required information is provided to that individual on a priority basis, and is also provided to selected additional people.[10]

Rockart points out that although the information systems of organizations are capable of producing large amounts of information, very little of it helps managers perform their jobs better. The problem is to identify critical information and separate it from the masses of data and less useful information. The CSF method highlights areas that should receive constant and careful attention from management; performance in these areas should be measured continually. In this way, the manager's information needs—both "hard" quantitative, factual data, and "soft" opinions, assumptions, and forecasts—can be identified and that information provided.[11] As Nobel laureate Herbert Simon of Carnegie-Mellon observed, the scarce resource today is not information but the capacity to process it. The information system that brings more information to the desk of the executive does him or her a disservice; what is needed are mechanisms to filter information and make sure that only the most important data reach the executive. For

---

[9] John F. Rockart, "Chief Executives Define Their Own Data Needs," *Harvard Business Review*, 57, No. 2 (March/April 1979), 85.

[10] V.E. Millar, "Decision-Oriented Information," *Datamation* (January 1984), 161.

[11] Rockart "Chief Executives," 85.

Table 18.1 Some Strategically Significant Environmental and Organizational Variables

Broader environmental variables	Industry structure variables	Market and consumer behavior variables
Economic conditions	Type of product	Stage of the life cycle
GNP trend	Degree of product	Market size
Interest rates	differentiation	Seasonality
Money supply	Equal products	Cyclicality
Energy availability	Price/cost structure	Market segmentation
Demographic trends	Economies of scale	Buyer concentration
Growth rate of	Degree of automation	Buyer needs
population	Degree of integration	Buyer loyalty
Age distribution of	Experience curves	Elasticity of demand
population	Marginal plant size	Purchase frequency
Regional shifts in	Optimal plant size	
population	Rate of product	*Organizational*
Sociocultural trends	technological change	*characteristics and*
Lifestyle changes	Rate of process	*resources*
Consumer activism	technological change	Market share
Career expectations	Transportation and	Degree of customer
Political/legal factors	distribution costs	concentration
Antitrust regulations	Barriers to entry	Quality of products
Environmental	Critical mass for entry	Value added
protection laws	*Competitor variables*	Length of the
Supplier variables	Degree of seller	production cycle
Degree of supplier	concentration	Newness of plant and
concentration	Aggressiveness of	equipment
Major changes in	competition	Labor intensity
availability of raw	Degree of	Relative wage rate
materials	specialization in the	Marketing intensity
Major changes in	industry	Discretionary cash
conditions of trade	Degree of capacity	flow/gross capital
	utilization	investment

Source: C.W. Hofer, "Toward a Contingency Theory of Business Strategy," *Academy of Management Journal*, 18, No. 4 (December 1975), 798. Reproduced by permission.

Table 18.2 An Example of Strategic Success Factors

Mission	Goals	Objectives	Strategies	Strategic Success Factors
To be the dominant textile products supplier to the most profitable domestic market segments and to provide a high-quality employee work life	Compete in profitable market segments	Identify and enter five new market segments with high-profit potential by 1996	Upgrade market research function to identify high-profit potential market segments	Effective market intelligence
		Increase market share 15 percent in high-profit market segments where we are not the dominant supplier, by 1997	Develop a product line that fits the requirements and needs of the high-potential market segments	New products
			Expand product distribution network	Market segment dominance
			Product differentiation	
	Be the low-cost producer in our market segments	Reduce total manufacturing costs by 10 percent per unit by 1996 and achieve 15 percent ROI	Review and upgrade all labor standards	High labor productivity
			Negotiate lower prices for raw materials and tighten control over yields	Low material cost
		Achieve 3 percent return above the cost of capital, by 1996		

Table 18.3 Information and Recipients for One Strategic Success Factor

	Strategic Success Factor: Low Material Cost	
	Information Recipients	
Key Performance Indicators	*Critical Individuals*	*Additional Recipients*
Material costs versus long-term target	Vice president, production	CEO; vice president, R&D; vice president, purchasing
Grayson percent material costs versus industry		
Material price as percent of standard price	Vice president, purchasing (fabric group)	CEO; vice president, purchasing; vice president, R&D
Change in material price as percent of consumer price index		

Source: Adapted from V.E. Millar, "Decision-Oriented Information," *Datamation* (January 1984), 161. Reprinted with permission of DATAMATION® magazine, Copyright © 1984 by Cahners Publishing Company (1984). All rights reserved.

top executives, this is largely information from outside the firm that enables them to answer the "what if" questions.[12]

It is information *needs* rather than information availability that drive the strategic information system. Information that is available but not related to the strategists' needs can be ignored; needed but unavailable information presents a problem that the firm may overcome by using judgment, outside sources of information, or competitor intelligence. Information needs specify the types of information to be included in the firm's planning data base, which "feeds" the company's planning system.

Strategic Information Sources

In general, strategic information needs relate to management's vision, viewpoint, and values; the organization's strengths and weaknesses; business and industry criteria for success; competitive information; and environmental opportunities, threats, and risks. Basil Denning has categorized the major sources of environ-

---

[12] "Simon Says," *Forbes* (December 20, 1982), 150.

mental information, as shown in Table 18.4. Information on the economy is available primarily from government, industry, and private sources, as well as through market research. Technological information is gleaned from information service firms, market research, and intelligence activities directed toward competitors' developments. A number of sources are required to obtain sociological information; political information can be obtained from various services and government reports. Information about competitors' potential actions can be gotten largely from intelligence efforts and "market signals," actions by competitors that indicate their intentions, motives, goals, strategies, or internal situations.[13]

Environmental Scanning and Monitoring

Scanning techniques and methods are used to search the environment for early evidence of changes. This involves looking for signals that may precede significant changes, *before* the changes assume economic, social, or strategic importance. Perhaps scanning could be better described as a task rather than a technique, although the result is intended to be an early warning system of important events. As such, it is an attempt to detect the weak signals of new trends early enough so that the business has sufficient lead time to develop a response strategy. Scanning involves looking for weak signals, because by the time there are clear signals, the change is widely known, and the early warning advantage is lost. Unfortunately, weak signals are difficult to discern above the "noise" in the system, and many of the changes never materialize.

There are several steps in implementing a scanning system.

1. Formation of a scanning network.
2. Development of scanning guidelines (what to look for).
3. Determination of sources.
4. Establishment of a synthesis/analysis process.

In addition to scanning, it is necessary to monitor changes or trends that have already been identified. Monitoring is concerned more with the immediate and the known than with the future and weak signals.[14]

---

[13] B.W. Denning, "Strategic Environmental Appraisal," *Long-Range Planning* (March 1978), 22.

[14] Ian Wilson, "Evaluating the Environment: Social and Political Factors," in *Handbook of Business Strategy*, eds. W.D. Guth (Boston, MA: Warren, Gorham & Lamont, 1985), 3-17—3-20.

Table 18.4 Environmental Information Sources

Type of Information	Sources	Techniques
Economic forecasts: national economy sector forecasts	Government and private forecasts Industry association, government, private forecasts Market research	Critical appreciation of published forecasts Development of models or relationships for sector forecasts Input-output analysis Large number of quantitative techniques
Technological forecasts	Technical intelligence service reports Technical market research Research into competitors' developments	Demand and conditional demand analyses Opportunity identification techniques Theoretical limits testing Parameter analysis Various systems analysis methods Discipline reviews Expert opinion
Sociological forecasts	Wide variety of sources of data, including government reports, educational forecasts, population forecasts, regional forecasts, skilled labor forecasts, institutional changes, etc.	National models such as built by Battelle (unlikely to be done in any one corporation) Expert opinion
Political forecasts	Political intelligence services and government reports	Expert opinion
Forecasting competitors' actions	Any intelligence about competitors	Any relevant technique to give information from intelligence

Source: Reprinted with permission from *Long-Range Planning* (March 1973), Basil W. Denning, "Strategic Environmental Appraisal," 22. Copyright © 1973, Pergamon Press, Ltd.

Intelligence Information

Much information about the environment, particularly about competitors, is "intelligence" information. This does not mean that a firm must use "spies" or clandestine means to gather the information. In fact, a good deal of it can be gleaned from a variety of media, while market signals and other types of intelligence information can be gathered from a variety of other sources, including colleagues; conferences, meetings of trade groups, and professional societies; and informal contacts. Thus, "boundary people" (managers and particularly engineers and salespeople) are valuable sources of advanced intelligence about competitors.[15] Michael Porter has compiled a list of field and published sources of intelligence information, and describes various options for compiling, cataloging, analyzing, and communicating such data to the strategic decision-maker, as shown in Figure 18.2.

Strategic Information Systems

Many firms—particularly large firms—of necessity employ systems for managing strategic data and information. This is where the strategic information system (SIS) comes into play. It is the SIS that incorporates the needs and sources of information: how information will be gathered, how and by whom it will be analyzed and interpreted, how and where it will be stored, and how it will be disseminated. Swanson and Digman have proposed designs for an SIS,[16] as have King and Cleland.[17]

Any SIS must provide an appropriate context for strategic management as well as meet the needs of strategic managers. As Figure 18.3 shows, critical success factors are key to determining the critical assumptions, information, and decisions for the firm. Related to these are the executive support system (ESS), the executive information system (EIS), and the decision support system (DSS). Information required for the critical assumptions, critical information, and critical decisions makes up the strategic data model.

Information Technology Trends. Information technology and systems are becoming increasingly important competitive tools, both as aids to strategic management and in creating competitive advantage. There are a number of informa-

---

[15] R.A. Thietart and R. Vivas, "Strategic Intelligence Activity: The Management of the Sales Force as a Source of Strategic Information," *Strategic Management Journal*, 2 (1981), 15.

[16] Swanson and Digman, "Conceptual Framework," 15.

[17] King and Cleland, *Strategic Planning and Policy*, Chapter 5.

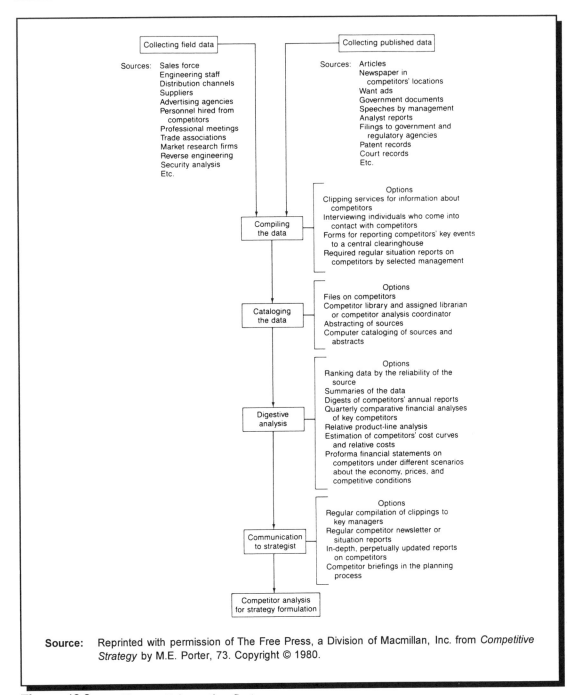

Figure 18.2 Intelligence Information System

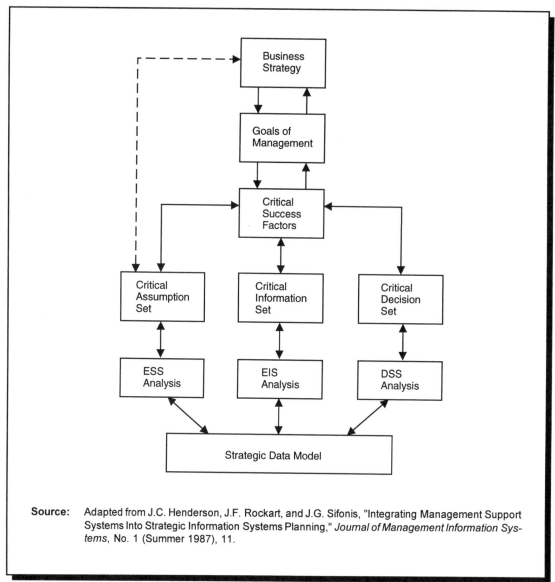

Source: Adapted from J.C. Henderson, J.F. Rockart, and J.G. Sifonis, "Integrating Management Support Systems Into Strategic Information Systems Planning," *Journal of Management Information Systems*, No. 1 (Summer 1987), 11.

Figure 18.3 Strategic Information and Support Systems

tion-related trends that are likely to have a major influence on organizations' strategic activities:

1. Widespread use of local area networks (LANs) to link computers and management users facilitates networking.

2. Graphic user interfaces (GUIs) make it easier for top managers to use computers, expanding the use of computers by executives.

3. PC-based networks make information technology systems more flexible.

4. New techniques make multi-dimensional modeling and analysis easier.

5. Inexpensive, off-the-shelf planning tools help small companies and novices. Customized and more sophisticated systems are contributing to appropriate users.

6. Collaborative software (e.g., intelligent electronic mail) will stimulate changes in information links in the organization.

7. New tools are cutting the cost of developing executive information systems (EIS).

8. Vastly more information is available at any level of the organization on CD-ROM.

9. Information technology will permit and facilitate changes in how organizations are structured, how they function, and how they learn—the ultimate competitive capability.[18]

Any SIS must be compatible with the decision-making processes and styles of the organization. It must also recognize the intersubjective nature of strategic information; that is, strategic information is interpreted subjectively, shared, and used to develop consensus. In contrast, MIS criteria are formal, structured, and objective. The SIS must also be flexible, providing personal access to sources and allowing easy modification of sources and perspectives as situations and managers change.[19]

STRATEGIC PLANNING SYSTEMS

One expert on strategic planning systems, Peter Lorange, has stated that far less is known about how to design formal planning systems than is known about effective strategies.[20] In other words, we know more about the strategies themselves than we know about the processes of formulating and implementing them in organizations. Nonetheless, we *do* know that planning is a learning process,

[18] Alistair Davidson, "Strategic Management Software and System Trends," *Planning Review*, 22, No. 4 (July/August 1993), 35-37.

[19] Paul Shrivastava, "Variations in Strategic Decision-Making Processes," in *Advances in Strategic Management*, Vol. 2, ed. R. Lamb, (Greenwich, CT: JAI Press, 1983), 188.

[20] Peter Lorange, "Formal Planning Systems: Their Role in Strategy Formulation and Implementation," in *Strategic Management*, eds. D. Schendel and C.W. Hofer (Boston, MA: Little, Brown, 1979), 237.

and organizations typically progress through several common stages in this learning or development process.

A System of Plans

For planning to be effective, a firm must have a system of plans, a planning process, a decision subsystem, and a planning-management subsystem. A system of plans describes the interrelated "subplans" that include the mission, goals, objectives, strategies, and other planning aspects of the firm's divisions, functional departments, and projects. Using a school district as an example, King and Cleland show how such plans comprise a system, illustrated in Figure 18.4. The mission plan, sometimes referred to as the strategic plan, outlines the "enterprise strategy" of the organization, and how goals, objectives, and specific area strategies support the mission or role. The development plan determines the activities necessary for creation of a new generation of products or services, and guides formulation of divestment, diversification, and R&D plans. The operations plan, in turn, focuses on activities geared to the manufacture and delivery of current products and services, as well as other current operations of the firm. Program and project plans support higher-level plans and specify what is to be done in specific task or functional areas.

The result of the organization's planning processes at the strategic, tactical, and operational levels should be a system of interrelated and interdependent plans that serve as the basis for detailed scheduling and dispatching. As the figure shows, mission plans are the longest range, with development plans geared to a one-to-five-year future. Operations plans usually are one year in scope, though occasionally longer. All of these plans, however, are supported by program and project plans, which can have various time horizons.

A difference between the strategic and operational aspects of the organization involves the number of levels in the hierarchy. A large, diversified firm such as GE may have four or more operational levels, as Figure 18.5 shows. In addition to the corporate level, there may be nineteen businesses, 150 departments, and 500 functional groups in a firm of this size. Four levels of plans are not required, however. As the figure shows, two to three levels of management are involved in planning reviews, and this reduction in levels often puts the CEO in contact with a department manager, for example. This streamlined planning hierarchy reinforces and emphasizes the importance of strategic planning throughout the organization.

Characteristics of Successful Systems

A successful planning system should encourage a congruence of people, rewards, information and decision processes, and structure. *Inc.* magazine, which is geared to new-venture managers, has suggested that successful business plans have five elements in common. They are, in order of importance:

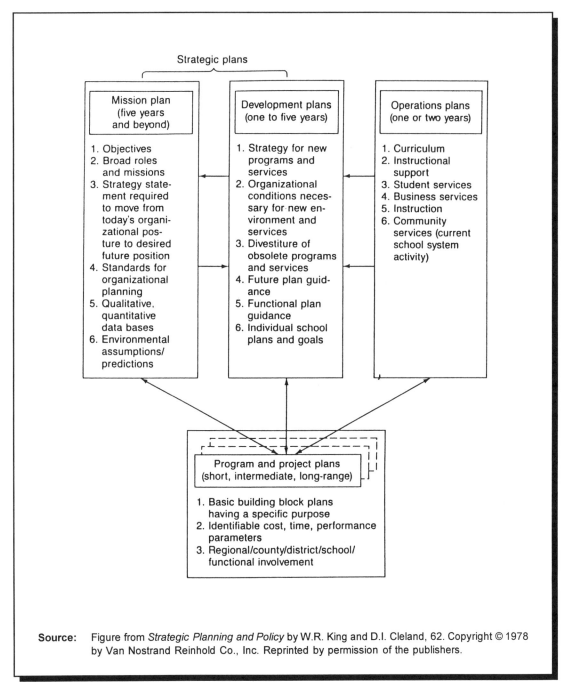

Source: Figure from *Strategic Planning and Policy* by W.R. King and D.I. Cleland, 62. Copyright © 1978 by Van Nostrand Reinhold Co., Inc. Reprinted by permission of the publishers.

Figure 18.4 A System of Plans

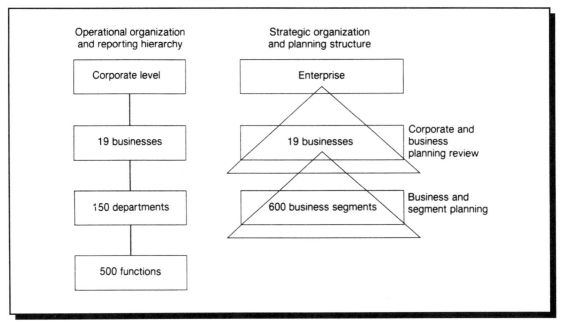

Figure 18.5 Planning and Operational Levels

1. The president serves and is recognized as the top planning officer in the company. This responsibility cannot be delegated.
2. The plan is prepared with input from all departments.
3. The primary goal is to create concise, easy-to-follow guidelines.
4. Resources are concentrated on achieving a limited number of major, quantified objectives rather than many insignificant ones.
5. Objectives are tested for compatibility with each other.[21]

Don Harvey contends that the experiences of managers and consultants show that eight factors are important to successful planning systems: (1) Invent the future; do not merely try to project the present. (2) Stay flexible; update the plan periodically, via people-to-people contact, stressing fast response times. (3) Avoid getting into a numbers game; broad goals are more important than specific, detailed targets. (4) Involve top managers; the real planners should be the CEO and his or her team. (5) Utilize contingency planning; develop scenarios and ask "what if" questions. (6) Realize that the plan is not an end in itself; it is a guide and a means to an end. (7) Anticipate future problems; reward—don't

---

[21] Ivan C. Smith, "Management Strategy: Five Tips for Making Plans Tick," in *Strategy: A Report From Your Partner* (1982), *Inc.* Magazine.

punish—the person who alerts the firm about bad news. (8) Planning should flow from long-range goals.[22]

CONCLUSIONS

Strategic information is essential to making strategic decisions. But what is strategic information? One approach to determining strategic information needs is to start with the critical success factors for the business, and specify the information required to judge how well the business is doing in terms of the CSFs. While there are numerous sources of strategic information, some items will probably not be available; in these areas, assumptions must be made. Also, it is necessary to scan the environment for weak early warning signals of trends and changes. In addition, existing changes must be monitored. It is advisable for firms to set up flexible strategic information systems around custom-designed guidelines to help them manage strategic information acquisition, analysis, dissemination, storage, and recall.

Again, management needs various types of external and internal information, available from a variety of sources. Management must ensure that important and essential information for strategic decisions is acquired through properly managed scanning and monitoring systems. The firm's MIS (which is internally and past-performance oriented) is not a sufficient source of such information. A present- and future-oriented strategic information system (SIS) is needed that incorporates the *pertinent* external and internal strategic decision information. In larger firms, the SIS may incorporate and draw from several data bases.

Many formal planning systems utilized by companies deal more with actions required to implement strategies than they do with formulating those strategies. However, firms use various approaches (systems) in formulating strategies. Such systems should be of a contingent nature, designed to fit the specific organization in question.

Relatively simple, less formal strategic decision and planning systems can work well in many firms, particularly in the less complex, smaller company. Systems should be no more complex than required, yet larger firms many times require more formal planning systems because of the organization's complexity, not because more sophisticated systems are better.

---

[22] D.F. Harvey, *Strategic Management* (Columbus, OH: Charles E. Merrill, 1982), 85-87.

Module
19

Implementation and Detailed Planning

LEARNING OBJECTIVES

After completing Module 19, you should be able to:

1. Discuss the steps involved in implementing a strategic planning process.
2. Describe the specific steps in implementing strategic decisions.
3. Realize the major factors required for successful implementation of strategic decisions.
4. Describe the types of managers appropriate for various types of strategic business-units.
5. Appreciate the effects of organizational climate, culture, and other social/political influences.

Experts have repeatedly cited strategy implementation, strategic performance evaluation, and international strategic management as being the "most intractable problems" of strategic management. This is the case because these problems are new, ill-defined, complex, and not amenable to study through traditional discipline-bound fields. In addition, these problems are among the most critical facing strategy practitioners.[1] What good is a brilliant strategy that can't be implemented; how can we evaluate strategic (versus operational) performance, both domestically and internationally?

Since the early 1970s, many companies have jumped on the strategic planning bandwagon and have acquired substantial and sophisticated strategic planning capabilities. However, relatively little attention has been given to the processes required to effectively implement the strategies.

But this is changing. As the new *Handbook of Business Strategy* states, "no area of change has been greater in strategic planning than the emphasis on linking strategy development with implementation. Management appears unwilling any longer to support large planning staffs that are divorced from operating management. Elaborate strategic planning processes are giving way to more focused efforts that tie together the plans themselves with the implementation needs of line management."[2]

In fact, "implementation" is now one of *the* buzzwords in strategic planning, pulling ahead of "market share" and "competitive analysis."[3] Frederick Gluck of McKinsey & Company has stated: "Planning without equal emphasis on what must be done to make plans work, is in trouble."[4] A poorly *executed* strategy can produce unsatisfactory results just as easily as can a strategy that was poorly *formulated*. It is difficult to question the value of good planning, but a number of companies have learned that if equal (or greater) attention is not given to executing strategy, failure is likely.

Unfortunately, implementation is often ignored in studies of decision making, quantitative methods, economic analysis, behavioral techniques, and organizational changes. Yet the way a decision is implemented determines its ultimate effectiveness. *How* the decision is put into practice is of critical, if not primary, importance. As King and Cleland have observed, "the greatest difficulties in instituting change . . . do not lie in the design and development of the changes

---

[1] Robert Lamb and Paul Shrivastava, eds., *Advances in Strategic Management*, Vol. 4 (Greenwich, CT: JAI Press, 1986), xi.

[2] Harold E. Glass, ed., *Handbook of Business Strategy*, 2nd ed. (Boston, MA: Warren, Gorham & Lamont, Inc., 1991), vii.

[3] D.R. Hykes, *Planning for Plan Implementation*, paper presented to Omaha Chapter, North American Society for Corporate Planning (November 7, 1984), 6.

[4] "Top Speakers Get Rave Reviews at Annual Conference," *The Planner* (May/June 1983), 1.

themselves. Rather, the greatest obstructions to positive change lie in the processes that are used to implement them."[5]

Implementation involves executing the strategic plan.[6] It is the process of:

- Designing the organization's structure and climate to match the strategy.
- Ensuring that divisional and functional managers have the right background, skills, and attributes to make the strategy work.
- Employing the right functional policies to make the strategy work.[7]
- Allocating resources to the operating units in support of the strategies approved for those units.

Every element of the company now comes into play—manufacturing, marketing, finance and accounting, purchasing, personnel, distribution, customer service, and so forth—to give life to the plan and accomplish the objectives.

Also, decision-making and planning processes are important, not only in implementing decisions and plans, but in formulating them as well. Therefore, we will first look at implementing planning *processes* likely to facilitate quality strategic decision-making. Next, we turn to implementing those *decisions*, which are described in terms of strategic *plans*, our final implementation topic.

Implementation is essentially an administrative and behavioral task, while strategy formulation is more conceptual and intuitive. Implementation occurs through the operational functions of the organization, while formulation is a product of the strategic function.

PROFILE

AM International, Inc.

Addressograph-Multigraph Corp., headquartered in Cleveland, was a marginally profitable manufacturer of old-fashioned duplicators and addressing machines. The company was being beaten in the marketplace by Japanese competition and producers of more advanced xerographic copiers. In 1976, Roy Ash, cofounder of Litton Industries and budget director in the administration of President Richard M. Nixon, was brought in as board chair and CEO.

Ash arrived with new strategies and promises of a new future for the company. He planned to remake the firm into a major supplier of word processors, small computers, and other components to be used in the "office of the future."

---

[5] W.R. King and D.I. Cleland, *Strategic Planning and Policy* (New York, NY: Van Nostrand Reinhold, 1978), 325.

[6] D.F. Harvey, *Strategic Management* (Columbus, OH: Charles E. Merrill, 1982), 236.

[7] W.F. Glueck and N.H. Snyder, eds., *Readings in Business Policy and Strategy from Business Week* (New York, NY: McGraw-Hill, 1982), 22.

Renaming the company AM International, his strategy was to use AM's older products as cash cows and to find new ventures, acquiring young companies and technologies to bring the company's products up to the level of Xerox, IBM, Wang, and other leaders in office automation. The strategy was appropriate and well conceptualized; the basic direction was correct and the strategy workable. However, in 1981, AM lost $245 million on sales of $857 million. In 1980, AM had equity of $232 million; in early 1982, the equity had fallen to $14 million. In February 1982, the board forced Ash to resign. What went wrong?

Under Ash, AM had a superb strategic plan that was poorly executed. Ash replaced 80 percent of the company's management and moved the headquarters from Cleveland to Los Angeles. He moved quickly into unfamiliar high-technology areas, buying a number of young companies that didn't have proven track records. Adequate financial controls to monitor performance of the divisions were not installed, nor were AM's older businesses—the cash cows— kept healthy enough to fund the new ventures. The changes in management caused too much instability in the company, and the skills of the new managers were not adequately matched to the needs of the divisions.

In short, investing in high-technology ventures can breathe new life into an old-line company when the investments are well thought out, experienced management is on board, and cash flow can support the ventures.

Unfortunately, that was not the case at AM, and the company had to fight for survival.[8]

PROFILE

Monsanto

Monsanto Company's Chemical Group conducted a benchmarking study of planning and implementation processes in 1992. Monsanto selected seventeen companies from nine industries (twelve U.S., three European, and two Japanese) from an initial list of over 100 "excellent" planners. Monsanto's findings fell into five areas:

1. *Formulating Plans.* The best companies start with a clear strategy and vision, and establish clear linkages between the strategy and their operational plans and budgets. They develop alternative scenarios and contingency plans, and establish "stretch" targets as goals.
2. *Review and Approval.* The best rely on review and approval processes to assure that plans and goals are objective, realistic, and consistent with the long-range strategy.

---

[8]"AM International: When Technology Was Not Enough," *Business Week* (January 15, 1982), 62.

3. *Managing Plan Implementation.* Effective implementation depends on acceptance or "buy-in" by the organization, and management of performance
to ensure conformance to the plan. Buy-in comes through communications
and clarity, and is helped by having plans formulated by those who have to
carry them out. However, some have good results—and buy-in—using a top-
down approach. The critical need is clarity of targets and expectations. Good
companies tell employees what they mean, mean what they say, and then do
it. It's not necessarily fatal to fail, but it *is* fatal to fail and not warn everyone as early as possible.

4. *Measuring Performance.* Plans are transformed into results through clear,
quantitative objectives and rigorous performance measurement and control.

5. *Rewards and Consequences.* Good companies have an understanding that
rewards for meeting targets and consequences of not doing so are clear and
certain. These rewards and consequences are clearly tied to results.

As the team concluded, a "*strategy* is worthless without a plan to implement it.
A plan is just as useless until it turns into action. Action is a waste of time and
energy unless it produces *results*. And that is the bottom line."[9]

IMPLEMENTING STRATEGIC PLANNING PROCESSES

As we observed earlier, effective implementation requires more than deftly
turning strategic decisions into reality. Implementation also includes developing
and using strategic planning processes and systems. These processes *aid* in the
implementation of strategic decisions, as well as in strategy formulation, analysis, and choice.

Businesses need planning systems to help them cope with the increasing
complexity and range of today's issues. Planning systems are vital to resource
allocation, and they help integrate and coordinate activities between business-
units and across organizational levels.[10]

Dale Hekhuis of GE has observed that CEO involvement is the key to effective planning systems. The most important contribution of the planning system
may be that it *forces* time for thinking about the future into the executive's
crowded calendar.[11]

---

[9] "What Good Planners Do: The Monsanto Study," *The Real World Strategist*, 1, No.
5 (July/August 1994), 4-5.

[10] Schendel and Hofer, *Strategic Management*, 221.

[11] *Ibid.*

Phases in System Implementation

Just as it is important to have a strategic plan, it also is important to have a plan for implementing the planning process. Consultants John Roach and Michael Allen have stated that implementation of planning systems occurs in six phases:

- *Phase I:* Assessment of the need for stronger planning, as evidenced by weak financial performance, eroding strategic performance, or mounting environmental challenges.
- *Phase II:* Making the strategic planning process (SPP) fit the company, reflecting company size, business type, structure, business elements, and environment.
- *Phase III:* Implementing the basic SPP.
- *Phase IV:* Integrating the SPP with the firm's basic strategies, such as production/technology resource strategies, budgeting strategies, and management selection strategies.
- *Phase V:* Auditing the SPP to keep the process "on course" and ensure that it operates effectively.
- *Phase VI:* Counseling on SPP problems to ensure that they do not render the system ineffective.[12]

Measures of System Effectiveness

But how does one measure the effectiveness of a planning system? Early studies of planning merely examined links between the degree of formality of planning and the firm's financial performance—a complex link at best. To evaluate planning systems, we need to think in terms of how well the system fulfills its objectives, how well it helps the organization perform, and the executives' satisfaction with the system. Planning system objectives include:

- Predicting future trends.
- Evaluating strategic alternatives.
- Avoiding problem areas.
- Enhancing management development.
- Improving short-term performance.
- Improving long-term performance.

---

[12] J.D.C. Roach and M.G. Allen, "Strengthening the Strategic Planning Process," in *The Strategic Management Handbook*, ed. K.J. Albert (New York, NY: McGraw-Hill, 1983), 7-22—7-44.

Problems and Pitfalls

Successful implementation and use of strategic management systems require that firms be fully aware of the problems and pitfalls associated with the system's use. In general, a company implementing a strategic planning system must be prepared to modify it to fit the "administrative realities" within the firm. Specifically, portfolio planning, the creation of strategic business-units (SBUs), and generic strategies for units often conflict with the way the firm operates.

Creation of strategic business-units may define a planning structure that conflicts with the operating structure already in place. The strategic business-units that exist only for planning purposes may be a meaningless concept offering little in the way of direction and motivation to employees of operating units. Further, management time demands often limit the number of units that can be reviewed adequately. Thus, many companies limit the number of SBUs to certainly no more than thirty or forty.

George Steiner surveyed 215 companies on their experiences with planning systems.[13] The study covered fifty pitfalls or mistakes related to the nature of strategic planning, implementing planning, doing the planning, and using the plans. The ten highest-ranking pitfalls or mistakes are shown in Table 19.1. Note that those ranked first, second, fourth, and ninth deal with inadequate involvement in the planning process by the CEO and line management.

IMPLEMENTING STRATEGIC DECISIONS

The purpose of implementation is ensuring that the planned results of the strategic decisions are realized. Implementation involves carrying out the chosen strategy—doing what must be done to make the strategy successful. As Harvard's Kenneth Andrews has observed, the corporate strategy must dominate the design of organizational structure and processes. That is, successful implementation requires that management shape the formal structure of the organization, its informal relationships, and the processes of motivation and control (which provide incentives and measure results) to the particular needs of the firm's strategy.[14] Stated another way, implementing strategy decisions results in the choice of organization structure, of information and measurement systems, and of reward-and- punishment systems; it also influences the style of management used to administer the organization.

---

[13] G.A. Steiner, *Strategic Planning* (New York, NY: The Free Press, 1979), 294.

[14] Kenneth Andrews, *The Concept of Corporate Strategy*, rev. ed. (Homewood, IL: Richard D. Irwin, Inc., 1980), 109.

Table 19.1 Strategic Planning Pitfalls

Rank	Description
1	Top management's assumption that it can delegate the planning function to a planner.
2	Top management becomes so engrossed in current problems that it spends insufficient time on long-range planning, and the process is discredited by other managers and staff.
3	Failure to develop company goals suitable as a basis for formulating long-range plans.
4	Failure to assume the necessary involvement in the planning process of major line personnel.
5	Failing to use plans as standards for measuring managerial performance.
6	Failure to create a climate that is congenial to and not resistant to planning.
7	Assuming that corporate comprehensive planning is something separate from the entire management process.
8	Injecting so much formality into the system that it lacks flexibility, looseness, and simplicity, and restrains creativity.
9	Failure of top management to review the long-range plans they have developed with departmental and divisional heads.
10	Top management's consistent rejection of the formal planning mechanism by making intuitive decisions that conflict with the formal plans.

Source: Reprinted with permission of The Free Press, A Division of Macmillan, Inc. from *Strategic Planning: What Every Manager Must Know* by G.A. Steiner, 294. Copyright © 1979.

The first step in implementation is identifying the activities, decisions, and relationships critical to accomplishing the strategy. For example, low-cost mass production may be critical to Ford, but ultra-high quality is the key to Rolls Royce. This phase of implementation requires that the strategy be broken down into specific and assignable tasks, usually according to specialized economic and technological factors. In addition, however, this series of specialized efforts must be reintegrated in a coherent fashion, which is largely a behavioral (as well as economic and technological) task. As a note of caution, unless consideration is given to reintegration of the tasks during the specialization step, it may be impossible to put the specialized tasks back together again—sort of like Humpty Dumpty.[15]

Key Implementation Tasks

Implementation of strategies is an administrative task performed by the operational organization. However, more is involved than just turning selected strategies over to those responsible for implementation and hoping for the best. The organization—its structure, processes, systems, and people—must be pointed toward what is needed to make the strategy work. Consequently, five critical administrative tasks emerge that are vital to successful implementation. These tasks are shown in Figure 19.1.[16]

1. Building an organization capable of carrying out the strategic plan. The organization must have the structure and skills necessary to turn the strategy into reality. As pointed out in earlier modules, the appropriate structure depends on a number of factors—the stage of the firm's development, the degree of diversification, the sector of the economy, to name a few—in addition to the needs of the chosen strategy. Furthermore, the firm's personnel must possess the skills necessary to make the strategy work. Related to this is the need to assign the responsibility for accomplishing key implementation tasks and for making related decisions to the right individuals or groups.

2. Allocating and focusing resources on strategic objectives. If the firm is to accomplish strategic objectives, top management must provide the resources needed. Management shows where its priorities are by how it allocates its resources: budgets, people, and support. The first step is to develop a corporate financial strategy that defines the boundaries within which resource allocations eventually will be made. After proposed strategies have been approved and top management has decided on how resources are to be applied, budgets can be prepared. Budgets should include the new capital expenditures required to implement the strategy, as well as the more difficult and less common estimation of the various incremental expenses associated with implementation. Further, once the strategy has been decided on, the key tasks to be performed and kinds of decisions required must be identified; plans must also be developed. The tasks should comprise a *formal plan*; they

---

[15] J.L. Bower, "Solving the Problems of Business Planning," *The Journal of Business Strategy*, 2, No. 3 (Winter 1982), 32.

[16] A.A. Thompson, Jr. and A.J. Strickland, III, *Strategy Formulation and Implementation: Tasks of the General Manager*, rev. ed. (Plano, TX: Business Publications, Inc., 1983), 314.

Building an Organization Capable of Carrying Out the Strategic Plan	Allocating and Focusing Resources on Strategic Objectives	Galvanizing Organizationwide Commitment to the Chosen Strategic Plan	Installing Internal Administrative Support Systems	Exerting Strategic Leadership
Key Recurring Issues: 1. How to match organization structure to the needs of strategy. 2. How to build and nurture a distinctive competence and to staff positions with the right talent and technical expertise. 3. What kind of core executive group is needed and who to select for each slot.	*Key Recurring Issues:* 1. What budgets and programs are needed by each organizational unit to carry out its part of the strategic plan. 2. How to focus the performance of tasks on achieving organizational objectives rather than on just carrying out the assigned duties.	*Key Recurring Issues:* 1. How to motivate organizational units and individuals to accomplish strategy. 2. What kind of strategy-supportive work environment and corporate culture is called for. 3. How to create a results orientation and a spirit of high performance. 4. How to link the reward structure to strategic performance.	*Key Recurring Issues:* 1. What kinds of strategy-facilitating policies and procedures to establish. 2. How to get the right strategic information on a timely basis. 3. What "controls" are needed to keep the organization on its strategic course. 4. How to create all the helpful administrative fits.	*Key Recurring Issues:* 1. What leadership actions to take in shaping values, molding culture, and energizing strategy accomplishment. 2. How to keep the organization innovative, responsive, and opportunistic. 3. How to deal with the politics of strategy, cope with power struggles, and build consensus. 4. When and how to initiate corrective actions to improve strategy execution.

Source: Adapted from A.A. Thompson, Jr. and A.J. Strickland III, *Strategic Management: Concepts and Cases*, 3rd ed. (Plano, TX: Business Publications, Inc., 1984), 198.

Figure 19.1 The Administrative Aspects of Strategy Implementation

should be arranged in a sequence comprising a plan of action with targets to be achieved at specific dates. Formal provisions for coordinating the tasksand activities of the plan must be made. Included in this is the need to develop substrategies in the functional areas of the firm, such as marketing, R&D, finance, production, personnel, and the like.

3. Galvanizing organizationwide commitment to the chosen strategic plan. People and departments of the firm must be influenced, through incentives, constraints, controls, standards, and rewards, to accomplish the strategy. This requires measuring the contributions of people and departments to the strategic objectives, and linking the reward structure to their strategic performance. Also, policies and procedures must be established that encourage attention and commitment to the strategy.

4. Installing internal administrative support systems. The management process, the way the managers in an organization work together, is the critical element in successful implementation and performance. Internal systems must support this process, as well as monitor strategic progress. Actual performance must be measured against planned performance in meeting strategic objectives, and corrective action taken where necessary. To acquire information on actual performance (as well as on changes in the external environment), strategic information systems must be designed and installed. In short, management must monitor the results of the strategy, adapt the organization to environmental changes, and ensure that the organization (and its people) work to carry out the strategy.

5. Exerting strategic leadership. Essentially, strategic leadership consists of obtaining commitment to the strategy and its accomplishment. This includes creating a climate and culture that causes the organization to work hard (and intelligently) toward the accomplishment of the strategy. While this requires management's personal leadership, it also involves the constructive use of power and politics in building a consensus to support the strategy.

Critical Senior-Level Abilities

Effective performance at senior levels in organizations requires abilities beyond and different from those needed at nonexecutive levels. Six such abilities identified by a recent New York University study are: knowing the business and markets; managing subunit rivalry; finding and overcoming problems; staying on strategy; being an entrepreneurial force; and accommodating adversity.[17]

---

[17] S.A. Stumpf, "Leadership and Beyond: The Need for Strategic Management Skills," in *Advances in Strategic Management*, eds. Robert Lamb and Paul Shrivastava, Vol. 5 (Greenwich, CT: JAI Press, 1988), 245-55.

The NYU study, as well as one by Harvard's John Kotter,[18] found that effective senior executives know their businesses well. They understand where it has been and where it is going and what the customers want. They also allow *productive* rivalry between subunits (functions and divisions); they don't try to eliminate rivalry or competition but *manage* it to improve performance. Effective executives are also adept at diagnosing issues before they become problems, as well as at assessing the implications of an issue. They tend to think several "moves" ahead in the competitive game.

A critical strategy-related skill is the ability to keep the organization focused on the strategy; the plan must be prominent in the thinking of management. For example, all too often managers "chase" ad hoc opportunities not related to the firm's strategy. Effective managers possess the ability to continually evaluate ideas, opportunities, and alternatives against the strategy.

Further, good executives possess an entrepreneurial spirit. Not only can they create a vision of what the company can be, but they are able to articulate that vision so others can understand it, share in it, and become excited about it—they are able to "build a dream" for people. Finally, they can deal with, learn from, and build upon setbacks—adversities. They are resilient and they don't dwell on setbacks; they move forward.

Management Selection, Development, Succession

Since strategic planning provides the link between the past, the present, and the future, executive succession—particularly CEO succession—is a vitally important strategic decision. In fact, some say that CEO succession is *the* most important strategic decision, because it determines all other strategic decisions for years to come (during the CEO's tenure).[19]

But CEO selection is not the only personnel decision with strategic importance. Selecting the best people to implement strategies is important in achieving the firm's strategic objectives. Today, there may be as many different types of managers and managerial styles as there are different types of businesses. Further, different types of businesses (such as cash cows, stars, question marks, and dogs) may require very different actions and leadership approaches for their strategies to be effective. Important to business-unit performance, then, is finding the right kind of manager for each type of business.

The managerial specialist best suited to handle a particular business situation can be identified and selected using the business screen matrix shown in Figure

---

[18] John P. Kotter, *The General Managers* (New York, NY: The Free Press, 1982).

[19] T.E. Comte and W.F. McCanna, "Progressive Differentiation: Improving the Strategic Act of CEO Selection," *The Academy of Management Executive*, 2, No. 4 (November 1988), 303.

19.2. Use of the matrix allows the business situation to be compared to its relative strategic position in the industry, allowing a manager or particular managerial style to be chosen to match the strategic situation. In the figure, suggestions are made about the types of managers most likely to be successful in each situation represented.

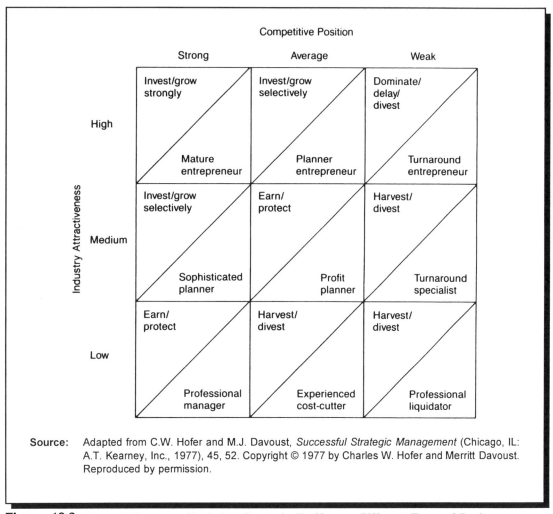

Source: Adapted from C.W. Hofer and M.J. Davoust, *Successful Strategic Management* (Chicago, IL: A.T. Kearney, Inc., 1977), 45, 52. Copyright © 1977 by Charles W. Hofer and Merritt Davoust. Reproduced by permission.

Figure 19.2 General Managers Needed to Strategically Manage Different Types of Businesses

Therefore, no one leader is best for every situation or stage of an organization's life cycle. Each type of leader needs a variety of talents. While leadership skills can be developed, this does not mean that any one leader can grow into every situation. A leader must know when his or her abilities fit the situation;

when they don't fit, they must step aside in favor of leaders with the right abilities. Bill Rothschild of GE has identified five criteria that affect this leader/situation fit. They are:

1. *Business Life Cycle Stage:* the age and maturity of the business as well as that of the market and industry.
2. *Customer Types:* characteristics of those buying the firm's products and services.
3. *The Competition:* the aggressiveness of the firm's competitors.
4. *Stakeholder Needs:* the attitudes and expectations of key stakeholders, whether they want security, dynamic growth, or high return.
5. *Technology:* the dominant technology of the industry or business requires a fit with leadership style and managerial abilities. A change in technology may require new leadership abilities.[20]

But, back to the question of whether managers should be selected or developed to fit the situation. Each approach has distinct costs and benefits and is therefore appropriate for different organizational contexts. Selection is congruent with a mechanistic view of organizations in which managerial traits and abilities are relatively fixed; it contributes to strategy implementation by matching managers with task demands. While a management development approach also aligns managers with strategies, it does so with a broader, longer-term perspective. Development is congruent with a more fluid, organic view of organizations in which both managers' abilities and the strategic demands of situations are seen as evolving over time.[21] Thus, selection and development are complementary approaches.

Michael A. Carpenter, GE's vice president for corporate planning, points out that a person rising through the ranks in a functional business typically has had no general management responsibility prior to becoming CEO. In a typical multibusiness company, the new CEO would have managed four or five business-units—out of these, maybe one or two will have had serious strategic issues that needed to be addressed. Therefore, the new CEO will have had very little experience in dealing with strategy. On the other hand, GE's approach has been to make a lot of general managers' jobs available; by the time someone makes CEO, he or she will have run twenty different businesses.[22]

---

[20] William E. Rothschild, *Risktaker, Caretaker, Surgeon, Undertaker: Four Faces of Strategic Leadership* (New York, NY: John Wiley & Sons, Inc., 1993), 30-31.

[21] J.L. Kerr and Ellen F. Jackofsky, "Aligning Managers with Strategies: Management Development versus Selection," *Strategic Management Journal*, 10, special Issue (Summer 1989), 157-170.

[22] "GE = Giant Entrepreneur?" *Planning Review*, 13, No. 1 (January 1985), 18-21.

Reward Systems

Managers, and people in general, tend to do what they are rewarded for doing. If the firm wants the professional liquidator employing a harvest/divest strategy to focus his or her efforts primarily on the present, the reward system (salary, bonus, promotions) must be so oriented. Likewise, reward systems for the turn-around and planner entrepreneur must be geared to future performance of the business-unit, rather than to short-term results. Hofer and Davoust have suggested present- versus future-focused reward and bonus levels for each of the positions on the grid, as shown in Figure 19.3. In fact, General Electric has utilized such an approach in developing performance measurements, compensation, and promotion criteria for its SBU managers. As shown in Table 19.2, social responsibility comprises 12 percent of the measurement and compensation weights for all SBU managers. However, future performance factors constitute 48 percent of the weight for the manager of invest/grow SBUs, 28 percent for selectivity/earnings SBUs, and just 16 percent for harvest/divest SBUs. Current results count 40 percent for invest/grow SBU managers, 60 percent for selectivity/earnings SBU managers, and a high 72 percent for harvest/divest SBU managers. In this way, GE influences the actions of the SBU managers by gearing the reward system to the focus it wants them to adopt.[23]

Other companies use modified forms of this approach. For example, Emhart Corp., Combustion Engineering (CE), Borden, and Sears have adopted compensation plans that tie executive pay to long-term performance measures, such as stock price or return on equity. As an indication that such approaches were needed at CE, prior to introduction of the new system, division general managers had been ignoring the company's strategic plans and focusing on what the bonus system rewarded them for doing—meeting short-term budget targets.[24, 25]

At Saturn Corporation, 80 percent of *everyone's* pay is salary, and 20 percent is sales-based bonus.

---

[23] C.W. Hofer, *Instructor's Manual to Accompany Strategic Management* (St. Paul, MN: West Publishing Company, 1981), 332.

[24] "Rewarding Executives for Taking the Long View," *Business Week* (April 2, 1984), 99.

[25] See also M. R. Hurwich, "Strategic Compensation Designs that Link Pay to Performance," *The Journal of Business Strategy*, 7, No. 2 (Fall 1986), 79-81; and P.J. Stonich, "Using Rewards in Implementing Strategy," *Strategic Management Journal*, 2, No. 3 (July/September 1981), 345-52.

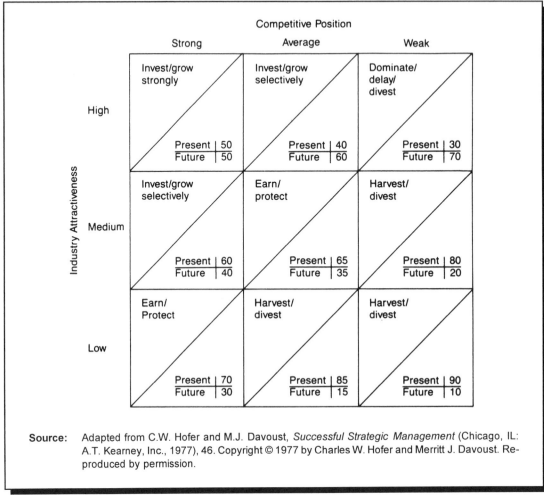

Figure 19.3 The Present/Future Focus of Compensation Bonuses for Business-Level General Managers

The Manager as an Organization Builder

The general manager is both a strategist and an "organization builder."[26] As a strategist, the general manager defines the corporate purpose and objectives, and the means to achieve them. As an organization builder, he or she must manage people as a cohesive unit in achieving the corporate mission and objectives

---

[26] H.E.R. Uyterhoeven, R.W. Ackerman, and J.W. Rosenblum, *Strategy and Organization*, rev. ed. (Homewood, IL: Richard D. Irwin, Inc., 1977).

Table 19.2 GE's Measurement, Compensation, and Promotion Criteria

Type of SBU	Manager's Key Characteristics	Measurement and Compensation Criteria and Weights		
		Future Performance Factors*	Current Financial Results†	Social Responsibility‡
Invest/grow	Entrepreneur	48%	40%	12%
Selectivity/earnings	Sophisticated/critical	28	60	12
Harvest/divest	Solid/experienced	16	72	12

*Strategy, programs, manpower, facilities; key checkpoints.
†Residual income (equals net income less a capital charge); last year versus this year.
‡Minority hiring, OSHA checks, environmental impact criteria, etc.

Source: Adapted from C.W Hofer, *Instructor's Manual to Accompany Strategic Management* (St. Paul, MN: West Publishing Company, 1981), 332

through strategies. In this light, the *process* of carrying out the strategies takes on great importance. It is not enough that the manager has embarked the organization on the proper mission, toward the proper objectives, employing optimal strategies. *How* these activities are carried out is likewise important.

Effects on the Organization. What does the manager really achieve if his or her objectives and strategies cause undue dissension in the organization, or if they—figuratively, if not literally—tear the organization apart? The goal of the general manager should be to strengthen—not weaken—the organization through the pursuit of objectives and strategies. What good are increased profits and market share and a better balance sheet if they result in a less conducive organizational climate and diminished human resources? The manager must consider not only what the strategies will do *for* the organization, but *to* the organization, as well. A less-than-optimal strategy that clearly strengthens the organization in terms of its climate, people, systems, and structure may be preferred over the "ideal" strategy.

In the final analysis, the policy and strategy job of the manager is to balance the relationships between the organization and its environment in such a way that the organization is strengthened. In fact, Sir Geoffrey Vickers sees the task as the "setting of governing relations or norms rather than the setting of goals, objectives, or ends."[27] The policymaker's job is to balance the desired relation-

---

[27] Sir Geoffrey Vickers, *The Art of Judgment: A Study of Policy-Making* (New York, NY: Basic Books, 1965).

ships, consisting of setting directions for the firm "bounded by recognizable constraints which originate from desired and inevitable relationships between the organization and its environment, *and from the organization's past.*"[28]

IMPLEMENTING STRATEGIC PLANS

Dennis Hykes, vice president of strategic planning services at Control Data Business Advisors, suggests that "implementable" strategic plans have, as minimum, three characteristics:

1. They are linked to the appropriate control system within the organization.
2. They are "owned" by operating management.
3. They are perceived as being achievable by those responsible for implementation.

Concerning the first characteristic, the plans must be tied to the budgeting, operational planning, and incentive compensation systems. There must be a smooth transition from the planning cycle to the budget cycle, and close interaction between the strategic and operational planning systems. This link is accomplished through *strategic programs* that connect a strategy with a responsible member of operating management, and are an integral part of an operational plan.

Plans are likely to be "owned" by operating management when the following occurs.

1. Strategic planning must be in the management mainstream; that is, it should be a regular, continuous process, as other management processes tend to be.
2. Plans, and the process, must be easily digestible; that is, relatively uncomplicated planning systems, techniques, and forms should be used to produce relatively brief (20- to 30-page) plans.
3. The line managers are the planners, with the planning staff concentrating on process design, facilitation, troubleshooting, and review and analysis.

Hykes' final point is that the plans must be achievable—neither too difficult nor too easy. Finding the optimal level of difficulty can be aided by using an

---

[28] K.J. Hatten, "Quantitative Research Methods in Strategic Management," in *Strategic Management: A New View of Business Policy and Planning*, eds. D. Schendel and C.W. Hofer (Boston, MA: Little, Brown, 1979), 461.

interactive, participative team approach in their development, coupled with a soundly constructed review program for the plan.[29]

The Plan Itself

Once the strategic decision has been made, detailed planning can begin. Now the chosen strategy is created in detail for each division or business-unit, and specific time-phased actions required to support the strategy, including budgets, are developed. The result is the strategic, long-range master plan, typically covering five years or more. From this plan, more specific and shorter-range tactical and operating plans are developed. But this module focuses on the longer-term strategic plan.

Many firms experience two problems in planning. They have difficulty in producing reasonably accurate forecasts, and they tend to misuse the strategic plan as an operating document. In fact, many strategic plans are little more than "financial hopes filled with 'nice' numbers." This is unfortunate, for a plan is of value only if it is realistic. However, specific ways to overcome planning problems have been proposed:

1. Emphasize the *process* of planning, not the financial details of the plan.
2. Differentiate between the more serious risks to the balance sheet and risks to the profit and loss statement.
3. Measure the total market and competitive market shares as accurately as possible.
4. Gear the plan, especially spending, to the occurrence of major *events*, rather than to time periods.
5. Plan to expend money step by step as events warrant, rather than up front.
6. Build a second plan based on time periods.
7. Decide in *advance* the criteria for abandoning a project.
8. Set up a monitoring system.
9. Make a new five-year plan every year.
10. Avoid excessive publicity about long-term financial goals. (They *may* not materialize.)[30]

[29] Hykes, "Planning for Plan Implementation," 5-12.

[30] R.N. Paul, N.B. Donavan, and J.W. Taylor, "The Reality Gap in Strategic Planning," *Harvard Business Review*, 56, No. 3 (May/June 1978), 124.

Remember, the goal of planning should be to speed up the organization's process of learning about its environment, not just to make plans.[31] Also, do not expect perfection in planning immediately; treat the initial try as just that—a first draft. Planning is a skill; no one ever became an expert golfer, musician, public speaker—or planner—on their first few tries.

The Plan's Process and Content

After strategic decisions have been made, more detailed planning occurs. Specific statements of policies and procedures, strategies and programs, priorities and schedules, and budgets and resources are developed. Figure 19.4 shows the process as practiced by the General Telephone Company of Illinois (GTI). In the GTI example, managers establish and maintain an "information bank" which they can draw from when setting performance goals and planning in their own areas of responsibility. This information bank is contained in a planning workbook with several interrelated sections so that individual planning efforts are coordinated and more supportive of the company's overall goals and objectives.[32]

Content and Format. There is no uniform format for a strategic plan; nearly every company has its own approach. As an example, strategic planning for a centralized company would differ from one that is decentralized. In the latter instance, each SBU may have its own strategic plans that would comprise the following elements:

- A statement of the SBU's mission.
- The key environmental assumptions summarizing the external environment and its opportunities and threats.
- Key competitor assumptions.
- A list of constraints imposed from either inside or outside the company.
- The desired future of the SBU—its *goals*.
- *Objectives*, stated as specific time-based measurements, that will be met in pursuing the goals.
- The course of action to be followed to achieve goals and objectives—*strategy*.
- The programs, development and investment, critical to the strategy.
- Contingency plans, which recognize that things might go wrong, and what can be done to correct the situation.

---

[31] A.P. DeGeus, "Planning as Learning," *Harvard Business Review*, 66, No. 2 (March/April 1988), 70.

[32] *MBO and the Planning Process in General Telephone Company of Illinois* (Bloomington, IL: GTC of Illinois, 1973).

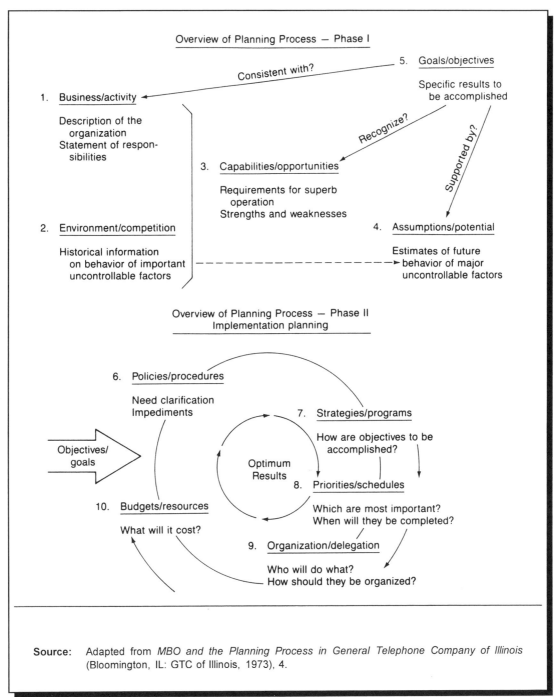

Overview of Planning Process — Phase I

5. Goals/objectives

Specific results to be accomplished

Consistent with?

1. Business/activity

Description of the organization
Statement of responsibilities

Recognize?

Supported by?

3. Capabilities/opportunities

Requirements for superb operation
Strengths and weaknesses

4. Assumptions/potential

Estimates of future behavior of major uncontrollable factors

2. Environment/competition

Historical information on behavior of important uncontrollable factors

Overview of Planning Process — Phase II
Implementation planning

6. Policies/procedures

Need clarification
Impediments

Objectives/ goals

Optimum Results

7. Strategies/programs

How are objectives to be accomplished?

8. Priorities/schedules

Which are most important?
When will they be completed?

10. Budgets/resources

What will it cost?

9. Organization/delegation

Who will do what?
How should they be organized?

Source: Adapted from *MBO and the Planning Process in General Telephone Company of Illinois* (Bloomington, IL: GTC of Illinois, 1973), 4.

Figure 19.4 GTI's Planning Process

- And finally, the financial components of the strategic plan in a form that will allow them to be integrated with the existing operational control system.[33]

STRATEGY AND STRUCTURE RELATIONSHIPS

Certain strategies are appropriate for certain types of organizations or stages of development. Likewise, the decision to compete in certain markets (e.g., to diversify into several product lines or to compete internationally) is a major one that requires an appropriate plan to implement the strategy successfully. But while an organization's strategy and structure are related and depend on one another, neither is an end in itself. Both are the means by which missions are fulfilled and goals and objectives are met. The strategy is the direction or route chosen to meet the goals and objectives, and the structure is the vehicle through which the strategies will be implemented. Structure here is defined broadly, to include not only the type of departmentation employed, but the organization's systems, procedures, and processes, as well.

"Good" organization structure, systems, and processes do not necessarily produce successful performance, any more than a safe car produces safe driving. However, poor or inappropriate structure can make successful performance more difficult, perhaps even impossible. The proper structure can permit or facilitate the organization and its managers achieving their best performance. The ideal organization structure does not frustrate, thwart, or otherwise prevent the firm's managers from doing their work.

Alfred Chandler found that when organizations adopted a new strategy, such as diversification, they tended to change to a structure appropriate for the new strategy (in this case, a divisional M-form). He concluded from his studies that structure follows strategy, perhaps as "form follows function" in design.[34]

Assuming the firm has been pursuing a certain strategy such as related diversification, using an appropriate centralized-functional (U-form) structure, a mismatch can occur if the firm changes its strategy. Under competitive conditions, adoption of a strategy change, such as unrelated diversification, while retaining a U-form structure can result in a performance decline. Therefore, the organization will need to adopt a structure appropriate to this strategy (an M-form structure) to restore its performance and take advantage of the new strategy. It is possible, however, that the company will judge the new strategy a failure and return to its previous approach (related-business strategy), reachieving the strategy-

---

[33] Robert M. Donnelly, "Strategic Planning for Better Management," *Managerial Planning*, 30, No. 3 (November/December 1981), 3-6.
[34] Alfred Chandler, Jr., *Strategy and Structure* (Cambridge, MA: MIT Press, 1967).

structure match. Or attempts may be made to influence or negotiate with the environment, perhaps restoring performance in spite of the mismatch. It should be noted that performance declines may occur because of strategy-structure mismatches only under competitive conditions. If little competition exists, as in the case of a monopoly or where the organization can influence its environment sufficiently, a performance decline may not occur. Therefore, this type of organization may not feel sufficient pressure to change its structure, and may retain the strategy-structure mismatch with few apparent ill effects.

Others have suggested that a reverse relationship also exists; that the firm's structure and processes influence its choice of strategies. The important point is that strategy and structure must be consistent and congruent with one another. The firm should *match* its strategy and structure, and should match the strategy with the environment.

Recent studies have indicated that it is this match—or interaction effect—that is the most significant factor in explaining an organization's performance. That is, it is not just the strategy *or* the structure or the environment that is most important in explaining performance, but the interaction between the factors.[35] In short, the relationships between the variables are more complex than most researchers have acknowledged.[36]

[35] Soen Tjan and L.A. Digman, "The Interaction Effects of Environment, Structure, and Strategy on Firm Performance," *Proceedings of the Midwest Decision Sciences Institute* (April 1989).

[36] D.B. Jemison, "Risk and the Relationship Among Strategy, Organizational Processes, and Performance," *Management Science*, 33, No. 9 (September 1987), 1087.

Module
20

Strategic Evaluation
and Control

LEARNING OBJECTIVES

After completing Module 20, you should be able to:

1. Understand the elements and types of strategic control.
2. Relate strategic performance measurement to the strategic control function.
3. Describe contemporary measurement approaches, such as activity-based management, economic value added, and the balanced scorecard.
4. Appreciate the roles and key elements of strategic audits.

In previous modules, we have studied what it takes to successfully formulate, select, and implement winning strategies. Another area—strategic evaluation and control (strategy analysis and corrective action during and after implementation)—is also very important and perhaps even more-neglected in studies. Strategic control focuses on two questions: Is the strategy being implemented as planned? and Is it producing the intended results?[1] The world (and the firm) are constantly changing, and it is not possible to forecast these changes with certainty. So the organization must be able to review the ongoing results of its strategic decisions and take corrective actions (modify the strategies, their implementation, and the firm's performance) as necessary.

PROFILE   Office Depot

When David Fuente became CEO of Office Depot in 1987, the company had ten stores. By 1995, the company had nearly 400. But the concept is essentially the same: no frills, warehouse stores selling brand-name office supplies 30 to 60 percent below list price. Office Depot has been successful; it is almost twice the size of its competitor, Office Max, a former Kmart subsidiary.

Office Depot grew by catering to small businesses (20 or fewer employees), but is starting to cater to bigger companies. Office Depot thinks it can compete on price because of their buying power and efficient distribution. In fact, Office Depot is connected to its suppliers through electronic data interchange, a la Wal-Mart.

Fuente says Office Depot and its competitors all sell the same products and they all buy from the same manufacturers. The difference comes down to price and service. "The difference is not in the strategy but in the execution."[2]

PROFILE   Mike Walsh and Union Pacific

Mike Walsh became head of the Union Pacific Railroad in 1986 and transformed the company prior to his departure for Tenneco in 1991 (he died of brain cancer in 1994). His approach to management was simple; set targets you can count, count the results, and hold people accountable.

With this approach, Walsh took a company headed for trouble (but didn't know it) and turned it into a star performer. Many at UP thought things were okay prior to his arrival; but if you asked questions like "how often do the trains

---

[1] Dan Schendel and Charles W. Hofer, *Strategic Management* (Boston, MA: Little Brown, 1979), 17.
[2] Zina Moukheiber, "A Lousy Day for Golf," *Forbes* (May 9, 1994), 60-64.

run on time?", you would be told that the company didn't measure such things—besides, that was someone else's job.

Walsh started measuring things, and found that:

- 20 percent of bills had mistakes.
- 14 percent of locomotives were typically out of service.
- 30 percent of freight cars were in "shabby" condition.

What's more, these kinds of "failure costs" were costing UP more than $600 million a year.

Walsh made numerous changes; new mission, strategy, structure, information technology, and control system. He made quantitative targets and measurement of results the core of strategy implementation. As a result, billing errors dropped to 6 percent, out-of-service locomotives declined to 8 percent, and so on. Walsh's system uses an "objectives and responsibilities matrix" to list key business objectives, specific individuals responsible for them, and timing. Top management develops the objectives (from the mission statement), and assigns responsibility for each to a senior executive. This person proposes quantitative measures and specific targets for each year. Each exec must account for results during annual performance reviews, and rewards mirror the results.

In short, people knew what was expected and treated their goals as commitments. In addition, they were motivated and empowered to achieve them. The approach would not work, however, without a good measurement and control system.[3]

STRATEGIC CONTROL

One of the key tasks in strategy implementation is strategic control: monitoring strategic progress and taking corrective action. Strategic control attempts to ensure that performance conforms to plans. Effective control requires the measurement of performance, an evaluation of that performance, an analysis of any deviations between planned and actual performance, and taking the appropriate corrective action to modify future performance, the plans, or both. Just as effective management depends on effective control, effective strategic management also requires strategic control.[4]

---

[3] Count, Count, and Account . . .," *The Real World Strategist*, 1, No. 5 (July/August 1994), 1-3.

[4] P. Lorange, M.F. Scott Morton, and S. Ghoshal, *Strategic Control* (St. Paul, MN: West Publishing Company, 1986).

Effective strategic control involves two key areas: has the strategy been implemented as planned (or have the implementation process and detailed planning unintentionally modified the strategy that was selected)? And, once implemented, is the strategy producing the desired results?

As is true of any effective control system, strategic control is not performed after the strategic plan has been fully carried out; instead, the results are evaluated *while* the strategy is being followed. Pilots flying from New York to Los Angeles make course corrections all along the way, allowing for winds and other forces. They do not wait until they are in San Francisco to determine that they somehow have gotten off course.

Basic Control Elements

Any control system consists of several basic elements:

- *Setting predetermined standards.* These are the desired states, goals, objectives, or results that the firm is attempting to achieve. In general, they are reflected in the plans—long, intermediate, and short range.
- *Measuring actual performance.* This includes sales, costs, profits, share of the market, and the like, that the firm experiences once the plan has been put into effect. Short-term performance indicates preliminary results in terms of longer-term plans.
- *Comparing planned versus actual performance.* Do the two differ and by how much? What is a significant or important deviation? What techniques of analysis should be used to make the determination?
- *Taking corrective action.* If there is a significant deviation between planned and actual performance, what should be done? Can changes be made to get future performance back on course? Or do the plans and objectives need to be changed? Or both? Also, performance equaling or exceeding that specified by the plan may indicate that the plan was not ambitious enough and so should be adjusted.

In general, the planning and control process is as shown in Figure 20.1.

Levels of Control

Three levels of control—organizational, internal, and strategic—are needed to fulfill a firm's mission and achieve its goals and objectives.

Organizational Control. This control over strategic matters is accomplished at the general management and functional levels and is assumed by the board of directors. Board members should periodically review an ongoing strategy, questioning its validity, modifying and recycling, and reconsidering critical strategic

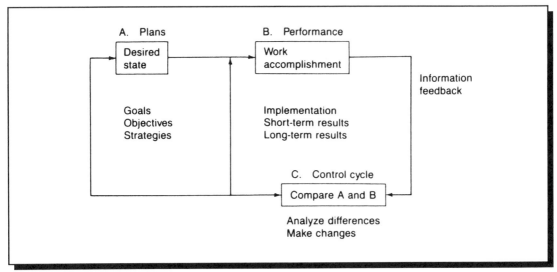

Figure 20.1 Planning and Control Cycle

issues.[5] At the general management level, the CEO and the president are responsible for overall strategic control, which includes establishing formats and criteria for a well-designed control system. However, they may designate the planning staff to act as the strategic control group for the organization.

Internal Control. Internal controls expand into more specific operating and functional areas. Operating managers use these as guides, concentrating on the internal actions necessary to keep the organization functioning. Internal controls can be described as techniques for keeping in touch with the progress of the various parts of the plan, assessing information received, and responding to a variety of functional and operational information inputs. There are five basic internal areas any firm should consider. While these areas center more on tactical than on strategic control, they need to be established before the changes affecting the company's strategic assumptions can be monitored. The internal controls include:

1. *Overall performance.* General managers are responsible for gathering operating, financial, and resource data to measure and evaluate the performance of the firm and its operations.

---

[5] Y.N. Chang and F. Campo-Flores, *Business Policy and Strategy* (Santa Monica, CA: Goodyear Publishing Co., 1980), 226.

2. *Organizational policies.* This type of control is maintained through additional policies established by the board of directors and policy executives.
3. *Financial activities.* Areas that should be strongly considered are assets management, cash budgets, tax planning, diagnostic surveys, interfirm comparisons, return on investment, and profitability.
4. *Budgetary control.* This involves departmental budgets and centrally prepared budgets relating to the total operation. Budgetary controls normally reflect costs and results.
5. *Operating.* Finally, line management can regulate departmental and program activities by using operating controls. Examples include: production, scheduling, and personnel control.[6]

Strategic Control. The final level of control complements the company's internal controls by instituting special controls over strategic activities. Strategic control is directed, first of all, at areas that must be visible to management. This ensures the flow of external and internal data and allows management to appraise environmental factors that may have an impact on the firm.

Also, management must specifically identify and assign responsibility for managing strategic programs and actions. These programs may be at any strategy level: R&D, new product/market, or acquisition and merger. Control over strategic activities is usually accomplished by periodic reporting or scheduled reviews.

Finally, strategic control provides a means of validating and adjusting strategies. The company's assumptions must be updated against evolving events, and its operations must be monitored to detect deviations. In any large organization, top management should be assured that each program can move efficiently toward its major goals.

The distinctive feature of strategic controls is that they are intended to *reassure* and allow those who are not close to the scene (such as top management) to see the strategic impact of functional and operating activities, and to evaluate them.[7]

A Contemporary View of Strategic Control

However, because of the uncertainty and complexity present in strategic management, the classic feedback model of control may be inadequate. Two West German scholars have recently proposed a new model of strategic control incorporating three elements: premise control, implementation control, and strategic surveillance. As shown in Figure 20.2, the three elements control both strategy

---

[6] *Ibid.,* 227

[7] S.J. Carroll, F.T. Paine, and J.B. Miner, *The Management Process* (New York, NY: Macmillan, 1977), 284.

formulation *and* implementation. In strategy formulation, a major consideration involves creating premises (assumptions, beliefs, scenarios) about the internal and external environments. *Premise control* has been designed to check systematically and continuously whether or not the premises set during the planning and implementation processes are still valid.

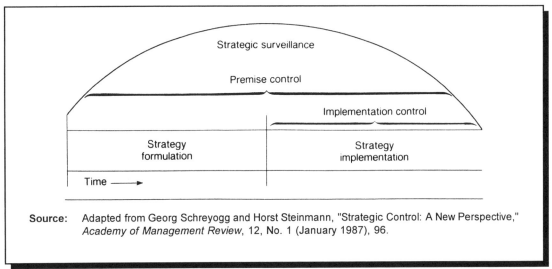

Source: Adapted from Georg Schreyogg and Horst Steinmann, "Strategic Control: A New Perspective," *Academy of Management Review*, 12, No. 1 (January 1987), 96.

Figure 20.2 Elements of Strategic Control

Not all important events and factors may be foreseen during strategy formulation; some of these may come to light during implementation. Thus, the implementation phase is an important source of additional information about the strategy and its likely results. Therefore, *implementation control* is used to assess whether or not the whole strategic course should be changed, given past, current, and likely future events which have come to light during implementation (note that implementation control is *not* designed to assure that implementation is proceeding as planned).

Finally, *strategic surveillance* is designed to monitor the full range of events, both inside and outside the firm, which could threaten the strategic action.[8] This type of control is more akin to scanning, whereas premise and implementation control are more focused, monitoring specific phases or elements of the strategy.

---

[8] Georg Schreyogg and Horst Steinmann, "Strategic Control: A New Perspective," *Academy of Management Review*, 12, No. 1 (January 1987), 95-97.

Strategic Control Processes

An important objective of strategic control is ensuring that performance is as near as practicable to the strategic plan. Four major steps can be identified in the strategic control process:

1. Evaluating the strategic plan and developing standard-of-performance criteria.
2. Measurement of actual performance.
3. Evaluating actual performance by comparing it to standards.
4. Taking corrective action and implementing contingency plans.

Step 1: Develop Performance Standards. The first step in the strategic control process is evaluating the plan and developing standards of performance. Strategic performance should be evaluated in terms of whether it will yield the desired objectives established by management and whether the goals, plans, or standards are realistic and well defined. Strategy evaluation provides a broad view of the interaction of various operations and helps create a balance between goals and tasks. The focus of evaluation should be on what must be done in the areas of organization structure, people, culture, and control systems to make the strategy succeed.

As the strategic plan is evaluated, key success requirements must be defined with sufficient specificity that strategic performance criteria or indicators can be developed. These are standards against which actual performance can be measured. A means for monitoring the execution of plans should be developed concurrently with standards of performance. Helpful measures of strategic performance include: sales (total, and by division, product category, and region); sales growth; net profits; return on sales, assets, equity, and investment; cost of sales; cash flow; market share; value added; product quality; employee productivity.

Step 2: Measurement of Actual Performance. Sensing (searching for and becoming aware of) and measuring actual conditions is the second step in the strategic control system. Data are collected and processed, functional controls are implemented, and environmental signals are monitored. The mechanism operates in a feedback network so that adjustments can be made to environmental changes.

Signals of change may be external or internal. External environmental signals are particularly significant since they are less predictable and their impact is more difficult to determine. Internal signals, on the other hand, tend to be more gradual, short term, and controllable. Knowledge of internal changes is more available and accessible than are details about external changes.

Environmental signals also can be classified as either strong or weak. Strong signals tend to have the following characteristics: (1) signal content is complete and clear, (2) response time is short, and (3) response options are limited.

Strong signals, analogous to surprise, may appear without warning. It is urgent that management act on them, even though the situation is probably unfamiliar. Strong signals often reflect discontinuous changes, the sudden appearance of an opportunity or threat with a significant impact.

Sensing enables management to scan the environment for these signals of change and to detect weak signals. Since weak signals often precede strong signals, correct and early detection reduces surprises and increases response time. The firm can respond gradually and position itself to act decisively and directly when the signal becomes more clear and complete. Once weak signals are detected, they can be monitored and planned for so that response options can be carefully developed and chosen.

Methods should be developed and evaluated to make certain that performance measures assess what they are supposed to measure. Areas of performance for which standards have been set should be measured as the strategic plans are implemented and at times corresponding to scheduled accomplishment of goals and objectives.

Step 3: Evaluating Actual Performance.
The third step in strategic control is to evaluate actual performance, as measured in step 2, by comparing it to the standards of performance developed in step 1. In this way, deviations from the strategic plan can be determined.

Step 4: Corrective Action and Contingency Plans.
Corrective action and implementation of contingency plans is the final step in strategic control. Once external environmental threats or opportunities have progressed to the point that a particular outcome is likely, corrective action may be necessary. Corrective action must also be taken when there is an undesirable deviation between the standard and actual performance.

There are three choices of corrective action:

1. *Normal mode*—follow a routine, noncrisis approach; this takes more time.
2. *Ad hoc crash mode*—saves time by speeding up the response process, geared to the problem at hand.
3. *Preplanned crisis mode*—specifies a planned response in advance; this approach lowers the response time and increases the capacity for handling strategic surprises.

Contingency plans should be developed to help counter the effects of strategic surprises. These plans can be applied quickly and help management face unfamiliar events.

In summary, the strategic control process attempts to ensure that performance will be as close as practicable to the plan. The objective of control is to take corrective action when actual and planned performance differ. In practice, strategic reappraisals are routinely conducted on an annual or biannual basis. In many companies, each SBU manager must completely reassess the unit's competitive position and strategy during an annual presentation to corporate management. At the same time, a staff review group evaluates and presents alternatives for the corporation's total portfolio of SBUs.[9]

MEASURING AND ANALYZING PERFORMANCE

Measuring performance is critical to strategic control. But which measure of performance? Peter Drucker says five basic measures of performance are necessary and sufficient for the manager:

1. *Market standing*—is share increasing? What is it doing in particular submarkets and niches?
2. *Innovative performance*—new products in growth areas.
3. *Productivity*—how much value has been added per resource input?
4. *Liquidity and cash flow.*
5. *Profitability.*

None of the measures is perfect, and none will give precise readings. However, the *trend*—not the absolute value—is most important.[10]

In recent years, a number of new approaches have arisen to help strategic managers evaluate and control their organizations' performance. Several of the more useful and promising are discussed here: activity-based management, economic value added, the balanced scorecard, and benchmarking.

Activity-Based Management

Activity-based management (ABM) is not just a system; it is a new way of planning and controlling an organization to achieve excellence. ABM has its roots in an accounting innovation called activity-based costing (ABC), an attempt to allocate costs to products more realistically than previous cost-accounting approaches. ABC attempts to focus on "drivers"; activities and factors which tend to drive costs up or down for a particular product. Costs are accumulated as they have traditionally been, then are allocated to products, territories or customers for example, based upon the presence of appropriate drivers. These drivers can be volume related (such as machine hours or floor space), product related (such

---

[9] W.K. Hall, "SBUs: Hot, New Topic in the Management of Diversification," *Business Horizons* (February 1978), 22.

[10] Peter F. Drucker, "If Earnings Aren't the Dial to Read," *The Wall Street Journal* (October 30, 1986), 15.

as size, weight, complexity, etc.), transaction related (set-ups, orders, inspections), or selling and administrative related (number of channels, warehousing, etc). A given product might be allocated 30 percent of the space costs, 20 percent of sales costs, ten percent of warehousing costs, and the like, depending upon how much of these various costs it creates.

Activity-based management *includes* ABC, but would also incorporate or facilitate a host of complementary concepts such as process improvement, modern manufacturing methods (focused, cellular, continuous flow, just-in-time), and employee empowerment. But it is rooted in the philosophy that management must focus on the performance criteria that *all* global competitors can use as common denominators—the productivity and efficiency of activities that support value-adding business processes, which must deliver the highest value at the lowest total cost. As in business process reengineering (BPR), ABM's focus is on activities that add value to business processes. Activities are the common denominator in the business process analysis. ABM, then, is a business process approach that focuses on the *activities* required to support the business *processes* for getting goods and services to the market. Like BPR, it strives to make fundamental modifications to organizational structures so that activities and business processes crossing functional boundaries can be managed more effectively.

As a measurement and control system, ABM strives to provide consistent measures of global competitiveness, using a balanced set of performance measures like those shown in Figure 20.3. Performance must be clearly defined and related to the firm's strategy before it should be measured and used as part of the strategic control system.[11]

Economic Value Added

Organizations tend to work to achieve what is measured. That is, if a particular aspect of firm performance is measured, managers will focus on improving performance in that area (especially if it is also part of the reward system). Therefore it is vitally important that an organization measure and reward what it *really* hopes to accomplish. For example, above all else, management should strive to increase the value of the company. Management can, in fact, be operating a business at a profit and increasing its net worth, but could be reducing the value of the company *in relation to what could be earned elsewhere on the capital employed in the business.*

One tool which provides this kind of information is a technique called economic value added (EVA). Companies using EVA—Coca-Cola, AT&T, Quaker

---

[11] John P. Campi, "It's Not as Easy as ABC," *Journal of Cost Management*, 6, No. 2 (Summer 1992), 5-11.

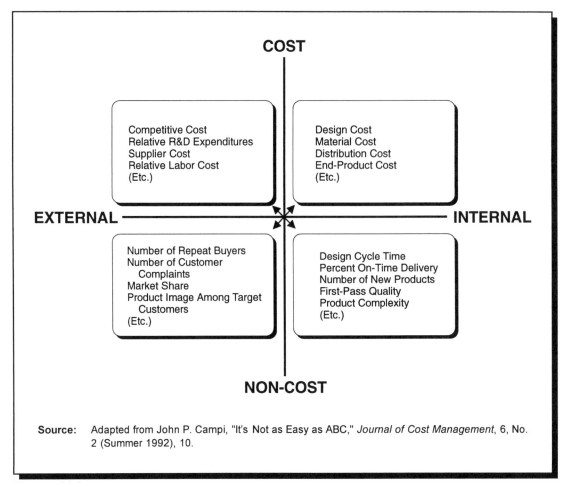

COST

Competitive Cost
Relative R&D Expenditures
Supplier Cost
Relative Labor Cost
(Etc.)

Design Cost
Material Cost
Distribution Cost
End-Product Cost
(Etc.)

EXTERNAL —————————————————— **INTERNAL**

Number of Repeat Buyers
Number of Customer
    Complaints
Market Share
Product Image Among Target
    Customers
(Etc.)

Design Cycle Time
Percent On-Time Delivery
Number of New Products
First-Pass Quality
Product Complexity
(Etc.)

NON-COST

Source: Adapted from John P. Campi, "It's Not as Easy as ABC," *Journal of Cost Management*, 6, No. 2 (Summer 1992), 10.

Figure 20.3 ABM Global Performance Measures

Oats, Briggs & Stratton, and others—have greatly increased their value. Briefly, EVA takes into account the *total* cost of capital. Thus, EVA is an indication of whether a business is creating wealth or, in fact, destroying capital.

Popularized by consultants such as Stern Stewart & Co. and McKinsey & Co., EVA works as shown in Table 20.1. First, after-tax operating profit is calculated. Next the *true* cost of *all* capital employed by the business is computed. The cost of borrowed capital is simply interest paid, adjusted for tax deductibility. Equity capital cost is calculated on the basis of opportunity cost; the total return stockholders could get (price appreciation plus dividends) by investing in companies about as risky as the one in question. Combining the two costs—debt and equity—based upon the amount of each, yields a weighted cost of capital.

Table 20.1 **Economic Value Added Examples**

	After-Tax Operating Profit	minus	Cost of Capital		equals	EVA
Anheuser-Busch	$1,756 OP - 617 Taxes $1,139 Million	minus	$ 8.0 Billion × 11.3 % $ 904 Million	67% equity @ 14.3% 33% debt @ 5.2%	equals	+$235 Million
Spiegel	$ 188 OP - 69 Taxes $ 119 Million	minus	$ 1.6 Billion × 11.1 % $ 178 Million	37% equity @ 18.3% 63% debt @ 6.8%	equals	-$59 Million

Source: Adapted from Shawn Tully, "The Real Key to Creating Wealth," *Fortune* (September 20, 1993), 44.

Next, the amount of capital tied up in the business is estimated. This includes real estate, machines, vehicles, etc., plus working capital. It also includes investments in R&D, training, and the like, figuring a useful life of five years or so. Multiplying the total capital employed by the opportunity cost of that capital gives the dollar cost of capital for the business. Subtracting this figure from after-tax operating profits yields EVA.

If the EVA figure is positive, wealth is being created; the firm is adding more capital than it is costing. If negative, the reverse is true; the firm would get a better return on its capital by investing it elsewhere. But, how can EVA be increased? There are basically three ways:

1. *Use less capital.* Cutting invested capital (perhaps by outsourcing, leasing, etc.) can be very effective.
2. *Increasing profits.* Profits can be increased in a variety of ways, but the trick is to do it without increasing capital invested; this usually means cost cutting.

3. *Invest in high-return projects.* Make sure any investment earns more than the total cost of capital required.[12]

The Balanced Scorecard

The balanced scorecard reduces the risks that result from controlling on the basis of short-term financial measures only. Traditional measures do not provide managers with the information they need to assess and manage the competencies that drive competitive advantage. Backward looking, aggregate financial measures like ROI, ROE, etc., cannot adequately capture the information needed to manage a process-oriented firm. As one executive said, "When I receive the financial reports, I'm either happy or upset, but rarely am I smarter." Financial-only information does not enable managers to assess the adequacy of their strategies and actions. Management needs performance measurement systems that incorporate non-financial as well as financial measures, and relate this information to the firm's strategies—in other words, a balanced strategic management "scorecard."[13] Using the balanced scorecard, companies like Apple Computer and Advanced Micro Devices feel that they have more meaningful feedback about their activities.[14] The company must first define key dimensions of performance for which specific measures can be developed. Often, these measures fall into the following categories: customers, business processes, human resources, and finance. Within each category or dimension, the firm should select performance measures that enable it to carry out its strategies and become more competitive. As shown in Figure 20.4, the dimensions are related and support one another:

- *Customer measures* usually consist of time, quality, service, cost, and market share, asking "how must we look to our customers in order to carry out our strategies?"
- *Process measures* are concerned with measuring rates of improvement and evaluating the return on technological resources and capital investments, in order to satisfy customers.

---

[12] Shawn Tully, "The Real Key to Creating Wealth," *Fortune* (September 20, 1993), 38-50.

[13] Mike Vitale, Sarah C. Maurinac, and Mark Hauser, "New Process/Financial Scorecard: A Strategic Performance Measurement System," *Planning Review* (July/August 1994), 12-16.

[14] Robert S. Kaplan and David P. Norton, "Putting the Balanced Scorecard Approach to Work," *Harvard Business Review*, 71, No. 5 (September/October 1993), 134-47.

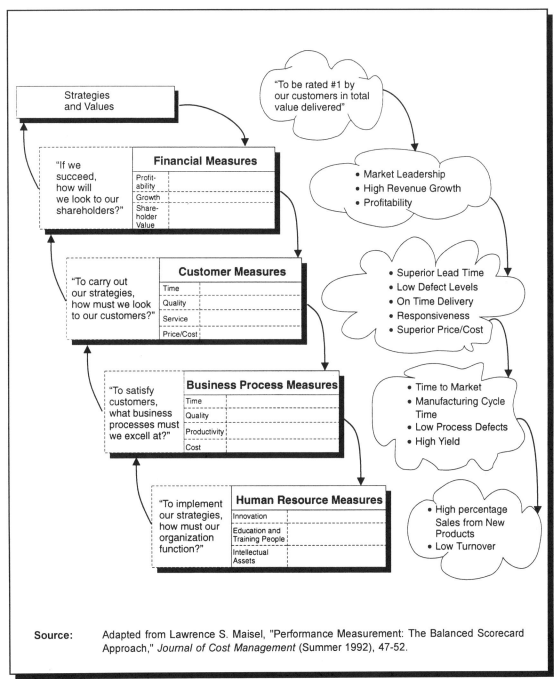

Source: Adapted from Lawrence S. Maisel, "Performance Measurement: The Balanced Scorecard Approach," *Journal of Cost Management* (Summer 1992), 47-52.

Figure 20.4 Strategy-Drive Balanced Scorecard

- *Human resource measures* assess the return on intellectual assets, education and training, innovation, morale, and other human resource measures to evaluate how the organization is functioning in implementing its strategies.
- *Financial measures* help the company evaluate how well it is performing for its shareholders, creditors, customers, and other stakeholders.[15]

Benchmarking

It is not good enough to compare your performance—and practices—against the best in your industry, because it is unlikely that you will surpass a competing firm by trying to imitate it. In addition, the competitor may not be excellent across the board, as compared to the best from other industries. Therefore, a recommended approach for those seeking to better the competition is to "benchmark" one's activities against the best—firms known to be excellent in a particular functional area, regardless of their industry. (Noncompetitors are much more likely to cooperate and share information, too.)

As an example of successful benchmarking, Xerox Business Systems' Logistics and Distribution unit was looking for ways to further increase its productivity growth, which was 3 percent to 5 percent per year. Xerox found the best warehousing and materials handling organization to be L.L. Bean in Freeport, Maine. With Bean's cooperation, Xerox studied their operation, and was able to improve its productivity growth to 10 percent per year[16]—and was able to "breakthrough" to a higher standard of performance.

Corrective Action: When to Pull the Plug

Why do decisions fail? Recent research has shown that failed decisions tend to be associated with imposing ideas on the decision process, using too limited a search for alternatives, and using power tactics to force implementation of the decision.[17]

A major source of decision failures is what some call decisional quicksand, where the organization is gradually drawn deeper and deeper into a losing project, hoping to turn it around and listening to pleas for additional resources to "save" the project, until it is too late and has become a major loss. Let's say your organization has spent several million dollars on a development project, and

---

[15] Lawrence S. Maisel, "Performance Measurement: The Balanced Scorecard Approach," *Journal of Cost Management* (Summer 1992), 47-52.

[16] F.G. Tucker, S.M. Zivan, and R.C. Camp, "How to Measure Yourself against the Best," *Harvard Business Review*, 65, No. 1 (January-February 1987), 8-10.

[17] Paul C. Nutt, "Why Decisions Fail," *Proceedings of Decision Sciences Institute Annual Meeting* (Atlanta, GA: DSI, 1987), 1127-29.

is already $500,000 over budget. This year, the project manager pleads that another $300,000 will "turn the corner" and result in success, whereas killing the project now will waste the several million already spent. What do you do? This is precisely how major projects (such as the Lockheed L-1011 and the Washington Public Power System) became major debacles—incrementally. Thus, decision failures are less likely to be gross miscalculations than they are to result from incremental decisions that seemed to be the lesser of two evils at the time; the trick is knowing when a particular project is going nowhere and when it should be terminated (versus those which do have a good chance of turnaround).[18]

STRATEGIC AUDITS

To aid in control, firms will occasionally perform audits to ensure that certain aspects of their operations are in order. It is a legal requirement, for example, that the financial books of a publicly held firm be audited by an outside CPA firm once each year. In addition, most larger firms have internal auditors who perform related audits for management. In recent years, periodic audits have been utilized by a number of firms to evaluate management activities, policies, systems, procedures, and performance. More recently, this concept has been extended to include operational audits (assessing the firm's operating health) and strategic audits (assessing the firm's strategic health). Such audits can be conducted regularly as needed when problems exist or significant changes have occurred either externally or internally.

Measures of Organizational Health

Measures or indicators of a firm's current operating and strategic health are shown in Tables 20.2 and 20.3. As the tables show, to assess a firm's current operating health, short-term financial, market, technological, and production position are used, while current strategic health is based on strategic market position, technological position, production capabilities, and financial health.

To determine a firm's vulnerability to financial trouble, some analysts use Altman's Z score (described in Table 20.4) or a refined but proprietary version, the Zeta score. The Zeta concept combines weighted key financial ratios to produce an indicator of financial vulnerability—the Zeta score. Ratios included are cumulative profitability (retained earnings and assets), leverage, earnings stability, return on total assets, fixed-charge coverage, liquidity, and total assets. A

---

[18] B.M. Staw and Jerry Ross, "Knowing When to Pull the Plug," *Harvard Business Review*, 65, No. 2 (March/April 1987), 68-74.

Table 20.2 Assessing Current Operating Health

Criteria	Current Operating Health		
	Weak	Average	Strong
Short-term financial position:			
Current ratio	< 1.0	1.5 to 3.0	> 4.0
Quick ratio	< 0.50	0.75 to 1.5	> 2.0
Pro forma breakeven	Volume < BE	BE < Volume < 1.2 BE	Volume > 1.4 BE
Altman's Z-score	< 1.8	2.0 to 3.0	> 3.5
Short-term market position:			
Σ Current product/market segments in relation to breakeven	PMS < BE volume	Be < PMS < twice BE	PMS > four times BE
Σ Volume all products in all markets	All < BE volume	BE < all < twice BE	All > four times BE
Short-term technological position:			
New or modified products available in less than one year	One or none	Two or three	Four or more
Relative product quality	Low	Average	High
Short-term production position:			
Variable costs versus competition's variable costs	Much higher	= Same	Much lower
Facilities replacement costs in next year	Substantially greater than depreciation	= Depreciation rate	Little or none
Facilities that could be sold in next year	None	Up to one fourth of fixed assets	More than one fourth of assets
Overall current operating health			

Source: C.W. Hofer, *Strategy Analysis at the Business-unit Level* (Chicago, IL: unpublished monograph, 1980). Copyright © 1980 by Charles W. Hofer. Reproduced by permission.

Table 20.3 Assessing Current Strategic Health

Criteria	Current Strategic Health		
	Weak	*Average*	*Strong*
Strategic market position:			
Relative industry attractiveness	Low	Medium	High
Relative market share	Low	Average	High
Stage of product/market evolution	High cost to change position	Moderate cost to change position	Low cost to change position
Distribution systems	Changing rapidly	Changing slowly	Not changing
Strategic technological position:			
New product concepts	Follower	Average	Leader
Major product improvements	Follower	Average	Leader
Product modifications	Follower	Average	Leader
Process improvements	Follower	Average	Leader
Strategic production capabilities:			
Experience curve position	Follower	Average	Leader
Strategy versus experience curve position	Inconsistent	Partially consistent	Consistent
Newness of production assets and technology	Old	Middle age	New
Strategic financial health:			
Long-term investment needs versus long-term internal cash flow	Needs $>>$ flow $+ \uparrow$ debt	Needs $\simeq$ flow $+ \uparrow$ debt	Flow $>>>$ needs
Long-term growth rate versus desired objectives	Objectives $>>$ growth rate	Growth rate $\simeq$ objectives	Growth rate $>$ objectives
Overall current strategic health			

Source: C.W. Hofer, *Strategy Analysis at the Business-Unit Level* (Chicago, IL: unpublished monograph, 1980). Copyright © 1980 by Charles W. Hofer. Republished by permission.

zeta score of less than zero suggests that the company may have trouble meeting its financial obligations, while positive values indicate fiancial health.[19]

Strategy Audits

A strategy audit may be needed under the following conditions: performance indicators show that a strategy is not working or is producing negative side effects; high-priority items in the strategic plan are not being accomplished; a significant change occurs in the external environment; management wishes to fine tune a

---

[19] "Corporate Finance: Companies that Face Financial Strain," *Business Week* (May 17, 1982), 110.

Table 20.4 Altman's Z Score

$$Z = 1.2x_1 + 1.4x_2 + 3.3x_3 + 0.6x_4 + 1.0x_5$$

where

x_1 = Working capital ÷ Total assets
x_2 = Retained earnings ÷ Total assets
x_3 = Earnings before interest and taxes ÷ Total assets
x_4 = Market value of equity ÷ Book value of total debt
x_5 = Sales ÷ Total assets

Z values range from -4 to $+8$; the higher the number, the healthier the company.
If Z exceeds 2.99, the company is financially healthy.
If Z is below 1.81, serious financial trouble exists.

Source: Adapted from J.R. Weston and E.F. Brigham, *Essentials of Managerial Finance*, 6th ed. (New York, NY: Holt, Rinehart & Winston, 1982), 110.

successful strategy; and to ensure that a strategy is in tune with external and/or internal changes.

Strategy audits should address the following key questions:

1. Is the strategy working?
2. Is the strategy practical?
3. Are objectives, goals, policies, and programs clear and consistent?
4. Are the assumptions valid?
5. Have contingencies been assessed?
6. Is the strategy still appropriate?
7. Is the strategy congruent with management's style, values, and preferences for risk?
8. Is the organization properly structured to implement the strategy?
9. Do systems and processes support the strategy and programs?
10. Does the information system monitor implementation?
11. Is there an appropriate balance between present and future performance?
12. Is there agreement regarding the strategy within the company?

In general, the audit concerns itself only with broad questions of competitive positioning and allocation of resources, and tries to uncover the reasons for past success or failure in strategy formulation and execution. Examples of the questions addressed in the audit are shown in Figure 20.5.

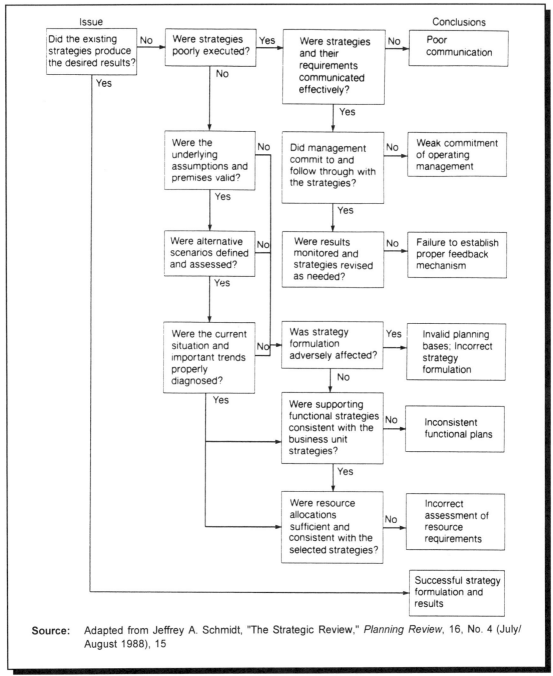

Figure 20.5 Strategy Audit Flow Chart

CONCLUSIONS

Good strategic management requires effective strategy implementation and control as well as effective strategy formulation (including planning decisions and processes). Strategic decisions result from strategy evaluation and choice activities, after which strategy implementation and detailed planning occur. Control activities ensure that the strategy is implemented and performing as planned; if it is not, corrective actions are required.

While the process of formulating and selecting strategies requires solid, objective quantitative analysis, social and political processes play a major role, too. One of the key tasks of the CEO is to manage these processes. Effective strategic management is truly the lifeblood of all organizations, and is the critical determinant of eventual success or failure.

Module 21

Entrepreneurial Start-Up and Small Business Strategies

LEARNING OBJECTIVES

After completing Module 21, you should be able to:

1. Describe the differences between the typical large business and smaller organizations.
2. Understand and describe the unique characteristics of start-up ventures.
3. Appreciate the strategy concerns and processes of small businesses.

The discussion of the process and content of strategic management, including the systems and techniques of strategic planning, is complete. Now several extensions, or special topics, will be explored. The primary perspective to this point has been that of the central type of organization in our economy, the medium-to-large, for-profit, well-established, private-sector corporation. While a good share of the material discussed is applicable not just to this typical corporation, but to organizations in general, certain organizations have unique characteristics. For this reason, attention in this module is devoted to two specific types of organizations commonly found in our economy: the start-up venture and the small business. Such organizations have many unique characteristics and needs that may significantly affect strategic decisions and processes. These are given special attention in this module.

We will first examine certain common characteristics of smaller organizations, and then look specifically at three types: the new venture internal to a larger organization, the start-up venture, and the small business.

PROFILE   Nebraska Furniture Mart

In 1917, Rose Blumkin, a Russian immigrant, funded a furniture store in the basement of an Omaha jewelry store run by her husband, Isadore, and relatives. In 1983, Warren Buffett's company, Berskshire Hathaway, bought her 80 percent stake in the Nebraska Furniture Mart—the country's largest furniture store—for $60 million. Several years later, Buffett, also from Omaha and the country's richest person, bought the jewelry store (by then the nation's largest jewelry store), Borsheims.

What was the secret to success of the Blumkins and Borsheims? Rose Blumkin—Mrs. B, as she is affectionately known to customers in Nebraska, Iowa, Missouri, and Kansas— always offered her customers better selection and better prices than they could get anywhere else. By 1989, the Nebraska Furniture Mart (NFM) was ringing up sales of nearly $160 million per year, and Mrs. B's personal wealth was estimated at $50 million. She says, "I sell good merchandise cheap. Competitors try to make $5 a yard profit on carpet. I'll sell for $1 a yard and make more." The numbers (the bottom line) never drove her; what's important she says, is making her customers happy.

After selling out to Buffett, she founded a competing 360,000 square foot store at age 95; this store—Mrs. B's Warehouse—is now part of NFM.[1]

---

[1] Dennis Rodkin, "Give 'em Hell, Granny," *Entrepreneur* (December 1990), 139-44.

PROFILE   ## Gateway 2000

Ted Waitt left the University of Iowa and founded Gateway 2000 to manufacture IBM-cloned personal computers in 1985 at age 22. By 1994, the mail-order seller had sales of close to $2 billion and close to 10 percent pre-tax profit; the company was still 100 percent owned by Waitt and his brother.

Gateway thrived in the mail-order niche, becoming the leader in the $7.5 billion market. Gateway pursued a low cost strategy, aided by its no-frills corporate philosophy and low-cost labor and tax environment in North Sioux City, South Dakota.

But, Gateway's work is cut out for it in the future. Where will growth come from as it outgrows its niche? As it grows larger, can it continue to excel in quality and service, and not lose control of costs? On the other hand, these are problems many less-successful start-ups wish they had.[2]

SMALLER ORGANIZATIONS

Start-up (new) ventures and small business often are discussed together, as if they have similar characteristics. In the broad sense, starting a small business is certainly a new venture of sorts, and most new ventures are relatively small. The differences, however, outweigh the similarities. Many small businesses are not "new;" they are family-run operations that have been around for 20 years or more. While they may still be called *ventures*, they certainly are not new. Also, forming a new business is only one type of venture. Many new ventures are begun *within* large firms, for example, as was discussed in a previous module. In addition, most small businesses have a goal that is very different from the goal of even recently formed new-venture firms. The venture firm has no intention of remaining small for very long; small size is a very brief phase through which this well-financed firm hopes to pass on its way to becoming a much larger firm. Most small businesses, on the other hand, are poorly financed and concern themselves with growth only after survival seems assured (if ever). However, once survival is established, some small businesses can become new ventures in the true sense of the word, with additional outside financing and a clear concept and plan for growth.

Karl Vesper, an expert in the new-venture field, has pointed out that those who run small businesses and entrepreneurs (people who form new ventures) differ in significant ways. Vesper observed that entrepreneurship is concerned with the *creation* of new businesses, some of which turn into substantial enter-

---

[2] Lois Therrien, "Why Gateway is Racing to Answer on the First Ring," *Business Week* (September 13, 1993), 92-94.

prises. Small business, however, mainly involves *operating* established firms that do not have many employees. He believes that entrepreneurs (many of whom previously worked for large, technically-oriented or marketing-oriented firms) work harder, more efficiently, "and generate more ideas and create more employment than established [managers of small businesses]."[3]

In addition, some of the claims made about smaller firms can be misleading. Dun & Bradstreet reports that 66 percent of the new jobs created in the United States in recent years came from concerns employing twenty or fewer people, and over 80 percent came from those with fewer than 100 employees.[4] This sounds impressive, but when you realize that 95 percent of all businesses have fewer than 20 employees, it becomes evident that 95 percent of the businesses create only 66 percent of the jobs. Put another way, 5 percent of businesses (i.e., those with over 20 employees) create 34 percent of the jobs. In addition, the 500 largest industrial firms alone contribute two thirds of U.S. output and three fourths of profits.[5]

In addition, recent commentaries have pointed out that the small business lobby has been very effective. Some researchers claim that there is little evidence to support the view that small business creates most of the new jobs. In fact, high-growth large companies add vast numbers of new jobs: over 50,000 at PepsiCo, 40,000 at UPS, 200,000 at Wal-Mart, not to mention Motorola, Home Depot, and a host of others. The main job creation activity is probably among the intermediate-sized firms with 500-5,000 employees.[6] Part of the controversy may lie at the feet of the studies that concluded that small business "created eight out of ten new jobs."[7] The problem is that the studies defined business size by the number of people working at a given *location* rather than by the number working for the *firm*. This technique means that if a new Wal-Mart outlet opened, its 200 employees would be counted as "small business growth" rather than as expansion by a large employer.[8]

The point of the above is not to deride small business, which is important and essential to our economy. Growth and jobs, however, come largely from

---

[3] S.N. Charkravrty, "Bashful Entrepreneurs," *Forbes* (June 20, 1983), 66.

[4] F.C. Klein, "Manageable Size: Some Firms Fight Ills of Bigness by Keeping Employee Units Small," *The Wall Street Journal* (February 5, 1982), 1.

[5] Norman Berg and R.A. Pitts, "Strategic Management: The Multi-Business Corporation," in *Strategic Management*, eds. D. Schendel and C.W. Hofer (Boston, MA: Little, Brown 1979), 339

[6] Gene Epstein, "The Real Engine of U.S. Economic Growth Might Be Bigger Than Many Believe," *Barron's* (May 23, 1994), 29.

[7] David Birch, "Who Creates Jobs?" *Public Interest* (Fall 1981), 3-14.

[8] Charles Brown, James Hamilton, and James Medoff, *Employers Large and Small* (Cambridge, MA: Harvard University Press, 1990), 2.

new ventures; both start-ups and those within larger firms. In contrast, most small firms are not particularly innovative; it is the *growth-oriented* small firms that are most likely to have this characteristic.[9]

Types of Smaller Firms

Several researchers have attempted to categorize the major types of smaller firms found in the economy. The frameworks of Cooper,[10] Sussbauer,[11] and Vesper[12] can be combined in the following typology:

1. *Survival firms.* These are the typical "mom and pop" businesses particularly found in retailing and service industries. Survival firms represent the vast majority of all U.S. businesses and often have no hired employees. The founders frequently lack managerial training and use intuitive methods. The firms are usually undercapitalized, undermanaged, and have very limited potential. This type of firm succeeds by surviving.

2. *Underachieving firms.* This type of firm may have established a profitable market niche and may provide the entrepreneur with a good standard of living. However, the firm has additional growth potential that either intentionally or unintentionally, is not being realized. In the intentionally underachieving firm, the entrepreneur may choose to keep the company small because he or she realizes an inability to manage a larger firm; because he or she values the leisure time and lifestyle possible with a small, profitable firm; or because the entrepreneur does not want to trade control of the business for the external capital required for growth. This type of stable, high-payoff company is often a small manufacturing firm. The unintentionally underachieving firm may be experiencing a mismatch between the market, technology, finance, and management skills.

3. *Potential growth firms.* This type usually possesses competitive advantages that result from growing markets, innovative methods or products, or managerial ability. Survival usually is a temporary concern as the firm searches out proper capitalization to permit growth and more substantial profits. This growth puts heavy demands on the founders, which they are willing to meet.

[9] A.C. Cooper, "Strategic Management: New Ventures and Small Business," in *Strategic Management*, eds. D. Schendel and C.W. Hofer (Boston, MA: Little, Brown, 1979), 322.

[10] Cooper, *Strategic Management*, 316.

[11] J.C. Sussbauer, "Commentary," in *Strategic Management*, eds. D. Schendel and C.W. Hofer (Boston, MA: Little, Brown, 1979), 327.

[12] Karl H. Vesper, "Commentary," in *Strategic Management*, eds. D. Schendel and C.W. Hofer (Boston, MA: Little, Brown, 1979), 332.

They are also willing to take the personal and company risks necessary for future growth.

4. *Successful growth firms.* These firms have survived and are achieving their growth potential. They have capitalized on their distinctive competencies, have adequate financial backing, and are pursuing proper strategies in their markets. They have taken (and survived) the necessary risks, and typically have their sights set on becoming a much larger company. Their management team, while entrepreneurial, is capable of managing a larger company and is willing to make the personal sacrifices and organizational (including personnel) changes to continue the company's growth. These are the Apple Computers, InaComs, COMPAQ Computers, Intels, Genentechs, Nikes, and so on that are likely to become the "darlings" of Wall Street.

The first two types—the survival firm and the underachieving firm—are the typical small businesses in our society. The latter two—the potential and successful growth firms—typify new ventures. Most small businesses are either unable or unwilling to reach these levels; most new ventures are not content to remain at the survival stage for long and have no intention of becoming underachievers. While any growing firm goes through several developmental stages—including start-up, early growth, and later growth—most start-ups do not progress through all three stages. In fact, most typical small businesses reach maturity *without* growth.

INTERNAL NEW VENTURES

Corporate entrepreneurship has created increased interest in recent years as companies try to develop an innovative spirit or culture. The desire to foster entrepreneurial behavior within organizations has resulted in a buzz-word of its own—*intrapreneurship.* Intrapreneurship refers to the activity resulting in successful entrepreneurial ventures within an established corporate framework.

Minnesota Mining and Manufacturing Co. (3M) is a widely-recognized innovative company. Perhaps the best-known successful internal new venture by a U.S. company in recent years is General Motors Corporation's Saturn subsidiary. Other successful intrapreneurial ventures have been undertaken by General Electric, IBM (the P.C.), Hewlett-Packard, and Poloroid, to name a few. Saturn, for example, is a General Motors *subsidiary*, not a GM division. This means that Saturn operates independently from GM, with its own culture, policies, goals, and strategies. This independence is important in the success of internal new ventures, as is the proper degree of structure. As Table 21.1 shows, corporate innovation and entrepreneurship *do not* thrive in a laissez-faire environment; explicit goals, individual responsibility, and rewards based upon results are critical.

Table 21.1 Elements Critical to Internal Ventures

Presence of explicit goals:	These goals need to be mutually agreed upon by employees and management so specific milestones are achieved.
System of feedback and positive reinforcement:	This feedback is necessary in order for potential inventors, creators, or intrapreneurs to realize there is acceptance and reward.
Emphasis on individual responsibility:	Confidence, trust, and accountability are key features to the success of any innovative program.
Rewards based upon results:	A reward system that enhances and encourages others to take calculated risks and to achieve must exist.

Source: Adapted from D.K. Kuratko, J.S. Hornsby, D.W. Naffziger, and R.V. Montagno, "Implement Entrepreneurial Thinking in Established Organizations," *SAM Advanced Management Journal* (Winter 1993), 57.

Innovation is most often the result of goal-directed behavior in which the innovator shares in the satisfaction and rewards generated by the innovation.

M.I.T.'s James Brian Quinn, an expert in the field of innovation, has noted that the following characteristics tend to be present in large corporations that develop successful internal ventures:

- **Atmosphere and vision:** innovative companies have a clear cut vision of an innovative company and the support necessary to sustain it.
- **Orientation to the market:** innovative companies tie their visions to the realities of the marketplace.
- **Small, flat organizations:** most innovative companies keep the total organization flat and project teams small.
- **Multiple approaches:** innovative managers encourage the parallel development of several projects.
- **Interactive learning:** within an innovative environment, learning and investigation of ideas cuts across traditional functional lines in the organization.

- **Skunkworks:** every highly innovative enterprise uses groups that function outside traditional lines of authority. This eliminates bureaucracy, permits rapid turnaround, and instills a high level of group identity and loyalty.[13]

START-UP VENTURES

In some ways, start-up ventures and small businesses are similar. For example, the goal-formulation and strategy-formulation processes are largely in the hands of the entrepreneur/founder. This person also divides his or her time between strategic and operating tasks, usually without the benefit of formalized systems or procedures. For both, the key to effective strategy is creating a unique match of skills and resources at the individual product or market level by filling a niche (providing a unique service or product to a small or specialized group of customers). Nonetheless, many new ventures fail. The major reasons for this include:

1. Lack of well-rounded experience in sales, production, and management by the founder (remember, the entrepreneur is now a general manager and no longer a specialist).
2. Lack of adequate financial controls.
3. Inadequate capitalization.[14]

In contrast to small business start-ups, the new venture typically has a new business plan that describes how the new firm plans to compete. This plan is essential in seeking the relatively large amounts of outside capital that the venture requires. Still, inadequate capital remains an important source of failures.

New Venture Strategies

Starting a business and surviving are two separate issues. It takes a lot more than a good idea to succeed; it takes money, planning, ability, hard work, and some luck. The National Federation of Independent Business Foundation reported that 876,000 businesses were founded in 1991, and 822,000 failed that year.[15]

---

[13] D.F. Kuratko, J.S. Hornsby, D. W. Naffziger, and R.V. Montagno, "Implement Entrepreneurial Thinking in Established Organizations," *SAM Advanced Management Journal* (Winter 1993), 33.

[14] D. Schendel and C.W. Hofer, eds., *Strategic Management* (Boston, MA: Little, Brown, 1979), 310.

[15] Wilma Randle, "Many Start-ups Lack Staying Power," *Omaha World-Herald* (May 22, 1994), 1-G.

Given these rather bleak survival odds what can a new venture do strategically to increase its chances of survival? One recent finding of interest is that most successful entrepreneurs try to minimize their risks. They are not risk averse, but they are very calculating about risks they do take. They try to minimize their investment by leasing instead of owning, and the like.[16]

Entry strategies for start-ups vary with the stage of the market life cycle during which the firm enters the industry. As shown in Table 21.2, while new start-ups are most likely to occur when a market is in the growth stage, their growth potential is the greatest when entry occurs for those entering emerging markets. Start-ups entering emerging markets have the greatest potential for growth because they can grow with the product class as the market develops. They also can select which market segments offer the best potential for growth. The main risk is entering too early; before the market "takes off."

Table 21.2 Start-Ups and Market Life Cycle

	Stage of Market Life Cycle		
	Emerging	*Growth*	*Maturity*
New start-ups	likely	most likely	least likely
Typical entry strategy	product class	product segment	specialized niche
Growth potential of entry strategy	highest	average	least

Source: Adapted from Stuart Slatter, "Successful Start-Up Strategies," *Engineering Management Review*, 20, No. 4 (Winter 1992/93), 72.

While the growth stage of the market is the most popular entry point for start-ups, the growing market often attracts firms with no real competitive advantage. They are often "shaken out" when growth slows and the market consolidates. The key to success for entry during the growth stage lies in selecting a segment of the product class on which to focus. Few start-ups occur during the mature stage. Those doing so should try to avoid direct competition with strong,

---

[16] Jeffrey A. Tannenbaum, "An Entrepreneur's Secret: Take No Risks," *The Wall Street Journal* (January 7, 1994), B1

established firms. New entrants need a specific competitive advantage to be successful. Success usually comes from following a specialized niche strategy.[17]

Finally, researchers at the Center for Creative Leadership found that start-ups progress through seven distinct stages as they grow and mature, as shown in Figure 21.1. Five of the stages are characterized as growth stages (conception, survival, stabilization, growth orientation, and rapid growth), followed by maturity and decline/regeneration. We know that business growth doesn't occur in a simple sequential progression; many firms fall back a stage or two, and others can jump ahead. Those that jump ahead can be called "hypergrowth" firms, and those that fall back experience "backsliding." Some can experience each at various times.[18] Descriptors of firm characteristics at each of the seven stages are listed at the bottom of the figure.

New-Venture Problems

Many start-up ventures grow rapidly—even spectacularly—for a time and then level off and even decline or fail. The reason is that the capitalization and narrow product lines that permit spectacular growth also permit disasters, sometimes almost overnight. To *continue* to grow and prosper, the start-up company must extend its initial idea as it matures through add-ons and variations, and continue to come up with additional viable ideas. Some are not able to do this and fail. Others find that their great idea soon attracts large competitors into their niche, such as Minnetonka, Inc. (creator of "Soft Soap"), leaving little profit for the innovator.

Many emerging growth companies peak and decline because their "shallow pockets" often force them to "bet the company" on the outcome of new moves. They don't always win the bet.[19]

New ventures, whether separate or internal, are a high-risk/high-reward strategy. While the entrepreneur is a critical element in the success of new ventures, appropriate strategies and financial backing are essential. The entrepreneur is a unique type of person, one with a high need for achievement, independence, confidence, and the ability to take calculated risks. It may not be true, however, that entrepreneurs are inherently risk-takers. What is more likely is that they have a different *perception* of risks than do nonentrepreneurs. For example, entrepre-

---

[17] Stuart Slatter, "Successful Start-Up Strategies," *Engineering Management Review*, 20, No. 4 (Winter 1992/93), 72-73.

[18] John H. Eggers and Kim T. Leahy, "Entrepreneurial Leadership in the U.S.," *Issues and Observations*, 14, No. 1 (1994), 3-5.

[19] G. Smith and P.B. Brown, "Emerging Growth Stocks—Why so Many Peak so Early," *Forbes* (January 28, 1985) 69.

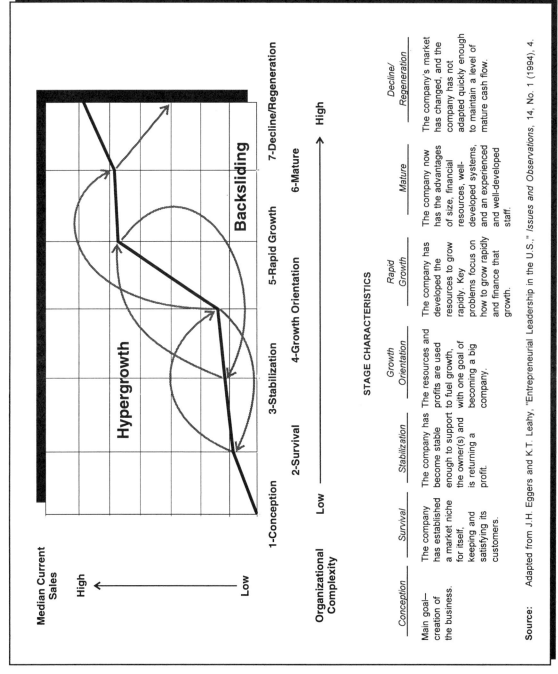

Figure 21.1 Development Stages of Entrepreneurship Start-Ups

STAGE CHARACTERISTICS

Conception	Survival	Stabilization	Growth Orientation	Rapid Growth	Mature	Decline/ Regeneration
Main goal— creation of the business.	The company has established a market niche for itself, keeping and satisfying its customers.	The company has become stable enough to support the owner(s) and is returning a profit.	The resources and profits are used to fuel growth, with one goal of becoming a big company.	The company has developed the resources to grow rapidly. Key problems focus on how to grow rapidly and finance that growth.	The company now has the advantages of size, financial resources, well-developed systems, and an experienced and well-developed staff.	The company's market has changed, and the company has not adapted quickly enough to maintain a level of mature cash flow.

Source: Adapted from J.H. Eggers and K.T. Leahy, "Entrepreneurial Leadership in the U.S.," *Issues and Observations,* 14, No. 1 (1994), 4.

neurs see the risk of "missing the boat"—letting an opportunity slip away—as a more threatening situation than the risk of failure, or "sinking the boat." In this light, entrepreneurs may be as risk averse as anyone else; they perceive failure as missing an opportunity. In addition, certain areas of the country seem to spawn an unusually high percentage of new ventures: Santa Clara County in California, Boston, New York, New Jersey, Minneapolis, Boulder, Austin in Texas, and North Carolina's "research triangle," to name a few. New ventures are the companies that have the potential to become the giants of the future, transforming whole industries in the process.

SMALL BUSINESSES

Here, the separate, already-operating and established small firm is the subject. It is typically a survival firm (such as a "mom and pop" business) or an under-achieving (either consciously or unintentionally) firm, although some small businesses may be potential-growth or even high-growth firms.

Characteristics of Small Business

In discussing "small" business, it is inevitable that the question of size must be addressed. Size has been explored and defined in terms of many dimensions. Common descriptions of small business include firms with annual sales of less than $25 million or firms with fewer than 500 employees. However, firms with fewer than 1,000 employees are sometimes considered small. Whatever the definition, most firms in the United States can be called *small*. Statistics supplied by the U.S. Department of Commerce show that 99.7 percent of U.S. companies in all industries have fewer than 250 employees, as shown in Table 21.3. In addition, these figures seem to be relatively constant over time.

Given that most businesses in our economy are small, what types of firms are these? A helpful categorization of small businesses is as follows:

1. *Rare success:* Firms evolving from small beginnings to substantial size under the founder's leadership. H. Ross Perot established Electronic Data Systems in 1962 with a $1,000 investment. Other examples are Winnebago, Dekalb Ag-Research, and Gateway 2000.
2. *Firms in "small business industries":* Industries in which the optimal scale of the individual firms is small. Metalworking, ethnic food production, printing, design consulting, and land development are just a few.
3. *Firms based on successful specialization:* Firms based on a unique innovation or the holding of a patent. Research instruments, gold-refining operations, and independent producers of coffee and beer are examples.

Table 21.3 Distribution of U.S. Companies by Numbr of Employees and Size of Company

	Companies with Fewer than 20 Employees		Companies with 20 to 249 Employees		Companies with 250 Employees or More	
	Percent of All Companies	Percent of All Employees	Percent of All Companies	Percent of All Employees	Percent of All Companies	Percent of All Employees
All industries	94.7%	21.7%	5.0%	26.3%	0.3%	52.0%
Manufacturing	71.0	4.5	26.3	19.8	2.7	75.7
Wholesale trade	88.0	40.7	11.8	46.1	0.3	13.2
Retail trade	96.3	39.4	3.6	25.8	0.1	34.8
Services	97.8	41.7	2.1	33.4	0.1	24.9
Construction	96.2	38.9	3.7	41.7	0.1	19.3

Source: Adapted from J. Deeks, *The Small Firm Owner-Manager: Entrepreneurial Behavior and Management Practice* (New York, NY: Praeger Publishers, 1976), 62.

4. *Satellite firms:* These are organizations linked to one or more large buyers. The industrial distributor who sells for a manufacturer on a commission basis is the classic example.

5. *Turnover firms:* These are firms whose activities consist of entry into a field followed by an exit from it in a few years or less. In the United States, a third of all small businesses are estimated to turn over every year.[20]

Small Business Strategy Formulation

Small businesses often experience scarcity of resources of every nature. To survive in the midst of significant problems, the manager of a small business has to stay in tune with the market and the environment. There is very little room for error. As Peter Drucker has pointed out:

> In the first place, [the small business] needs strategy. The small business cannot afford to become marginal. Yet this is its perennial danger. It must, therefore, think through a strategy which gives it distinctions. It must, to speak in biological terms, find its specific ecological niche in which it has an advantage and can therefore withstand competition. This specific niche may be leadership in a distinct market, whether it is defined by geography, consumer needs, or consumer values. The strategy may lie in a specific excellence, such as a capacity to give service. Or it may lie in a specific technology. . . . For the typical small business has no strategy. The typical small business is not "opportunistic," it is "problematical"—it lives from problem to problem. But the typical small business is also, as a result, not a successful business.[21]

Drucker also has stated that it is more important for a small business to do the right things than to do things right. This stresses the need for effective tactics in a small business. With limited resources, the company has to be effective. If the firm is not effective, efficiency cannot even be considered. In a sense, the ineffective firm does not get the chance to be efficient. Rather, it becomes a business failure statistic.

Small firms are in a unique strategic situation compared to large firms. They must find a market niche and operate within this niche. Their distinct competitive advantage is often flexibility in production or service. Changes in demand that alter product or service properties are seen as an advantage because of the firm's flexibility. Specialization also can be a distinct advantage.

---

[20] Lee E. Preston, "The World of Small Business: A Suggested Typology," *American Journal of Small Business*, 1, No. 4 (April 1977), 13.

[21] P.F. Drucker, *Management: Tasks, Responsibilities, Practices* (New York, NY: Harper & Row, 1974), 649, 651.

The strategy formulation process must fit the characteristic mold of small businesses and the manager of a small business. The process therefore must be simple, practical, and easy to use. It must be functional and be in line with the user's personality traits and decision processes.

How Small Businesses Plan

Large corporations typically start their strategic planning process with an examination of future economic and competitive conditions in relation to the company's existing businesses. Then they consider potential new businesses in terms of their companies' strengths, weaknesses, and needs. A strategic plan is developed from this analysis, followed by a projection of resources needed to accomplish the plan. Next, more specific plans and resource budgets are developed to implement the strategic plan.

This process is different in a smaller company. The large corporation can recruit people and raise money almost at will. The smaller company is much more restricted. Resources must be considered much earlier in the process, as must personal planning of the owner. While the larger firm often can *create* its own opportunities, the small firm cannot. It must plan to be able to seize opportunities if and when they arise. Thus, its strategies must be more flexible, adaptive, and opportunistic.[22] Small firms should strive to excel in *short-term*, not long-term, planning, remaining as adaptable and flexible as possible. But the small firm does need a planning process and discipline, just as does its larger counterpart.

In spite of this, only one third of small businesses have a written strategic plan defining long-term objectives (about 50 percent of those over 50 employees had written plans, while one fourth of those with under 50 people did).[23] Table 21.4 contrasts strategic planning in small versus large companies, in terms of administration, procedures, and substance.

While executives of small firms are intimately familiar with their own operations, they are often too busy to update their knowledge of factors outside the company, such as: the prices charged by the major competitors; the *real* attitude of major customers toward the product and service; the market share of each product; the various ways customers use their products; or the potential impact of pending legislation.

The manager of a small company should realize that he or she cannot do all things for the firm. Planning may require the assistance of others, outsiders or insiders. In any case, survival is "job one" for the small firm, and nothing—in-

---

[22] Neil C. Churchill, *Planning in Smaller Companies: An Argumentative View*, Case No. 9-179-014 (Boston, MA: HBS Case Services, 1978).

[23] "Long-Range Plans," *The Wall Street Journal* (October 31, 1986), 29.

Table 21.4 Strategic Planning in Large and Small Companies

Strategic Factor	Typical Large Company	Typical Small Company
Company Administration and Strategic Decisions:		
Strategy, operations, and management	Complex	Relatively simple
Operations	Tactics (distinct from strategy)	Intertwined with strategy
Dealings with customers and vendors	Via lower-level employees	Personally by owner
Administration of company	Formal planning and delegation	Owner's personal overview
Organizational design	Based on tasks to be accomplished	Based on capabilities of incumbents
Desired qualification of employees	Specialized expertise	Mainly versatility
Attractiveness to employees	Maintenance factors exceed motivational incentives	Motivational incentives exceed maintenance factors
Regulations	Heavy	Though burdensome, enjoys many exemptions
Typical life span	Perpetual	Brief
Strategic Planning Procedures:		
Pervasiveness of strategic planning	In general use	Most firms abstain
Where used, plan's format	Written (formal)	Oral
Organization	Decentralized planning. Coordinator needed	Owner conducts centralized planning
Strategic subunits	Divisions or SBUs	Functions
Perceived financial burden	Almost negligible	Substantial
Specialized assistance	Board of directors and planning experts	None
Tools, techniques	Management information systems, sophisticated models, portfolio analyses, scenarios, and other planning routines	Much improvisation
Alignment of functions and projects	Numerous special meetings	Frequent routine contact
Financial analysis	In-depth cost accounting, adjustments for time differences, inflation, etc., many other techniques	Superficial
Beneficiary	All stockholders	Owner-manager
Strategic Planning Substance:		
Company mission	Formal statement	Not defined
Environment	Proactive	Passive
Environmental scanning	Formal efforts	Haphazard, mainly owner's chance contacts
Assessment of strengths and weaknesses	Realism (documented)	Optimism (opinion)
Forecasts	Causal methods	Extrapolation
Options	Analyses in depth	Few considered: little analysis
Feedback	Reports	Boss's inspection
Financial objective	Return on investment	Amount of profit
Financial planning	Main quest is quarterly growth in sales and profit	Main problem is insufficient cash
Type of strategy	Multiple approaches (differentiation strategies)	Concentration (focus strategy)
New products	Strong in marketing	Strong in development

Source: Harold N. Fox, "Strategic Planning in Small Firms," in *Strategic Planning and Management Handbook*, eds. W.R. King and D.I. Cleland (New York, NY: Van Nostrand Reinhold, 1987), 576-77.

cluding planning—should be permitted to detract from the small firm's primary advantages: customer service and product customization.[24]

Problems of Small Businesses

Many small businesses fail each year. Poor management has been cited most often as the reason for these failures, along with lack of resources (both financial and human). However, many observers postulate that a lack of strategic planning is also responsible for a growing number of small-business failures. Studies have shown that small firms with a higher level of formal planning tend to show better performance in terms of five-year annual growth rates. Other evidence indicates small firms that plan are more successful than those that do not.

The major strategic causes of small-business failure include:

1. *Faulty research.* Starting the business on a hunch or feeling instead of using market research.
2. *Wrong skills.* Running a small business requires more than just engineering, sales, manufacturing, or management experience obtained by working for a larger company.
3. *Undercapitalization.* Most new businesses are not profitable for several years, and significant cash is required to start and stock the business. Will the business be able to withstand early mistakes, operational problems, contingencies, or a possible recession?
4. *Poor franchises.* Many franchises promise more than they can deliver and may be more interested in collecting the franchise fee than assisting the franchisee. Also, many franchises do not have well-developed criteria and guidelines to help the owner succeed.[25]

Family Businesses

The family-owned and run business is a special type of small business. Many exist, but those that survive the founder are still the exception, according to Peter Drucker. He states that if the family business is to survive—let alone prosper—it must adhere to four rules:

1. Those family members who work in the business must be *at least* as capable and hard-working as any other employee.

---

[24] R.B. Troxel, "How Small Companies Can Plan Effectively," *Management Focus* (September/October 1978), 13.

[25] "How to Start a Sideline Business," *Business Week* (August 6, 1979), 94.

2. Except for the very smallest, family-run businesses need to staff more and more key positions with non-family professionals.
3. One top job must be filled by a non-relative, *regardless* of how many family members are managers and how effective they are.
4. *Before* the situation requires it, the issue of management succession should be entrusted to an outsider—someone who is neither a family member nor an employee.[26]

An important problem for family-run businesses is management succession. The founder is often reluctant to relinquish control to his or her children. A successor should be trained in the same way executives are groomed in big corporations, by working his or her way through important areas such as marketing or sales, production, and finance. Children should work outside the family business first, making their mistakes away from their parents and learning how other businesses and managers operate. Ideally, children should enter the family business when they are in their 30s and the founder is close to retirement. However, the question of which members are to take over the top spots can be a source of family conflict and resentment. Individuals—family or otherwise—who are unable or unwilling to earn their keep should not be kept on the payroll. As indicated, the family firm has unique problems and concerns.[27] For example, when a company is operated largely as a vehicle for the family—to provide jobs, security, and goals geared as much to the family as to the market—then conventional financial rules don't always apply.[28]

CONCLUSION

To summarize, most literature on strategic planning (indeed, most business literature in general) focuses on the large, multiproduct corporation and ignores the small business. For this reason, owners of small businesses may feel that they simply are not big enough to have to worry about strategic planning. But they need it, too. Many small firms have relatively few products, or rely heavily on a few major customers, so that demand shifts away from their products or loss of a major customer may be catastrophic. Small businesses face more risk than larger businesses due to their lack of diversification and smaller resource "cush-

[26] Peter F. Drucker, "How to Save the Family Business," *The Wall Street Journal* (August 19, 1994), A10.
[27] S.L. Jacobs, "Small Business: It's Often Hard in a Family Firm to Let the Children Take Over," *The Wall Street Journal* (March 14, 1983), 23.
[28] R.I. Levin and V.R. Travis, "Small Company Finance: What the Books Don't Say," *Harvard Business Review*, 65, No. 6 (November/December 1987), 30-36.

ion." Consequently, strategic planning is perhaps *more* critical to the success of a small firm than to that of a large one.

Yet, Sexton and Van Auken found that a minority of the small businesses they studied employed strategic planning.[29] Possible reasons for this include:

1. Lack of enough management expertise to do strategic planning.
2. Attitude: many owners of small businesses feel they must pay attention to the present, rather than worrying about the situation several years in the future.
3. Limited resources: management in many small firms simply doesn't think it has the financial and/or human resources to develop a strategic planning process.
4. Lack of relevant information: a significant amount of data is available on the relevant environment facing large corporations; much less has been made available for small firms.

Basically, the study found that the small firm that planned was more dynamic, proactive, and successful (as measured by return on assets). The emphasis in the small firm is on simplicity and manageability. It is not necessary for the small firm to "burden itself with a detailed formal planning document, an extensive reporting system, or an avalanche of paperwork" to engage in strategic planning. If the basic steps are followed to the degree appropriate for the firm, the result will be the same benefit a more elaborate process provides for a larger firm—better control over the company's destiny.[30]

[29] D.L. Sexton and R.M. Van Auken, "Prevalence of Strategic Planning in Small Business," *Journal of Small Business Management*, 20, No. 3 (July 1982), 20-26.

[30] W.D. Jones, "Characteristics of Planning in Small Firms," *Journal of Small Business Management*, 20, No. 3 (July 1982), 15-19.

Module
22

Service, Not-for-Profit,
and Professional Applications

LEARNING OBJECTIVES

After completing Module 22, you should be able to:

1. Realize the important role and strategic aspects of service organizations.
2. Discuss characteristics unique to service organizations, including not-for-profits and professional services organizations.
3. Describe the various types of NFP organizations, including government, public service, and public-interest organizations.
4. Understand the unique characteristics of third-sector organizations and institutions.

Having completed our discussion of strategic management processes, content, systems, and techniques, we now focus our attention on a vitally important part of our economy, the service sector. We will look first at types and unique characteristics of service organizations in general, regardless of their sector of the economy or whether they are for-profit or not-for-profit (NFP).

Not-for-profit organizations, concentrating initially on public-sector organizations such as government, public-service, and public-interest organizations, will then be examined. Other not-for-profit groups, such as third-sector organizations (amalgams of private organizations with a public charter) and institutions (education, health care, religious, etc.), will also be discussed. Finally, attention will be directed toward an increasingly important service organization, the professional services organization (such as consulting firms, law firms, and professional practices).

There are important distinctions between for-profit firms and not-for-profit organizations. First, there is a basic difference in purpose. Different missions are likely to result in different goal structures, as well as in differences in the strategies formulated to reach those goals. Economic goals act as a powerful constraint on for-profit firms, while such constraints have much less immediacy in the not-for-profit organization and play less of a role in the selection of strategies. Furthermore, the nature of the environments is different for each of the organizational types. However, all are similar in that the roles and responsibilities of general managers differ from those of functional managers. In short, the major differences are found in the areas of strategy substance and *content*, while the main similarities—and there are many—occur in the area of strategic *processes*. Nonetheless, this module's intent is to point out the unique features and concerns of each type of organization, stressing how they differ from the "typical" medium-to-large, for-profit business firm.

PROFILE

The HMO Industry

Health maintenance organizations (HMOs) provide health services to an enrolled group of patients for a fixed, prepaid fee. From its fees and any outside support, the HMO must cover all its patients' expenses, including hospital stays, when necessary.

While HMOs may appear to be a relatively recent phenomenon—and an attempt to hold down the rapidly rising costs of medical care—the first HMO began in 1929. Growth of the concept accelerated when Kaiser Industries began an HMO for its employees, opening enrollment to the public in 1945. Since that time, and largely in recent years, various forms of HMOs have arisen, ranging from not-for-profit to profitmaking concerns, to company-operated plans (to reduce the cost of company-paid health insurance premiums), to community-operated plans. Today, there are hundreds of HMO plans in operation in the

United States with millions of members. Not all are successful; however, a number have failed.

Ideally, HMOs are suppose to save money by encouraging preventive medicine; that is, keeping their patients healthy and out of the hospital. In reality, there is little evidence to show that HMO patients are healthier. While HMOs do cut hospitalization rates by 15 to 30 percent, no one is sure just why. Some say they are more economical; others say that HMO physicians are pressured to skimp on medical care, that doctors have been overusing hospitals, or that HMOs tend to have younger members who need less medical care. In addition, some people balk at the HMO concept because of the loss of the patient's right to choose his or her own doctor.

Whatever its form or future, HMOs have proliferated recently as an attempt to reduce burgeoning health-care costs. To succeed, their overall concept and mission must be sound, they must provide quality medical care of the type demanded by the public, and their operating strategies must be sound. Whether operated privately or publicly, for-profit or not-for-profit, in the long run their costs cannot exceed their revenues—a condition any organization must meet.

SERVICE ORGANIZATIONS

Service industries and the providing of "service" by all organizations have become the buzzwords of the latter 80s. As part of this phenomenon, the service industries have become widely accepted as the future strength of advanced industrialized nations (or, for some, an example of their *lack* of strength). Yet most serious study in the areas of business strategy and practices has ignored the service industries and focused on the manufacturing sector.

This is unfortunate, because the production of services currently exceeds 68 percent of U.S. gross national product and employs over 72 percent of the work force.[1] Again, strategic management of service organizations has received limited attention in the business literature, and many misconceptions abound concerning services; for example, some have expressed fears that the United States is fast becoming a nation of people who are "serving each other hamburgers or taking in each other's laundry,"[2] with the real engines of economic growth moving offshore. We will take a look at the role of services in our economy, some characteristics and types of service organizations, including some suggestions for strategies and operations of service organizations.

---

[1] Mack Ott, "The Growing Share of Services in the U.S. Economy—Degeneration or Evolution?" Review, Federal Reserve Bank of St. Louis, 69, No. 6 (June/July 1987), 5.

[2] Alan Murray, "The Service Sector's Productivity Problem," *The Wall Street Journal* (February 2, 1987), 1.

Role in the Economy

The view that a move toward services signals a decline in the U.S. economy is not based in fact; it has been the *strength* of the U.S. manufacturing sector—not weakness—that has precipitated the shifts in employment and output toward services. In fact, high-productivity growth in manufacturing and agriculture, plus the long-term effects of American investment in education, have made faster growth of the service sector possible. What's more, these trends have been occurring for a century or more with no significant recent changes in the trends. Also, an appreciable share of these services aid in the production of goods, making their production more efficient.[3] Remember from an earlier module that the U.S. private sector is 167 percent as productive as Japan, including being 771 percent as productive in agriculture, 127 percent in manufacturing, and over 150 percent in services.

As Table 22.1 illustrates, most of the growth in services has occurred at the expense of other commodities, not manufacturing, with productivity increases in almost all areas. The biggest growth in services output has occurred in finance, insurance, and real estate; business services; and health services; with declines in a number of other areas (the segments containing hamburger cooks and laundry workers have not increased).

Characteristics of Service Organizations

Service organizations (the types listed in Table 22.1) and the delivery of services in general have certain unique features. One is that service jobs (with certain notable exceptions, such as utilities and communications) tend to be located where and when the customer wants them, rather than centralized, as in manufacturing. This means more and decentralized workplaces, with fewer people at each. Also, in many services, the service is produced, marketed, and delivered at the same place and time, often by the same person; there is no "inventory" that can be accumulated for later delivery. Many are "information driven," beginning with familiarity between the server and the served.[4]

There is a tendency for service companies to view themselves as unique, and consequently they tend to not promote operations management and efficiency techniques with the same vigor as the manufacturing sector; they need to realize that they are not merely unique entrepreneurial entities, but can learn from other industries (and other segments of the service sector). In addition, they are not necessarily labor intensive; many are quite capital intensive, such as utilities,

---

[3] Ott, "The Growing Share of Services."

[4] J.L. Heskett, "Lessons in the Service Sector," *Harvard Business Review*, 65, No. 2 (March/April 1987), 118-26.

Table 22.1 Percent of U.S. Labor and Output by Various Sectors

	1948		1972		1985	
	Labor	GNP	Labor	GNP	Labor	GNP
Commodities (total):	46.2	41.2	33.9	35.8	28.1	32.4
Agriculture	11.4	5.5	3.9	2.7	2.9	2.6
Manufacturing	27.4	21.3	23.6	21.5	18.7	21.6
Mining	1.8	6.5	0.8	5.2	0.9	3.6
Construction	5.7	8.0	5.6	6.4	5.7	4.5
Services (total):	53.8	58.8	66.1	64.2	71.9	67.6
Transportation	5.2	6.8	3.5	4.2	3.1	3.5
Communications	1.3	0.8	1.4	1.8	1.2	2.6
Utilities	0.9	1.2	0.9	2.5	0.9	2.9
Wholesale trade	4.9	5.0	5.3	6.7	5.6	7.4
Retail trade	13.5	9.5	14.1	9.2	15.5	9.5
Finance, insurance, real estate	3.2	9.6	5.0	13.5	6.2	14.6
Government	11.7	13.8	18.3	13.1	16.3	11.1
Personal services	2.1	1.3	1.6	0.9	1.5	0.6
Business services	0.7	1.0	2.3	2.0	4.5	3.3
Auto repair	0.6	0.4	0.7	0.7	1.1	0.8
Health services	1.9	2.2	4.3	3.4	6.0	4.3
Legal services	0.4	1.0	0.5	0.9	0.9	1.0
Miscellaneous professional	0.4	0.7	1.0	1.1	1.6	1.5
Other	7.1	4.9	7.4	3.4	7.7	3.3

communications, and even hospitals. In fact, the most labor intensive tend to be brokerage houses, insurance, and business services.[5]

Franchising seems to be a growing trend in services; not just for fast food and other outlets, but for *professional* services as well, such as optical, medical, legal, real estate, and other services.

The Service Profit Chain. Customers and front line workers are the center of concern for many service organizations, whether they be restaurants, hospitals, or CPA firms. The relationship between the customer and the front line worker in large measure drives the customer's experience and determines the organization's success. The relationships between factors influencing the performance of

[5] R.W. Schmenner, "How Can Service Businesses Survive and Prosper?" *Sloan Management Review* (Spring 1986), 21-32.

service organizations comprise the *service profit chain*. Shown in Figure 22.1, the service profit chain is analogous to the value chain, discussed in an earlier module.

Developed from analyses of successful service organizations, the service profit chain portrays relationships between organizational performance, customer behavior, and employee behavior. That is, between profitability, customer loyalty, and employee productivity, satisfaction, and loyalty. Specifically, the chain links the factors as follows:

- Revenue growth and profits are strongly influenced by customer loyalty.
- Customer loyalty is the result of customer satisfaction.
- Customer satisfaction is determined by the value of services received by customers.
- Value results from the efforts of satisfied, loyal, and productive employees.
- Employee satisfaction, loyalty, and productivity result from high-quality support services plus policies encouraging and enabling employees to satisfy customer wants.[6]

The service profit chain, then, illustrates what drives performance for the service firm and highlights what needs to be done to achieve long-term profitability. Organizations, whether private or public sector, can conduct a service profit chain audit to determine how they "measure up" in each of the important links in the chain.

Types of Service Organizations

A closer look at two types of service institutions—hospitals and higher education—sheds some light on their operations and strategies.

Hospitals. As Drucker observed, managing a hospital is one of the most difficult managerial tasks. One reason is that major controllers of the use of the hospital's facilities—the physicians—are typically not employees and are not under management's supervision or control. In addition, many of the hospital's employees, especially the nurses, are responsible both to the hospital and to the physician on an ad hoc basis. A hospital also involves very diverse functions that entail very different skill levels and types of operations, including:

---

[6] J.L. Heskett, T.O. Jones, G.W. Loveman, W.E. Sasser, Jr., and L.A. Schlesinger, "Putting the Service-Profit Chain to Work," *Harvard Business Review*, 71, No.2 (March/April 1994), 164-174.

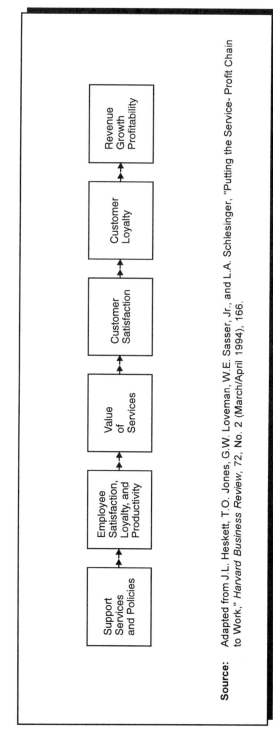

Source: Adapted from J.L. Heskett, T.O. Jones, G.W. Loveman, W.E. Sasser, Jr., and L.A. Schlesinger, "Putting the Service- Profit Chain to Work," *Harvard Business Review*, 72, No. 2 (March/April 1994), 166.

Figure 22.1 The Service Profit Chain

1. Medical services, such as surgery, obstetrics, anesthesiology, radiology, and the like, which are performed by nonemployees often reporting to a nonemployee (the chief of medicine or surgery), but using the hospital's facilities.
2. Hospital services, such as pharmacy, nursing, laboratory, and the like.
3. The "hotel" function, including housekeeping, laundry, food service, and others.
4. Administrative services, such as records, accounting, and billing.

In addition, hospitals are forced to mix several types of production/operations approaches in the same facility, which is not an ideal situation. For example, patient care is typically of the "unique product" category, while many of the administrative services are "process production." On the other hand, hospital and hotel-services functions most often function as "flexible mass-production" units.

Hospitals also typically have very high fixed costs, with 40 to 50 percent of their budget going to salaries. For the NFP hospital, excess capacity *raises* its prices—the amount it must charge for use of its facilities (such as room rates)—since these charges are set so that the hospital will break even.

With all of the changes facing the health-care industry, a shakeout is coming. Experts says that 30 percent of U.S. hospitals are likely to close by the year 2000, particularly those general care facilities with fewer than 200 beds. The very large hospitals are likely to shrink in size, with an increase in the number in the 200-400 bed range—large enough to enjoy economies of scale, small enough to be flexible and to adapt to changes. The very nature of the business will be transformed as hospitals become part of a network of health-care providers—no longer the hub of the health care delivery system.[7]

Colleges and Universities. Most colleges and universities have traditionally done very little strategic planning. Even when warned as long as ten years ago that declining enrollments were imminent, most seemed to assume that the other institutions would be affected. Today, however, higher education is being forced to think in terms of distinctive competencies, niches, and missions, but their strategic decision processes still appear to be primarily ad hoc; most have not implemented a regular strategic management process.

Some schools, such as Carnegie-Mellon, Stanford, Houston, George Mason, and Miami, are exceptions. In 1981, Carnegie-Mellon developed a plan to seek academic excellence in selected areas of comparative advantage. This focus has catapulted departments such as computer science and cognitive psychology into national prominence, and has increased the applicant pool by 15 percent. Miami

---

[7] Maggie Mahar, "Tomorrow's Hospital," *Barron's* (January 10, 1994), 12-18.

uses a modified portfolio model to focus its programs and allocate its resources.[8]

NOT-FOR-PROFIT ORGANIZATIONS

The not-for-profit (NFP) area includes a host of organizational types: publicly funded organizations (such as government, service, and public-interest organizations); institutions (such as most schools, hospitals, and charities); and "third-sector" organizations (research institutes, cooperatives, and government- chartered private organizations such as the Federal National Mortgage Association). A "fourth sector" could be discussed—the publicly chartered for-profit firm, such as COMSAT, CONRAIL, and AMTRAK.

Many business students are likely to find themselves employed by NFPs. Some schools have colleges of business and public administration, others have departments of public administration, and some teach public administration in departments such as political science. In such schools, the student is exposed to the workings of "public organizations," primarily government. However, many NFPs are neither "business" nor "government," but institutions or third-sector organizations. Thus, the study of a large percentage of NFPs tends to be totally ignored in colleges and universities.

Types and Characteristics of Not-for-Profits

Max Wortman has written extensively on strategic management in NFPs. Table 22.2 is a modification of a typology of different NFPs that Wortman proposed. As can be seen from the table, the term NFP indicates much more than a simple public versus private dichotomy. There are types of NFPs in both sectors, and some private NFPs have more in common with certain types of public-sector organizations than they do with other private for-profit firms. Thus, the term *nonprofit* is not very descriptive; it tells only what an organization is *not*, not what it is. The NFP designation covers a whole spectrum of organizations, as different from each other in some cases as they are from for-profit firms.

Norman Waks, of the MITRE Corporation (a third-sector research institute), concluded that NFPs seem to be *services* enterprises, rather than producers of goods. In contrast, most enterprises that provide *goods* for sale seem to be for-profit enterprises. (Some services enterprises that require expensive capital equipment must also be profit making to provide a return on the capital.) In general, though, NFP means simply that no individual or group realizes profit or personal

---

[8] "How Academia Is Taking a Lesson From Business," *Business Week* (March 26, 1990), 58.

Table 22.2 A Typology of NFPs

Public organizations:
A. Governmental executive agencies and departments at the federal, state, and local levels, including the military.
B. Public-service organizations
   1. Urban services, such as law enforcement, fire, and public housing.
   2. Rural services, such as rural electrification, agricultural services, and county agents.
   3. General services, such as postal, transportation, social services and welfare, human resources, medicare and medicaid, and the FBI.
C. Public-interest organizations, such as those involved with conservation, water resources, energy resources, and air pollution.

Institutions:
   Education (public and private)
   Hospitals and health care
   Labor unions
   Political parties
   Churches
   Libraries
   Performing arts
   Voluntary associations
   Organized charities
   Foundations

Third-sector organizations:
   Publicly chartered private firms (e.g., Federal National Mortgage Association and Government National Mortgage Association).
   Research institutes.
   Not-for-profit consultants, including American College Testing and Educational Testing Service.
   Consumer cooperatives.

Source: Modified from Max S. Wortman, Jr., "Strategic Management: Not-for-Profit Organizations," in *Strategic Management: A New View of Business Policy and Planning*, eds. D. Schendel and C.W. Hofer (Boston, MA: Little, Brown 1979), 353. Reproduced by permission.

financial gain (other than salary) from the organization's operations.[9] NFPs, then, tend to be service oriented and people based, rather than product oriented and capital-equipment based.

Also, many organizations could be classified one of several ways. Hospitals, for example, can be either for-profit or not-for-profit, and are considered to be

---

[9] Norman Waks, *Strategic Planning in Private Non-Profit Organizations*, MTP-201 (Bedford, MA: The MITRE Corporation, 1979), 3.

service organizations. Colleges and universities are also service organizations, and can find themselves either in the public sector or private sector.

An enterprise will be likely to operate as NFP for one or more of the following reasons:

1. *Cannot make profits.* By law or the nature of its services, the organization is not permitted to make a profit. This type of organization has no choice; it *must* be NFP. (Others may have the option of being NFP or for-profit.) Organizations required to be NFP include government agencies, voluntary organizations (religious, social welfare, and so on), stock exchanges, unions, and consumer cooperatives.
2. *Should not make profits.* These organizations are permitted to make a profit, but are involved in activities where it is considered improper to do so. Examples are most hospitals, schools, most institutions, and privately operated public-interest organizations.
3. *Should make but not retain profits.* These organizations try to make as much money as possible, but do not retain it. Their very purpose is to give such money away. Foundations and charitable organizations are obvious examples.
4. *Optional NFP.* These are firms that can and should make and retain profits, but have elected not to as an element in their strategy. They see themselves being significantly aided in their mission by choosing to be an NFP. Many research institutes fall into this category (such as Battelle, SRI, Brookings), as do federally funded R&D centers and organizations such as American College Testing (ACT) and the Educational Testing Service (ETS).

Differences between NFPs and for-Profits

The basic difference between NFPs and for-profit firms is their missions. In addition, goals and objectives may differ considerably. For-profit firms tend to seek profits, by definition, whether or not you agree that they actually try to maximize profits. Thus, profit is a basic consideration in their need hierarchy, while it is not for the NFP. NFPs tend to focus on goals and objectives such as improving the quality and coverage of their service, increasing their reputation and influence, increasing their responsiveness and prestige, containing costs within budget, and increasing their budget. However, the use of planning in many NFPs is in its infancy, and goals frequently are short range and poorly defined. In addition, some types of NFPs pose particular problems.

Additional unique features of NFPs include:

1. *Governing boards.* Boards of NFPs are often made up of individuals with varying interests, backgrounds, and expertise, who frequently act as fund raisers or public relations people for the organization, rather than as true "directors."

2. *Measures of success.* The for profit can simply compare revenues and costs, and conclude that the market values its goods or services accordingly. But service is intangible and hard to measure. Also, outputs (services) are in different units than inputs (dollars), making it difficult to "prove" that the organization is efficient or effective.

3. *Planning initiatives.* NFPs tend to be skill based, and their degree of activity is a function of needs and problems that may (or may not) arise. Attempts to plan and forecast often take the form of simple extrapolations of the past. Marketing to "create" needs may be expressly forbidden for many NFPs.

4. *Weak customer influence.* The NFP's budget may be largely independent of customer or client need for the service.

5. *Commitment to cause or profession.* Employees may identify more with a movement, cause, or profession than with the NFP organization itself.

6. *Undue contributor influence.* Funding sources, private and public, may attempt to exert undue influence over goals, operations, and management, putting management in a compromising position.

7. *Charismatic leaders.* The organization may rise and fall with the fortunes and credibility of the founder or director.

8. *Reward constraints.* NFPs tend to have no "profit centers," but only cost centers. How, then, is service improvement rewarded as opposed to cost cutting? The tendency is to pay salaries that are independent of results and input resources employed.

9. *Culture and values.* Many NFP employees tend to discount any trade-off possibilities between resources (time and money) and performance. An attitude of spending whatever it costs to do the job, as well as doing whatever one's value system requires may predominate.

John R. Garrison, president of the National Easter Seal Society, observes that management was once regarded as near-obscenity by some nonprofit purists; the term seemed to put them into the same category as profit-seeking private sector managers. "Some nonprofit people used to think that if you're doing good, somehow God will provide. But almost everyone now realizes that commitment isn't enough anymore. You also have to have professionalism, or you're going to go out of business."[10]

Strategic Management in NFPs

In sum, the primary goals of the NFP are noneconomic and difficult to measure. An NFP manager is primarily involved in operations, and is more of an "admin-

---

[10] John A. Byrne, "Profiting From the Nonprofits," *Business Week* (March 26, 1990), 67.

istrator" or implementer than an entrepreneur. Many NFPs have goal structures and policies to guide their operations, but no explicit strategies to tie the two together. They tend to be managed much more in terms of short-term operations than in a strategic sense. Management control is based on inputs, rather than on objectives or intended outcomes. This is not an indictment of NFP managers, however, because their task and environment is different from those in the for-profit firm, and perhaps more difficult, as well. Formulating and implementing long-term strategies and plans in such organizations may be difficult (and, in some instances, fruitless) because of the imposition of goals and objectives by a frequently changing group of outside stakeholders.

The quality of resources, particularly management and personnel, is frequently more varied in the NFP organization than in the for-profit organization. Also, financial resources tend to be more widely dispersed. In spite of such factors, consistent and effective strategy formulation is possible for the NFP, following a process similar to that used by the for-profit (careful strategy assessment; evaluation of the fit between the environment, the organization, and the strategy; and changes in strategy if needed). While these tasks may be *more* complex for the NFP manager as he or she monitors the varied constituency and objectives, they are not impossible. Testing the consistency of the current strategy with the environment and the resources and values of the organization spotlights strengths and weaknesses. Comparing a proposed future strategy with the expected future situation helps to ensure that strategies are appropriate for the organization's upcoming needs.[11]

Also, many NFPs are regulated organizations. The more regulated an organization (or even an industry in the for-profit sector), the less leeway or freedom the organization has. Therefore, fewer strategic options are open to regulated organizations. For highly regulated or constrained organizations (such as in the public sector), few true "strategic decisions" may exist, as compared to the typical unregulated, for-profit firm. By comparison, public-sector organizations' "strategies" are more akin to the for-profits' tactics or operating strategies.

Public-Sector Management

Management in the public sector is different from corporate management not just in degree; it is also qualitatively different. For example, in contrast to the case in the private sector, managers in the public sector must frequently accept goals that are set by groups or organizations other than their own. Also, the managers must often operate with structures designed by outside groups. Further, they must commonly work with, for, and manage people whose careers are in many

---

[11] M.L. Hatten, "Strategic Management in Not-for-Profit Organizations," *Strategic Management Journal*, 3 (1982), 103.

respects outside of their control. As if these factors weren't enough, public sector managers must often accomplish their goals and objectives in less time than is allowed to corporate managers.[12]

Government. Management's task in managing governmental organizations differs from business organizations in many important ways. For example, businesses strive to make a profit, whereas governmental organizations are often left to provide services which cannot be provided profitably by the private market. Additional differences are as follows:

- Government administrators pursue goals and objectives which are more difficult to measure; the *appearance* of success may be as important as the reality.
- A government agency's performance is often judged in terms of effort, or inputs, rather than results.
- Government managers typically receive little credit for effective administration, since its benefits are hard to measure.
- Because they are evaluated on the basis of effort rather than on results, government managers are often reluctant to delegate responsibility to subordinates.
- Government managers are often accused of being "inconsistent" if they change their positions, even if their response is a reasonable reaction to changing events.
- Actions of government top managers are exposed to intensive scrutiny by the media.
- While shareholders' interests are typically consistent with those of business managers, government managers must often report to hostile and varied constituencies.
- Government managers usually have less control over their subordinates and, because of the difficulty of measuring output, find it more difficult to set goals and evaluate the performance of subordinates than do private-sector managers.
- Political leaders and high-level government managers often have not been prepared for their responsibilities by either formal training or pertinent experience.[13]

---

[12] J.L. Bower, "Effective Public Management," *Harvard Business Review*, 55, No. 2 (March/April 1977), 134.

[13] P.E. Morrison and J.R. Fox, *How Management in Government Differs from Business*, 9-386-085 (Boston, MA: HBS Case Services, 1985), 1-2.

Charitable Organizations. Certain charitable organizations, such as the United Way, utilize well-developed strategic planning and management by objectives approaches. In fact, their progress and sophistication may cause some resentment on the part of certain of their agencies and donors. As shown in Figure 22.2, United Way's long-range planning model is a logical modification of the basic strategic planning model, adapted to United Way's situation. In addition, United Way develops alternative scenarios of the future, based on predicted events in the environment. These predicted events are interpreted to determine the likely key implications for United Way. Thus, charitable organizations, as well as other NFPs, can make effective use of strategic management concepts.

The Process in the Public Sector. As noted above, United Way's strategic planning process looks startlingly similar to that used by businesses. On the other hand, public-sector organizations *are* different from businesses. It may be that United Way is independent enough to be able to operate more like a business than like a government agency. For an actual government agency, however, our business model may need to be modified. A modified model of the process for public organizations is shown in Figure 22.3.

The main difference between this model and other strategic management models is the modified model's increased emphasis on the identification of important outside stakeholders and their role during the entire strategic planning process. In many ways, the strategic management process in public organizations revolves around the values, views, and expectations of the organization's most important outside stakeholders. To be successful at strategic management, top management must realize this and take action to at least indirectly include the outside stakeholders in virtually all stages of the strategic management process. This is why the stakeholders' value analysis stage of the strategic management process dominates or overshadows the other elements of the new model.

Additionally, policies and procedures take on a more important role in this model, flowing directly from and reflecting the stakeholders' values and expectations. The policies and procedures also function at least partially as proxies for the stakeholders. However, should the policies and procedures fail to adequately or properly influence their respective elements in the process, the stakeholders have the power to override them and exert direct influence, as shown by the dotted lines. Therefore, the stakeholders exert direct or indirect influence over virtually all of the elements in the process; some flow through policies and procedures, but the possibility of secondary or exception basis direct control exists.

Therefore, the more central role of stakeholders' values and expectations facilitates direct and indirect communication between important stakeholders and public managers during each stage of the strategic management process. This gives outside stakeholders the opportunity to give valuable input and feedback to public managers at each stage of the strategic management process. As stated earlier, top management's careful consideration of feedback from outside stake-

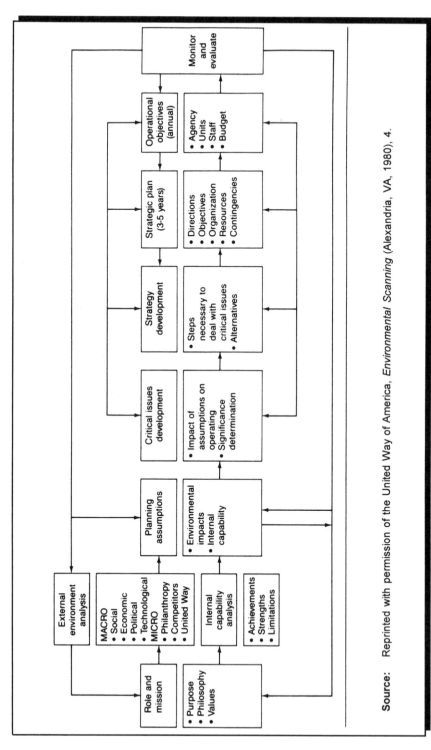

Source: Reprinted with permission of the United Way of America, *Environmental Scanning* (Alexandria, VA, 1980), 4.

Figure 22.2 Long-Range Planning Model for United Way

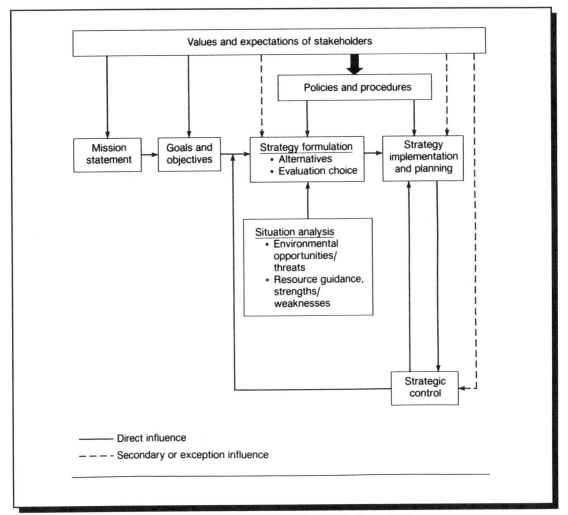

Figure 22.3 Modified Strategic Management Model for Public Organizations

holders at each stage of the planning process is generally crucial for the strategic management process to work in a public setting, due to the greater amount of power held by the outside stakeholders versus the for-profit setting. Other models that attempt to describe the strategic management process do not allow for this type of direct feedback at each stage of the process. But then again, this type of direct feedback is not as crucial for success in a for-profit setting where much more discretion is allowed its top management as compared to its outside stakeholders.[14]

PROFESSIONAL SERVICES ORGANIZATIONS

Another largely overlooked type of organization from a strategic perspective is the professional services firm, including legal, CPA, and management (and other) consulting firms, medical and dental practices, and advertising agencies. Many business school graduates find themselves employed by such firms. Professional service firms differ in important ways from the traditional corporation, and are also unlike most types of not-for-profit organizations.

Most professional service firms are relatively small, and are either incorporated or operate as partnerships. The choice of organizational form, however, has little to do with size. For example, many large law, CPA, and consulting firms operate as partnerships (the giant CPA firm, Arthur Andersen, for example, operates as a partnership), while even very small medical and dental clinics tend to incorporate. An important strategic decision, then, concerns the form of organization—an aspect of enterprise strategy.

A second key decision is scope of services—how specialized or general does the firm want to be? A management consulting firm may choose to specialize in manufacturing planning, or personnel selection, or executive development, for example.

A third consideration is how large does the firm want to become? For many, this is a function of available business, but some feel that it is better to remain small and busy (and able to select desirable clients and projects) than to grow and become concerned with searching for clients. In a way, the decisions concerning size and specialization are related. A firm could grow while remaining specialized, or grow by broadening its services.

A fourth strategic decision involves whether or not to advertise, and, if so, how. Recent legal changes have permitted certain types of professional services firms to advertise, something that is foreign to many professionals. Should a CPA firm advertise in the media or market its services through seminars and public service, as has been the traditional approach? This decision depends upon how well established the firm is, as well as the image (the degree of "professionalism") it wishes to project.

Another strategic decision involves financial and operational policies. How will the firm charge for its services? How will the profits be distributed among

---

[14] James J. Hoffman, L.A. Digman, and William Crittenden, "A Paradigm of the Strategic Management Process for Voluntary Nonprofit Organizations," *Journal of Managerial Issues*, 3, No. 3 (Fall 1991), 357-371.

the members of the firm? And what will the pay scale be? What percentage of a firm member's time will be required to be "billable"? What arrangements exist if a member decides to leave the firm? Mistakes, miscalculations, or oversights in any of these areas can spell problems for an otherwise promising professional services firm.

Operations in a professional services firm tend to be very different from those in traditional organizations. Most professional firms operate as committees, with the partners or officers acting as a group of equals. For example, the president of a medical group is not a "superior" to the others in the practice. He or she is merely a firm member who acts as head of the firm for a specified period of time—usually one or two years. The other firm members have "delegated" speaking for the firm and handling administrative tasks for the specified period. Typical levels of practitioners in such firms are shown in Figure 22.4. A principal is typically a senior firm member responsible for obtaining projects or clients and supervising all work in his or her area of expertise. A senior associate is usually in charge of a particular project or case, whereas associates usually work on a given project or case under the direction of a senior associate. Interns tend to be newer employees in a training and probationary period. If the firm is a partnership, senior associates *may* be elected to partner status, while principals are almost always partners. (A partner shares in the profits of the firm and has a vote in major decisions.`

The key resources in any professional firm are its specialists—the accountants, consultants, doctors, architects, lawyers, or engineers—who actually generate the client services and create a reputation for the firm. But how do you manage these people? If you pull the best into management, you lose your best producers; but the specialists won't accept less than the best producers as superiors. The solution is often the "producing manager"; that is a person responsible for *both* management activities and client services. With producing managers heading small business units as a "playing manager," the firm can stay productive and nonhierarchical, permitting it to grow and change while retaining its competitive edge.[15]

In short, professional services firms are distinctly different from most other types of organizations, both strategically and operationally. They tend to be less formal and more egalitarian, and depend on the knowledge, skills, abilities, and charisma of relatively few key people. In the final analysis, success lies in the ability of the key people to work as a team in acquiring jobs and satisfying the clients.

---

[15] J.W. Lorsch and P.F. Mathias, "When Professionals Have to Manage," *Harvard Business Review*, 65, No. 4 (July/August 1987), 78-84.

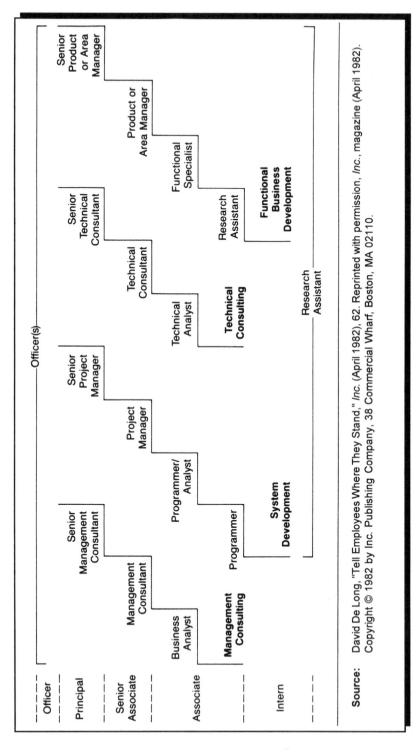

Source: David De Long, "Tell Employees Where They Stand," *Inc.* (April 1982), 62. Reprinted with permission, *Inc.*, magazine (April 1982). Copyright © 1982 by Inc. Publishing Company, 38 Commercial Wharf, Boston, MA 02110.

Figure 22.4 Titles, Ranks, and Career Paths in Professional Services Firms

SERVICE SECTOR LESSONS

Successful service organizations tend to have several strategies in common. They include:

- Close coordination between marketing and operations, since marketing, production, and delivery of the service tend to occur together.
- Development of a *strategic service vision*—identification of a target market segment, development of service concepts geared to the targeted customers' needs, an operating strategy to support the service concepts, and an efficient and effective delivery system.
- Employee understanding of the service vision; because the employees are vital to productivity and quality of service, their internalization of the concept is vitally important.
- A stress on quality control of service, through generous incentives, pride, teamwork, and customer contact.
- A close look at economies of scale; service firms, particularly delivery points, can easily become too large to deliver superior service.
- Recognition that information about customers is important to providing service to existing customers as well as in attracting new ones.[16]

We can conclude, then, that service organizations, including not-for-profits, and professional service organizations, are sufficiently different from the traditional organization to warrant special attention and unique approaches.

---

[16] Heskett, "Lessons in the Service Sector."

Module
23

Strategic Management
Trends and Directions

LEARNING OBJECTIVES

After completing Module 23, you should be able to:

1. Assess the current state of the art of strategic management, including current developments.
2. Discuss emerging trends in the field.
3. Speculate on several key trends as the field matures.

Modules 1 through 22 represent a summary of the state of the art of the strategic management field, as it has developed over the past 20-25 years. As noted, strategic management is more than strategic planning; it includes formulation, implementation and planning, and control. In addition, an organization may be required to make strategic decisions at several levels: at the enterprise (or mission) level; at the corporate level, relating to its selection of businesses and their interrelationships; at the business-unit level; and at the functional and operations levels.

Strategic management is a logical—but creative—process. The process includes an assessment of the strategic situation facing the organization, including environmental analysis, resource analysis, management's vision, and consideration of the values and expectations of stakeholders. The environmental analysis involves diagnosing the general environment as well as the competitive environment, including a look at markets that can range from local, to regional, to national, to international, to global in scope.

Another important part of the process includes strategic decision-making—formulating, evaluating, and selecting strategies. We saw that the manager may choose from certain generic business-level strategies, such as strategies for positioning the business, distinguishing the business (including differentiation and scope), plus those for increasing, redefining, and reducing scope. At the corporate level, general-purpose differentiation, concentration, and restructuring strategies exist. In contrast, certain strategies must be specific; the appropriate approach can vary by phase of the life cycle, type of business, and certain other factors.

Certain strategic planning systems and techniques are helpful. For example, determining a business's competitive advantages and critical success factors can greatly assist in formulating and evaluating strategies, as well as in determining management's information needs. Preparation of scenarios and contingency plans can help the manager deal with an uncertain and risk-laden environment.

Organizations sometimes structure themselves differently for strategic decision purposes (using strategic business units) than for operational purposes. Also, strategy is implemented through the operational organization, which can sometimes result in a lack of continuity and puts a premium on strategic control activities.

Finally, strategy processes and content are different and less developed in organizations other than the medium-to-large, for-profit corporation. These differences must be realized and taken into account when dealing with other increasingly common types of organizations.

CURRENT STATE OF THE ART

A number of practices currently exist in leading organizations that represent the latest "best-business practices," or state of the art. These include the points described in the following paragraphs.

Creating a Vision

Strategic management is not a mechanistic, "by the numbers" exercise in analyzing forecasts and evaluating alternatives. It begins with the creation of a "vision" by top management of what *can* be, what the future can bring, and results in developing plans for how to get there. It is not enough to create a vision; management must "build a dream" for people in the organization by articulating that vision so that others can understand, appreciate, and commit to it. Forward thinking management teams today are beginning the process with "vision statements," so that key stakeholders and others can share the dream.

Fostering Organizational Learning

It is not only the individual manager who must develop; the organization must "learn" as well. In this light, the role of corporate planning departments and systems is becoming less one of "preparing plans" than it is one of enhancing the organization's ability to learn. That is, making the organization's managers aware and appreciative of significant environmental and competitive changes and trends early—often using scenarios—so that timely action can be taken. The key is management's "quick study" understanding of the trends and their implications. The realization that planning is more about fostering learning processes than it is about developing specific plans is beginning to take hold in leading corporations.

Interorganizational Strategies

Strategies involving joint ventures, or "strategic alliances," have started to become more common and may continue to grow more so in the future. Such arrangements can exist between two firms, such as Apple and IBM for personal computer system development, or between several firms. Actually, such strategies exist in organizations ranging from trade associations, lobbying groups, and industry committees to joint ventures and even collusions and cartels. OPEC is an example. Another, perhaps less threatening, is the sharing of automatic teller machine networks by banks, as is the creation of Sematech and the Microelectronics and Computer Technology Corp. to perform research for various firms in the semiconductor industry.

Flexible Planning Processes

In line with the above processes, leading companies appear to be downplaying the highly formal, structured planning process in favor of more flexible, creative, qualitative, and intuitive processes. The emphasis is on creative strategic thinking, developing the vision of where the company should go and how it should get there.

Restructuring and Internal Growth

Diversified growth through acquisitions is on the decline, replaced by restructuring and internal growth. Many past acquisitions have been disappointing, and corporate raiders have forced many companies to refocus and concentrate their corporate portfolios. In addition, related-diversified firms have been shown to outperform others, and internal growth seems to avoid a number of merger-related problems. The emphasis on total quality management and business process reengineering are manifestations of this practice.

Strategic and Operational Harmony

The approach of creating market-oriented strategic business units to serve as the structure for corporate- and business-level planning in multibusiness companies has some disadvantages. While it provided a common denominator for defining separate businesses for which separate plans had to be developed, the SBUs did not always coincide with operating divisions. Thus, this approach required two separate structures—one for strategic planning and one for operations. If the SBUs and operating divisions could not be reconciled, this dual structure may have been a necessary evil. Some organizations, however, are forcing a merger of the strategic and operating organizations—resulting in one set of "businesses"—and a single structure for both. To the extent that this harmony is possible, a more efficient process of planning *and* implementation can result.

Improved Strategy Frameworks

The generic strategy classifications of Derek Abell, Michael Porter, and others have contributed greatly to our understanding of the principal types of strategies available to and appropriate for business units and corporations. Analysis of these frameworks by notable scholar/experts such as Hofer and Mintzberg have pointed up deficiencies in the options, and improved classifications have been proposed. This evolutionary process is likely to continue until a commonly accepted "general theory" of basic strategies is developed and supported by research. The framework presented in this book represents an emerging view of generic strategies.

Better Information and Tools

Efforts such as the profit impact of market strategies (PIMS) project are making a definite contribution to the practice of strategic management. As relationships between decision variables and actual results are examined, specific decisions are becoming more objective and less dependent on rules of thumb, mythical relationships, and unproven hypotheses. Specific guidelines are being provided concerning the *content* of strategic decisions, rather than placing an overreliance on process-related suggestions. One problem with PIMS data in particular has been the proprietary nature of the research findings; however, the Strategic Planning Institute has been liberal in allowing publication of general findings. Better information is also becoming available to decision-makers who utilize custom designed strategic information systems geared to critical success factors for the organization and the industry.

Providers of goods and services are looking more to the ultimate consumer for feedback information and in designing their offerings for the marketplace. For example, Goodyear's ultimate customer is not Ford or General Motors, but the person who buys the automobile. However, some suppliers have tended to lose sight of the final customer. As an illustration, fireplace manufacturers have tended to consider lumber stores, home improvement centers, and the like as their customers, assuming that the public buys the product largely for fuel savings, energy saving, and related reasons. A study of the final customers revealed that nostalgia is the number one reason for purchase, and that Florida ranks high in the number of fireplace sales per capita.[1]

Many of the tools used for strategic management are being refined both in terms of their mechanics and their role in the process. There is less a reliance on simplistic portfolio models and a greater realization that the picture they provide is just one input to the decision process.

Focus on Core Competencies and Competitive Advantage

The work of C.K. Prahalad and Gary Hamel has taken hold; firms are concentrating on developing competitive advantages that are sustainable by concentrating on their core competencies and core businesses. Along with this practice, they are "outsourcing" many non-core activities through joint ventures and partnerships with other firms.

---

[1] Michael Kami, *Strategic Planning for Changing Times* (Dayton, OH: Cassette Recording Co., 1984).

EMERGING TRENDS

A number of trends are currently evident, as strategic management progresses from its first generation to a more mature field. Many of these trends are confusing to some observers, but they need not be. While the majority of such trends were mentioned in the preceding modules, they are highlighted here for perspective and emphasis.

Rewarding Strategic Performance

Traditionally, managers have been rewarded primarily on the "bottom line," profit and cash-flow measures of an organization's performance. As seen in earlier modules, reward systems that *do not* treat all business-unit managers equally are starting to be developed with the realization that different units can and do have very different goals and objectives. Also, measures and rewards are becoming more closely tied to the costs and results of implementing a particular strategy, rather than strictly to operational results.

Development of Strategic Managers

Companies have long indulged in transferring employees from one division, plant, function, or location to another to develop management. The emphasis has been on "learning the business" by gaining experience in various facets—usually operational entities—of the organization. But what of strategic experience? Why not transfer future top strategic decision-makers between business units possessing differing strategic characteristics? In this way the manager's on-the-job development would be specifically orchestrated to expose him or her to a preselected range of *strategic* situations, rather than to differing *operational* situations that may (or may not) result in optimum exposure to strategic learning. Further, we have come to realize that the skills required by top-level managers (including strategic management and general managers) are not the same as those required by managers in general. The abilities discussed in this text are difficult to learn in the classroom as well as on the job, and may require special developmental techniques and approaches.

Contingent Strategy Processes

It was shown that top-down strategies, determined by the corporate level, are best if coordination between business units is critical, and bottom-up (business determined) strategies are best if financial performance is most important. Corporations are beginning to employ approaches contingent on the needs of their particular situations, rather than "one size fits all" prescriptions. Likewise, planning systems contingent on the type of environment have been proposed. The use of structured processes in "high-velocity" environments has been found to be associated with high-performing firms, for example. Such advances in pre-scribed processes are likely to continue.

Managing Global Integration

The term *global* has begun to appear so frequently that it has become a buzz-word. Buzzword or not, the concept is likely to be one that strategic managers will have to live with (and pursue) for the foreseeable future. And global does not mean Japan, Europe, China, and a few other countries. In 1970, North America and Western Europe generated over 60 percent of the world's manufac-turing output; by 2000 it will likely be less than 40 percent. Most of the growth will come from a host of newly industrialized countries (NICs).[2]

Managers are reorienting their concepts of industry structure and strategic groups to incorporate relevant international variables; that is, a firm's "relevant environment" may contain global variables and intercultural dimensions. The firm's (particularly multibusiness firms) structure, systems, processes, and strate-gies will be affected. Specifically, strategic managers will likely be affected by European integration, Pacific Rim competitors, the demise of communism, and the emergence of 24-hour capital markets. Defensively, domestic (niche) sup-pliers will need to develop means of beating or neutralizing the global strategies of the multinationals.

Emergence of "Micro-multinationals"

The term "multinational"—MNC—suggests a large, far-flung corporation. Prahalad and Hamel point out a new reality; we are starting to see very small (less than $10 million in sales), highly-specialized firms with global scope. Such firms have started to appear in professional services, software, high technology (such as biotechnology), and other industries.[3] These "micro-multinationals" are small, yet global in scope, and may be better known in foreign countries than in their home town. How does one best serve this type of market and operate this type of firm? What are its unique strategic challenges and contributions?

---

[2] R. Lamb and Paul Shrivastava, eds., *Advances in Strategic Management*, Vol. 4 (Greenwich, CT: JAI Press, 1986), xvii

[3] C.K. Prahalad and G. Hamel, "Strategy as a Field of Study: Why Search for a New Paradigm," *Strategic Management Journal*, 15, Special Issue (Summer 1994), 14.

Strategies for NFPs and Services

The not-for-profit sector has consistently lagged behind the for-profit sector in strategic thinking and the use of up-to-date approaches. It is in many of these organizations that planning is an ad-hoc process still in Phase I or II (financial planning or forecast-based planning), resulting in voluminous budget and operationally-oriented documents. In the foreseeable future, many such organizations, including those in the service sector, will be forced to think strategically, bringing themselves into the modern-day world of flexible, externally-oriented plans and processes.

Improved Performance Measures

Along with the need to maximize stakeholder value (or returns) from the firm will come the need for improved performance measures. Such measures will likely include yardsticks to best measure the welfare of each major stakeholder group, as well as means of assessing firm performance on a multistakeholder basis. The latter goal resulted in the development of completely new performance measures. Improved measures such as Economic Value Added and the Balanced Scorecard allow the firm to better assess the performance of diverse business units, building on the recent promise shown by value-added performance measures.[4] Finally, better measures aid management in evaluating the results of strategic decisions and in other aspects of strategic control.

Activity-Based Management

Growing out of activity-based costing from the field of accounting is a new, umbrella-like family of approaches called "activity-based management" (ABM). ABM focuses on activities and processes, and is, therefore, compatible with business process reengineering. ABM enables management to focus on strategically-relevant value-adding core processes.

AS THE FIELD MATURES. . .

Strategic management is maturing. As is true of any adolescent, the field has had some growing pains, inconsistent behavior, and confusion in terms of the future,

---

[4] N.E. Swanson and L.A. Digman, "A Value-Added Management Support System," *International Journal on Policy and Information*, 12, No. 2 (December 1988), 1-15.

while showing potential and long-term promise. We may speculate on future directions of the field.

Practical, Contingent Research Data

Medical practitioners look to research-oriented medical schools for the latest findings in their field. The case of management is not yet similar. Hopefully, as strategic management matures, less time and effort will be spent studying the practitioner, and more will be spent on underlying disciplines and relationships. As we have seen, appropriate strategies depend on the measures of performance, type of industry, life-cycle stage, and other factors. Consequently, creation of a set of contingent relationships would appear to be a logical next step for research in the field. This would highlight the major areas where research voids exist. In addition, the practicing manager could use such contingent relationships and their research findings as a guide in the formulation of strategy alternatives.

For example, we have recently learned that in many instances, internal growth is preferable to growth by acquisition. Also, related diversification produces superior financial returns, as compared to unrelated diversification. However, the M-form of organization (divisionalized) works better for the unrelated-diversified firm than for the related (which performs best with the U-form). At the business-unit level, researchers are attempting to learn correlation and cause/effect relationships between an appropriate group of generic strategies and business performance. Additional studies are investigating the roles of environment, structure, and strategy on performance, and some recent results indicate that interactions between the variables are the dominant influences on performance.[5] This means that managers will need to consider the interaction, or fit, between the combination of variables when making strategic decisions. Thus, we are seeing the beginnings of a contingency-based set of research data and prescriptions, which will become increasingly valuable to strategic decision-makers in the future.

Contributions from DSS/AI/ES

Decision support systems (DSS) are making contributions to many management decisions, via the organization's management information system. Artificial intelligence (AI) and expert systems (ES) are also beginning to assist in certain decision tasks. As more strategic research data is gathered, analyzed, and structured into data bases and contingent relationships, computer-based tools and systems

---

[5] S.E. Tjan and L.A. Digman, "The Interaction Effects of Environment, Structure, and Strategy on Performance," *Proceedings of the Midwest Decision Sciences Institute* (April 1989).

will gradually help the strategic decision-maker as well. It is not likely, however, that major portions of strategic decisions will be "automated" through these approaches, but certain amenable analyses and subdecisions will likely lend themselves to this approach (e.g., multiple scenario analysis)[6], allowing the decision-maker to focus on the more judgmental, intuitive, and creative aspects of the task.

Sustaining Networks and Cooperation

Competition has been a byword in the strategy field. However, there are numerous instances where cooperation may be beneficial to the "competitors." Interorganizational strategies, such as joint ventures and strategic alliances, are already a step in this direction. However, collective, cooperative strategies could be formulated to respond to environmental challenges and to influence, through an interorganizational network, the nature of the environment itself. In the future, we are likely to see more collective endeavors, whether at the national level in the form of an industrial policy or at the unit level between two or more businesses.[7]

Virtual Organizations

The roots of virtual organizations are already in place. We have seen joint ventures, are currently experiencing strategic alliances, and have studied the related concepts of core competencies and outsourcing. These trends, coupled with the growing sophistication of information systems enabling supply chain management (SCM) systems to function, make the virtual organization a likely possibility for the future. Given the various specialized roles a firm can elect to perform, strategic choice of role is likely to be critical, as is one's desirability as a partner. Finally, firms may have more "virtual employees;" temporary, independent contractor-like human resources.[8]

[6] Ruth S. Raubitschek, "Multiple Scenario Analysis and Business Planning," in *Advances in Strategic Management*, eds. Robert Lamb and Paul Shrivastava, Vol. 5 (Greenwich, CT: JAI Press, 1988), 181-205.

[7] Charles Fombrun and W.G. Astley, "Strategies of Collective Action," in *Advances in Strategic Management*, ed. R. Lamb, Vol. 2 (Greenwich, CT: JAI Press, 1983), 125.

[8] Tom Peters, "Employees Must Begin Thinking Like Independent Contractors," *Lincoln Journal* (December 22, 1993), 22.

Hypercompetitive Markets

The pursuit of sustainable competitive advantage may be impossible in software, soft drinks, fast foods, microchips, and other industries. In hypercompetition, the pace of change is so rapid that sustaining advantages is nearly impossible. The grand, long-term strategy that sustained itself for long periods is replaced by rapid moves and countermoves intended to neutralize or destroy a competitor's advantage.[9] That is, a business may need to seek a series of temporary, unsustainable advantages as the basis for its competitive battles. Obviously the type of planning required in high-velocity, chaotic environments, coupled with rapid decision-making, is likely to be at a premium here. Traditional "long range planning" is likely to be useless at best.

CONCLUSIONS

In this, the final module, the main points in strategic management were summarized, with the conclusion that the end of the first generation of development in the field has occurred. Currently there is a transition to a new generation offering more focus and maturity to the practitioner and the researcher. But the field is not diminishing in importance. While responsibility for strategic planning in company after company has been taken out of the hands of the planning departments and given to the general managers, the role is growing. In short, the consensus among top executives in major corporations is overwhelming: "You won't become a top manager unless you learn to manage strategically."[10] You will also need to think strategically to work for and with such individuals. Strategic management is not primarily a set of concepts and models; it is a way of thinking and acting. A strategy, then, can be thought of as the firm's "vision in action."

---

[9] Richard D'Aveni, *The Whittemore Conference on Hypercompetition* (September 8-10, 1994).

[10] J.W. Patten, *How to Become a Strategic Manager*, Business Week Executive Program Brochure (1985).

Appendix A

Financial Ratios

Liquidity Ratios

$$\text{Current ratio} = \frac{\text{Current assets}}{\text{Current liabilities}}$$

$$\text{Quick ratio} = \frac{\text{Current assets} - \text{Inventory}}{\text{Current liabilities}}$$

$$\begin{array}{c}\text{Defensive interval} \\ \text{(days)}\end{array} = \frac{\text{Cash} + \text{Short-term marketable securities} + \text{Accounts receivable}}{\text{Daily operating expenses}}$$

Leverage Ratios

$$\text{Debt ratio} = \frac{\text{Total debt}}{\text{Total assets}}$$

$$\text{Debt/equity ratio} = \frac{\text{Total debt}}{\text{Stockholders' equity}}$$

$$\begin{array}{c}\text{Long-term} \\ \text{debt/equity ratio}\end{array} = \frac{\text{Long-term debt}}{\text{Stockholders' equity}}$$

$$\text{Times interest earned} = \frac{\text{Net income before taxes} + \text{Interest expense}}{\text{Interest expense}}$$

Profitability Ratios

$$\text{Profit margin} = \frac{\text{Net income}}{\text{Net sales}}$$

$$\begin{array}{c}\text{Return on investment} \\ \text{(ROI)}\end{array} = \frac{\text{Net income}}{\text{Average stockholders' equity}}$$

$$\text{Return on assets (ROA)} = \frac{\text{Net income}}{\text{Average total assets}}$$

$$\begin{array}{c}\text{Return on capital} \\ \text{employed (ROCE)}\end{array} = \frac{\text{Net income}}{\text{Average long-term debt} + \text{Stockholders' equity}}$$

$$\begin{array}{c}\text{Return on value} \\ \text{added (ROVA)}\end{array} = \frac{\text{Net income}}{\text{Value added}}$$

Activity Ratios

$$\text{Accounts receivable turnover} = \frac{\text{Credit sales}}{\text{Average accounts receivable}}$$

$$\text{Average collection period} = \frac{\text{Average accounts receivable} \times 365}{\text{Credit sales}}$$

$$\text{Inventory turnover} = \frac{\text{Cost of goods sold}}{\text{Average inventory}}$$

$$\text{Days of inventory} = \frac{\text{Average inventory} \times 365}{\text{Cost of goods sold}}$$

$$\text{Working capital turnover} = \frac{\text{Sales}}{\text{Average working capital}}$$

$$\text{Fixed asset turnover} = \frac{\text{Sales}}{\text{Average net fixed assets}}$$

$$\text{Total asset turnover} = \frac{\text{Sales}}{\text{Average total assets}}$$

$$\text{Fixed assets per sales dollar} = \frac{\text{Average net fixed assets}}{\text{Sales}}$$

$$\text{Total assets per sales dollar} = \frac{\text{Average total asset}}{\text{Sales}}$$

Common Stock Ratios

$$\text{Earnings per share} = \frac{\text{Net income available for common}}{\text{Common shares outstanding}}$$

$$\text{Cash flow per share} = \frac{\text{After-tax profits} + \text{Depreciation}}{\text{Common shares outstanding}}$$

$$\text{Book value per share} = \frac{\text{Shareholders' equity}}{\text{Common shares outstanding}}$$

$$\text{Market to book value} = \frac{\text{Market price per share}}{\text{Book value per share}}$$

$$\text{Dividend yield} = \frac{\text{Annual dividends per share}}{\text{Market price per share}}$$

Coverage Ratios

$$\text{Cash flow coverage} = \frac{\text{Cash flow}}{\text{Interest} + \dfrac{\text{Principal payments}}{1 - \text{Tax rate}}}$$

$$\text{Fixed charge coverage} = \frac{\text{Earnings before interest and taxes} + \text{Lease obligations}}{\text{Interest} + \text{Lease obligations}}$$

Appendix
B

Strategic
Planning Worksheet

The strategic planning worksheet, shown as Figure 1, is designed to facilitate use of the simple, flexible planning process described in the text. It is particularly useful in organizing one's strategic thinking regarding a given business-unit, and provides the basis for development of the complete strategic plan.

This completed form is the core of the strategic plan for the business. The form is self-explanatory, and forces management to think through the business unit's broad goals and specific objectives, as well as its critical success factors. Next, the five most critical environmental factors likely to affect the business over the next five years are listed, followed by the five most promising actions (strategies) to deal with each. Finally, implementation responsibility and schedule are listed for each of the actions.

Business Unit	Critical Environmental Factors	Action Items	Implementation Responsibility	Implementation Schedule
Name _____	1.	1. 2. 3. 4. 5.		
Broad Goals 1. 2. 3. 4. 5.	2.	1. 2. 3. 4. 5.		
Specific Objectives 1. 2.	3.	1. 2. 3. 4. 5.		
	4.	1. 2. 3. 4. 5.		
3. 4. 5. Critical Success Factors 1. 2.	5.	1. 2. 3. 4. 5.		
3. 4. 5. 6.	6.	1. 2. 3. 4. 5.		

Figure 1 Strategic Planning Worksheet

Appendix C

How to Value a Business

Often the most difficult step in buying, acquiring, selling, or divesting a business is determining its value. Many judgment decisions must be made. There is no "fixed price;" it is a lot like buying a used car. There is a retail average book, and a wholesale price (both for an "average" vehicle, which must be adjusted for condition, mileage, options and the like). Finally, it is only worth its *value* to a certain buyer.

For businesses, there are two basic methods of determining value; one is the earnings-based method, relying on expectations of future profits and return on investment. The other is asset-based, depending on the appraised value of assets at the time of the sale. Manufacturing firms value the asset method more, while service industries give greater importance to earnings. Keep in mind that buying and selling a business is an art—there is no fixed price. It depends upon perceived worth, or value, and negotiation. Therefore, there is typically an "asking price" and an "offering price," with any possible "deal" negotiated between these two upper and lower bounds.

Following are some "ballpark"ways of estimating the value of a business:

1. Book value times 125 percent (book value should be adjusted for worth of assets to buyer).
2. Average three-year earnings capitalized at some current opportunity-cost rate of return, usually in the range of 10-20 percent.

3. Five-year payback. Total estimated earnings for the next five years.
4. Present value of estimated earnings over the next ten years, discounted at the opportunity-cost rate of return.
5. Stock market value multiplied by two or less.
6. Price/earnings ratio times past three-year average earnings.
7. Earnings before interest and depreciation times 3 (lower limit) to eight (upper limit).

These methods of valuation are for cash purchase. Stock Trades and other considerations are more complex. Tax considerations add additional factors.[1]

---

[1] R.G. Murdick, R.C. Moor, R.H. Eckhouse, T.W. Zimmerer, "Business Policy: A Framework for Analysis (Columbus, OH: Grid Publishing, Inc., 1984), 88-89.

Index

—A—

Abell, Derek F., 6-5
Acquisition growth, 9-3
Acquisition-related strategies, 16-20
Acquisition results, 16-28
Acquisitions, 16-1, 16-18 to 16-19, 16-33
Action strategies, 3-18
Actions, 3-12
Activity ratios, A-2
Activity-based costing (ABC), 20-10
Activity-based management (ABM), 20-1, 20-10
Aging and declining markets, 13-30
Alignment of business-units, 10-4
Alliances, 9-1, 9-16
Altman's Z score, 20-17
AM International, Inc., 19-3
Analysis of competition, 4-13
Analytical vs. political decisions, 17-5
Andrews, Kenneth R., 2-18, 3-7, 12-7, 19-7
Ansoff, H. Igor, 1-20, 2-18, 3-7, 13-15
Anticipatable and unanticipatable surprises, 5-9
Asset mass efficiencies, 8-4
Asset-reduction strategies, 13-29

—B—

Balanced scorecard, 20-1, 20-14
Bargaining power, 11-17
Bargaining power of customers, 11-6
Bargaining power of suppliers, 11-6
Basic financial planning, 3-6

BCG matrix, 16-10
Benchmarking, 20-16
Bendix, 2-4
Berbiglia Liquors, 13-4
Best-business practices, 23-3
Board,
    role of, 12-8
Board of directors, 6-3, 12-1, 12-5
Boston Consulting Group (BCG), 8-12
Bottom-up, 3-22
Boulton, William R., 13-3
Bower, J.L., 19-9
Branch operations, 14-13
Breakthrough, 2-9
Buffett, Warren, 21-2
Business definition, 2-10
Business development strategies, 13-15
Business level, 3-17
Business process reengineering, 8-2, 8-19
Business profile matrix, 16-14, 16-35
Business strategy, 6-6, 6-3
Business synergies, 8-7
Business-unit/level strategy, 1-11, 13-1 to 13-2, 15-1
Business-unit strategy formulation, 12-13
Buyer switching costs, 13-10
Buzzell, Robert, 11-12

—C—

Cash cows, 16-10
Cash flow, 4-9

Cash generating businesses, 16-11
CEO succession, 19-12
Chandler, Alfred, Jr., 19-22
Change, 2-16
Chaos theory, 5-3
Chaotic environments, 5-1
Chief executive officer (CEO), 6-3
Chief operating officer (COO), 6-3
Chief staff officer (CSO), 6-3
Christensen, C.R., 2-18
Chrysler Corp., 9-17
Climate, 7-1, 7-15
Coca-Cola, 14-2
Collaborative strategies, 9-1
Colleges and universities, 22-8
Combination strategies, 13-30
Committees of the board, 12-9 to 12-10
Common stock ratios, A-2
Communication, 10-4
Comparative, 8-1
Comparative advantages, 8-4
Competencies, 8-1
Competition, 11-3
Competitive advantage, 1-21, 3-2, 8-1, 8-3
Competitive environment, 3-15, 11-1 to 11-2
Competitive forces, 11-3
Competitive or industry environment(s), 10-9
Competitive position objectives, 17-15
Competitive positioning, 14-11
Competitor analysis, 11-7 to 11-8, 17-11
ConAgra, 3-2
Concentration, 16-17
Concentric acquisition, 16-22
Conceptual and synthesis skills, 6-9
Conglomerate(s), 9-4 to 9-5, 16-5
Consultant,
    role of, 12-13
Consultants outside, 12-1, 12-13
Content of the strategies, 10-3
Contingency planning, 5-12 to 5-13
Contingency plans, 5-14, 20-9
Contingent strategy processes, 23-6
Continuous improvement, 8-19
Contraction, 13-2
Contrarian preemptive strategies, 13-19
Control, 3-1, 20-1
Control elements, 20-4
Cooperation, 23-10

Cooperative strategies, 9-1
Core competencies, 8-1, 8-5, 9-1, 16-5, 16-9
    and competitive advantage, 23-5
"Core" portfolios, 16-5
Corporate concentration and restructuring
    strategies, 16-30
Corporate governance, 12-5
Corporate level, 3-18
Corporate-level decisions, 16-1
Corporate-level processes, 16-9
Corporate-level strategy, 16-1
Corporate planning, 6-1
Corporate portfolio and resources, 8-7
Corporate portfolio models, 16-9
Corporate renewal, 9-10
Corporate restructuring, 16-32
Corporate strategy, 1-11, 6-6, 8-7
Corporate strategy formulation, 12-13
Corporate value added, 16-5
Cost-cutting strategies, 13-29
Cost leadership, 13-2
Cost minimization, 15-9
Cost-push factors, 4-18
Costs, 4-9
Costs of entry, 11-18
Coverage ratios, A-2
Creativity, 2-8
Critical dimensions, 2-3
Critical failure factors, 4-12
Critical success factors (CSFs), 4-1 to 4-2, 4-8,
    8-7, 18-6
CUC International, 9-2
Culture, 3-13, 7-1, 7-4
Current strategic efforts, 4-18
Customizing strategies, 13-14

—D—

D'Aveni, Richard, 17-8
Decision "blind spots," 17-6
Decision speed, 17-4
Decision support system (DSS), 18-12
Decisional quicksand, 20-16
Decline stage, 11-23
Declining demand, 13-31
Deere & Company, 10-2
Defense and renewal, 13-1

Defense and renewal strategies, 13-24
Defensive responses, 13-25
Defining and redefining the business, 7-7
Defining the market, 11-11
Definition of strategic management, 2-2
Definitions of quality, 15-7
Deliberate strategy, 2-7 to 2-8
Delivery strategies, 15-3
Demand conditions in the home market, 15-4
Demographic influences, 10-23
Design differentiation, 13-8
Design strategies, 15-3
Detailed planning, 19-1
Development of strategic managers, 23-6
Development stages of entrepreneurship
     start-ups, 21-20
Devil's advocate, 3-24
Dialectic inquiry, 3-24
Differentiation strategies, 4-9, 13-1 to 13-2, 13-8
Digman, L.A., 11-16
Discontinuous change, 2-13, 5-10
Discontinuous environment, 2-13
Distinctive and core competencies, 8-1, 8-7
Distinctive competencies, 2-10, 3-2, 8-7
Distinguishing the business, 13-1 to 13-2
Diversification, 9-3
Diversification and performance, 16-26
Diversification into unrelated industries, 16-22
Diversification results, 16-26
Diversification strategies, 16-17
Diversified company, 9-3 to 9-4
Diversified firm, 16-4
Diversified majors, 9-4 to 9-5
Diversity, 6-11
Divestiture strategies, 16-30
Divestitures, 16-1
Division managers, 6-3
Dog businesses, 16-11
Domestic versus international growth, 9-3
Dominant-product business, 9-3 to 9-4
Downsizing, 8-2
Drucker, Peter, 8-2
DSS/AI/ES, 23-9

—E—

Economic factors, 3-15

Economic value added (EVA), 20-1, 20-11
Economies of scale, 8-14
Economy, 3-16, 10-10
Educational acquisitions, 16-19
Efficiency improvements, 13-25
Eisenhardt, Kathleen, 17-5
Emergent strategy, 2-8
Emerging trends, 23-1, 6
Endgame strategies, 13-1, 13-31
Enterprise strategies, 1-9, 6-6, 12-1, 12-3
     and stakeholders, 1-9
Enterprise strategy components, 12-3
Entrepreneurial start-up, 21-1
Entry strategies, 16-18
Environmental analysis, 3-15, 10-4
Environmental fit, 1-18
Environmental influences, 8-7, 10-1
Environmental information sources, 18-11
Environmental scanning, 4-10
Environmental scanning and monitoring, 18-10
Essence of strategy, 2-9
Evaluating alternatives, 17-1, 17-14
Evaluation techniques, 17-19
Evolution of strategic planning, 3-5
Executive information system (EIS), 18-12
Executive support system (ESS), 18-12
Exit barriers, 16-31
Experience curve, 8-12
Experience curve position, 8-17
Experience curve pricing, 8-14
External environment, 1-17, 3-15, 10-4
Externally oriented planning, 3-6
Extrapolation of trends, 5-12

—F—

Factor conditions, 15-4
Factors essential to success, 4-3
Family businesses, 21-17
"Fast-follower" strategy, 15-9
Financial resources, 8-9
Financial services, 11-18
Firm, 10-9
Firm strategy, structure, and rivalry, 15-4
Firms based on successful specialization, 21-12
Firms in "small business industries," 21-12
First-mover advantages, 13-10

First to market, 15-9
Fit, 1-17, 3-2
Five forces model, 11-6, 11-18
Flexibility, 15-11
Flexible planning processes, 23-4
Focus on continuous improvement, 8-5
Focus strategies, 13-2
For-profit firms, 22-2
Forces driving industry competition, 11-5
Ford Motor Co., 3-20
Forecast, 5-8
Forecast-based planning, 3-6
Forecasting, 5-8
Forecasting techniques, 5-1, 5-11
Formal planning, 3-7
Formal planning systems, 1-20
Formulating strategy, 1-22
Forums, 10-27
Forward versus backward integration, 9-3
Functional manager, 6-7
Functional strategy, 1-11, 13-2, 15-1, 15-3
Functions, 13-2

—G—

Galbraith and Nathanson Model, 9-7
Gallup organization, 7-5
Gateway 2000, 21-3
General Electric, 1-8, 4-2, 21-6
General Electric's nine-cell business screen,
    16-12 to 16-13
General environment, 10-1, 10-6, 10-9
General environment: opportunities and threats,
    3-15
General managers, 6-1, 6-7 to 6-8, 19-16
General Motors (GM), 2-3, 21-6
"Generic" business strategies, 13-2
Generic strategies, 17-8
Generic value chain, 15-6
Geographical expansion, 13-1 to 13-2, 13-21
Global, 14-1, 14-4, 14-8
Global business, 9-9, 14-1, 14-4, 14-8
Global competition, 14-1, 14-4
Global competitor, 14-5
Global industry, 14-3
Global strategies, 14-1
Global trends and risks, 14-12

Gluck, Frederick, 19-2
Glueck, William F., 3-7
Goals, 3-9, 3-11, 7-1, 7-4
Goals and objectives, 3-14, 17-3
Goodyear, 13-19
Governance, 12-1
Government, 22-1
Greiner's Evolution and Revolution Model, 9-7
Group approaches, 3-24
Group consensus approaches, 3-24
Growth, 13-1
Growth and evolutionary patterns, 9-1
Growth of served market, 4-18
Growth strategies, 13-17
Guerrilla warfare strategies, 13-13

—H—

H-form organizations, 9-11
Hambrick, Don, 12-13
Hamel, Gary, 3-21, 8-8, 16-9, 23-5
Harley-Davidson, 3-20
Harrigan, Kathryn Rudie, 13-31
Harvard University, 4-16
Hax, Arnoldo C., 2-2, 13-16
Health maintenance organizations (HMOs), 22-2
Hesselbein, Frances 1-5
Hewlett-Packard, 21-6
Hierarchical, or vertical, organization, 9-12
Hierarchy of objectives, 7-13
High performance strategic planning, 3-19
High-velocity environments, 17-1, 17-3
History and evolution of strategic management,
    2-12
HMO industry, 22-2
Hofer, Charles W., 3-9, 13-3, 17-13
Holding, 9-9
Holding companies, 9-11
Honda, 3-20
Horizontal, 9-3
Horizontal acquisition, 16-22
Horizontal corporations, 9-12
Horizontal growth of existing businesses, 16-17
Hospitals, 22-6
Human resources, 7-16, 8-9
Hypercompetition, 17-8

—I—

IBM (the P.C.), 21-6
IBM, 1-8, 2-7
Image differentiation, 13-8
Implementation, 2-10, 3-3, 3-18, 19-1, 19-3
Implementation control, 20-6 to 20-7
Implementing strategy, 1-22
Implementing strategic decisions, 19-1, 19-7
Implementing strategic planning processes,
    18-1, 19-5
Implementing strategic plans, 19-18
Improved strategy frameworks, 23-4
InaCom, 2-7
Increased penetration, 13-2
Increasing scope, 13-14
Increasing the scope, 13-1
Incremental planning, 3-7
Industry, 11-13
Industry analysis, 17-11
Industry/business experts, 4-13
Industry chain or stream, 13-4
Industry environment,
    competitive factors, 3-16
Industry or operating environment, 10-6
Industry structure, 3-17, 11-6, 11-9, 11-13
Industry structure analysis, 4-10
Information and tools, 23-5
Information resources, 8-9, 18-1
Information technology trends, 18-12
Infrastructure, 4-4
Initiating actions, 3-18
Innovation and/or differentiation, 4-18
Innovation strategies, 15-1
Institutions, 22-1
Integrated organization, 9-13
Intelligence Information, 18-12
Intended strategy, 2-7 to 2-8
Intensity of competition, 11-1
Internal control, 20-5
Internal development, 16-18 to 16-19
Internal development and venture strategies,
    16-23
Internal/joint-venture strategies, 16-23
Internal new ventures, 21-6
Internal situation, 1-17
Internal ventures, 16-18 to 16-19, 25
International, 14-1, 14-4

International competitor, 14-4
International factors, 10-14
International markets, 14-1
International strategies, 14-6
Internationalization, 14-11
Interorganizational strategy, 1-10, 23-3
    collective behavior, 1-10
    competitive behavior, 1-11
    cooperative actions, 1-10
Intrapreneurship, 21-6
Introductory and growth stages, 11-20
Investment intensity, 4-17
Investment strategies, 17-15
Issue, 10-3
Issue and surprise management, 5-1
Issues analysis, 5-22
ITT Corp., 16-2

—J—

Jackson, Susan, 6-11
Japan, 10-13
Joint venture, 14-13, 16-25
    alliances, 16-19

—K—

Kami, Michael, 1-7, 3-20
Key implementation tasks, 19-9
Kotter, John, 6-5
Kustom Electronics, 10-2

—L—

Learned, Edward P., 2-18
Learning-curve concept, 8-12
Levels of control, 20-4
Levels of sales,
    profits, and rate of growth, 7-13
Leverage ratios, A-1
Leveraged buyouts, 16-34
Levi Strauss, 12-2
Licensing, 14-13, 16-18 to 16-19
Life-cycle stage, 4-10, 8-17
Line and staff, 6-5

Line and staff managers, 6-1
Liquidity ratios, A-1
Local, 14-1, 14-8
Long-range planning, 2-4
Long-range planning model, 22-23
Lorange, Peter, 18-15

—M—

M-form (for Multidivision), 9-5, 9-11
M, H, and P2-forms, 9-11
Macro- and microeconomic influences, 10-1
Macroeconomic factors, 10-12
Management information systems (MIS), 18-4
Management selection, development,
    succession, 19-12
Managing global integration, 23-7
Market, 11-9
Market development, 13-1 to 13-2
Market development strategies, 13-15, 13-21
Market/industry factors, 8-7
Market segmentation, 15-9
Market share, 4-9, 4-17
Market share and ROE, 11-15
Market structure, 11-1
Martin-Marietta, 2-4
Maturity stage, 11-22
McKinsey & Company, 1-22, 3-5, 7-5
Measures of system effectiveness, 19-6
Measuring and analyzing performance, 20-10
"Me-too" strategy, 11-17
Mergers, 16-1, 16-33
Micro-multinationals, 23-7
Microeconomic factors, 10-11
Miles and Snow's types of organizational
    adaptation, 13-2
Miller Brewing, 2-11
Minnesota Mining & Manufacturing Co. (3M),
    15-2
Mintzberg, Henry, 1-7, 2-7, 6-6, 13-3
Mission, 2-10, 3-9, 3-13, 7-1 to 7-2, 7-4, 17-3
Mission for an individual business, 7-8
Mission of the firm, 7-8
Mission statements, 7-1
Mobility barriers, 11-17
Model of strategic management, 3-10
Monitoring, 18-4

Monitoring the environment, 18-1
Monopolistic competition, 10-12
Monopoly, 10-12
Monsanto Corp., 19-4
Motorola, Inc., 13-3
Multi-industry company, 9-3 to 9-4
Multibusiness firms, 8-6
Multibusiness organization, 16-3
Multibusiness strategies, 16-1
Multidomestic, 14-4
Multidomestic competitor, 14-4
Multilocal, 14-4, 14-8
Multimission organizations, 7-8, 16-2
Multinational, 9-9, 14-1, 14-4, 14-8

—N—

National, 14-1
National Broadcasting Company (NBC), 17-2
NCR, 6-2
Nebraska Furniture Mart, 21-2
Need for planning, 2-12
Networks, 9-1
New product development, 15-1 to 15-2
New product development/innovation strategies,
    15-9
New venture strategies, 21-8
New ventures, 16-1, 21-6
New-venture problems, 21-10
NFPs
    typology of, 22-10
NFPs and for-profits,
    differences between, 22-11
Niche strategies, 13-13
Not-for-profit organizations, 22-1 to 22-2
Not-for-profits types and characteristics of, 22-9

—O—

Objectives, 3-9, 3-11
Office Depot, 20-2
Oligopoly, 10-12
Operating health, 20-24
Operational planning, 1-12
Operations strategies, 1-11
Opinion quantification techniques, 5-12

Opportunities, 1-19
Organization builder, 19-16
Organization structure, 19-22
Organizational control, 20-4
Organizational culture, 7-14
Organizational form, 14-13
Organizational governance, 12-4
Organizational health, 20-17
Organizational learning, 23-3
Organizational planning processes, 1-12
    strategic planning system, 1-12
Organizational resources, 8-9
Organizations, 5-3
Outsourcing, 9-1, 9-16

—P—

P2-form organizations, 9-11
Penetration strategies, 13-1, 13-15
Pepsi, 14-2
Perfect competition, 10-12
Performance, 1-21
Peters, Thomas, 1-7, 4-4
Philip Morris, 2-14, 13-19
Physical resources, 8-9
Plan implementation, 19-5
Planning, 2-1
Planning systems, 3-2, 18-1
Plans, 7-4
Plan's process and content, 19-20
Players, 10-27
Polaroid, 21-6
Policies, 3-1, 3-9, 17-3
Political allocation problem, 7-15
Political/legal considerations, 3-16, 10-27
Political/legal environment, 10-28
Political-legal factors, 3-15
Political/legal strategy, 10-28
Political risk and economic forecast chart,
    14-16 to 14-19
Political risks, 14-15
Porter, Michael, 3-23
Porter's generic strategies
    cost leadership, 13-5
    focus strategies, 13-6
    product or service differentiation, 13-5
Portfolio models, 16-1, 16-14

Portfolio planning techniques, 16-5
Portfolios, 16-1
Positioning the business, 13-1 to 13-2, 13-4
Positions of competitive advantage, 8-7
Potential growth firms, 21-5
Pralahad, C.K., 8-8, 16-9, 23-5
Predictions, 5-9
Preemption of assets, 13-10
Preemptive opportunities and characteristics,
    13-19
Preemptive strategies, 4-9, 13-18, 13-20
Premise control, 20-6 to 20-7
Preparedness strategies, 3-18
Price differentiation, 13-8
Primary activities, 15-6
Problems of small businesses, 21-17
Procedures, 17-3
Process improvement, 8-1, 8-19
Process quality management (PQM), 3-21
Process technology, 10-19
Processes, 20-11
Processing strategies, 15-3
Product development, 13-1 to 13-2
Product development strategies, 13-15, 13-18
Product extension strategy, 13-18
Product life cycle, 11-26
Product line proliferation, 13-18
Product/market life cycle, 11-1, 11-20
Product/service development activities, 13-2
Product termination, 13-2
Product timing, 13-11
Productivity, 4-17
Productivity-related influences, 10-1
Professional partnerships, 9-11
Professional services organizations, 22-1, 22-5,
    22-18
Profit impact of market strategies (PIMS),
    4-1 to 4-2
Profitability ratios, A-1
Profits, 4-9
Projections, 5-9
Public-interest organizations, 22-1
Public-sector management, 22-13
Public-sector organizations, 22-2
Public service, 22-1

—Q—

Qualitative techniques, 5-12
Quality differentiation, 13-9
Quality improvements, 13-25
Quality strategies, 15-7
Question marks, 16-11
Quinn, James, 17-11

—R—

R&D/technology strategies, 15-8
Rare success, 21-12
Rate of change, 2-17
Realized strategy, 2-8
Redefining the business, 13-1
Reducing the scope, 13-1
Reengineering, 8-2, 15-2
Regional, 14-1, 14-8
Regulatory influences and processes, 10-1
Related and supporting industries, 15-4
Related diversified, 16-4
Related or unrelated industries, 9-5
Relevant environment, 10-9
Renewal, 4-7, 4-9, 13-2
Resegmentation, 8-7
Resource allocation problems, 16-5
Resource audit, 1-19, 8-10
Resource capabilities, 10-4
Resource properties and advantage, 8-6
Resources, 4-4, 8-1, 8-9
Resources and competencies, 3-17
Response actions, 3-18
Restructuring, 8-7, 16-5, 16-33
Restructuring and internal growth, 23-4
Retreat, 13-2
Retrenchment, 13-2, 13-26
Retrenchment and turnaround, 13-1
Retrenchment and turnaround strategies, 13-26
Return on capital, 7-13
Return on shareholders' capital, 7-13
Revenue-increasing strategies, 13-29
Reward systems, 19-15
Rewarding strategic performance, 23-6
Risk analysis, 5-1, 5-6
Risk and uncertainty, 5-6
Rivalry, 11-3 to 11-4, 11-18
Rothschild, Bill, 12-12

Rubbermaid Corp., 15-11

—S—

Satellite firms, 21-14
Scale, 11-18
Scanning, 18-1, 18-4
Scenario-based planning, 5-1, 5-18
Schendel, Dan E., 3-9 17-17
"Schools" of strategic management, 2-11
Schumpeter, Joseph, 10-21
Schwartz, Peter, 5-19
Scope, 3-17, 13-1 and 13-2
Second to market, 15-9
Sector of the economy, 4-8
Segmentation, 4-9
Segmentation strategy, 13-12
Segmentation tactics, 13-25
Selecting a strategy, 17-14
Senior-level abilities, 19-11
Served market, 11-13
Service organizations, 22-1, 22-3 to 22-4
    types of, 22-6
Service profit chain, 22-5
Service technology, 10-19
Service vision, 22-21
Shakeout stage, 11-21
Share-building strategies, 13-17
Shareholders, 12-6
Simon, Herbert E., 18-6
Simulation and cause and effect techniques, 5-12
Single-product business, 9-3 to 9-4, 9-9
Situation audit, 17-7
Small business
    characteristics of, 21-12
Small business strategies, 21-1
Small business strategy formulation, 21-14
Small businesses, 21-1, 21-4, 21-12
Social factors, 3-15 to 3-16, 7-1, 10-23
Societal analysis, 17-11
Sources of comparative advantage, 8-7
Sources of information, 18-1
Sourcing strategies, 15-3
Southwest Airlines, 11-13
Stable environments, 3-4
Stakeholder groups, 6-1

Stakeholder values and expectations, 6-12
Stakeholders, 3-9, 6-1, 12-6
Star businesses, 16-10 to 16-11
Start-up ventures, 21-1, 21-8
Statements of strategy, 1-14
Steiner, George, 17-7
Stockholders, 6-14
Strategic advantage, 8-1
Strategic alliances, 9-1, 9-17
Strategic and operational harmony, 23-4
Strategic architecture, 18-2
Strategic assumption surfacing and testing
    technique (SAST), 6-14
Strategic assumptions analysis technique, 6-16
Strategic audits, 20-1, 20-17
Strategic business-units, 16-1, 16-4, 16-9
Strategic choice, 17-11
Strategic control, 2-4, 3-9, 20-1, 20-3, 20-6
Strategic control processes, 20-8
Strategic decision, 1-7, 2-6, 5-1, 6-2
    characteristics of, 2-6
Strategic decision support systems, 18-3
Strategic decision-makers, 6-9
Strategic decision-making, 17-3
Strategic evaluation, 20-1
Strategic group, 3-17, 4-8, 11-1, 11-3, 11-14
Strategic health, 20-19
Strategic information, 18-3
Strategic information needs, 18-5
Strategic information sources, 18-9
Strategic information system (SIS), 18-1, 18-4
Strategic infrastructure, 18-1 to 18-2
Strategic issues, 10-4
Strategic leaders, 12-12
Strategic leadership, 6-5
Strategic management, 1-3, 1-7, 2-4, 3-2, 3-6
Strategic management in NFPs, 22-12
Strategic management model for public
    organizations, 22-17
Strategic management process, 3-1, 3-7
Strategic managers, 6-1 to 6-2
Strategic options, 13-1, 17-9
Strategic performance measurement, 20-1
Strategic planning, 1-6, 1-12, 2-4, 3-1, 3-9, 12-6
Strategic planning pitfalls, 19-7 to 19-8
Strategic planning systems, 18-1, 18-15
Strategic planning worksheet, B-1
Strategic Planning Institute (SPI), 4-16

Strategic position, 17-7
Strategic profile, 17-7
Strategic service vision, 22-21
Strategic situation, 17-6
Strategic success factors, 18-7
Strategic surveillance, 20-6, 20-7
Strategic, tactical, and operational planning,
    operational planning, 1-14
    strategic planning, 1-13
    tactical planning, 1-13
    scheduling and dispatching, 1-14
Strategic thinking, 1-3, 1-7, 3-22
Strategic versus operating management, 1-16
Strategies, 2-5, 3-12, 7-2
Strategies for aging and declining markets,
    13-30
Strategies for redefining and reducing scope,
    13-22
Strategies of scope, 13-12
Strategy alternatives, 10-1, 16-1, 17-1, 17-3,
    17-11, 17-13
Strategy and structure relationships, 19-22
Strategy audit flow chart, 20-21
Strategy audits, 20-19
Strategy clusters, 14-11
Strategy committees, 12-9
Strategy concept, 16-5
Strategy content, 12-2, 17-18
Strategy dimensions, 14-11
Strategy formation, 3-3
Strategy formulation, 3-17, 17-3, 17-8
Strategy formulation system, 18-2
Strategy-making modes, 6-12
Strategy patterns, 14-10
Strategy process, 1-21
Strategy types, 14-7
Stratport, 17-19
Strengths, 1-9
Strengths and weaknesses, 8-1, 17-11
Structure, 7-16, 9-1, 19-22
"Stuck in the middle", 13-6
Subsidiary operations, 14-13
Substitute products, 11-18
Successful growth firms, 21-6
Successful internal ventures, 16-25
Supply chain management (SCM), 9-16
Support activities, 15-6
Support differentiation, 13-8

Supporting strategies, 15-3
Surprise and crisis management, 5-14
Surprise events, 5-16
Surprise matrix, 5-24
Surprises, 5-14
Survival firms, 21-5
Sustainable competitive advantage, 2-10, 3-4, 8-3
Sustainable growth, 17-17
Sustaining networks, 23-10
Swatch, 5-2
Synergies, 3-2, 16-18
System implementation phases in, 19-6

Trends and directions, 23-1
Turbulent environments, 3-4
Turnaround, 4-9, 13-2
Turnaround options, 13-28
Turnover firms, 21-14
Types of acquisitions, 16-21
Types of business organizations, 9-1
Types of international strategy, 14-8
Types of strategies, 1-8
    business-unit strategy, 1-8
    corporate-level strategy, 1-8
    enterprise strategy, 1-8
    functional/operational strategies, 1-8
    interorganizational strategy, 1-8

—T—

Tactical planning, 1-12
Tactics, 2-5
Takeovers, 16-33
Task environment, 10-9, 11-2
Technical and analytical skills, 6-10
Technical design problem, 7-15
Technological factors, 3-15
Technological leadership, 13-10
Technology, 3-16, 8-9, 10-1, 10-17
Technology-based strategies, 15-1
Technology strategies, 15-8
The growth/share matrix, 16-10
The Institute of Electrical and Electronic
    Engineers (IEEE), 1-4
Third-sector organizations, 22-1
Threat of new entrants, 11-3
Threat of substitution, 11-6
Threats, 1-19
Thurow, Lester, 10-17
Time, 8-1, 8-4
Time-based competition, 15-2
Time compression, 8-5
Timing, 8-1, 8-11
Timing differentiation, 13-9
Top-down strategy making, 3-23
Total quality management (TQM), 8-2, 15-2, 15-7
TQM Implementation, 4-16
Trade risk, 14-15
Transnational, 14-4 to 14-5, 14-8
Transnational business, 14-1

—U—

U-form (for Unitary), 9-11
Uncertain futures, 5-1
Underachieving firms, 21-5
Undifferentiated products, 13-9
Union Pacific, 20-2
Union Pacific Railroad, 8-2
Unitary, multidivisional, and professional
    forms, 9-1
Unrealized strategy, 2-8
Unrelated diversification (conglomeration), 13-16
Unrelated diversifiers, 16-4
Unsegmented strategy, 13-12
US West, 7-2
USX Corp., 14-2

—V—

Value-added chain, 15-5
Value analysis, 3-9
Value based planning concepts, 16-5
Value chain, 9-17, 15-1 to 15-2, 15-5
Value of strategic management, 1-19
Values, 12-2
Valuing a business, C-1
Venture capital, 16-24
    nuturing, 16-19
Venture characteristics, 16-23
Venture merging and melding, 16-25
Venture nurturing, 16-24

Venture spin-off, 16-25
Versus strategic planning and long-range
    planning, 2-3
Vertical acquisitions, 16-21
Vertical integration, 4-17, 9-3, 16-17
Vertically integrated, 16-4
Video rental industry, 11-2
Virtual organization, 9-1 to 9-2, 9-15, 23-10
Vision, 2-8, 2-10, 3-9, 3-13, 7-1-3
Vision statements, 7-5

—W—

Walsh, Mike, 20-2
Weaknesses, 1-19
Welch, Jack, 4-2
"World class" competitor, 8-8
World-class industries, 15-4
World market, 11-12
World scenarios, 14-20

—XYZ—

Zajac, Ed, 17-6